JMH
1/14/98

FIFTH EDITION

ADJUSTMENT & GROWTH IN A CHANGING WORLD

FIFTH EDITION

ADJUSTMENT & GROWTH IN A CHANGING WORLD

Vince Napoli

James M. Kilbride

Donald E. Tebbs

MIAMI-DADE
COMMUNITY COLLEGE
MIAMI, FLORIDA

WEST PUBLISHING COMPANY

Minneapolis/St. Paul   New York   Los Angeles   San Francisco

PRODUCTION CREDITS

Composition   Parkwood Composition

Copyeditor   Jan Krygier

Text Design   Roslyn Stendahl

Index   Sandy Schroeder

Production, Prepress, Printing, and Binding   by West
Publishing Company

Photo credits on page xxxi.

British Library Cataloguing-in-Publication Data. A catalogue
record for this book is available from the British Library.

Library of Congress Cataloguing-in-Publication Data

Napoli, Vince.
    Adjustment and growth in a changing world / Vince
Napoli, James M. Kilbride, Donald E. Tebbs. -- 5th ed.
        p. cm.
    Includes index.
    ISBN 0–314–04557–0(hard)
    1. Self-actualization (Pyschology)   2. Adjustment (Psy-
chology)   3. Identity (Psychology)   4. Interpersonal relations.   I. Kilbride, James M.   II. Tebbs, Donald E.
III. Title
    BF637.S4N365   1995   94–32602
    158—dc20   CIP

WEST'S COMMITMENT TO THE ENVIRONMENT

In 1906, West Publishing Company began recycling materials
left over from the production of books. This began a tradition
of efficient and responsible use of resources. Today, up to 95
percent of our legal books and 70 percent of our college and
school texts are printed on recycled, acid-free stock. West also
recycles nearly 22 million pounds of scrap paper
annually–the equivalent of 181,717 trees. Since the 1960s,
West has devised ways to capture and recycle waste inks, sol-
vents, oils, and vapors created in the printing process. We
also recycle plastics of all kinds, wood, glass, corrugated
cardboard, and batteries, and have eliminated the use of Sty-
rofoam book packaging. We at West are proud of the longevity and the scope of our commitment to the environment.

CONTENTS

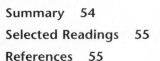

PART TWO

INFLUENCES ON ADJUSTMENT AND GROWTH   97

CHAPTER 5
The Physical Self   147

Features

CHAPTER **7**
**Emotional
Influences   239**

Features

CHAPTER **8**
The Social Self   285

Features

PART THREE

ADJUSTMENT AND GROWTH IN INTERPERSONAL RELATIONSHIPS   333

Features

Features

PART FOUR

ADJUSTMENT AND GROWTH THROUGH LIFE MANAGEMENT AND THE WORLD OF WORK   421

Features

PREFACE

FOCUS

To lead an effective and fulfilling life, a person must do two things—*adjust* and *grow*. This book deals with adjustment and growth on two levels—the level of people in general and the level of *you* in particular. The material that deals with people in general tends to be theoretical, although specific devices have been used to ground this theoretical material in reality. The material that deals with you in particular is practical; it should help you in your own adjustment and growth.

Adjustment and Growth in a Changing World, Fifth Edition, is a text on the psychology of adjustment. It is concerned with the practical application of psychological principles to everyday life.

The book is organized on one level in a topical progression from a consideration of the individual to a consideration of interpersonal relationships. On another level a second organizational pattern is interwoven with the first: a progression from personal awareness to evaluation to change. This developmental pattern—from awareness to evaluation to change—is consistent with the general pattern of problem solving. That is, first we become aware of a problem; then we decide what to do about it; and finally we design and carry out specific action plans geared to solve the problem. Hence, the book helps you first to become aware of and to evaluate your own patterns of adjustment and growth, and then to make changes as you deem necessary or desirable.

ORGANIZATION

The book contains introduction and five major parts. The introduction is particularly useful because it deals with a topic that can be applied to any textbook you might use: study techniques. In addition, the introduction shows how a distinctive approach to learning, the SQ3R study method, has been employed in this book. We suggest that you read the introduction carefully before moving to Part I.

Part I presents an overview of the psychology of adjustment. It includes considerations of the processes of adjustment and growth, personality theories, and the concept of self-esteem. Part II surveys health psychology by examining stress and the influences of the physical, thinking, feeling, and social aspects of your well being. Part III considers adjustment and growth in interpersonal relationships. This section should help you to understand the impact of intimacy on your personal growth, as well as to understand your communication style. Life management and the world of work are the subjects of Part IV. Here you will consider the processes of goal setting and decision making, and the impact of career decisions and choices on your life. Part V focuses on a variety of factors involved when things go wrong for the individual. It includes a survey of maladjustive responses and of approaches that may be used to facilitate a return to healthy functioning.

MAJOR CHANGES IN THIS EDITION

We have made several major changes in the fifth edition, and all have received positive critical reviews from both students and teachers. Changes in organization and topic coverage including the following: The chapter on stress and health is now included with chapters on physical self, thinking self, feeling self, and social self in a part on health psychology, and the chapter on the world of work is now paired with the chapter on life management. The chapter on self-esteem contains a new section on parenting skills. The chapter on stress and health has new material on personal coping and the power of positive thinking. New information on aging, the exaggeration of sex differences, and energy and enzymes in fat reduction appears in the chapter on the physical self. The chapter on the thinking self has a new section on deductive and inductive reasoning and the use of heuristics in adjustment. The discussion of depression has been extended and new information on happiness and anger has been added to the chapter on the feeling self. The chapter on the social self contains a new section on the life cycle, and the chapter on the world of work has a new section on human relations skills in the workplace. Finally, the chapter on problems in adjustment has new sections on mood disorders and eating disorders, and the entire chapter has been rewritten to conform with DSM-IV. We have updated research and statistics throughout the book and attempted to retain the quality and level of writing of the fourth edition.

A new feature, Cultural Crosscurrents, has been added to each chapter. It is designed to emphasize the role of culture in the psychology of adjustment and to stimulate student interest. Also new is the inclusion of "warm up" questions to the Critical Review questions. These are intended to prime the student for the recall and critical thinking required to answer the Critical Review questions. Both of these new features have been enthusiastically received by reviewers.

ANCILLARY MATERIALS

There are two companion pieces to *Adjustment and Growth in a Changing World*—one for the student and one for the instructor. The *Study Guide to Accompany Adjustment and Growth in a Changing World*, written by the text authors, includes a listing of the major terms and concepts from each chapter and several exercises, including short quizzes, designed to help students master the concepts. We have found that students who complete these exercises tend to make relatively good class grades (C or better); therefore, we recommend the use of the study guide.

The *Instructor's Manual* is given to each instructor who adopts the text. It includes a chapter overview, suggested teaching activities, questions for reflection/discussion, and suggested audiovisual materials for each chapter. It also includes a complete test bank, authored by Ed Lamp, professor of Psychology at Terra Technical in Fremont, Ohio. The test bank is also available in computer disk form.

ACKNOWLEDGMENTS

This book is the product of the efforts of literally hundreds of people. Many students and teachers have helped us by offering constructive criticism. We also have been helped by many in the editorial and production departments of West Publishing. We thank all of you for your help.

We offer special thanks to the following individuals who acted as principal critical reviewers:

Anne Louise Dailey
Community College of Alleghany County

Dorothy DiCola
Stark Technical College

Dan Dougherty
Northcentral Technical College

George Hughston
Arizona State University

Ed Lamp
Terra Community College

Lou Maris
Milwaukee Area Technical College

John Nield
Utah Valley State College

Nicholas Santilli
John Carroll University

Margaret Thibodeau
Southeast Missouri State University

Vince Napoli
James M. Kilbride
Donald E. Tebbs

STUDYING TO UNDERSTAND, CHALLENGE AND REMEMBER

How much will you have to adjust your schedule to meet the demands of this course on adjustment? Your answer will depend on the level of your **study skills.** Below are four definitions of studying. Check the one that best describes your present approach. Studying is:

1. _____ Reading the pages over and over until the information sinks in.
2. _____ Reading the text until I understand what I am reading.
3. _____ Reading the chapter and underlining the important parts.
4. _____ Using my mind to acquire knowledge.

The goal of using special study techniques is to learn as much as possible in the shortest time and to retain what is learned. Let's look at how psychologists evaluate the definitions listed above in light of that goal.

1. **Reading and rereading.** Passive reading—simply looking at the words while "waiting for good things to happen." (Locke, 1975)—is of little help in learning. Repeating the process simply adds frustration and wastes time.

2. **Reading for understanding.** The task of learning is to understand and remember what you read so that you are able to explain it to others or to apply it when necessary. Many college students confuse understanding what they are reading with being able to recall what they have read—a fatal error. We must go beyond what we read as we are reading it. We must literally make the new information a part of ourselves.

3. **Reading and underlining.** Underlining is perhaps the most used, and abused, study method. It is a useful tool for noting what is important to make learning and review easier. However, it is not learning. It is an I.O.U., a promise of future learning. "Underlining says, 'Look, I'm picking out the real meat so I can concentrate on it—some other time'" (Elliott, 1966, p. 48).

4. **Using the mind to acquire knowledge.** This definition offers little specific help in teaching us how to study, but it does give us a starting point. We can use our minds to improve our ability to learn. We can learn good study methods, incorporate them into our system of study, and monitor our study behavior in terms of these methods until they become a part of us.

ELEMENTS OF A STUDY PLAN

The following suggestions can form the basis of a personal action plan for studying that can improve performance while allowing more time for activities other than studying. Samuel Smith (1970) reports that "students can save from one-quarter to one-third of their time if they systematize their efforts in accordance with the chief principles of learning." Each element in this plan has merit, and each should be given consideration, *but the plan should not be used in a mechanical fashion.* Select from these elements and build a personal plan to meet your unique needs. Any plan is better than no plan at all.

Before Studying

I. **A time for study.** Robinson (1970) reports that "students may actually be strangers to their own relative abilities" (p. 5). Most students underestimate the time they need to learn, work, play, and in general enjoy whatever it is they are doing while they are attending college. Planning pays. (A Personal Action Plan on managing time can be found on page 18.)

II. **A place for study.** Study in a well-equipped workplace. Create a situation that will prompt you to go to work quickly, concentrate fully, and perform effectively. A suitable study place should provide:

A. Freedom from external distractions.

1. Low levels of noise and no unexpected noises. Even background music increases inattention and decreases performance. "For everyone, there's a level of distraction which is too low to be noticed and identified as a distraction but high enough to interfere and make you feel bored." (Laird, 1991) For this reason students who study in the library generally outperform those who study in the dorm.

2. Good lighting, free from glare or flicker. Invest in a study lamp—it will last for decades.

3. Infrequent interruptions. Choose a place away from the flow of traffic and out of eye contact with others.

B. Freedom from internal distractions.

1. Internal distractions such as boredom, fear, or confusion may invade even the best workplace. (See IV: A climate for study.) "It's not that boredom is the reason you can't concentrate. Instead, feeling bored lets you know that you're not concentrating the way you should be. It's the way one part of the mind tells the rest of the mind it's not doing a good job." (Laird, 1991)

2. Do not complain about the lack of a "perfect place to study." Just change what you can, and then try to study only at that place. Also, *only* study at that place: eat, daydream, and so on elsewhere.

III. **Equipment for study.** In addition to the text, keep the following on hand: calendar, clock, college dictionary and thesaurus, loose-leaf notebook and scratch paper, pen and pencil, reading stand (to hold your place and free your hands for note taking), bookshelf, and, if possible, typewriter and/or printer and personal computer. Do not allow the lack of needed supplies to become a source of distraction. Restock regularly.

IV. **A climate for study.** There is no substitute for high interest and motivation when it comes to learning something. A positive, confident, and determined attitude toward the task at hand produces a climate in which knowledge and personal satisfaction about.

The Personal Action Plans, as well as class discussions and activities, will give you opportunities to gain self-awareness, clarify values, set goals, and in general reduce the number and intensity of internal distractions that can be so destructive to study. Your skill in studying should grow as the course unfolds.

V. **A unit of study.** How may pages of text should you attempt to cover during one study effort? Some factors to consider when selecting the size of your study unit include the following:

A. The amount attempted should be the most you can permanently learn in one continuous sitting. "The measure of study is the amount permanently learned" (Elliott, 1966).

B. Studying is not like reading; it is *work*. Therefore, fatigue, boredom, and memory span limit the amount of learning to be attempted.

C. Small units are more easily learned than large units.

1. You can make each small unit a piece of a larger, meaningful unit, not an arbitrary chunk.

2. You can overlearn small, manageable units. *Overlearning* means continuing to rehearse and review material that you understand and remember. *Overlearning* is good, because practicing material already learned reduces forgetting.

Time yourself as you study to learn exactly how long it takes you to permanently learn a given number of pages of text. Ehrlich (1976) reports that ten pages an hour is not an uncommon rate.

During Study

Active study, involving your body as well as your mind, will help you to understand and remember what you read. The suggestions that follow are drawn from the work of many study theorists. In turn, all writers on effective study have been influenced by the pioneering work of F. P. Robinson. In 1941 Robinson introduced the famous *SQ3R* (survey, question, read, recite, review) study method:[1] Each of Robinson's elements follow, along with suggestions that confirm and extend his system. **We encourage you to select from these elements and increase your range of study skills.** When you find yourself in your place of study at the appointed time, in a positive mood, surrounded by the proper equipment and supplies, and committed for a limited time to learn and remember a definite unit of work, you have already begun well. Here are some suggestions to help you complete your study task.

SQ3R TECHNIQUES

Steps in Studying

I. **Survey.** Complete the Critical Thinking Issue that appears in the beginning of the chapter. This material is designed to encourage *critical and creative thinking* and the application of *personal values* to the topic under study. Such emotional and mental *involvement* greatly aids retention. Next, read the chapter overview (at the beginning of each part—see page 1, for example), and then focus to learn the five or six major ideas of the chapter and to become involved with its contents. These few minutes provide you with knowledge of the major theme of the chapter, its important ideas, and how they flow together. This knowledge will give you a permanent framework of "tags" or "pegs" around which you can cluster the myriad details that are to come.

---

1. Now known as the *PQ4R* method. Survey has become Preview, and a fourth R, *relate*, has been added.

II. **Question.** This text has been carefully constructed to present meaningful "chunks" of information under three levels of headings. *Convert the heading into a question!* For example, the heading "Diseases of Adaptation" can be quickly turned into the question, What are the diseases of adaptation, and how do they come about? Such questions will direct your reading.

III. **Read.** Now, carefully read the information under the heading *with the intention of answering the question that you have just posed.* This step gives purpose and direction to your reading and makes it possible for you to be selective in what you commit to memory.

As you read:

A. **Actively challenge the material.** Each paragraph, at times each sentence, contains an idea you can support or question from your own background. According to Locke (1975), it is essential that you "make a habit of understanding each concept the first time you encounter it" (p. 23). Then, make an effort to learn the idea immediately. Classify the information, for example, in some way that is meaningful to you and related to the topic under study. Integrate it into what you already know. This creates a rich network of associations that makes the information easier to recall.

B. **Allow time to respond emotionally and intellectually to what you are reading.** What prior experience have you had with the ideas you have just read? Prior exposure often improves our ability to remember new information (Chawarski and Sternberg, 1993). How do you feel about it? What is its significance? What are its implications? Try to take a stand for or against the ideas under discussion. This will get your ego involved and make recall easier.

C. **Involve your whole body in active participation by marking your textbook.** Why mark up a textbook? Because if done correctly, marking identifies important ideas and makes reviewing easier. It is essential that you understand what is important before you mark up your text. *Do not underline as you read.*

    1. Finish reading the entire passage before making any marks.

    2. Wait a brief period to allow for your analysis and reaction.

    3. Mark only the essential idea and its supporting detail.

    4. When taking notes, use your own words, plus key phrases from the text. Symbols and abbreviations are useful, as are color codes. Use marginal notes to emphasize material that your professor has elaborated on in class.

IV. **Recite.** Stop reading at intervals and summarize what you have just read. "Say aloud the full idea in your own words," advises Walter Pauk (1974). Then restate the same idea using the technical terminology of the text.

A. **Why recitation?** Because active responding is a form of self-test.

    1. It keeps you focused on your task.

    2. It gives you knowledge of your progress.

    3. It reduces anxiety.

    4. It allows you to reconstruct the new material, to make it a part of you.

    5. It gives you helpful practice.

B. **How much recitation?** Spend at least half your total study time in active recitation (Pauk, 1974).

C. **What should be recited?** Everything you think important enough to be understood and remembered should be recited. Try to reproduce your recorded notes without looking at them.

D. **What type of recitation?** Every possible type of recitation, using as many of your faculties as possible, should be employed. Speak, write, and act. In your imagination, challenge yourself to recite accurately and completely by playing the role of a debater, teacher, or consultant. After reciting, *revise* your notes and underlinings to make later review more effective.

After Studying

V. **Review.** Do you quickly forget? Most of us forget as much as 50 percent of what we read immediately after reading. After completing your study unit, *critically review* the information you wish to remember. Review is most effective at three times: just after study, just before rest, and just before examinations.

Why is review so necessary? It is essential because:

■ It takes a while after learning for information to be stored in our memories. Immediate recall prevents its being lost prior to storage.

■ Mental review can effectively replace worrying and so reduce anxiety.

■ Review is a form of practice, which promotes retention.

■ Review helps you concentrate on your central task of understanding and remembering.

■ Review gives you knowledge of what you still need to know, suggestions for revision of notes, and directions for rereading.

At the end of each unit of study:

A. **Set high standards for your immediate recall.** Do not try for perfect recall, but demand recall of the main idea and its supporting details. After all, you will never be able to remember what you did not commit to memory in the first place. *Do not confuse understanding what you read as you read it with knowing the material.*

B. **Distribute your practice sessions.** Space your reviews at intervals prior to exams. Eliminate cramming as your only review activity.

Consider these ideas when reviewing:

1. Use mnemonic devices. These are memory tricks. Making the first letters of the names of the Great Lakes into the word HOMES, for example is a mnemonic device for remembering the names of the lakes. You just think of the letter H in the word *home,* and Lake Huron comes to mind, and so on.

2. Use active recall. Do not engage in another session of passive reading or looking at your notes.

3. Practice first without notes, then with notes. Revise your notes and underlinings as needed.

4. Avoid mental mumbling. Recall specifics using complete sentences.

5. State the relationship among the details you have learned under each major topic, along with the main ideas you learned from the chapter overview.

At the end of the study session:

> This is the time for you to reflect, to consolidate your progress and your approach by asking yourself two final questions:
>
> A. **What is the meaning of what I have just learned?**
>
> 1. Does this new information challenge an existing belief that I hold?
> 2. Is this new information based on reliable sources and sound reasoning?
> 3. Is the required new belief consistent with my other beliefs?
> 4. Am I being fair-minded in evaluating this new information?
>
> B. **Have I followed the process for studying that is best for me?**

After an examination:

> After each examination, review your study methods in light of their results so that your knowledge, understanding, and study skills will continue to grow. Learning is a lifelong joy that goes far beyond this textbook or this course.

ELEMENTS OF YOUR SQ3R TEXT

This text has been written with your study needs in mind. If you are aware of its unique style and structure, you can build its features into your study plan. Your *SQ3R* text includes:

1. **A table of contents** to provide you with an outline of the entire work and access to its parts.

2. **A preface and an introduction** to make you aware of the approach, general assumptions, and central values of the authors of the text.

3. **Sectional introductions** to help you focus on the major themes to be explored in the chapters that immediately follow.

4. **Fourteen individual chapters** to present major ideas, principles, and practices in the psychology of human adjustment.

5. **Critical Thinking Issues** at the beginning of each chapter to get you thinking about problems and issues early in your study of each subject area.

6. **Questionnaires** in each chapter to help you to understand yourself better and to give you examples of psychological measures and their application.

7. **Critical Reviews** at several points in each chapter to prime your recall of newly read information, and to encourage you to ask questions, summarize, and understand the material under review.

8. **Cultural Crosscurrents** to emphasize the important role that culture, the learned and shared portion of our existence, plays in our understanding of the psychology of adjustment.

9. **Personal Action Plans** in each chapter to allow you to put theory into practice in areas of your own personal growth. These exercises make it possible for you to actively direct your behavior toward a more satisfying and effective lifestyle. See "Managing Growth" in chapter 1 for an overview of the theory supporting the construction of these exercises.

10. **Selected readings** at the end of each chapter to provide you with resources for greater understanding of the concepts presented.

11. **A conclusion at the end of the text** to relate the information presented in the chapters to the text's central theme—adjustment and growth in a changing world.

12. **An index and a running glossary** to provide you with ready access to authors, subjects, and terms presented in the text. New terms appear in boldface type when introduced in the text, and definitions of all these terms appear in the margin.

13. **References** to give the sources of information cited in the text.

14. **Typefaces** of different colors and sizes to draw attention to important ideas or facts.

15. **Pictures, charts, and graphs** to depict visually information presented in the chapter.

A Study Guide is also available. This workbook provides behavioral objectives, questions for reflection/discussion, student response exercises, vocabulary lists, and practice tests. Students who elect to use the Study Guide have been found to outperform those who do not by significant margins. We strongly recommend its use.

CHAPTER FORMAT

Each chapter contains these elements of the *SQ3R* plan:

SURVEY   1. A **critical thinking issue, focus,** and a **summary** to interest and involve you in the topics to be presented.

QUESTION   2. **Headings** designed to be converted into questions to give purpose and direction to your study. The **summary** is also drawn from the chapter headings, so that you can use it to turn each of the major portions of the chapter into questions for a final self-quiz.

READ   3. **Questionnaires, anecdotes and selected boxes** to provide further insight into the psychology of adjustment. Each *anecdote* describes a fictional incident suggested by the text material, while each selected box is either: (a) a research-based example, (b) a real-life case study, or (c) an insight-provoking exercise. **Cultural Crosscurrents** to help you become more aware of the diversity of human nature and the limitations of single culture research. **Selected readings** are included to encourage you to read further in areas of interest developed in the body of the text.

RECITE   4. **Critical review questions** are built into each major section to prime your memory and to encourage you to think reflectively as you study your text. Research on procedural memory has indicated that priming, a type of procedural memory, occurs whenever the perceptual processing of previously studied information is better than that of nonstudied information. Memory researchers have found that such prior exposure often improves people's performance on perceptual memory tasks (Chawarski & Sternberg, 1993).

5. **Personal Action Plans** that allow you to apply your new understandings to your own individual concerns.

REVIEW   6. A **summary** to draw together the ideas and supporting facts presented in the chapter. **Illustrations** highlight important information or provide human interest.

REFERENCES

Apps, J. W. *Study Skills for Adults Returning to School,* Second Edition. New York: McGraw-Hill, 1982.

Chawarski, M. C., and Sternberg, R. J. Negative priming in word recognition: A contextual effect. *Journal of Experimental Psychology:* General, 122, 195–206, 1993.

Ehrlich, E. *How to Study Better and Get Higher Marks.* New York: Thomas Y. Crowell, 1976.

Elliott, H. C. *The Effective Student: A Constructive Method of Study.* New York: Harper & Row, 1966.

Harris, M. T. *How to be Successful in Reading, Studying, Taking Exams, and Writing in College.* Warminster, PA.: Surrey Press, 1983.

Lock, E. A. *A Guide to Effective Study.* New York: Springer Publishing Company, 1975.

Mahoney, M. J. *Cognition and Behavior Modification.* Cambridge: Mass.: Bollinger, 1974.

Pauk, W. *How to Study in College.* Boston: Houghton Mifflin, 1974.

Robinson, F. P. *Effective Study,* Fourth Edition. New York: Harper & Row, 1970.

Watson, D. L., and Tharp, R. G. *Self-Directed Behavior: Self-Modification for Personal Adjustment.* Monterey, Calif.: Brooks/Cole, 1972.

PHOTO CREDITS

PART ONE

OVERVIEW OF ADJUSTMENT AND GROWTH

art I provides an overview of the psychology of adjustment by looking at the processes of adjustment and growth, at personality theories, and at the concept of self-esteem.

Chapter 1 analyzes the process of adjustment and growth. It examines criteria for the adequacy of any individual response and any adjustment strategy and points out significant differences between the adjustment of humans and that of other living organisms. It also introduces an approach to behavior management that will be extremely useful in your own adjustment and growth.

Chapter 2 provides an overview of personality—one of the fundamental concepts upon which the psychology of adjustment is built. Early in the chapter, we suggest that body, mind, emotions, and behavior are interdependent.

Chapter 3 examines a critically important part of our self-concept—self-esteem, the degree to which we value ourselves or feel worthy. This examination is particularly important because our level of self-esteem may influence our adjustment and growth patterns more than any other personality factor.

1

ADJUSTMENT AND GROWTH

Chapter Outline

FOCUS

Although all of us would perhaps agree that personal adjustment and growth are requirements for effective living, we might disagree on what constitutes good adjustment and growth. Many questions might be raised and debated. For example, can good adjustment and growth ever include self-deception? Should good adjustment and growth be measured only in relation to the self (as opposed to other people or the environment)? Is personal happiness always a criterion by which good adjustment and growth can be measured? Are good adjustment and growth states of being or ongoing processes? Can we speak of good adjustment and growth without the intrusion of value judgments? Are there universal standards by which good adjustment and growth can be measured?

In this chapter we will consider these and other questions. We will focus on adjustment and growth in general, on the adjustment and growth of living organisms, and, most particularly, on the adjustment and growth of human beings.

ADJUSTMENT AND GROWTH

adjustment   the individual's response to the physical, psychological, and social demands of the self, other people, and the environment

growth   the process by which the individual changes his or her thoughts, feelings, or behaviors regarding the self, others, or the environment

Adjustment refers to the individual's response to the physical, psychological, and social demands of the self, other people, and the environment. Thus, adjustment is concerned with how we respond to stimuli. For example, learning to meet the demands of a college environment is a matter of adjustment.

Growth refers to the individual's changing his or her thoughts, feelings, or behaviors regarding the self, others, or the environment. Growth involves internal change. Learning to control my temper so that I may improve the quality of my interpersonal relationships is a matter of growth.

The concepts of *adjustment* and *growth* are complementary, but each has a different emphasis. Adjustment emphasizes the impact of the environment on our attempt to meet our needs. Growth emphasizes internal motivation. We adjust because we sense that environmental demands will overwhelm us if we do not adjust; we grow because we are not satisfied with our responses to ourselves, others, or the environment.

> Both Sam and Helen were shocked to find that their fifteen-year-old son, Michael, had become addicted to cocaine. What had happened? They knew this kind of thing occurred in other families, but they never believed it could happen in theirs. How could Michael have done such a thing?
>
> After the initial shock, they placed Michael in a drug counseling program to help him give up drugs and cope effectively with his problems. At the same time, Sam and Helen joined another therapy group designed to help them deal with Michael and their feelings toward him.
>
> Today, five years later, Michael has completely given up his drug habit and is well on his way to becoming an honors student at the state university. He has learned from his mistakes and is determined not to make the same errors again.
>
> Sam and Helen are trying to provide Michael with as much support as they can. They are proud of his achievements and have accepted completely the financial burden of seeing him through school. Deep down, however, both of them fear that he will again turn to drugs. Sam and Helen have adjusted; Michael has grown.

Evaluating Adjustment and Growth

value   an idea of something being intrinsically desirable. Examples: honesty, freedom, beauty

Scholars have not been able to agree on a universal standard by which to evaluate adjustment and growth. Rather, they have adopted a variety of standards, each reflecting the theoretical orientations and **values** of its proponents. For example, Sigmund Freud viewed good adjustment as the individual's effective use of self-deception to satisfy simultaneously the demands of his or her desires and conscience. Carl Rogers, on the other hand, saw self-deception as maladjustment, because it interferes with the fulfillment of one's potential. Behaviorists such as B. F. Skinner tend to view good adjustment from a third perspective. They emphasize learned behavior that allows the individual to cope successfully with situational demands.

There are many other conceptions of good adjustment and growth. Those of several scholars—including Freud, Rogers, and Skinner—are dealt with in other chapters of this book. The important point here is that each scholar's conception rests upon his or her theoretical orientation and values.

It is impossible to evaluate good adjustment without making value judgments. In fact, the very use of the word *good* tells us that value judgments are being made. That, however, is not a condemnation of any definition of good adjustment and growth, for value judgments may be based on logic. For example, if, as Freud suggested, there are inevitable conflicts between the demands of desires and conscience, and if these conflicts produce great (and potentially psychologically disabling) tensions for the individual, then self-deception (which can reduce the tensions) can only be defined as good adjustment. This is not to say that Freud necessarily liked the idea of lying to oneself. Rather, he saw self-deception as the only means available to avoid maladjustment. Hence, in Freud's view, self-deception must be valued for a logical reason. In like manner, other scholars have come to hold their values for similar, logical reasons.

Social Values and Adjustment

Although it appears true that some conceptions of good adjustment are based on logically derived value judgments, it also seems true that others are based on socially and culturally determined values. We in the United States, for example, tend to place great emphasis on winning through competition. Thus, it would not be unusual to find Americans defining good adjustment in the following terms: The more one is able to compete successfully, the better adjusted one is. Other cultures, however, may place little or no emphasis on competitive prowess. The Zuni Indians, for instance, do not allow habitual winners to run in their footraces. Therefore, when considering the adequacy of an adaptive response, we must consider social and cultural factors as well as individual needs.

CRITICAL THINKING ISSUE
Happiness and Personal Adjustment

Happiness is the primary standard by which personal adjustment should be measured.

Happiness is not the primary standard by which personal adjustment should be measured.

Well-adjusted persons are happy persons. They enjoy life, whether or not difficult circumstances prevail. They have developed the ability to feel good about themselves and to look with optimism to the future, regardless of the circumstances.

Well-adjusted persons are not always happy persons. They do not enjoy life when difficult circumstances prevail. They have developed the ability to accept negative as well as positive feelings, depending on the circumstances.

I take the position that:

Being "number 1" might be important to many, but some cultures do not place such great emphasis on winning.

A few of the values Americans have traditionally used as barometers of good adjustment are trust, self-reliance, self-control, personal happiness, and an ability to get along well with others. However, living up to these values would not necessarily make a person well adjusted. A consideration of cultural and social factors may be useful in making judgments concerning adjustment, but individual needs must be considered, too. For example, although it may generally be true that Americans value trust in others, in some situations, a display of trust could be maladjustive for the individual. (Would you, for instance, trust a stranger with your life's savings?) Thus, a person who *never* displays trust in others might be considered somewhat maladjusted from the American point of view, but a person who *always* displays trust might be considered equally maladjusted.

Critical Review 1

1. Scholars have not been able to agree on a universal standard by which to evaluate adjustment. T F

2. When considering adjustment, behaviorists emphasize the role of learning. T F

3. It is easy to decide what comprises good adjustment without making value judgments. T F

4. One must take into consideration social and cultural factors as well as individual needs when considering the adequacy of an adaptive response. T F

5. A person who never displays trust in others is remarkably well adjusted from the American point of view. T F

6. How are adjustment and growth different from one another?

7. Why is it impossible to evaluate good adjustment without making value judgments?

8. How do social and cultural values affect personal adjustment?

$\mathcal{Q}uestionnaire$ *Ranking Your Values*

Below is a list of eighteen values. The list was made up by Milton Rokeach, who has surveyed Americans to find out the relative importance of these values to them.

After considering each of these values, determine which of the eighteen is most important to you and write a "1" in the space provided in the column. Then determine your next most important value and write a "2" in the appropriate space. Continue this process until you have ranked all eighteen values. You may then compare your rankings to those of a survey sample that appear on page 17.

Value

A Comfortable Life   *a prosperous life*   _____

An Exciting Life   *a stimulating, active life*   _____

A Sense of Accomplishment   *lasting contribution*   _____

A World at Peace   *free of war and conflict*   _____

A World of Beauty   *beauty of nature and the arts*   _____

Equality   *brotherhood, equal opportunity for all*   _____

Family Security   *taking care of loved ones*   _____

Freedom   *independence, free choice*   _____

Happiness   *contentedness*   _____

Inner Harmony   *freedom from inner conflict*   _____

Mature Love   *sexual and spiritual intimacy*   _____

National Security   *protection from attack*   _____

Pleasure   *an enjoyable, leisurely life*   _____

Salvation   *saved, eternal life*   _____

Self-respect   *self-esteem*   _____

Social Recognition   *respect, admiration*   _____

True Friendship   *close companionship*   _____

Wisdom   *a mature understanding of life*   _____

SOURCE: Copyright © 1967 by Milton Rokeach. Permission to reproduce granted by Holgren Tests, 873 Persimmon Avenue, Sunnyvale, CA 94087.

ADJUSTMENT AND INDIVIDUAL NEEDS

Perhaps the most basic criterion we can use to judge the adequacy of any response is its ultimate survival value. Does the behavior contribute to the ultimate survival of either the individual or his or her gene pool? If so, it may be considered adjustive; if not, it may be considered maladjustive.

In this view, one must take into account not only what an individual is doing at the moment but the long-term implications of this behavior. Delaying, avoiding, distorting, or retreating from reality may seem dysfunctional at first glance but may ultimately ensure survival. For example, running away from danger might prove to be a much better response than facing up to it.

By analyzing the transactions that actually take place between the individual and the environment in the light of ultimate survival value, we begin to real-

Many people remember the Great Depression of the 1930s as a time of economic compromise.

ize that many situations can be dealt with successfully only through compromise or even resignation. "Events may occur that require us to give in, relinquish things we would have liked, perhaps change direction or restrict the range of our activities. We may have no recourse but to accept a permanent impoverishment of our lives and try to make the best of it" (White, 1976, p. 20). In this view, compromise becomes essential for survival.

Growth

Survival value is not the only criterion by which to judge an individual response. Another fundamental criterion is personal growth. Does the behavior contribute to the personal growth of the organism? If so, then it may be considered adjustive; if not, it may be considered maladjustive.

One aspect of growth is the expansion of the organism at the expense of its environment. That is, a growing organism is constantly taking materials from outside itself and transforming them into parts of its own. This expansion may be physical, like the bodily growth that takes place when a person eats food. It may be psychological, like the mental growth that takes place when a person learns from experience. Or it may be social, like the interpersonal growth that takes place when a person acquires communication skills.

Autonomy

autonomy   self-governance

Another aspect of growth is **autonomy** (self-governance). Living organisms are to a degree governed from within. Environmental forces may impinge on them, but they have an internal tendency to resist these forces. In this sense, growth becomes the movement toward an increase in autonomy.

Thus, all adjustment involves a kind of compromise—an attempt to balance the effects of internal and external demands so that personal growth as well as survival is achieved. Note that adjustive compromise does not mean abandoning everything we believe is important simply in order to survive. A strategic retreat today may ensure the drive forward tomorrow. Note also that adjustive compromise not only permits survival and personal growth but ensures that both the individual and the environment will be changed as a result of their interaction.

> Susan is pleased with herself. At twenty-eight she has a challenging job, her own apartment, money in the bank, and a variety of creative pursuits. In short, she is managing her life well. However, things have not always gone so smoothly.
>
> Just a few years ago Susan was caught in the seeming dilemma so many young people face these days. At twenty-two she had been accepted into the law school at the university in her hometown. Her parents, who were willing to pay the expenses for her schooling, insisted that she live at home in order to save money.
>
> Susan, an adult by virtually any standard, wanted the personal freedom that typically accompanies adulthood. Her parents, on the other hand, wanted her to follow the somewhat rigid guidelines they had set for her. If she pressed for personal freedom, she would lose the financial backing she so desperately needed to get through school. If she submitted to the guidelines, she would retain the financial backing but lose her personal freedom.
>
> After much soul searching she decided to accept her parents' financial backing and their guidelines as well. In the long run it appears she chose correctly, for today she has the benefits of both her education and her personal freedom.

ADJUSTMENT STRATEGIES

A Choice of Strategies

We can imagine few situations in which no choice among responses is available. In essence, each potential choice may be viewed as a strategy of adjustment, and the adequacy of each may be judged according to certain criteria. Consider, for example, the following situation. You are alone at night, camping out in a tent. You are fairly deep in the woods, and, to your knowledge, there are no people within shouting distance. You hear a strange noise coming from some nearby bushes. What are your potential adjustment strategies?

One strategy is to approach the bushes directly. In that case, an immediate confrontation with whatever is making the noise is likely. Another strategy is to look closely and listen carefully to find out what is making the noise, while at the same time maintaining some distance so that an immediate confrontation is less likely. A third strategy is to turn and run away to avoid confrontation altogether. A fourth strategy is to hide quietly in your tent, thus also avoiding confrontation.

Evaluating Strategies

Three criteria are particularly useful in judging the adequacy of an adjustment strategy. The criteria involve the strategy's value in helping the organism: (1) to secure adequate information about the environment, (2) to maintain the internal conditions necessary for action and for processing information, and (3) to maintain autonomy, or freedom of movement (White, 1976, p. 20). Generally all three criteria must be met for an organism to interact successfully with the environment, and all must be met simultaneously. Let's consider each of the criteria and then apply them to the four adjustment strategies suggested in the preceding example.

It seems obvious that the organism must have adequate information about the environment to respond adequately. Certainly all of us recognize that action based on too little information can be disastrous. But too much information may be just as harmful. The flooding of our senses with information often leads to confusion that, at least temporarily, immobilizes us. Thus, behavior geared to obtain more information when we do not have enough and behavior geared to cut down on information when we are receiving too much are both adjustive.

Maintaining the internal conditions necessary for action and for processing information is also critical. If, for example, you become so anxious about your performance on your final biology exam that you cannot concentrate when taking the test, you may flunk the test even though you know the material well. Hence, behavior such as remaining calm in the midst of an intense situation is adjustive.

It is also of critical importance to maintain autonomy and freedom of movement. How can any organism adjust if it cannot move? Generally, behaviors that allow the greatest freedom of movement are the most functional, provided they do not interfere with either the securing of adequate information about the environment or the maintaining of the internal conditions necessary for action and for processing information.

Now let us apply these three criteria to the example given earlier. The first adjustment strategy mentioned in the example is to approach the bushes directly on hearing the strange noise. From the standpoint of securing adequate information, this appears to be a good strategy. It also seems to imply that you, the actor, are relatively calm. Remember, however, that all three criteria must be applied simultaneously. From the standpoint of maintaining autonomy, this appears a poor strategy, because it restricts rather than enhances freedom of movement. Can you imagine approaching the bushes only to find a grizzly bear waiting for you?

The second adjustment strategy is looking and listening while maintaining some distance. This appears to be a good strategy, because it seems to meet all three criteria. You are obtaining needed information, remaining calm, and keeping options open.

The third strategy is to turn and run away. Clearly, this is a poor choice. You do not have adequate information, and you have already panicked. The fourth strategy—to sit quietly and hide—is also poor. You have not obtained adequate information, and you have become totally immobile.

Critical Review 2

1. Two criteria by which to judge the adequacy of any response are its ultimate _____ value and its contribution to the personal _____ of the organism.

2. A particularly important process that leads not only to the survival but to the growth of organisms is _____.

3. One aspect of growth is the _____ of the organism; another is movement toward an increase in _____.

4. It is useful to think of each potential choice by the organism as a _____ of adjustment.

5. The three criteria for judging the adequacy of an adjustment strategy involve: (1) securing _____ _____ , (2) maintaining _____ necessary for action and for processing information, and (3) maintaining _____ , or freedom of _____ .

6. Why is compromise necessary for survival?
7. How is autonomy related to growth?
8. What criteria are useful in judging the adequacy of adjustment strategies?

PSYCHOLOGICAL AND SOCIAL ADJUSTMENT AND GROWTH

Adjustment and growth occur on biological, psychological, and social levels. In the preceding section we focused primarily on biological adjustment as we applied adjustment criteria to specific behaviors and strategies. The discussion was universal in that the principles given may be applied not only to humans but to animals as well. In this section we will consider human psychological and social adjustment and growth.

Human Adjustment and Growth

Human adjustment and growth are different from those of animals with regard to three significant dimensions: time, language, and morality. Humans have the unique ability to relate to events in terms of the past and the future as well as the present. We can make judgments about today's behavior in the light of goals we hope someday to attain. Similarly, we can use yesterday's successes or failures as standards by which to judge today's or even tomorrow's behavior. Thus, effective time management, the subject of this chapter's Personal Action Plan, (see p.   ) is crucial to human adjustment and growth. We have the ability not only to sort out current information and respond to the current situation but also to set goals, to plan actions, to act in accordance with those plans, and to evaluate actions in terms of their effectiveness in achieving our goals.

CULTURAL CROSSCURRENTS
Teaching For Broad or Narrow Purposes?

Sometimes our best intentions go unappreciated when trying to operate in a culturally different environment. While living in Ethiopia during the 1960s, the author met two Peace Corps teachers assigned to a secondary school in Makele located in Tigre Provence. Even though both volunteers were well-trained, enthusiastic, and highly motivated teachers, they found themselves in the center of a controversy with their students. In fact, matters became so serious that the students went on strike, refusing to attend classes until certain changes were made in the classroom. The communication problems occurred because the teachers brought their own set of cultural assumptions about teaching into their classrooms in Ethiopia. Like any good educator in the United States, these two Peace Corps teachers wanted to go beyond their subject matter by teaching certain "carryover" skills such as critical thinking, debate skills, written forms of expression, and the capacity to see rela-

tionships between phenomena. In their own university training they had learned well the value of logic, the Socratic method of teaching, rational thought, the scientific method, and the need to seek reasons behind actions. Unfortunately, they assumed, quite uncritically, that these values were equally appropriate in northern Ethiopia. But the Ethiopian students came from a vastly different cultural tradition that does not necessarily value individual intellectual development. The students, confronted with highly competitive national exams for entrance into the university, wanted the teachers to stick as closely as possible to the set curriculum so as to maximize their chances of scoring well on these standardized exams.

SOURCE: Taken from G. Ferraro, *Cultural Anthropology: An Applied Perspective*. St. Paul, MN: West, 1992, p. 67.

The language capabilities of humans allow us to accumulate, store, and transmit an enormous amount of information of many types and qualities. We can express opinions ("I believe it is going to rain"), feelings ("I love you"), and facts ("George Washington was the first president of the United States"). We can talk about something without it being present ("Last summer I visited the Grand Canyon, which was an awesome experience"), and we can refer to entities whose very existence cannot be objectively verified—that is, known to our senses ("God is omnipresent"). Animals may communicate with one another on a rudimentary level, but none can begin to compare with humans with regard to length, depth, and breadth of language use.

As human beings, we also are capable of making moral judgments; we differentiate between good and evil. The culture of every human society contains a code of ethics that guides and directs behavior. Through the socialization process, we learn and come to accept an ethical code and, eventually, to experience guilt when we violate it. No one has been able to demonstrate that animals have such moral capabilities.

Thus, time, language, and morality provide human beings with a world of experience eminently larger than that of animals, and to the degree that our experiential world is larger, our adjustment and growth strategies are more intricate and complex.

Human Adjustment and Growth Strategies

Securing Information   Animals are restricted to their immediate cognitive field when searching for information, but humans can secure information about things even when those things are not present. Thus, a person may obtain information that will help him or her solve an interpersonal problem he or she is having at work by talking with other people, by reading a book, or even by taking a course in the psychology of adjustment. When evaluating human adjustment and growth, we must consider the variety of informational strategies available as well as how well those strategies are being carried out.

self-esteem   the degree to which one values oneself and feels necessary and useful in the world

Internal Conditions   Human beings must maintain and, if possible, enhance their level of **self-esteem.** However, no one has been able to demonstrate clearly that animals have a conscious idea of who and what they are, much less a need to maintain a positive evaluation of themselves. Hence, self-esteem is a factor that separates humans from animals.

defensive behavior (defense) an attempt to cope through some form of self-deception. For Freud (see chapter 2), the unconscious ego process by which we reduce tension from moral anxiety by deceiving ourselves

When a person begins to believe that he or she is incapable, unfit, or unworthy, that person invariably adopts one of two mental postures: emotional depression or **defensive behavior** (an attempt to cope through some form of self-deception). Either is likely to upset the person's internal equilibrium to the point that efficiency in both action and information processing is impaired.

David had been working at the firm for only a few months when the United Way campaign was launched. Because the firm was so small, it did not take long before each person knew the amount of every other person's pledge.

Unfortunately, David could not afford to pledge as much as most of the others because he had recently lost money on several bad investments in the stock market. All of this left him in a mild state of depression and, in an attempt to convince himself that he really was just as good as the next person, David made the largest pledge of all.

Moreover, the ramifications of maintaining self-esteem are so wide that any adaptive strategy that fails to take it into account is unlikely to succeed.

> Almost any situation that is not completely familiar, even casual and superficial contacts with new people, even discussing the day's news, can touch off internal questions like, "What sort of impression am I making?" "How well am I dealing with this?" "What kind of a person am I showing myself to be?" When self-esteem is tender or when the situation is strongly challenging, such questions, even if only vaguely felt, can lead to anxiety, shame, or guilt with their threat of further disorganization (White, 1976, p. 31).

Autonomy or Freedom of Movement   Our strategy for maintaining autonomy, or freedom of movement, is unique in two ways: (1) it involves an *expanded time factor,* and (2) it involves powerful *psychological* and *social factors.* One aspect of the expanded time factor is its *future dimension.* We can plan for the future in such a way that we are likely to have more options. It is quite possible, for example, that you are now selecting and preparing for some future occupation. Your planning can take into account projected income and job opportunities, as well as the anticipated capacity of a particular job to meet your growth needs and/or to be a stepping stone to other jobs that will meet those needs.

Another aspect of the expanded time factor may be called the *duration dimension*—the "things-take-time" concept. In many instances, adjustment strategies are not devised instantly but develop and change over time. For example, grieving for a time immediately following the death of a loved one may enhance adjustment more than attempting too quickly to resume one's usual activities. A person can move more effectively toward greater freedom of

A period of grief immediately following the death of a loved one may facilitate adjustment and growth.

movement in the long run by consciously choosing less freedom of movement at the moment.

morality   a concern with good as opposed to evil

The psychological and social factors related to autonomy, or freedom of movement, are connected with self-esteem and **morality.** If our self-esteem is to be high, we must believe our actions are correct and/or moral. Conversely, if we believe our actions are incorrect and/or immoral, our self-esteem will be low. Generally, high self-esteem is a liberating factor that leads to greater autonomy, and low self-esteem is a debilitating factor that leads to less autonomy.

Because societies define correct and moral behavior in terms of their rules, it would appear that all we need do is conform to the rules of our society to attain high self-esteem and, thereby, autonomy. The problem here, though, is that each person has the ability to define morality on his or her own terms, regardless of what society preaches. Suppose, for instance, that your society had evolved as its major criterion of personal success the acquisition of material goods (that is, a successful person is one who has accumulated a lot of things, particularly expensive things). But suppose that material goods hold little value for you and that you define personal success in terms of qualities such as honesty, integrity, fidelity, and so on. (In other words, you define a successful person as one who is honest, regardless of whether he or she is wealthy.) In this case, it appears that you would attain high self-esteem and autonomy by *not* conforming to your society's rules.

Autonomy, however, is not attained merely by either blindly conforming to or steadfastly deviating from society's rules. Rather, autonomy is attained by making independent judgments in light of personal needs. In some instances, these judgments may coincide with the rules; in others, they may not. In any case, the chronic nonconformist is no more autonomous than the person who always conforms.

Critical Review 3

1. Human adjustment is different from that of animals with regard to three significant dimensions: time, language, and morality. T F

2. Only humans transmit information from one member of the species to another. T F

3. Many animals seem to plan their futures. T F

4. Humans are different from animals in that they maintain and, if possible, enhance their level of self-esteem. T F

5. Adjustment strategies often develop and change over time. T F

6. It is necessary to become a social deviant to attain autonomy. T F

7. How are human adjustment and growth different from those of animals?

8. What is the relationship between self-esteem and adjustment and growth?

9. How is autonomy related to self-esteem and morality?

MANAGING GROWTH

Thus far, this chapter has provided an overview of the processes of adjustment and growth. It has discussed the general nature of adjustment and growth and the relationship of adjustment to both social values and individual needs. It has also dealt with adjustment strategies and human psychological and social adjustment and growth. Now we will consider a specific approach you may use to manage your own growth.

ABCs of Behavior

The approach called the **ABCs of behavior** comes from Watson and Tharp (1993), and it is their version of *cognitive-behavioral theory*. Let's begin with *B*, your behavior itself. This category includes everything you think, feel, or do. Eye blinks, hunger pangs, fear responses, and problem solving are all behaviors. Such behaviors can be observed or inferred, and some can be evaluated *by you* as: (1) excessive—too much eating, worrying, daydreaming, and so on; (2) deficient—too little studying, smiling, exercising, and so on; and/or (3) inappropriate—eating the wrong foods, mistaking intentions, talking negatively about yourself, and so on.

The approach holds that all behavior comes under the immediate control of *C*, its *consequences*. Consider the effect your behavior has on you and your environment. Pleasurable consequences strengthen or maintain behavior. For example, the smile that evokes a warm hug will likely be repeated, as well as the smile that softens another person's anger.

In the long run, however, our behavior comes under the control of *A*, its *antecedents*. Antecedents—stimuli present just prior to the behavior being emitted—may evoke or maintain that behavior. For instance, hearing a strange noise while camping in the woods might cause us to "freeze." In time, control may shift from immediate consequences to *anticipated consequences*, which depend on our perception of the situation in which the behavior unfolds. Our memories allow us to interpret present situations in terms of the past. Thus, we come to respond, or behave, in terms of what we expect to happen, based on our beliefs about past events. For example, we may hear a noise, believe it signals danger (it could be the grizzly bear), and resort to screaming because we have come to view ourselves as too slow and weak to run or fight. In this way our behavior may come under the control of its antecedents.

Knowing about the *ABC* approach can help you direct your own behavior in three ways. First, it explains why you behave as you do (the *A* and *C* parts). Second, it gives you three specific areas (*A, B,* and *C*) to consider when creating a plan for changing your behavior. Third, it allows you to regulate your motivations, beliefs, and actions by monitoring your *ABCs* in specific situations and altering them in terms of your progress toward whatever goals you have selected.

Applying the ABCs

Suppose you are dissatisfied with your excessive display of anger. You keep a record of your outbursts (*behavior*) and discover that they occur under certain conditions (*antecedents*) at home: in the evening; in the presence of your parents; after much negative thinking about what you see as the unfair pressure your parents are placing upon you; and during discussions of household duties or social activities. Moreover, you find that your anger supports your negative thoughts, relieves your tension, intimidates your parents, and frequently helps you to get your way—even though it destroys the warmth and closeness between you and your parents and leads to remorse (*consequences*).

You decide to attack this unwanted anger on three fronts: (1) *To change antecedents,* you reduce the stimuli that trigger your anger by avoiding certain topics in the evening and by **cognitively restructuring** your thoughts to exclude

ABCs of behavior the antecedents of behavior, the behavior itself, and the consequences of behavior. These are determined by a critical analysis of the situation

cognitive restructuring altering thoughts that needlessly produce negative emotions and inappropriate behaviors

incompatible response a response that prevents unwanted behavior from being emitted. For example, you cannot drink water and inhale smoke at the same time

contingency a specified relationship between a given response and the occurrence of a reinforcer. If, then statements are contingency statements

reinforcement the process by which a perceived reward is associated with an emitted behavior. The perceived reward is called a reinforcer

the notion that your parents are placing excessive pressure on you. (2) *To change behaviors*, you select a response that is **incompatible** with anger—such as a sincere compliment—and use the evening appearance of your parents as a signal for you to search for such a compliment and deliver it sincerely. (3) *To change consequences*, you arrange (contract) with yourself to make some reward **contingent** on your carrying out A and B above. For example, you may grant yourself one half hour of free time if, and only if, you avoid excessive negative thoughts during the evening. Further, you may grant yourself one half hour of listening to your favorite music *if*, and only if, that evening you notice something positive about your parents and communicate that observation to them.

As you gain skill and success in directing your behavior, you will raise the standards by which you judge success (you will strive for even less frequent, less intense, and less prolonged anger, for example), and you will change your earned pleasures (**reinforcers**) to include more self-praise. You will also increase the number of times you must meet your standards before you may earn and consume your reinforcers. In this way you can establish a new, less angry pattern of interacting with your parents, and more satisfying evenings will emerge as easy as *ABC*.

Critical Review 4

1. Watson and Tharp call their approach to cognitive-behavioral theory the _____.

2. This approach holds that all behavior comes under the *immediate* control of its _____.

3. Watson and Tharp maintain, however, that in the long run our behavior comes under the control of its _____.

4. Problem behaviors may be evaluated as _____, _____, or _____.

5. Explain the ABCs of behavior. Provide examples in your explanation.

SUMMARY

■ Adjustment refers to the individual's response to the physical, psychological, and social demands of the self, other people, and the environment. Growth refers to the individual's changing of his or her thoughts, feelings, or behaviors regarding the self, others, or the environment. Thus, adjustment emphasizes the impact of the environment, while growth emphasizes internal motivation.

■ There is no universal standard by which to evaluate adjustment. Scholars have adopted a variety of standards, each reflecting the theoretical orientations and values of its proponents.

■ When judging the adequacy of an adaptive response, we must consider social and cultural factors as well as individual needs. Perhaps the most basic criterion we can use to judge the adequacy of a response is its ultimate survival value.

■ Another fundamental criterion by which to judge a response is its contribution to the personal growth of the organism.

■ Growth includes both the expansion of the organism at the expense of its environment and its movement toward an increase in autonomy (self-governance).

■ We may view each potential adjustive choice as a strategy of adjustment, and the adequacy of each may be judged according to whether it helps the organism (1) to secure adequate information about the environment, (2) to maintain the internal conditions necessary for action and for processing information, and (3) to maintain autonomy, or freedom of movement. Generally, all three criteria must be met for an organism to interact successfully with the environment, and all must be met simultaneously.

■ Human adjustment is different from that of animals with regard to three significant dimensions: time, language, and morality. As a result, our world of experience is eminently larger than that of animals, and our adjustment strategies more complex.

■ Unlike animals, humans (1) are not restricted to their immediate cognitive field when securing information, (2) must maintain and, if possible, enhance their level of self-esteem, and (3) can consciously set goals and modify long-range adjustment strategies.

■ The autonomous person is one who makes independent judgments in the light of his or her own needs, regardless of what society dictates.

■ We can manage our own personal growth. A useful approach to self-management is Watson an Tharp's ABCs of behavior.

SELECTED READINGS

Glasser, W. *Take Effective Control of Your Life.* New York: Harper & Row, 1984. This book contains practical suggestions for meeting one's internal demands and, thus, taking control of one's life.

Grasha, A. F. *Practical Applications of Psychology.* Boston: Little, Brown, 1983. A consideration of how psychology can be applied practically.

Lauer, R. H., and Lauer, J. C. *Watersheds.* Boston: Little, Brown, 1988. An examination of several life crises as opportunities for growth.

Stanovich, K. E. *Thinking Straight about Psychology,* 3rd ed. New York: Harper Collins, 1992. A book that will help you to think critically about psychology.

Stock, G. *The Book of Questions.* New York: Workman Publishing, 1985. A consideration of questions that may stimulate growth.

Zimbardo, P. G. "The Age of Indifference." *Psychology Today* (August 1980): 71–76. A noted psychologist's warning of the destructive influence, both to the individual and to society, of the trend toward isolation and indifference.

REFERENCES

Ball-Rokeach, S. J., Rokeach, M., and Grube, J. W. "The Great American Values Test: Can Television Alter Basic Beliefs?" *Psychology Today* (November 1984): 34–41.

Watson, D. L., and Tharp, R. G. *Self-directed Behavior: Self-modification for Personal Adjustment,* 6th ed. Pacific Grove, CA: Brooks/Cole, 1993.

White, R. W. "Strategies of Adaptation: An Attempt at Systematic Description." In *Human Adaptation: Coping with Life Crises,* edited by R. H. Moos, 131–149. Lexington, MA: D. C. Heath, 1976.

■ *Questionnaire Scoring Key*

Ranking Your Values—Comparison with National Sample

A national sample of adults responded to the values questionnaire with the following rankings:

Family security 1
A world at peace 2
Freedom 3
Self-respect 4
Happiness 5
Widsom 6
A sense of accomplishment 7
A comfortable life 8
True friendship 9
Salvation 10
Inner harmony 11
Equality 12
National security 13
Mature love 14
A world of beauty 15
Pleasure 16
An exciting life 17
Social recognition 18

How do these rankings compare with yours?

SOURCE: Ball-Rokeach, Rokeach, and Grube, 1984, p. 40.

■ *Answers to Critical Review Questions*

Critical Review 1 1. T   **2.** T   **3.** F   **4.** T   **5.** F
Critical Review 2 1. survival, growth   **2.** compromise   **3.** expansion, autonomy
   4. strategy   **5.** adequate information; internal conditions; autonomy, movement
Critical Review 3 1. T   **2.** F   **3.** F   **4.** T   **5.** T   **6.** F
Critical Review 4 1. ABCs of behavior   **2.** consequences   **3.** antecedents   **4.** excessive, deficient, inappropriate

PERSONAL ACTION PLAN
Time Management

Perhaps the most practical first step in meeting the demands of college is to construct a time schedule, a budget of your time. In college you spend less time in class, and class time counts little toward your final grade. What does count is performance on tests, papers, and examinations. Therefore, study time really counts. You should consider constructing a formal plan for allocating your time, because such a plan frees you from worry and makes time for pleasurable pursuits. It also improves your performance. The very act of planning encourages you to:

■ Focus attention on your future.

■ Reflect on your present values.

■ Select short-, intermediate-, and long-term goals.

■ Establish priorities among your competing goals.

■ Give consideration to obligations arising from non-college demands.

■ Set realistic standards for work, play, and study.

   Carrying out a planned schedule provides many benefits, too:

■ It gets you started.

■ It keeps you busy on task-centered behavior rather than occupied with worry or daydreams.

■ It allows you to do one thing at a time.

■ It keeps you progressing toward your selected goals.

■ It systematically varies your activities.

■ It prepares you for special events, from exams to weekends.

Step I. Time Log

If you wish to construct a time schedule for use during this term, it is best to begin with a realistic notion of how you are now spending your time. For one week record your actions in the time frame in which they occur. Be complete and accurate.

   After finishing your time log, complete the classification of time log data and the analysis of time log classification below.

Name _____ Class _____ Date _____

Hours	Monday	Tuesday	Wednesday	Thursday	Friday	Saturday	Sunday
AM 7:00							
7:30							
8:00							
8:30							
9:00							
9:30							

Name _____ Class _____ Date _____

Hours	Monday	Tuesday	Wednesday	Thursday	Friday	Saturday	Sunday
AM 10:00							
10:30							
11:00							
11:30							
12:00							
PM 12:30							
1:00							
1:30							
2:00							
2:30							
3:00							
3:30							
4:00							
4:30							
5:00							
5:30							
6:00							
6:30							
7:00							
7:30							
8:00							
8:30							
9:00							
9:30							
10:00							
10:30							
11:00							

Name _____ Class _____ Date _____

Hours	Monday	Tuesday	Wednesday	Thursday	Friday	Saturday	Sunday
PM 11:30							
12:00							
AM 12:30							
1:00							
1:30							
2:00							

Step II. Classification of Time Log Data.

Using the information contained in your time log, fill in the hours spent in the following pursuits.

A. Fixed obligations
   1. Class and lab   _____
   2. Job   _____
   3. Transportation   _____
   4. Required meetings and so on   _____
B. Variable obligations
   1. Individual needs
      a. Meals   _____
      b. Sleep   _____
      c. Rest   _____
      d. Exercise   _____
      e. Grooming   _____
      f. Other   _____
   2. Scholastic needs
      a. Study   _____
      b. Review   _____
      c. Research   _____
      d. Writing   _____
      e. Discussion   _____
   3. Social needs
      a. Family   _____
      b. Friends   _____
      c. Others   _____
C. Obligation-free time
   1. Recreation   _____

   2. New interests   _____
   3. Travel   _____
   4. Other   _____
                    Total   _____

The total hours should equal 168, the number of hours in a week.

Step III. Analysis of Time Log Classification

Use your experience and the results of your time log classification to make reasonable evaluations of your present use of time.

Analyze the results by answering these questions.

What hours were spent in activities you value highly or consider essential? _____
_____

What hours were spent in activities that constitute a waste of your time? _____
_____

What hours were insufficient to complete what needed to be done? _____
_____

Record possible alternative allocations of time.

List activities that are low on your priority list and could be omitted or reduced. _____
_____

List activities that were omitted from the week's schedule but are important to you. _____
_____

List activities that could replace the wasteful or less essential activities. _____
_____

Now prepare your own time schedule.

Step IV. Construction of a Time Schedule

Using your analysis of the time log, construct a tentative schedule for your time this term. Consider these suggestions.

A. Keep study hours close to class periods. Schedule study time before class if you are expected to perform (class recitation or examination) and after class if the professor is expected to perform (class lecture or demonstration).

B. Allocate specific hours for each subject, not simply study time.

C. Maximize the use of daylight hours and minimize the use of dead hours when you are least alert.

D. Give attention to what follows what. One subject can interfere with the learning or remembering of another.

E. Allow ample time for eating, resting, exercising, and sleeping. Know your physical needs and respect them.

F. Schedule a quiet review period just before sleep.

G. Build in spare time each day and week to allow for any opportunity or emergency that may arise.

H. List points you want to keep in mind while constructing your time schedule.

1. _____
2. _____
3. _____
4. _____
5. _____
6. _____
7. _____
8. _____
9. _____
10. _____
11. _____

A workable time schedule contains three parts. The first is a calendar covering the entire semester and listing important dates for exams, papers, holidays, and so on. The second is a weekly calendar (one for each day) recording daily tasks to be accomplished. The third is a note (one for each day) recording daily tasks to be accomplished. All three should be placed where they cannot be overlooked. The daily note can be carried with you. Once you have constructed your schedule, commit yourself to living by it and enjoy the returns in increased security, peace, and accomplishment.

Good Grades!

Time Schedule

Name _____ Class _____ Date _____

Hours	Monday	Tuesday	Wednesday	Thursday	Friday	Saturday	Sunday
AM 7:00							
7:30							
8:00							
8:30							
9:00							
9:30							
10:00							
10:30							
11:00							
11:30							
12:00							

Name _____ Class _____ Date _____

Hours		Monday	Tuesday	Wednesday	Thursday	Friday	Saturday	Sunday
PM	12:30							
	1:00							
	1:30							
	2:00							
	2:30							
	3:00							
	3:30							
	4:00							
	4:30							
	5:00							
	5:30							
	6:00							
	6:30							
	7:00							
	7:30							
	8:00							
PM	8:30							
	9:00							
	9:30							
	10:00							
	10:30							
	11:00							
	11:30							
	12:00							
AM	12:30							
	1:00							
	1:30							
	2:00							

Chapter Outline

Who am I? This question is as old as human questioning. It has been asked by philosophers, theologians, writers, artists, and scientists, as well as by you and me and almost anyone who has ever lived. Within the last hundred years many psychologists have attempted to investigate this question scientifically. The concept of *personality* has emerged from their work.

In this chapter we will explore this pattern of adjustment called personality. We will focus primarily on three approaches to personality and six specific models of personality, two for each approach.

PERSONALITY

personality   the individual's unique and dynamic pattern of thoughts, feelings, and actions

Personality may be defined as the individual's unique and dynamic pattern of thoughts, feelings, and actions. Most psychologists agree that at least three characteristics of personality should be taken into account: (1) *uniqueness* (no two personalities are exactly alike), (2) *organization* (a personality is not just a collection of behaviors; it is a patterned response to the environment that shows some degree of consistency), and (3) *adaptability* (personality can change).

Describing Personality

personality trait   a personality characteristic consistently expressed by an individual

personality type   a set of interrelated personality traits that form a consistent pattern

Psychologists describe personality in much the same way most of us do: by **traits** and by **types.** Suppose, for instance, you are asked to describe the personality of a girl you know. One approach is to list some of the consistent characteristics of her personality—her traits. You might say she is honest, loyal, fun-loving, persistent, and so on. Generally, the description that emerges from the trait approach emphasizes the uniqueness rather than the organization of the personality. If you compare the personality of the girl with that of a boy who is also honest and loyal but who is relatively indifferent to having fun and who is not especially persistent, you are struck by the uniqueness of each person.

Another approach is to describe personality as a type: a set of interrelated traits that seem to form a consistent pattern. For example, you might refer to people who are sociable, good-natured, humorous, and impulsive as extraverted personalities. Notice that the traits mentioned seem relatively consistent with one another. The type approach emphasizes organization rather than uniqueness.

Although each of these two approaches emphasizes a different attribute of personality, neither does so to the exclusion of the other. Even though the trait approach emphasizes uniqueness, it is still possible to find some degree of consistency among the traits expressed in a given personality, and even though the type approach emphasizes organization, it is possible to find inconsistency among the traits expressed in a given type of personality. The same principle holds true for the third personality characteristic mentioned above—adaptability. Personality can change, but the amount and kind of change may vary from one individual to the next. We might also note that although some traits (such as self-esteem) seem to be subject to great change, others (such as introversion/extraversion) appear to be relatively stable. Thus, personality is both stable and adaptable.

Factors That Influence Personality

One factor that may influence personality is **genetic inheritance.** For example, the genetically controlled production of certain hormones may cause a person to display certain behavioral or emotional reactions. We can see this when we consider that the thyroid glands secrete a hormone called thyroxin, which governs the rate of metabolism. If your body had secreted too little thyroxin when you were a child, you would be short, have a pot belly and a protruding tongue, and be mentally retarded. If your body secreted too little thyroxin in adulthood, you would be physically sluggish, less alert, and have a lower degree of motivation than other people. If your thyroid produced too much thyroxin, you would be nervous and irritable and probably would eat large amounts of food without gaining weight.

Diet, exercise, rest, and general physical health are other factors that may influence personality. Indeed, scientific research suggests that an intricate relationship exists among body, mind, emotions, and behavior, with each affecting the others in their functioning. For example, a man who fails to get enough sleep may eventually begin to experience a kind of depression that causes him to become irritable and to behave erratically. His fellow workers, in turn, may begin to respond to him as though he were nothing but a grouch, which may further depress him, and so on. As you can see, many factors, both learned and unlearned, influence personality.

> **genetic inheritance** the unique physical characteristics of the individual (such as eye color, body frame, blood type) that are biologically transmitted from parents to child

Personality Development

We are not born with personalities completely formed. The newborn must mature and must have many interactions with the environment before personality development is complete. Indeed, although some scholars believe our personality development is completed while we are relatively young (about six years old is the low figure), others take the position that personalities never stop

---

CRITICAL THINKING ISSUE
Personality Dynamics

The process of living is basically one of conflict

We are who we are primarily because of the conflicts we have faced and the ways in which we have resolved them. Sometimes we are at odds with society. Sometimes we are at odds with individuals. At still other times, we are involved with internal struggles in which part of us moves in one direction and part of us moves in the opposite direction. That is the nature of life. We cannot escape conflict, and conflict is the predominant force that shapes our personalities.

The process of living is basically one of learning.

We are who we are primarily because we have learned to approach the world in certain ways. Yes, all of us face conflicts in our lives, but our personalities do not represent conflicts nearly as much as they represent habits—habits in thinking, feeling, and behaving that we have learned. Learning is the crucial force that shapes our personalities.

The process of living is basically one of becoming.

We are who we are primarily because we have seized opportunities to grow and to become what we are capable of becoming. We do have conflicts from time to time, and learning does play a role in our development. But the process of becoming, the process by which we fulfill our unique potential, is by far the most significant force that shapes our personalities.

I take the position that:

developing. In this chapter and the next we examine several positions taken on this issue.

Personality Models

personality model   a logically organized general description of what a personality is and how it works

A **personality model** is a logically organized general description of what a personality is and how it works. It contains basic assumptions about the nature of people and provides clues to predict how people will respond under given circumstances. In a sense, all of us rely on personality models from time to time. For example, we may believe that people are basically good or bad, selfish or giving, honest or dishonest, smart or stupid; our actions are often based on these assumptions.

Scholars construct personality models that are much more detailed and more logically consistent than the models most of us have devised. However, scholars who have constructed personality models disagree widely on at least four major issues: (1) *determinants* (what factors determine, or cause, personality); (2) *structure* (what its component parts are); (3) *dynamics* (how these parts interact with each other and how the personality interacts with the environment); and, as we have briefly mentioned, (4) *development* (how the personality grows and changes).

Although there is a great variety of personality models, each differing in some aspects from all the others, they may be divided into three basic approaches: *conflict, learning-centered,* and *fulfillment*. Each approach rests on a particular assumption about the nature of human beings. On the following pages we will introduce the general characteristics of each approach and survey six models of personality—two for each approach. In discussing these models, we present the views of the persons who constructed them. In all cases the ideas presented are not ours but theirs, and we offer them without criticism or comment.

Critical Review 1

1. Personality includes thoughts, feelings, and actions. T F

2. Genetic inheritance, diet, exercise, and learning may all affect personality. T F

3. The two main approaches to personality description are trait theories and behavior theories. T F

4. Scholars often disagree on how personality is structured. T F

5. One characteristic of personality is that once it is formed, it cannot be changed. T F

6. A personality model is a logically organized general description of what a personality is and how it works. T F

7. Use the concepts of personality traits and personality types to describe your personality.

8. How may both learned and unlearned factors influence personality? Provide examples.

A CONFLICT MODEL—PSYCHOANALYSIS

Freud and Psychoanalysis

The basic assumption of the conflict approach is that a clash between two opposing forces shapes personality. Older versions of the conflict approach identified a clash between good and evil; modern versions identify conflicts between social and psychological forces, such as conflict between social rules and the individual's personal desires. Many scholars have constructed personality models based on the conflict approach, but the most influential is Sigmund Freud (1856–1939), the originator of **psychoanalysis.**[1]

Freud's impact on the field of psychology has been enormous. Although many have come to challenge the basic concepts of psychoanalysis, both as personality theory and as psychotherapy, some of these concepts—unconscious functioning, including defensive behavior; the critical influence of the relationship between parent and child on the child's development; and the role of transference in the therapeutic relationship—are essential to a general understanding of psychological adjustment and maladjustment.

psychoanalysis Sigmund Freud's system of psychological thought. It includes both a theory of personality and a therapeutic method (see chapter 14).

Drives

The opposing forces Freud saw as shaping personality are the self-serving demands of the individual and the **communal** demands of society. Freud believed that when we are born, we are, in a psychological sense, a mass of drives that demand immediate gratification.[2] In the beginning, our most pressing drive is to obtain the air, food, and water we need for physical self-preservation. Most of us are able to meet our self-preservation demands relatively easily; they usually do not cause great conflict for us, because society does not oppose our gratifying them. Our other major drives, however, do cause great conflict, because society places many restrictions on their gratification. These are our drives for sex and aggression. Like the self-preservation drive, the drives for sex and aggression are with us when we are born; but unlike the self-preservation drive, they are not fully developed and take time to mature.

communal pertaining to the people of the community

Freud believed all drives have four characteristics: a *source*, an *energy*, an *aim*, and an *object*. The source is always biological. The energy is the tension caused by the source. The aim is to reduce the tension, and the object is the means by which the tension is reduced. Consider an example: The hunger drive emanates from biological functioning in the gastrointestinal tract. When you have not eaten, the fluid level in the mucous membranes of your gastrointestinal tract goes down (source). This drying up creates a bodily tension experienced mentally as hunger pains (energy). You want to reduce the tension (aim), and you will do so by seeking and eating food (object).

---

1. The volume of Freud's work is large, and his later thought varies, sometimes considerably, from his earlier thought. Our discussion attempts to present the mainstream of his ideas concerning personality in a reasonably consistent and coherent fashion. It is drawn primarily from the following works (title and year originally published are given): *The Interpretation of Dreams* (1900), *The Psychopathology of Everyday Life* (1904), *Beyond the Pleasure Principle* (1920), *The Ego and the Id* (1923), *Civilization and Its Discontents* (1930), *New Introductory Lectures on Psychoanalysis* (1933), and *An Outline of Psychoanalysis* (1940). It is perhaps appropriate to emphasize that the ideas presented in this section are Freud's. These ideas may or may not be consistent with other theorists' views of personality or with what today's scholarship generally concedes to be correct with regard to personality functioning. Our purpose here is to provide an example of a conflict model of personality. Models representing other approaches appear later in this chapter and in other chapters of this book.
2. There are many translations of Freud's writings into English. Sometimes the German word *Trieb* is translated as *drive;* other times, as *instinct.* We have chosen to use drive rather than instinct because we believe it is closer to what Freud meant.

We should note that Freud saw a very close connection between the body and the mind. He believed the source and the object of a drive manifest themselves in a person's mind as a *wish* and that the energy and the aim of a drive are experienced as *uncomfortable emotions*. Our wishes and uncomfortable emotions are therefore expressions of biological requirements.

We should also note that in Freud's view the basic thrust of our biological requirements is to avoid pain and enhance pleasure. Our drives create painful tension, and we seek pleasure through tension reduction. To eat food when we are hungry, for example, is pleasurable. In this sense, Freud saw the basic nature of the individual as self-serving.

Personality Structure—Id, Ego, Superego

id our personality at birth, which consists of the biologically based drives for preservation, sex, and aggression. The id is inherently self-serving and irrational

Freud referred to all of our basic drives collectively as the **id.** Because the id is only a collection of drives, it is not rational. It cannot think, perceive, remember, or act to gratify its own demands. If the personality were only an id, we would not have the power to recognize our drives or to direct ourselves to act in ways that would gratify them. But Freud recognized that there is more to a personality than just self-serving drives. People do possess rational faculties. These faculties develop as we mature physiologically and learn to fend for ourselves. Freud referred to our rational faculties collectively as the **ego.** With both an id and an ego we have the means to experience our wishes and emotions and to act on them. (When the ego functions to help gratify the id, it is operating according to what Freud called the *pleasure principle*.)

ego the rational part of our personality, which develops as we mature physiologically and learn to fend for ourselves. Thinking, perceiving, and remembering are aspects of ego functioning

The id and the ego do not compose a complete personality. A third component depends on what we learn from others. We are reared in a society—a web of relationships with rules and regulations that will not permit us to do whatever we want whenever and however we want. As we grow up, we learn these rules. When we break them, we are punished by other people. Punishment, or even the threat of punishment, increases tension within us; we experience this tension mentally as anxiety (a general fear or apprehension). Freud called this fear of punishment **reality anxiety.** Like all tension, it is painful. In this case we reduce the tension by obeying the rules. (When the ego functions to help reduce tension and anxiety by using realistic, problem-solving methods, it is operating according to what Freud called the *reality principle*.)

reality anxiety a fear that we will be punished for breaking the rules

As time goes by, we learn the rules, remember them, and finally accept them. When this happens, the third and last part of the personality is complete. Freud calls this part the **superego.** It is a set of moral ideas that reflect society's rules, or what Freud referred to as the "internalized values of society." The superego allows us to make moral judgments about our thoughts and actions. When we think or do something opposed to the superego, we experience a guilty conscience, the kind of tension Freud called **moral anxiety.** As with reality anxiety, we reduce moral anxiety by obeying the rules.

superego the part of our personality that represents society's rules and regulations

moral anxiety a fear caused by guilt

Conflict and Defense

Freud believed that we invariably find ourselves in situations in which our desires conflict with our moral beliefs. For example, suppose you are a young man who has been taught and has accepted the belief that it is immoral to have sexual intercourse outside marriage. However, both you and your girlfriend want to have sexual intercourse. In essence, your id would say, "I want her so badly it hurts." But your superego would say, "You will be hurt by terrible guilt feelings if you go to bed with her." In this case, if you do have sexual intercourse, you will reduce the tension of your sex drive, but you will also experience pain in the form of moral anxiety. If you do not have sexual relations, you will not experience moral anxiety, but you will feel pain in the form of increasing sexual tension.

Freud believed that tension from the id and the superego could be reduced simultaneously in only one way—through **defense.** Defense involves deceiving ourselves so that we remain unaware of our true wishes. Reconsider the example just given. Suppose you actually go to bed with your girlfriend. Having committed what you believe is an immoral act, you can escape the pain of moral anxiety by convincing yourself that it was she and not you who really wanted sex. Furthermore, you can convince yourself that if you had not satisfied her sexual desire, you would have lost the relationship you have with her. If you really believe either of these things, you will have less reason to feel the pain of guilt.

> **defense** the process by which we reduce the tension from moral anxiety by deceiving ourselves. It is an unconscious function of the ego

The Nature of Defense

The foregoing explanation of defense presents a problem: How could you tell yourself a lie and believe that lie if you were aware you were lying? The answer is that you would not know you were deceiving yourself. According to Freud, the mind operates on three levels: the **unconscious,** the **preconscious,** and the **conscious.** The unconscious is composed of the aspects of our functioning of which we are totally unaware. Unconscious behavior is so far removed from our awareness that, even if the behavior were pointed out to us, we would deny that it existed. The preconscious is composed of the aspects of our functioning of which we are not immediately aware but which are accessible if we concentrate on them. For example, people with nervous habits such as tapping a pencil on a desk when taking a test are often unaware of this behavior. However, if you point out the behavior to such a person, he or she will become aware of it. Finally, the conscious is composed of everything of which we are immediately aware.

> **unconscious** the part of the mind containing the aspects of our functioning of which we are totally unaware
>
> **preconscious** the part of the mind containing the aspects of our functioning of which we are not immediately aware, but which are accessible if we concentrate on them
>
> **conscious** the part of the mind containing everything of which we are immediately aware

Defense takes place in the unconscious. In the situation involving you and your girlfriend, you would be able to believe your own lie because you would be totally unaware that you were deceiving yourself. The form of defense used in this example is called *rationalization* (offering reasonable and acceptable explanations for unreasonable and unacceptable behavior). Freud's work has been extended considerably in this area; consequently, many forms of defense have been identified, some of which will be discussed in chapter 4. The important point here is that defense is an unconscious process and, according to Freud, a function of the ego. Defense is essential in that it allows us to resolve the apparent dilemma we face when what we wish is in direct conflict with what we believe to be morally right. Without defense, we would be unable to reduce tensions sufficiently to maintain adequate adjustment.

Critical Review 2

1. The basic assumption of the _____ approach is that a conflict between two opposing forces shapes personality.

2. According to Freud, the three structural components of personality are _____, _____, and _____ .

3. Freud argued that the basic nature of the individual is _____ , while the basic nature of society is _____ .

4. The kind of unconscious functioning by which we deceive ourselves about our true wishes is called _____ .

5. What are the id, ego, and superego, and how do they interact with each other?

6. How does defense work?

Psychosexual Stages of Development

psychosexual stages of development five successive levels of personality development identified by particular personality traits. The first three stages are dominated by conflicts related to sexual gratification

Freud believed personality emerges in a series of **psychosexual stages of development.** The first three stages are dominated by conflicts related to gratification of the sexual drive. According to Freud, if these conflicts are adequately resolved, a mature and relatively well-adjusted personality will develop; if not, the resultant personality will be immature and maladjusted. Each stage is identified by distinctive characteristics and forms of defense.

Oral Stage   The first stage begins at birth and lasts approximately one year. It is called the *oral* stage because it is primarily through oral activities (sucking, chewing, eating, and so on) that infants obtain sexual gratification. Infants who

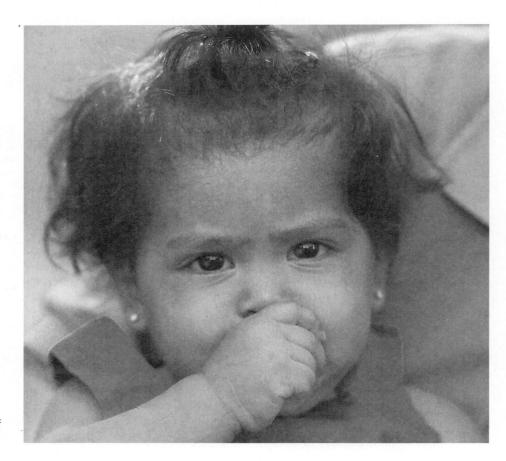

Is thumb-sucking really a means of obtaining sexual gratification?

receive the optimal amount of sexual gratification will develop adjustive personality traits and will proceed to the next stage of development with their personalities unharmed. If either too indulged or too frustrated in oral activities, however, infants will become **fixated** in the oral stage; although they will proceed to subsequent stages of development, they will retain the unresolved psychological conflicts of the oral stage. Fixations can occur in any of the first three stages, according to Freud, and they always produce adjustment problems in adult life. For example, oral characters (persons fixated in the oral stage) with a background of overindulgence might display gullibility as adults; that is, their pleasure from oral overindulgence might be translated into their "swallowing" almost anything they are told. Conversely, an oral fixation caused by frustration might lead to suspiciousness. *Projection* (attributing to others one's own objectionable characteristics and motives) is a major defense of the oral character.

fixation arrestment in a particular psychosexual stage of development

Anal Stage   The *anal* stage begins at the end of the oral stage and lasts until the child is approximately two to three years old. During the anal stage the child obtains sexual gratification primarily through voiding or withholding the voiding of the bowels. Toilet training becomes the primary area of potential conscious conflict between parent and child. Anal fixation is associated with stinginess/overgenerosity, stubbornness/acquiescence, and orderliness/messiness. For example, the anal character with a background of frustration might be particularly stubborn as an adult. A major defense of the anal character is *reaction formation* (replacing true wishes and impulses with directly opposite wishes and impulses). For example, the meticulously clean person might really be renouncing a tendency to be messy.

Phallic Stage   The third stage is the *phallic* stage, which lasts from about age three to age five or six. The emphasis here is on genital activity. The child obtains gratification primarily through heterosexual interactions (usually with other children in the form of "show and tell") and through masturbation. During the phallic stage the child experiences the **Oedipus complex,** in which the child competes with the parent of the same sex for the affection of the parent of the opposite sex.[3] Children's feelings about their parents may become very intense during this period. The boy, although he is unaware of it, and probably does not know quite how to do it, wants to possess his mother sexually. He views his father, who is infinitely more powerful than he, as the major competitor for his mother's affection and fears that his father will punish him for his desires.

Oedipus complex   conflict during the phallic stage in which the child competes with the parent of the same sex for the affection of the parent of the opposite sex. Freud considered this the major conflict in each person's life

The boy's growing resentment and fear of his father eventually lead to **castration anxiety,** a fear that his father will castrate him or mutilate his genitals (the source of his lustful feelings). In turn, castration anxiety leads to **identification** with the father, a process through which the boy incorporates the father's characteristics into his own personality. Through this identification, the boy is able to reduce the tension that stems from castration anxiety and, ultimately, to resolve his Oedipal conflict. By identifying with his father, he comes to accept his father and the relationship between his parents. His father is no longer a competitor but a kind of hero, a model after which to pattern his behavior. Now the boy can treat his mother with harmless, tender affection.

castration anxiety   a young boy's fear that his father will damage his genitals

identification   the process of incorporating the characteristics of another person into one's own personality

---

3. Freud used the term *Oedipus complex* to identify the major conflict in the phallic stage for both boys and girls. Some scholars use the term *Electra complex* to identify the conflict for the girl, but Freud did not care for the use of this term.

penis envy a young girl's feeling of inadequacy at her lack of a penis

A girl may also have intense feelings, particularly when she experiences **penis envy,** a feeling of inadequacy at her lack of a visible sexual appendage. Holding her mother responsible for her castrated condition, the girl rejects her positive feelings for her mother. At the same time, she transfers her love to her father, because he has the organ she lacks, and she wants him to share it with her. Freud believed, however, that the daughter's love for her father (and, ultimately, for all men) is tainted by envy precisely for the reason she is attracted to him in the first place—because he has something she lacks. Freud believed women are able to compensate somewhat for the lack of a penis when they give birth, particularly if the baby is a boy. Like boys, girls resolve the Oedipal conflict through the process of identification. However, unlike boys, girls do not experience the intense fear associated with castration anxiety. Rather, it is an awareness of the realistic barriers that prevent sexual gratification with her father that leads the girl to identify with her mother.

As in the oral and anal stages, the individual may become fixated in the phallic stage. Phallic fixation is associated with vanity/self-hatred, pride/humility, and stylishness/plainness. Thus, the phallic character who was overindulged might be vain as an adult. The major defense of the phallic character is *repression* (blocking out unpleasant memories or impulses from awareness).

For Freud, these first three stages are so important that the major part of what we might call our character is developed by the time we are about six years old. However, he also believed that part of our development takes place after six years of age.

Latency   The *latency* stage lasts from approximately age six until puberty. During this time, the sexual drive becomes temporarily inactive. Consequently, no major new conflict related to the sexual drive takes place, and there can be no fixation.

Genital Stage   The fifth and final stage lasts from puberty until death. The sexual drive is active once again, but in a more mature fashion. The self-centered gratifications expressed in the oral, anal, and phallic stages give way to mutual gratifications expressed through caring and responsibility in heterosexual relationships. The individual matures into a responsible and productive member of society. Conflicts occur from time to time, but they are not as severe as in the first three stages, and no new fixation can take place. Of course, fixations from earlier stages may cause adjustment problems, sometimes severe. The major defense in the genital stage is *sublimation* (substituting a socially acceptable activity for an unacceptable one). A person with a very strong aggressive drive, for example, might divert the aggressive energy into volunteer work rather than picking fights with other people.

Table 2–1 summarizes Freud's psychosexual stages of development.

Erikson's View

life cycle the general sequence of events in our physical, psychological, and social development as we progress from infancy through old age

Freud did not identify substages within the genital stage, but other scholars have postulated a **life cycle** that includes additional stages during adulthood. Erik Erikson (1902–1994), a student of Freud, modified Freud's view by adding three stages of development and by emphasizing the social rather than the sexual nature of the conflicts we must contend with in each stage. Thus, Erikson spoke of eight *psychosocial* stages of development. Table 2–2 lists the major con-

	ORAL STAGE	ANAL STAGE	PHALLIC STAGE	LATENCY	GENITAL STAGE
Approximate age	Birth to 1 year	1 year to 2 or 3 years	3 years to 5 or 6 years	6 years to puberty	Puberty to death
Sexual gratification	Sucking, chewing, eating	Voiding or with-holding voiding of bowels	Masturbation, heterosexual interaction	Inactive	Mature heterosexual sexual relationships
Possible fixation	Yes	Yes	Yes	No	No
Major defense mechanism	Projection	Reaction-formation	Repression	None	Sublimation

TABLE 2–1
Freud's Psychosexual Stages

flicts (Erikson called them *crises*) associated with each stage and the age range within which the stage occurs.

Trust Versus Mistrust   During the first year, the infant is totally dependent on others. If the infant's caretakers are relatively consistent and generous in the love, care, and attention they provide, the infant develops a basic trust with which to approach life. If the love, care, and attention are inconsistent or inadequate, then the infant develops mistrust. Erikson maintained that the amount of trust or mistrust developed in this stage affects the way the individual approaches all later relationships.

Autonomy Versus Doubt and Shame   During the second and third years, the child, although still dependent, learns to do some things for himself or herself. To walk, talk, and comply or refuse to comply with directions are all actions within the child's prerogative. During this same period, the child is expected to master the social demands of bowel and toilet training. When these skills are mastered, the child develops a sense of autonomy (self-governance). Failure to achieve such mastery produces a sense of shame and self-doubt. The self-assurance that accompanies success or the shame and doubt that accompany failure affect the person's self-concept throughout life.

CRISES (CONFLICTS)	AGE RANGES
Trust versus mistrust	First year
Autonomy versus doubt and shame	Second and third years
Initiative versus guilt	Preschool age (4–5)
Industry versus inferiority	School age (6–11)
Identity versus identity confusion	Adolescence (12–18)
Intimacy versus isolation	Young adulthood
Generativity versus stagnation	Middle age
Integrity versus despair	Old age

TABLE 2–2
Erickson's Psychosocial Stages

Initiative Versus Guilt   Preschool children are well on their way toward social independence. Fully capable of initiating their own behavior, they can make independent decisions—a process that involves risk. The problem here for the child is to make decisions that are correct, or at least acceptable. Correct or acceptable decisions are approved by others, encouraging the child to risk future initiatives. But incorrect or unacceptable decisions are not approved and often bring punishment, leading to a sense of guilt that can inhibit future initiatives.

Industry Versus Inferiority   With school comes work, and school-age children may be rewarded in a variety of ways, from praise to A's, for doing their school-work well. These rewards lead to the development of personal industry and a sense of accomplishment. Children who do not do well in school invariably suffer from the negative feedback they receive. The result is a sense of inadequacy and inferiority.

Identity Versus Identity Confusion   Adolescents attempt to forge a complete self-concept through integrating various aspects of self with the images others have of them. In other words, they seek a complete physical, psychological, and social identity. Erikson believed three areas are of crucial importance here: (1) the sexual area (How well do I meet the requirements of my adult sex role?); (2) the vocational area (What will I be when I grow up?); and (3) the social values area (What are the appropriate moral principles by which I should conduct my life?). Firm answers to these questions provide the basis for a firm identity. Fragmented or confused answers lead to identity confusion.

Intimacy Versus Isolation   Young adults seek intimate relationships with both opposite-sex and same-sex partners. By intimacy, Erikson (1963) meant commitment to "concrete affiliations and partnerships and the ethical strength to abide by such commitments, even though they may call for significant sacrifices and compromises" (p. 263). Failure to form intimate relationships results in a sense of isolation.

> Carol, well into her fifties, has never been married and believes she never will be. She has had few intimate relationships in her life and seems to shy away from any man who attempts to become emotionally close to her. Now, few men even try. It was not always that way. When Carol was younger, more than one man tried to form an intimate relationship with her, but her inability to make a commitment kept the relationships at a superficial level. Even then, she sensed that she would always be lonely.

Generativity Versus Stagnation   During middle age, persons become concerned with conditions beyond their own immediate development (How can I make this a better world for future generations?). This seems an obvious concern for parents, but Erikson maintained it is a problem for nonparents as well. The failure to give of oneself to create better conditions for all human beings results in stagnant self-absorption, a kind of self-centeredness dysfunctional both for the individual and for society.

Integrity Versus Despair   Old age is primarily a time to reflect on one's life and to integrate all past life experiences. Erikson (1968) referred to integrity as the ego's accrued assurance of its proclivity for order and meaning. . . . It is the acceptance of one's one and only life cycle and of the people who have become significant to it as something that had to be and that, by necessity, permitted of no substitutions. It thus means a new and different love of one's parents, free from the wish that they should have been different, and an acceptance of the fact that one's life is one's own responsibility. (p. 139)

People who achieve integrity are therefore able to accept life and, when it comes, death. Failure to achieve integrity results in despair—a feeling of disgust with one's life and a belief that it is too late to start over. The person in despair is afraid of death.

Critical Review 3

1. A person who becomes psychologically arrested in a stage of development is said to be _____.

2. The great conflict associated with Freud's phallic stage is the _____ _____, which we eventually resolve through the process of _____.

3. Erikson defined the major conflict of old age as _____ versus _____.

4. Why are the first three of Freud's psychosexual stages of development considered to be more important than the last two?

5. In what ways do you think Erikson's view is an improvement over Freud's?

A LEARNING-CENTERED MODEL—BEHAVIORISM

Skinner and Behaviorism

The basic assumption of the learning-centered approach is that learning shapes personality. Many scholars who have constructed personality models based on this approach pay scant attention to biologically based drives inferred from people's behavior or to emotional conflicts in people's minds. Instead, they focus on observable behavior and the observable conditions that may cause or determine it. Although some of these **behaviorists** consider internal determinants of behavior (perceptions, motives, attitudes, and so on) as well as external determinants (events in the physical and social environments), others are more extreme in their exclusive emphasis on environmental conditions. The most influential of these *radical behaviorists* is B. F. Skinner (1904–1990).[4]

behaviorist a psychologist who focuses on observable behavior and on the observable conditions that may cause behavior. Behaviorists often experiment with animals such as rats and pigeons to identify behavioral principles that can be applied to human behavior. Sometimes they experiment with humans as well

Heredity Versus Environment

Skinner recognized that genetic factors can affect behavior. He argued, however, that no matter how much we learn about genetics, no adequate explanation of behavior can be achieved without a thorough understanding of how the envi-

4. Skinner produced many important books from the 1930s through the 1970s. Our discussion is based on his work in general and in particular on *Science and Human Behavior* (1953), *Verbal Behavior* (1957), *Contingencies of Reinforcement* (1969), *Beyond Freedom and Dignity* (1971), and *About Behaviorism* (1974).

CULTURAL CROSSCURRENTS
Child-Rearing Environments: Do They Make a Difference?

Most of you were raised in a fairly standard American home. You slept under your parents' roof each night. Your contact with peers was limited—at least in the early years. Your primary associations were with parents and siblings. All your friends were brought up the same way. But what if you were raised in a completely different environment, perhaps a communal home? Would your personality and social relationships be much different?

This was one question that Rachel Levy-Shiff and Michael Hoffman tried to answer in their study of urban and kibbutz-raised children. In Israel, some children are raised on communal agricultural establishments called kibbutzim. These children sleep in a children's house with other preschoolers, instead of in their parents' quarters.*

The kibbutz-raised children were compared with preschoolers raised in the modern city of Tel Aviv. The parents of all the children in the study were born in Israel, were middle class, had similar educational backgrounds, and enjoyed similar standards of living. The fathers of the kibbutz-raised children were involved primarily in agricultural work or worked in light industry, while the mothers held jobs in social services or education. The parents of the urban preschoolers held white-collar jobs in business and social services. Previous research had reported that older children raised in the communal environment showed better group-oriented skills but less warmth and personal intimacy in interpersonal contact. Perhaps these behaviors have their roots in this early arrangement, where children are likely to have to depend on one another and do not develop the same intense relationship with parents.

Both groups of children were observed in free-play situations, either at the urban nursery school or in the kibbutz children's house. An assortment of play materials was provided, and observers used a checklist to indicate the type of interpersonal behavior shown by the subjects, such as responding positively to a playmate's initiatives, showing cooperative and coordinated play, competitive behaviors, and the like.

The results showed that even at the early preschool stage the differences were apparent. Among the most important findings were that the kibbutz preschoolers—compared with the urban children—were less competitive, engaged more frequently in coordinated play, displayed less warmth toward their peers, and were more verbally aggressive. They also showed more solitary play. Urban preschoolers spent more time exchanging toys and objects and struggling over who would get the toys.

The researchers conclude that the larger amount of coordinated play, reduced competition, and avoidance of physical conflict shows greater group-oriented skills and enhanced group cohesion. The increased amounts of verbal aggression, reduced warmth in interpersonal relations, and more solitary play demonstrate greater emotional distancing in kibbutz-raised children, compared with their urban peers.

These findings parallel those found for older children in kibbutzim, showing that the roots of these behaviors can be found even in very young preschoolers. In the United States, the typical upbringing is quite different from kibbutz upbringing. In other areas of the world, especially in Africa and Asia, children are raised in environments that are very different from the standard American nuclear family. The results of this study, as well as other similar studies, suggest that the child-rearing arrangement itself may help shape the child's behavior and orientation toward others. The roots of the person's personality may be found in the child-rearing environment of the society or subculture that structures the child's early peer and parental interactions.

SOURCE: Levy-Shiff, R., and Hoffman, M. A. Social Behavior of Urban and Preschool Children in Israel. *Developmental Psychology*, 1985, *21*, 1204–1205.

*Not all kibbutzim are structured this way. In some communal establishments, children sleep in the same house as their parents.

Taken from P. S. Kaplan, *The Human Odyssey: Life-Span Development*. St. Paul, MN: West, 1988, p. 211.

ronment affects it. In other words, both heredity and environment affect behavior, but Skinner preferred to concentrate on environment. In fact, he argued that environment ultimately determines a species' genetic characteristics. According to the principle of natural selection, he pointed out, it is the environment that determines what behaviors will allow members of a species to survive. When the successful members breed with one another, they transmit their adaptive characteristics to the next generation. So a species' genetic characteristics are ultimately determined by the environment. It appears that Skinner had good reason to emphasize environmental factors.

Conditioning

Environmental factors affect learning in two important ways, according to Skinner: One produces *respondent* behavior, the other produces *operant* behavior. Respondent behavior is a reflexive type of behavior preceded by and elicited by a stimulus. For example, if someone placed a lit match directly under your hand, you would quickly pull your hand away. The sensation of extreme heat (the stimulus) would cause the respondent behavior of your pulling your hand away (the reflexive response). Early in the twentieth century, behaviorists discovered that respondent behavior could be *conditioned.* Suppose, for instance, each time the lit match were placed under your hand, someone rang a bell. Eventually, you would so strongly associate the heat (the original stimulus) with the sound of the bell (a neutral stimulus) that if the bell were rung, you would jerk your hand, even if the lit match were not present. Skinner called this process **respondent conditioning.** It is also called **classical conditioning.**

Perhaps the most famous of the early behaviorists was Ivan Pavlov, a Russian physiologist whose experiments with dogs led to the first demonstration of how learned reflexes are acquired. Soon, two other important discoveries were made. First, conditioned responses would gradually diminish and eventually disappear if the neutral stimulus was never again paired with the original stimulus. For example, if you never again burned your hand when a bell was rung, eventually you would not jerk back your hand at the sound of a bell. This process is called **extinction.** Second, the early behaviorists found that the conditioned response tended to generalize to similar but neutral stimuli (that is, you might jerk back your hand upon hearing a buzzer or a whistle as well as a bell). This is called **stimulus generalization.**

Respondent conditioning is obviously important in understanding how and why we display certain learned behavior, and Skinner recognized its validity. However, he believed another concept, **operant conditioning,** explains our most significant responses to the environment.

Operant conditioning is the process in which an emitted behavior produces consequences that either increase or decrease the probability that the behavior will be repeated under similar circumstances in the future. Suppose, for example, you are visiting Las Vegas and you decide to try your luck with a slot machine. You have never been much of a gambler, so you decide to limit your gambling to a dollar. You put a quarter in the machine and pull the handle on four successive occasions. Each time, you win a dollar. The odds are that you will play again, regardless of your previous decision to gamble only one dollar. Why? Because each time you behaved in a particular way (played the machine), you were rewarded (the machine paid off), and you anticipate that if you display the same behavior again, you will be rewarded again. You have been operantly conditioned to play the machine because your behavior produced positive consequences. The process by which a behavior is made more likely to occur is called **reinforcement.**

> Oscar's heart was pounding as he walked toward Sylvia. This was his first dance, and Sylvia was the prettiest girl in the room. Would she dance with him? He thought he would die if she refused. At the least, he would never go to another

respondent conditioning a kind of learning in which a neutral stimulus is substituted for a stimulus that causes a reflexive response; the neutral stimulus comes to cause the same reflexive response. Also called classical conditioning

extinction the gradual dying out of a conditioned response

stimulus generalization the repetition of a response conditioned by one stimulus in the presence of similar but neutral stimuli

operant conditioning a kind of learning in which an emitted behavior produces consequences that either increase or decrease the probability that the behavior will be repeated under similar circumstances in the future

reinforcement the process by which a perceived reward is associated with an emitted behavior. The perceived reward is called a reinforcer. Skinner held that reinforcement always increases the probability that an emitted behavior will be repeated

dance. It had taken him a full half hour to muster the courage to approach her. Several other boys had done so, and she had turned each of them down. Now, the moment of truth had arrived. He asked. She said yes. Now, Oscar can't wait until the next dance.

The Nature of Reinforcement

Although it may appear simple at first glance, operant conditioning has many ramifications. To begin with, let us note an important difference between respondent conditioning and operant conditioning. In respondent conditioning, the stimulus always precedes the response; in operant conditioning, the stimulus follows the response. Thus, we may conclude that an organism that displays respondent behavior is essentially passive. It simply reacts to environmental stimuli. But an organism that displays operant behavior is essentially active. It emits behavior to produce consequences that, in turn, may serve as stimuli for future responses.

Skinner recognized that human beings, even from early infancy, are active behavior emitters who produce a great variety of responses. Those that are reinforced are woven into conditioned-response patterns that represent our more significant everyday responses. For example, reading, writing, carrying out a particular work routine, and interacting in certain ways with friends are more significant than respondent behaviors such as jerking one's hand away from a flame or displaying fear on hearing an unexpected loud noise. Thus, Skinner considered personality to be primarily based on the operantly conditioned responses of the individual.

Types of Reinforcement

Reinforcement works in two ways: One has to do with the type of reinforcement, and the other concerns its regularity. Two types of reinforcement occur in operant conditioning—positive and negative (see Table 2–3). Both increase the probability that a response will be repeated. **Positive reinforcement** occurs when something perceived as pleasant follows a response. For example, playing the slot machine in the previous example led to the accumulation of money, a positive result. It is important to realize, however, that the learner must perceive the payoff as a reward; if he or she does not, the probability of the response being repeated is not increased.

positive reinforcement the introduction of something perceived as pleasant following a response

Negative reinforcement occurs when something perceived as unpleasant is removed after a response is emitted. For example, suppose you are in the library trying to study for an exam and are distracted by loud talk from two people nearby. If you leave the room to get away from the noise, and thus are able to concentrate, you increase the probability that the next time you are in a similar situation, you will respond by leaving the room.

negative reinforcement the removal of something perceived as unpleasant from a situation after a response is emitted

The second consideration with regard to reinforcement is its regularity. Some behaviors are **continuously reinforced,** that is, there is a payoff each time the behavior is emitted. For example, flicking the light switch in your bedroom results consistently in the light going on. Flicking the switch has been continuously reinforced; therefore, you continue to do it. Skinner found that when the usual reinforcement is not forthcoming in such situations, the result is often disturbing and sometimes humorous. Thus, if you flick the switch and the light does not come on, your initial reaction might well be anger or laughter. Skinner also found that continuously reinforced behaviors are extinguished rapidly if

continuous reinforcement reinforcement that occurs each time a particular behavior is emitted

POSITIVE REINFORCEMENT	NEGATIVE REINFORCEMENT
Occurs when something perceived as pleasant follows a response.	Occurs when something perceived as unpleasant is removed after a response is emitted.
Example: You play the slot machine and win (see text).	Example: You escape the noise by going to another room (see text).

*Reinforcement increases the probability that an emitted behavior will be repeated under similar circumstances in the future.

TABLE 2–3
Types of Reinforcement*

reinforcement ceases. If, for instance, the light does not turn on when you first flick the switch, you will not keep flicking the switch for long.

Many behaviors are not continuously reinforced; their reinforcement is said to be **intermittent.** When we engage in conditioned behavior that has been maintained by intermittent reinforcement, we are not disturbed when reinforcement is not forthcoming; so intermittently reinforced behaviors take longer to extinguish. Suppose, for example, you know your light switch isn't dependable. In this case, you will not become disturbed if you flick the switch and the light does not go on. After all, you do not expect it to go on every time. You may flick the switch for a long time before you give up on it. Thus, intermittent reinforcement is particularly important in repeated-response patterns.

intermittent reinforcement reinforcement that does not occur each time a particular behavior is emitted

Critical Review 4

1. Skinner argued that environment ultimately determines a species' genetic characteristics. T F

2. Our most significant responses to the environment are caused by respondent, or classical, conditioning. T F

3. In operant conditioning, the stimulus follows the response. T F

4. Reinforcement is the process by which a behavior's occurrence is made more likely. T F

5. Compare and contrast respondent and operant conditioning.

6. Explain the two ways reinforcement works.

Reinforcement Schedules

Not all intermittent reinforcement is the same. The timing may vary considerably, as may the results. Different ways of delivering reinforcers are called *reinforcement schedules* (see Table 2–4). One kind of intermittent reinforcement is based on the passage of time, or what Skinner called an **interval schedule.** If the time interval between reinforcers is constant, the schedule is called a *fixed-interval* schedule. The couple that has sex once a week on Saturday night operates on a fixed-interval schedule. They tend to become amorous as Saturday night approaches but not to feel very sexual early in the week, particularly on Sunday morning. This pattern—a low rate of response that immediately follows each reinforcement and a gradual increase of response rate as the next reinforcement approaches—is typical of behavior reinforced at fixed intervals. On the other hand, if the time inter-

interval schedule a pattern of reinforcement based on the passage of time. If the interval is constant, it is called a fixed-interval schedule; if the interval varies, it is called a variable-interval schedule

TABLE 2–4
Intermittent Reinforcement
Schedules

	INTERVAL	**RATIO**
Fixed	Behavior is reinforced at regular time intervals. Reinforcement is followed immediately by low rate of response; a gradual increase of response rate occurs as next reinforcement approaches.	Based on amount of behavior emitted. The number of responses required for each reinforcement is constant. Generally, high response rates are typical.
Variable	Behavior is reinforced at irregular intervals. Rate of response is more consistent than behavior reinforced on fixed-interval schedule.	Based on amount of behavior emitted. The number of responses required for each reinforcement varies. A high, sustained rate of response is maintained.

val between reinforcers varies, the schedule is called a *variable-interval* schedule, and the behavior is emitted more constantly. Thus, the couple that has sex on an average of four times a month (the same average as in the previous example) but does not know when the next sexual encounter will occur will display amorous behavior more often.

Another kind of intermittent reinforcement is based on the amount of behavior emitted; it is administered on a **ratio schedule.** If the number of responses required for each reinforcement is constant, the schedule is called a *fixed-ratio* schedule. The salesperson who works on commission operates on a fixed-ratio schedule. He or she must make a predetermined number of sales to earn a given commission. A large number of sales results in a very good living, so the commissioned salesperson often works very hard. Such high response rates are typical of behavior reinforced at fixed ratios (assuming that the required number of responses for reinforcement is not too large and that the individual does not become fatigued). If the number of responses required for reinforcement varies, the schedule is called a *variable-ratio* schedule. Here, because any response might result in reinforcement, a high, sustained rate of response is maintained. Our old friend, the slot machine, operates on a variable-ratio schedule, as it does not pay off predictably. Each failure increases the probability of subsequent success; thus, the more we lose, the more we play.

Skinner has identified a great variety of schedules that combine variable and fixed elements in many configurations. In a *concurrent* schedule, for example, two or more schedules operate at the same time, and reinforcement can be received from any of them. You could, for instance, study tonight or go to the movies, either of which may ultimately be reinforced. According to operant psychologists, many of our behaviors are related to concurrent schedules.

Another common schedule is the *chained* schedule. Here, behavior reinforced by one stimulus produces a second stimulus; behavior reinforced by the second stimulus produces a third; and so on until a final payoff is received. For example, suppose you have decided to go to the movies tonight. A friend has told you about a movie she described as great. You have always enjoyed the movies your friend has recommended, so you look in the newspaper to see if this particular movie is playing, and it is. The paper has always been correct on such matters, so you go to the theater. The theater is open, so you buy your ticket, and so on until you have seen the movie.

The first stimulus in the chain is a **discriminative stimulus.** A response is very likely to follow this stimulus, because it has been associated with rein-

ratio schedule   a pattern of reinforcement based on the amount of behavior emitted. Ratio schedules may be fixed or variable

discriminative stimulus   a stimulus that elicits a response associated with a high probability of reinforcement in the past

forcement in the past (that is, you have been rewarded for following your friend's recommendations in the past; if you had not, you might not bother to look at the newspaper). Each succeeding stimulus in the chain is both a discriminative stimulus and a **conditioned reinforcer** (that is, looking at the newspaper is reinforced by finding an ad, which has in the past been associated with going to the theater to see the movie, and so on). Chaining accounts for many of our complex behaviors.

Punishment

According to the **law of effect,** a principle formulated by Edward Lee Thorndike, responses that lead to satisfying consequences are strengthened and therefore tend to be repeated, and responses that lead to unsatisfying consequences are weakened and therefore tend not to be repeated. Certainly punishment qualifies as an unsatisfying consequence; hence, punishment as well as reinforcement can condition behavior.

Skinner recognized two types of punishment. One occurs when unpleasant consequences follow a response (for example, your request for a date is turned down); the other occurs when a reinforcer is removed after a response (that is, a child's allowance is taken away because she has misbehaved). However, Skinner had grave reservations regarding the use and effectiveness of punishment. He believed both types of punishment tend to suppress behaviors temporarily rather than weaken the overall tendency to respond. Thus, when punishment ceases, the behavior is likely to return. In addition, punishment may produce secondary consequences that are ultimately undesirable (as, for example, when a child punished for talking back to his parents later avoids standing up for his rights even when it is appropriate to do so).

A related Skinnerian concept is *aversive control,* in which threats are used to encourage expected behaviors. Thus, the boss threatens to fire the worker, the parent threatens to spank the child, the teacher threatens to fail the student, and so on. Skinner contended that aversive control, like punishment, is ultimately ineffective and may lead to undesirable secondary consequences. Skinner preferred the use of reinforcement to condition behavior.

Shaping

Many behaviors are so complicated that they must be learned in a series of steps. **Shaping** is the process of reinforcing at each step only those responses that come closest to approximating the desired behavior. For example, the student learning to write a high-school-level term paper might initially be rewarded just for putting some thoughts on paper. Eventually, however, more precise writing behavior (use of correct grammar, spelling, punctuation, sentence structure, paragraph structure, and so on) will be necessary for reinforcement to be received. Ultimately, only the production of a high-school-level term paper will be rewarded. A great many of our behaviors are shaped in this manner.

Thoughts and Feelings

Skinner recognized thoughts and feelings as well as external behavior, but he believed that they, like external behavior, result from environmental conditions. According to Skinner, there are internal stimuli that arise from biological functioning and physical movement. These stimuli, unlike our overt behavior, are private experiences; they are directly experienced only by us as individuals. It is other people, however, who interpret these internal stimuli for us and who teach us the labels for them. Our parents, for example, observe our external behaviors, then tell us we are angry, embarrassed, loving, or indisposed. A child, for instance, may experience sensations of arousal and exhilaration when standing at the edge of a balcony. The parents, however, observing the child's external behavior, may label his feelings as fear or excitement. Children later use these labels and superimpose them on their internal sensations, because they receive parental attention, sympathy, and praise for doing so. In this way, we are conditioned to think and feel as we do.

As you may see, this process often leads to confusion. If, for instance, we have learned to label several slightly different internal sensations as *anger,* it will be difficult for us to express, and for others to understand, exactly what we are feeling when we say, "I'm angry." Similarly, when we make such statements as "I love my car," "I love my dog," "I love my parents," "I love my spouse," and "I love my God," do we really express the same feeling each time? It is no wonder that many of us know more about our external environments than we do about our own thoughts and feelings.

Another problem with internal sensations relates to whether they cause us to respond in certain ways. Have you ever heard statements such as "I lashed out at him (or her) because I was angry," or "I did poorly on the test because I felt depressed"? These statements indicate that the emotions caused the behavior. Skinner disagreed. He believed that if we look for what causes the emotion, we will also find what causes the behavior—and the answer is in the consequences. For example, the angry person experiences sensations that he or she has been conditioned to label *anger,* then lashes out because this behavior has produced a payoff in similar situations in the past. In like manner, the depressed person may feel low because of a general lack of reinforcement for his or her behavior. A lack of reinforcement for previous test-taking behavior may explain poor test results.

Skinner also denied that *drives* (in the sense Freud uses the word) can explain behavior. We do not behave a certain way because we have a strong (or weak) sex drive; we behave that way because we have been conditioned to behave that way. Thus, according to Skinner, thoughts, feelings, and actions all are controlled by environment.

Critical Review 5

1. Intermittent reinforcement occurs every time a particular stimulus occurs. T F

2. Extinction is the gradual dying out of a conditioned response. T F

3. Punishment occurs when unpleasant consequences follow a response or when a positive reinforcer is removed after a response. T F

4. Shaping is another name for the law of effect. T F

5. Skinner argued that a person's internal processes, such as thoughts and feelings, are conditioned, as a person's actions are. T F

6. What are the four types of intermittent reinforcement schedules?

7. Explain the two types of punishment.

8. How may our thoughts and feelings be conditioned?

Bandura and Walters's View

Modeling   Two behaviorists, Albert Bandura and Richard H. Walters, have proposed a *social learning theory* that emphasizes internal as well as environmental factors in behavior. The theory focuses on **modeling** as the principal technique through which we learn; that is, we learn by observing the behaviors of other people who serve as models for us. In this view, what the observer primarily acquires from the model is a symbolic representation of a behavior, not stimulus-response connections. A child learning to swim, for example, does not just watch someone swim and then begin to swim herself. She observes, asks questions, receives information, and eventually, under supervision and with criticism, begins to take her first awkward but successful strokes. Thus, our uniquely human capacity to interpret reality, to formulate ideas and make judgments about what we observe, is more important than mere stimulus-response connections.

Of course, trial and error accounts for some learning, but our most complex behaviors are learned through verbal instructions and the observation of models. In learning to speak a language, for example, the learner must have a model:

modeling   the process in which a learner observes a behavior, formulates ideas and makes judgments about the behavior, and attempts to imitate the behavior

We learn many significant behaviors through the process of modeling.

A child who is unfamiliar with the Polish language would never emit the Polish phrase for "expectancy" even though the probability of reinforcement was 100 percent and the contingent reinforcer was exceedingly attractive. Obviously, in this particular example, the introduction of an important social variable—a verbalizing model—is an indispensible aspect of the learning process. (Bandura and Walters, 1963, p. 2)

The Nature of Learning   Learning requires more than exposure to a model, however. Attention, retention, reproduction, and motivation are needed as well.

To begin with, the learner must direct *attention* to relevant cues and perceive those cues accurately (Bandura, 1969, 1971b). In other words, we must pay attention to what is important in the modeling situation.

The learner must also *retain* symbols of the modeled behavior. We could not imitate a behavior if we had forgotten it. We recall the behavior by coding it into symbolic form (words or images).

Next, memory is used to guide *reproduction* of the behavior. Merely acquiring and retaining an idea of what to do does not ensure skillful or even adequate performance. The learner must practice the behavior and make necessary adjustments as dictated by self-observation and feedback.

Finally, the learner must be *motivated* to display the behavior. Rewards and punishments play a paramount role. If, for instance, you could dance the tango but were ridiculed each time you began to do that dance, then you would likely give up the tango.

Vicarious Rewards and Punishments and Their Effects on Behavior   Bandura and Walters agree with Skinner that rewards and punishments may operate directly on the learner's behavior; however, they believe rewards and punishments may also operate vicariously; that is, the learner may be affected by what he or she sees happening to a model. For example, if you observe a model being rewarded immediately after he or she displays a particular behavior, then you are more likely to imitate that behavior. Conversely, if the model is punished, you will not be likely to imitate the behavior.

According to Bandura (1971a, 1971b), the effects of vicarious rewards and punishments are regulated by six mechanisms:

1. *Information*—the observer may discover how to behave in ways that will be rewarded and how to avoid behaving in ways that will be punished.

2. *Incentive motivational effects*—the observer may begin to expect rewards similar to what the model has received when he or she displays behavior similar to the model's.

3. *Emotional arousal*—the observer may experience a general heightening of responsiveness that extends beyond the specific responses of the model. For instance, fear generated from observing a model being punished may not only keep the observer from imitating the model's behavior but may also keep the observer from displaying any response. In this case, the observer may direct attention elsewhere or otherwise attempt to get away from the situation.

4. *Increased susceptibility to direct reinforcements*—the observer may become more accurate in his or her imitation in order to obtain direct reinforcement in the future.

5. *Modification of social status*—the observer may become aware that the model's (and, if the behavior is imitated, his or her own) social status may be increased or decreased through rewards and punishments.

6. *Alteration of valuation of reinforcing agents*—the observer may change his or her psychological posture toward a reinforcing agent if the agent is perceived to be abusing power. For example, if you observe a model receiving what you believe is unjust punishment, you may become aggressive toward the person dispensing the punishment.

Through these six mechanisms, the observational learner feels the effects of the model's rewards and punishments and modifies his or her own behavior accordingly.

Critical Review 6

1. Bandura and Walters claim that motivation has nothing to do with learning. T F

2. Information is one of the mechanisms that regulate the effects of vicarious rewards and punishments. T F

3. Explain the roles of modeling, attention, retention, reproduction, and motivation in social learning theory.

Expectancy for Success

Questionnaire

Social learning theorists such as Albert Bandura emphasize the influence of expectancies on our behavior. For example, when we expect that personal effort will be rewarded, we tend to persist, even when confronted with difficult circumstances.

The following scale by Bobbi Fibel and W. Daniel Hale is designed to give you some indication as to whether you expect future success. The scoring key on page 56 will tell you how your expectancy for success compares with other students taking undergraduate psychology courses.

Directions: Indicate the degree to which each item applies to you by circling the appropriate number, according to this key:

    1 = highly improbable
    2 = improbable
    3 = equally improbable and probable, not sure
    4 = probable
    5 = highly probable

In the future I expect that I will

1. find that people don't seem to understand what I'm trying to say   1   2   3   4   5

2. be discouraged about my ability to gain the respect of others   1   2   3   4   5

3. be a good parent   1   2   3   4   5

4. be unable to accomplish my goals   1   2   3   4   5

5. have a stressful marital relationship   1   2   3   4   5

6. deal poorly with emergency situations   1   2   3   4   5

Questionnaire
—continued

7. find my efforts to change situations I don't like are ineffective   1   2   3   4   5
8. not be very good at learning new skills   1   2   3   4   5
9. carry through my responsibilities successfully   1   2   3   4   5
10. discover that the good in life outweighs the bad   1   2   3   4   5
11. handle unexpected problems successfully   1   2   3   4   5
12. get the promotions I deserve   1   2   3   4   5
13. succeed in the projects I undertake   1   2   3   4   5
14. not make any significant contributions to society   1   2   3   4   5
15. discover that my life is not getting much better   1   2   3   4   5
16. be listened to when I speak   1   2   3   4   5
17. discover that my plans don't work too well   1   2   3   4   5
18. find that no matter how hard I try, things just don't turn out the way I would like   1   2   3   4   5
19. handle myself well in whatever situation I'm in   1   2   3   4   5
20. be able to solve my own problems   1   2   3   4   5
21. succeed at most things I try   1   2   3   4   5
22. be successful in my endeavors in the long run   1   2   3   4   5
23. be very successful working out my personal life   1   2   3   4   5
24. experience many failures in my life   1   2   3   4   5
25. make a good first impression on people I meet for the first time   1   2   3   4   5
26. attain the career goals I have set for myself   1   2   3   4   5
27. have difficulty dealing with my superiors   1   2   3   4   5
28. have problems working with others   1   2   3   4   5
29. be a good judge of what it takes to get ahead   1   2   3   4   5
30. achieve recognition in my profession   1   2   3   4   5

SOURCE: Reprinted with permission from B. Fibel and W. D. Hale, 1978, p. 931.

A FULFILLMENT MODEL—HUMANISM

Rogers and Humanism

The basic assumption of the fulfillment approach is that personality is shaped by a single force from within the person. Like the conflict and learning-centered approaches, the fulfillment approach has many adherents and many variations. Generally, fulfillment theorists reject the basic **determinism** of the other two approaches—the notion that behavior is caused by and can be explained by factors over which the individual has no control. Rather, they emphasize both freedom of choice for the individual and responsibility for one's own behavior.

determinism   the doctrine that behavior is caused by and can be explained in terms of factors over which the individual has no control

Scholars who support this position are often referred to as **humanists.** One of the most influential fulfillment theorists was Carl Rogers (1902–1987).[5]

Freedom and Control

You may recall that the conflict approach assumes that behavior is determined by and can be explained in terms of the conflict of two opposing forces. For Freud, the conflict is between the id and the superego. Through defense, the ego maintains equilibrium for the personality. In this view, about the best we can do is lie to ourselves to maintain adequate adjustment.

Behaviorism assumes that behavior is determined by and can be explained in terms of learning. For Skinner, learning is synonymous with conditioning, and our most significant learned responses are controlled by the environment through operant conditioning. In this view, concepts such as freedom of choice and responsibility for behavior are ultimately meaningless.

Rogers and other humanists are much more optimistic about the possibilities for human beings. They believe there is much more to human functioning than self-deception or responses to environmental stimuli.

Rogers did not deny that the ultimate causes for human behavior lie outside the individual's control. However, he believed that we have freedom to choose from among responses, within the limits of the factors that determine our behavior. We can, for instance, choose either to become aware of and to understand the factors that determine our behavior, or to ignore them. Through this kind of choice we can exercise responsibility for our behavior. Rogers accepted both determinism and freedom of choice, and he believed both concepts are useful in understanding human functioning.

The Actualizing Tendency

The force Rogers saw as shaping personality is the drive to actualize potentialities, to become what we are capable of becoming. Rogers believed that all living organisms possess this **actualizing tendency.** Like Freud's self-preservation drive, the actualizing tendency aims at maintaining life by pushing the organism to meet its needs for oxygen, food, and water. In addition, however, the actualizing tendency aims at enhancing life as it pushes the organism to grow. Growth can have involuntary aspects (biological changes that automatically take place over time, such as the development of a fetus from an embryo) and voluntary aspects (such as your conscious decision to become better educated by going to college).

There are fundamental differences among Freud, Skinner, and Rogers on this issue. All three would agree that involuntary growth takes place, but there is no notation of voluntary growth in the Freudian and Skinnerian views. For Freud, unconscious functioning dominates our behavior, while Skinner's theory holds that our choices are determined by environment.

humanist   scholar who views humans as having free choice of and responsibility for their own behavior

actualizing tendency   the biologically based drive to become what we are capable of becoming

---

5. Like Freud and Skinner, Rogers produced a large volume of work over an extended period. The following books and articles were particularly useful to our discussion of his ideas: "A Theory of Therapy, Personality, and Interpersonal Relationships, as Developed in the Client-Centered Framework" (1959, pp. 184–256); *On Becoming a Person* (1961); "Actualizing Tendency in Relation to 'Motives' and to Consciousness" (1963, pp. 1–24); and *Person to Person: The Problem of Being Human* (1967).

Potentialities

potentialities the inherent capacities with which the individual is born

Potentialities are the inherent capacities of the individual. Because Rogers viewed human beings as dynamic, growing, and free organisms, he did not believe it possible to specify what these potentialities are. However, he did indicate that all inherent potentialities of humans function to maintain and to enhance life. Again, we see a significant difference among Freud, Skinner, and Rogers. The Freudian view holds that the aggressive drive may be turned inward and may ultimately result in suicide; therefore, suicide may be a function of human nature. The Skinnerian view holds that the only significant human potentiality is the ability to respond differentially to environmental stimuli. In contrast, the Rogerian view holds that we have many significant inherent potentialities and that these work toward positive growth. Thus, a person may choose to commit suicide, but suicide (and other destructive behavior) is an expression of psychological maladjustment rather than an expression of human nature.

The Nature of Conflict

Unlike Freud, Rogers rejected the idea that conflict between the individual and society is inevitable. He believed that the maintenance and enhancement of the individual are consistent with society's communal requirements. Conflict, when it does occur, is an expression of maladjustment. For example, we lash out at people and act destructively in other ways only when we feel insecure, unworthy, depressed, and so on. Conversely, when we feel good about ourselves (secure, worthy, happy) we cooperate, reach out, and lend a helping hand. Therefore, we maintain and enhance our own lives when we maintain and enhance the lives of others. In this view, aggressiveness is an expression of maladjustment because it is not an expression of the basic life force, the actualizing tendency.

Critical Review 7

1. The doctrine that behavior is caused by and can be explained in terms of factors over which the individual has no control is called _____.

2. The _____ _____ is the biologically based drive to become what we are capable of becoming.

3. Rogers referred to the inherent capacities of the individual as _____.

4. How do Rogers's concepts of potentialities and the actualizing tendency differ from Freud's drives?

The Self-Actualizing Tendency

self-actualizing tendency the drive to become what we think we are

self a conscious idea of who and what we are; may also be referred to as self-image or self-concept

The actualizing tendency is our biological drive to become what we can become. As previously mentioned, all living organisms have this drive. Rogers assumed, however, that living organisms do not have identical potentialities; hence, the actualizing tendency does not express itself in the same way for all species. Human beings, for instance, experience psychological aspects of the actualizing tendency that do not occur in other life forms. One such aspect is the **self-actualizing tendency,** the drive to become what we think we are.

Rogers asserted that each of us has a **self**—a conscious idea of who and what we are. Unlike the actualizing tendency, the self is not part of us when we are born. It develops over time as we gain the approval and disapproval of significant others in our environment (such as our parents). In other words, people make judgments about us and our behavior and tell us that we are good (or bad), smart (or stupid), kind (or mean), and so on. Eventually, we integrate this feedback into a conscious idea of who and what we are. Once we have developed this self-concept, we begin to make judgments about our own behavior, which, in turn, further defines our self-concept. We may, for example, evaluate our own thoughts, feelings, and actions as being more or less consistent with our self-concept. In this manner, we push to become what we think (and what others have originally taught us) we are. Thus, the self-actualizing tendency is manifested in our attempts to live up to our self-concept.

Potentialities and Self

Sometimes we strive to live up to standards that are outside the range of our potentialities. In these instances we may feel guilty and anxious and begin to behave defensively. Consider, for example, a boy who has been taught from early childhood that he has a superior intellect. He has incorporated the idea of being a little genius into his self-concept, but he really does not have extraordinary intellectual capacity. When he learns that his grade on a school test is less than A, he experiences guilt and anxiety for not living up to his expectations. In an attempt to maintain his self-concept, he will tell himself a lie. For instance, he may convince himself that he did not feel well when he took the test, that the test was poorly constructed, or that it was unfair because it dealt with material not covered in the book. The boy in our example is maladjusted because, in his attempt to maintain a distorted self-concept, he works against the drive to actualize his potentialities. If he continues to display such maladjusted behavior, he will prevent himself from becoming all he could become.

Rogers provided a general description of the process by which inconsistencies between potentialities and self-concept arise. Significant others begin the process by giving us **conditional positive regard.** This means they accept, support, and respect us only some of the time (for example, when we behave the way they want us to behave). Our self-concept develops in accordance with their idea of who and what we should be. Soon we translate their "shoulds" into standards by which we judge the value of our thoughts, feelings, and actions—**conditions of worth.** Once we have established conditions of worth, we must meet them or display the guilt, anxiety, and defensive behavior previously mentioned. At this point, we find ourselves in a state of **incongruence,** in which we restrict the full expression of our potentialities. Thus, we are maladjusted.

If, however, we receive complete acceptance, support, and respect from significant others **(unconditional positive regard),** we will not develop conditions of worth. Without conditions of worth, we will not experience the guilt and anxiety or display the defensive behavior associated with them. We will be in a state of **congruence,** which will not restrict the full expression of our potentialities. Under these circumstances, there will be no inconsistency or conflict between our potentialities and our self-concept; on the contrary, our self-concept will reflect our potentialities. We will be adjusted. Rogers referred to this type of person as the *fully functioning person.*

Rogers recognized that it is highly unlikely that fully functioning people exist; however, ideally it is possible that they could. This position is, of course, an extreme departure from the determinism and inherent pessimism of the Freudian view, in which conflict is inevitable. Moreover, Rogers argued that

conditional positive regard partial acceptance, support, and respect from significant others

conditions of worth standards by which we judge our own value, taught to us by other people

incongruence the state in which the full expression of one's potentialities is restricted

unconditional positive regard complete acceptance, support, and respect from significant others

congruence the condition in which there is no conflict between potentialities and self-concept

even if we display maladjusted behavior from time to time, we can do something about it. We can examine our thoughts, feelings, and actions. We can explore our own potentialities and be creative. We can learn to trust our own judgment and to reject inappropriate standards set for us by other people. Indeed, we can rearrange our self-concept so that it reflects our potentialities, thus eliminating the cause of our defensive behavior. And we can do all these things by conscious *choice,* a course of action unavailable to us in both the Freudian and Skinnerian views.

Critical Review 8

1. When we receive the complete acceptance, support, and respect of significant others, we are receiving _____ _____
_____ .

2. Conditions of worth typically lead to _____ ,
_____ , and _____ .

3. Rogers called our conscious idea of who and what we are our _____ .

4. How do inconsistencies between potentialities and self-concept lead to maladjustment?

Maslow's View

Abraham Maslow (1908–1970), another humanist, concentrated on human needs and their relationship to the development of a person's full potential. According to Maslow, human needs unfold in a pyramidlike structure (see Figure 2–1). Each level of need in the pyramid emerges as the requirements of the preceding level are met.

The Lower Levels of the Pyramid of Needs   At the base of the pyramid are our physiological needs—our needs for food, air, rest, and so on. These are *unlearned* needs related to physical survival. Failure to meet them results in death. As previously mentioned, the aid of other people is initially indispensable in meeting

FIGURE 2–1

Maslow's perception of human needs.

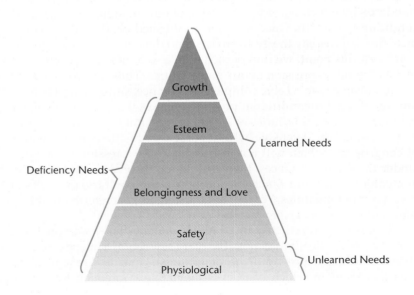

physiological needs. When we have met these needs sufficiently, the next level of need emerges—the need for *safety*. We seek physical safety and psychological security so that we may feel free to act within our environment without fear or threat.

Note that needs for safety are *learned*, as are all of the needs above the physiological level in the pyramid. For example, if you had been placed in a room with a poisonous snake when you were only a year old and you had not yet learned that poisonous snakes are dangerous, you probably would have approached the snake out of curiosity. You might have tried to hold it and perhaps to put it into your mouth. Contrast that image with the behavior you would display now if you were placed in a room with a poisonous snake. You have learned to fear poisonous snakes for safety's sake. Indeed, if you are like many people, this particular fear may have become generalized to include non-poisonous snakes as well. Although it is possible to learn safety needs through observation of and reflection on direct life experiences, it is likely that you have learned many ideas related to safety through communication with other people.

When needs for safety have been satisfied, needs for *belongingness* and *love* arise. We want affection and appreciation from others, and we want to feel wanted as a social group member. Satisfaction of the needs for belongingness and love directly depend on interaction with others; failure to satisfy these needs results in inadequate development.

The fourth level of the pyramid contains needs for *esteem*. We want respect, both from other people and from ourselves. These two types of needs for esteem have something in common, but they also differ. Both are concerned with meeting standards for achievement. However, we gain the respect of others by meeting *their* standards, while we gain self-respect by meeting *our own* standards. Generally, when we satisfy our needs for esteem, we feel good about ourselves and are confident that we can do whatever we choose to do. When we do not satisfy these needs, we feel frustrated, discouraged, inferior, and helpless.

Need Conflict   In Maslow's view, we can attend to only one level of need at a time, so the needs cannot conflict. The person with unsatisfied needs for love and belongingness must attend to them before needs for esteem can be satisfied. Perhaps that is why the unloved superstar is such an unfulfilled person. He or she may be striving for self-respect or the respect of others without having first fulfilled the more basic need to get love and acceptance from others. Thus, although we do not have need conflicts, we may very well have a confusion of needs.

It is important to understand that, in Maslow's view, we always function on the lowest level of unmet need at any given time. If, for example, you usually eat three meals a day and you miss breakfast, then by lunch time you will not be concerned with whether you are respected or loved. You will be concerned with satisfying your hunger. In such a situation, your needs for love and esteem are suspended until your need for food has been satisfied.

Needs for Growth   Maslow identified several needs related to growth, including needs for *self-actualization, understanding,* and *aesthetics*. Maslow used the term *self-actualization* in virtually the same sense Rogers used the term *actualizing tendency*. Hence, our need for self-actualization is our desire to fulfill our potential. Our need for understanding is our desire to reach the greatest levels of meaning and awareness of ourselves, others, and all aspects of the external environment. Our desire for beauty is reflected in our aesthetic need.

We need the affection of others in order to become complete persons.

There is a significant difference between the needs of the lower levels of the pyramid and the needs for growth. Maslow referred to the lower needs as *deficiency needs;* we act to meet these needs because we lack something. Once we have fulfilled the deficiency needs, we are free to become, to understand, and to appreciate all that we are capable of becoming, understanding, and appreciating. When we are actively engaged in fulfilling growth needs, we have reached the highest level of human development. Finally, we should note that at this level, as at all levels of the pyramid, human contact plays a vital role. We must have human contact if we are to become all we are capable of becoming.

Critical Review 9

1. Maslow's growth needs include the needs for _____ , _____ , and _____ .

2. How are human needs related to the development of a person's full potential?

SUMMARY

■ Many psychologists have attempted to investigate scientifically the question "Who am I?" The concept of personality has emerged from their work.

■ Although scholars often disagree on specific definitions of personality, they do agree that at least three characteristics should be taken into account: uniqueness, organization, and adaptability.

■ We may define personality as the individual's unique and dynamic pattern of thoughts, feelings, and actions.

■ Modern scientific information suggests that an intricate relationship exists among body, mind, emotions, and behavior, with each affecting the others in their functioning. Many factors, both learned and unlearned, influence personality.

■ Psychologists use two primary approaches to describe personality: by traits and by types. Generally, the trait approach emphasizes uniqueness, while the type approach emphasizes organization.

■ Psychologists also often provide broader, more general descriptions in the form of personality models. The major issues they address are the determinants, structure, dynamics, and development of personality.

■ The various personality models may be divided into three basic approaches: conflict, learning-centered, and fulfillment. The conflict approach (psychoanalysis) assumes that a conflict between two opposing factors shapes personality. The learning-centered approach (behaviorism) assumes that learning shapes personality. The fulfillment approach (humanism) assumes that a force that comes from within the individual shapes personality.

■ Sigmund Freud viewed the conflicts between the self-serving demands of the individual and the communal demands of society as the determinants of personality.

■ Freud postulated a personality structure consisting of id (selfish demands), ego (rational functioning), and superego (society's rules). The conflict between the id and the superego is managed by the ego through its defensive functioning.

■ According to Freud, personality development proceeds through a series of five psychosexual stages, the first three of which are critical in the individual's character formation.

■ Erik Erikson modified Freud's view by adding three stages of development and placing emphasis on the social rather than the sexual nature of the conflicts encountered in each stage. Erikson's stages are called psychosocial stages.

■ B. F. Skinner asserted that personality is determined primarily through learning.

■ Although he did not write about personality structure, Skinner believed the important structural component in human behavior is the ability to respond differentially to environmental stimuli.

■ Skinner treated personality dynamics in terms of respondent and operant conditioning; the more important of these is operant conditioning, because it explains our most significant responses.

■ Skinner explained development in terms of the individual's history of reinforcements.

■ Albert Bandura and Richard H. Walters have proposed a social learning theory that focuses on modeling as the principal technique through which we learn.

■ Carl Rogers held that personality is determined by the degree of consistency between the individual's potentialities and self-concept.

■ Rogers believed personality structure consists of the actualizing tendency, the potentialities, and the self-concept. The individual pushes to behave consistently with his or her self-concept.

■ Conditional positive regard and conditions of worth lead to guilt, anxiety, defensive behavior, a state of incongruence, and, ultimately, maladjustment.

■ Unconditional positive regard and an absence of conditions of worth lead to a state of congruence, which in itself represents adjustment.

■ Rogers asserted that although initial development is heavily influenced by significant others, later development is a matter of conscious choice.

■ Abraham Maslow concentrated on human needs and their relationship to the development of a person's full potential. Our needs unfold in a pyramidlike structure, with each higher level of need emerging as the requirements of the preceding level are met.

SELECTED READINGS

Feshbach, S., and Weiner, B. *Personality*, 3rd ed. Lexington, MA: D. C. Heath, 1991. A highly readable, eclectic overview of personality.

Gay, P. *Freud: A Life for Our Time*. New York: Norton, 1988. An outstanding biography of Freud.

Hall, C. S., Lindzey, G., Loehlin, J. C., Manosevitz, M., and Locke, V. O. *Introduction to Theories of Personality*. New York: Wiley, 1985. An excellent general introduction to personality theory.

Nye, R. D. *Three Psychologies: Perspectives from Freud, Skinner, and Rogers*. Pacific Grove, CA: Brooks/Cole, 1992. A brief introduction to the views of three theorists, including comparisons, contrasts, and criticisms.

Pervin, L. A. *Personality: Theory and Research*. New York: Wiley, 1989. An overview of personality theory and research.

REFERENCES

Bandura, A. *Principles of Behavior Modification*. New York: Holt, Rinehart and Winston, 1969.

_____. "Analysis of Modeling Processes." In *Psychological Modeling: Conflicting Theories*, edited by A. Bandura. Chicago: Aldine-Atherton, 1971(a), 29–43.

_____. Social Learning Theory. Morristown, NJ: General Learning Press, 1971(b).

Bandura, A., and Walters, R. H. *Social Learning and Personality Development*. New York: Holt, Rinehart and Winston, 1963.

Erikson, E. H. *Childhood and Society*, 2nd ed. New York: Norton, 1963.

_____. Identity: Youth and Crisis. New York: Norton, 1968.

Fibel, B., and Hale, W. D. "The Generalized Expectancy for Success Scale—A New Measure." *Journal of Consulting and Clinical Psychology* 46 (1978): 924–931.

Freud, S. *Beyond the Pleasure Principle*. Revised, translated, and edited by J. Strachey. New York: Liveright, 1961. First German edition, 1920.

_____. *Civilization and Its Discontents*. Translated and edited by J. Strachey. New York: Norton, 1961. First German edition, 1930.

_____. *The Ego and the Id*. Translated and edited by J. Strachey. New York: Norton, 1961. First German edition, 1923.

_____. *The Interpretation of Dreams*. Translated and edited by J. Strachey. New York: Avon, 1965. First German edition, 1900.

_____. *New Introductory Lectures on Psycho-Analysis*. Translated and edited by J. Strachey. New York: Norton, 1965. First German edition, 1933.

_____. *An Outline of Psycho-Analysis*. Revised, translated, and edited by J. Strachey. New York: Norton, 1969. First German edition, 1940.

_____. *The Psychopathology of Everyday Life*. Translated by A. Tyson; edited with an introduction and additional notes by J. Strachey. New York: Norton, 1966. First German edition, 1904.

Maslow, A. H. *Motivation and Personality*, 2nd ed. New York: Harper & Row, 1970.

Rogers, C. R. "Actualizing Tendency in Reaction to 'Motives' and to Consciousness." In *Nebraska Symposium on Motivation*, edited by M. R. Jones, 1–24. Lincoln: University of Nebraska Press, 1963.

_____. *On Becoming a Person*. Boston: Houghton Mifflin, 1961.

_____. "A Theory of Therapy, Personality, and Interpersonal Relationships, as Developed in the Client-Centered Framework." In *Psychology: A Study of a Science*, vol. 3, edited by S. Koch, 184–256. New York: McGraw-Hill, 1959.

Rogers, C., and Stevens, B. *Person to Person: The Problem of Being Human*. Lafayette, CA: Real People Press, 1967.

Skinner, B. F. *About Behaviorism*. New York: Knopf, 1974.

_____. *Beyond Freedom and Dignity*. New York: Knopf, 1971.

_____. *Contingencies of Reinforcement: A Theoretical Analysis*. New York: Appleton-Century-Crofts, 1969.

_____. *Science and Human Behavior*. New York: Macmillan, 1953.

_____. *Verbal Behavior*. New York: Appleton-Century-Crofts, 1957.

■ *Questionnaire Scoring Key*

Expectancy for Success

To figure your score: Calculate your total score by first reversing the scores for the following items: 1, 2, 4, 6, 7, 8, 14, 15, 17, 18, 24, 27, and 28. For example, change a 5 to a 1; a 4 to a 2, etc. After reversing scores for these items, add all scores.

The highest possible total score is 150; the lowest is 30. The higher your score, the higher your expectancy of success, and the more likely you are to persist, even when confronted with difficult circumstances.

Fibel and Hale found that both male and female students taking undergraduate psychology courses averaged 112, although the range of scores for men (81–138) was narrower than that of women (65–143).

■ *Answers to Critical Review Questions*

Critical Review 1 1. T 2. T 3. F 4. T 5. F 6. T
Critical Review 2 1. conflict 2. id, ego, superego 3. self-serving, communal 4. defense
Critical Review 3 1. fixated 2. Oedipus complex, identification 3. integrity, despair
Critical Review 4 1. T 2. F 3. T 4. T
Critical Review 5 1. F 2. T 3. T 4. F 5. T
Critical Review 6 1. F 2. T
Critical Review 7 1. determinism 2. actualizing tendency 3. potentialities
Critical Review 8 1. unconditional positive regard 2. guilt, anxiety, defensive behavior 3. self
Critical Review 9 1. self-actualization, understanding, aesthetics

PERSONAL ACTION PLAN
Personality Description

The exercises in this Personal Action Plan are designed to provide you with information you can use to become more aware of your personality. Later Personal Action Plans will encourage you to make judgments about your behavior patterns and help you change those behaviors you would like to change. At this point, however, it is most useful to focus on description.

In this Personal Action Plan, you will acquire most of the information through introspection or self-examination, although some of the information will be provided by others. The first exercise is relatively simple, and you will probably finish it in five minutes or less. Take more time if necessary.

I. Directions.

Think about some of the enduring characteristics of your personality. Then, complete the following ten sentences by filling in some of your more important personality traits.

Example. A person who usually relies on himself or herself to get things done might write: I am self-reliant.

1. I am _____
2. I am _____
3. I am _____
4. I am _____
5. I am _____
6. I am _____
7. I am _____
8. I am _____
9. I am _____
10. I am _____

In their attempts to study personality, psychologists often use two methods: inventories or questionnaires, and projective tests. A few of the more commonly used inventories or questionnaires are the Minnesota Multiphasic Personality Inventory, Cattell's Sixteen Personality Factor Questionnaire, and Edward's Personal Preference Schedule. Possibly the two most commonly used projective tests are the Rorschach Test and the Thematic Apperception Test. These devices purport to measure a variety of personality dimensions. Contact your psychology instructor or the college or university counseling department for

more information about them. You may even arrange to take one or more of them. In the meantime, we would like you to concentrate on the next exercise, which is an adaptation of the characteristics measured by Cattell's Sixteen Personality Factor Questionnaire.

II. Directions.

The following is a list of sixteen pairs of opposing personality characteristics, with each pair separated by a five-point rating scale. Rate your personality according to these characteristics by circling the point on each scale that you believe best represents your personality with regard to that characteristic.

Example. A person who believes he or she is moderately serious would mark the scale as follows:

Serious   __ /(__)__ / __ / __   Happy-go-lucky

Yourself:

Reserved	__ / __ / __ / __ / __	Outgoing
Concrete thinking	__ / __ / __ / __ / __	Abstract thinking
Easily upset	__ / __ / __ / __ / __	Calm
Flexible	__ / __ / __ / __ / __	Stubborn
Serious	__ / __ / __ / __ / __	Happy-go-lucky
Gives up easily	__ / __ / __ / __ / __	Persistent
Shy	__ / __ / __ / __ / __	Uninhibited
Self-reliant	__ / __ / __ / __ / __	Dependent
Trusting	__ / __ / __ / __ / __	Suspicious
Conventional	__ / __ / __ / __ / __	Unconventional
Forthright	__ / __ / __ / __ / __	Calculating
Confident	__ / __ / __ / __ / __	Worried
Respects status quo	__ / __ / __ / __ / __	Critical of status quo
Follower	__ / __ / __ / __ / __	Leader
Undisciplined	__ / __ / __ / __ / __	Disciplined
Relaxed	__ / __ / __ / __ / __	Tense

Rating your own personality characteristics is useful; however, it only tells you what you think about yourself. What about others? How do they perceive your personality? Duplicates of the exercise you have just completed follow. Think of three people you believe know you well. (Try to include at least one person who is either a generation older or younger than you.) Then, ask each of these people to rate your personality characteristics and return the ratings to you. When you receive these ratings, compare them with your own. You may want to discuss these ratings with the people who did them. Whether you just compare the ratings or both compare and discuss them, you should keep the purpose of the exercise in mind. What you are attempting to do is get a description of your personality from several different perspectives. As previously mentioned, evaluation and action plans designed to facilitate desired change will come later.

Person #1:

Reserved	__/__/ __/ __/ __	Outgoing
Concrete thinking	__/__/ __/ __/ __	Abstract thinking
Easily upset	__/__/ __/ __/ __	Calm
Flexible	__/__/ __/ __/ __	Stubborn
Serious	__/__/ __/ __/ __	Happy-go-lucky
Gives up easily	__/__/ __/ __/ __	Persistent
Shy	__/__/ __/ __/ __	Uninhibited
Self-reliant	__/__/ __/ __/ __	Dependent
Trusting	__/__/ __/ __/ __	Suspicious
Conventional	__/__/ __/ __/ __	Unconventional
Forthright	__/__/ __/ __/ __	Calculating
Confident	__/__/ __/ __/ __	Worried
Respects status quo	__/__/ __/ __/ __	Critical of status quo
Follower	__/__/ __/ __/ __	Leader
Undisciplined	__/__/ __/ __/ __	Disciplined
Relaxed	__/__/ __/ __/ __	Tense

Person #2:

Reserved	__/__/ __/ __/ __	Outgoing
Concrete thinking	__/__/ __/ __/ __	Abstract thinking
Easily upset	__/__/ __/ __/ __	Calm
Flexible	__/__/ __/ __/ __	Stubborn
Serious	__/__/ __/ __/ __	Happy-go-lucky
Gives up easily	__/__/ __/ __/ __	Persistent
Shy	__/__/ __/ __/ __	Uninhibited
Self-reliant	__/__/ __/ __/ __	Dependent
Trusting	__/__/ __/ __/ __	Suspicious
Conventional	__/__/ __/ __/ __	Unconventional
Forthright	__/__/ __/ __/ __	Calculating
Confident	__/__/ __/ __/ __	Worried
Respects status quo	__/__/ __/ __/ __	Critical of status quo
Follower	__/__/ __/ __/ __	Leader
Undisciplined	__/__/ __/ __/ __	Disciplined
Relaxed	__/__/ __/ __/ __	Tense

Person #3:

Reserved	__/__/ __/ __/ __	Outgoing
Concrete thinking	__/__/ __/ __/ __	Abstract thinking
Easily upset	__/__/ __/ __/ __	Calm
Flexible	__/__/ __/ __/ __	Stubborn
Serious	__/__/ __/ __/ __	Happy-go-lucky
Gives up easily	__/__/ __/ __/ __	Persistent
Shy	__/__/ __/ __/ __	Uninhibited
Self-reliant	__/__/ __/ __/ __	Dependent
Trusting	__/__/ __/ __/ __	Suspicious
Conventional	__/__/ __/ __/ __	Unconventional
Forthright	__/__/ __/ __/ __	Calculating
Confident	__/__/ __/ __/ __	Worried
Respects status quo	__/__/ __/ __/ __	Critical of status quo
Follower	__/__/ __/ __/ __	Leader
Undisciplined	__/__/ __/ __/ __	Disciplined
Relaxed	__/__/ __/ __/ __	Tense

Chapter 2 of your text introduces three approaches to personality: conflict, learning-centered, and fulfillment. The next three exercises are related to those three approaches, respectively.

III. Directions.

Below are listed three periods of your life: childhood, adolescence, and now. Think about significant conflicts associated with each period. Try to recall your specific thoughts, feelings, and actions in dealing with those conflicts. Then, write a brief description of the conflicts, how you have dealt with them, and how they have contributed to your personality as it currently is.

Example. Childhood: During childhood, I had a continuing conflict with my brother over the attention of our father. Each of us wanted his attention very much and each tried to outdo the other in order to get it. I would even go so far as to wish that negative things would happen to my brother. I remember feeling elated one time when he was punished for coming home very late for dinner. Dad always wanted us to be prompt. At other times, I had fantasies of bringing home a report card with all A's (a feat that neither of us ever accomplished), or being elected captain of the little league baseball team (another achievement that eluded both of us). As time passed, I gradually came to realize that our father loved us for ourselves, not for our achievements or for what we thought he wanted us to be. From my own experience, I have learned that it is unnecessary to prove my worth to other people. At the same time, I have become compassionate and understanding with people who have not yet learned this valuable lesson.

Childhood:

Adolescence:

Now:

IV. Directions.

Many of our habitual thoughts, feelings, and actions are conditioned responses to the environment. Complete the following sentences by filling in some of your habits.

Example. When I am interacting with my parents, I often (think/feel/act) *think they really don't understand me.*

1. When I am interacting with my parents, I often (think/feel/act) _____
_____

2. During school classes, I often (think/feel/act)
_____

3. With my good friends, I usually (think/feel/act)
_____

   With acquaintances, I often (think/feel/act)
_____

4. When riding in a car, I often (think/feel/act)
_____

5. When I interact with others at a large party, I often (think/feel/act) _____
_____

6. At work, I usually (think/feel/act) _____
_____

7. With my brother(s) and/or sister(s), I usually (think/feel/act) _____

_____
_____

8. When I am alone, I often (think/feel/act)
_____
_____

V. Directions.

Some of our personality traits are directly related to particular talents we have developed and/or particular choices we have made at some point in our lives. Write a brief description of some of the talents you have and how they have contributed to your personality. Then, write a brief description of a few important decisions you have made and how each has been important in the formation of your personality.

Example. Talents: I have liked music for as long as I can remember. When my parents allowed me to take piano lessons, I was very happy. When I discovered I had musical talent, I was overjoyed. Over the years, I have explored my musical talent, and today I can play the guitar, the drums, and the bass, as well as the piano. Playing these instruments always provides an outlet for my tension whenever I begin to feel uptight. As a result, I am usually a pretty loose person.

Talents:

Decisions:

This Personal Action Plan has focused on personality. The foregoing exercises have helped you focus on many facets of your unique and dynamic pattern of thoughts, feelings, and actions. Now, in the final exercise, you are asked to summarize what you have learned about your personality.

VI. Directions.

After referring to the responses to the previous exercises in this Personal Action Plan, write a descriptive essay about your personality. Include a consideration of your characteristic thoughts, feelings, and actions. Use as many circumstances and as many people as you can. Entitle the essay "Who Am I?"

3

SELF-ESTEEM

Chapter Outline

FOCUS

For decades, psychologists have known that self-esteem is the major factor determining our ability or inability to adjust both psychologically and socially. The effects of low self-esteem can be seen in poor achievement among schoolchildren and teenagers, teenage pregnancy, low productivity among the nation's workers, drug abuse, alcoholism, welfare dependency, crime, murder, and suicide. This evidence has begun to influence government agencies to consider the possibility that the self-esteem of society's individuals may be the root of many problems.

DEFINING SELF-ESTEEM

self-esteem   the degree to which one values oneself and feels useful and necessary in the world

The range of feelings described in the preceding Focus section results from what psychologists call the level of **self-esteem**. We know that some people exhibit characteristics of low self-esteem for long periods. We also know that other people enjoy long periods of high self-esteem. Still others (probably most of us) are somewhere between, with occasional fluctuations from high to low, low to high, and back again. We can experience these ups and downs in a single day or even in a moment. In this chapter we will discuss the characteristics of various levels of self-esteem, the effects of earlier development on our level of self-esteem, and, most important, the maintenance of positive self-esteem as a lifelong process.

Self-esteem is perhaps the most important part of our self-concept (see chapter 2 for discussions of personality and self-concept). More specifically, it is the degree to which we value ourselves, or the degree to which we feel worthwhile. Psychological development throughout life is greatly affected by this self-judgment. It is probably the single most important factor determining our feelings, attitudes, values, behaviors, and goals (Branden, 1969); Canfield and Wells (1975) believe that the enhancement and preservation of our self-esteem is our highest value.

Abraham Maslow (1970) wrote that all people in our society (with a few pathological exceptions) have a need or desire for a stable, firmly based, usually high evaluation of themselves—in other words, for self-respect and self-esteem—as well as for the esteem of others (see the discussion of Maslow in chapter 2).

■ The need for *self-respect and self-esteem* is the desire for strength, achievement, adequacy, mastery and competence, confidence in the face of others, independence, and freedom.

■ The need for the *esteem of others* is the desire for reputation or prestige (defined as respect or esteem from other people), status, fame and glory, dominance, recognition, attention, importance, dignity, and appreciation.

These needs require *feedback* from others assuring us that we are highly regarded and appreciated. As our need for self-esteem is satisfied, we begin to realize that our lives have meaning, and we begin to feel more useful and better able to make choices for ourselves and to direct our own lives.

The best indicator of the level of your self-esteem is the way you behave. Behavior is an acting out of the basic attitudes (beliefs) we hold and of the feelings we are experiencing. In turn, our behavior reinforces our attitudes and affects the way we view ourselves and, hence, the way we feel. It also greatly affects our relationships with others. Others are often more aware of our behavior than we are; we can learn much about ourselves by objectively viewing our behavior through their eyes.

The intent of this chapter is to help you sharpen your awareness of yourself so you can identify personal characteristics that affect your level of self-esteem. We hope you will discover how your level of self-esteem affects the way you live your life and what you can do to maintain positive self-esteem.

DEVELOPMENT OF SELF-ESTEEM

The present condition of our self-esteem results most from the psychological environment in which we grew up and matured. Within this environment, other people (adults) had the greatest effect on the development of our self-esteem. The people who influence us serve as *models* for the development of our *attitudes, values,* and *behaviors* (see the discussion on modeling in chapter 2). The development of our self-esteem depends not only on what we learn from others, however; it also results from what we learn from experiencing life independently.

Shaping Influences

Our models include parents, siblings, close relatives, schoolteachers, and playmates. Some of these people may still influence us. Others may no longer be directly involved in our lives, but what we learned from them may have a dramatic effect on our self-perceptions. The foundation for self-esteem seems to be constructed very early in life, and it is believed that some children have a negative self-image prior to entering school.

Parents   For most of us, parents are the most significant influence in shaping us as people. They are, with few exceptions, our major source of security, love, and other need fulfillment. When parents love us as we need to be loved and treat us as human beings of worth and value, we grow up in psychologically healthy environment and probably will enjoy positive self-esteem in later life. However, when parents are too involved in their own problems to be able to love us, or even to conceive of us as unique individuals, it is difficult for us to develop positive self-esteem. Conflict and tension within the family often result in an envi-

---

CRITICAL THINKING ISSUE
Loving Self Versus Loving Others

You cannot love others until you first learn to love yourself.

Love is a feeling to be shared with others, not with ourselves.

This is viewed by some as a prerequisite to loving others. Loving yourself may mean that you give yourself the same respect and appreciation that you would your dearest and most cherished friend. In this way, you are genuinely more able to love others.

Humility is one of life's greatest virtues. People who love themselves are narcissistic, that is, full of conceit and vanity. We should put the needs of others ahead of our own. The world has too many people who think only of themselves. It would be a better place if we learned to put others first.

I take the position that:

ronment that negatively affects the developing child. The influential and still relevant view of Karen Horney (1956) suggests that parents often unknowingly impede their children's psychological development by being erratic, dominating, overprotective, intimidating, irritable, overexacting, overindulgent, partial to other siblings, hypocritical, or indifferent.

Low self-esteem usually develops as a result of parents and others failing to understand the needs of children. This lack of understanding often makes children confused about how and when to let their needs be known. The confusion results in a serious dilemma. Children—impressionable, vulnerable, and dependent on adults for their survival—are seldom able to understand that sometimes adults make mistakes, too.

Sullivan (1953) believes that for some people this childhood dilemma develops into a survival attitude toward life that profoundly affects the individual's interpersonal relationships and self-esteem. His still useful concept refers to this survival attitude as the **malevolent attitude**—the belief that one really lives among enemies. Sullivan believes it is perhaps the greatest disaster that can happen in the childhood phase of personality development. The child comes to personify himself or herself as something detestable that will always be treated badly, and these beliefs often result in failure to achieve life goals. "I don't deserve this" or "I am unlovable" are examples of unconscious decisions that affect moods, relationships, physical health, and ability to succeed.

malevolent attitude the belief that everyone, to a greater or lesser degree, is an enemy

> Keith grew up in a home where he was treated as a nuisance. His father and mother worked six days a week and often came home tired and unhappy. Consequently, they spent very little time and energy helping Keith meet his needs. The rare expressions of affection or love shown toward him usually resulted from their feel-

The chances of developing a positive self-worth are greater in a healthy, loving environment.

ings of guilt. Out of desperation, Keith occasionally reached out to his mother, who frequently screamed, "Get away! Can't you see I'm busy?" His father usually responded to his requests by saying, "I can't now! Wait 'til later." Unfortunately, "later" usually became "never."

These repeated responses taught Keith that he could not depend on his mother or father for love and affection. He soon learned that it was disadvantageous to show any need for affection. In response to his unfulfilled needs, Keith lashed out at his parents, teachers, and peers. Their negative responses to his behavior only reinforced his feelings of being unloved.

As an adult, Keith makes it practically impossible for anyone to show him tenderness and affection. His untrusting behavior keeps others from giving him the love he so desperately needs.

Some parents may not want children, but they have at least one because they believe childbearing is expected of them. "Our parents are eager to be grandparents. We really can't disappoint them" or "All our friends have children" represents beliefs that compel many couples to have children. Other parents who do want children often want them for reasons detrimental to the development of the child. Bernard Berelson (1979) lists several reasons why some parents choose to have children—reasons that reflect parent-centered motives:

■ *Personal power*: Parents have nearly absolute power during the early years of childhood. Fathers or mothers may have little power over their authority figures (employers) or peers, but they have power over their children. Children may be used to bind one parent to another ("You can't leave me. What about the children?"). Children also are used to increase political and economic power where marriage alliances are arranged.

■ *Personal competence*: The ability to produce a child demonstrates personal competence and virility. ("See what I made. She looks just like me.")

■ *Personal status*: Children can enhance one's social status and influence one's opportunities. ("It is good for business for me to have a beautiful wife and well-behaved children.")

■ *Personal extension*: Children represent a form of immortality. ("I am going to live on through my children. After all, someone must carry on the family name.")

■ *Personal experience*: Parents may live through their children. A parent may be challenged by the possibility of shaping another human being into "perfection." ("My child is going to have all the opportunities I never had—whether he likes it or not.")

■ *Personal pleasure*: There can be much pleasure in loving, caring for, and enjoying children. It can be a tremendously fulfilling experience for a parent. Unfortunately, some parents tend to smother their children with love and overprotectiveness. ("I can never do enough for my children.")

■ *Moral responsibility*: Childbearing is compatible with religious and other beliefs. ("My religion says that every married couple should have children.")

Understanding our reasons for having children is a step in the direction of healthy child rearing. Understanding that children are individuals in their own right, with no responsibility to fulfill our needs, is another step in the right direction. Further, we must understand that children need a secure, cohesive and loving environment in which to grow and develop.

Population Control

Some Third World countries are concerned about overpopulation and their ability to feed their populaces. The People's Republic of China has recently decided to limit nearly all families to just one child. The state penalizes couples for having more than one child by cutting off money for the support of the children and their education. In the face of such penalties and the high value traditionally placed on having sons, some families practice female infanticide.

Today, more couples are deciding not to have children. Bernard's (1975) survey cites ten reasons why people make this choice:

1. *Dual careers*: Both spouses are free to pursue meaningful careers without the conflict that exists when a working couple has children.

2. *Freedom*: Couples are free to come and go as they please and live spontaneously.

3. *Time together*: Couples have more time together to develop a more intimate relationship.

4. *Financial security*: Couples do not face the financial burdens that come with having children.

5. *Difficulty*: Parenting is demanding. It requires sacrifice of time, money, and energy. Not everyone makes a good parent.

6. *Choice, not mandate*: Motherhood should be a choice, not a psychological or social requirement.

7. *Community welfare*: Couples have more opportunities to become involved in civic and community organizations.

8. *Other children available*: Couples can enjoy the children of others. Adoption is always a possibility.

9. *Strain on resources*: The world has limited resources, and it is wrong to place additional strain on these resources.

10. *Overpopulation*: More children will only geometrically increase the problems of overcrowding and overpopulation.

In another survey conducted by Ayers Campbell (1975), more than two thousand people were asked to respond to questions pertaining to life satisfaction. The results indicated that when couples had children their stress increased and their life satisfaction decreased. Many couples with children reported feeling "tied down." It was further discovered that those who decided not to have children showed few signs of regret. These findings were confirmed later in a *Ladies Home Journal* survey of more than thirty thousand women. Women without children (65 percent) reported being happier than women with children (55 percent) (Schultz, 1980). The survey also showed that women without children were better adjusted in specific areas such as optimism about the future, degree of control of their lives, feelings of anger or irritability, level of energy, happiness with their sex lives, and general happiness with their marriages (Figure 3–1).

It is apparent that more couples are feeling less pressure to have children. This may be viewed as a positive sign with respect to the psychological health and self-esteem of future generations of children, who may have a greater

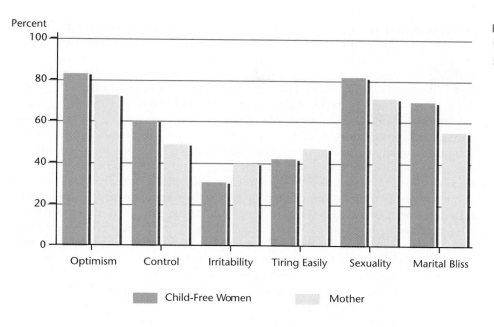

chance of growing up in an environment where they are wanted rather than tolerated.

Growing Beyond the Dysfunctional Family   David Hamburg (1994) cites a longitudinal study conducted by University of California–Davis Professor Emmy Werner that featured seven hundred children, all of whom came from a less than normal family environment. Werner reports that even under adverse conditions, some children are able to develop healthy personalities. These *resilient children* recover from and adjust completely to misfortune and stress. She found that resilient children have four central characteristics in common: *(1) an active, vigorous approach to solving life's problems; (2) a tendency to perceive their experiences constructively even if they involved pain or suffering; (3) the ability to gain other people's positive attention;* and *(4) a strong ability to maintain a positive vision of the meaning of life.*

Many of us have come from dysfunctional family environments such as those described previously. There are several things we can do to grow beyond our past and become healthy individuals. First, we must overcome the notion that we are victims. Our parents may have made many mistakes. Perhaps they were functioning as a result of what they had learned from observing their parents and also from their own low self-esteem. Second, we can learn much from observing others (our parents) and behaving in healthier ways. Sadly, our parents have been the best models of what not to be. Third, we can use the contents of this book to help us overcome some of our feelings by changing our thinking and our behavior. Fourth, we can seek professional counseling, which may help us effectively deal with some of the concealed anger or hurt that burdens us while finding ways to channel our energy in growthful and productive ways (see chapter 14, "Getting Help").

Parenting Skills   Raising children is a mutual learning experience. Parents are viewed as omnipotent models early in a child's life. But, as the child grows, parents can learn many things by observing and listening to the child. This mutual learning environment can enhance the self-esteem of all family members in part because family cohesion and harmony have been determined to be significant variables in the development of positive self-esteem in children (Cooper, Holman, and Braithwaite, 1983). The classic research of Coopersmith (1967, 1975) studied self-esteem patterns of fifth- and sixth-grade boys. Boys with high self-esteem often came from families where parents were strict but not harsh. These parents expressed more affection, were involved in the boy's activities, were accepting, used consistent discipline, and seemed to have high self-esteem themselves. Boys with low self-esteem came from homes where the parents were more permissive but were harsh when they did use discipline. The strict parents were perhaps more demanding, but their involvement in their sons' activities communicated a sense of love and caring. The encouragement these boys received from their parents motivated them to develop competencies in areas that enhanced self-esteem. Coopersmith also discovered that once self-esteem is established, it seems to persist. When checked at three-year intervals, his subjects exhibited stable levels of self-esteem over time. Even if they had momentary swings, it appears that their self-esteem continued to meet the strains of life successfully.

Diana Baumrind (1971, 1991) defines three basic *parenting styles* that she believes affect the development of children: *authoritarian, authoritative,* and *laissez-faire* (permissive). Other developmentalists (Maccoby and Martin, 1983) believe that permissive parenting takes two forms: *permissive-indifferent* and *permissive-indulgent.*

authoritarian parenting   a restrictive, punitive style of parenting

Authoritarian parenting is a punitive and restrictive style that demands that the children follow the orders of the parent with little or no opportunity to communicate their wishes or feelings. The basic assumption is that the child is incompetent. The communication style is one way: "You will do it because I said so!" Children raised in this environment often are afraid of social interaction (the fear of rejection), afraid of taking risks (the fear of being wrong), and have undeveloped communication skills (the inability to say what they need or want).

permissive-indifferent parenting an uninvolved style of parenting

The opposite of authoritarian parenting is **permissive-indifferent parenting**. This style conveys that the child is unimportant: "I don't care what you do. Just don't defame the family name." The parent is uninvolved in the child's life and rarely shows concern if the child does something wrong or something wonderful. The child believes that everything and everyone is more important. These children often grow up with little sense of values or goals. They see themselves as socially incompetent and demonstrate little self-control.

permissive-indulgent parenting an involved style of parenting but with few demands or controls

Another form of permissiveness is **permissive-indulgent parenting**. These parents let their children do whatever they wish without restraint. Some parents adopt this style because they believe it will teach their children to be creative and confident. The penalty is that the children always expect to get their way often by threatening the parents with temper tantrums. As a result, they develop a self-centered attitude. Consequently, they lack self-control, never learn respect for others, and develop few friendships.

authoritative parenting   a warm and nurturing parenting style that encourages independence with limits and controls

The most effective parenting style is **authoritative parenting**. The assumption here is that the parent, through experience, is more knowledgeable about life in many ways than is the child. The parent, therefore, places limitations and controls on the child's behavior, yet also encourages creativity and independence. An authoritative parent would say, "I was unhappy about what you did. Let's talk about how you could handle it differently the next time." The child grows up to be independent, competent, and responsible.

Authoritative parents can also help their children become more resilient (Hamburg, 1994) if they:

- accept their children's temperamental idiosyncrasies and offer them some experiences that challenge but do not overwhelm their coping abilities;

- convey to the children a sense of responsibility and caring and in turn reward them for helpfulness and cooperation;

- encourage their children to develop distinctive interests that can serve as a source of gratification and self-esteem;

- model a conviction that life makes sense despite the inevitable adversities that each of us encounters;

- encourage their children to reach out beyond the nuclear family to a sympathetic relative or friend.

Teachers Schoolteachers, too, have an impact on children's development. However, too often teachers are not fully aware of and responsive to children. Much like the child, the teacher is caught in a system of external and extraneous purposes and goals, a system of authorities, and a canned curriculum that defines appropriate behavior, success, and failure. The teacher is often guided by experts and authorities who remain anonymous and invisible and who are seldom in contact with a classroom or a child.

> Erica, who is brighter than most of her classmates, has become quite bored with the slow pace at which she and the other children are being taught. However, the teacher only notices that Erica is either always looking out the window, apparently daydreaming, or getting out of her seat to sharpen her pencil. Annoyed with this lack of attention, the teacher tells Erica that she will have to sit in the principal's office until she decides she "wants to learn."

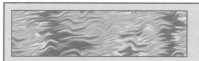

CULTURAL CROSSCURRENTS
Misunderstanding can Negatively Affect Self-esteem

The scene is a classroom in an inner-city elementary school in Richmond, Virginia, Pedro, the nine-year-old son of a recent immigrant family from Puerto Rico, leaves his seat to sharpen his pencil. When the teacher, Ms. Harkins, asks Pedro where he is going, Pedro casts his eyes downward and tries to explain that he was going to the pencil sharpener. Ms. Harkins, thinking that Pedro has something to hide by not looking her in the eye, becomes so annoyed with him that she lifts up his chin and says, "Look at me when I'm talking to you!" Pedro cannot understand what he did wrong that made his teacher so angry.

This unfortunate scenario—played out all too often in our multicultural schools—is a classic example of how cross-cultural communication can be short-circuited. This needless escalation of ill will between student and teacher could have been avoided if Ms. Harkins had understood a fundamental feature of nonverbal communication in Pedro's Puerto Rican culture. In the teacher's mainstream U.S. culture, the student is expected to maintain a high level of eye contact with the teacher as a sign of respect. But in Puerto Rico, Pedro learned not only a different meaning of eye contact but also an opposite meaning. That is, in Puerto Rican culture, children are taught to *avoid* eye contact as a sign of respect for high-status people, such as teachers, priests, grandparents, and adults in general. Thus, while Pedro was trying to show the greatest respect for his teacher by avoiding eye contact, Ms. Harkins mistook his downcast eyes as a sign of disrespect or disinterest. This cross-cultural misunderstanding—stemming from a lack of knowledge about other cultures—hardly contributed to student-teacher rapport.

SOURCE: Ferraro, G., *Cultural Anthropology: An Applied Perspective*. St. Paul, MN: West Publishing Company, 1992.

Moustakas (1969) believes that in many cases, such as Erica's, it is the child who suffers when he or she comes into conflict with rules that interfere with his or her development and growth; it is the child who is belittled and shamed, and inevitably frightened and defeated. The child sees himself or herself as unimportant. The irony is that such children pay a double penalty by being told that the rules exist for their own good. It is understandable why many students feel burned out by the educational process by the time they reach high school and college.

There are teachers, however, who seem to be able to work with or around the system and who never lose sight of children's needs. Even though they teach hundreds of children, they make each child feel important and special, even without reference to achievement and "good" behavior.

> The teacher, noticing that Roberto appears bored, discovers that he has some special interest in the terrarium. The teacher asks him if he would like to be in charge of its operation and also finds several books on terrarium animals for him that are written at his reading level. This special concern for Roberto teaches him that he is important, and learning continues to be rewarding.

It is important for teachers not only to help raise and protect a child's self-esteem but to help the child earn a higher self-esteem through achievement. Lerner (1986) believes that if teachers focus only on making children happy, the result may eventually be unhappy children. A lack of knowledge and success through achievement will someday erode the child's self-worth by causing restlessness, boredom, and dissatisfaction. For example, in Florida, 80 to 90 percent of the black high-school students failed the first statewide minimum-competency test. Lerner says they may have had a momentary blow to their self-esteem, but they did not quit. By the fifth try, 90 percent passed. It is not difficult to imagine the long-term effect this success will have on their self-esteem.

Idealistic Expectations

Perfectionism   The unrealistic expectations of some adults are actually idealistic, perfectionistic demands on children's behavior. As young children, we are often expected to act as our parents do only in their best moments, or to try to match the feats of characters in storybooks. Later we are encouraged to hold as models a few historical figures, the descriptions of whom are totally unrealistic (for example, George Washington, who never told a lie). Our goal seems to be perfection, something we rarely see demonstrated but something for which we are told to strive. Striving for perfection is a self-defeating process, though. As human beings, we are destined to fail, often constantly, although as children (and even as adults) we constantly try to succeed. Some common notions of perfection taught to us as children are:

Not crying when we feel the need.

Accepting the fact that our parents are always right, even if what they tell us today is the opposite of what they told us yesterday.

Always doing what we are told, even if it is unreasonable and detrimental to our self-esteem.

Guarding what we say so as not to embarrass our parents, even if what we say is true.

Giving in to others at the expense of our own needs and wants.

Knowing what our mothers and fathers expect of us, even if they do not tell us.

Always being kind and loving, never angry.

Getting all A's in school.

Conflict between Ideal Self and Real Self These idealistic expectations result in a conflict between our **ideal self** (the self we should be) and our **real self** (the self we actually are) (Rogers, 1959). The wide chasm that exists between the real self and the ideal self presents an impossible obstacle to overcome—an obstacle that we view as a failure to achieve what is expected by others and, consequently, ourselves (see the discussion of irrational beliefs in chapter 6).

Denial of Self Unfortunately, the child can only believe that he or she is in some way morally and intellectually deficient when his or her performance is inadequate. This often robs the child of the opportunity to learn new things for fear of not being able to do them perfectly from the start. "I don't want to play softball" means "What if I can't hit the ball?" "I don't like to bowl" means "I've never bowled before, and I'm afraid I will look stupid." Even as adults we continue to strive toward the unrealistic and impossible goal of perfection.

Fear of Failure, Fear of Success Procrastination seems to be a way of life for many students. According to psychologist Jane B. Burka, this behavior is really "a strategy, a defensive mechanism that protects a shaky self-esteem" (Fields, 1981). Surprisingly, almost all chronic procrastinators are perfectionists. Many of

ideal self a set of beliefs that result in self-expectations concerning what one should be or could be, or the optimal self

real self that which a person identifies honestly as being his or her actual self

Assessment of Perfectionism

Some people are not sure if they suffer from the unrealistic demands of perfectionism. Perfectionism may have become so much a part of their motivation that they no longer notice its effects.

The following assessment may help you become more aware of how perfectionism may be affecting your life. Use the following scale to measure your agreement or disagreement with the assessment statements. Try to respond to the way you usually think, feel, and behave.

+2 = Very much like me
+1 = Sometimes like me
0 = Neutral
−1 = Usually not like me
−2 = Definitely not like me

_____ I should be able to excel at anything I attempt.
_____ If I cannot do something really well, there is no point in doing it at all.
_____ People will think less of me if I make mistakes.
_____ If I do not set very high standards for myself, I will never be successful.

_____ An average performance is unsatisfying to me.
_____ If I get angry with myself for failing to live up to high standards, it will help me to do better in the future.
_____ I should be upset when I make a mistake.
_____ It is wrong to make the same mistakes several times.
_____ I am less of a person when I fail at something important.
_____ It is shameful when I display weakness or foolish behavior.

Add up your score. My score is _____.

If your score is +20, you possess a very high degree of perfectionism. If your score is −20, you are relatively unaffected by perfectionism. This assessment has been used with several classes of college students. The results indicate that many of us tend to be affected, to varying degrees, by perfectionistic demands.

them "expect top performance all the time. Any performance that is not up to their standards is a failure." Their insecurity requires that only an outstanding performance is acceptable. By procrastinating, it is possible to avoid any realistic assessment of their true abilities. Students who wait until it is too late to complete a project or study for a test can always say to themselves that they could have done better if they had spent more time. It is better to view themselves as lazy or disorganized rather than stupid. The thought is that someday they will finally do their best at something and test their true ability. Unfortunately, the potential for learning by doing their best at each moment is lost.

Students also procrastinate because they fear success. This may seem like a paradox. Some students are fearful of being too successful because it is lonely. If they appear successful, they must be more responsible for what they do and can no longer blame others or circumstances for what happens. They also fear they may lose friends, lovers, or spouses, and they may feel guilty if their lives become more successful than their friends' or families.'

Critical Review 1

1. The value we place on ourselves is referred to as self-perception. T F

2. Our attitudes, behaviors, and feelings are indicators of our level of self-esteem. T F

3. Canfield and Wells believe that our highest value is the enhancement and preservation of relationships to others. T F

4. Children who grow up believing that they are unacceptable to others may develop what Sullivan calls a malevolent attitude. T F

5. Parents are the only ones who are influential in shaping us as adults. T F

6. Studies show that children raised in strict environments develop low self-esteem. T F

7. The reasons why people decide to have children can affect the children's self-worth. T F

8. Permissive-indulgent parents help prepare their children for a productive and fulfilling future. T F

9. Authoritative parents are usually rigid and unfeeling. T F

10. The ideal self is the self that we believe we should be. T F

11. Describe what influences the development of our self-esteem.

12. In what ways does the conflict between the real self and the ideal self influence our self-esteem?

CHARACTERISTICS OF LOW SELF-ESTEEM

All kinds of things happen to us that result in our feeling bad about ourselves. Sometimes, thoughtless people influence our feelings of worth, at least temporarily. We may feel worthless because of our race, sex, physical appearance, creed, religious beliefs, political beliefs, aptitudes, or income. Failure also can be very damaging to our self-esteem, whether it is a failure at school, failure as a spouse, failure as a parent, failure at work, or a past failure that seemingly cannot be overcome.

It appears that many people suffer from low self-esteem, probably as a result of growing up with some of the problems discussed in the preceding section. The best evidence of low self-esteem comes from behavior.

Behaviors

People who experience low self-esteem have little self-respect. Their insistence on degrading themselves clearly demonstrates this lack. We hear people say, "I can never do anything right," or "I'm stupid," or "I'm no good." These frequent devaluations do nothing to enhance self-respect and often drive away others who could meet the need for friendship. These individuals also frequently blame others for their condition, which leads us to a second behavioral problem: They often behave irresponsibly. For example, they may be late for appointments yet invariably blame something or someone else for their tardiness, or they may seldom follow through on tasks they have agreed to do. With a defeatist attitude and a lack of self-confidence, they seem to arrange for failure by producing low-quality work; this further verifies their belief that they can seldom do anything well. These beliefs become a **self-fulfilling prophecy**, which severely limits their future achievements and further supports their negative views about themselves. Robert Merton's classic work (1957) defines *self-fulfilling prophecy* as a "false definition of a situation evoking a new behavior which makes the originally false conception come true" (p. 423). (Self-fulfilling prophecies can also be positive, as when we do surprisingly well at something and so develop confidence that we can do it.)

self-fulfilling prophecy   an originally false prediction of the future that comes true because of the influence of the prediction itself

People with low self-esteem often appear to be guarded and withdrawn. When their friends try to help by offering praise or constructive criticism, they behave defensively by negating the feedback or attacking the people who offer them help. These attacks may be projections directed at behaviors in the other people that the attackers dislike in themselves. They may say, "Well, you are like that too," or "You're not perfect either." They see others' attempts to help as ego-threatening. Hence, they not only reject themselves, they also reject others.

People with low self-esteem are often unable or unwilling to be open with others, to give important personal information about themselves. Sidney Jourard (1974) refers to the process of letting oneself be known to others as **self-disclosure.** Self-disclosure is one means by which the healthy personality is achieved and maintained (Jourard, 1971)—but only if the self-disclosure meets the condition of **authenticity,** a term used by Jourard (1968) to mean honest self-disclosure. People with low self-esteem, if they self-disclose at all, tend to say things about themselves that they do not mean. Their disclosures seem to have been chosen more for cosmetic value than for truth.

self-disclosure   letting oneself be known honestly to others

authenticity   honest self-disclosure

The consequence of a lifetime of lying about themselves is the loss of contact with their real selves, what Karen Horney (1950) refers to as **self-alienation.** She describes self-alienated people as having:

self-alienation   detachment from self and from others

■ An inability to recognize themselves as they really are, without minimizing or exaggerating.

■ An inability or unwillingness to accept the consequences of their actions and decisions.

■ An inability or unwillingness to realize it is up to them to do something about their difficulties.

People who are self-alienated believe that others, fate, or time will solve these difficulties. This is a further indication of their irresponsible behavior; they do not see themselves as directing their own lives.

People with low self-esteem usually resist change. They seem to prefer the safety of stagnant and unfulfilling patterns of behavior over the risk of trying new behaviors, environments, and relationships. Richard Leider (1994) suggests that the evidence for resistance to change is characterized by *always taking the safe way; reacting instead of taking risks; avoiding decisions;* and *daydreaming and talking rather than taking action.* If people continue to avoid the risks of change, their lives may never be fulfilling, and they may continually suffer from low self-esteem.

People with low self-esteem have many regrets. We may wonder why they behave as they do. This question is often difficult to answer, for as we mentioned earlier, people with low self-esteem are usually guarded about themselves. However, they appear to have a fear of failure that results from feelings of inadequacy. They attempt to present a false image of themselves as a means of preserving their self-esteem; however, this facade results in a confused and distorted self-image, further contributing to their low self-worth. In addition, they often try to diminish the self-esteem of those they really admire in an attempt to lessen the imagined gap between the self they see and the self they would like to be (see chapter 7 to learn about depression).

Attitudes

Clearly, then, people suffering from low self-esteem have a dim and murky view of themselves. This negative self-image stems from the general attitude that "I am not worthwhile, hence I do not count for much in the world." They believe themselves neither useful nor necessary. Many believe that it is wrong to think positively about themselves—that they should only think positively about others. A suggestion that they should feel good about themselves leads to a response like "That would be conceited."

People with this self-diminishing attitude see no clear purpose for their existence and often question their reason for being. Unable to trust their own judgments, they believe there is little they can do to change and continue to search desperately for answers outside of themselves. Therefore, they are easily persuaded by the beliefs and values of others. This vulnerable position causes them to talk and act in ways suited more to others' needs and desires than to their own. This further confuses the organization of values and attitudes.

The confusion and frustration of not having found self-satisfaction often result in their "giving up." They accept the notion that the world is a miserable place and that there is not much anyone can do about it, least of all themselves. It follows that people with low self-esteem see the world through the same eyes as they view themselves and adopt the same untrusting attitude toward others as they have toward themselves. Sullivan (1953) believes that for some people this untrusting attitude develops early. A child may learn to deal with apparent contradictions by concealing what he or she is thinking or feeling. For example, a mother may tell a child that being honest is the most important quality, then punish the child for telling the truth. The resulting lack of trust may greatly reduce the child's chances for achieving satisfying relationships.

Feelings

Fear has much to do with our untrusting attitude toward others. The fear of being known and of being rejected, and the fear of knowing ourselves and rejecting ourselves, leads to another cause of low self-esteem: the feelings we have about ourselves. These negative feelings seem to lend support to the attitudes we hold and the behaviors we exhibit. However, it is often difficult to know what the person with low self-esteem is feeling. Many of us are more aware of our thoughts than our feelings, perhaps because many of us have difficulty expressing our feelings honestly. Hence, we have learned to place little importance on them. Psychotherapists find that helping people to feel and to feel good about feeling is a major task. Simple human emotions are still disapproved by many of us (Brennecke and Amick, 1978).

People experiencing low self-esteem feel unloved even when others express or show love for them. They often perceive such demonstrations as insincere, because they believe they are unlovable. They ask themselves, "Why would anyone want to love me?" They see themselves as unlovable because they do not love themselves. Moreover, they reject the concept of self-love because they believe it is an expression of conceit. Although they raise no objection about applying the concept of love to various objects ("I love my shoes," "I love my diamond," "I love nature"), and while they believe it is virtuous to love others, they consider it sinful to love themselves. They further believe that the greater their self-love, the less their capacity to love others. On the contrary, the author of *The Art of Loving*, Erich Fromm (1956), believes that if people are to love productively, they must love themselves first; if they can love only others, they cannot love at all.

If our basic need for love and belonging is not met, deep hurt and resentment often result; these feelings are, in turn, directed back onto ourselves. If there is no apparent outlet for these feelings of self-rejection, an even greater problem develops—the problem of depression. Deep, negative feelings that are not expressed in a healthy way but are kept inside will continue to erode self-esteem, resulting eventually in self-pity and self-hatred. The belief that asking for help from others or sharing concerns with others is an admission of weakness leaves the person with low self-esteem even more vulnerable. This denial of need may cause negative, self-destructive feelings—the person may become purposeless, indifferent, helpless, and, eventually, hopeless. Suicide may seem a reasonable, as well as the only, alternative (see chapter 7 for a discussion of depression).

Figure 3–2 shows low self-esteem as a circular, self-defeating process in which negative feelings cause negative attitudes, negative attitudes cause negative behaviors, negative behaviors support the negative feelings, and on and on, with each part affecting and being affected by self-esteem. In effect, a person with low self-esteem becomes a psychological prisoner of his or her own negative self-image (Branden, 1969). At this point, it may appear that there is little hope for such a person. On the contrary, there is hope. Later in this chapter we discuss how to overcome negative self-esteem and how to acquire and sustain more positive self-esteem.

Critical Review 2

1. Robert Merton defines _____ _____ as a false definition of a situation that results in a new behavior that makes the previously false conception come true.

2. _____ is the process of letting one's self be known to others.

3. _____ is only healthy and useful if it meets the condition of authenticity.

4. Karen Horney believes that _____ is a consequence of a lifetime of lying about oneself to others.

FIGURE 3–2
The development of self-esteem
may be seen as a circular process.

SOURCE: Adapted from Brockner and Guare, 1983.

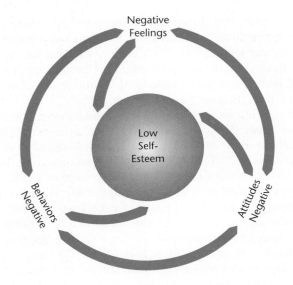

5. The person experiencing low self-esteem and often suffers from feelings of
_____ , _____ , and _____ .

6. Always playing it safe, avoiding decisions, and fear of risk-taking are characteristic behaviors associated with _____ _____ .

7. Give some examples of how the concept of the self-fulfilling prophecy negatively affects self-esteem.

8. What are the benefits of self-disclosure to the process of growth?

CHARACTERISTICS OF HIGH SELF-ESTEEM

Behaviors

Leider (1994) believes that to engage life, we must take the *initiative*. We must be responsible for ourselves and behave in responsible ways. This sense of responsibility contributes to our feelings of worth. It requires that we overcome a number of common fears: *criticism, rejection, betrayal, failure,* and even *success.*

People with high self-esteem relish the challenge of experiences in which they can grow and learn more about themselves, and they use their creativity in constructive ways. We can say that persons with high self-esteem strive for congruence; that is, they want their behavior to be congruent with their feelings, thoughts, attitudes, and experiences. They are free to act on their feelings and express their love for others by demonstrating affection, encouragement, and support.

People with high self-esteem are able to take a greater variety of risks—the more chips they have, they more they can afford to lose. It is better to choose the calculated risk of a positive decision than to let outside events force other less-welcomed outcomes (Leider, 1994). Positive people, therefore, are free to be open to the risk of new experiences and to others because they are capable of accepting failure and rejection as part of growth. They seldom see failure and rejection as a reflection upon their self-worth. When they excel, they are able to accept praise for their accomplishments without pretense or false modesty. In so doing, they allow themselves to continue to build their self-esteem.

Another quality of positive people is that they trust themselves. Leider (1994) believes that we must *rescript* ourselves to trust our own judgments. This trust frees us to be spontaneous and live fully at the moment of experiencing, rather than in the past ("I really messed that up") or future ("I hope I can get this right when the time comes"). It is no wonder that people enjoy being with those who exhibit positive levels of self-esteem—they are confident, exciting, and comfortable to be around. Their behavior indicates to others that they possess positive and healthy attitudes about themselves and the world around them. Table 3–1 lists several characteristics of people with positive self-esteem.

Attitudes

The most important attitude of people with high self-esteem is their belief that they are worthwhile and valuable. They need no particular credentials to support this feeling; they believe they are worthwhile because they belong to the society of human life. It is not necessary for them always to be important to others, for they are important to themselves. They do not have to strive continuously for perfection to prove themselves but can function productively within their presently known limitations. If they do accomplish extraordinary things and become important to others, they experience even greater feelings of worth.

People with positive self-esteem also have the attitude that it is important to continue to learn and grow psychologically. Therefore, they are open to what they can learn from others as well as what they can learn from more fully knowing themselves. They continually seek out and involve themselves in activities and relationships that have the potential for enhancing their self-esteem, even though involvement may mean conflict and disappointment.

This involvement stems from their belief that people are the sum of all of their experiences. Because they like who they have become, they value all of the experiences that helped make them the people they are today. Therefore, they continue to use their experiences to grow, and they also encourage others to grow and learn from their life experiences. Knowingly and unknowingly, they become models for others. Though they may not be teachers, they often teach.

People who feel worthwhile experience a personal freedom that is seldom controlled by guilt. In other words, they do not allow regrets to get in the way of their experiencing now in a positive and growing way.

Responsibility: They can be depended on to do what they have agreed to do.

Honesty, integrity, and congruence: They are accountable for their values, beliefs, and opinions.

Personal growth: They search for opportunities to grow, learn, and realize their potential and creativity.

Positive attitude: They are optimistic about themselves, others, and the world.

Expression of feelings: They express feelings openly without fear of rejection.

Risk taking: They are open to new and challenging experiences.

Acceptance of failure and rejection: They view failure and rejection as part of growing.

Acceptance of praise: They can accept compliments without negating responses.

Trust in themselves and others: They trust their own and others' competency.

TABLE 3–1

Characteristics of People with Positive Self-Esteem

The person with a healthy self-esteem has a positive influence on others.

Mary Hudson Vandegrift was born in Texas and went to elementary school and high school in Texas and Oklahoma. In 1933 she was widowed at twenty with a six-month-old daughter. She borrowed $200 and established $600 credit to buy a gas station and went on to become the first woman to found an oil trade group (Society of Independent Gasoline Marketers). Today, she is the president of Hudson Oil Company. During an address at Wichita State University in 1979, she stated, "the genius of living is to carry the spirit of a child into old age. What is the spirit of a child? That of wide-eyed open wonder, excitement and zest; the optimistic attitude that nothing is too good to be true and that the world literally is a wonderful place!" (Schwartz, 1980, p. 7)

Many people spend too much time and energy fretting over the past; each tomorrow is spent worrying about what should have been done better today. People with high self-esteem do not accept responsibility for events beyond their control—especially the actions of others. They do accept responsibility for their own choices. They believe that "life is what you make it" and that, within reason, we can be whatever we choose to be. In this way, we are all free.

As you might expect, people who experience a high degree of self-worth usually have very positive feelings about themselves and others. These positive feelings set the stage for them to live full, productive, and rewarding lives.

Feelings

Generally, people whose self-esteem is high feel happy and contented with themselves and their lifestyles. They feel loved and appreciated by others and

Conditions of Self-Esteem

Characteristics of High Self-Esteem:

■ seeks the stimulation and challenge of worthwhile and demanding goals;

■ welcomes the opportunity to engage in growthful experiences even at the risk of failure;

■ does things for the joy of doing them without the need to prove anything (sports, learning new skills, etc.);

■ accepts responsibility for actions taken without the need to blame or make excuses;

■ acknowledges the strengths and accomplishments of self and others;

■ acknowledges one's personal power without the need to abuse and manipulate others;

■ engages in meaningful communication both as a clear message giver and as an active listener;

■ develops loving and nurturing relationships with others;

■ focuses on the quality of life experiences rather than the quantity (friendships, etc.);

■ enjoys teamwork and sees the value of it in getting a job done or in maintaining interpersonal relationships;

■ finds a balance in life (work, pleasure, solitude, others, etc.).

Characteristics of Low Self-Esteem

■ inability to accept constructive criticism and use it to grow;

■ inability to make decisions and implement values creatively, must rely on clearly defined rules;

■ inability to take risks that may lead to failure;

■ inability to change, locked into the same foods, entertainment, behaviors, etc. ("This is the way I am.");

■ inability to focus on the strengths of others;

■ inability to focus on own personal strengths;

■ tendency to live vicariously through the accomplishments of others (hero worship);

■ tendency to do things for appearances (date the most attractive person on campus, drive the flashiest car, etc.);

■ tendency toward being excessively compulsive about such things as cleanliness, eating, order, etc.;

■ tendency toward fadism as a way to be "included" in the "in" group;

■ tendency to be highly competitive (must win at everything, be ahead of everyone else on the highway, and get in line ahead of others to make themselves feel important);

■ tendency to be poor losers, and to see losing as confirmation of personal worth;

■ tendency to be highly critical of others (finding fault);

■ tendency to be prejudiced toward others, even in their own group; their shaky self-image causes them to denigrate others;

■ tendency to be workaholics in order to prove to themselves and to others that they are worthwhile.

can share feelings of warmth and affection with others. Although they experience positive feelings most of the time, they are able to feel, accept, and express a wide range of feelings, from sorrow to anger to joy. They do not attempt to avoid unpleasant feelings but accept all of their feelings as natural and human.

Critical Review 3

1. The positive person demonstrates his or her self-worth to others by sharing the responsibility for their behavior. T F

2. The only way a person can reach a high level of self-esteem is through achievements and accomplishments. T F

3. Congruence, integrity, and risk-taking are qualities characteristic of a person with high self-esteem. T F

4. The only problem faced by people with positive self-esteem is that they often feel guilty about negative behaviors from the past. T F

5. The positive person's feelings are characterized most by the love and respect shown for self and others. T F

6. Defend what you believe to be the greatest characteristic of the person with high self-esteem.

BUILDING AND MAINTAINING SELF-ESTEEM

Two of our most time-consuming and important tasks are building and maintaining self-esteem. Perhaps the greatest challenge in life is maintaining self-esteem in healthy and growth-encouraging ways that are beneficial both to ourselves and to others.

Although it is theoretically possible, maintaining high self-esteem continuously may seem a difficult task. However, even if we have grown up in a negative environment, we can, if we choose, achieve a satisfying level of self-esteem. For most of us, high self-esteem may serve as a goal. It is important to realize that personal growth is a lifelong process in which we proceed slowly, experience after experience, decision after decision, toward becoming the person we have the potential to be. Each of us, no matter how young or how old, has time to grow toward becoming the person he or she would like to be. Each new day presents opportunities to try healthier behaviors and to grow through new experiences.

Each day also may bring things that get us down. As we confront the hassles of everyday life, we must realize that the world is a less-than-ideal place to live. We must also realize that the way we view the world is greatly affected by our past interpretations of our life experiences. These interpretations become the basis for our present level of self-esteem. Influenced by this present level of self-esteem, we have at least two ways to view the experiences of everyday life—positively and negatively.

> Marie is pretty and has always attracted male attention. In high school, she did more dating and cheerleading than studying. Her first job was as a typist in a posh insurance office. During the first six months, she came to realize how inadequate her skills and background were. She began to think of herself as stupid and to feel that her good looks were the only reason she had been hired. Consequently, she began to resent both the man who had hired her and other people in the office. She assumed that others saw her as she saw herself. Whenever a male co-worker stopped to chat, she cut him off or insulted him. Soon, she had the reputation of being a bad-tempered snob.
>
> When an executive assistant position was created, Marie asked her boss if she could have it and was told she was not ready for the job yet. Her boss thought her sometimes offensive behavior toward others could create problems in this new position. However, Marie assumed he did not think she was smart enough, so she quit her job.

It may be that in Marie's past, her beauty was emphasized at the expense of her intellectual development. She may have had little chance of knowing which qualities were important or of realizing other possibilities for growth. Marie may be partially correct in her assessment of how some people see attractive women, but it dominates her thinking, with detrimental results.

Understanding Irrational Beliefs

The classic works of Ellis and Harper (1975), Beck (1976), Meichenbaum (1977), and other cognitive therapists view negative interpretations of experiences as problems in our thinking. They also believe that our perceptions of our worth result from the collection of expectations and beliefs we have acquired during our development. The effect is determined by what we say to ourselves about a particular experience. According to Ellis and Harper, those of us who are greatly disturbed by the behavior of others toward us may make such *negative self-statements* as the following:

Irrational Beliefs

Questionnaire

Albert Ellis and others have described the way irrational beliefs influence the way we feel about ourselves. The following is a partial list of some of the irrational beliefs people may have about themselves. Look through the list. If a statement fits you, even occasionally, place an X in the space next to that statement. This exercise may not be able to help you overcome some of these beliefs, but it may help you increase the knowledge you have of yourself and give you some insight into what may be getting in the way of your positive feelings.

_____ **1.** I am a terrible person because others get angry with me.

_____ **2.** I must not be good enough when others don't recognize my accomplishments.

_____ **3.** It is important that everyone who knows me likes me.

_____ **4.** My family never had very much, so I will have great difficulty being successful.

_____ **5.** A female (girlfriend, mother, etc.) treated me badly, therefore I can never trust another female.

_____ **6.** A male (boyfriend, father, etc.) treated me badly, therefore I can never trust another male.

_____ **7.** I never know the answer when a teacher calls on me, so I must really be stupid.

_____ **8.** I must always please others and never disappoint them.

_____ **9.** I would be a nicer person if I were more beautiful or handsome.

_____ **10.** I never seem to get ahead even though I work harder than others. I should stop trying so hard.

_____ **11.** I don't like to try new activities unless I can do them perfectly the first time.

_____ **12.** I had a terrible childhood. Therefore, I will never be well adjusted.

_____ **13.** The harder I study, the worse I perform. I will never be able to get the grades I want.

_____ **14.** Other people are always luckier than I am.

_____ **15.** Because I cannot find the right mate, I am going to stop looking.

_____ **16.** I must be invisible; other people never seem to notice me.

_____ **17.** Other people always ignore my ideas.

_____ **18.** I am the only one who has this many problems.

_____ **19.** I should be more like other people.

20. If I can do it, anybody can.

I must be loved and approved of by every significant person in my life; if not, that is awful.

I must not make errors or do poorly; if I do, that is terrible.

People and events should always be the way I want them to be.

Marie assumes she is unintelligent. She also assumes her boss hired her for her good looks and refused her the new position because he thought she did not have the ability to do the job. In Marie's mind, this confirms her beliefs about herself. Her feelings, thoughts, and attitudes influenced her behavior. Her behavior results in negative responses from others, and these responses, though misinterpreted, confirm her beliefs. This process, diagrammed in Figure 3–3, may severely limit our chances for success in trying new esteem-building behaviors.

Marie could have handled this situation in a healthier way by asking her boss why he believed she was not ready to take the executive assistant position. She would have found his reasons quite different from her assumptions. Marie also might have been able to work on changing her offensive behavior. Instead of quitting, for example, she could have taken some courses to help her improve her skills. Marie's feelings, thoughts, attitudes, and behaviors were unhealthy and kept her from viewing her job as an opportunity for growth.

The negative beliefs described by Ellis and Harper are quite common. Many of us were taught unrealistic beliefs such as these. That is why we have such terrible feelings when someone does not like us or when we fail. In spite of their commonness, though, these beliefs are *irrational*. They are based on the belief that our self-worth is solely determined by the approval of others and by continual strivings for perfection. According to Ellis and Harper, the negative self-statements based on this belief must be replaced by *positive self-statements* such as the following:

> It is definitely nice to have people's love and approval, but even without them, I can still accept and enjoy myself.
>
> Doing things well is satisfying, but it is human to make mistakes.
>
> People are going to act the way they want, not the way I want.

FIGURE 3–3
The way we feel, think, and behave is influenced by others and influences others' responses to us.

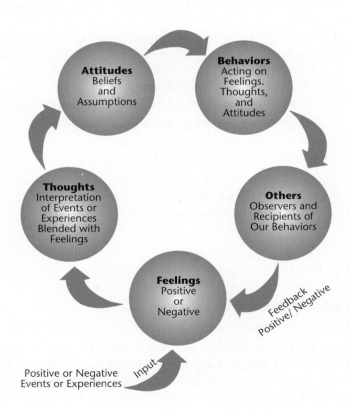

Changing Beliefs People with low self-esteem are able to change their beliefs about themselves. Low-self-esteem individuals tend to attribute their failures to *internal* causes (weaknesses and shortcomings), reflecting their doubts about self-worth. On the other hand, such individuals attribute successes to *external* claims such as "I got lucky," "Someone helped me," and "It will probably never happen again." Brockner and Guare (1983) took these facts and hypothesized that by inducing people with low self-esteem to attribute their failures to possible external causes (factors beyond their control) and their successes to internal causes (abilities and traits), the effects of low self-esteem could be reduced. In addition, they hypothesized that people with low self-esteem may be encouraged to try harder and consequently become more successful, further elevating their self-esteem.

In Brockner and Guare's study, college students were administered personality inventories to determine their levels of self-esteem. Two groups were identified: students who had low self-esteem and students who had high self-esteem. After the students were identified, they were given an insolvable task so that each student experienced failure. After this failure experience, each student worked on an anagrams task that was solvable. Prior to undertaking this task, however, some individuals in both the high and low self-esteem groups were provided with information suggesting that their previous failure experience stemmed from external causes. In contrast, others were provided with information suggesting that their previous failure was due mostly to internal causes. Some subjects received no information about what had contributed to their failure. The result of the study showed that when people with low self-esteem are able to realize that sometimes failure is due to external causes rather than to internal causes, they are able to take more personal risks and try harder, which leads to more successful endeavors. In fact, the results were more dramatic than had been anticipated. The students with low self-esteem who had been told that the previous failure was due to external causes solved more anagrams than any other group; the students with high self-esteem who had been told that the previous failure was due to external causes solved the least number of anagrams. Perhaps this result indicates that when the high self-esteem students discovered that their effort was not the only factor in their success, they felt less of a need to do their best on the task (see Figure 3–4).

The significance of this study may be that, for low self-esteem people, the need to prove their worth through perfectionistic achievement and the consequential fear of failure may result in the self-fulfilling prophecy of failure. The predictions and findings of this study suggest that performance and, consequently, self-esteem can be enhanced by inducing individuals with low self-esteem to interpret failure as stemming, at least partially, from external causes. Of course, it is not wise to induce low-self-esteem people to attribute all of their failures to external causes. On some occasions, poor performance does indeed result from internal causes.

Many of us have had negative interpersonal experiences and may be somewhat sensitive to the judgments of others. Most of us want to be well thought of and, consequently, may be too concerned with what others are thinking about us. Sherod Miller (1983), a communication specialist, responds to this concern by noting that most of the time no one is thinking about us—other people are too busy thinking about themselves. If on occasion people say things about us that sound derogatory, we can find out whether we have cause for concern by asking them what they meant by what they said (see chapter 10 for more about communication).

FIGURE 3–4

Self-Esteem and Success—Beliefs
About Previous Failure—Internal vs.
External Causes

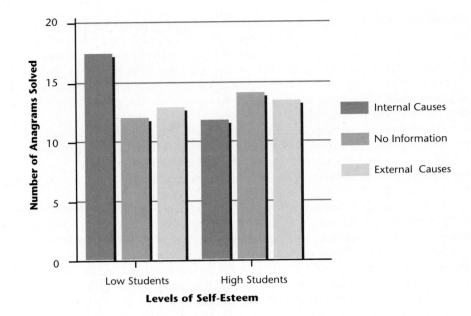

FIGURE 3–4

Self-Esteem and Success—Beliefs About Previous Failure—Internal vs. External Causes

Developing Significant Relationships

We can begin to develop significant relationships by more positively communicating about ourselves to others. We constantly give clues about how we value ourselves. These clues influence how others value us, which in turn reinforces the value we place on ourselves, and on and on. Let's look at an example. A group discussion is taking place. Bob, in a vibrant voice, exclaims, "I just had a great idea. Let me tell you about it!" Paul, in a quiet monotone, says, "I had an idea a little while ago, but it really wasn't very good. Let me see if I can remember it." You can easily see who values himself more. Chances are the group members will be more interested in Bob's idea.

Appreciating Ourselves

Another way we can positively influence our relationships is by showing more genuine appreciation for ourselves and for others. To be self-accepting is to be compassionate and respectful toward ourselves even when we do not like our feelings or behavior (Branden, 1994). In other words, we should treat ourselves like we do our best friend. By doing this, we build our own esteem and the esteem of others. Self-confident women and men are usually attracted to each other and form healthy and lasting relationships.

Problems in relationships usually develop when people feel insecure and unappreciated by each other. They tend to forget their purpose for being together, and soon their positive feelings for themselves and for each other are obscured. The self-esteem of each begins to suffer, and the relationship gradually loses its value. Unfortunately, insecurity and low self-esteem draw men and women together as does high self-esteem. Such individuals often form destructive relationships that reflect and increase their lack of self-worth.

The possibility of our maintaining high-quality relationships is greatly increased when we regularly express our appreciation to ourselves and our significant others. Then our need for mutual nurturing and supportive relation-

---

Appreciations

Take a few moments to think about some of the things you appreciate about yourself. List them in the spaces below. These appreciations need not reflect what you think others appreciate about you, just what you appreciate about yourself.

I appreciate the following things about myself:

_____
_____
_____

When was the last time you expressed these appreciations?

_____
_____
_____

Now spend a few moments thinking of what you appreciate about another significant person in your life.

I appreciate the following things:

_____
_____
_____

When was the last time you shared your appreciations with this person?

Would you be able and willing to share your appreciations with three people?

_____
_____
_____

---

ships in which we can learn and grow will be satisfied (see chapter 9 for a discussion of intimate relationships).

Changing Our Behavior   It seems as though many of the negative experiences in life are associated with people's attempts to develop relationships. Previously, we stated that negative interpretations of experiences often involve a problem with behavior. When we discover that repeated negative experiences have affected our self-worth, we certainly need to examine what we may be doing to contribute to these experiences. Such examinations may indicate that we are punishing ourselves as a way of emphasizing our lack of self-appreciation and self-respect. We may also feel trapped by the way we have approached our problems in the past—our behavior.

Aaron Beck (1976) suggests that if we change our behavior with regard to a particular situation, the outcome of the change may allow us to examine and eventually change our thinking.

> José, a twenty-five-year-old man, had had only one date in his life, and that had been seven years earlier, in high school, when a friend had "fixed him up." The evening had turned out to be a disaster, at least for José. At the encouragement of a friend, José finally sought professional counseling from a qualified psychologist. Several sessions passed before José reluctantly agreed to do one of the things he feared most—ask a woman for date. When José appeared for his next session, he happily reported that he had asked a young lady to go out with him. She had, and they both had had a great time. They had planned another date for the following weekend, and he no longer believed he was an undesirable creature.

By risking a change in his behavior, José not only changed his thinking about his behavior, he also changed, at least partly, his outlook on life. José took the first step toward achieving more positive self-esteem.

When we have a purpose for changing our behavior, we can set goals to help us work toward accomplishing the change. Once we have set behavioral goals, we can perform specific actions that will allow us to keep on track and move toward their fulfillment. Branden (1994) believes we must be *self-responsible*, that is, "to recognize that you are the author of your own choices and actions. You are the source of your own fulfillment. No one is going to make your life right for you . . . or make you truly happy . . . or give you self-esteem."

Developing Realistic Expectations   There is nothing wrong with having an ideal self-image as a source of motivation for personal goals and personal growth. But when we believe we *must* be perfect to feel good about ourselves, we destroy our sense of worth. Perfectionistic expectations rob us of the ability to accept ourselves as fallible but worthwhile human beings. When we judge ourselves by perfectionistic standards, our appreciation of our actions and achievements is replaced by frustration, compulsiveness, and defeat.

> Evelyn, having become aware of how her perfectionistic standards had been affecting her, remarked, "I've been trying to be bright, witty, popular, pretty, and successful at everything I do. I've been trying very hard to be all these things to please others and feel better about myself instead of just being me. It's no wonder I've been feeling so little joy in my life."

The irony is that in trying to be all these things, Evelyn missed the very thing she hoped to gain—more joy in her life. Certainly, recognition of our achievements contributes to our self-esteem. But when the drive to achieve and accomplish becomes excessive, it can detract from our joy and satisfaction.

Activities and Experiences

Many activities we often treat as essential to our lives may actually detract from our self-worth. Some examples are participating in the latest fads and socializing with the "in" crowd. A closer look at the real importance of some of these involvements may reveal that they not only are unimportant in relation to our values but actually diminish our self-worth.

> Six months had passed since Juan's acceptance into the most prestigious fraternity on campus. The feeling of excitement at having survived the initiation process had died months ago. His experience so far had been quite unlike what he had expected. Instead of providing a warm, friendly environment with the goal of brotherhood, the fraternity was plagued with cliques one entered by wearing the most expensive clothes and knowing the most influential people. Juan realized that to remain a "brother" would mean denying his needs and values and diminishing his feelings of self-esteem. He decided to leave the fraternity.

Everyday experiences may test our self-esteem. Picture yourself riding along in your car on an uncrowded highway. It is a sunny autumn afternoon and you are feeling happy and alive. You look into the rearview mirror expecting to see an empty stretch of highway behind you. Instead, you see a black and white car with a blue flashing light on top; the person inside is motioning for you to pull over and stop. Your training tells you to obey immediately. In the few moments (which seem like hours) it takes for the police officer to get out of her car and appear at your side window, you notice several things happening to you. First, your legs begin to shake and your heart begins to beat rapidly. Second, you notice that your entire body feels both hot and cold. When the officer arrives and asks to see your driver's license, you notice that your hands are shaking so much that you can hardly remove your license from your wallet. This is truly a stressful event. Soon you are on your way, traveling at a slower speed and in possession of a speeding citation. You are no longer aware that it is a beautiful day, and even though you are alive, you certainly do not feel happy. Your self-esteem appears to have taken a temporary plunge. Quietly, you berate yourself for the "stupid" thing you did.

If your self-esteem is generally positive, you will soon be able to admit, "Yes, I was going over the speed limit, and yes, occasionally I am careless and break the law." You will be able to view this experience as an unfortunate happening from which you have learned something. If your self-esteem is generally negative, you may deny your responsibility by making excuses and blaming the officer. You may also use the experience to confirm your low self-esteem (see chapter 6 for a discussion of cognitive dissonance theory).

Dealing with People

We have to deal with all kinds of people every day: store clerks, supervisors, co-workers, car mechanics, teachers, lawyers, and doctors, to name a few. The confrontation that comes with dealing with others can present problems. Public embarrassment caused by an instructor or boss who singles us out in the presence of others as an example of what not to do or say can be devastating. Sometimes, others may attempt to put us down to make themselves feel more important. Every day contact with co-workers who are always looking for an opportunity to improve their self-esteem at our expense can take much of the joy out of the work we do. Of course, the degree to which these interactions affect our self-esteem depends on how high our self-esteem is in the first place. Someone who already feels negative about himself or herself will either lash out or withdraw when a conflict arises. This person may also attempt to avoid most conflicts, even though it is difficult and even unhealthy to do so. On the other hand, a person who generally feels positive will confront the conflict in an assertive way and not interpret the outcome as a reflection on his or her self-worth. Branden (1994) believes we must honor our wants and needs and find

The consequences of being human often affect our worth temporarily.

ways to express them. We must stand up for our convictions, values, and feelings; be willing to be who we are; and let others see it.

Our Environment

Our environment, though safe and secure, may be so unstimulating that it begins to affect us in negative ways. This may be the case when we become bored with the familiarity or the routine associated with our surroundings: A feeling of stagnation often develops. Our work or school environment can affect us in this way, as can the room, apartment, or house we live in. Although the way we feel about our environment may actually be a reflection of how we feel about ourselves, it is important not to allow our surroundings to produce feelings of stagnation. For some of us, a good place to start positive change in our lives is to change something in our environment. That does not necessarily mean we should quit our jobs, drop out of school, or move into a new apartment or house. Making drastic changes without first considering other factors may cause further problems with self-esteem.

We can assess our environment by first analyzing our situation to discover what conditions are affecting our feelings. A few minor changes (asking for a change in responsibilities at work, involving ourselves in more stimulating activities at school, or redecorating our surroundings at home) may create a more desirable atmosphere. In addition, such simple changes as taking a new, more scenic route to school or work may add zest to our lives. The important thing is that we use our creativity to change our negative feelings.

Physical Health

Our physical health and how we feel about the condition of our bodies greatly affect our feelings about ourselves. Conversely, the value we place on physical well-being is often a reflection of our self-worth in general. A person who does not value himself or herself often places little value on physical upkeep. Leaving the core of the body to chance often results in its not receiving proper nutrition, exercise, stress management, and monitoring (McCamy and Presley, 1972). This lack of care may result in the body's losing its resistance to ever-present attackers (viruses, etc.). Unable to defend itself, the body give in, and we become ill.

When we are ill, we usually feel miserable and defeated. If illness occurs often or becomes chronic, the feelings of misery are prolonged, and our self-esteem often suffers. Even if we do not become seriously ill, a lack of appreciation for our bodies becomes evident in a lessening of energy and stamina. This may severely limit our actions and performance in many ways, further lowering our self-esteem.

If we wish to grow and to enhance our self-esteem, we must place equal value on emotional, intellectual, and physical well-being. We discuss more about the physical self in the next chapter.

Critical Review 4

1. It is important to realize that we maintain our self-esteem by continuing the _____ process of personal _____.

2. Ellis and other cognitive therapists view negative interpretations of experiences as resulting from problems with our _____.

3. Our behavior is usually caused by our beliefs and/or _____ about ourselves.

4. The statement, "People are going to act the way they want, not the way I want," is an example of a _____ self-statement.

5. Our dealings with _____ usually affect our self-esteem more than any other factor.

6. Ellis and Harper believe that it is an _____ belief to think that our self-worth is solely determined by the approval of others.

7. Our unrealistic and _____ expectations often rob us of the ability to accept ourselves as fallible yet worthwhile human beings.

8. Aaron Beck suggests that we can often change our way of thinking by risking a change in our _____

9. If we are feeling stagnant and unstimulated, it may be important to analzye the quality of our relationships and/or our _____.

10. We are often referred to as our "own worst enemy." Considering this possibility, how can we establish a plan to ensure that we continue to develop and maintain a high level of self-esteem?

SUMMARY

■ One of the most important factors determining our feelings, attitudes, values, behaviors, and life goals is self-esteem—the degree to which we value ourselves and feel useful and necessary in the world.

■ Various levels of self-esteem may be experienced. Some people may be described as having high, or positive, self-esteem, while others are described as having low, or negative, self-esteem.

■ Three major factors affect and are affected by self-esteem: attitudes, behaviors, and feelings.

■ The way we develop as children greatly affects our self-esteem in later life.

■ Parents are the greatest influence on the development of their children's self-esteem; teachers, relatives, and peers are other shaping influences.

■ Parents are most effective when they mix limits and controls with the necessary love, support, and nurturance required to foster creativity and independence in their children.

■ A child who grows up feeling loved, accepted, and valued will enjoy a higher level of self-esteem and live a happier life. On the other hand, a child who grows up without these feelings may suffer from low self-esteem and live an unhappy and unfulfilled life.

■ The malevolent attitude—the belief that everyone is an enemy—severely affects personality development and the ability to live a satisfying life.

■ The development of self-esteem is a lifelong process in which the level of self-esteem tends to rise or fall as the discrepancy between the real self (actual self) and the ideal self (desired self) narrows or expands.

■ We can achieve a satisfying level of self-esteem even if our personality development was influenced by a negative environment. People with low self-esteem are usually characterized by such behaviors as putting themselves down in the presence of others, blaming themselves and others, acting irresponsibly, procrastinating, being guarded and withdrawn, acting defensively, attacking others, rejecting themselves and others, being unable to disclose themselves to others, and resisting desirable change.

■ The following attitudes characterize low self-esteem: I do not count for much; the world is a miserable place; it is dangerous to reveal myself to others; my ideal self is so far removed from reality that there is no use trying to achieve it.

■ Low self-esteem is characterized by such feelings as fear, hurt, rejection, depression, anger, self-hatred, and a sense of being unloved.

■ People with positive self-esteem are usually characterized by such behaviors as enjoying being by themselves and with others, showing love and respect for themselves and for others, behaving responsibly, demonstrating honesty and integrity, demonstrating assertiveness and congruence, taking risks, trusting themselves and others, accepting praise and criticism, and being spontaneous and free.

■ The attitudes that characterize people with positive self-esteem include beliefs in the worth and value of themselves and others, the importance of learning and growing, the importance of seeking out and developing significant interpersonal relationships, the importance of viewing all life experiences in terms of their contribution to growth, the necessity of taking responsibility for their own decisions and behaviors, and the freedom to become whatever they desire.

■ The feelings that characterize people with positive self-esteem include love and appreciation for themselves and others. They can express and accept a wide range of feelings, from sorrow to anger to joy. A general feeling of happiness and contentment prevails. We can maintain our self-esteem by increasing our awareness of ourselves and of the effects of our relationships and surroundings on our self-esteem.

■ The way we have interpreted our experiences dramatically affects the way experiences presently influence our self-esteem.

■ The achievement of high self-esteem should serve as a life-long goal for each of us to work toward.

SELECTED READINGS

Branden, N. *The Six Pillars of Self-Esteem.* New York: Bantam Books, 1994. Branden describes the six virtues or practices on which self-esteem depends: living consciously, self-acceptance, self-responsibility, self-assertiveness, living purposefully, and personal integrity.

Cooper, J. E., Holman, J., and Braithwaite, V. A. "Self-Esteem and Family Cohesion: The Child's Perspective and Adjustment." *Journal of Marriage and the Family* (February 1983): 153–158. An investigation of the relationship between children's self-esteem and their perceptions of family cohesion.

Hamburg, D. A. *Today's Children: Creating a Future for a Generation in Crisis.* New York: Time Books, 1994. A survey of important recent research in child development focusing on early childhood and early adolescence. Specific examples are given on how to help children grow and develop in healthy and productive ways.

Helmstetter, S. *What to Say When You Talk to Yourself.* New York: Pocket Books, 1986. An exploration of how beliefs that control our thinking about ourselves can be changed. Changing our conversation about our behavior, feelings, attitudes, and beliefs can help us change the self-defeating things we think about and do.

Leider, R. J. *Life Skills: Taking Charge of Your Personal and Professional Growth.* Pfeiffer and Company, 1994. Leider helps people of all ages deal with inevitable change and risk taking. He helps the readers assess their quality of life by looking at ten fundamental life management areas.

McKay, M., and Fanning, P. *Self-Esteem.* Oakland, CA: New Harbinger, 1987. Using the cognitive therapy approach, the authors help the reader learn how to patiently and rationally build a higher level of self-esteem over a lifetime.

Sanford, L., and Donovan, M. *Women and Self-Esteem.* New York: Penguin Books, 1984. An examination of how women's harmful attitudes about themselves are shaped. It offers concrete, step-by-step exercises to help women resolve the dilemma of building a higher self-esteem.

REFERENCES

Baumrind, D. "Current Patterns of Parental Authority," *Developmental Psychology Monographs,* 4 (1, Pt. 2), 1971.

_____. "Effective Parenting During the Early Adolescent Transition." In *Advances in Family Research* (Vol. 2), edited by P. A. Cowen and E. M. Hetherington, pg. 28–41, Hillsdale, NJ: Erlbaum, 1991.

Beck, A. *Cognitive Therapy and Emotional Disorders.* New York: International Universities Press, 1976.

Berelson, B. "The Value of Children: A Taxonomical Essay." In *Current Issues in Marriage and the Family,* 2d ed., edited by J. G. Wells, pg. 143–156. New York: Macmillan, 1979.

Bernard, J. "Note on Changing Life Styles, 1970–1974." *Journal of Marriage and the Family* 37 (August 1975): 582–593.

Branden, N. *The Psychology of Self-Esteem: A New Concept of Man's Psychological Nature.* Los Angeles: Nash, 1969.

_____. *The Six Pillars of Self-Esteem.* New York: Bantam Books, 1994.

Brennecke, J. H., and Amick, R. G. *Psychology and Human Experience,* 2d ed. Encino, CA: Glencoe, 1978.

Brockner, J., and Guare, J. "Improving the Performance of Low Self-esteem Individuals: An Attributional Approach." *Academy of Managerial Psychology* 26 (1983): 642–656.

Campbell, A. The American Way of Mating: Marriage Si, Children Only Maybe. *Psychology Today* (August 1975): 37–43.

Canfield, J. T., and Wells, H. C. "Self-Concept: A Critical Dimension in Teaching and Learning." In *Humanistic Education Source Book,* edited by D. A. Read and S. B. Simon, pg. 92–105. Englewood Cliffs, NJ: Prentice-Hall, 1975.

Cooper, J. E., Holman, J., and Braithwaite, V. A. "Self-Esteem and Family Cohesion: The Child's Perspective and Adjustment." *Journal of Marriage and the Family* 45 (February 1983): 153–158.

Coopersmith, S. *Antecedents of Self-Esteem.* San Francisco: Freeman, 1967.

_____. "Studies in Self-Esteem." In *Psychology in Progress: Readings from Scientific American,* edited by R. C. Atkinson, pg. 64–71. San Francisco: Freeman, 1975.

Ellis, A., and Harper, R. A. *A New Guide to Rational Living.* Englewood Cliffs, NJ: Prentice-Hall, 1975.

Fields, C. M. "Student Procrastinators May Fear Failure—or Success." *The Chronicle of Higher Education* 2 (September 1981): 10.

Fromm, E. *The Art of Loving.* New York: Harper & Row, 1956.

Gelman, D., and Raine, G. "Pondering Self-Esteem." *Newsweek* 2 (March 1987): 70.

Hamburg, David A. *Today's Children: Creating a Future for a Generation in Crisis.* New York: Time Books, 1994.

Horney, K. *Neurosis and Human Growth: The Struggle Toward Self-Realization.* New York: Norton, 1950.

_____. "The Search for Glory." In *Self-Explorations in Personal Growth,* edited by C. Moustakas, pg. 86–95. New York: Harper Colophan Books, 1956.

Jourard, S. M. *Disclosing Man to Himself.* Princeton, NJ: D. Van Nostrand, 1968.

_____. *Healthy Personality: An Approach from the Viewpoint of Humanistic Psychology.* New York: Macmillan, 1974.

_____. *The Transparent Self.* New York: Van Nostrand, Reinhold, 1971.

Leider, Richard J. *Life Skills: Taking Charge of Your Personal and Professional Growth.* New York: Pfeiffer and Company, 1994.

Lerner, B. "Student Self-Esteem and Academic Excellence." *Educational Digest* 52 (September 1986): 32–35.

Maccoby, E. E. and Martin, J. A. "Socialization in the Context of the Family." In *Handbook of Child Psychology* (4th ed., Vol. 4), edited by P. H. Munsen, pg. 181–197. New York: Wiley, 1983.

Maslow, A. H. *Motivation and Personality,* 2d ed. New York: Harper & Row, 1970.

McCamy, J., and Presley, J. *Human Lifestyling: Keeping Whole in the Twentieth Century.* New York: Harper & Row, 1972.

Meichenbaum, D. *Cognitive-Behavior Modification: An Integrative Approach.* New York: Plenum Press. 1977.

Merton, R. K. *Social Theory and Structure.* New York: Free Press, 1957.

Miller, S. "Worry About What Others Think of You?" *New Relationships* 1 (October 1983): 1.

Moustakas, C. *Personal Growth: The Struggle for Identity and Human Values.* Cambridge, MA: Howard A. Doyle, 1969.

O'Connell, V., and O'Connell, A. *Choice and Change: An Approach to the Psychology of Growth.* Englewood Cliffs, NJ: Prentice-Hall, 1974.

Rogers, C. R. "A Theory of Therapy, Personality and Interpersonal Relationships as Developed in the Client-Centered Framework." In *Psychology: A Study of a Science,* vol. 3, edited by S. Koch., pg. 33–51. New York: McGraw-Hill, 1959.

Schultz, T. "Does Marriage Give Today's Women What They Really Want?" *Ladies Home Journal* (June 1980): 89–91, 146–155.

Schwartz, D. *Introduction to Management: Principles, Practices, and Processes.* New York: Harcourt Brace Jovanovich, 1980.

Sullivan, H. S. *The Interpersonal Theory of Psychiatry.* New York: Norton, 1953.

■ *Answers to Critical Review Questions*

Critical Review 1 **1.** F **2.** T **3.** F **4.** T **5.** F **6.** F **7.** T **8.** F **9.** F **10.** T
Critical Review 2 **1.** self-fulfilling prophecy **2.** self-disclosure **3.** self-disclosure **4.** self-alienation **5.** rejection, fear, hurt **6.** low self-esteem
Critical Review 3 **1.** F **2.** F **3.** T **4.** F **5.** T
Critical Review 4 **1.** life long, growth **2.** thinking **3.** attitudes **4.** positive **5.** people **6.** irrational **7.** perfectionistic **8.** behavior **9.** environment

PERSONAL ACTION PLAN
Assessing Self-Esteem

The exercises in this section are designed to provide you with information you can use to (1) assess your present level of self-esteem; (2) trace the development of your self-esteem to this point; and (3) continue to grow toward a satisfying level of self-esteem.

I. In this assessment exercise, you will have an opportunity to examine some possible discrepancies between your real self (actual self) and the ideal self (desired self). This assessment is a good measure of how you view your worth as a person.

On this page and the next are listed several personal traits and some space for you to add your own. Using the following scale, rate each trait according to how you honestly view your real self and your ideal self. Place the difference between the two ratings in the right-hand column.

Scale

1	2	3	4	5	6	7	8	9	10
Very Little					Somewhat				Very Much

Real Self	Trait	Ideal Self	Difference
	Honesty		
	Giving love		
	Receiving love		
	Receiving criticism		
	Receiving praise		
	Openness to views of others		
	Awareness of self		
	Assertiveness		
	Listening to others		
	Sensitivity to others		
	Loving oneself		
	Responsibility		
	Openness to new experiences		
	Acceptance of self		
	Acceptance of others		
	Loyalty to friends		
	Expressing feelings		
	Dealing with conflict		
	Intellectual ability		
	Trusting self		
	Trusting others		
	Other Traits:		

If the difference for any trait was 5 or more, perhaps this is an area that is detracting from your self-esteem. In the space below, list those traits that you believe represent possible areas of growth. After each trait, describe some ways you might be able to act on modifying this discrepancy (change in behavior, change in thinking, change in feeling, and so on). Use all of your creativity, intuition, and hunches to help yourself.

Trait Area	Possible Alternatives

II. Striving for perfection often interferes with our feelings of worth. The following statements are designed to help you identify ways in which perfectionism may be affecting your appreciation of yourself. Complete each of the following statements.

1. With regard to perfection, I am too hard on myself by

2. With regard to not meeting my expectations for myself, I react by

3. My expectations for myself come from

III. We mentioned in this chapter that other people probably have the greatest influence on us when it comes to the development of our self-esteem. Below, list as many people as you can remember by name and relationship who you believe have influenced you and your worth as a person. Indicate specifically how they were influential.

Name of the Person	Relationship	How He/She was Influential

IV. Reviewing past accomplishments and peak events (experiences that resulted in positive feelings) in our lives is important for two reasons:

1. It helps us put into perspective the activities and experiences from the past that have contributed to our self-esteem, and

2. It helps us see ways in which we can continue to plan for future self-esteem-enhancing experiences.

In the spaces provided on this page, list as many accomplishments and peak events as you can and the ways you might plan for such future experiences.

The following is a list of my past accomplishments and peak events:

The following examples are some ways I might be able to plan for future self-esteem-building experiences:

V. People, activities, experiences, and/or environmental conditions often affect our self-esteem, at least temporarily. Increasing our awareness of these factors may help us maintain a more positive level of self-esteem. Think about those times when you feel most and least happy about yourself and your abilities. Then, in the spaces below, describe how certain people, activities, experiences, and environmental conditions either negatively or positively influence your feelings of worth.

	Negative Influences	Positive Influences
People:		
Experiences:		
Activities:		
Environmental Conditions:		

Modified from Martin L. Seldman and David Hermes, *Personal Growth Through a Collection of Methods*. San Diego, CA: We Care Foundation, 1975.

VI. Many of us have learned how to live in a fast and complex society. However, in our pursuit of life, we often lose sight of our own personal appreciations and qualities. The continual awareness of this vital data becomes the basis on which we build significant relationships with others as well as reaffirm our belief in ourselves. (For example, I feel good about my personal qualities and I share them with you through my statements, behavior, and so on.)

In the space below, list as many personal strengths and qualities as you can. Do not let words such as "conceit" or "bragging" (words often meant to discourage us from feeling good about ourselves) detract from this positive experience. If you get stuck, some areas in which to look for strengths and qualities may include: relationship strengths; emotional strengths; intellectual strengths; health, sports, and other physical activities; hobbies; survival skills; creativity strengths; organizational strengths; vocational strengths; special aptitudes; and educational training. Use these areas as a guide. Do not be limited by them. Here is a chance to finally blow your own horn.

The following is a list of my personal strengths and qualities:

INFLUENCES ON ADJUSTMENT AND GROWTH

Part II gives recent information on several influential factors that affect our adjustment and growth, including physical, cognitive, emotional, and environmental influences.

Chapter 4 describes the demands that life places on us and describes our mental, emotional, and physical responses to those demands. It explores the strain on our mental and physical health caused by the constant need to adjust and grow in our complex and changing world.

Major life events such as marriage and daily concerns such as getting to class on time produce changes in our bodies that may make us more vulnerable to disease and more susceptible to injury and death. Chapter 4 reviews some of the interesting new information being learned about the complex relationships among our behaviors, stress, and physical and mental illness.

How we view life, how we see our role in it, how effectively we see ourselves filling that role, and how many personal and social resources we can call on in times of trouble all have been found to be good predictors of successful adjustment. Chapter 4 includes an exploration of coping methods along with its analysis of stress.

Chapter 5 explores physical influences. It begins by describing the effects of body type and stereotype on human social behavior. Attributions of others, which may be based on our physical attractiveness, also are given attention, along with proper nutrition, weight control, strength, aerobic fitness, health, and life extension. We continue the exploration of physical influences by concentrating on the psychological impact of our gender identity and roles.

Chapter 6, which discusses factors that influence our thinking, presents a broad spectrum of information, from how the mind functions to new techniques for altering thinking styles and even specific thoughts. Special attention is given to applying these new techniques to improving study skills.

Chapter 7 investigates a necessary and precious aspect of our existence—our feelings. Internal bodily changes, unconscious mental evaluations, and external physical expressions associated with emotion are described in terms of their adaptation and survival value. Emotional growth is presented in terms of its being appropriate to the situation, authentic, suitably intense, and effectively expressed. Two failures in emotional growth—aggression and depression—are given extended coverage.

Chapter 8 examines social and physical environmental influences, including a consideration of groups and how they affect our adjustment and growth. It also focuses on density, crowding, and other aspects of city life that influence our adjustment and growth.

4

STRESS AND HEALTH

Chapter Outline

FOCUS

The human being is the only animal that is forever unfinished. All of us face the challenge of constantly developing ourselves during our lifetime. This is an awesome task. Our genes and our families are necessary but insufficient factors in our development. At any moment our emerging selves reflect choice and chance far more than the unfolding of a grand design. Our unique responses to life are not determined for us at birth or at maturity. We must grow and change to meet the continuing demands of our imperfect world.

Fortunately, we are constituted to do just that. Our central nervous system and our immune system can perceive minute changes in our environment and change their cellular structures to better challenge the demands of each new reality. This coordinated bodily response to any perceived demand is termed *stress*. Stress makes it more likely that we will be able to cope successfully with whatever life has to offer.

HEALTH PSYCHOLOGY AND BEHAVIORAL MEDICINE

Western men and women have long dreamed of existing within a garden; strived to gain access to a garden spot; prayed to reenter a lost garden. The mystery and magic of the garden is that there it would be possible to live and simply allow one's personality and self-esteem to unfold—without blemish, without distortion. Our American garden, however, is not so perfect. There are multiple forces at work here to cause us strain and to threaten us with maladjustment.

As this is being written, America is engaged in a great debate over **health care reform.** Our desire for universal coverage and a lifetime guarantee of affordable medical services is clashing with the realities of exploding medical costs, an entrenched provider system, and attempts by all concerned to protect their own advantages—while shifting the costs onto anyone other than themselves. This behavior is all too human, as are the very behaviors, cited by the *American Medical Association* (1993), responsible for the health crisis:

1. criminal violence
2. bad habits
3. legal and illegal drug use

These are not war, pestilence, and disease, the scourges of ancient times, but *habits*—behavior patterns learned and practiced within contemporary social settings! In response, the new discipline of **health psychology,** begun by the *American Psychological Association* in 1978, has become a major player in this human drama. Psychologists now study the ways people stay healthy, the reasons they become ill, and the ways they respond to illness (Taylor, 1992). A **biopsychosocial model** has replaced the older biomedical model used to explain health and illness. This model sees health as a result of the interplay of *biological, psychological, and social* factors.

Behavioral medicine, a new medical specialty, shares the same goals and much the same point of view as the biopsychosocial model—it researches behavioral factors associated with health and illness, and encourages active patient participation in the diagnosis and cure of their illnesses (Blanchard, 1992). Both groups are interested in helping us to move toward individual **wellness** and to work together toward the improvement of our health care system.

health care reform   a movement to improve the delivery of health care services to all Americans

health psychology   a field within psychology devoted to understanding psychological influences on how people stay healthy, why they become ill, and how they respond when they do become ill

biopsychosocial model   model of health and illness that holds that links between the nervous system, the immune system, behavioral styles, cognitive processing, and environmental factors can put people at risk for illness

behavioral medicine   an approach to treatment that follows the biopsychosocial model of illness. Emphasis is on prevention as well as cure, and the patient assumes an active role in nurturing a lifestyle that is health producing

wellness   optimal health, including the ability to function fully over the emotional, environmental, intellectual, physical, and spiritual domains of health

Psychology and medicine are becoming formal partners in precisely those areas of health in which sanitation, surgery, or drugs do not as yet cure or control a health problem. As of this writing, for example, science and medicine have not developed a vaccine to inoculate us against **AIDS**, nor have they developed drugs to cure this acquired immunodeficiency syndrome.

AIDS acronym for Acquired Immune Deficiency Syndrome, a lethal syndrome caused by a virus that damages the immune system and weakens the body's ability to fight bacteria

Responding to a Crisis

The **HIV virus,** which claimed the lives of more than 300,000 Americans in 1994, is typically transmitted by bodily fluids being exchanged between people engaged in *voluntary behaviors,* such as sharing—sharing sexual partners, sharing sexual practices, sharing drug needles, and sharing toothbrushes!

HIV virus a virus that attacks white blood cells, weakens the immune system and in many cases develops into AIDS

How do you change the **risky behaviors** of hundreds of thousands of people, when the behaviors that place them at risk are pleasurable, social, and/or addictive? Health psychologists find that four conditions must be present if prevention programs are to work.

risky behaviors styles of acting and thinking that produce an increased possibility of premature injury, illness, or death

1. People must be informed about the dangers associated with their risky behavior.

2. People must believe that they are *personally at risk* (Cochran et. al., 1992).

3. People must believe that they can perform the new response that will reduce the risk.

4. People must believe that the new response will work—that it will reduce or eliminate the risk (Bandura, 1986).

Adjusting to Reality

Although some at-risk behaviors have changed for the better (e.g., sexual promiscuity has declined and safer sex practices have increased), we are now much more aware of the array of forces acting to prevent significant shifts in our personal and social behavior. Perhaps the most devastating barrier to change is

---

CRITICAL THINKING ISSUE
Stress Without Distress

We can cope best by striving for self-fulfillment.

Self-fulfillment is not just everything in life— it is the only thing. Knowing who you are, being faithful to your true self, and striving to be all that you can be—these activities alone give life its special meaning. We must not let any person, cause, or couse of events stop us from investing our precious growing years in self-absorption, self-reflection, and self-mastery. Only by maintaining a personal orientation to life can we hope to survive the stress of daily living.

We can cope best by striving to be useful and helpful to others.

"Alone and afraid in a world I never made." This terrible sense of isolation awaits those who think they are in the world solely for themselves. Such a belief leaves them tense, harsh, intensely competitive, and greedy—a perfect formula for short-term success and long-term desolation. Only by having a conventional orientation to life, that is, by being useful and helpful to others, can we find joy in living, true meaning in life, and the support and love we need to embrace the stressful challenges of living.

I take the position that:

What Makes Sally Cry?

At first it was sheer terror. In terror Sally urinated and was forced to swallow her urine. Her vaginal and anal areas were torn by the gun barrel repeatedly thrust into her—her breasts were burned by cigarettes . . . As her physical wounds healed, her fear remained—but now became mixed with anxiety and self-blame. "Did I ask for it? Did I lead him to think I meant 'Yes' when I said 'no'?" Anger followed. Through all this inner turmoil, Sally maintained a mask of controlled composure. But six years is a long time to fear being hurt again, and Sally, tired of the nightmares, contemplated suicide. Instead she "did away" with herself

by leaving town. Even after moving away, Sally is nervous to be outdoors or in a crowd—even more nervous to be alone. And she is alone in a very fundamental sense; the very idea of gaining enjoyment from sexual activity is now enough to bring Sally to tears. . . .

It is clear that rape is among the most stressful affronts to human dignity. It is good to know that early and compassionate treatment can be highly effective for the victims of rape (Calhoun and Atkeson, 1989). It is very important that colleges develop procedures so that the victims of "Date Rape" can receive such restorative care.

the knowledge that at present we socialize our children to accept certain harmful stereotypes, for example, that "real men" are violent, hard drinking, sexually exploitive, heavy smokers. "Real men" don't worry about risky behavior! (Kimmel and Levine, 1992)

Cultural stereotypes extend to women as well. For example, the incidence of AIDS is *increasing* most among Latin populations, in part because of the cultural conflict young women must resolve. On the one hand, they desire to please themselves, their family, their religion, and their society by remaining virgins until marriage; at the same time, they wish to please themselves and their boyfriends by being sexually active. Increasingly, they resolve this conflict through a dangerous compromise: They engage in anal intercourse, which allows them to protect their technical virginity but at the price of placing themselves and their future children at the *highest single risk* for **HIV transmission** (Singer et. al., 1990, Sanchez and Fernendez, 1993). Although anal intercourse is believed to create an especially high rate of transmission, vaginal intercourse is actually a greater source of transmission because it is practiced more widely (Ironson and Schneiderman, 1991). Recent research indicates that psychological stressors are also associated with the progression from HIV Positive status to full-blown AIDS (Ickovics and Rodin, 1992).

Being under **stress** seems to make us more likely to revert back to risky behaviors that we are trying to control. We eat, drink, do drugs, and smoke more while under stress, for example. It is stress and **coping** strategies that have received the most attention from health psychologists during the past decade.

HIV transmission   the virus is not airborne. It is passed from one person to another by 1) the exchange of semen or blood during sexual contact, especially anal intercourse, and 2) the sharing of needles and syringes used for drug injection

stress   reaction to any demand placed on a person

coping   means of dealing with a situation seen as being threatening

stressor   a physical or psychological stimulus that creates a demand within a responding organism

Human Stress

Stress may be studied from any one of three perspectives: (1) as **stressors**—stimulus events such as earthquakes or hurricanes; (2) as *responses*—bodily reactions to stressful events; or (3) as *transactions*—interactions between events and our personal cognitive appraisal of those events (Lazarus and Folkman, 1984). In this chapter we examine stress from each of these points of view and describe how our adjustments have an impact on our physical and mental health.

Human Stressors   Anything that humans can sense can be stress provoking. We can, for instance, learn to swell with pride or cringe in terror at the sight of a colored cloth (a flag). We can learn to respond with stress to almost anything—divorce, sex, final exams, or even ideas.

Stress and Major Events

Catastrophic events have long been recognized as dangerous to to our emotional as well as our physical health. The shell shock of World War I, the battle fatigue of World War II and Korea, and the posttraumatic stress disorder, or PTSD, of Vietnam and Operation Desert Storm all represent the prolonged, disruptive impact of extreme stress on young, healthy members of our fighting forces.

In 1991, United Nations soldiers were mistakenly identified as the enemy and killed by "friendly fire" from United States pilots who were flying in support of our ground troops. Such tragic decisions are frequently made under the stress of combat (Adler, 1993) and the combatants frequently relive the trauma in flashbacks, dreams, or daytime fantasies. Fortunately, most of our soldiers remain healthy after the stress of the Gulf War (Bartone et. al., 1992).

Although American women are only now taking their place in combat air- and seacraft, all too many have experienced *sexual abuse* and a form of posttraumatic stress disorder known as the **rape trauma syndrome,** as detailed in the accompanying "What Makes Sally Cry."

rape trauma syndrome a post-traumatic stress response to having been raped

What could possibly be more stressful than rape? Perhaps the chronic rape brought about by intolerance and social injustice. In America certain ethnic groups are likely to experience major stressors (prejudice and discrimination) that are made more intolerable by the simple fact that they are not being felt by other groups, and they never end (Lopez and Takemoto-Chock, 1992).

Disastrous earthquakes, floods, and hurricanes, such as those of the early 1990s demonstrate clearly that our safety and security can never be certain. On a more personal level, individual life events can just as devastatingly rock our sense of security. It is in our personal life that the link between events and physical and mental health has been most carefully charted. Thomas Holmes and Richard Rahe ranked each of forty-three critical life changes on a scale ranging from 0 to 100 (the stress of one's wedding day was established as a midpoint and ranked 50). "Death of a spouse" ranked at the top of the scale. These values are termed **life-change units (LCUs).** When the LCUs for one person totaled between 150 and 190 (mild-life crisis), 37 percent of those people were found to have undergone an appreciable deterioration in health. Between 200 and 299 LCUs (moderate life crisis), the figure rose to more than 51 percent; and among those suffering major life crisis, 79 percent fell ill within the following year (Holmes and Rahe, 1967).

life change units (LCUs) the amount of change experienced by an individual during a one-year period

Stress and Life's Daily Hassles

Lazarus (1981) and Delongis and associates (1982) maintain that it is daily hassles, rather than major events, that result in cumulative stress. For college students minor hassles, rather than major life events, tend to maintain stress at unhealthy levels. The hassles of college life revolve around three themes: (1) wasting time, (2) meeting high standards, and (3) experiencing personal loneliness. Because college students differ from the general population, a special version of Holmes and Rahe's Social Adjustment Scale has been prepared for them and tested on college freshmen. The amount of stress reported by them

habituate   a decrease in responding when a stimulus is presented repeatedly

was found to directly relate to their general health. (The scale is reproduced in Table 4–1, see how you compare with your fellow scholars.) As daily hassles lessen, general well-being improves (Chamberlain and Zika, 1990).

We tend to **habituate** to most daily stressors; we get used to them, thus their negative impact lessens. However, interpersonal conflicts must be dealt with effectively when they first occur, as they tend to recur and grow worse over time (Bolger et. al., 1989).

How stressful life has been for you seems to predict how well you will perform academically in college (Lloyd, Alexander, Rice, and Greenfield, 1980): the higher the LCUs, the lower the GPAs (grade point averages) for the next two years. Results from the Lloyd et. al. study shed light on a value system that might explain why some students do poorly in college. It seems that play and a job mean more to the poorer student than to the better one. At a minimum, changes in work (either new responsibilities or a new job) and changes in recreation are two factors that produce the greatest negative effect on the grades of the already poorly performing student. Many of you may have friends who have chosen a car and play over college itself. They work to support a car that they see as necessary for the good life and have no time left for their classes.

College as a Stressor

Attending college is a full- or part-time job for the majority of readers of this text. In what ways is college itself a stressor? Shaw and Riskind (1983) identify four factors associated with job stress:

1. Environment—physical and social conditions of the workplace.

2. Job complexity—the nature of the tasks to be done.

3. Role conflict—the complications of the status positions we hold because of our job.

4. Job responsibility—the consequences that flow from our doing or not doing the job.

Freshmen often have difficulty adjusting to college life—so many changes occurring so fast. The dropout rate among college freshmen is high, as is the rate of alcohol abuse and suicide. Such escape and avoidance tactics deprive people of the opportunity to learn more adaptive ways of coping with stressful environments, including college (Cooper et. al., 1992).

To your professor, the college environment is a "stress factory" (McMillen, 1987). College professors also are confronted with too many tasks in too little time. Your instructor has classes to teach, papers to grade, grant applications to write, committee work to complete, students to advise, and books and articles to write and publish. He or she works under increasingly tougher competition for fewer positions that often offer low pay and poor working conditions. And you thought that professors had it easy!

Because it would be unethical to manipulate catastrophic events, the link between stressful life events and illness has been documented through the use of prospective studies, in which the life event measure is obtained at one time and the health outcome measure at a later time. These findings, or **correlations** typically fall in the .20–.30 range (Rodin and Salovey, 1989). The modest results we are discussing are impressive for their consistency, not their strength.

correlations   measurements of the degree of relationship existing between two or more variables

You can get an idea of how much stress you have experienced lately by (1) multiplying the value for each event by the number of times it happened to you during the past year (maximum of four times) and (2) totaling your results. Scores below 347 are considered to fall in the low stress category, and scores above 1,435 are classified as representing high stress.

TABLE 4–1
The College Schedule of Recent Experience

EVENT	NUMERICAL VALUE
(1) Entered College	50
(2) Married	77
(3) Trouble with your boss	38
(4) Held a job while attending school	43
(5) Experienced the death of a spouse	87
(6) Major change in sleeping habits	34
(7) Experienced the death of a close family member	77
(8) Major change in eating habits	30
(9) Change in or choice of major field of study	41
(10) Revision of personal habits	45
(11) Experienced the death of a close friend	68
(12) Found guilty of minor violations of the law	22
(13) Had an outstanding personal achievement	40
(14) Experienced pregnancy or fathered a pregnancy	68
(15) Major change in health or behavior of family member	56
(16) Had sexual difficulties	58
(17) Had trouble with in-laws	42
(18) Major change in number of family get-togethers	26
(19) Major change in financial state	53
(20) Gained a new family member	50
(21) Change in residence or living conditions	42
(22) Major conflict or change in values	50
(23) Major change in church activities	36
(24) Marital reconciliation with your mate	58
(25) Fired from work	62
(26) Were divorced	76
(27) Changed to a different line of work	50
(28) Major change in number of arguments with spouse	50
(29) Major change in responsibilities at work	47
(30) Had your spouse begin or cease work outside the home	41
(31) Major change in working hours or conditions	42
(32) Marital separation from mate	74
(33) Major change in type and/or amount of recreation	37
(34) Major change in use of drugs	52
(35) Took a mortgage or loan of less than $10,000	52
(36) Major personal injury or illness	65
(37) Major change in use of alcohol	46
(38) Major change in social activities	43
(39) Major change in amount of participation in school activities	38
(40) Major change in amount of independence and responsibility	49
(41) Took a trip or vacation	33
(42) Engaged to be married	54
(43) Changed to a new school	50
(44) Changed dating habits	41
(45) Trouble with school administration	44
(46) Broke or had broken a marital engagement of a steady relationship	60
(47) Major change in self-concept or self-awareness	57

SOURCE: M. B. Marx, T. F. Garrity, and F. R. Bowers. "The Influence of Recent Life Experiences on the Health of College Freshmen." *Journal of Psychosomatic Research* 19 (1975): 97.

THE HUMAN STRESS RESPONSE

fight-or-flight response a sequence of internal changes triggered by threat, prepares the body for combat or running away

According to Selye's *The Stress of Life* (1976), although the number and types of stressors are infinite, we give a single psychophysiological response to all of them.[1] When we are stressed, a host of internal changes take place to enable us to react with anger, fear, or lust and so that we can be ready either to confront our stressor or to flee from it. This **flight-or-fight response** (Cannon, 1929) mobilizes energy so that we may survive by confrontation or escape (see Figure 4–1). The amount of electrical activity in our brain increases, our vision and hearing improve, our blood clots faster, and we become less sensitive to pain. All of these factors and more are helpful in combat.

In combat or in daily life, stress can disrupt a number of our normal response patterns— the usual ways in which we think, feel, and act. Under the influence of moderate to severe stress we may find ourselves exhibiting any or all of the following:

1. *Excessive and compulsive behaviors,* such as nail biting, teeth clenching, overeating, pacing, picking, scratching, and talking. Or we may find ourselves not responding at all!

2. *Illogical and noncoherent thinking,* as evidenced by memory loss, concentration loss, repetitive thoughts, nightmares, and/or reduced ability to solve day-to-day problems.

3. *Negative emotions,* such as anger, anxiety, depression, guilt, irritability, or shame.

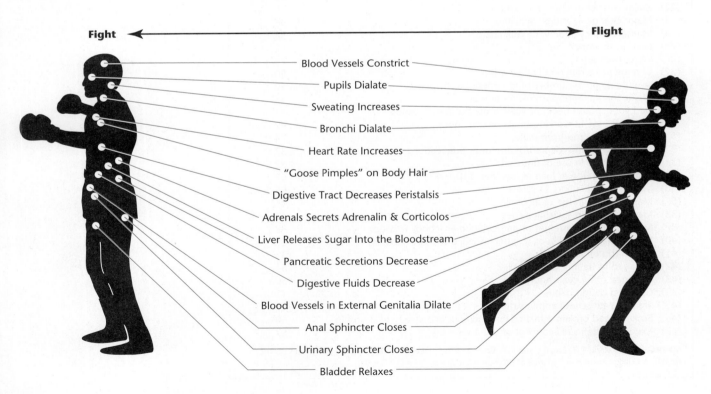

Fight ←————————————————————————————→ Flight

- Blood Vessels Constrict
- Pupils Dialate
- Sweating Increases
- Bronchi Dialate
- Heart Rate Increases
- "Goose Pimples" on Body Hair
- Digestive Tract Decreases Peristalsis
- Adrenals Secrets Adrenalin & Corticolos
- Liver Releases Sugar Into the Bloodstream
- Pancreatic Secretions Decrease
- Digestive Fluids Decrease
- Blood Vessels in External Genitalia Dilate
- Anal Sphincter Closes
- Urinary Sphincter Closes
- Bladder Relaxes

FIGURE 4–1
The Body's Reaction to Stress

The common factor in these disruptive response patterns is **biochemistry.** Our body and brain respond to a stressor by communicating with each other via neuropeptides, small amino acid chains found both peripheral to and in the brain (Spector and Arora, 1993). These neuropeptides allow for direct intercellular communication among the systems that have evolved to enhance our survival.

biochemistry the chemical process necessary to create and sustain life forms

THREE SYSTEMS FOR SURVIVAL

Our survival requires that our nervous system, endocrine system, and immune system function harmoniously. Under stress this complicated rhythm is regulated by increased activation levels in our brain. Ursin (1986) holds that all physiological processes, including all hormone secretions, are affected by brain (i.e., psychological) factors. Stress reactions "center on a biological pathway known as the 'HPA axis' or 'stress circuit'" (Asher, 1987). This is a feedback loop connecting the brain's hypothalamus with the pituitary and the adrenal glands. (See Figure 4–2: The Brain Body Pathways of the Stress Reaction.)

central nervous system the brain and spinal cord

The Neural Response

Our **central nervous system** regulates our somatic nervous system, which controls the level of tension in our skeletal muscles. It also regulates our **autonomic**

autonomic nervous system part of the peripheral nervous system that governs activities not usually under conscious control, such as temperature regulation

FIGURE 4–2
The Adrenal Glands and the Hormones They Secrete

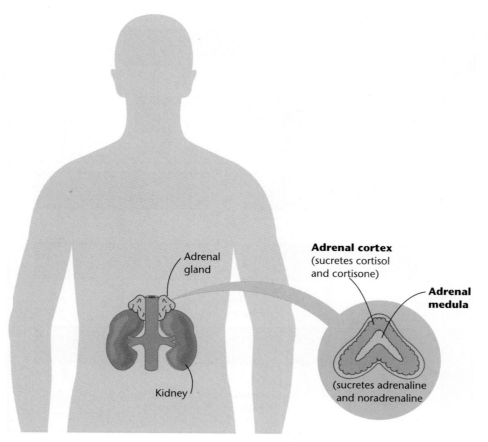

Adrenal gland

Kidney

Adrenal cortex
(sucretes cortisol and cortisone)

Adrenal medula

(sucretes adrenaline and noradrenaline

nervous system, which controls our internal visceral organs and glands (heart, bladder, etc.). This regulation is done via direct neural messages. There is also a second messenger system that is controlled by our central nervous system.

The Endocrine Response

endocrine system   glandular system transferring information between cells in different parts of the body by way of hormonal messengers

Our **endocrine system** secretes hormones directly into our bloodstream via a series of glands. The *adrenal glands,* located on top of each of our kidneys, are called the stress glands because of the hormones they produce. Each adrenal medulla, or inner cove, when stimulated by the sympathetic branch of our autonomic nervous system, secretes *adrenaline* (epinephrine), which flows to and increases the activity level of our heart, liver, and muscles. It also secretes our *adrenaline* (norepinephrine), which flows to and constricts the blood vessels in our skin, diverting blood to our muscles so that we may run or fight.

corticosteroids   stress hormones released by the adrenal cortex that have long lasting effects on the body

Each *adrenal cortex,* or outer shell, secretes a family of stress hormones known as **corticosteroids,** including *cortisol* and *cortisone,* which help us during an emergency. They flow to body cells and reduce inflammation while releasing cellular energy. The *pituitary* also emits bursts of the hormone *prolactin,* a

FIGURE 4–3
The Brain-Body Pathways of the Stress Reaction

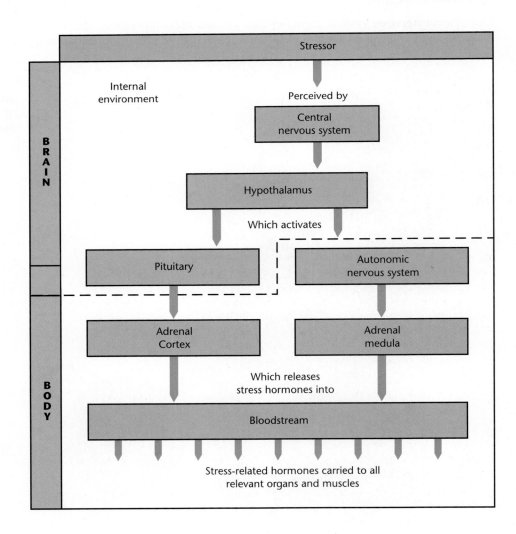

painkilling substance. Our tears of emotion contain prolactin, perhaps explaining why we feel better after a good cry. **Endorphins,** morphinelike chemicals, also occur naturally within our brain in response to painful stimuli. In all, more than thirty hormones are produced during stressful encounters.

The Immune Response

The most exciting area of recent research involves our **immune system,** which must be efficient if we are to defend ourselves. Bacteria, viruses and other potentially harmful organisms are abundant in the environment, thus the human body must develop defense mechanisms to guard against them.

Nonspecific defenses such as skin form barriers against outside invaders. Mucus shields your mouth, nose, and other passages.

Specific defenses, based in white blood cells, send specialized cells to resist bacteria and fight viruses that get past your nonspecific defenses.

Immunosuppressants are substances that decrease the efficiency of our immune system. There is growing evidence that our bodies release natural suppressants when under stress. A new branch of study, **psychoneuroimmunology,** examines the role of our nervous system in regulating these protective responses. Our white cells comprise "a liquid nervous system" (Locke, 1985) that can chemically recognize foreign cells and then attack and destroy them. Having done so, these immune-system cells change their very structure to build a faster and more efficient defense against subsequent invasion.

Our body's remarkable adaptive response worked well for us when our enemies were lions, tigers, and bears. We could use our anger to direct our attack or our fear to effect our escape. Having done so, we could return to a calm and restful state until the next crisis.

Today our stressors are taxes, freeways, and social pressures. Consider your bodily response to the threat of speaking in public—sweaty hands, pounding heart, shortness of breath, etc.

Sweat is our cooling mechanism, and sweaty palms provide a better grip. Cold hands and trembling legs reflect a massive blood shift toward the body's vital centers— its brain, heart, and large muscles. Some muscle groups tighten and others relax so that you can move and breathe more effectively. The blood flows away from your digestive tract and genitals. You do not need to waste energy while in combat; thus, you experience the lump in the throat, the dry mouth, and nausea. Nor do you need to carry excess baggage into battle, so your bladder and bowels automatically empty when you are under extreme stress. Even fainting may be seen as a physical defense mechanism, for it prevents further pain and brings a stillness that might help avoid detection.

Many additional, unfelt changes are also taking place. For example, your spleen is increasing its production of red corpuscles to improve blood clotting, fat is increasing in your bloodstream for ready energy where needed, and your liver is supplying glycogen for energy. This massive mobilization and redirection of energy, termed **catabolism,** takes place unconsciously. You do not have to will your heart to beat faster or your breathing to quicken. Our discomfort is unfortunate in that few of these changes aid us in public speaking. It is a price we have paid for leaving the cave.

endorphins neurotransmitters involved in many reactions to pleasure and pain

immune system a specialized cellular defense against bacteria and viral invasion. Immune cells can learn and can communicate with nerve cells

immunosuppressants substances that decrease the efficiency of the immune system

psychoneuroimmunology a science that examines the role of our nervous system in regulating our protective responses to bacterial or viral invaders

catabolism changes in living cells that provide energy for vital processes

Critical Review 1

1. College students are more "stressed out" by catastrophic events than by daily hassles. T F

2. Our three biological systems for survival are (1) the nervous system, (2) the endocrine system, and (3) the immune system. T F

3. In what important ways does our "unfinished nature" as human beings increase the amount of stress we encounter in life?

4. In what ways does this unfinished nature reduce the number of stressors we encounter throughout life?

5. Describe how the physical and emotional changes we experience while under stress prepare us to fight or run.

6. In what ways are such modern realities as income taxes, expressways, and acid rain similar to the ancient realities represented by lions, tigers, and bears?

7. In what ways are they different, and how do these real differences change the way we must learn to respond to stressors?

Prolonged Stress

The dry throat and other symptoms of distress are not the only price we pay for our civilized existence. In ancient times when danger passed, a deep calm descended on us. The relief that slowed our breathing also reduced the amount of oxygen we consumed and the carbon dioxide we produced. Our brain activity slowed and our sweating ceased. Blood pressure and heart rate decreased, and even the chemistry of our blood altered. These changes had a profound restorative effect on our minds and bodies. The stress response, necessary for survival, was balanced by the **restorative response,** equally necessary.

restorative response a state of profound calm

We cannot run away or fight today's stressors, even though we are well prepared to do so. We therefore cannot directly and completely discharge the energy we have mobilized. We cannot experience the deep calm of the restorative response. Stress remains within us in the form of glandular secretions, muscle contractions, and neural discharges. We feel these states as anxiety, anger, or depression.

When Stress is Harmful

Stress is harmful when we respond to it by becoming nervous and withdrawn, or irritable and antagonistic. These behaviors hinder our growth, our potential for becoming a finished animal, a complete human being. Hans Selye describes many of our modern physical ills as **diseases of adaptation.** We are being injured or destroyed by our own defense systems, which have not been able to keep up with the times.

diseases of adaptation diseases that have their roots in attempts to adapt to stressors

The Body's Responses to Persistent Stress

Stress can play a crucial role in the entire spectrum of physical illnesses, from the common cold to cancer, heart disease, and sudden death (Cohen and Williamson, 1992).

Selye describes our responses as a group of changes that occur together, a **general adaptation syndrome (GAS).** These involve the entire body and are intended to help us survive. The GAS can be divided into three stages—the *alarm reaction,* the *stage of resistance,* and the *stage of exhaustion.*

general adaptation syndrome (GAS) the body's pattern of reaction under continued stress

The alarm reaction is the flight-or-fight response. If we are unsuccessful in warding off an illness, for example, we display general symptoms such as a loss of sleep, aching joints, loss of appetite, headaches, and low-grade fevers. All of these occur in response to any illness.

The stage of resistance occurs if the stressor continues. Our bodies then develop a resistance to that specific stress, and the earlier symptoms disappear. We may regain our sleep and eating patterns, for example, but still feel tired and not interested in eating. Our neural and glandular systems remain hyperactive, and we remain overstimulated and constantly mobilized for defense.

The stage of exhaustion occurs when the stressor continues despite our best defenses. Glands must rest and restore their balance. If they cannot rest, they overtax themselves, resistance stops, and symptoms reappear; if the stressor persists, we may die. After such a death, an autopsy usually reveals enlarged adrenal glands, a wasted **lymphatic system** (part of the system that defends against disease), and peptic ulcers. All this is found in addition to the failed organ, such as the heart, that is officially listed as the cause of death.

Our knowledge about these stages and about the consequences of persistent stress is growing rapidly. For example, people who have lived near the nuclear reactor at Three Mile Island since the 1979 radiation leak there show increased levels of the stress hormones cortisol, epinephrine, and norepinephrine in their urine—an indication that these individuals remain in a chronically stressed state. They find themselves in a situation that exceeds their ability to adapt; they can't hide and can't (or won't) run. As the residents attempt to adjust to life under the threat of a peaceful nuclear cloud, their physiological defense systems are working against them in two important ways—overloading of the endocrine system and suppressing of the immune system.

lymphatic system body system that includes the ducts that discharge white blood cells to protect against infection

Direct Self-Destruction: Endocrine-System Overload

As you know, our brain responds to stress by directing the sympathetic branch of our autonomic nervous system to stimulate our adrenal medulla to quickly secrete stress hormones into our bloodstream. The pituitary is directed to produce chemicals that more slowly cause our adrenal cortex to secrete similar hormones. When these hormones are excessive and prolonged, headaches, mood swings, muscle tension, and similar felt changes result. Unfelt changes also occur. For example, when blood samples were regularly taken from working accountants, their cholesterol levels rose at the times that they considered themselves to be under the greatest amounts of stress (Orlebeke and Van Dooren, 1982). At such times, our acid and lipid (cholesterol) levels increase, as does our blood pressure. It is these unfelt changes that can cause serious illness and even death.

An increase in slow-acting cortisol and/or fast-acting adrenaline increases our blood pressure and blood-platelet stickiness. This is good for raising our metabolism and our blood-clotting ability during a fight. Unfortunately, battles such as Three Mile Island appear endless. Hypertension (high blood pressure) is the silent killer for our age. Elevated pressure, combined with high serum cholesterol (blood fats) and small blood clots, lead to **atherosclerosis.** The fats and clots are forced into the arterial walls, clogging and stretching them and bringing about hardening of the arteries (Benson, 1975). When arteries become clogged, the blood supply to vital organs decreases, and **angina** and **cardiac infarction** may result. If a clot breaks loose, it may circulate and block blood flow to any part of the body. Blocked blood flow in the brain results in neural tissue death—a **cerebral stroke.**

Ulcers, spastic colon, and similar gastrointestinal disorders are the result of elevated acidity brought on by cortisol, the stress hormone associated with emotional responses such as anger, hostility, and rage. For those who are ulcer prone, reducing the stress response, not spicy food, is the preferred treatment (Weiss, 1972).

atherosclerosis thickening of the interior walls of the arteries

angina pain in the chest, not caused by heart-muscle damage

cardiac infarction an area of dead or dying heart tissue resulting from obstruction of the blood vessels normally supplying the area

cerebral stroke a sudden trauma with the brain itself

Indirect Self-Destruction: Immune Suppression

Cortisol reduces the activity of our immune system as part of its function of controlling inflammation. Cortisol is secreted at higher levels when events are perceived as threats. This increases our chances of becoming ill. Infections, allergies, and even cancers are found to be more prevalent in populations that are under stress. How can this be so? The specific answer to that question occupies the new science of psychoneuroimmunology. Our immune system is very complex, and its workings are poorly understood. It is a remarkable system that is diffused throughout our bodies.

Science once believed that the immune system operated independently, isolated from other physiological systems. We were very slow to give up this belief.

In the 1920s it was repeatedly demonstrated that immune responses could be elicited, in the absence of any **antigen,** by a neutral stimulus being repeatedly paired with an antigen in classical conditioning experiments (Spector and Arora, 1993). These Pavlovian experiments provided evidence that there must be neural connections between our central nervous system and our immune system. In 1975, Robert Adler and Nicholas Cohen rediscovered this phenomenon while trying to condition rats to a taste aversion to saccharin. The bad tasting substance that they paired with saccharin was (cyclophosphamide) an immunosuppressant. Their rats learned to avoid saccharin, and to suppress their own immune system. They began dying! (Adler and Cohen, 1993).

It wasn't until the 1980s, however, when neurohormones were identified and matched with receptor sites on human immune cells, that the biological linkages between mind and body could be confirmed and the quest for specific practical health applications could receive the blessings of legitimacy by psychology and medicine! In 1979, Norman Cousins was laughed at when he described the role of humor in his recovery from a usually incurable disease of the connective tissue. In 1989, researchers were not laughing; they reported that people who used humor to deal with stress had the highest baseline levels of **immunoglobulin A** (Dillon and Totten, 1989) and significant reductions in the stress hormone cortisol (Berk et. al., 1989).

The same opiumlike peptides (hormones) that help us by reducing our pain perception and increasing our tension tolerance also endanger us by dampening our immune response. In the distant past we may have had to reign in our powerful immune system by reducing the helper cells and increasing the suppressor cells so that it did not attack us in case we received an injury in battle. We all know and fear AIDS, the suppression of our immune system brought about by different strains of the HIV virus. What we are beginning to understand and respect is the fact that certain kinds of stress can temporarily produce AIDS-like immunosuppression. During exams or similar periods of academic pressure, students in general show lower levels of salivary immunoglobulin, a defense against respiratory infections (Jemmott et al., 1985). Even the teenage curse, **acne,** worsens under stress (Sizer and Whitney, 1994).

The idea that mental activity such as worrying about an exam can affect our ability to ward off disease was buttressed by the finding that when sections of the left side of the cerebral cortex are surgically removed, T-cell and natural killer-cell activity is reduced throughout the body (Melmed, 1986). Stress can alter the brain's regulation of our immune response.

antigens   substances, such as viruses, bacteria, or cancer cells, which induce the formation of antibodies when introduced directly into the body

immunoglobulin A   one of a group of blood serum proteins capable of acting as an antibody

acne   an inflammatory disease of the oil glands, characterized by pimples on the face

Critical Review 2

1. In the animal world, the stress response is usually followed by the fight-or-flight response after the danger has passed. T F

2. The first stage of Selye's General Adaptation Syndrome is the resistance stage. T F

3. Our central nervous system and our immune system are connected by both neural and hormonal receptor sites. T F

4. In what ways does prolonged stress hinder our growth (1) emotionally; (2) socially; (3) intellectually?

5. Describe how prolonged stress can lead to physical illness and death (1) directly (through heart attack or stroke) and (2) indirectly (through allergies, infections, and cancers).

STRESSFUL TRANSACTIONS

A critical link is missing from the mind-body connection, however. Unhappy mental states may lead to immune system changes, but it's not known whether those changes, which are small, affect health. In spite of the theories mentioned in the previous section, no biomedical sequence connecting a specific stressor with a specific illness has yet been demonstrated (Grady, 1992).

The search is complicated first by the fact that there are great individual differences in the way we respond to given stressors. Some of us raise our blood pressure; others raise the heart rate. The identical stressor may produce different intensities of response in different subjects. A third complication is our differing genetic makeup. **Psychosomatic** illnesses are thought to attack the weakest link in our chain of organs, muscles, and glands. For some it is the heart, for others it is the pancreas. Under stress, one group may develop heart trouble, and another may develop diabetes. A fourth complication is the profound effect learning has on visceral responding. If you received attention for stomachaches as a child while your friend received more of a response for headaches, under stress you might develop ulcers while your friend might complain of migraines.

psychosomatic   relating to physical symptoms attributable to psychological disturbances

Stress and Physical Illness

Stress can best be understood from the perspective of interactions described in the **diathesis-stress perception model** (a diathesis is a vulnerability, or predisposition to a disorder).

Stressful transactions are interactions between events and our emotional and physical response to our **cognitive appraisal** of those events. Under stress, systems involved in cognition and emotion are activated. Dantzer (1986) reports "that emotional arousal in conscious subjects exposed to stressful situations was responsible for the pituitary-adrenal response to such events" (p. 37).

diasthesis-stress model   the idea that one becomes vulnerable to diabetes for example, with age and obesity, but one only becomes diabetic if subjected to stresses that are too much to handle

cognitive appraisal   an assessment of the situation in terms of personal well being, a step in the creation of an emotional-stress response

Primary and Secondary Appraisal

The degree to which our central nervous system (CNS) will be activated by any stressor is dependent upon the meaning we attach to it. Do we view the stressor as positive or negative? Does it represent damage already done? Is it a threat to us or those we love? Could it present us with an opportunity, a challenge? These and other questions represent facets of the primary question What does this mean to me? Our secondary appraisal considers the question What can I do about it? (Lazarus and Folkman, 1984)

Perceptions That Increase our Vulnerability

It is the answers to these questions that determine the length and level of our arousal. For example, the following perceptions increase our level of plasma corticoids and lower our immunity:

1. The greater novelty in an event
2. The greater threat of an event
3. A greater sense of being helpless or hopeless
4. Lower administrative or social support at work or home.

Perceptions That Decrease our Vulnerability

The following perceptions decrease our level of plasma corticoids and increase our immunity:

1. A greater sense of control over an event
2. A greater ability to predict a stressful event
3. A greater ability to emit an effective coping response—even via displacement. (An example of such coping is children who respond to the stress of having to sit still in school by swinging their legs [Dantzer, 1986; Ursin, 1986].)

As we might expect, we suffer less stress and less illness from negative events that are *highly predictable, readily controllable,* and for which we can receive appropriate *emotional* or *informational supports* (Cohen and Wills, 1985; Katz and Wykes, 1985).

Central Values and Severity of the Stress Response

Stress is value laden. The danger of any stressor is influenced by our system of learned beliefs and values. We are most vulnerable to stress in the areas we hold most dear. **Central stressors** are those that threaten us with a loss of self-esteem or a loss of a significant other (Fisher, 1984). Because of this, an individual's negative perception of events is a good predictor of psychological stress (Zukerman et al., 1986). Richard Lazarus (1981) reports such central stressors to be five times as significant as the number or intensity of the daily hassles we experience.

central stressors   events that threaten us with a loss of self-esteem or the loss of a significant other

Personality Traits and Vulnerability to Stress

A *personality trait* is an underlying attribute, such as shyness, that we seem to bring with us and project onto each situation we face; such traits are thought to partially determine our behavior. Certain personality traits, such as optimism and high self-esteem, are associated with increased resistance to infectious illnesses and superior success in fending off the chronic diseases of middle age (Seligman, 1991, 1992). Seligman believes optimism can be learned.

Other personality traits, such as anxiety and pessimism, have been found to be associated with high activation levels, high stress-hormone levels, and high levels of illness and disease. The effect seems to work both ways; highly stressed students report greater levels of anxiety, depression, and somatic (bodily) discomfort (Lustman et al., 1984).

anxiety   a fear response to a perceived future threat

Anxiety   Our primary response to a situation appraised as threatening is **anxiety.** When a person reacts with excessive anxiety in situations that others regard as only mildly stressful, the assumption is that the primary source of the threat is a predisposition toward anxiety that magnifies the strength of the stressors present.

Depression   If we can't cope with a continuing stressful situation, we may respond first with apathy and then with **depression.** This mood disorder is characterized by sadness, negative thoughts, and low self-esteem. These traits endanger our health by increasing the probability of our physiologically over-reacting. Recent research results support the idea that *loneliness* is an important contributor to depression among college students (Rich, 1987), having more of an impact than stressful life events or attributional style. Learned helplessness is an example of a stress-provoking attributional style.

depression   a mood disorder characterized by excessive sadness

Learned Helplessness   Each of us has a characteristic way of explaining bad events when reality is ambiguous. For example, you might ask yourself, "Why did I miss the date when the term paper was due? Was it because I honestly forgot? Or was it that I always mess up on important events?" Perhaps you would end up thinking, "It was all my fault. I always screw up. I'm incapable of doing anything right" (see chapter 6 for an explanation of this cognitive style).

If we believe bad events happen to us because of global faults that we have and can't change, then we suffer from a personality trait that has been termed **learned helplessness.** The belief that you have no control over stressful events can lower your self-esteem, cause you to give up, and impair your body's ability to fight disease by increasing its production of *suppressor cells* (Peterson and Seligman, 1986). According to Martin Seligman, it is our explanation of an event, more than the event itself, that determines the extent to which we will be helpless or depressed. [Critical Note: There is no convincing evidence to date that successful therapeutic treatment for anxiety or depression results in significant increases in immune responses (Grady, 1992). Changing our beliefs may make us feel better, but we may not be any healthier.]

learned helplessness   occurs when a person has learned to be helpless in one situation and transfers that appraisal to a new situation in which an adequate response is possible

Hostility   A cynical, hostile attitude toward life appears to make one's life more fearful, brutish, and short. A research team, headed by Redford Williams, Jr., of Duke University Medical School, examined the health records of 255 male physicians. Twenty-five years earlier, when they were in medical school, they had taken the **hostility** (HO) subscale of the Minnesota Multiphasic Personality Inventory. Resentful, jealous, bitter, and suspicious people score high on this subscale, one that is a measure of trust. Williams found a striking link between cynical mistrust and an early demise from heart disease (Williams, 1985). The total mortality rates for the high-scoring physicians were found to be five to six times higher than the rates of low scorers. Repressed anger also has been found to signal high heart-disease risk (Friedman, 1991).

hostility   a state of antagonism or enmity

Hostile, angry people tend to be **hot reactors** who have very intense physiological reactions to stress. For example, when given an arithmetic test or asked to hold one of their hands in ice water for sixty seconds, such people respond by pumping a greater number of liters of blood per minute at a higher rate and through more rigid small arteries. The result is much higher blood pressure (Buell, 1985). (Note: In 1993, Natalie Angier of the *New York Times* reported a series of "negative" studies that indicate that hostility, as it is now measured, is *not* a strong predictor of the later development of heart disease.)

hot reactors   people who have sensitive and excessive outpouring of the Sympathetic Nervous System in response to stimulation

Self-absorbed   The personality trait of being egocentric, or **self-absorbed,** can also be a risk factor in stress-related disorders. Schwartz (1977) found that men who used twice as many self-references (I, me, my, or mine) during a

self-absorbed   excessively engrossed in one's self or one's affairs

structured interview had higher blood pressure, more blocked arteries, and more second heart attacks. He believes that self-involvement leads to a feeling of isolation and incompleteness, which promotes hostility, aggression, and the inability to give and receive social support. Interpersonal mistrust also increases our chances of becoming depressed (Rich, 1987).

vigilance   alert watchfulness

Vigilance   Mistrust, coupled with hostility and cynicism, causes people to be forever on guard. Eternal **vigilance** means that we are forever "stirred up," forever emitting the "flight-or-fight" response. This may well be the link between personality and illness. People who believe that others will mistreat them if given a chance to do so maintain higher adrenaline, cholesterol, cortisol, and testosterone levels. They are at greater risk with less protection due to immune suppression (Williams, 1985).

Personality Types and Vulnerability to Stress

Personality types are classes of people who have characteristics (more than one personality trait) in common that set them apart.

Type A   a personality type characterized by impatience and work addiction; thought susceptible to premature heart disorders

Type B   personality type characterized by patience, trust, good nature, and an easy going style that is thought to protect them against premature heart disorders

Type A Personality   **Type A** people are aggressive, competitive, overcommitted to achieving, and rushed. **Type B** people are more relaxed, easygoing, and flexible. They have lower needs for achievement and acquisition and so feel less pressure (see the discussion later in this chapter on Type A individuals and job stress). Type A people are considered to be at risk for heart disease. Hyperactive children display the Type A traits of being impatient and aggressive (Whalen, 1986).

The urgent behavior of the Type A personality in the adult is based on a set of beliefs and fears, many of which are irrational. For example, Type A individuals would say that the following statements are true:

My self-esteem is based on my material accomplishments.

I am worthless if I do not achieve worldly success.

There are no universal moral principles.

All human and natural resources are limited.

Furthermore, Type A persons commonly express the following fears:

Good may not prevail over evil; therefore, I cannot expect justice in this world.

I may not get my fair share of worldly goods.

A lack of success will cause me to be judged as worthless.

You can sense why such people are driven and why they are hard on themselves and others and unable to relax. Type A people recover more slowly from stress, and they have higher blood pressure, higher anxiety, and more upper respiratory tract illnesses (Stout and Bloom, 1982). They are also thought to have higher rates of coronary heart disease.

From 1973 until 1982 the U.S. National Heart, Lung and Blood Institute ran a "Multiple Risk Factor Intervention Trial" (MRFIT) on more than twelve hundred American men who smoked and who had both high cholesterol and high blood pressure. Being Type A was considered an additional risk factor for fatal and nonfatal heart problems. MRFIT failed to show Type A men more likely to develop heart disease! Redford Williams, Jr., examined this long-term study and others and concluded that only the trait of "hostility" appears to be related to heart disease (1986). Busy Type A men who are less cynical and less angry appear no more at risk than their relaxed Type B counterparts.

Hardy Personality Type   Suzanne Kobasa, coauthor of *The Hardy Executive: Health Under Stress* (1984), believes that there are "distinct, measurable personality traits that buffer the negative effects of stress." According to Kobasa, people who possess the following cluster of traits have a **hardy personality:**

1. A commitment to self, work, fun, and other important values;
2. A sense of personal control of their lives;
3. The ability to see change in their lives as a challenge to master.

Such optimistic people can handle conflicts better, accept the help of others, and use such help to master stresses instead of feeling overwhelmed by them (Scheier and Carver, 1992). Pessimists are more likely to give up. Thus, the "power of positive thinking" gains its power from the way thinking influences behavior (Greer, 1991).

A hardy personality provides more stress protection than does a strong constitution (good genes), physical exercise, or social supports (Kobasa, 1985). She found four times as much sickness among Type A men who were not "hardy." Unlike the typical Type A, a hardy Type A views his or her job and boss in a positive light and is friendly with co-workers. To assess your own cluster of traits, complete the questionnaire "How Hardy Are You?"

hardy personality   a personality type with certain traits, such as a commitment to work, a sense of personal control, and a view of life as a challenge, that makes them less vulnerable to the negative consequences of stress

---

How Hardy Are You?

Questionnaire

Below are twelve questions designed to measure hardiness. Evaluating someone's hardiness requires more than this quick test, but this simple exercise should give you some idea of how hardy you are.

Write down how much you agree or disagree with the following statements, using this scale:

0 = strongly disagree
1 = mildly disagree
2 = mildly agree
3 = strongly agree

_____ **A.** Trying my best at work makes a difference.
_____ **B.** Trusting to fate is sometimes all I can do in a relationship.
_____ **C.** I often wake up eager to start on the day's projects.
_____ **D.** Thinking of myself as a free person leads to great frustration and difficulty.
_____ **E.** I would be willing to sacrifice financial security in my work if something really challenging came along.
_____ **F.** It bothers me when I have to deviate from the routine or schedule I've set for myself.
_____ **G.** An average citizen can have an impact on politics.
_____ **H.** Without the right breaks, it is hard to be successful in my field.
_____ **I.** I know why I am doing what I am doing at work.
_____ **J.** Getting close to people puts me at risk of being obligated to them.
_____ **K.** Encountering new situations is an important priority in my life.
_____ **L.** I really don't mind when I have nothing to do.

To figure your score, turn to page 140.

Stress Response in Primates

Baboons are highly social primates that are physiologically similar to humans in a number of ways. Robert Sapolsky examined the difference in stress response in a troop of sixty baboons. One of the most important characteristics of the dominant male was that it stood up well under stress. Blood samples showed that high-ranking males had lower resting levels of cortisol than did lower-ranking males. They also exhibited the highest rises in cortisol when under stress. These hardy animals, having good control and social support, apparently could respond fully and completely when presented with a challenge within their primate world (Sapolsky, 1984).

Critical Review 3

1. Stressful transactions are interactions between the event and our cognitive appraisal of the event. T F

2. According to Martin Seligman, optimism can be learned. T F

3. How do our primary and secondary cognitive appraisals of an event act as a transformation between the event itself and our bodily response to it?

4. What kinds of stressors are you particularly vulnerable to because of the values you hold?

5. What Type A and/or hardy psychological traits (if any) form a consistent part of your personality?

6. Can you change those traits you consider a weakness in your battle against stress?

THE SURVIVAL UTILITY OF STRESS

culture shock a condition of confusion and anxiety that can affect a person suddenly exposed to an alien culture or milieu

Our unfinished nature seems to indicate that we have not survived by finding an unchanging niche and conforming to it. We do not seem content to remain idle until hunger forces us to attack or to hide until forced to forage for food. Nor are we content to graze continuously in large, protective bands. We seem

CULTURAL CROSSCURRENTS
Culture Shock

Going away to college is stressful. Can you imagine the stress associated with being a college freshman in a foreign land? **Culture shock** is the term used to describe the overwhelming stress of finding yourself alone among strangers. Foreign freshman feel lonely and often become suspicious of others. They report stomachaches, insomnia, diarrhea, headaches, loss of sex drive, mild depression, a general tiredness, and a lack of enthusiasm for life (Brislin, 1993).

Barbara Oropeza and her colleagues (1991) identify five "*Special Stressors*" that affect foreign students: They are:

1. *Culture Shock* (Primary and secondary appraisal becomes almost impossible.)

2. *Change in Social Status:* (Much lower prestige, power, and privilege)

3. *Change in Economic Status:* (Relative poverty hurts absolutely)

4. *Change in Expectations About Academic Performance:* (What is expected?—Is the expected possible?)

5. *Family Pressures:* (Families want them to grow, but not to change.)

What Makes Johnny Jump?

"When the mixture becomes 51 percent excitement and 49 percent fear, that's when you can go out the door." The person speaking is no teenager, but Gordon Riner, a veteran parachutist who operates Parachutes Are Fun, Inc., near Easton, Maryland. His unusual customers need varied, novel, and complex experiences to get high on life.

Such sensation seekers are, in a sense, addicts. They crave constant high levels of stimulation and seem to thrive on levels of stress that would crush most of us. Interestingly, each develops his or her own area of adventure. Other people's thrilling avocations seem to them to be unduly stressful. It is unlikely that Gordon would voluntarily spend his time exploring underwater caves, for example.

to have a need for new experiences, mild uncertainties, and moderate risk taking. *We need stress.* Adult volunteers who attempt to remain in a completely stress-free environment (a sightless, soundless, weightless, motionless body of liquid heated to body temperature) soon begin to have disturbances of mood, thought, and action; they ask to be released.

Stress and Growth

To be perfect, our garden for children—kindergarten—should contain some imperfections, some minor stressors. The complete absence of stress in childhood results in poor development (Levine, 1959). Both moderate distress and stimulating **eustress,** or beneficial stress, produce more competent offspring. Stress demands that we adjust. Adjustment can mean growth, as when we learn more effective ways of gaining the support of others. A lack of response, or the wrong kind of response, can alert us to the possibility that we may need to redirect our energies.

> **eustress** a state of high arousal induced by a pleasurable stressor, for example, an award or honor

We might note that gaining strength through overcoming a stressor can be overdone. The lives of death-camp and death-march survivors were generally shortened, not prolonged, by their successful coping experience (Bettelheim, 1943). Hans Selye (1976) spoke of a fixed amount of "deeper" adaptive energy, which, when exhausted, leaves us without resources to continue living. He believes we can replenish "superficial" adaptive energy by eating, but we can only preserve our original store of survival energy. Tolerable levels of stress preserve this vital store by helping to immunize us against future, more traumatic experiences.

Stress and Optimal Performance

Stress can facilitate our behavior as well as distort it. **Optimal stress** levels can improve concentration, prolong endurance, build strength, and reduce errors (Hebb, 1958). Have you ever waited just the correct amount of time before studying for an exam and been amazed at how much you accomplished in a short time without undue worry or guilt? A mobilization of energy was working for you. Writers, poets, inventors, and musicians speak of stress as an intensity of feeling that accompanies the times they are at their creative best. They long for a quiet retreat but generally do their best work in places like Los Angeles and New York City, where they are surrounded by stressors.

> **optimal stress** most favorable level of stress as it relates to task efficiency

Thrill Seekers

Psychologist Frank Farley speaks of thrill seekers, "men and women whose temperament drives them to a life of risk-taking, stimulation, and excitement seeking." Such **Type T personalities** show little relationship between life changes and physical disorders (Cooley and Keesey, 1981). Farley (1990) makes a distinction between Creative Type T's, who act within the bounds of common decency, and Destructive Type T's, who engage in delinquency, vandalism, crime, and substance abuse, mostly just for the thrill of it.

Most of us may not need high levels of sensation, but we do need some stress in our lives. Most of all, we need positive stress. Giving and receiving love, a state of arousal, is thought to be necessary for emotional well-being (Glasser, 1965; Rogers, 1971). Recognition and moderate responsibility, forms of positive stress, are believed to be necessary for reducing anxiety and for building self-esteem (Erikson, 1968; Selye and Cherry, 1978).

EMOTIONAL AND PROBLEM-SOLVING COPING STRATEGIES

A reasonable position regarding stress is to recognize that it is natural, an inevitable part of our lives. We have no choice but to respond to the strain of living. We do, however, have a number of choices with respect to how we will respond to stressors and to stress. There is no one best way to cope. Each person and situation is different. Stress is a complex interaction between the specific nature of the demand, the emotional and mental state of the individual, and the strength of the coping resources that individual can bring together to combat the stressor. What we can benefit from accepting is that we do not have to be passive recipients of stress. There is much we can do to reduce its noxious effects and to take advantage of its potentials.

Type T personality a cluster of traits centering around an excessive need for high levels of arousal, a sensation seeker

Stress is an inevitable part of our lives.

We can begin by focusing on the interaction between coping capabilities and environmental demands. A belief in **self-efficacy,** or our ability to master life's stressors, appears to be central to successful coping (Bandura, 1986). You can learn such self-mastery techniques by yourself or with the help of a support group. For example, on four consecutive nights, college students spent fifteen minutes writing about a traumatic event in their lives—both describing the event and reporting their feelings surrounding it. A comparison group also wrote, but not about anything personal. Immediately after writing, the students felt sad and had elevated blood pressure. However, during the remainder of the semester the students who shared their innermost feelings reported being ill less often and making fewer visits to the university health center. Having someone to confide in seems to be a major component of the benefits of social support (Pennebaker et. al., 1990).

self-efficacy a belief in one's own power to produce a desired effect

TYPES OF COPING

Coping can be divided into two types. **Problem solving** is acting to alter the environment that caused the stress (for example, after being fired, you find a better job). These active coping efforts activate the flight-or-fight response. **Emotional coping** is acting on yourself to alter the significance of the stressor. (You intellectualize your firing as a statistical certainty given the current state of the economy.) This indirect style makes use of **defense mechanisms.** Defensive coping efforts, triggered by a perception of helplessness, activate the conservation-withdrawal response (Ursin, Boode, and Levine, 1978).

problem solving attempts to change the conditions that produce stress

emotional coping altering of oneself to reduce stress

defense mechanisms unconscious tactics, such as projection, that help the ego deal with high levels of anxiety

There are *costs* and *benefits* associated with both emotional and problem-solving coping (see Table 4–2). In general, problem solving and social support work are associated with stable adjustment to stressors; emotion-focused strategies that involve avoiding feelings or taking things out on other people predict depression and poorer adjustment (Holahan and Moos, 1990).

Taking some direct action is generally better than changing ideas of reality. (But some forms of direct action may be harmful—you might attack the boss after he has fired you or rob a bank to recover your lost income.) Emotional coping acts are not always emotional. Smoking, getting drunk, overeating, and abusing drugs are all defensive coping strategies. They reduce the symptoms of stress in the short run but do not act directly on the stressor. They may act directly on you, however. Two and one-half cups of coffee will double the amount of epinephrine in your blood. Stress and cigarette smoking combine to impair your motor performance, increase your adrenergic activity, and heighten your risk of coronary disease. Three times as many women as men turn to food to chase their stress away.

Gary Schwartz (1977) calls such actions **disregulators** because they interfere with the function of the brain as a natural health-care regulator. *Negative information* from our peripheral organs concerning the effects of stress is used by our brain to regulate our behavior to maximize health. Successful defensive coping—through drugs or denial, for example—is dysfunctional because it perpetuates our stressful lifestyle and continues the accumulation of stress that will eventually produce exhaustion, breakdown, and premature death. Schwartz finds little comfort in the fact that *chemical coping*, the use of drug therapy, is the method of choice for most doctors today for handling diseases of adaptation. Just as stress-related disorders make up 50 to 80 percent of a typical medical practice, major and minor tranquilizers still make up the major

disregulators a mechanism or medicine designed to reduce symptoms and delay the recognized need to adjust for proper functioning

TABLE 4–2
The Costs and Benefits of Direct or
Indirect Coping Strategies

PROBLEM-SOLVING COPING

Benefits

1. Your action may be appropriate and eliminate the stressor.
2. You can give vent to your aroused emotions.
3. You may come to terms with an unrecoverable loss.
4. You increase your self-esteem.
5. You increase your sense of control.

Costs

1. You may engage in a great deal of nonproductive worry.
2. You may misdiagnose the problem.
3. You may increase your distress via inappropriate actions.

EMOTIONAL COPING

Benefits

1. You may reduce your stress response.
2. You may maintain increased hope and courage.
3. You may restore your self-esteem.

Costs

1. Denial may interfere with appropriate action.
2. You may become emotionally numb.
3. Intrusions of threatening material into awareness may disrupt your ongoing activities.
4. You may remain unaware of the relationship between your symptoms and their source.

SOURCES: S. Roth and J. L. Cohen, "Approach, Avoidance and Coping with Stress." *American Psychologist* 41 (1986): 813–19. R. Lazarus and S. Folkman. "Stress, Appraisal, and Coping," (1984) New York: Springer Press.

portion of patients' prescription drugs. The three best-selling drugs in the country are an ulcer medication (Tagamet), a hypertension drug (Inderal), and a tranquilizer (Valium). Ninety percent of the prescriptions for minor tranquilizers are written by general practitioners.

Doctors often administer such drugs because it is less time consuming than helping a patient work out a more healthful lifestyle which doctors are not trained to do. Drugs do offer symptom relief, and that is what we expect when we go to the doctor. They lower blood pressure, reduce heart rate, neutralize acidity, produce a calming effect, and relax muscles. Drugs may have some other positive effects. If we stay on the medication, the chance of a more serious disorder is lessened. More important, drug therapy at times makes possible a tolerance of stressful reactions while more permanent behavioral adjustments are being incorporated and a natural restoration of healthy functioning is occurring (Wolpe, 1978).

In light of the apparent disadvantages of defensive coping, you may wonder why people use it. Defensive coping is less complex, more accessible, and promises quicker results than problem solving. The function of defensive coping, a Freudian concept, is to defend the self against threats to self-esteem.

Helping Children Combat Stress

Is it possible to inoculate your child against stress? Not protect them from it, but provide them with effective measures to combat it? Saunders and Remsberg (1984) believe that you can. They suggest that you give them a *sense that they are doing their best and that you love them* by:

- Touching and hugging them
- Listening to them
- Being consistent with them
- Being honest and open and accepting of them
- Giving them approval and encouragement

- Teaching them a relaxation response
- Encouraging them to be active

They suggest a "good night formula." During the bedtime ritual, get your children to tell you something they like about themselves, something they did that day that they feel good about, and something they are looking forward to doing tomorrow.

SOURCE: A. Saunders and B Remsberg, *The Stress-Proof Child.* New York: Holt, Rinehart & Winston, 1984.

Such coping also serves to protect against feelings of anxiety. Anxiety itself is a defense against anger, the trigger for the direct but dangerous coping tactic of aggression. In our modern world, it is almost never prudent to attack whomever is pressuring us, frustrating us, or causing us injury. That is why our times have been termed the "age of anxiety." We will examine anxiety more closely later in the chapter.

> Joe is a friendly and outgoing person. He seems to have a good sense of humor, and he likes to help people. Because he is a hard worker, Joe is able to combine a part-time job with a full schedule of college classes.
>
> But Joe is not so friendly when things aren't going well. When complications set in, the ready smile and helpful demeanor turn quickly to rage. Today is one of those complicated days. Just after Joe is "chewed out" by his supervisor at work, his parole supervisor arrives and wants to "chat." Joe is upset and embarrassed. The people he works with don't even know he is on parole. Joe sullenly agrees to talk in the back room. Soon talk turns to shouts and curses:
>
> "Leave me alone! Get off my back or I'll kill you!" screams Joe.
>
> Joe doesn't "kill" the parole supervisor, but he does smash him in the face. With surprising calm, the parole supervisor holds his reddened cheek. "That's enough. That's direct assault. Call the police."
>
> Joe seems quite calm when the police arrive. He tells them how well he is doing in college, and how his parole supervisor just won't leave him alone.
>
> "Yes," Joe said, "I know what assaulting a parole officer means. I didn't have any choice. I had to hit him."
>
> The same lack of normal anxiety that lets Joe be so outgoing and friendly during good times lets him explode impulsively during bad times.

DEFENSIVE COPING TECHNIQUES

More than thirty specific techniques of **defensive coping** appear in the literature; here we will describe only a few of the basic mechanisms. All defensive coping techniques are substitutes for direct forms of behavior aimed at reducing distress by gaining love, security, esteem, or recognition. When direct means appear threatening, inaccessible, or unproductive, alternative approaches are used to reduce, direct, or control the energy mobilized to respond to stress. We also use defensive coping techniques when we are faced with intangible foes and cannot tell who or what is threatening us. The aim is

defensive coping   to defend against difficulties by the use of unconscious mechanisms that protect the ego but do not eliminate the source of difficulty

The Benefits of Being Childlike

Is it possible to inoculate ourselves against stress? It might just be possible if we are able to reawaken the "child" that is in all of us. The following childlike personality traits have been found to protect children against the strain of daily life:

- flexibility
- a playful nature
- a sense of curiosity

- an open mind

Such traits allow children the rapid growth they need to meet the ever increasing demands placed upon them. Such traits can also serve us well as we attempt to meet the demands that come with responsibility and age. Think of the opposite of each of these traits and notice how they make us less able to cope—not mature, but more vulnerable.

denial   a refusal to accept the reality of a threat

rationalization   a socially acceptable excuse

repression   exclusion of uncomfortable thoughts or feelings from awareness (largely unconscious forgetting)

procrastination   to postpone or delay needlessly

always the same: to reduce stress by maintaining self-esteem and controlling dangerous impulses. When under stress, people tend to fall back on approaches that have worked for them in the past: Fighters fight, fleers flee.

Fighting defense mechanisms include **denial** (acknowledging a stressor but minimizing its importance) and **rationalization** (generating reasons for not taking problem-solving action ["It would only make things worse."]). Fleeing defense mechanisms are exemplified by **repression** (conveniently forgetting that exam on Monday morning). **Procrastination** is a good example of defense mechanisms at work. This unconscious belief that "something will happen" so that I won't have to complete the hard or nasty task (problem-centered coping)

Defensive coping may cause a person to become emotionally numb.

Twenty Tips for Personal Coping

The Roper Institute reports that being served a home-cooked meal makes us feel loved, especially when it is enjoyed with family and friends, includes extra helpings, and isn't served on paper plates. Makes sense, doesn't it? Each day, include one or more of the following sensible tips toward handling stress.

- Eat a good breakfast.
- Plan ahead.
- Write things down.
- Do one thing at a time.
- Do things now.
- Savor your tasks.
- Calm your inner critic.
- Fight fairly.
- Limit worrying.
- Breathe slowly.

- Take a walk.
- Listen to soothing music.
- Seek quiet.
- Exercise.
- Enjoy nature.
- Reflect before eating.
- Eat nutritious meals.
- Read something joyful.
- Relish a soothing bath.
- Get a good night's sleep.

Such good habits help produce physical fitness. Brown (1991) found that physically fit people were much less likely to become physically ill following stressful events than people who were not fit.

leads to constant rationalization (emotion-centered coping) and increased stress.

Critical Review 4

1. Which, if any, of the following "shocks" have accompanied your role as a college student: lowered social status _____, lowered economic status _____, family pressure _____, academic expectations _____, loneliness _____.

2. Is it possible that any of the above might be good for you, that is, result in personal growth and improved performance?

3. Do you notice more "Destructive Type T" personalities in high school or college? Why do you believe this is so?

4. Are you an optimist or pessimist? Support your choices with a brief review of the defensive coping mechanism you most often employ.

5. Is it possible to adapt the "good night formula" found on page 121 and use it to help you handle stress? Write a short bedtime ritual for yourself that can give you a sense of self-acceptance and self-efficacy.

6. Which coping style do you use most often, emotional or problem-solving? Write specific examples to support your personal perception.

ANXIETY AND ITS CONTROL

Anxiety, a vague, unpleasant feeling accompanied by a premonition that something bad is about to happen, is a major component of most adjustment problems. Kidney problems, sleep-onset disorders, speech pathologies, and even hyperactivity can result from prolonged anxiety. Understanding and control of

Risk Reduction

Burt was both unlucky and lucky. He was unlucky to find himself eligible to be included in a scientific medical experiment. To be included, he had to be in the the top 5 percent of the U.S. population in terms of blood cholesterol level—and he was aware of the connection between high blood fats and increased heart disease. He was lucky because when he volunteered to participate in the long-term study of the possible benefits of a new anticholesterol drug, he was placed in the diet-plus-drug-therapy group. Loving life and wanting to prolong his good health, Burt faithfully adhered to his prescribed diet and faithfully took his prescription drug.

Ten years later, Dr. Basil Rifkind, director of the study, reports that anticholesterol drug therapy, combined with a low-calorie, low-fat, low-salt, high complex-carbohydrate diet, can lower the risk of coronary heart disease by as much as 50 percent (Schorr, 1984). Burt is lucky indeed. This report is the first to demonstrate conclusively that the risk of coronary heart disease can be reduced by diet plus cholestyramine, a cholesterol-lowering drug.

anxiety, therefore, are central to successful adjustment. We conclude this chapter on stress with a description of anxiety and a look at some old and new methods of gaining personal control of anxiety. Gaining control will allow us to tolerate stressful situations so as to confront the stressor and successfully adapt to or change this situation. Table 4–3 presents a scale that measures roughly the amount of anxiety you are currently experiencing. On the average, college students score 14 to 15 on this scale.

The Roots of Anxiety

The physical symptoms of anxiety are associated with the activity of a small part of our brain called the *locus coeruleus* (Henry and Stevens, 1978). Pearson and Shaw (1980) report that taking thirty to forty milligrams of *propranolol,* a drug that blocks receptor cells in the locus coeruleus from being stimulated by sympathetic nervous system activity, can reduce the amount of anxiety we feel prior to performing in public. During anxiety the brain produces extra stress hormones such as CRH (corticotropin-releasing hormone) and prolactin (Brown, 1986). Under stress, such peptides block the binding action of natural anxiety-inhibiting drugs and induce increased anxiety (Miller, 1983). Physical symptoms aside, many believe that anxiety is rooted in our basic human condition. Freud believed anxiety to be a product of *unresolved conflicts* between the id and superego.

Karen Horney (1950) postulates an *inadequate or unworthy self-concept* as the root of anxiety. She holds that we construct an ego ideal designed to gain the unconditional approval of our parents. Comparing ourselves with this too-perfect, too-rigid ideal self results in a constantly poor self-evaluation. **Self-censure** is the worst form of stress, for it is the most difficult to avoid, escape, or satisfy.

self-censure   one's own activities; a cognitive style characterized by severe criticism and blame directed inward

Social learning theory holds that *anxiety can be taught* to the infant by the environment and by significant others as well as by the parents. Constant verbal instructions to "watch out" and premature exposure to adult problems are sources of learned anxiety. We can model anxiety by worrying constantly in front of our children. Once learned, worry and other forms of anxiety can become generalized and elicited by a wide range of conditions.

The same situations that threaten self-esteem produce anxiety. These are typically social situations in which competition, hostility, rejection, and guilt are part of the expected pattern of interaction. The singles bar is such a social situation (see chapter 3 for more about self-esteem).

Score one point each time your response corresponds with the answer—True or False—keyed at the end of a statement.

1. I do not tire quickly. (F)
2. I am troubled by attacks of nausea. (T)
3. I believe I am no more nervous than most others. (F)
4. I have very few headaches. (F)
5. I work under a great deal of tension. (T)
6. I cannot keep my mind on one thing. (T)
7. I worry over money and business. (T)
8. I frequently notice my hand shakes when I try to do something. (T)
9. I blush no more often than others. (F)
10. I have diarrhea once a month or more. (T)
11. I worry quite a bit over possible misfortunes. (T)
12. I practically never blush. (F)
13. I am often afraid that I am going to blush. (T)
14. I have nightmares every few nights. (T)
15. My hands and feet are usually warm enough. (F)
16. I sweat every easily even on cool days. (T)
17. Sometimes when embarrassed, I break out in a sweat which annoys me greatly. (T)
18. I hardly ever notice my heart pounding and I am seldom short of breath. (F)
19. I feel hungry almost all off the time. (T)
20. I am very seldom troubled by constipation. (F)
21. I have a great deal of stomach trouble. (T)
22. I have had periods in which I lost sleep over worry. (T)
23. My sleep is fitful and disturbed. (T)
24. I dream frequently about things that are best kept to myself. (T)
25. I am easily embarrassed. (T)
26. I am more sensitive than other people. (T)
27. I frequently find myself worrying about something. (T)
28. I wish I could be as happy as others seem to be. (T)
29. I am usually calm and not easily upset. (F)
30. I cry easily. (T)
31. I feel anxiety about something or someone almost all the time. (T)
32. I am happy most of the time. (F)
33. It makes me nervous to have to wait. (T)
34. I have periods of great restlessness that I cannot sit long in a chair. (T)
35. Sometimes I become so excited that I find it hard to get to sleep. (T)
36. I have sometimes felt that difficulties were piling up so high that I could not overcome them. (T)
37. I must admit that I have at times been worried beyond reason over something that really did not matter. (T)
38. I have very few fears compared with my friends. (F)
39. I have been afraid of things or people that I know could not hurt me. (T)
40. I certainly feel useless at times. (T)
41. I find it hard to keep my mind on a task or job. (T)
42. I am usually self-conscious. (T)
43. I am inclined to take things hard. (T)
44. I am a high-strung person. (T)
45. Life is a strain for me much of the time. (T)
46. At times I think am no good at all. (T)
47. I am certainly lacking in self-confidence. (T)
48. I sometimes feel that I am about to go to pieces. (T)
49. I shrink from facing a crises or difficulty. (T)
50. I am entirely self-confident. (F)

College students, on average, score 14 to 15 on this scale.

TABLE 4–3

Taylor Manifest Anxiety Scale

"My emotions are running wild," Jane said to her girlfriend as she sat in the singles bar trying to sip her free drink casually. "I don't know if I'm excited, frightened, disgusted, or bored."

"Well, I know how I feel," her friend replied without trying to hide the anger in her voice. "I'm damn mad at having to be here at all. I feel like a commodity. This 'free drink' just adds insult to injury."

"Mine is almost gone," Jane said quietly as she began to glance around without any apparent concern. "Look at Harry over there, posing by the piano. He looks like a fish in the moonlight—he shines and stinks!"

"That's good. Let's get out of here," said her friend. "All I see around this place are strumpets, or I guess I should say trollops. I feel guilty just being here."

"The music's good. OK. I guess it's not working out," sighed Jane. Then, frozen in sudden interest, she anxiously whispers, "Don't look up. Here come those two fellows we were noticing last night. They're coming right toward us. . . ."

As you can see, anxiety can be caused by *conflicting motives,* such as a desire to leave the bar and a desire to stay. It can also be produced by a conflict between a motive (to find companionship or excitement) and an inner standard (not to be a "trollop"). Finally, anxiety can *alter our social behavior.* Apprehension concerning possible rape can prevent a woman from seeking recreation or a career outside the home. Apprehension concerning possible rejection can prevent a man from initiating contact with an attractive female.

Anxiety and Fear

The body responds to anxiety and fear in the same way. A fear response is associated with a real and present danger, however, and we quiet down after the danger has passed. Anxiety is dread of the unknown, and the danger may never pass. An anxiety attack is a panic response that often begins with spasms or weakness in the abdomen, then affects the entire visceral system. Heart palpitations, rapid breathing, nausea, and even fever rush together during an attack. A victim, trying to make sense of this extreme response in the absence of a clear stressor, often fears a mysterious illness or experiences the more terrifying fear of "going crazy." People who have panic attacks are more likely to have parents who suffer from anxiety or depressive disorders. There appears to be a genetic link to stress vulnerability.

secondary anxiety   a fear of the bodily changes associated with fear

The fear of fear itself, known as **secondary anxiety** (Cameron, 1963), conditions people to go to any lengths to avoid the pain of another anxiety attack. They are often left with a sense of insecurity and unreality about themselves and their world. Their anxiety is so severe, so out of proportion to any visible danger, that they feel as if they are in the midst of a bad dream.

trait anxiety   chronic fear that is part of the makeup of an individual

Anxiety is not pathologic; we all experience it at times. We tend to forget (repress) the moments of panic from childhood. Highly anxious people are not going crazy, but they do tend to live in a constant state of tension with restless, irritable activity during the day and poor sleep patterns at night. Spieberger (1966) differentiates between trait and state anxiety. **Trait anxiety** is a constant facet of a personality. Each of us is characteristically highly, minimally, or moderately anxious. People do not move from highly anxious to mentally ill. However, highly anxious individuals are less communicative, less optimistic, and make poorer grades than their less anxious counterparts. Anxiety hurts their chances for intimacy, concentration, and flexibility in responding to a crisis.

state anxiety   fear produced by an identifiable stressor

State anxiety is a response to a specific event—a vague fear of the pending final exam, for example. A growing number of researchers (Jacobson, 1978) feel that most forms of disruptive behavior are rooted in anxiety (see the discussion of intimacy in chapter 7).

MODULATION OF ANXIETY

Personal control of anxiety can be achieved through learning or relearning ancient capabilities—specifically, the capacity for producing the restorative response at will, in appropriate circumstances, for maximum health and effectiveness. The difficulty does not lie in learning the restorative response; several techniques have been developed to master deep relaxation. It is the application of such learning prior to or just at the appropriate moment of a stressful encounter that constitutes the learning problem. Ideally, a stressor should become a signal for deep relaxation. Because anxiety can be partially controlled via escape and avoidance behavior, learning to approach anxious situations to develop skill in responding with relaxation is most difficult to do. Ironically, what is needed is new learning in the face of strong incentives to avoid new learning.

Because anxiety is an asset as well as a curse, it is wise to approach changing our response patterns with caution. Words such as *control, eliminate,* and *regulate* suggest a finality and rigidity that can be dysfunctional. We have elected to talk about *modulation of anxiety* in an attempt to express the flexibility and sensitivity in responding that are needed to handle stressful situations.

We can modulate anxiety by bringing it into our consciousness and directing its course. The term *altered states of consciousness* is popular today. The idea of getting into a different state of awareness is intriguing, and humankind has sought such an experience in a thousand ways—through religion, philosophy, drugs, and physical exhaustion, for example. Here we will discuss ways to achieve and maintain an altered state of consciousness that is incompatible with anxiety and that blocks the ravaging effects of prolonged stress and allows restoration. This altered consciousness is based on a new awareness that we can modulate the workings of our autonomic nervous system. In the 1960s, Dr. Neil Miller and his associates (Di Cara and Miller, 1968) were successful in training a rat to direct and control the functioning of its autonomic nervous system (ANS). This demonstration was exciting, for ANS functions are the very ones implicated in stress-related disorders in humans.

Along with this awareness of unity of body and mind, a new technology of electronic sensors, amplifiers, computers, and display devices was soon developed. New awareness and new technology were combined with a renewed belief in preventive medicine to open up novel approaches to the reduction of stress-related mental and physical ills. These new approaches differ from older methods of stress management in three respects. First, they do not depend solely on medication, surgery, or faith to produce a cure. Second, they depend on the active involvement of the person in directing and being responsible for his or her own improvement. The third difference is found in the radical assumption that often the symptom is the problem and that symptom removal is a cure. How do these new approaches relate to anxiety modulation? If you assume anxiety is a symptom of unresolved conflict, of childhood separation, or of existential fear, then successful therapy is directed toward identifying specific causes and structuring potentially cathartic experiences. However, you may view anxiety as being a learned response, conditioned by direct or vicarious experiences to many stimuli. You may also believe that autonomic nervous system functions that characterize anxiety responses can be altered via voluntary control. These beliefs suggest directly attacking and modulating the symptom (the anxiety response) to cure anxiety. One way to do this is through biofeedback training.

Biofeedback

biofeedback   a method of getting information from our own bodies

In 1985 **biofeedback** was being presented as a successful treatment for patients suffering from a number of neuromuscular disorders, motion and space disorders, and urinary and fecal incontinence (Miller, 1985). It was also being categorically denounced: "There is absolutely no convincing evidence that biofeedback is an essential or specific technique for the treatment of any condition" (Roberts, 1985, p. 940).

George Fuller, of the Biofeedback Institute of San Francisco, reports on the many applications of biofeedback training. For example, electromiograph (EMG) training in forehead muscle relaxation is effective in alleviating anxiety symptoms and conditions such as tension headaches and bruxism, the gnashing of teeth. We can learn to relax our minds as well as our bodies. *Electroencephalograph* (EEG) training is effective in insomnia cases in which muscle tension is not a problem. Such training enables insomniacs to allow sleep to come rather than encouraging them to drug themselves into a sleeplike state. EEG is also effective in enhancing concentration and attention—problems of cognition often suffered by the highly anxious. Obsessive-compulsive worriers are also helped. Many stress-related disorders, from hemorrhoids to menstrual cramps, are related to blood-volume changes. Vasomotor activity—the expanding and contracting of blood vessels—can be modulated by the aid of the *thermister*, or temperature trainer. Migraine headaches, asthma, and high blood pressure are conditions in which skin-temperature training is useful.

The EDR, or *electrodermal response,* has application in the treatment of hypertension and hyperhydrosis (excessive sweating in anxiety or arousal) and indirectly in the treatment of many fear disorders when used as part of systematic desensitization training (Wolpe, 1973). Heart-rate feedback, along with desensitization, is applicable to reducing anxiety concerning heartbeat irregularity that is not medically dangerous.

Physical pain, in many cases, is reduced by biofeedback training. Anxious, tense people are less tolerant of pain. We are all more sensitive to pain while under moderately high stress. Sexuality and anxiety are incompatible. Biofeedback equipment is useful in monitoring genital muscle contractions and blood flow in both men and women and is thus helpful in treating sexual dysfunctions such as impotence in men and low genital arousal in women. Finally, Fuller reports that *closed circuit television and videotape recorders* are feedback devices helpful in the development of social skill training. Such behavioral feedback is helpful to highly anxious individuals.

Biofeedback training is brief and inexpensive when compared with more traditional forms of therapy for anxiety. It is best used in conjunction with a trained counselor, however, so a cost is involved. The training is necessary until you have learned (1) to produced deep relaxation at will and (2) to become sensitized to internal and external clues that signal a need for your antianxiety response.

Biofeedback is not the only way to modulate anxiety. Ancient forms of self-modulation, such as *yoga* and *Zen Buddhism,* and newer forms, such as *transcendental meditation,* can also be paths to the restorative response. Meditational techniques such as yoga and Zen follow different roads toward unity of body and

Biofeedback: An Answer to Anxiety?

Can you control your internal bodily activity? Up until the 1960s, most psychologists believed that our systems for regulating temperature and blood pressure, for example, were involuntary—beyond conscious control. Now several electronic devices have been developed that provide external linkages from our neurons, muscles, and glands to our higher brain centers, the voluntary control devices of our minds.

Training on any or all of the devices listed below can increase your awareness of your body's internal functions and, in most cases, allow you to increase control over them. Such awareness and control are now part of many health-related programs, including the modulation of anxiety.

The four devices that have received the most research application to date measure:

- Electrical activity on the surface of the brain (electroencephalograph, or EEG).
- Electrical activity associated with the contraction of muscles (electromiograph, or EMG).
- Resistance to electrical activity associated with sweat-gland activity (electrodermograph or EDG).
- Electrical activity that reflects thermal (temperature) changes due to alterations in surface blood flow (thermister).

mind. Physical exercise, rhythmic exercise, mental activity and its absence, restful postures, and direct breathing and thought control are all to be found among the Eastern approaches. None of these depends on the technology of biofeedback.

A careful review of contemporary research on the effects of meditation on somatic arousal—heartbeat, blood pressure, skin resistance, and so forth—reveals a surprising pattern. Those who meditate show no lower somatic arousal while they are meditating than others who are simply resting (Homes, 1984). However, meditation seems to produce protective changes in our body chemistry. Although we may be just as aroused, our "end organs" (pupils, heart, lungs, etc.) are less *responsive to adrenergic stimulation* if we are trained in the techniques of relaxation (Lehmann et al., 1986). We are less responsive to stress.

All of these techniques involve a *state of mind* quite foreign to the value system of the West. The common element is passive attention, a process of doing without effort or final goal (Peper, 1977). But attending to the means, not the outcome, and not striving go against all our value training. "Letting it flow" and "allowing it to happen" are phrases attempting to capture this noncompetitive, process-focused approach to the cultivation of low arousal. Anticipation and evaluation kill progress in learning deep emotional calm. A restful, relaxed body and an alert but passively attentive mind form the base for the restorative response. For some pointers on developing coping skills, see Table 4–4.

Four Methods for Training in Low Arousal

The West has produced several meditational methods that are promising for training in low arousal. A very brief description of four of them follows. If a particular method appears promising to you, details may be obtained by reading the works cited at the end of this chapter. The four methods are the following:

The Relaxation Response   Herbert Benson (1975) found no significant difference between the metabolic benefits to be derived from transcendental meditation, the popular yoga style, and this simple procedure. All that is necessary to produce the relaxation response is a few minutes, twice a day, in which you experience:

A quiet environment (no unexpected noises).

A passive attitude (the most important factor).

TABLE 4–4
Tips for Good Coping

1. To gain physical hardiness:
   a. Maintain good nutrition and excercise.
   b. Reduce smoking and alcohol consumption.
   c. Eliminate drug consumption.
2. To gain mental hardiness:
   a. Cultivate a positive perspective on life.
   b. Increase your belief in self-efficacy.
   c. Challenge your problem-solving skills.
3. To gain social hardiness:
   a. Become more trusting.
   b. Schedule more fun.
   c. Make commitments; become involved.
4. To gain physiological hardiness:
   a. Practice a relaxation response.
   b. Become less self-centered, less hostile.
   c. Reduce cynical vigilance.

A comfortable position (but not so comfortable as to produce sleep).

An object to dwell on (the number 1, for example).

Now, while remaining passive, breathe slowly in and out. Repeat this number 1 or its equivalent on each "out" breath. Benson reports this procedure to be associated with reduced drug and alcohol use, both of which are costly coping techniques often used to reduce anxiety.

Progressive Relaxation   In more than seventy years of clinical testing, Edmund Jacobson (1978) found that every thought is accompanied by muscle tension, and that the path to deep calm lies in emptying your mind of thoughts and systematically relaxing your voluntary muscles. He believes the involuntary muscles will then follow, involuntarily. A brief version of progressive relaxation includes these steps:

Lie quietly on your back with your eyes gradually closing.

Recognize contraction (tension) in a muscle group by bending or tightening the appropriate muscles.

Observe the sensation of tension in the selected muscle. Learn to distinguish muscle tension from other sensations.

Realize that what you are feeling is the result of doing. What you want to accomplish is not doing—"going negative."

Relax. Let the muscles go limp. Do not gradually release tension.

Permit yourself a half hour of continuous relaxation without movement, but also without rigidity.

On the days to follow, learn to recognize tension in your body in the following order:

Right arm

Left arm

Right leg

Left leg

Trunk

Shoulders

Neck

Brow

Eyes

Forehead

Cheeks

Jaws

Lips

Tongue

Throat

Muscles associated with visual imagery

Muscles associated with negative self-talk

You can sense tension and let it go while you are active as well as while you are lying down. Fear and worry are modulated when you relax the tensions you sense while engaged in fear and worry. "If you relax these particular tensions, you cease to imagine or recall or reflect about the matter in question" (Jacobson, 1978, p. 251).

Autogenic Training   While Jacobson advocates letting your mind go negative, Luthe and Schultz (1970) advocate using your mind, or at least that portion that controls voluntary speech, to achieve the opposite of stress, the neutral autogenic state. Again, regular training in a tranquil atmosphere without disturbance is considered essential. While in this restful environment, passively concentrate on following the suggestions contained in these six phrases.

My arms and legs are heavy.

My arms and legs are warm.

My heartbeat is calm and regular.

My body breathes itself.

My abdomen is warm and regular.

My forehead is cool.

The reference to a cool forehead is important, because blood rushes to and warms the forehead in times of worry. During these mental exercises, your skeletal and visceral muscles begin to relax in response to your passive concentration on the sensations of being heavy and warm.

Self-Hypnosis   Reports of subjects who have been successfully hypnotized describe the following: a sense of deep relaxation, a narrowing of attention, and an increased level of suggestibility (Hilgard and Hilgard, 1975). These sensations are identical to the passive concentration or passive attention considered essential to success in biofeedback, progressive relaxation, and autogenic training. Relaxing self-talk forms the basis for self-hypnosis, as this example demonstrates.

In a comfortable sitting or lying position, say to yourself: "I am becoming more and more relaxed. I let my whole body relax. I let my muscles go limp. I feel my arms (and legs, and so on) relaxing even more. Now I direct my attention to my forehead (and shoulders, and so on). I let it relax more and more. My body is beginning to feel rather heavy. I feel myself sinking into the chair (or bed, or floor). My shoulders, neck, and head are more and more relaxed. My mind is relaxing along with my body. I set all worries aside. My mind is calm and peaceful. As I count from twenty backwards toward one, I will feel myself going down further and further into this deeply relaxed hypnotic state." After the backward count, make a suggestion to yourself concerning your worry or fear. Example, "When I awake I will be able to concentrate on my studies" or "I am going to awake very calm and refreshed and able to control my worries." Before ending the experience, say to yourself, "Now I am going to count backward from five to one. At the count of one I will awake relaxed, alert, and beautifully refreshed."

Herb Benson, in a recent comparison of hypnosis with the relaxation response, reports that individual differences in gaining beneficial effects from the relaxation response in the treatment of anxiety might be related to responsiveness to hypnosis. That is, anxious people who can be easily and deeply hypnotized derive substantial relief from anxiety when they practice the relaxation response without hypnosis. The state of being hypnotized is considered identical to the state of being deeply relaxed in both mind and body (Benson, Arns, and Hoffman, 1981).

Combining Methods for Anxiety Modulation

The various methods just described may be combined. Biofeedback stresses an experimental approach in which you may try any combination of techniques. The equipment will inform you instantly what works for you. Empirical data, rather than faith in an authority, help you to improve your ability to combat anxiety. The mastery of any of these techniques to the extent necessary for modulating anxiety requires a great deal of disciplined work. Some positive results usually occur with your initial attempts, however, and encourage you to practice. The function of this skill is to allow you to use your increased tolerance for stress to cope directly with the situation that produced the stress in the first place. Its major benefit is that it allows a clear mind and a calm body to consider and put into action some rational coping techniques.

Relax and Do What?

In April, 1993, clinical psychologist Mihaly Csikszentmihalyi, writing for the APA (American Psychological Association) newspaper, noted that, "Humans seem to be biologically programmed to enjoy confronting challenges, using their skills and developing their potential." He finds that both coercive work and empty leisure seem to stifle this essential pleasure.

His subjects were contacted at random hours, both day and night, and asked to report on their activities and their emotional state. When people were contacted while working, they reported feeling generally strong, creative, and satisfied; when asked to report their feelings during times when they were free to do whatever they wanted to, they acknowledged themselves to be feeling weak, dull, and dissatisfied. It isn't enough to learn to relax. We must also learn to work and to play. Both Sigmund Freud and John Dewey noted that existence is most rewarding when it involves the seemly contradictory traits of rigor and playfulness.

THE JOB AS A STRESSOR

With the possible exception of the home, no institution shapes our personality as much as the workplace. Our job and the rewards we derive from that job affect our self-esteem, our social relations, and our physical and mental health.

Although Selye (1977) maintains that we were made to work, the design and location of work can have serious effects on our well-being. If job-related health disorders were given consideration by our legislatures, we would all be able to depreciate ourselves during our work life for income-tax benefits. Some could qualify for greater deductions than others. In addition to such pollutants as chemicals, asbestos, tobacco, coal, and similar noxious materials, noise itself is a pollutant of great significance. Glass and Singer (1971) found that a measurable amount of stress occurs every time noise is introduced into a workplace. Loud, soft, predictable or not, all noise causes stress, even when the workers think they have adapted to it.

On the job, anxiety and the number of health-related problems have been found to vary with the frequency at which stressful events are encountered. Also, as time on a job lengthens, workers report less stress from both their jobs and homes (Weiss, 1972). Apparently, a longer tenure allows people more time to establish predictability and control. The number of jobs held at the same time and the hours and conditions of work are related to stress. Dr. Mark Russek, professor of cardiovascular disease at New York Medical Center, reports that 91 of 100 heart-attack victims he studied were holding two or more jobs and working more than sixty hours a week, or they were experiencing unusual job insecurity, discomfort, or frustration. Long hours, low pay, routine tasks, pollution, insecurity, and little opportunity for increased responsibility or advancement are stressors common to low-level jobs.

Stress Related to Types of Jobs

High job stress itself does not account for stress-related illnesses. The nature of the stressful job is what makes the difference. High job stress with little job latitude or job flexibility is the problem. For example, a bus driver—who must frequently give up lunch breaks to maintain an impossible timetable, endure city traffic while dealing politely with passenger hassles, and keep on the lookout for roving plain-clothes supervisors—is a candidate for "high blood pressure, musculoskeletal disorders and gastrointestinal problems" (Syme, 1986). Dr. Michael Smith (1977) of the National Institute of Occupational Safety and Health reports that rank-and-file workers get just as sick as, if not sicker than, industry tycoons and professional overachievers as a result of on-the-job stress. The "simple" jobs

---

The Worker of the 90s Speaks

- Victims of burnout deserve disability pay. 82%
- I expect to burn out in the near future. 33%
- Job stress causes me frequent health problems. 70%
- I thought seriously of quitting my job last year. 34%

"Job-related stress has created a crisis that largely goes unrecognized by employers."

SOURCE: Knowlton Scott. "Stress Exacts a Toll in Workplace." *The Miami Herald* (May 8, 1991).

Warning: Work May Be Hazardous to Your Mental Health

The National Institute for Occupational Safety and Health warns that the U.S. workplace could grow even more stressful during the 1990s. Consider these facts:

- Economists predict a 26 percent increase in employment in the health services, an area associated with high stress.
- Computers and robots are expected to affect 7 million factory and 39 million office jobs by replacing workers or creating work that requires lower skills. Lower skills traditionally mean lower pay.

- Nine of 10 new jobs will be in the service sector, where jobs often offer lower pay and fewer benefits.
- Six of 10 new jobs will be filled by women, who often face added responsibilities at home and more limited opportunities at work.

SOURCE: *The Miami Herald* (March 16, 1987).

"Emerging trends in technology, the economy, and demographic characteristics of the work force may lead to increased risk for psychological disorders."

are not stress free, and the rich and powerful do not pay for their success by having stress-linked breakdowns, as was once thought to be the case (Tanner, 1976).

Women and poor people, who hold a disproportionate number of undesirable jobs and are less able to use anger to their advantage, report more stress and more health problems. In fact, women in general report more perceived stress at work. Those who report high job stress and high life-changing units experience a greater number of symptoms of stress-related health disorders. This holds true for high- or low-salaried women in positions of high or low responsibility (Pepitone-Arreola-Rockwell et al., 1981). The most stressful jobs for women include inner-city high school teacher, customer-complaint person, intensive-care head nurse, waitress, garment stitcher, and data-entry clerk.

According to Robert Karasek (1983), "The greatest stress occurs in jobs where the individual faces heavy psychological demands, yet has little control over how to get the work done" (p. 45). More than 25 percent of all jobs fall in this "high-demand, low-control" category. Librarians, professional technicians (who do research and nonroutine work), stock handlers, store checkout workers, repairpersons, architects, and dentists were found to be in the least stressful occupations.

Stress in Jobs Open to College Graduates

College graduates expect fulfilling and rewarding careers. Such positions are not plentiful, and much stress is experienced in training for and obtaining them. People with a high need to achieve are often torn between being aggressive and being liked. Both of these attributes are thought to be necessary in top management. People who believe it necessary to hide their anger during this drive for power are prime candidates for stress disorders (McClelland, 1976). Glamorous jobs in the communications and entertainment industries are chained to time (deadlines, air times, and so on). Friedman and Rosenman (1974) report that it is better to work twelve or fourteen hours a day without time pressure than four hours with time pressure.

For the young executive, too much responsibility, too heavy a workload, and too many decisions to be made that affect the lives of others are particularly stressful (Burke, 1976). Not enough information to get the job done, not being able to influence superiors, and too-slow personal progress on the job all

A high stress job with little job latitude or job flexibility may cause stress-related health problems.

create occupational stress without increasing performance or profits. Even profits or other sources of annual income of $100,000 or more do not ensure stress-free living. "Jumbo mortgages and college tuition bills, and trying to save for lengthy and costly retirements" place a large part of the upper middle class under pressure (Spiers, 1993).

In our culture, not having a job or being unable to replace a lost job (job-lessness) is so profound a stressor that our government is giving serious consideration to becoming the employer of last resort.

SIGNS OF JOB STRESS

How can we tell if job stress is present? From the standpoint of the worker, a pattern of tiredness, nervousness, sleeping difficulties, loss of appetite, depression, general dissatisfaction with the job or with life—any or all of these can signal job-related stress. If you find yourself taking tranquilizers, alcohol, or other mood-changing drugs to stay on—or on top of—the job, you can suspect job stress.

From the standpoint of management, figures indicating increases in absenteeism, on-site accidents (especially where employee substance abuse is suspected), compensation claims, and personnel turnover are signs of job stress. Decreases in productivity, quality control, and profit margins are bottom-line indicators of stressful working conditions.

WHAT TO DO ABOUT JOB STRESS

You can cope in three ways:

1. You can attempt to make changes on the job—a problem-solving strategy.

2. You can try not to let the job "get to you"—an emotional strategy.

3. You can tell your boss to "take this job and shove it"—an escape strategy.

Latack (1986) found that individuals employing a *problem-solving strategy* are less likely to report job anxiety, job dissatisfaction, or to leave the company. She also found that workers need *strong social supports* and *few personal-life stressors* to employ such a strategy. Women are more likely to seek social support as their first strategy (Placek, Smith, and Zanas, 1992).

Men have fewer social supporters to fall back on. The way we have organized work has placed every man in competition with every other man. According to Alvin Baraff, clinical psychologist of the MenCenter in Washington, DC, rarely does a man have two or more really good friends. In fact, few men even have a best friend.

Many people consider it a sign of weakness to speak of being under stress. In fact, it is a weakness not to. If your co-workers report similar distress, it is important to work with management to redesign the workplace and/or the nature of the task itself so that stress is reduced. Stress is cumulative, that is, it builds up over time. Constantly complaining to fellow workers will neither reduce stress nor increase your abilty to tolerate it. If changes can't be worked out, a job transfer or job change should be given careful consideration. However, note that the loss of a job is very stressful also. It produces higher levels of adrenaline (elevation of the heartbeat rate and of blood pressure) and noradrenaline (resulting in a reduced immune response). Many people belive they can't afford to leave their jobs. You might think that the well-paid, well-trained professional would have the greatest opportunity to flexibly change jobs if conditions were stressful. However, McKenna, Oritt, and Wolff (1981) found this not to be the case. They did find that job satisfaction and company commitment are negatively correlated to occupational stress—that is, the more stress, the less satisfaction and commitment. The surprising finding is that extensive education and training lead to a lessened probability of leaving a job, even under severe stress and dissatisfaction.

Critcal Review 5

1. According to Karen Horney, an idealized self-concept leads to anxiety. T F

2. Self-censure is the worst form of stress, because we carry it with us. T F

3. Do you believe that your social adjustment has been hindered by anxiety concerning your personal safety? If so, in what way?

4. What states or specific conditions make you anxious?

5. Do you believe that anxiety is largely a learned response that can be helped by the cultivation of low arousal? Why or why not?

6. What were/are the stressors that you have experienced in jobs that you have held to date?

7. What strategies did/do you use to reduce your stress response? How well did/do your strategies work?

8. What stressors are you aware of that are associated with your career choice?

9. What coping resources (social skills, family, problem-solving skills, etc.) do you have that will allow you to thrive in your chosen career?

SUMMARY

- We have survived by being able to change our behavior to meet the changing demands placed on us.

- The new disciplines of Health Psychology and Behavioral Medicine are helping us to reduce risky behaviors and to establish improved health care systems.

- The demands on us are termed *stressors* and are present without limit in our environment.

- Our response to any demand is termed *stress*. Our body changes in order to energize us and to direct that energy toward confrontation or escape.

- Both major life changes and daily hassles are sources of continuing stress.

- Excessive stress or a failure to cope with stress leads to "diseases of adaptation." Selye describes the stress sequence in terms of a general adaptation syndrome consisting of three stages: alarm, resistance, and exhaustion.

- We have three bodily systems—neural, endocrine, and immune—that must function together to keep us healthy and well adjusted.

- Herbert Benson emphasizes the direct link between stress and high blood pressure, strokes, and heart attacks.

- Immunosuppressants, both physical and mental, indirectly affect our well-being.

- A failure of the immune system, related to prolonged stress, results in reduced ability to defend against disease cells.

- Cognitive appraisal of the meaning of an event is a transaction between the event and the nature of our response to it.

- Both personality traits and personality types work for and against our ability to cope with stressful events.

- Albert Bandura finds that certain forms of stress are necessary for personal growth and change.

- Eustress also requires adjustment but is less damaging physically and is not emotionally damaging at all.

- Stress is best viewed as a natural, inevitable part of daily living. We are capable of modulating stress so that it works for us, not against us.

- Emotional coping mechanisms are indirect methods of regulating stress. They serve to protect the ego and reduce the probability of destructive aggression.

- Drugs, from alcohol and valium to cocaine and heroin, are termed *disregulators* because they hinder the functioning of the brain's coping mechanisms.

- Anxiety is a response to a perceived threat that produces chronic fear and irritability.

- Anxiety has roots in early childhood experiences and in the realities of human existence. It may become a conditioned response and be transmitted to others.

- The restorative response, a profound state of low arousal, is incompatible with anxiety. It has been produced by both Eastern and Western approaches, from yoga to biofeedback.

- An attitude of passive attention appears to be central to both Eastern and Western approaches that have been successful in producing a prolonged state of low arousal.

- The restorative response reduces the ravages of stress and allows us to use a clear mind in a calm body to select and use rational, direct coping techniques in response to stress.

- Jobs are among the chief stressors in modern America.

- Individuals employing a problem-solving strategy are less likely to report job anxiety, job dissatisfaction, or to leave the company.

SELECTED READINGS

Benson, H. *The Relaxation Response.* New York: Morrow Press, 1975. A beautiful book that describes behavior patterns that provoke premature heart attacks and offers a simple relaxation technique for combatting stress.

Calhoun, K. S. and Atkeson, B. M. *Treatment of Rape Victims.* New York: Pergamon Press, 1989. An excellent description of effective methods of treating victims of rape.

Kobasa, S. C. "How Much Stress Can You Survive?" American Health Magazine (September 1984): 64–77. A discussion of ways you can change your personality in order to be a survivor.

Lecron, L. *Self-Hypnotism.* Englewood Cliffs, NJ: Prentice-Hall, 1964. A lively and professional description of relaxation through self-suggestion.

Luthe, W., and Schultz, J. *Autogenic Therapy,* vols. 1, 2, and 3. New York: Grune and Stratton, 1969; 1970. A description of the systematic use of verbal phrases to induce a deep, restorative calm.

Selye, H. *Stress Without Distress.* Philadelphia: Lippincott, 1976. A philosophical work that contains the wisdom gained by Selye in a lifetime of studying stress.

Tubesing, Donald A. *Kicking Your Stress Habits.* New York: Whole Person Associates, Inc. 1989. This how-to workbook, which features personal examples, deals with ways to cope with stress. The first half of the book discusses how change, life stages, and grief can cause stress. The second half is devoted to stress-management skills. Teaches you to manage your time, relationships, physical stamina, and outlook on life.

Watson, D. L., and Tharp, R. G. *Self-Directed Behavior.* Pacific Grove, CA: Brooks/Cole, 1993. This book is designed to help you help yourself. By regulating your own behavior, you can learn to manage stress and improve the quality of your life.

REFERENCES

Adler, R., and Cohen, N. "Psychoneuroimmunology: Conditioning and Stress." *Annual Review of Psychology* 44 (1993): 53–85.

Adler, T. "Bad Mix: Combat Stress, Decisions." *APA Monitor* (March 1993): 1.

Asher, J. "Born to Be Shy." *Psychology Today* 21 (April 1987): 56–64.

Bandura, A. "Self-efficacy: Toward a Unifying Theory of Behavioral Change." *Psychological Review* 84 (March 1986): 191–215.

Bartone, P., Gifford, R., Wright, K., Marlowe, D., and Martin, J. "U.S. Soldiers Remain Healthy Under Gulf War Stress." Paper presented at the 4th annual convention of the American Psychological Society, San Diego, 1992.

Benson, H. *The Relaxation Response.* New York: Morrow, 1975.

Benson, H., Arns, A. A., and Hoffman, J. W. "The Relaxation Response and Hypnosis." *International Journal of Clinical and Experimental Hypnosis* 29 (1981): 259–270.

Berk, L. S., Ian, S. A., Fry, W. F., Napier, B. J., Lee, J. W., Hubbard, R. W., Lewis, J. E., and Eby, W. C. "Neuroendocrine and Stress Hormone Changes During Mirthful Laughter." *American Journal of Medical Science,* 298 (1989):390–396.

Bettelheim, B. "Individual and Mass Behavior in Extreme Situations." *Abnormal and Social Psychology* 38 (1943): 417–452.

Blanchard, E. "Introduction to the Special Issue on Behavioral Medicine: An Update for the 1990s." *Journal of Counseling and Clinical Psychology,* 60 (1992): 491–492.

Bolger, N., DeLongis, A., Kessler, R. C., and Schilling, E. A. "Effects of Daily Stress on Negative Mood." *Journal of Personality and Social Psychology* 57 (1989): 808–818.

Brislin, R. *Understanding Culture's Influence on Behavior.* Fort Worth, TX: Harcourt Brace Jovanovich, 1993.

Brown, J. "Psychological Distress, Depression and Prolactin Response in Stressed Persons." *Journal of Human Stress* 12 (Fall 1986): 113–118.

_____. "Staying Fit and Staying Well: Physical Fitness as a Moderator of Life Stress." *Journal of Personality and Social Psychology* 60 (1991): 555–561.

Buell, J. C. "Stress: It's Not Worth Dying For." *Reader's Digest* (January 1985): 76–80.

Burke, R. J. "Occupational Stress." *Journal of Social Psychology* 100 (1976): 235–244.

Calhoun, K. S. and Atkeson, B. M. *Treatment of Rape Victims.* New York: Pergamon Press, 1989.

Cameron, N. *Personality Development and Psychopathology: A Dynamic Approach.* Boston: Houghton Mifflin, 1963.

Cannon, W. B. *Bodily Changes in Pain, Hunger, Fear and Rage,* 2d ed. New York: Appleton-Century-Crofts, 1929.

_____. "Voodoo Death." *American Anthropologist* 44 (1942): 169–181.

Chamberlain, K., and Zika, S. (1990). "The Minor Events Approach to Stress: Support for the Use of Daily Hassles." *British Journal of Psychology* 81 (1990): 469–481.

Cochran, S. D., Mays, V. M., Ciarletta, J., Caruso, C., and Mallon, D. "Efficacy of the Theory of Reasoned Action in Predicting AIDS-related Sexual Risk Reduction Among Gay Men." *Journal of Applied Social Psychology* 22 (1992): 1481–1501.

Cohen, S., and Williamson, G. G. "Stress and Infectious Disease in Humans." *Psychological Bulletin* 109 (1992): 5–24.

Cohen, S. and Wills, T. A. "Stress, Social Support, and the Buffering Hypothesis." *Psychological Bulletin* 98 (1985): 310–357.

Cooper, M., Russell, M., Skinner, J., Frone, M., and Mudar, P. "Stress and Alcohol Use: Moderating Effects of Gender, Coping and Alcohol Expectancies." *Journal of Abnormal Psychology* 101 (1992): 139–152.

Dantzer, R. "Psychobiology of Adaptive Behavior: A French Contribution to the Issue of Stress, Coping, and Health." *Advances: Institute for the Advancement of Health* 3(4) (Fall 1986): 36–44.

Delongis, A., Coyne, J. C., Dakof, G., Folkman, S., and Lazarus, R. S. "Relationship of Daily Hassles, Uplifts, and Major Life Events to Health Status." *Health Psychology* 1 (January 1982): 119–136.

Di Cara, L. V., and Miller, N. E. "Instrumental Learning of Vasomotor Responses by Rats: Learning to Respond Differentially in the Two Ears." *Science* 159 (1968): 1485–1486.

Dillon, K. M., and Totten, M. C. "Psychological Factors Affecting Immunocompetence and Health of Breast Feeding Mothers and Their Infants. *Journal of Genetic Psychology* 150 (1989): 155–162.

Erikson, E. H. *Identity: Youth in Crisis.* New York: Norton, 1968.

Farley, F. "The Type T Personality, With Some Implications for Practice." *The California Psychologist* 26 (1990): 29.

Fisher, K. "Berkeley Study Finds Stress Is Value Laden." *APA Monitor* 15 (1984): 30.

Friedman, H. S. (Ed.). *Hostility, Coping, and Health.* Washington, DC: American Psychological Association.

Friedman, M., and Rosenman, R. F. *Type A Behavior and Your Heart.* New York: Knopf, 1974.

Glass, D. C., and Singer, J. E. "Behavioral Consequences of Adaptation to Controllable and Uncontrollable Noise." *Journal of Experimental Social Psychology* 7 (March 1971): 244–257.

_____. *Urban Stress: Experiments on Noise and Social Stressors.* New York: Academic Press, 1972.

Grady, Denise. "Think Right. Stay Well?" *American Health* (November 1992): 50–54.

Greer, S. "Psychological Response to Cancer and Survival." *Psychological Medicine* 21 (1991): 43–49.

Hebb, D. O. *A Textbook of Psychology.* Philadelphia: Saunders, 1958.

Henry, P. J., and Stevens, P. M. *Stress, Health and the Social Environment: A Sociobiological Approach to Medicine.* New York: Springer, 1978.

Hilgard, E. R., and Hilgard, J. R. *Hypnosis in the Relief of Pain.* Los Altos, CA: William Kaufmann, 1975.

Holahan, C. J., and Moos, R. H. "Life Stressors, Resistance Factors, and Improved Psychological Functioning: An Extension of the Stress Resistance Paradigm." *Journal of Personality and Social Psychology* 558 (1990): 909–917.

Holmes, T. H., and Rahe, R. H. "The Social Readjustment Rating Scale." *Journal of Psychosomatic Research* 11 (March 1967): 213–218.

Homes, D. S. "Meditation and Somatic Arousal Reduction." *American Psychologist* 39 (January 1984): 1–10.

Horney, K. *Neurosis and Human Growth.* New York: Norton, 1950.

Ickovics, J., and Rodin, J. "Women and AIDS in the United States: Epidemiology, Natural History, and Mediating Mechanisms." *Health Psychology* 11 (1992): 1–16.

Ironson, G., and Schneiderman, N. (1991). "Psychoimmunology and HIV-1: Scope of the Problem." In *Psychoimmunology and HIV-1*, edited by N. Schneiderman et al. Geneva: World Health Organization, pp. 24–28.

Jacobson, E. *You Must Relax.* New York: McGraw-Hill, 1978.

Jemmott, J. B., III, Borysenko, M., McClelland, D. C., Chapman, R., Meyer, D., and Benson, H. "Academic Stress, Power Motivation, and Decrease in Salivary Secretory Immunoglobulin: A Secretion Rate." *Lancet* 1 (1985): 1400–1402.

Karasek, R. "Jobs Where Stress Is Most Severe." *U.S. News and World Report* 5 (September 1983): 45–46.

_____. Quoted in *The Miami Herald* (27 April 1986): 7G.

Kimmel, M. S., and Levine, M. P. "Men and AIDS." In *Men's Lives*, 2nd ed., edited by M. S. Kimmel and M. A. Messner, pp. 318–329. New York: Macmillan, 1992.

Knowlton, S. "Stress Exacts a Toll in Workplace." *The Miami Herald* (May 8, 1991): 5B.

Kobasa, S. C. "How Much Stress Can You Survive?" In *Psychology 85/86*, edited by M. G. Walraven and H. E. Fitzgerald, pp. 122–130. Guilford, CT: Dushkin, 1985.

Latack, J. C. "Coping With Job Stress: Measures and Future Directions for Scale Development." *Journal of Applied Psychology* 71 (August 1986): 377–385.

_____. "Little Hassles Can Be Dangerous to Health." *Psychology Today* 15 (July 1981): 58–62.

Lazarus, R. S., and Folkman, S. *Stress, Appraisal, and Coping.* New York: Springer, 1984.

Lehmann, J., Goodale, I. L., and Benson, H. "Reduced Pupillary Sensitivity to Topical Phenylephrine Associated with the Relaxation Response." *Journal of Human Stress* 12 (Fall 1986): 101–104.

Levine, S. "The Effects of Differential Infantile Stimulation on Emotionality at Weaning." *Canadian Journal of Psychology* 13 (April 1959): 243–247.

Lloyd, G., Alexander, A. A., Rice, D. G., and Greenfield, N. S. "Life Events as Predictors of Academic Performance." *Journal of Human Stress* 6 (September 1980): 15–26.

Locke, S. "Stress May Damage Cell Immunity." *Science News* 113 (March 1978): 151.

_____. Personal Interview. Fort Lauderdale, Florida: December 1985.

Lopez, M., and Takemoto-Chock, N. "Assessment of Adolescent Stressors: The Adolescent Life Events Scale." Paper presented at the meetings of the Western Psychological Association, Portland, OR, April 1992.

Lustman, P., Sowa, C., and O'Hara, D. "Factors Influencing College Student Health: Development of the Psychological Distress Inventory." *Journal of Human Stress* 31 (Spring 1984): 28–35.

Luthe, E., and Schultz, J. *Autogenic Therapy*, vols. 1, 2, and 3. New York: Grune and Stratton, 1969; 1970.

Maddi, S. R., and Kobasa, S. C. "The Hardy Executive: Health Under Stress." Homewood, IL: Dow Jones-Irwin, 1984.

Marx, M. B., Garrity, T. F., and Bowers, F. R. "The Influence of Recent Life Experiences on the Health of College Freshmen." *Journal of Psychosomatic Research* (January 1975): 87–98.

McClelland, D. C. "Sources of Stress in the Drive for Power." In *Psychopathology of Human Adaptation*, edited by George Serban, pp. 224–5. New York: Plenum Press, 1976.

McKenna, J. F., Oritt, P. L., and Wolff, H. K. "Occupational Stress as a Predictor in the Turnover Decision." *Journal of Human Stress* 7 (December 1981): 12–18.

McMillen, L. "Job-Related Tension and Anxiety Taking a Toll Among Employees in Academe's 'Stress Factories.'" *Chronicle of Higher Education* 33 (21) (February 4, 1987): 1, 10–11.

Melmed, R. N. "Biobehavioral Research in Israel." *Advances: Institute for the Advancement of Health* 2 (Fall 1986): 77–82.

Miller, J. A. "Brain Peptides in a Chemistry of Anxiety." *Science News* 123 (June 1983): 388.

Miller, N. E.. "Rx: Biofeedback." *Psychology Today* 19 (February 1985): 54–59.

Orlebeke, K. F., and Van Dooren, L. "Stress, Personality and Serum Cholesterol Level." *Journal of Human Stress* 8 (December 1982): 12.

Oropeza, Barbara, Clark, A., Fitzgibbon, Maureen, and Baron, Augustine, Jr. "In the Field, Managing Mental Health Crises of Foreign College Students." *Journal of Counseling and Development* 69 (January/February 1991): 280–283.

Pearson, D., and Shaw, S. *Life Extensions.* New York: Warner Books, 1980.

Pennebaker, J. W., Colder, N., Sharp, L. K. "Accelerating the Coping Process." *Journal of Personality and Social Psychology* 58 (1990): 528–537.

Peper, E. "Passive Attention: The Gateway to Consciousness and Autonomic Control." In *Psychology and Life*, 9th ed., edited by P. G. Zimbardo and F. L. Ruch, pp. 82–83. Glenview, IL: Scott, Foresman, 1977.

Pepitone-Arreola-Rockwell, F., Sommer, B., Sassenrath, E. N., Rozee-Koker, J., and Stringer-Moore, D. "Job Stress and Health in Working Women." *Journal of Human Stress* 7 (December 1981): 19–26.

Peterson, C., and Seligman, M. E. P. "Causal Explanations as a Risk Factor for Depression: Theory and Evidence." *Psychological Review* 91 (July 1986): 347–374.

Placek, J. T., Smith, R. E., and Zanas, J. "Gender, Appraisal, and Coping: A Longitudinal Analysis." *Journal of Personality* 60 (1992): 747–770.

Rich, A. "Causes of Depression in College Students: A Cross-Lagged Panel Correlational Analysis." *Psychological Reports* 60 (February 1987): 27–30.

Roberts, A. H. "Biofeedback: Research, Training, and Clinical Roles." *American Psychologist* 40 (August 1985): 938–941.

Rodin, J., and Salovey, P. "Health Psychology." *Annual Review of Psychology* 40 (1989): 533–579.

Rogers, C. R. "A Theory of Personality." In *Perspectives on Personality,* edited by S. Maddi, pp. 195–206. Boston: Little Brown, 1971.

Roth, S., and Cohen, J. L. "Approach, Avoidance, and Coping with Stress." *American Psychologist* 41 (July 1986): 813–819.

San Francisco Chronicle. "Bad Habits, Violence Raise Health Costs." (February 1993) 4:1.

Sanchez, J. I., and Fernandez, D. M. "Acculturative Stress Among Hispanics." *Journal of Applied Psychology* 23 (April 1993): 654–658.

Sapolsky, R. "Stress and the Successful Baboon." *Psychology Today* 9 (April 1984): 62–66.

Saunders, A., and Remsburg, B. "The Stress-proof Child: A Loving Parent's Guide." New York: Holt, Rinehart, and Winston, 1984.

Scheier, M. F., and Carver, C. S. (1992). "Effects of Optimism on Psychological and Physical Well-being: Theoretical Overview and Empirical Update." *Cognitive Therapy and Research* 16 (1992): 201–228.

Schorr, B. "Anti-Cholesterol Treatment Can Cut Risk of Heart Disease Up to 50% a Study Shows." *Wall Street Journal* (January 13, 1984): 4.

Schwartz, G. E. "Behavioral Approaches to Stress Management and Correction of Disregulation." Paper presented at the Stress and Behavioral Medicine Symposium sponsored by BioMonitoring Applications, New York, 1977.

Selye, H. *The Stress of Life,* rev. ed. New York: McGraw-Hill, 1976.

_____. Stress Without Distress. New York: Lippincott, 1974.

_____. "Man Made to Work." Presented at Stress and Behavioral Medicine Symposium sponsored by BioMonitoring Applications, New York, 1977.

Selye, H., and Cherry , L. "On the Real Benefits of Eustress." *Pschology Today* 11 (March 1978): 60–63.

Seligman, M. E. P., *Learned Optimism.* New York: Norton, 1991.

_____. *Omni* interview 14 (12) September, 1992: 59–65.

Shaw, J. B., and Riskind, J. H. (Eds.). "Predicting Job Stress Using Data From the Position Analysis Questionnaire." *Journal of Applied Psychology* 68 (May 1983): 253–261.

Singer, M., Candida, F., Davidson, L., Burke, G., et. al. "SIDA: The Economic, Social, and Cultural Context of AIDS Among Latinos." *American Anthropology Quarterly* 4(1) (1990): 72–114.

Sizer, F. S., and Whitney, E. N. *Nutrition: Concepts and Controversies.* St. Paul, MN: West, 1994.

Smith, M. J. "Occupational Stress." Proceedings of the Conference on Occupational Stress 3, Los Angeles, 1977.

Spector, Novera Herbert, and Arora, Kumar. "Science, History, and Psychoneuroimmunology." *The Quarterly Review of Biology* 68 (2) (June 1993): 233–237.

Spielberger, C. D. (ed.). *Anxiety and Behavior.* New York: Academic Press, 1966.

Spiers, J. "Upper-middle-class woes." *Fortune* 126 (16) (December 27, 1993): 80–86.

Stout, C. W., and Bloom, L. J. "Type A Behavior and Upper Respiratory Infections." *Journal of Human Stress* 8 (June 1982): 121–126.

Syme, L. Quoted in *The Miami Herald* (April 27, 1986): 7G.

Tanner, O. *Stress.* New York: Time-Life Books, 1976.

Taylor, S. E. *Health Psychology,* 3rd ed. New York: Random House, 1992.

Ursin, H. "Behavioral Medicine in Norway." *Advances: Institute for the Advancement of Health* 2 (Fall 1986): 105–113.

Ursin, H., Boode, E., and Levine, S. *Psychobiology of Stress: A Study of Coping Men.* New York: Academic Press, 1978.

Weiss, H. M. "Effects of Life and Job Stress on Information Search Behaviors of Organizational Members." *Journal of Applied Psychology* 67 (February 1982): 60–66.

Weiss, J. M. "Psychological Factors in Stress Disease." *Scientific American* 226 (June 1972): 106.

Whalen, C. K. "Type A Personality in Hyperactive Children: Evidence of Overlapping Constructs." *Child Development* 57 (June 1986): 688–699.

Williams, R. B. "An Untrusting Heart." In *Annual Editions: Psychology,* edited by Michael G. Walraven, 86–92, Guilford, CT: Duskin, 1985.

Wolpe, J. *The Practice of Behavioral Therapy,* 2nd ed. New York: Pergamon Press, 1973.

_____. "The Training Programs of the Behavioral Therapy Unit at Temple University." *Journal of Behavioral Therapy and Experimental Psychiatry* 9 (December 1978): 295–300.

Zukerman, L. A., Oliver, J. M., Hollingsworth, H. H., and Austrin, H. R. "A Comparison of Life Events Scoring Methods as Predictors of Psychological Symptomatology." *Journal of Human Stress* 12 (Summer 1986): 64–70.

■ *Questionnaire Scoring Key*

How Hardy Are You?

To figure your score: These questions measure control, commitment, and challenge. For half of the questions, a high score indicates hardiness; for the other half, a low score indicates hardiness.

To figure your scores on control, commitment, and challenge, first write in the number of your answer—0,1,2, or 3—above the letter for each question on the score sheet below. Then add and subtract as shown. (For example, to figure your control score, add your answers to questions A and G; add your answers to B and H; and then subtract the

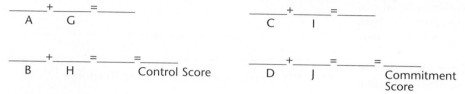

_____+_____=_____   _____+_____=_____
   A   G   C   I

_____+_____=_____=_____   _____+_____=_____=_____
   B   H   Control Score   D   J   Commitment
                                                               Score

second answer from the first.)

Add your scores on commitment, control, and challenge together to get a score for total hardiness.

A total score of 10–18 shows a hardy personality. A score of 0–9 shows moderate hardiness. Below 0: low hardiness.

_____+_____=_____
   E   K

_____+_____=_____=_____
   F   L   Challenge Score

_____+_____+_____=_____
 Control Commitment Challenge   Total Hardiness Score

SOURCE: S. Kobasa. *American Health* (September 1984): 66.

■ *Answers To Critical Review Questions*

Critical Review 1 1. False   **2.** True
Critical Review 2 1. False   **2.** False   **3.** True
Critical Review 3 1. True   **2.** True
Critical Review 5 1. True   **2.** True

PERSONAL ACTION PLAN
Stress Reduction

The purpose of this plan is to give you an opportunity to select and put into action alternative responses in situations that are emotionally stressful. These new transitions between yourself and recurring stressors will potentially reduce the frequency, duration, and intensity of your stress response. Such coping strategies may extend the satisfying and healthy portion of your life.

The first half of this stress reduction plan is to be found at the end of chapter 7. Locate and complete steps I through V of this action plan if you have not already done so. When you have the information for these steps at hand, you are ready to begin.

Step VI. Alternatives to My Problem Emotional Response Pattern

You are now ready to consider problem-solving coping responses when you find yourself in these circumstances.

Get comfortable, relax, and when you feel deeply relaxed, repeat the following statement slowly and calmly five times: "No one can make me _____; I can only choose to become_____." Just as no one can make you fat, because you have to choose to take in more energy than you expend, no one can make you. You have to choose to mobilize and expend your energy in that fashion.

Review your emotional log and list situations in which a more productive and rewarding emotional response on your part might have been:

A. Humor:

B. Empathy:

C. Compassion:

D. Patience:

List situations in which a more rewarding and productive attitude on your part might have altered the situation constructively: "I could have viewed the situation as. . . ."

A. One calling for reason and constructive thought:

_____

_____

_____

_____

B. A problem to be solved rather than a personal threat: _____

_____

_____

_____

_____

C. A sign that additional support on my part was needed:_____

_____

_____

_____

_____

D. Other: _____

_____

_____

_____

Step VII. Practicing an Alternative Response

As you know, your problem emotion is, at least internally, a state of high arousal. A state of low arousal, or deep calm, is incompatible with that emotion. You cannot be deeply relaxed and angry at the same time. The skill of deep relaxation can be learned and called on in stress-provoking situations. To practice this response:

A. Set aside a five- to fifteen-minute period when you are not likely to be disturbed.
B. Sit or lie in a comfortable position.
C. Breathe slowly and regularly. Let your body "breathe itself."
D. Let your mind be still.
E. Beginning with your toes, concentrate on contracting muscles in an area, be aware of the tension, breathe out, and quickly let the tension go.
F. Concentrate only on the tension and and the release of tension. Notice what it feels like to have your muscles completely relaxed.
G. Continue concentrating on and relaxing each set of muscles from your toes to the top of your head. Do not omit your genitals.
H. When you have finished, focus your attention on any areas that retain some tension or pain and repeat the process there.
I. Let your mind be still. If thoughts arise, let them go and refocus on your tension. Do not become annoyed at yourself.

Try to practice this procedure twice a day, every day, for five to fifteen minutes. You will gain skill as the days go by. While you are practicing, arrange for another person to help you modulate your emotional response. Perhaps you can work together to help each other.

Step VIII. Rehearsing Behavior

Using your daily log as a guide, construct brief, typical scenes that usually produce your unwanted emotion. Be specific as to time, place, events, and other details. With these scenes, prepare for future encounters by rehearsing alternate ways of looking at the situation or the people involved, alternate ways of feeling, and alternate ways of acting. Take care not to look for support or justification for your old behavior; rather look for suggestions for new responses. Evaluate these in terms of staying relaxed, rational, and on task. Be sure to ask your partner to model appropriate, useful responses and then discuss them with you. Do not just talk. Act. It is also important for you to rehearse what you say to yourself during these practice episodes so that you can begin to monitor your self-talk and improve it.

Step IX. Using Positive Self-Statements

Thoughts lead to feelings, which lead to behavior. Review your log to be sure of what you typically say to yourself during emotional entanglements. "This is a catastrophe!" is an example of negative self-talk that leads to uncomfortable feelings and unfortunate behavior. As a direct coping technique, write out and rehearse one or more positive statements that are appropriate to your typical problem situation and that will help you modulate your response to it. Examples of such statements include "I can handle this; I can stay on task."

Step X. Responding on Cue

You now have an understanding of your typical response patterns, their costs, and their benefits. You also have insight into direct coping techniques available to you in problem situations. You have, or soon will have, skill in producing the relaxation response at will. Review your log one last time to refresh your memory concerning the specifics of the incidents that provoke your unwanted emotion. Study them so that you are sensitized to any subtle cues that seem to occur just before you respond inappropriately. It is imperative that you be able to identify such cues, because you are now ready to make productive use of them.

There is a certain beauty in this step because, instead of attempting to ignore or escape people or situations that were troublesome in your past, you are going to actively look for them so that you may use them as cues or signs that tell you it is time to respond with one or more of your new skills.

Step XI. Positive Reinforcement Log

Identifying a problem situation early, maintaining composure, and acting to reduce stress while staying on task are all reinforcing in themselves. It is important to realize that you will not always be able to do all of these things all of the time. Do not wait for perfection to feel good about yourself, but rather set up a system of small rewards for each of the components of emotional modulation that you successfully produce under real-life conditions.

Set up a daily log as you did in Step II. Add the following entries:

A. I was able to recognize the provoking signs early.

B. I was able to initiate the relaxation response.

C. I was able to maintain patience or composure.

D. I was able to maintain a problem-solving, nondefensive attitude.

E. I was able to be aware of and modulate my self-talk.

F. I was able to decide whether humor, anger, empathy, support, or another response was called for.

G. I was able to produce the response deemed appropriate.

H. I was able to stay on task.

I. I was able to prevent the escalation of the situation into unfortunate dialogue or actions.

J. I was able to control the situation so that a need for my unwanted emotion never developed.

As you can see, there is plenty of room for partial success and little likelihood of complete success during any one encounter. Reward your partial successes, rehearse alternatives to your partial failures, and build on your increasing skills. The result can be a sense of self-mastery and a feeling of positive personal control.

CHAPTER

5

THE PHYSICAL SELF

Chapter Outline

If you have not done so already, take a moment to determine your stand on the critical issue of free will versus determinism found on page 149, an issue that cuts to the very core of our human experience. After you have taken a stand, close your eyes and relax.

As you relax, permit moving portraits of yourself to flood your mind. Do not be selective; just let your relaxed mind turn out image after image. Enjoy a few moments of this soothing mental exercise.

Were you able to see yourself? Could you watch without evaluating your self-image? Do you believe your size, sex, race, or shape gives others reliable clues to your personality? Has your personality been shaped by others' reactions to one or more aspects of your physical self? Finally, do you believe that your anatomy seems to control a large part of your destiny?

There is widespread disagreement among psychologists on the relative impact of three forces—inborn biological factors, personal life experiences, and individual choices— on human personality and behavior. The debate is known as the *nature-nurture controversy*. We all know that both nature and nurture interact to shape differences *within* individual personalities. We could not survive without both our biological and environmental hosts. The question is the extent to which differences between people reflect choice, chance, or genetic inheritance!

To what extent can we exercise choice in adjusting to this world? If we can freely choose, can our choices improve our health, fitness, and length of life?

BIOLOGICAL DETERMINISM (THE NATURE POSITION)

behavioral genetics   the discipline that studies the relative effects of heredity and environment on behavior and ability

Behavioral genetics is casting new light on this old controversy. For example, in a seven-year study of 350 pairs of monozygotic twins who were reared apart, Tellegen and Lykken of the University of Michigan (1988) found that key *personality traits* were mostly inherited! Leadership and obedience to authority are both considered to be traits important to success, and, if found in one twin, are largely shared by the other. A zest for life, so important in mental health, was also found to be highly shared. On the down side, identical twins at risk were also likely to share mutual alienation, risk-seeking tendencies, and a general vulnerability to stress.

Plomin (1990) reported that "activity level, emotional reactivity (neuroticism) and sociability-shyness *(extroversion)* have accumulated the best evidence for significant genetic influence" (p. 185). Altruism and aggression, empathy and nurturance, as well as assertiveness seem the more strongly influenced by heredity (Rushton et al., 1986). Even social traits such as obedience to authority and love of tradition have been found to be under genetic influence (Martin et al., 1990). In chapter 4, "Stress and Health," we learned how important it is to perceive life events as controllable and how our general sense of well-being is critical to our secondary assessment of the threat posed by any stressor. Both of these hardy personality traits appear to be strongly influenced by our genes (Plomin and Rende, 1991). In fact, the common environment shared by twins raised together contributes very little to their personality as reported by Bouchard and McGue (1990). Other events, such as birth order, gender differences, accidents, and illnesses, do influence personality (Plomin, 1989). This does not mean that environment doesn't count, or that we will one day find a single gene for the production of leadership or obedience, for example. It does seem, however, that many genes, working together in complex and indirect ways, and influenced by the environment, express themselves by influencing our behavior.

Personality and Physique

Many observers have come to the conclusion that our physical selves come in three **phenotypes:** the broad, heavy person; the narrow, tall person; and the person in between (Eysenck, 1973). Further, for more than 2,500 years of recorded history, physicians, poets, and philosophers have noted a **correlation,** or relationship, between body type and personality type. We expect tall, lean people to be introvertish, muscular people to be aggressive, and stout people to be sociable. Our phenotype is largely a function of our genes. Although nutrition, exercise, and our general style of life can affect our physique, such visual dimensions as bone structure, fat-cell distribution, hormone levels, and height are largely inherited. The slight connection between body build, temperament, and predisposition to certain illnesses remains fairly consistent throughout a person's lifetime and could be an indication that part of our **constitution** is determined by genes. In 1991, it was reported that "Left-Handedness [was] a Marker for Decreased Survival Fitness." By 1994 the survival differences were found to be the result of statistical errors, not genetic makeup (Coren and Halpern, 1991).

phenotype   the body type displayed by an individual

correlation   a reciprocal relationship between two measures (for example, the height of fathers and sons)

constitution   basic physical and psychological tendencies that remain fairly constant throughout a person's lifetime

---

CRITICAL THINKING ISSUE
Self-Determination

Human behavior is an expression of free will.

A rock makes a nice pet; it's beautiful, cheap, clean, and dependable. Why then do humans reject rocks as pets and prefer living organisms such as dogs? The reason is that nothing about the rock can reflect our unique human qualities; it has no warmth, no empathy, no uncertainty, no spontaneity—nothing to identify with and respond to. We train our pets to be more human—to stand up, to offer their forelimbs, even to speak. We love them most when they are most like ourselves.

As humans, we are not just victim-spectators of a process that is determined by natural law. The causes of our behavior arise from within each of us, not from blind, mindless obedience to environmental laws expressed in genetic codes. Our identity, our feelings of guilt, and our personality traits are all evidence that we can choose. In fact, we must exercise choice to stay mentally healthy. Our belief in the possibility of choice—our free will—is not an illusion but an affirmation of our unique humanness.

Human behavior is an expression of cause and effect.

A rock makes a nice pet; it's beautiful, cheap, clean, and dependable. Its behavior is predictable because it obeys natural laws. Everyone knows that, but did they always? Long before Sir Isaac Newton, people had observed that rocks fall toward the earth and that their speed increases as they approach the ground. The early observers explained this behavior of rocks by indicating that the earth was the mother of all rocks, and her children would rush to be by her side! The nearer to the breast of mother earth, the stronger would be their desire and the faster they would rush. The theory fit the facts. It was based on granting a rock free will and a purpose. The observed behavior of these rocks was goal-directed and purposeful and evidenced choice. How human!

Progress in physics was not made until we removed "purpose" and "free will" from the rocks and gave them no choice but to obey natural laws. Strides in physics were also made when we removed the earth from the center of the universe and placed it on the fringe of a minor solar system.

Psychology today still grants free will and purpose to people and places them at the center of their discipline. If we apply the lessons of physics to the study of human adjustment, we will abandon the notion of free will and choice as an explanation of behavior and at long last place men and women in their rightful place in the universe, as natural organisms obeying the laws of nature.

I take the position that:

Genes Influence Behavior Through Protein Synthesis

The role of genes in directing behavior is very indirect. There is no little genetic ghost within us pulling strings! Genes are simply **DNA** molecules that become the code for building the proteins that make up our sensory, motor, neural, and other cellular systems. A change or omission in the code can produce changes in the structure or performance of a system and change how we respond or are responded to by others.

---

dna deoxyribonucleic acid; the chemical substance of which genes are composed

sociobiology the study of the biological bases of social behavior. Sociobiology applies the theory of natural selection and fitness to social behavior.

genetics the biological study of heredity

homo sapiens the only living species of the genus Homo; humans

adaptation a change in structure, function, or form that makes an organism better able to survive in its environment

procreative proficiency adeptness at producing large numbers of offspring who share a common gene pool

BEHAVIORAL GENETICS

Sociobiology

Sociobiology is a discipline that is attempting to discover the extent to which our behavior is genetically determined. The existence of biological foundations for social behavior is well accepted with reference to the social insects and the social animals below humans (Hamilton, 1972). The concept meets with fierce resistance when it is applied to modern humans, however.

The field of sociobiology came to national attention in 1975 with the publication by Harvard zoologist Edward O. Wilson of the book *Sociobiology: The New Synthesis*. This fusion of **genetics** and population biology extended neo-Darwinian evolutionary theory into the study of social behavior among insect and animal societies. The last chapter applied the same general principles to our species, **Homo sapiens.** The notion that our behavior could be theoretically linked to that of Old World monkeys and apes, for instance, unleashed a fury from some elements within the social sciences.

What are the bases for believing human behavior is affected by human biology? To the biologist, adjustment is termed **adaptation.** Our physical selves represent a successful adaptation to a wide variety of environments. As humans, we are basically like all other living organisms. The kind of body we have is an indication of the kind of behavior of which we are capable. *Our capacity to adjust is thus limited.* There are sounds we cannot hear, frequencies of light we cannot see, and topical features we cannot feel. Most important, the construction of our brain sets limits and perhaps gives direction to the ways we mentally see and solve problems of everyday living. (For more on this topic, see chapter 4, "Stress and Health," and chapter 6, "The Thinking Self.")

David Barash (1977) maintains that behavior arises from the structure and function of the nervous system and is inherited. In this context behavior does not mean specific acts but rather predispositions that may be expressed in diverse and complex behavior patterns. The effect of testosterone levels on aggressive acts is one such example.

Our human body is an ancient structure, millions of years old, that has been constantly shaped by its interaction with the physical world, even as it has more recently begun to shape the world. However, the idea that our genes may give direction to our behavior is disturbing to many. Most can accept the idea that there are physical limits on their potential for behavior. However, the related idea that their bodies may partly direct their thoughts and actions is more foreign, and more frightening.

Procreative Proficiency Survival of the fittest now means **procreative proficiency**—the ability to reproduce the most of one's kind. The unit of survival has shifted from the individual to the genes that carry the code for reproducing similar individuals.

Such a shift provides an explanation of some otherwise perplexing behavior observed among all social creatures. For example, wasps sting attacking enemies at the cost of their own lives; birds risk death to warn other birds of an impending threat; and sterile soldier ants die to protect a reproductive queen. Such **altruism,** or self-sacrifice, does not make sense in terms of individual survival. Why then does it exist? Darwin had no answer.

Sociobiologists believe individuals act not only on the basis of individual fitness but also on the basis of **inclusive fitness,** which involves the genetic representations of individuals through their close relatives. **Kin selection,** and kin protection, become the keys for survival. Organisms are motivated by a tendency to protect their own genes (Dawkins, 1976). Thus, you protect yourself so you may pass on your genes through reproduction. You also protect your relatives, because they share your gene pool, and they too may pass it on. Your chance for immortality is thus enhanced, because "genes are forever" (Dawkins, 1976, p. 37). Altruism has evolved because it favors survival of one's genes (Rushton, 1991).

Wilson (1975, 1978) cites research indicating that genes establish predispositions, set emotional curbs, and direct hormonal messages that act upon such human behaviors as learning modes, mental and neuromuscular abilities, and personality traits. Differential sex roles and such specific practices as aggression and **nepotism** (showing favoritism to relatives in hiring practices and the like) are seen as examples of genetic effects on human behavior patterns.

Critics of Sociobiology

Critics of sociobiology, such as Harvard's Sociobiology Study Group, maintain that cultural evolution, individual experience, and socialization are far better vehicles for understanding human behavior. All of these depend on our capacity to learn. In this view, we learn the roles we are to play, the rules that shape these roles, and the ways we are expected to relate to the world and to each other. Sociobiology is seen as offering simple explanations for behaviors that are quite complex. For example, altruism may have its roots in **empathy,** the ability to put oneself in the place of another (Batson and Shaw, 1991); **Negative State Relief,** a simple desire to reduce the pain of seeing someone in distress (Cialdini, 1993); **egoism,** the expectation of gain; negative state relief (Cialdini, 1993); or all of that and more. The altruistic behavior of the Eskimo elders can be seen as having cultural roots. Perhaps there are no genetic differences between the Eski-

altruism   performance of acts intended to help another. Such acts may stem from emotional distress or intellectual understanding of another's needs, or a desire to protect one's gene pool

inclusive fitness   the genetic representation of the individual through surviving relatives; emphasis is on survival of the gene pool rather than the gene-bearing individual

kin selection   the tendency to protect most those persons with whom one shares the most

nepotism   the practice of favoring relatives, as by appointing them to office regardless of their qualifications

empathy   the condition of feeling someone else's emotion

negative state relief   the conscious or unconscious removal of pessimistic and self-blaming views of one's experiences

egoism   self-centered focus

Altruism Among the Eskimos

During the harsh winters, Eskimo family groups must move constantly in order to survive. Aged grandparents of some groups willingly stay behind on ice floes when it becomes apparent they might slow down the group on the long and dangerous journey because of their infirmities. They die so that their families might live. According to sociobiologists, this is a clear case of sociobiological evolution. The altruistic gesture increases the inclusive fitness of those who die. Family groups with fewer altruistic genes, slowed down by their old members, may not live to reproduce. (Read further for an alternate explanation of why an ancient Eskimo may choose self-sacrifice.)

mo families, in which case the gift of the grandparents is adaptive. It may well be offered because offering it is the thing to do, a learned cultural trait. The honor and glory of giving such gifts to loved ones may be taught from childhood, to be acted on in old age. The Harvard Sociobiology Study Group, and most psychologists, believe that to try to reduce the richness of human behavior to an elaboration of a limited set of biologically determined dispositions is absurd and dangerous (see chapter 7 for more about socialization).

Critical Review 1

1. The study of the relative contributions of heredity and environment to human behavior and ability is called behavioral genetics. T F

2. Bouchard and McGue found that the identical environment of identical twins reared together contributed greatly to their personalities. T F

3. Although activity level and emotional reactivity may be strongly influenced by genetics, such social attitudes as empathy and shyness are predominately the result of deliberate child-raising practices. T F

4. Try to use kin selection to explain how homosexuality within human groups can persist over time even though copulation between members of the same sex will produce no offspring.

5. Explain the differences between *inclusive fitness* and *the survival of the fittest.*

SEXUAL DETERMINISM

David Barash (1977) flatly states that "sociobiology relies heavily upon the biology of male-female differences and upon the adaptive behavioral differences that have evolved accordingly. Ironically, Mother Nature appears to be a sexist" (p. 283). Now read "Angelica-Angelo" below.

If you can imagine such an experience, how would you complete this tale of sexual transformation—first woman, then man? Would you project future happiness and success for this new man, or a life of confusion, frustration, and despair? Would your projections differ if the change was from male to female?

Angelica-Angelo

Imagine yourself to be a beautiful, slim, brown-eyed little girl. You live in a remote village in Santo Domingo and you are dreaming of your fifteenth birthday, your Quince! This magic day, still a few years away, marks the end of childhood and the beginning of young womanhood, and you have been preparing for it since the moment of birth when your parents knew they had been graced with a little girl.

You visualize yourself in a lovely white gown, a symbol of the virtue and purity that has been so carefully taught to you by your grandmothers and protected by your father and brothers. All eyes are upon you as you glide across the floor in the arms of your proud father. You shyly catch the eye of a handsome . . .

Now imagine that you enter puberty and your dreams are shattered as your slim, little-girl body takes on its adult proportions. Instead of the beautiful breasts, narrow waist, and rounded hips of your dreams, you watch in horror as your body becomes muscular, your shoulders widen, and your hips and waist form into a straight line. Dreams of feminine romance and the fulfillment of motherhood vanish as you observe your genitals change from those of a female to those of a male.

Angelica-Angelo is a fictitious name, but not a fictional character. Angelo and at least sixteen others like him live in Santo Domingo. A local Spanish term, *penis-at-twelve,* describes the essence of their shared genetic disorder. Angelo was conceived a male, with the XY male chromosome, but the hormones necessary for the formation of male genitals were not present when he was a six-week-old developing fetus (a critical period of development, as you will see later). At birth, he looked like a girl. He was christened Angelica and raised as a girl. At puberty, male hormones rushed through his body and initiated the completion of his sexual self as directed by his original genetic code.

Julianne Imperato-McGinley (1980) wrote about eight children from the United States with the same genetic disorder. Now, as young adults, these North Americans all consider themselves to be women, even though they must receive injections to maintain their feminine forms.

In the United States there is a greater opportunity for medical intervention in such cases. The eight Americans were given no chance to allow their genitals to become masculinized at puberty. They were all castrated shortly after birth, and a functional vagina was constructed for each of them. In this way, **coitus** and orgasm, if not conception and biological motherhood, were retained as possibilities. In Santo Domingo, nature was allowed to run its course.

coitus   sexual intercourse

Apparently, Mother Nature knows best. Five of the eight U.S. women are reported to have serious psychological problems, while all of the seventeen men from Santo Domingo made a relatively smooth transition from the female to the male sexual identity and role. None of them needs injections to maintain his new status.

Gender Identity

Sex refers to the biologically based categories of female and male. **Gender,** in contrast, *refers to the culturally constructed distinctions between femininity and masculinity.* **Gender identity** *is the sense of being female or male,* which most children acquire by the time they are three years old. **Gender role** *is a set of expectations that prescribe how females and males should think, act, and feel.*

Although socialized as females, the Santo Domingo youths readily adopted the culturally accepted male gender role. Their gender identity is now male as well. Their occupational aspirations, sexual orientation, and sexual activity are those of the traditional Hispanic male. As the sociobiologists suggest, perhaps their male genes helped direct them in overcoming their earlier gender training. Perhaps the less restricted lifestyle of the Hispanic male meant a new threshold of opportunity for these former girls, which they readily accepted. Their local culture was supportive, with several parents proud that their daughter was, in reality, their son.

Although unaware of their sixth-week fetal mishap, the Americans may have experienced difficulties because of the knowledge of their castration and the adjustments during puberty. Also, their inability to bear children and their need for constant injections to keep them physically feminine may also be psychologically stressful. Another possibility is that their original genetic and hormonal codes created in each of them a male brain (see page 155), which predisposes them to male, rather than female, imagery, temperament, and activity.

sex   a biological motive, not essential for individual survival. The cerebral cortex plays a major role in human sexual development.

gender   one of three classes: masculine, feminine, or neuter. In French, there are only two classes; masculine and feminine

gender identity   a person's sense of being male or female

gender role   the patterns of behavior expected, regulated, and reinforced based on gender

Carol and Robert are best friends. Best friends are lifesavers in junior high. "Jack and Jill" is what their other friends call them. "Jack" is Carol Stevens, a husky, square-built girl of thirteen who is head and broad shoulders above her classmates. "Jill" is

Bob Carmichael, a slightly built, fine-featured young man of fourteen, without the shadow of a chin whisker.

Jack and Jill are friends in mutual suffering and self-defense. Each knows how bad it feels—especially in junior high—to display physical traits that everyone "knows" belong to the opposite sex.

Sex-Linked Differences in Human Behavior

Sexuality can be viewed as a way of seeing ourselves and a way of relating to others. These change as we progress through our life cycle. The single most salient factor in shaping the nature of our interpersonal relations is our sex. Grady (1977) found that sex is a social label associated with widespread ideas of sex differences (see **attribution theory,** page 162) Maccoby (1990) holds that there *are few natural male or female differences in behavior.* Not all agree.

It is certain that females, and not males, **menstruate, gestate,** and **lactate.** It is equally certain that males, and not females, **impregnate.** In line with these adaptive functions, aggressive behavior seems to be a more intense and stable trait for males from birth (Moyer, 1974). Aggression contributes to inclusive fitness; it protects genetic relatives and ensures that the stronger male will reproduce (Loehlin, 1992). **Nurturing** behavior is found to be more stable among females (Kagan and Moss, 1962). These sex differences, while real, have been exaggerated (Benbow, 1992). For example, the natural superiority of women in verbal ability, accepted as biological in 1974, has now virtually disappeared (Maccoby, 1987), and male mathematical superiority, based on their being better able to rotate objects in mental space, is now found only among gifted males compared to gifted females (Benbow, 1992).

What is certain and constant is that there are wide variations in aggression, nurturance, and verbal and mathematical ability *within each sex,* and at present it is impossible to attribute the small, real differences between each sex that are observed to the exclusive influence of biology, socialization, or choice.

The Brain, Hormones, and Sexual Differentiation

The role of hormones and sex-linked behavior is under intensive study. John Money and Anke Ehrhardt (1972) reported the effect of **androgens** (a class of male hormones) on the behavior of females. In the 1940s several women were given shots of an androgen to help prevent miscarriage. Some gave birth to girls with malformed genitals. These organs were surgically corrected, and the androgenized girls were raised from birth as females. Their behavior as children was tomboyish—they were much more energetic and competitive than a matched set of normal girls. When young, they were less interested in dolls and infants; when adolescent, they were less interested in romance and dating. Today, only two-thirds want to have children, and the majority value a career above marriage and family. Such behavior is, at present, atypical among American girls and suggests to some a link between prenatal hormones and gender differences.

A congenital defect that exaggerates the hormone output from the adrenal glands—**congenital adrenal hyperplasia (CAH)**—produces similar effects when it is present in a female (XX) embryo. Such children also are more tomboyish and aggressive; they prefer masculine toys, playing with cars (rather than dolls) at about the same rate as do boys (Kimura, 1992). CAH girls also outper-

attribution theory   a body of theory that seeks to explain how the ordinary person attempts to make sense of events that occur within and about him.

menstruate   a discharge of the periodic flow of blood from the uterus through the genital tract.

gestate   carry in the uterus during pregnancy

lactate   give milk; suckle young

impregnate   to make pregnant, to fertilize a viable ovum by introducing sperm cells

nurture   feed; cherish

androgens   male sex hormones that can give rise to masculine characteristics

congenital adrenal hyperplasia (CAH)   a birth disorder characterized by an abnormal increase in the number of adrenal tissue cells

form typical girls on the cognitive tasks measuring spatial ability, such as the mental rotation task!

In like manner, Reinisch and Sanders (1992) reported that males who were exposed to high levels of the female hormone estrogen before birth scored lower on tasks of spatial ability when tested between the ages of nine and twenty-one. Can prenatal hormones affect gender differences?

In the first six weeks after conception, the sex organs of all embryos are identical; they have the capacity to develop either way, regardless of the make-up of the sex chromosomes (Gorski, 1979). The embryonic sexual glands begin to develop into testicles at six weeks *if instructed to do so by the male (XY) chromosome*. In females, at about twelve weeks, the female (XX) chromosomes order the gonads to take the form of ovaries. After the development of either testicles or ovaries, the powerful gonadotrophic hormones take over and control the development of the external sex organs. A surplus of androgen causes the external structure to form a penis. Without this surplus, the same structure forms into a clitoris. Another fetal structure, the labioscrotal swelling, either remains open to form the vaginal opening and labia or, under the influence of androgens, fuses in males to form the scrotum (see Figure 5–1).

Under normal conditions, an inhibiting agent excreted by the testes or ovaries will cause the unused, opposite-sex structures present in the fetus to wither away. We are thus born with internal and external sex organs that correspond to our genetic sex. Later, at puberty, further hormone secretions control the appropriate secondary sexual characteristics such as facial hair and a deeper voice in males and enlarged breasts and wider hips in females.

In the first weeks after conception, the brains of males and females are thought to be identical. If the brain receives a surplus of androgen from the newly forming testes in a male, a region of one brain center, the hypothalamus, will be altered and a male brain will develop (Reinisch, 1981). This brain directs the adrenal glands and the testes to produce larger amounts of the hormones epinephrine and testosterone in the male. These hormones in turn produce a higher energy output and a greater tendency to act on the environment to force changes. You will remember that a more active, more competitive nature has been ascribed to males. The behavior aroused by female hormones (estrogens) seems to involve tendencies toward material responses (Money and Ehrhardt, 1972). Males are typically more sexually active than females. This difference is under the influence of androgens (Reichlin, 1971). The sexual activity levels of females are also regulated by androgens. This is possible because the adrenal glands and the ovaries produce small amounts of the male hormones. Similarly, the testes produce small amounts of the female hormone. Thus, in all of us, male and female traits are under at least partial control of estrogens (feminizing hormones) and androgens (masculinizing hormones), as well as progesterone (pregnancy hormones). Our gender identity and role appear to be in part regulated by the amount of these three hormone groups present within our systems from day to day, as well as at critical periods in the development of our physical selves.

Sex Hormones Versus Environmental Learning

The masculine behavior of the androgenized girls appears to be due to changes in their fetal brains plus the constant, brain-regulated production of higher levels of androgens as their bodies grew and changed. These powerful physical effects

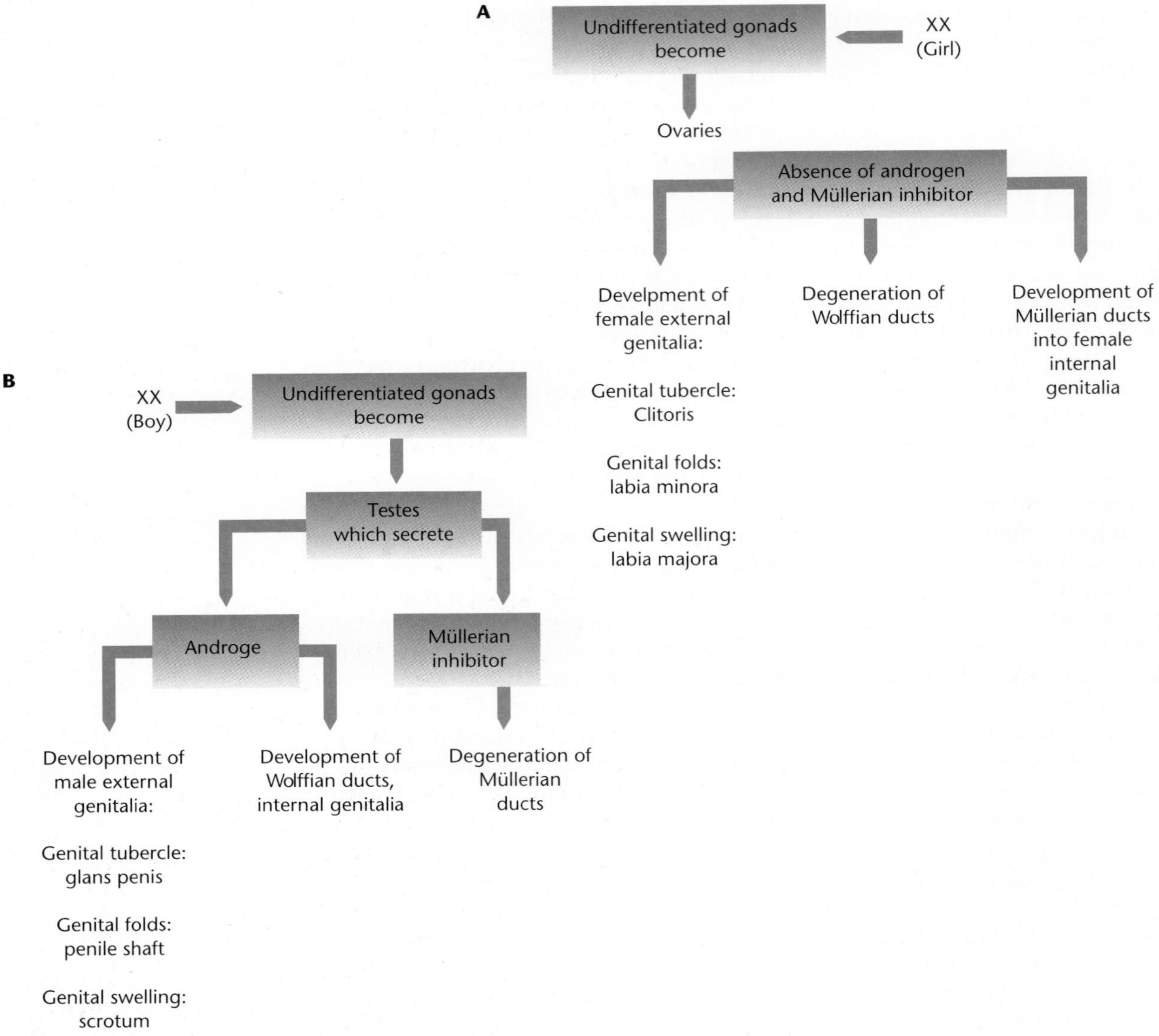

A

Undifferentiated gonads become ← XX (Girl)

↓

Ovaries

Absence of androgen and Müllerian inhibitor

Develoment of female external genitalia:

Genital tubercle: Clitoris

Genital folds: labia minora

Genital swelling: labia majora

Degeneration of Wolffian ducts

Development of Müllerian ducts into female internal genitalia

B

XX (Boy) → Undifferentiated gonads become

↓

Testes which secrete

Androge

Müllerian inhibitor

Development of male external genitalia:

Genital tubercle: glans penis

Genital folds: penile shaft

Genital swelling: scrotum

Development of Wolffian ducts, internal genitalia

Degeneration of Müllerian ducts

FIGURE 5–1

Pathways for differentiation of the (A) female genital system and (B) male genital system.

seem to have more than offset the effects of social learning about appropriate gender roles (see chapter 8, "The Social Self," for more about socialization).

A dramatic example of social versus physical effects on gender differences is unfolding at present. In 1972, Money and Ehrhardt reported the case of an infant boy whose genitals were mutilated by accident. It would have been impossible for him to function as a normal male, so surgery was performed and the child was raised as a girl. At four the child behaved like a typical girl. At the same time, her identical twin brother was behaving like a typical boy! Upbringing appeared more powerful than genetics in shaping gender identity and gender role. In 1982, however, Diamond reported that by thirteen years of age, the child had developed a manly gait, wanted to become an automobile mechanic, and was not happy with her female role. Her peers began calling her "cave woman." By sixteen she was under the care of a psychiatrist, trying to adjust to life as a female.

Conflict between the physical self and social learning can arise for all of us. We inherit a physical structure that predisposes us to precocious sexual activity. At puberty, pleasure centers in the brain are sensitized by sex hormones. This makes us more receptive to erotic stimuli—visual stimuli in males, tactile stimuli in females (Wolman and Money, 1980). Once sensitized, these centers are stimulated by androgens from the adrenal as well as from the sexual glands. (This is thought to be the reason female humans are sexually receptive throughout their menstrual cycle, rather than only during estrus, the fertile period, as is the general case among mammals.) Social rules, especially traditionally held **gender stereotypes** are embedded in our culture and society and influence our sexual activity. It can be comforting to know what is expected of us in terms of sexual values, attitudes, and actions. On the other hand, it can be distressing to find ourselves unable or unwilling to conform to these expectations. These stereotypes perpetuate a society that values males more than females (Bem, 1993). We may or may not value males more; after all, we do teach them a masculine stereotype that shortens their lives. In addition to aggression, other actions that validate this spurious masculinity include engaging in risky behaviors such as smoking, premarital sex, excessive alcohol and drug consumption, and delinquent acts. Although not yet a part of the dominant feminine stereotype, such "You've come a long way, baby" validations as heavy smoking, alcohol consumption, narcotic addiction, and exposure to STDs can not only reduce a female's chances for health and long life, but also place her unborn children at risk. (See chapter 9, on "Intimacy and Sexuality," for more about gender expectations, and chapter 4, "Stress and Health," for health-threatening lifestyles.)

gender stereotype   typical beliefs of society relating to the nature of males and females

Critical Review 2

1. All of the young men from Santo Domingo made a relatively smooth transition from their female to male gender identity and role. T F

2. While sex refers to the biologically based categories of female and male, gender *refers to the culturally constructed distinctions between femininity and masculinity.* T F

3. The biologically caused differences between males and females are many, large, and underestimated. T F

4. Support your belief that the documented differences in male-female performances are primarily the result of nature (genes and hormones, etc.), nurture (family pressures, cultural ideals, etc.), or choice (individual decisions, freely made).

5. Do you believe that the androgenized girls will maintain their masculine views as they continue to develop throughout their life span? Why or why not?

ENVIRONMENTAL DETERMINISM: (THE NURTURE POSITION)

The association of body type and behavior has had its greatest impact on theories of childhood development. Frances Ilg and Louise Bates Ames (1961) of the famed Gesell Institute of infant care believe that babies act as they do largely because of their phenotypes and that parents should not try to make them over.

Attribution

Not all psychologists share Ilg and Ames's extreme biological point of view. Most firmly believe that differences between people are likely to be the result of the impact on our psyche of events in our personal history, rather than the maturation and unfolding of our genetic endowment. We will now take the kindergarten view of adjustment. This equally radical view holds that if children (kinders) are allowed to grow freely in fertile soil (gartens) they will all blossom into wonderfully positive and competent adults. In this view the seeds are constant; the soil is the variable to be understood and cultivated.

The Looking-Glass Self

looking-glass self   the socially constructed self; self-image based on the perceived reactions of others

As early as 1905 Charles Horton Cooley (1864–1929) argued that the human mind is actually a product of a person's interaction with the world. Cooley believed that our sense of self is a mirror reflection of how we think others judge the way we look and act. This **looking-glass self** is made up of (1) what we think others see in us, (2) how we think others react to what they see, and (3) how we evaluate ourselves in response to these perceived reactions from others.

Stereotypes and Self-Image

stereotype   a fixed idea of the nature of members of a group

What sort of person do you see when you look in the mirror? How is such a person expected to act? Very clear and consistent **stereotypes** exist in the minds of most people concerning phenotypes and expected behavior. These stereotypes develop early and are held to be true for individuals of different races, classes, and cultures (Montemayor, 1978). For example, we all "know" that fat people eat and drink more; muscular people are the best soldiers; thin people smoke more and are nervous; females are soft and delicate; and males are strong and silent. You may see yourself, and be seen by others, as being fat and jolly precisely because everyone "knows" all fat people are jolly.

Stereotyping also changes how we act toward other people. Bandura and Walters (1963) attribute much of our personalities to the effects of social learning. People positively reinforce our behavior *when we act as we are expected to act.* If you are thin, being shy is expected and rewarded. If you are male and muscular, being sensitive is unexpected and less likely to be rewarded. By such con-

---

Mirror, Mirror on the Wall . . .

Look at yourself in a full-length mirror and describe your reflection.

- When I view my face I see
- I see my body as
- My best physical attribute is

- The part of my physical self I hate the most is
- People who look as I look are expected to be
- People who look as I look are expected to act
- I believe the stereotypes about the way I look are

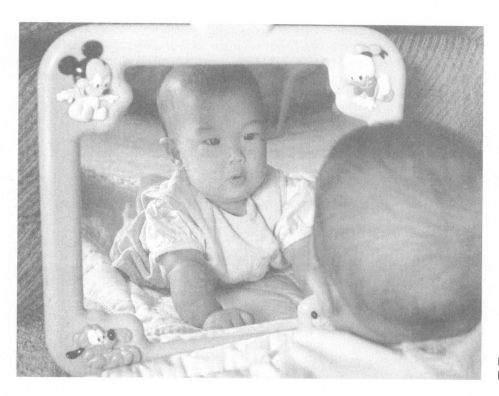

How is a person who looks like I look expected to act?

tinuous shaping, our personalities may come to mirror our body types. In other words, perception of sex and body type, not the phenotype itself, may be what is correlated with observed behavior patterns.

The "Bodily Me"

We come to see ourselves as we think others see us. Zastro (1979) believes that our sense of identity is the key element of our personality. A central part of this sense of identity is achieved through recognition and exploration of our physical selves, our bodies: "The child, the adolescent, the adult—each observes his own body and the bodies of others in order to compare and evaluate himself" (Diamond, 1957). **Gender-role stereotypes** *are broad categories that reflect our impressions and beliefs about females and males.* Stereotyping is pervasive across all cultures, however, male and female stereotypes are more similar in developed countries, which can produce a major adjustment problem for immigrants from the developing world (Williams and Best, 1989).

Although children make bodily-based inferences about each others' activities, emotions, and even future occupations (Ross and Martin, 1993), the onset of puberty produces rapid changes in height, weight, musculature, sex organs, and voice and makes adolescence the time of the bodily me—and thee. People view us differently. We become obsessed with what others think of us and spend hours in front of a mirror (the looking-glass self). We must revise our body image in recognition and acceptance of these changed perceptions and reactions.

Pregnancy alters the self-image of the young woman, and so often does male-pattern baldness in the young man. Both require acceptance if self-esteem is to be maintained. The passing years demand that we adjust our idea of a

gender-role stereotypes typical beliefs of society pertaining to patterns of behavior that are expected, regulated, and reinforced based only on gender

healthy body to the realities of advancing age. The despair of the sixty-year-old who clings to a twenty-year-old body image is real, and ridiculous. Gordon W. Allport (1960) believes that the **bodily me** is made up of the many sensations that exist within us and that this "bodily sense remains a lifelong anchor for our self-awareness" (p. 42).

bodily me one's perception of one's physical self

Self-Fulfilling Prophecy

Finally, our perception of other people's reactions to our physical attributes, or lack of them, can influence our subsequent behavior, thus creating a self-fulfilling prophecy. For example, the muscular male, who is expected to be an athlete, or the slender female, who is expected to be a model, find general support for their efforts in these directions and may thrive in spite of perhaps only ordinary talents. Such persons do well precisely because others think well of them. (For more information on this topic, see chapter 3, "Self-esteem.")

The Eye of the Beholder

Sociobiology suggests that radiant health, vigor, and *symmetrical features* are standards of universal beauty. Most authorities, however, maintain that there is no universal standard for physical attractiveness. Each age and every culture defines itself by redefining beauty. For example, being tall is often valued (Feldman, 1971). Kagan (1966) reported a height anxiety developing in children as early as the third grade. Individuals classified as dwarfs or midgets are so stigmatized that they tend to associate primarily with each other (Wineberg, 1968).

Another study found that in selecting prospective dates and/or mates, males consistently ranked physical attractiveness higher than did females. There seems to be some empirical support for the commonly held belief that it is more important for a woman to be good-looking than it is for a man (Bersheid, Walster, and Bohrnstedt, 1973). Being attractive, however, may not ensure that you will attract the person you prefer. Extroverts tend to prefer mates who are larger in the chest, breast, and buttocks than the ideal; introverts do not. When we feel good about ourselves, we tend to be attracted to a more physically imposing mate. When we feel insecure about ourselves, the physically unattractive mate actually makes us more sexually aroused (Kielser and Baral, 1970). Early-maturing girls become too attractive too soon and seem to incur such ambivalent responses from teachers as well as from classmates that their attitudes toward school and learning suffer (Davis, 1977).

The Matching Hypothesis

We can't all be handsome or beautiful. Fortunately, when we select friends, dates, and mates, we realistically take into consideration our own perceived level of attractiveness. The **matching hypothesis** suggests that people of similar levels of physical attractiveness gravitate toward each other (Riedal and McKillip, 1979).

matching hypothesis the idea that persons of approximately equal physical beauty are attracted to one another

Being perceived as attractive depends on more than height, color, or breast size. The body image we project to others includes physical features, voice patterns, dress, grooming, and impressions of health and energy. We are seldom seen as a still life, posed against an appropriate backdrop. We are observed in motion, acting within a situation. The way we move and communicate also creates first impressions, as does the role we play. A man was introduced to one college class as a student, to another as a senior lecturer, and to a third as a professor. Each class gave written estimates of his height. As he grew in academic status, he also grew in estimated physical stature (Wilson, 1978). Competence and intelligence, warmth and sincerity, and similar nonphysical dimensions of self become increasingly important as we come to know each other.

Stereotypes and Stigmas

Evaluation by physique is seen by many psychologists as just another form of **prejudice.** As you know, stereotypes are attitudes held toward a whole group of people. They may be positive or negative. Some are so negative that they are termed **stigmas** and result in their victims' being avoided or unnaturally treated. The physically disabled are at times stigmatized, and such prejudice can become an important factor in the development of emotional disturbances among them. It is also possible to stigmatize yourself. Loss of control or of functioning of a person's bowel, bladder, or sexual organs is often accompanied by deep shame and a loss of self-confidence. If such a disability is accepted by those who are important to the afflicted individual, however, that disabled person is not more likely than others to be maladjusted.

> **prejudice**   an unreasonable or hostile attitude based on negative attributions
>
> **stigma**   a mark of disgrace or reproach

Not all stereotypes are untrue, but all are unjust. Rosenthal (1970) found criminals as a group to be lower in IQ, more muscular, and more frequently brain damaged as measured by the electroencephalograph. But to respond to any former prison inmate as if he or she were an irrational, brutish idiot is unwarranted, because a given individual may fall *anywhere within the range used to compute the average.* In addition, your stereotyped response just might produce the behavior you fear.

Discrimination   Negative behavior that reflects stereotypical thinking about the physical self is all too frequently observed in America. Such unwarranted behavior is termed **discrimination** and extracts an enormous cost in lost performance and unfulfilled lives. Simply being left-handed used to be considered a

> **discrimination**   the showing of partiality or prejudice; negative distinctions in treatment

People of equal attractiveness seem attracted to each other.

physical disability of such severity that children were beaten or bound to force them to become normal—that is, right-handed.[1]

The Brain and Social Labels   We label people because we are verbal, conceptual animals. After experiencing an object (for example, a knife) in its many forms, we develop a mental image (concept) of a knife. Our culture usually provides us with a word or phrase to identify the concepts we form. From then on, we respond to the concept "knife," rather than constructing a novel response for each knife with which we come in contact. It is a matter of economy. We grant to that conceptual knife the characteristics or traits that were associated with the knives we have experienced in our past. A knife is sharp, hard, pointed, and so on. Any object that we perceive as "knife" we expect to be sharp, and we react to it accordingly. Life is more easily managed when we can toss people, too, into labeled boxes when deciding whom to approach or avoid. Concepts (stereotypes) can also be *vicariously* learned. We do not have to be cut to know that a knife is sharp. In the same way, we can "know" that skinny people are nervous or that females are passive.

Why We Make Attributions

Attribution theory is the formal body of information pertaining to the use of inferences and implied causality under conditions of minimal information. This application of stereotyped thinking, although at times very damaging, may simply reflect the most basic structure of human information processing (Bodenhausen, 1988).

Fritz Heider (1958) holds that we use attributions so as to understand and control the world we live in. It is not enough that we observe the behavior of ourselves or others. We need to figure out why the behavior occurs. We especially need to know if something was done because of force or because of choice. For example, your friend does not show up for a date. Was this action **dispositional**—that is, caused by internal, personality factors? Or was it **situational**—that is, due to circumstances beyond the friend's control? Your feelings and reactions will depend on your answer to this question. Kelly and Michel (1980) reviewed current studies of this **locus of control** question and concluded that we test others and ourselves in three ways before making a decision.

The first test involves **consistency.** Does the fact being judged display a stable trait? Does your friend regularly miss dates? The second test involves **consensus.** Is the trait in conformity with the norm? In your crowd, is it common not to show up for dates? The third test involves **distinctiveness.** Is this a global trait? Does your friend only miss dates, or are classes, tests, and appointments also missed? Table 5–1 gives the most likely attributions for three different sets of answers to these questions.

The table indicates that the first set of answers adds up to a situational attribution—your friend was just following tradition. The second attribution is dispositional, because missing the date is seen as constant, but it violates the social norm. The third attribution is situational and unique. Something must have come up unexpectedly.

Another central factor in making attributions is what Kelly (1980) terms the **discounting principle.** We tend to discount, or give less importance to, one fac-

attribution theory   the formal body of information pertaining to the use of inferences and implied causality under conditions of minimal information

dispositional   stemming from stable personality traits

situational   based on the assessment that environmental forces caused the observed behavior to occur

locus of control   responsibility for success or failure; may be seen to reside within or outside the self

consistency   in attribution theory, the degree to which a person is seen to act similarly under similar conditions

consensus   in attribution theory, the degree to which the behavior in question is shared by others

distinctiveness   in attribution theory, the degree to which actions are peculiar to a given set of circumstances

discounting principle   a principle that states that people tend to have less confidence in an explanation for an action if other plausible explanations exist

1. The term *sinister* is from the Latin *sinisteri*, or left-handed.

INFORMATION			ATTRIBUTION
Consistency*	Consensus*	Distinctiveness*	
1. High—always misses dates	High—everyone misses dates	High—doesn't miss other appointments	(External) SITUATIONAL
2. High–always misses dates	Low—few miss dates	Low—misses other appointments	(Internal) DISPOSITIONAL
3. Low—seldom misses dates	Low—few miss dates	High doesn't miss other appointments	(External) SITUATIONAL

*In practice, we do not give equal *intensity* to each of these factors. Therefore, we do not simply average the answers in making our decision.

TABLE 5–1
Why Did Your Friend Stand You Up?

tor if other likely factors are present. For example, you would discount the possibility that your friend had deliberately missed the date if you remembered that the time and place had not been firmly agreed upon in advance.

An attribution is a perception and may not always be fair, impartial, or just. Perception is basically self-serving. Consider the following four statements:

1. There is a pervasive tendency for us to attribute our actions to situational requirements if our behavior is unacceptable.

2. There is a similar tendency for us to attribute the same unacceptable behavior to a stable personal disposition when we see someone else doing it.

3. If we catch ourselves doing something praiseworthy, we attribute it to the positive values we hold and the intelligent strategies we use.

4. If we observe others doing something exceptional, we tend to attribute their action to the demands of the situation (Jones and Nisbett, 1972).

In short, we tend to make a **fundamental attribution error,** to believe our bad behavior is situationally determined and our good behavior is dispositionally determined (Jones, 1990). We hold just the reverse to be true for others. Such distortions do much to enhance and preserve our self-esteem. At times they produce a double victim. We often blame welfare recipients for their failure to have a job, for example. The situational factors that lead to poverty and joblessness are complicated, and the more simple act of blaming the victim for his or her misfortune helps us to maintain our belief that we live in a just world, where bad things only happen to bad people (Frazier, 1990).

fundamental attribution error the systematic mistake of attributing good acts we do to character traits, and bad acts we do to environmental factors—and doing just the opposite to others

Attribution Theory and Physical Attractiveness

We have spent a great deal of time discussing attribution in a chapter on physical influences. We have done so because it is on the basis of physical appearance that we first judge others and are judged by them. Physical appearance is more important than similarity or physical nearness in determining interpersonal attraction (Jackson, 1992). Each year 100,000 American women undergo surgery to increase the size of their breasts, and millions follow dangerous diets to conform to cultural demands for thinness (Wolf, 1991). Looking good, in a new evolutionary hypothesis (Angier, 1994a) increases the probability of being chosen for a mate because symmetrical beauty indicates a state of health, a vigor of the immune system, and an ability of the genes to withstand the assaults of the environment.

College students with the most symmetrical faces were considered the most appealing by fellow college students, and, when compared to asymmetrical classmates, lost their virginity earlier and had a greater number of sexual partners (Thornhill, in Angier, 1994b). Looking good and being good are linked in our minds; thus, we attribute to the beautiful person other traits we consider good. We take for granted that the beautiful person is intelligent, successful, competent, and pleasant, for example (see chapter 9, on intimacy, for the roles played by similarity and propinquity in romantic love.)

Even among the mentally ill, the beautiful are more often diagnosed as being less disturbed and are given a better prognosis with more personal suggestions for improvement (Cash et al., 1977). If physically unattractive, such patients are more likely to be placed on drug therapy. If attractive, greater opportunity for personal counseling is offered.

For an absolutely chilling account of the disastrous effect of the negative attributions connected with being mislabeled schizophrenic (a severe mental disorder now thought to have both biological and environmental roots), read "On Being Sane in Insane Places" by D. L. Rosenhan (see "suggested readings," at the end of this chapter.) "Once a person is designated abnormal, all of his other behaviors and characteristics are colored by that label . . . [and people look upon him with an attitude that is] . . . characterized by fear, hostility, aloofness, suspicion, and dread" (Rosenhan, 1973, p. 262). Incidentally, if a counselor is female, clients will be more likely to perceive her as being effective if she is physically attractive (Lewis and Walsh, 1978).

On the other hand, being physically attractive can be a handicap at times. If you are found guilty of using your physical assets to cheat an innocent victim, your exceptional beauty will likely earn you a more severe sentence. Similarly, if you act immorally, you will be judged more harshly if you are attractive. A beautiful woman who has intercourse on a first date is more likely to be seen as immoral than a homely woman who acts in the same way.

Attractive people are often seen as vain and egotistical (Dermer and Thiel, 1975). This negative attribution, plus the tendency of plain people to bypass attractive people and instead seek out equally plain partners, makes it more difficult for beautiful people to develop relationships. Finally, the discounting principle, mentioned earlier, works against the peace of mind of attractive individuals. Good-looking people, like wealthy, successful, or socially prominent people, can never be sure why others are attracted to them: "Am I loved for myself, or is it my body (or wealth, or position, or fame, or the like)?" There is always a plausible reason for attractive people to discount attention and affection when it comes their way. At least one counseling couple, Jerry Lipkin and Bliss Kalet, stand ready to help such unfortunates. They run a "stress and trauma clinic" open only to exceptionally attractive people. They report that such people "often suffer guilt and anxiety syndromes related to their being better looking than anybody else and they need to get together and talk about it" (Maeder, 1983, p. 2A).

Gary seems to have everything going for him. Tall and handsome, intelligent and well educated, he is considered a "sure bet" for success. But another six months have passed, and again Gary has been passed over for promotion.

It isn't his job performance. That is excellent. The problem is that Gary is too good-looking! His movie-star profile and exquisite taste in clothing have produced envy among his co-workers and in his immediate superior.

Gary feels confused and excluded. Higher-level managers are confused as well. "Gary certainly makes a great first impression. It's a shame his evaluations are so ordinary. Well, I guess nobody has everything."

You can see that attribution theory is revealing, but attribution research is limited by the fact that it is largely confined to first encounters, where first impressions can be managed and manipulated.

"I am me, the me I am right now." This is the motto of a person who monitors his or her projected self constantly, and "becomes" the person the situation seems to call for (Snyder, 1980); consult Table 5–2 to test your self-monitoring tendencies). Although such constant self-monitoring is exceptional, impression management—presenting ourselves so as to shape the attributions of others—is commonplace during first encounters.

How successful is impression management? Schwibbe (1981) succeeded in manipulating information about "attractiveness." Highly attractive persons were seen as having positive qualities. The same people, differently presented, were seen as unattractive and as having negative qualities.

Women may have some difficulty managing impressions, however. Sex-typing seems more powerful than physical attractiveness in determining positive or negative attributions. Cash and Smith (1982) reported that men who on first impression were seen as attractive were evaluated as having more self-determination. They were also expected to achieve more and to suffer less anxiety and depression. However, such qualities as success, emotional stability, and internal locus of control were not projected as being significantly higher for attractive women than for their less-attractive male counterparts.

TABLE 5–2
Monitor Your Self

If you would like to test your self-monitoring tendencies, follow the instructions and then consult the scoring key.*

These statements concern personal reactions to a number of different situations. No two statements are exactly alike, so consider each statement carefully before answering. If a statement is true, or mostly true, as applied to you, circle the T. If a statement is false, or not usually true, as applied to you, circle the F

1. I find it hard to imitate the behavior of other people.   T   F
2. I guess I put on a show to impress or entertain people.   T   F
3. I would probably make a good actor.   T   F
4. I sometimes appear to others to be experiencing deeper emotions than I actually am.   T   F
5. In a group of people I am rarely the center of attention.   T   F
6. In different situations, and with different people, I often act like very different persons.   T   F
7. I can only argue for ideas I already believe.   T   F
8. In order to get along and be liked, I tend to be what people expect me to be rather than anything else.   T   F
9. I may deceive people by being friendly when I really dislike them.   T   F
10. I'm not always the person I appear to be.   T   F

SCORING: Give yourself one point for each question 1, 5, and 7 that you answered F. Give yourself one point for each of the remaining questions that you answered T. Add up your points. If you are a good judge of yourself and scored 7 or above, you are probably a high self-monitoring individual; 3 or below, you are probably a low self-monitoring individual.

*The Self-Monitoring Scale measures how concerned we are with the impressions we make on others, and our ability to control and modify our behavior to fit the situation of the moment.

SOURCE: Mark Snyder, *Psychology Today,* March 1980.

The Job Interview   Looking attractive while interviewing for a job is a form of impression management. The results of Cash and Smith's study imply that, for a woman, looking strikingly attractive may not create a favorable impression during an interview for a responsible job, however. The stereotyped impression that women are weak and passive hurts them during job interviews. Impression management during a job interview is tricky for men as well as women. If you present yourself in formal dress, appear unresponsive, and confine yourself to the use of professional terms, you will probably receive high ratings and be considered an expert in your field. If you dress casually, are responsive, and use a good deal of jargon in your speech, you will be rated as less of an expert, but as warmer and more attractive (Dell and Patkin, 1982). The difficulty lies in the fact that in order to be hired you must appear both expert and attractive—no small feat of impression management.

Critical Review 3

1. Cooley believes that our "looking glass self" reflects the way we feel others react to our physical image. T F

2. Zastro believes that the key element of our personality is our self-identity. T F

3. Developed countries greatly exaggerate differences in gender stereotypes. T F

4. Sociobiologists hold that symmetrical features are a universal sign of beauty that signals an increased prospect for successful gene transmission. T F

5. What are the stereotypes (positive and negative) that are associated with your physical self at this time? Do you fit any of these? If so, do you think it is the result of chance, genes, or choice?

6. It has been said that there is no prejudice among front-line soldiers during battle. What are the battle conditions that force the breakdown of stereotyping? Can you think of a way to establish similar (but not dangerous) conditions that could inoculate young children against becoming prejudiced?

PERSONAL DETERMINISM (THE CHOICE POSITION)

Physical Fitness

If we see our bodily self as being healthy, well-proportioned, and active, anxiety is reduced and self-esteem is elevated. If others perceive us in the same way, they will make many positive attributes about us. The primary physical attraction between men and women is sexual in nature, and a strong, flexible, healthy body is a definite plus in terms of our sexuality. Physical fitness also enables and encourages us to join in social and work activities that allow us to be perceived as an active and involved individual—a most significant positive attribution.

Choosing Fitness

A comprehensive notion of physical fitness includes body weight, posture, musculature, and endurance. Most people consider a lean, erect, and well-proportioned body to be fit. Fitness also includes muscle strength, muscle endurance, flexibility, and perhaps most important in the long run, cardiovascular and respiratory fitness. These last dimensions of fitness are not self-evident. They are, however, associated with youth and vigor, traits our culture values highly. They are also associated with an increased capacity to cope with stress and to resist the infirmities and illnesses of old age. We all value health and vigor at any age.

Work, Study, and Physical Fitness   If your job keeps you physically active for prolonged periods of time, it might keep you fit. Few jobs do. Study is difficult but not strenuous. The same might be said of most sedentary jobs that the majority of college students train for and hold after graduation. For most Americans, the job fails us when it comes to maintaining our fitness. Our leisure activities fail us as well. In order to have a physical self that is fit, we must train. Training implies a comprehensive, intensive, and sustained fitness program. Kenneth Cooper (1986, pp. 37–38) gives the following dividends to be gained from such a program:

1. More personal energy and stamina
2. More enjoyable and active leisure time
3. Greater ability to handle domestic and job-related stress
4. Less depression, less hypochondria, less anxiety
5. Fewer physical complaints
6. Better self-image and more self-confidence
7. More restful sleep
8. Stronger bones
9. A more attractive, streamlined body
10. Better concentration
11. Greater productivity
12. Lower risk of heart disease.

Choosing to Improve Posture

Posture is the alignment of our body. Our posture is a result of genetics, early experiences, and long-established habits. Kurtz and Prestera (1976) believe that rigid muscular patterns reflect emotional blocks. We create muscle tensions to deaden impulsive wishes or to block fear and pain. These *defensive postures* become unconscious and habitual. For example, our jaws may become set to help us stop crying. For some of us, adjustment requires active intervention by trained body therapists. For most of us, awareness and continuous attention to and practice of correct posture is all that is required for a relaxed, flexible, and balanced bodily state to become habitual as we stand, sit, and walk. If you are dissatisfied with your posture, a program of daily posture checks and possible realignment is necessary until your muscle re-education becomes habitual. Periodic checks are then called for. Be sure to check yourself while you are under tension. How do you sit while studying for an exam or while writing a term paper? See chapter 4, "Stress and Health," for a discussion of the health consequences of habitual, high-tension lifestyles.

Choosing to Improve Flexibility

Flexibility is the capacity to move the joints of the body through their full range without excessive strain or pain. Age, size, sex, diet, and medical history are related to flexibility. The extent and range of our daily physical activity is most important in this regard. We must move every joint through its full range several times a day if we are to maintain maximum flexibility (Miller and Allen, 1979). Flexibility training consists of gently and slowly stretching (extending), and holding and then turning each joint. Swimming and cross-country skiing are good general exercises for flexibility because they require total bodily movement. Our rear upper leg muscles and our neck, shoulder, and back muscles tighten in response to general stress and respond well to systematic exercise. The payoff is less fatigue, less stiffness and soreness, greater mobility, and greater protection against injury.

Choosing to Improve Strength

Strength refers to the size and contractile forces of our muscle system, including its tendons, ligaments, and bony structures. Strength is a powerful label. People tend to attribute positive character traits to those who possess obvious strength and vigor. A person labeled as weak is seen as less attractive and is less trusted. To label ourselves as weak reduces our ability to cope as well.

In addition to improvement in strength, muscle work increases *definition*, or the form of specific muscle groupings. A firm, well-defined torso is considered youthful and attractive for both men and women. Women who train need not fear excessive growth in size or definition of muscles; they will remain feminine looking but more trim and with a finer-toned body. The fit, active look is now popular for both men and women in America.

Miller and Allen (1979) suggest you follow these steps in a muscle training program:

1. Consult your doctor before starting on any exercise program.

2. Select the specific muscle groups you wish to work on. Select more than one group so you may vary your training.

3. Consult an authority to determine the appropriate "lifts" to use in stimulating these muscles.

4. Use the maximum weight you can handle and do a set consisting of five or six repetitions of the lift.

5. Do three sets for each lift, varying the lifts.

6. When you are able to do three sets, and exceed the number of repetitions on the third set, increase the weight for that lift at the beginning of the next training session.

7. Train three times a week on nonconsecutive days.

8. In addition, we suggest that you avoid steroids (see Figure 5–2)

Choosing to Improve Aerobic Fitness

Aerobics refers to a variety of exercises beneficial to our oxygen- and blood-transportation systems—our heart, lungs, and blood vessels. This portion of our physical self is largely invisible to others, so few attributions are made in terms of aerobic fitness. However, our aerobic capacity is the best index of overall physical fitness.

Aerobic fitness is the ability to breathe large amounts of air, to deliver large volumes of blood, and thus be able to transport oxygen to all parts of the body.

FIGURE 5–2

What steroids do to the body

In Men
Large doses decrease the production of testosterone, causing breasts to grow, testes to shrink, and impotency.

In Women
The drugs bring out male characteristics: decreased breast size, deeper voices, the growth of facial and body hair, and an enlarged clitoris.

In Men and Women
Steroids can cause acne, and hasten the balding process in men.

In Men and Women
They promote atherosclerosis by increasing blood levels of cholesterol, thereby promoting the artery-clogging disease. They likewise decrease levels of the "Good cholesterol" the body uses to fight heart disease.

In Teenagers
Steroids can stunt growth by closing the epiphyseal growth plates, the spongy parts of the bones that allow expansion.

In Men and Women
The drugs can cause psychological effects like aggressive behavior, mood swings, and depression.

SOURCE: *The Miami Herald* (May 17, 1987), p. 20A.

If you are dissatisfied with your aerobic power, a program of strenuous exercise that involves your large muscle groups in *continuous, rhythmic contractions* will result in increased cardiovascular and respiratory efficiency. We recommend that you see a doctor prior to entering an aerobic program. Because fitness requires almost daily activity, the best exercise is one you love or can become positively addicted to. Any number of exercises will produce the desired physical effect. The *intensity, frequency,* and *duration* of the exercise are as important as the type of exercise. Naturally, a physical activity that requires less energy to perform (such as slow walking) will require more duration and greater frequency to produce practical results. A level of intensity necessary to produce measurable gains in aerobic capacity is approximately 50 percent of your maximum heart-rate change. This should be your minimum target heart rate for training. (See the Personal Action plan at the end of this chapter for a simple procedure to determine your training heart rate.)

A *frequency* of three times a week, evenly spaced, seems desirable. Duration depends on intensity, but to be effective an exercise period must consist of a minimum of five to ten minutes of warm-up exercises (including stretching and flexing), twenty minutes of sustained aerobic exercise, and five to ten minutes of cool-down exercises (walking, stretching). Cycling, jogging, cross-country skiing, swimming, and walking are well-researched methods of aerobic exercise, and group aerobic dancing is now very popular, whereas the trend is moving away from jogging. (See the "Selected Readings" section at the end of this chapter for additional information on fitness testing, exercise programs, and medical cautions.)

Doing nothing and overdoing are both unwise. Aerobic programs are now shifting from high-impact to low-impact exercises—from running and jumping to bicycling and walking, for example. There appears to be no significant health advantage in excessively vigorous exercise (Levine, 1986). Remember, you can be fit but unhealthy. Jim Fixx, author of *The Complete Book of Running*, died of a heart attack at age fifty-two while jogging on a back road in Vermont. He was fit but had diseased arteries. Vigorous exercise does give us more energy and better subjective feelings (self-attributions) but it also gives us the potential for more injuries, heart-attack risks, and for women, hormone changes that disrupt menstruation if the exercise results in an extreme loss of body fat. (However, such women may still ovulate and become pregnant.)

Exercise and Your Heart

A sedentary lifestyle, under conditions of increased stress and inappropriate diet, is considered to be a factor in the high incidence of early heart attacks in this country. Aerobic exercise boosts your lung capacity, strengthens your heart muscle, increases your blood level of HDL cholesterol (the beneficial type) and promotes less clotting in the blood—all of which are associated with less heart disease (Cooper, 1986).

Lars Ekelund (1986) used a treadmill to obtain repeated precise measurements of the fitness of 3,106 men. He found during eight years of continued observations that those who were not physically fit (bottom 25 percent) were 4.3 times more likely to die of heart attacks (see chapter 4 for more about stress).

Critical Review 4

1. A comprehensive notion of physical fitness includes body weight, posture, musculature, and endurance. T F

2. For most Americans, *the job fails us* when it comes to maintaining our fitness. T F

3. We must move every joint through its full range at least once a week if we are to maintain maximum flexibility. T F

4. Why is it true that the jobs sought after by college graduates so often fail them when it comes to providing physical fitness?

5. What choices on the job can you make that will allow you to be successful at work and fit and healthy as well?

6. What can you do in your free time to bridge the fitness gap (if any) that you see as being built into your career choice?

REGULATION OF BODY WEIGHT

America is a nation on a diet. This is not the eternal fast of the developing country but the result of eating patterns that turn our bountiful harvests into a national health problem. We eat too much, so we are too fat. In 1980, 28 percent of us were obese, in 1994, 34 percent of us can make this dubious claim (Schute, 1994). We accomplished this feat while consuming less fat—but a great deal more sugar and protein. Weight is considered a crucial variable in any assessment of our physical self. To be obese, or to be considered obese, profoundly affects our perception of our self-worth and provokes largely negative attributions from those around us.

Obesity and Health

Obesity has a devastating effect on health. It increases our chances of contracting serious illnesses by 100 to 1,200 percent (Wurtman, 1987). These illnesses include heart disease, diabetes, hypertension, and some cancers. Such findings impressed the National Institutes of Health so much that the NIH classified obesity as a disease in 1985. Obese people also have less muscular proficiency on some measures, such as dynamic strength, gross body coordination, and stamina (Brady, Knight, and Berghage, 1977).

Women and Obesity

Nature and culture have conspired to make it doubly difficult for women to lose weight.

> The cultural prescriptions for ideal weight . . . have an obsessional nature that have made women's lives miserable. . . . Evidence is beginning to appear that moderately over-weight women are **not** at greater risk than so-called "normal women" and that they do not have shorter life spans, as do over-weight men. However, it remains significant that the prevalence of obesity among women is 70% higher than men (Haremustin, 1983, pp. 597–598).

The sociobiologist would say that the theory of inclusive fitness and our culture's "ideal woman" are incompatible. Fashion modeling, for example, actually requires women to maintain weights at anorexic levels. At the same time, a critical ratio of body fat is necessary for successful childbearing, thus nature promotes its reproductive efficiency by defending women against losing weight. (The metabolic rate is lowered, and fat and sugar craving is increased). Physical pressure to maintain weight and cultural pressure to lose weight add up to a real problem for many overweight women. No wonder diet books are perennial best-sellers!

Obesity and Overweight

It is important to distinguish between obesity and overweight. If your doctor wanted to know if you were obese as opposed to overweight, he or she would take your weight in kilograms (1 kilogram = 2.21 pounds) and divide that figure by the square of your height in meters (1 meter = 39.37 inches). This would give you your doctor your Body Mass Index (BMI). If your BMI is over 30, you are obese. Ideally, your BMI should fall between 23 and 25.

A Superachiever

Jane Collins is fat. There is no way around it. But Jane is also sparkling. She radiates charm and has a vibrant personality. Always well groomed and always on the go, Jane stands in proud defiance of the notion that fat represents failure. On the job, she is a superachiever.

Jane represents the ideal of NAAFA (the National Association to Assist Fat Americans) support group. Jane accepts herself and doesn't worry about gaining or losing weight. She is not alone. More than 3,000 members of NAAFA agree that you don't have to be skinny to have self-esteem. Headquartered in Bellerose, New York, the group helps members to build self-confidence for their never-ending struggle to combat the belief that fat people are poor workers and poor employment risks.

Ideal Weight

Overweight is not necessarily the same as overfatness. Whether the weight comes from fat or from lean muscle tissue is more important than the weight itself. Athletes can be overweight without being fat, while older, less-active people can be at the "low-mortality" weight while carrying too much fat. Normal weight *for fit people* is 15% body fat for men and 22% body fat for women (Baily, 1993). Excess body fat accumulates under the skin, so lifting a fold of skin and measuring its thickness is one way of identifying overweight due to overfatness.

Causes of Obesity

The chief cause of obesity is an imbalance of calories. Excessive intake of any or all of the three energy nutrients—carbohydrates, fats, or proteins—causes obesity. When energy intake exceeds the body's needs, the extra is stored as body fat. This is a survival mechanism that is, in America, a threat to survival.

Obese people, then, eat more than they need and have done so consistently for a long time. Some indirect causes are rooted in feelings; others are rooted in eating habits and activity patterns. A few may be rooted in brain chemistry. Wurtman (1987) reports that some people are obese as a result of self-medication. A deficiency in brain serotonen leaves them with feelings of anxiety and depression. They may have found by trial and error that by "carbing out"—adjusting by consuming large amounts of carbohydrates—they can elevate their mood. Antidepressant drugs, which increase serotonen within brain synapses, are now under study as potentially promising drugs for such obese patients.

Obesity may also be due to genetic factors or to early feeding patterns that produce a permanent excess of fat cells that the body defends by maintaining a constant, moderately strong degree of hunger (Nisbett, 1972). If these researchers are correct, people may be no more directly responsible for their weight than they are for their height.

Brain Hunger Regulation and Obesity

As millions of dieting Americans know, the problem with weight control is not only losing the weight but keeping it off. Most of us keep within a few pounds of our normal weight each year despite great variation in the foods we eat and the exercise we do (Keesey and Powley, 1975). We manage to do this by unconsciously monitoring our food intake. Receptor cells in our brains monitor substances in the blood that fluctuate with food consumption. This information, in

CULTURAL CROSSCURRENTS
Is There a Genetic Basis for Obesity?

When you see obese children walking with their obese parents, do you ever wonder whether their weight problem is due to genetic factors or environmental factors—or both? We cannot conclude that just because obese parents tend to have obese children (correlation) that genetics has anything to do with it (causation). Eating habits and exercise may be the cause.

Adoption studies help us discover the involvement of genetics in obesity. Albert Stunkard and his colleagues surveyed the weight and height of more than 3,500 Danes who grew up with adoptive parents. The weights and heights of their natural parents were obtained from the Danish Adoption Register.

The results showed a "clear relation between adoptee weight class (thin, medium, overweight, and obese) and that of their *biologic* parents: there was no apparent relation between adoptee weight class and that of the adoptive parent." In other words, a clear genetic basis for weight was found. It held true for all weight classes! This study in Denmark says nothing about the effectiveness of restricting caloric intake, or increasing exercise in the control of weight. The fact remains that if the results of this study are correct, we must appreciate the genetic basis for weight and perhaps target programs to prevent obesity in children who are at risk.

SOURCE: A. J. Stunkard, et al. "An Adoption Study of Human Obesity." *New England Journal of Medicine* 314 (January 23, 1986): 193–197.

turn, allows part of the brain to act as a thermostat—or appestat—for our appetite.

Apparently, in obese people, the appestat is set too high, demanding more food than is needed. When this demand is met by overeating, other physiological changes take place that compound the problem. As fat cells increase in size, they also increase in ability to store fat. These fatter fat cells are associated with high insulin levels. Insulin helps convert sugar into fat, again making the obese person able to store fat better. Diabetic patients say that when their insulin levels are too high, they "feel hungry," even if they have just eaten. Obese patients often report the same distressing urge.

When overweight people try to lose weight, they find that fat cells give up their stores with great reluctance. Muscle cells may be weakened by diets to reduce fat cells. When people feel fat, weak, and hungry, they are less likely to be physically active. But physical activity, along with diet, is the key to weight loss.

Is it possible to change this set point? If we reduce stress, are more physically active, require our body, not our clothing, to keep us warm, and reduce our fat and sugar consumption, we just might be able to adjust it downward.

Choosing to Lose Weight

There is no magic way to lose weight. Quick-weight-loss diets are *not* recommended, as they do not rest on a base of sound nutrition, do not teach altered eating patterns or altered attitudes toward food and eating, and often present medical risk. In the long run, they do not work. The good news is that there is no physiological reason why you can't lose weight. The long cherished excuse of overweight Americans—that they are victims of a genetically determined, underactive metabolic system—has been taken away by recent research. A three-year study of food intake and energy output gives no "evidence that there is any difference in people's efficiency in the way food is metabolized" (Moe, 1991). One hundred subjects each spent twenty-four fours in a calorimeter, a box that measures heat, oxygen, and carbon dioxide output. The sample demonstrated that when the subjects received the same food, and did the same exercise, in the same environment, they "burned up" calories at the same rate: "If you reduce calories, exercise and start eating like a 120-pound person, you can become a 120-pound person . . . the bad news is, once you lose the weight, you can't go back to what you were eating like a 150-pound person or you'll gain it right back." Medical supervision is recommended if you are contemplating an extensive loss of weight. The best way to lose body fat is to cut calories while increasing bodily activity. We'll talk about activity first, then turn to diet.

Energy and Enzymes

Covert Bailey, a nutritional biochemist, suggests that we choose the ultimate cure for obesity—*exercise*. He maintains that *muscle chemistry* is the real difference between being fat and being fit (Bailey, 1991), and that fasting and dieting harm, rather than improve our muscle chemistry.

His suggestion is based on the relationship between energy and enzymes. The human body is very efficient; it expends its energy wisely and throws nothing away. What is not immediately used is stored as fat. The difficult part is getting our bodies to release these fat stores. What does it really mean to "burn up calories?"

When we burn up a calorie, we literally *take it apart and get the energy out of it*. This disassembly is done by **enzymes** located inside each cell body.

Getting energy from glucose (sugar or grain calories) is a two-step process. The first step, from glucose to pyruvic acid, requires enzymes that need very little oxygen to function. Complete burning, however, requires that this acid be broken down into water and carbon dioxide, a process that demands a second set of enzymes that require much more oxygen.

Getting energy from fats is also a two-step process that requires two sets of enzymes, but all of these enzymes require large quantities of oxygen.

If we have a large number of the right kind of enzymes, we can store and use energy efficiently, we can eat well and stay slim. The key to building and maintaining the *right kind* of these enzymes is the *right kind and amount of* exercise! Enzymes are large, and cannot enter or leave a cell; they must be manufactured inside under the direction of the cellular DNA. Further, they break down quickly and need constant repair. Muscle cell DNA only responds to these needs when it is stimulated.

Exercise stimulates DNA to produce and repair energy burning enzymes. The questions now become which cells? What enzymes? The answers seem straightforward. Which cells? Muscle cells. They use more energy, even at rest. When in action, their specialized enzymes can increase calorie burning 50 times over (active brain cells only double their burning rate). By far the largest portion of our body is composed of muscle.

What enzymes? Here the answer is also straightforward. We want to produce and repair the high oxygen-demanding enzymes involved in burning the calories from fat. This leads directly to the answer to a third question, Which exercises?

Aerobic exercises make our muscles work hard enough to demand large amounts of energy. If this energy is to come from fat cells, the exercise must be an aerobic activity, that is, one not so hard to make us short of breath (anaerobic). Remember: Fat-digesting enzymes of the muscles require oxygen. Any exercise that involves large muscles, keeps them in continuous and constant

enzymes   protein catalysts; a catalyst is an agent that promotes a chemical reaction without itself being altered in the process

aerobic exercise   training in which the heart and lungs are able to supply enough oxygen to the muscles so that glucose is completely burned.

motion, and lasts for a minimum of 12 minutes after warm-up will build fat-burning enzymes.

Moderate amounts of *weight lifting,* an **anaerobic exercise,** should be included in any plan to lose weight because it builds muscle mass, maintains muscle tone, and prevents muscle mass from being replaced with fat mass as we age. Although exercise does not burn up a great many calories, it does change muscle chemistry so that the muscles burn fat more efficiently and we may have the pleasure of eating, the pleasure of exercise, and the pleasure of being slim.

Calories and Chemistry

Dieting makes no sense metabolically. "All dieting does is disturb the system" (Leibowitz, in Marano, 1993). Skipping or skimping meals disturbs the natural daily rhythm of bodily neurochemicals that maintain our life and reproductive proficiency. Our bodies work on routines, and ground-breaking work by Sara Leibowitz is demonstrating that a specific part of our brain, the **paraventricular nucleus** of the **hypothalamus,** monitors our energy needs from minute to minute and makes specific suggestions to our stomach as to what we should eat.

The idea that eating preferences are not simply an example of free will, but rather a response to chemical signals from our brain, is gaining acceptance from health psychologists. Whether it be carbohydrates for immediate fuel, fat for energy reserves or reproduction, or protein for growth and muscle maintenance, our cravings follow the lead of cascading neuropeptides (Marano, 1993).

Neuropeptide Y turns on our taste for carbohydrates. Both the burning of carbohydrates and the stress hormone **cortisol** stimulate the hypothalamus to increase neuropeptide Y production. High levels of neuropeptide Y lead to weight gain by cueing us to eat sugars.

Another neuropeptide produced in the paraventricular nucleus, **galanin,** turns on our taste for fat. When we burn stored fats for fuel, galanin production is turned on. It is also turned on by the production of estrogen, the female hormone. Fat reserves are needed for reproduction.

Our natural craving rhythm makes sense. In the morning, after the long night's fast, we have high levels of both cortisol and neuropeptide Y—signals to eat a breakfast of simple and complex carbohydrates, which provide quick fuel for initiating the day's activities. Carbohydrate intake increases the brain production of **serotonen,** a peptide that shuts off neuropeptide Y and allows us to increase our appetite for protein-rich food—both to sustain our day's activities and to repair our bodies. In the afternoon, increased secretion of galanin prompts us to desire fatty foods, so as to prepare our bodies for the coming night's fast.

We ignore these signals at our peril. Eating a fat-filled breakfast, for example, prompts premature galanin production, increases our craving for fat the rest of the day, and lays the groundwork for obesity.

Prior to puberty, neither boys nor girls crave fat. Girls develop a craving for sweets, boys for protein. Again, this pattern serves the sociobiological function of reproduction and protection. Sweets make fat palatable for the girls, protein makes for larger muscle growth. When puberty strikes, estrogen drives up the production of galanin in girls, and the craving for sweet-fats, chocolate cake, for example, takes over.

Amazingly, Leibowitz (Leibowitz, in Marano, 1993) is able to determine individual taste preferences in the very young: "Those constituted to favor fat consume the most calories and weigh the most" (p. 35). This pattern, complete

anaerobic exercise training in which the heart and lungs are not able to supply sufficient oxygen to the muscles to completely burn glucose

dieting eating a special selection of food or drink, especially for losing weight

paraventricular nucleus a dense cluster of nerve cells deep in the hypothalamus, involved in the regulation of hunger.

hypothalamus A brain structure controlling many body processes, including hunger, thirst, and sexual drive

neuropeptide Y a neurochemical released from the hypothalamus that turns on and off our desire for carbohydrate-rich food

cortisol this chemical messenger of alarm marshalls forces of energy needed for fight or flight

galanin a neurochemical released from the hypothalamus that turns on and off our desire for fat

serotonen a compound made from the amino acid tryptophan, it is one of the brain's principal neurotransmitters

with food cravings late in the day, continues into adulthood. Neurons are very "plastic" in the very young, implying that the brain production of sweet and fat-craving neuropeptides can possibly be shaped, perhaps prior to weaning! Eating disorders, from anorexia and bulimia, to obesity can be treated by early intervention.

Farewell to the Diet   The impact of this new awareness is profound. The major task of adjustment becomes twofold. For most of us, it means *never going on a diet*, for fasting increases sugar and fat signals from the brain. Rather, it means coordinating our meals and their content with our body's caloric and rhythmic demands. For our children, it becomes one of predicting (perhaps by age two) who is in danger of obesity, and then regulating what they eat and when in the day they eat it so as to change the routine of their chemical signals and perhaps save them the trauma of anorexia, bulimia, or obesity.

Most health professionals now recommend that, in lieu of a diet, you eat small, balanced meals and exercise often.

Men who say they are always on a diet were found to have dramatically higher rates of heart disease and diabetes than men who say they never diet (Blair, 1994). Those whose weight varied had higher health risks than those whose weight was steady, providing yet another reason not to diet.

The only proven way to lose weight successfully and permanently is to adopt an eating plan that provides balanced nutrition at the appropriate energy level and to stay with such a plan for life" (Whitney and Hamilton, 1977, p. 252). "Balanced nutrition" means avoiding fad diets. The average American should lose weight and keep it off. The World Health Organization recommends that we:

1. Choose a diet low in fat, from 15 to 30 percent of total calories from fat.
2. Choose a diet low in saturated fat, 0 to 10 percent total calories from saturated fat.
3. Choose 3 to 7 percent of total calories from poly- or monounsaturated fats.
4. Choose to eat no more than five grams of table salt a day.
5. Choose less refined sugars (no more than 10 percent of our daily intake).
6. Choose more complex carbohydrates (starch) and naturally occurring sugars (such as in fruit) until they comprise a full 48 percent of our daily intake.

All That It Can Be

A fatty acid can be:

1. Saturated. All points containing hydrogen atoms. Animal fats are generally the most saturated.
2. Monounsaturated. One point of unsaturation (no hydrogen atom). Some vegetable oils, especially olive oil, are monounsaturated.
3. Polyunsaturated. Two or more points of unsaturation. Vegetable and fish oils are polyunsaturated.
4. Trans-saturated. One or more points of hydrogen added to an unsaturated fatty acid to give it hardness. Cookies and similar baked goods use hydrogenated oils.

**Saturated and trans-saturated fats have been associated with high blood pressure, cancer, and heart disease.
***Fats in food provide energy reserves, lend satiety to meals, enhance food's aroma and flavor, cushion the vital organs, protect the body from temperature extremes, carry fat-soluble nutrients, and provide the material from which all cell membranes are made (Sizer and Whitney, 1994). No "No Fat" diets, please.

In everyday terms, these goals require us to eat more fruits, vegetables, and whole grains and less refined sugars, red meats, high-fat dairy products, and salt. We should consume more potatoes and fewer potato chips, more whole-wheat bread and less white bread, more plain breakfast cereals and less bacon and eggs or sugar-coated cereals, and more skim milk and less whole milk.

Vegetarians

Not so long ago, American doctors believed that a diet consisting only of plants couldn't supply enough protein and would be unhealthy. Today many doctors are advocating a modified vegetarian diet. Medical research (Shealey, 1986) seems to indicate that when modest amounts of dairy products are added to an all-plant diet, the results include:

1. Less diabetes
2. Lower blood pressure
3. Less osteoporosis
4. Less heart disease
5. Less sex hormones in the blood (high levels are associated with breast and prostate cancer).

In 1994, Dr. Paul Talalay of Johns Hopkins University isolated a compound from broccoli (**sulforaphane**) that blocks or reduces the growth of tumors in laboratory mice (Angier, 1994a). Sulforaphane is found in other cruciferous vegetables, as well.

sulforaphane   an antipromotor substance that opposes cancer, recently identified in broccoli

Formula for Losing Weight

If you keep active, drink a lot of water, eat sensibly sized servings, and limit your calories from fat to 30% of your total calories, *you should slowly lose weight and keep it off.* The following formula will allow you to determine if a particular food item falls within your limits.

Formula: (1) Total grams of fat in one serving × 9 (number of calories per gram of fat) = X

(2) X ÷ number of calories in one serving = % of fat

(3) If % of fat < 30, then it is OK to buy, eat, or serve!

Critical Review 5

1. Although a burden, obesity has never been classified as a disease by the National Institute of Health. T F

2. According to Sara Leibowitz, our taste for a sugar-, fat-, or protein-rich meal is an example of free choice. T F

3. By sampling infants' tastes, it will be possible to predict weight control problems. T F

4. The normal, rather than ideal, weight for a fit person will include from 15 percent to 22 percent body fat. T F

5. Give reasons why you agree or disagree with the idea that America's "ideal feminine form" is incompatible with the sociobiological concept of inclusive fitness.

6. Are we more personally responsible for our weight or our height? Why?

7. Why does dieting make no sense metabolically?

Questionnaire

Can You Live to Be 100?

The following test gives you a rough guide for predicting your longevity. The basic life expectancy for males is age 67, and for females age 75. Write down your basic life expectancy. If you are in your 50s or 60s, you should add 10 years to the basic figure because you have already proved yourself to be a durable individual. If you are over age 60 and active, you can add another 2 years.

Basic life expectancy

Decide how each item below applies to you and add or subtract the appropriate number of years from your basic life expectancy.

Family history

Add 5 years if two or more of your grandparents lived to eighty or beyond. _____

Subtract 4 years if any parent, grandparent, sister, or brother died of a heart attack or stroke before 50. _____

Subtract 2 years if anyone died from these diseases before 60. _____

Subtract 3 years for each case of diabetes, thyroid disorder, breast cancer, cancer of the digestive system, asthma, or chronic bronchitis among parents or grandparents. _____

Marital status

If you are married, add 4 years. _____

If you are over 25 and not married, subtract 1 year for every unwedded decade. _____

Economic status

Add 2 years if your family income is over $40,000 per year.   _____

Subtract 3 years if you have been poor for the greater part of your life.   _____

Physique

Subtract 1 year for every 10 pounds you are overweight.   _____

For each inch your girth measurement exceeds your chest measure-ment deduct 2 years.   _____

Add 3 years if you are over 40 and not overweight.   _____

Exercise

Regular and moderate (jogging three times a week), add 3 years.   _____

Regular and vigorous (long-distance running three times a week), add 5 years.   _____

Subtract 3 years if your job is sedentary.   _____

Add 3 years if it is active.   _____

Alcohol

Add 2 years if you are a light drinker (one to three drinks a day).   _____

Subtract 5 to 10 years if you are a heavy drinker (more than four drinks per day).   _____

Subtract 1 year if you are a teetotaler.   _____

Smoking

Two or more packs of cigarettes per day, subtract 8 years.   _____

One to two packs per day, subtract 2 years.   _____

Less than one pack, subtract 2 years.   _____

Subtract 2 years if you regularly smoke a pipe or cigars.   _____

Disposition

Add 2 years if you are a reasoned, practical person.   _____

Subtract 2 years if you are aggressive, intense, and competitive.   _____

Add 1 to 5 years if you are basically happy and content with life.   _____

Subtract 1 to 5 years if you are often unhappy, worried, and often feel guilty.   _____

Education

Less than high school, subtract 2 years.   _____

Four years of school beyond high school, add 1 year.   _____

Five or more years beyond high school, add 3 years.   _____

Environment

If you have lived most of your life in a rural environment, add 4 years.   _____

Subtract 2 years if you have lived most of your life in an urban envi-ronment.   _____

Sleep

More than 9 hours a day, subtract 5 years.   _____

Temperature

Add 2 years if your home's thermostat is set at no more than 68° F.   _____

Questionnaire
—continued

Health care

Regular medical checkups and regular dental care, add 3 years. _____

Frequently ill, subtract 2 years. _____

Your life expectancy total _____

SOURCE: From *The Psychology of Death, Dying and Bereavement* by Richard Schultz. Copyright © 1978 by Newbury Award Records, Inc. Reprinted by permission of Random House, Inc.

CHOOSING LONGEVITY

Ponce de Leon is said to have discovered Florida while searching for the legendary fountain of youth. The search goes on. We have been discussing diet and exercise in terms of looks and fitness; now we turn our attention to increasing the length of our life as well as its quality.

Many believe there is no adjustment they can make to prolong their "allotted" number of years. Recent research may turn that "truth" into a myth. According to Richard Walford (1983), a professor of pathology at the University of California, laboratory animals are routinely raised to increase their maximum life span by 50 to 100 percent, and "biologists agree that there's a very high order of probability—about 98 percent—that [similar methods] will work on human beings." Walford (1987) maintains that we can all achieve longevity with a high-nutrient diet that is low in calories. He suggests that we stay leaner than acceptable weight tables would allow and that we exercise with moderation.

Another myth is the assumption that our life span is largely determined by fate in the form of accidents, disease, war, or other catastrophes beyond our control. For the most part, we are born healthy and become sick as a result of our own choices, environmental conditions, and hereditary conditions, all of which may interact. Lifestyles that increase personal risk, occupational and recreational conditions that ignore public health and safety, and environmental contaminants that plague us all—these, and a medical delivery system that demands illness before intervention, are the major contributors to illness and early death. As Pogo said, "We have met the enemy, and it is us."

Aging and Ageism

ageism discrimination or negative stereotyping formed solely on the basis of age

Ageism is prejudice against older people. It can lead to discrimination that limits the opportunities of the elderly, isolates them, and fosters their negative self-image. Negative attributions based on age alone, and the irrational fear of growing old that it fosters, punish both victim and perpetrator.

Useless, Toothless, Sexless In cultures like ours, a loss or decline of strength, speed, endurance, or quickness is feared and often denied, even to ourselves. Other cultures, such as those of Japan and China, provide greater opportunity for their elderly to age successfully.

Several factors predict relatively high status for the elderly and increased opportunities for successful aging. They include:

1. A veneration of experience and wisdom

2. A system of age-related norms in which a person rises toward greater responsibility and authority throughout life—with role changes shifting toward advisory duties with advancing age

3. A norm of wise elders engaging in useful family and community functions

4. An economic system in which scarce resources are controlled by the elderly

5. A social system that emphasizes the extended family

6. A veneration of a collective, rather than individualistic, orientation to life.

A moment's reflection reveals that American values and institutions make successful aging a challenge. The sad truth is that Japan is rapidly moving toward our industrial model, with China not far behind. Elderly men in Japan are now going back to work in lesser jobs at lower pay, and elderly women are entering the work force in rapidly increasing numbers.

Aging in America

To be elderly means different things to different Americans. African-Americans, Asian Americans, and Hispanic Americans have more negative stereotypes about the old, have more health problems among their old, and fear growing old more than do Anglo-Americans. On the other hand, Anglo-Americans feel less respected, have higher suicide rates, and actually have higher mortality rates after the age of 75. It appears that minority *ethnicity* provides the ethnic elderly in America with a source of esteem that prolongs life.

To be elderly means different things if you are male or female in America. Women are older longer and outlive men in America. Elderly men enjoy more social status, income, and sexual partnerships than women. (Elderly females represent one of the lowest income levels in American society.) Women are much less lonely, have more friends, and are more involved in family and community affairs. The decline of strength, speed, and physical endurance are much less threatening to females, while the decline in physical attractiveness remains a greater female concern.

Physiological Aging: A Synonym for Decline

In America, to be elderly generally means to be in physical decline. However, these physical changes arrive slowly and at different times for each of us. As we age, our skin begins to wrinkle, our hair begins to thin out and turn gray, our hearts and lungs become less efficient, our immune system declines, our senses dull, and we become shorter! The following is a universality of physical decline that is wonderfully American in its democratic application.

Activity level: Humans become less active as they mature.

Vision: The vast majority of Americans over 65 report a loss of visual ability, particularly close vision and poor recovery from glare (Fozard, 1990).

Hearing: Three-quarters of Americans over 75 report significant hearing loss, especially for high-pitched tones under conditions of confusing background noise (Fozard, 1990).

Sleep: Delayed, disturbed, and dissatisfying sleep is reported by increasingly large numbers of Americans as they age.

Sex: Age-related hormone changes bring about *menopause* in women, and slower and less intense physiological responses in both sexes.

Senile dementia: The usual estimate of senility among Americans rises from 4 to 6 percent at age 65 to about 25 percent in Americans over 85.

Psychological Aging: Not Synonymous With Decline

The changes that come with age come slowly, and we typically have plenty of time to make psychological and social adjustments. Successful adjustment depends on several personal and environmental factors that vary greatly from individual to individual. Aging thus is quite different for each of us.

Visual Adjustment   Corrective lenses for night driving and bifocals for close work allow most of us to handle weakened vision without difficulty.

Hearing Adjustment   Hearing aids, and loved ones who enunciate clearly and use lower tones help adjustment, as do selective efforts to reduce background noise.

Sexual Adjustment   Belief in the stereotype of a sexless old age proves to be a greater obstacle to experiencing satisfying sex than do physical limitations. Rather than being a universal trauma, menopause produces reactions that vary greatly among American women. Many find it liberating. Maintaining "healthy pleasures" such as regular sexual activity enhances successful aging—it provides arousal, aerobic exercise, fantasy, and positive social interaction (Ornstein and Sobel, 1989). It is also possible. In a survey of men and women between the ages of 80 and 102 *who were not taking medication,* 70 percent of the males and 50 percent of the females reported that they "fantasize about intimate relations often." Sixty-three percent of the men and 30 percent of the women reported having sexual intercourse recently (McCartney, 1989).

Cognitive Adjustment   Americans' fear of losing their intelligence to age is unfounded. There is little evidence of a general cognitive decline among the healthy elderly. Although the number of active neurons in the brain declines with age, and elders acquire new information more slowly, these facts have little functional significance. Memory loss is not universal, is largely confined to short-term memory, and does not compromise our problem-solving ability as we age. Accumulated knowledge can become wisdom (Baltes, 1990) and we can maintain high performance by being selective in what we do, by practicing more, and by making use of new technologies. Productive mental work peaks in our forties, stays quite stable through our sixties and even well into our seventies (Dennis, 1966). The onset of senility due to chronic alcoholism, hardening of the arteries, and small strokes can be reduced and/or delayed by adjustments in our lifestyle. **Alzheimer's disease** and the *"terminal drop"* in intelligence often found just before death are more resistant to our present capabilities to adjust. (The genetic component of Alzheimer's is under intense study at present, and screening and preventative measures seem to be a possibility in the near future.)

Alzheimer's disease   chronic, organic brain disorder, characterized by a gradual loss of thinking abilities and the deterioration of personality

Emotional Adjustment   Twenty years ago, a *social disengagement theory* regarding aging was widely accepted as valid. In this view as people aged, they universally desired to distance themselves emotionally from activities and individuals so that they could prepare themselves for death. Others were to respect this nearing-death wish. This view has been discredited. Although the elderly are less socially active, this may simply reflect the wisdom of selectivity whereby the elderly enhance positive relationships and conserve energy. A single human relationship, a pet, and even a plant have been found to be essential for emotional health. Elders can adjust and minimize emotional losses by staying active, involved, and close to people. Others can respect this lifelong need for involvement.

Mental disorders are actually at their lowest after age 65. The exceptions are depressions and dementias, and both of these disorders have been found to be more related to health, choice, and activity levels than to chronological age.

Why Humans Age

Reproductive Efficiency Why do we grow old? The sociobiologists would say to maximize "inclusive fitness." The gene seeks immortality; the genetic container is disposable. This theory holds that our brain monitors the number of harmful gene mutations within our system. When the mutants present a danger to the gene pool (the possibility of too many defective infants being produced by the aging parents), then the brain may program the **pituitary** gland to release a death hormone, **DECO** (for "decreased oxygen consumption hormone").

According to the theory, the gradual loss of oxygen produced by the effects of DECO causes a deterioration of the body. However, no such hormone has as yet been isolated. Based on the rate at which human cells divide, biologists place the upper limits of the human life cycle at 115 to 120 years.

Free Radicals Oxygen also figures in a related theory of aging. **Free radicals** are chemicals produced by radiation and by normal metabolism that react with oxygen and that can disrupt and destroy living cells. Gout and arthritis are thought by some to be products of free-radical damage, as is normal aging (Harmon, 1962). Excessive free radicals are associated with an oxygen imbalance. The average life span of animals has been extended by giving them special nutrients (antioxidants) that protect against free-radical damage. **Antioxidants** protect cell fats against oxidation by offering themselves for destruction.

Autoimmune Reactions Part of aging may involve our immune system failing to recognize our own cells and acting to defend against them (called an autoimmune reaction). Or, as we get older, our system may fail to recognize foreign organisms (such as cancers) and thus fail to reject or destroy them. If we can assist our immune system, we can prolong life. White blood cells and antibodies are being made and dismantled rapidly, and their maintenance requires a continuous supply of nutrients (Sizer and Whitney, 1994).

DNA Repair Our immune system defends us. We also have a DNA repair mechanism. As our cells divide, strands of DNA (which carries genetic information) often break, and enzymes rush in to repair them. As we age, repair work falls behind, and like computer disks with too many error tracks, our cells can no longer make accurate copies of themselves.

pituitary the "master gland" of the endocrine system. It secretes hormones that influence other tissue or glands. It also produces a growth, and perhaps a death, hormone

DECO in theory, a pituitary hormone that causes decreased oxygen consumption and a deterioration of the body

free radicals a class of chemicals that damage tissue by combining with other molecules to form harmful mutations

antioxidant a compound that protects other compounds from oxygen by itself reacting with oxygen

Sources of Antioxidants

Beta carotene is found in bright orange and dark green vegetables such as carrots, sweet potatoes, pumpkin, cantaloupe, spinach, greens, and broccoli.

Selenium is an essential mineral that helps Vitamin E act as an antioxidant by taking its place, thus sparing Vitamin E. It is plentiful and found in meats, shellfish, and grains grown in selenium-rich soil.

Vitamin C, which works as an antioxidant for water-absorbing substances, can be found in orange juice, broccoli, cantaloupe, and green pepper. There is no shortage of Vitamin C.

Vitamin E works as an antioxidant for fat-absorbing substances; it breaks the oxidant chain of destruction, and can be readily found in vegetable oils, fruits, and meats. There is no shortage, but Vitamin E can be destroyed by heat, so diets high in processed foods and low in fresh vegetables may be low in this essential vitamin.

Note: A 1994 study of lifelong smokers in Finland demonstrated no protection against lung cancer or heart disease from daily supplements of Vitamin E or beta carotene, or both. Use natural antioxidants as part of a healthy lifestyle, not supplements to allow yourself to continue an unhealthy one.

thymus   a ductless gland situation in the upper thorax near the throat; part of the immune system

somatotropin   a hormone released by the pineal gland that stimulates growth in the young

Hormones   When we are young (under thirty-five), our **thymus** gland, located behind our breastbone, produces a hormone that instructs our immune system to attack foreign targets. After thirty-five, the thymus shrinks, its hormones decline, and our defense system suffers. To the extent that we can prevent or reverse this shrinkage we can prolong life.

Another gland, the pituitary, also plays a role in aging. When we are young, it produces and releases a growth hormone **(somatotropin)** that allows us to eat more and stay lean, increases the benefits of exercise, and stimulates our immune system. The first major study reported on supplements of this growth hormone given to healthy elderly subjects reported a 9 percent increase in lean body mass, and a decrease in fat tissue of 14 percent (Echtixial, *The Lancet*, 1991). By 1993 the *Journal of the American Medical Association* was publishing a letter to the editor entitled "Growth Hormone Therapy for the Elderly: The Fountain of Youth Proves Toxic (Yarasheski and Zachwieja, 1993). This wonder treatment may not be so wonderful afterall! Our "aging clock" may be located in our pituitary. Menopause, male-pattern baldness, and similar signs of aging appear to be the result of a built-in mechanism. The theory suggests that if we can prolong the natural production of this growth hormone, we can prolong youth.

Longevity as a Personal Choice

Generally, research doesn't indicate that we can rejuvenate the body or reverse the aging process. There is support for the idea that we can slow aging and prolong the youthful portions of our lives, however. Health psychologists are now beginning to study wonderfully healthy men and women as vigorously as they once studied the sick. New doctors in training spend a much greater part of their time with healthy patients. These thriving people routinely report that the joy of living is to be found in the vigorous use of a healthy mind and body, working toward valued goals with people they love or respect. Playing valued roles helps prolong life and make life worth living.

We all can begin accepting responsibility for our choices concerning our own style of life, what we do and don't do to ourselves. For example, we can increase the pleasure of living and working while reducing stress, calories, stim-

---

An Experiment in Life Extension Choices

Sandy and Durk live well. Basically they read and write for a living. They exercise regularly, but not for long. No aerobic exercises are included in their brief routines. They are childless and are in their mid-thirties.

Such a sedentary lifestyle may appear common; however, Sandy and Durk are not your ordinary next-door neighbors. They have committed themselves to living younger longer and are using themselves as human guinea pigs to test diet and exercise routines suggested by several contemporary theories of aging.

They read the latest literature on aging, select potentially helpful programs, and, with the help of a friendly physician, program themselves for a maximum life span. Their routine consists of preparing and consuming, at regular intervals during the day, dietary supplements that may offer protection or relief from the ravages of daily living. (Researcher Roy Walford cautions that megadoses of vitamins, drugs, and nutrients do not prolong life and can lead to kidney damage, headaches, and intestinal problems.)

They write and intend to keep writing about their attempts and the results they obtain as measured by exhaustive medical tests. Although the medical profession considers them profoundly unscientific, their dramatic adventure has sparked national interest in extending the quality and quantity of our "allotted years." Hopefully, we will be hearing from them both for a long time.

---

ulant abuse, smoking, excessive drinking, and overexposure to direct sunlight. Each of these good habits is associated with expanded longevity (Pearson and Shaw, 1980).

Lifestyle and Physical Health

Lifestyle choices can affect the incidence of cancer and heart disease, major causes of premature death in America. Diet is believed to be the major environmental cause of cancer; smoking, the second (Doll, 1983). Quayle (1983) reports that "alcoholism is gaining on heart disease, cancer, and diabetes, and in a decade may become American's number one killer." Bruce Ames, a cancer specialist, writes that "there are large numbers of mutagens and carcinogens in every meal, all perfectly natural. . . . Foods naturally contain a range of cancer-preventing chemicals, or 'anti-carcinogens' as well" (1983, p. 14E). High-fat foods may increase the risk of cancer, and such foods as fruits and vegetables may confer protection. Our job is to identify carcinogenic (cancer-causing) foods and determine if they present a major health risk. The National Cancer Institute has established the Chemoprevention Program to explore the use of natural and synthetic agents in preventing cancer.

Diet is also correlated with heart disorders. "At least 25 to 30 percent of American five- to 18-year-olds have 'dangerously high' cholesterol levels caused mainly by eating too many fats," reports the American Health Foundation (Cohn, 1984, p. 14A). Lowering cholesterol by the use of drugs has resulted in lowered heart-attack rates. It is assumed that lowering cholesterol levels by diet will have a similar effect. The foundation believes that heart-attack prevention should begin early, with low-fat diets introduced when children first begin to eat regular foods. Dr. Dean Ornish has documented the benefits of diet and stress-reduction techniques for people with heart disease (1990). He reports that he can reduce the blockage in coronary arteries in patients who go on a very low-fat diet, give up smoking, take moderate exercise, use stress-reducing techniques, and cultivate style of life choices such as altruism and forgiveness of enemies (Tasker, 1991). In 1987 a combination of two drugs was found to lower blood cholesterol levels dramatically. Scott Grundy reports that Lovastatin and Colestipol, taken together, lower LDL by 48 percent and raise the level of beneficial HDL by 17 percent.[2] Finally, eliminating the use of stimulants and depressants can help increase our ability to ward off disease and repair tissue damage.

Lifestyle and Life Extension

Health vigilants pursue health with a vengeance and believe that diet and exercise can conquer any health threat. **True believers** think that illness can best be combated through positive thinking, prayer, optimism, and friendships. **Fatalists** believe that health is determined by fate, luck, or genetic endowment. When studied, the fatalists were the most unhappy and the vigilants were physically and psychologically the healthiest (Rubinstein, 1982). This is no surprise as the single greatest threat to happiness among the elderly is ill health.

The central beliefs of the vigilants and the true believers seem to point toward an adjustment plan for a happy and healthy old age. Maintaining *close family relationships* and being involved in an *effective exercise program* predict successful aging (Valliant and Valliant, 1990).

Choosing Life Extension

Nature does seem to have a plan for us to age and die. Is it possible for us to have other plans and to make them stick? Many believe we can slow the aging process. Maintaining involvement with our family helps us psychologically by elevating our status, reducing our stress, and giving life purpose and meaning. Becoming involved with an effective exercise program helps us psychologically by improving our bodily image and encouraging positive attributions from others. Physical exercise helps longevity because:

1. Activity level, not metabolic rate, goes down with age; therefore,

2. The proportion of our body fat tends to increase with age. We become infirm with age because, without exercise,

3. Up to 50 percent of our muscles can atrophy, to be replaced by fat. Exercise makes us fit, not fat, and,

4. The fitter you are the longer you live (Bailey, 1991). Thus exercise can keep us younger even as we get older.

Diet may also extend our life. Walford (1983) claims that if we reduce our caloric intake by 60 percent over a number of years, while being sure we get superior nutrients, we can prolong life. That seems drastic. There are less extreme choices that may be effective. Reducing intake of polyunsaturated fats (fats susceptible to free radicals) and increasing use of quenchers (nutrients found in fruits and vegetables that quench, or terminate, certain chemical reactions) may slow free-radical damage and prolong life. Using sun-blocking ointments reduces the risk of skin cancer, and following a higher-fiber diet may protect against certain cancers as well. Good sleeping patterns promote growth-hormone production. Low stress levels also help. Because drug abuse and smoking are associated with reduced immune-system effectiveness, lower

2. HDLs are fatty substances in the bloodstream associated with coronary disease. "It takes several months to increase the HDL level but only a short time to lower it. So exercise should not be used as a handy medication, to be taken only when needed. It should be a lifelong habit" (J. Patsch, 1983).

growth-hormone production, and impaired tissue repair, the elimination of these habits can increase our life span. There is much we can do. But there is no guarantee. (See the "Selected Readings" at the end of this chapter for more information on life extension.)

The Quality of an Extended Life

Would life extension be worth the effort that appears necessary? The best prediction is, "Yes, it would." The over-eighty age bracket is proportionally the fastest-growing population subgroup in our nation (Briley, 1983). One study found more than 90 percent of a representative group of seventy-five to eighty-four-year-old Americans fully independent. The vast majority were self-sufficient and satisfied with life. The study reported that "persons with a positive attitude and high morale tend to be those whose health and physical function are best" (p. 97).

At age seventy-nine, the very practical B. F. Skinner, along with his associate M. E. Vaughn, brought us insight into the many things we can do to shape our environment so that we can enjoy old age. How to keep in touch with the world, think clearly, keep busy, get along with others, and feel good are some of the areas explored in their writing (Skinner and Vaughn, 1983). They make a strong case for a well-planned old age. The payoff seems to be worth the investment.

An Example of Positive Choice

California Seventh-Day Adventists who (1) do not use tobacco, alcohol, or caffeinated beverages and (2) follow a lacto-ovo-vegetarian diet (milk, eggs, plants) have an average life expectancy that is twelve years longer than our U.S. average (Snowden, 1986). California Seventh-Day Adventists who do not make these choices help us to understand that (1) meat eating is associated with heart attacks and diabetes, (2) fried foods (especially fried eggs) are associated with ovarian cancer, and (3) coffee is associated with colon and bladder cancer. Surprisingly, Snowden finds that healthy (conforming) Adventists derive few extra longevity benefits from vigorous physical exercise.

In this chapter we have discussed the possibility of choosing a fit and attractive physical self. In the next chapter, we will explore our thinking or cognitive self. Both a positive mental attitude and a positive lifestyle seem necessary for a full and flourishing life.

Critical Review 6

1. Negative attributions based on age alone, and the irrational fear of growing old that they foster, punish both victim and perpetrator. T F

2. Elderly women enjoy more social status, income, and sexual partnerships than do elderly men. T F

3. Alcoholism is gaining on heart disease, cancer, and diabetes, and in a decade may become America's number one killer. T F

4. Maintaining *close family relationships* and being involved in an *effective exercise program* predict successful aging. T F

5. Why do you think the Vigilants were found to be superior physically and psychologically to the Fatalists?

6. We speak of DECO and free radicals as possible killers. We know for certain that alcohol and tobacco are killers—both of these abused substances reflect an illusion of individual choice and the reality of social pressure, and both seem to devastate some abusers while leaving others unscathed. Review the nature-nurture-choice positions to bring this phenomenon into perspective.

SUMMARY

■ We are physical organisms that adjust to a changing environment. There is a constant interaction between psychological and physiological adjustment.

■ There appears to be a small, positive correlation between phenotype and temperament. Such personality traits as leadership and shyness have been found to be mostly inherited.

■ Sociobiology is a discipline that attempts to discover the biological foundations of human social behavior. It includes such central concepts as procreative proficiency, inclusive fitness, and kin selection.

■ Sexuality is a way of seeing ourselves and relating to others.

■ *Gender identity is the sense of being female or male,* which most children acquire by the time they are three years old.

■ Chromosomes combine at conception to form the genetic male or female. Differentiation begins during the prenatal period, when antigens program the gonads to form testes or ovaries. Later, the external genitals differentiate under the control of prenatal hormones.

■ Excessive testosterone causes a male-differentiated brain to develop.

■ Sex-linked behavior differences are largely illusions, but levels of sexual and aggressive activity seem higher in the male, and nurturing levels appear higher in the female.

■ The theory of the "looking-glass self" offers an alternate explanation of the phenotype-temperament relationship. This theory is based on the notion of shared stereotypes. Social learning theory adds the idea that social reinforcement of expected behaviors shapes temperament to conform with phenotype.

■ Our physical self is made up of bodily images and sensations and remains a lifelong anchor for our self-awareness.

■ We regularly associate character traits with physical characteristics. Attribution theory studies this phenomenon.

■ Sociobiology suggests that radiant health, vigor, and *symmetrical features* are standards of universal beauty. Most authorities, however, maintain that there is no universal standard for physical attractiveness. Each age and every culture defines itself by redefining beauty.

■ Physical attractiveness is the most important factor in first impressions. A good appearance leads others to think well of us. We are most attracted to highly attractive people when our own self-esteem is high.

■ A positive body image is associated with low anxiety and increased self-esteem.

■ Negative stereotypes, or stigmas, cause psychological pain. Discrimination arising from negative stereotypes extracts an enormous cost in lost performance and unfulfilled lives.

■ We tend to attribute our good behavior to dispositional determinants and our bad behavior to situational determinants.

■ We generally make just the opposite attributions about the behavior of strangers. Mental tests of consistency, consensus, and distinctiveness help us confirm these attributions.

■ Impression management allows us to positively influence the attributions that others make of us.

■ Our job and leisure activities fail us in terms of providing for fitness.

■ Physical fitness includes posture, strength, flexibility, and endurance. Appropriate tests and exercises are available to each of us to become fit.

■ Aerobic fitness is the single best index of physical fitness and can be obtained through a pattern of sustained, rhythmic muscle contractions.

■ Intensity, frequency, and duration of exercise have to be coordinated with specific muscle stimulation if muscle fitness is to be achieved.

■ Obese people are seen as being less attractive, and they have more medical complications. Obesity is directly caused by an imbalance between energy in (calories) and energy out (activity).

■ The brain's rhythmic production of neuropeptide Y sheds new light on our preferences for sugar, protein, and fat. The work of energy-burning enzymes helps us to understand why exercise, not dieting, is the real cure for overfatness.

■ Slow, constant, aerobic exercise, involving our large muscles, affords the best adjustment for reducing weight and keeping it off.

■ An eating plan that provides balanced nutrition at an appropriate energy level is needed to maintain healthful living. This plan should be followed for life.

■ People who are not physically fit are four times more likely to die of a heart attack.

■ Ageism, with its negative attributions based on age alone, and the irrational fears of growing old that it fosters, punish both victim and perpetrator.

■ There are several theories of aging, including those related to DNA repair, immune-system failure, free radicals, and thymus and pituitary-gland secretions. Some scientists believe aging is programmed by changes in the brain.

■ Physiological, but not psychological aging, is a synonym for decline.

■ Diet, exercise, a positive attitude, and good lifestyle habits can extend the healthful, pleasurable portion of our lives.

SELECTED READINGS

Bailey, C. A. *The New Fit or Fat,* Boston: Houghton Mifflin, 1991. Based on the latest discoveries in fat metabolism and exercise physiology, this easy-to-read work clarifies the fitness/fatness relationship and shows how to lay the groundwork for an enjoyable exercise plan.

Cooper, Kenneth. A name synonymous with aerobic exercise. Any of his works is recommended. His charts of exercise programs for various age groups, covering several exercises, are especially helpful.

Cooper, Robert K. *The Performance Edge.* Boston: Houghton Mifflin Company, 1991. This well-written book helps us make the most of what we have, physically, mentally, and emotionally. The section on quick stress reduction techniques is especially helpful.

Durden-Smith, J., and Densimone, D. *Sex and the Brain.* New York: Arbor House, 1983. A controversial yet thoroughly researched study of how and why sexual pleasure evolved.

Kimmel, D. C. *Adulthood and Aging: An Interdisciplinary, Developmental View.* New York: Wiley Press, 1990. An engaging, personal style makes this look at life extension profitable reading.

Kugler, H. *Doctor Kugler's Seven Keys to a Longer Life.* New York: Fawcett Crest, 1978. A collection of practical suggestions for increasing our life span while enjoying life.

Legwold, Gary. "Steroids Build Muscle but Big Problems, Too." *Consumers Digest* (January-February 1985): 10–11, 24. A mature look at a choice often made by those who want to build up strength and bulk at any cost.

Logue, A. W. *The Psychology of Eating and Drinking.* New York: W. H. Freeman, 1986. Why do some people gain weight while others do not? If you want to know more about how genetic, physiological, and social factors interact to determine what and how much we eat, read this comprehensive text.

Marino, Hara E. "Chemistry and Craving," *Psychology Today* (January/February, 1993): 30–36, 74. "We eat what we are," rather than "We are what we eat," is the thesis of this ground-breaking research article. Two brain chemicals are reported to control our appetite for carbohydrate-rich and fat-rich foods.

Pelletier, K. *Longevity.* New York: Delacorte, 1981. An interesting account of communities in which many members live past the century mark. The conditions of life within these communities are examined with an eye toward application in contemporary America.

Rosenhan, D. L. "On Being Sane in Insane Places," *Science* (January 19, 1973): 250–259. The title says it all.

Sizer, Frances S., and Whitney, Eleanor N. *Nutrition: Concepts and Controversies,* 6th ed. St. Paul, MN: West Publishing Company, 1994. This completely updated text helps us to bring the science of nutrition into our lives and into the grocery store. The importance of nutrition in body composition, obesity, longevity, immunity, and disease prevention is presented in a scholarly and interesting way.

Skinner, B. F., and Vaughn, M. E. *Enjoy Old Age.* New York: Norton, 1983. An authoritative guide to changing our environment so that we can be joyful and productive in our old age.

Snyder, M. "The Many Me's of the Self-Monitor." *Psychology Today* (March 1980): 60–64.

Wood, P. *The California Diet and Exercise Program.* Mountain View, CA.: Anderson World, 1983. A good expression of the idea that one can self-manage health and physical fitness through nutrition and aerobic exercise.

REFERENCES

Allport, G. W. *Becoming.* New Haven, CT: Yale University Press, 1960.

Ames, B. N. Quoted by P. Hilts. In "Foods Naturally Contain Cancer-Causing Chemicals. *The Miami Herald* (September 22, 1983): 14E.

Angier, N. "Eating Veggies: Mom Was Right After All." *The Miami Herald* (April 12, 1994): 1A.

Bailey, C. *The New Fit or Fat.* Boston: Houghton Mifflin, 1993.

Bandura, A., and Walters, R. H. *Social Learning and Personality Development,* p. 59. New York: Holt, Rinehart and Winston, 1963.

Baltes, P. B. "Toward a Psychology of Wisdom." Address given at the annual convention of the Gerontological Society of America, Boston, MA, November 1990.

Barash, D. P. *Sociobiology and Behavior.* New York: Elsevier, 1977.

Batson, C. D., and Shaw, L. L. Evidence for Altruism: Toward a pluralism of prosocial motives. *Psychological Inquiry,* (1991): 2, 107–122.

Bem, S. L. *The Lenses of Gender.* New Haven, CT: Yale University Press, 1993.

Benbow, C. P. "Academic Achievement in Mathematics and Science of Students Between Ages 13 and 23: Are There Differences in the Top One Percent of Mathematical Ability?" *Journal of Educational Psychology* 84 (1992): 51–61.

Bennett, D. D. "Of Berries and Bison: Stone Age Standards for Modern Diets." *Science News* 87 (February 9, 1985): 127.

Berscheid, E., Walster, E., and Bohrnstedt, G. "The Happy American Body: A Survey Report." *Psychology Today* (November 1973): 119–123.

Blair, S. N. "Study: Men Who Always Diet Have Higher Rate of Heart Disease, Diabetes." *The Miami Herald,* (March 20, 1994): 4A.

Bodenhausen, G. V. "Stereotypic Biases in Social Decision Making and Memory: Testing Process Models of Stereotype Use. *Journal of Personality and Social Psychology* 55 (1988): 726–737.

Bouchard, T. J., Jr., and McGue, M. "Genetic and Rearing Environmental Influences on Adult Personality: An Analysis of Adopted Twins Reared Apart." *Journal of Personality* 58 (1990): 263–292.

Brady, J. I. Knight, D. H. R., and Berghage, T. E. "Relationship Between Measures of Body Fat and Gross Motor Proficiency." *Journal of Applied Psychology* (April 1977): 224–229.

Briley, M. "Over 80-and Doing Fine." *Modern Maturity* (October-November 1983): 96–97.

Cash, T. F., Kehr, J. A., Polyson, J., and Freeman, V. "Role of Physical Attraction in Peer Attribution of Psychological Disturbances." *Journal of Counseling and Clinical Psychology* 45 (December 1977): 87–93.

Cash, T. F., and Smith, E. "Physical Attractiveness and Personality Among American College Students." *Journal of Psychology* 3 (1982): 183–191.

Cialdini, R. B. *Influence. Science and Practice,* 3rd ed. New York: Harper Collins, 1993.

Cohn, V. "Doctors Urge Low-Cholesterol Diet for Kids to Prevent Heart Disease." *The Miami Herald* (March 15, 1984): 14A.

Cooper, K. H. *The New Aerobics.* New York: Bantam Books, 1970.

_____. "Re-shape Your Body and Re-charge your Heart." *Prevention* 38 (May 1986): 33–42.

Coren, S., and Halpern, D. F. "Left-Handedness: A Marker for Decreased Survival Fitness." *Psychological Bulletin* 109 (1) (1991): 90–106.

Davis, B. L. "Attitudes towards School among Early and Late Maturing Adolescent Girls." *Journal of Genetic Psychology* 131 (December 1977): 261–266.

Dawkins, R. *The Selfish Gene.* New York: Oxford University Press, 1976.

Dell, D. M., and Patkin, J. "Effects of Certain Behaviors on Perceived Expertness and Attractiveness." *Journal of Counseling Psychology* 29 (May 1982): 261–267.

Dennis, W. "Age and Creative Productivity." *Journal of Gerontology* 21 (1) (1966): 1–8.

Dermer, M., and Theil, D. "When Beauty May Fail." *Journal of Personality and Social Psychology* 31 (1975): 1168–1176.

Diamond, M. "Sexual Identity, Monozygotic Twins Reared in Discordant Sex Roles and a BBC Follow-up." *Archives of Sexual Behavior* 11 (April 1982): 181–186.

Diamond, S. *Personality and Temperament.* New York: Harper & Row, 1957, p. 95.

Doll, R., a British epidemiologist. Quoted in "Food's Link to Cancer: Cause and Protection." *The Miami Herald* (August 31, 1983): 1E.

Eysenck, H. L. *Eysenck on Extroversion.* London: Crosby Lockwood Staples, 1973.

Feldman, S. D. "The Presentation of Shortness in Everyday Life—Height and Heightism in American Society: Toward a Sociology of Stature." Paper presented to the American Sociology Association meeting, Washington, D.C. 1971.

Fozard, J. L. "Vision and Hearing in Aging." In *Handbook of the Psychology of Aging,* 3rd ed. edited by Birren and K. W. Schaie (Eds.), San Diego: Academic Press.

Frazier, P. A. Victim Attributions and Post-rape Trauma. *Journal of Personality and Social Psychology,* 59, (1990): 293–311.

Gorski, R. A. Quoted by R. Kotulak in "Gender: What Makes You Male or Female?" *The Miami Herald* (March 9, 1979): 181–190.

Grady, K. E. "Sex as a Social Label: The Illusion of Sex Differences." *Dissertation Abstracts* 38 (June 1977): 416.

Hamilton, W. D. "Altruism and Related Phenomena, Mainly in Social Insects." *Annual Review of Ecology and Systematics* 3 (1972): 193–232.

Haremustin, R. "Problems Associated with Eating." *Journal of the American Psychological Association* 38 (May 1983): 597–598.

Harmon, D. "Role of Free Radicals in Mutation, Cancer, Aging, and the Maintenance of Life." *Radiation Research* 16 (1962): 753–764.

Heider, F. *The Psychology of Interpersonal Relations.* New York: Wiley, 1958.

Ilg, F. L., and Ames, L. B. *The Gesell Institutes' Child Behavior.* New York: Dell, 1961.

Imperato-McGinley, J. "Sex Hormone Overrides Upbringing." *Science News* 117 (June 28, 1980): 406.

Jackson, L. A. *Physical Appearance and Gender.* Albany: State University of New York Press, 1992.

Jones, E. E. *Interpersonal Perception.* New York: Freeman, 1990.

Jones, E. E., and Nisbett, R. E. "The Actor and the Observer: Divergent Perceptions of the Causes of Behavior." In *Attribution: Perceiving the Causes of Behavior,* edited by E. E. Jones, D. E. Kanouse, H. H. Kelly, R. E. Nisbett, S. Valins, and B. Weiner. Morristown, NJ: General Learning Press, 1972.

Kagan, J. "Body Build and Conceptual Impulsivity in Children." *Journal of Personality* 34 (1966): 118–128.

Kagan, J., and Moss, H. A. *Birth to Maturity: A Study in Psychological Development.* New York: Wiley, 1962.

Keesey, R. E., and Powley, T. L. "Hypothalamic Regulation of Body Weight." *American Scientist* 63 (September-October 1975): 558–565.

Kelly, H. H., and Michel, J. L. "Attribution Theory and Research." *Annual Review of Psychology* 31 (1980): 457–501.

Kielser, S. B., and Baral, R. L. "The Search for a Romantic Partner: The Effects of Self-Esteem and Physical Attractiveness on Romantic Behavior." In *Personality and Social Behavior,* Edited by K. Gergen and D. Marlowe. Reading, MA: Addison-Wesley, 1970.

Kimura, D. Sex Differences in the Brain. *Scientific American* 267(3), (1992): 118–125.

Kurtz, R., and Prestera, H. *The Body Reveals.* New York: Harper & Row/Quicksilver Books, 1976.

The Lancet, "Growth hormone therapy in elderly people" (editorial), May 11, 1991.

Levine, A. "New Rules of Exercise." *U.S. News and World Report* (August 11, 1986): 52–57, 101.

Lewis, K. N., and Walsh, W. B. "Physical Attractiveness: Its Impact on the Perception of a Female Counselor." Journal of Counseling Psychology 25 (May 1978): 210–16.

Loehlin, J. C. *Genes and Environment in Personality Development.* Newbury Park, CA: Sage, 1992.

Maccoby, E. E. "Gender Differentiations." Paper presented at the meeting of the American Psychological Society, Dallas, TX, June 1990.

Maeder, J. "The Jay Maeder Column." *The Miami Herald* (November 19, 1983): 2A.

Marano, H. E. "Chemistry and Craving" *Psychology Today,* (January-February 1993): 30–36, 74.

Martin, G. M., Schellenberg, G. D., Wijsman, E. M., and Bird, T. D. Dominant susceptibility genes. *Science,* (1990): 347, 124.

McCartney, P. "Ageless Sex. *Psychology Today,* (March 1989): 62.

Miller, D. K., and Allen, T. E. *Fitness: A Lifetime Commitment.* Minneapolis: Burgess, 1979.

Moe, P. In "Metabolic Magic Doesn't Hold Weight in Diet Study," by Angelia Herrin of the Herald Washington Bureau. *The Miami Herald* (May 24, 1991): 24A.

Money, J., and Ehrhardt, A. A. *Man and Woman, Boy and Girl.* Baltimore: Johns Hopkins University Press, 1972.

Montemayor, R. "Men and Their Bodies: The Relationship between Body Type and Behavior." *Journal of Social Issues* 34 (1978): 48–64.

Moyer, K. E. "Sex Differences in Aggression." In *Sex Differences in Behavior,* (pp. 335–372). Edited by R. C. Friedman, R. M. Richart, and R. L. Vande Wiele. New York: Wiley, 1974.

Nisbett, R. E. "Hunger, Obesity, and the Ventromedial Hypothalamus." *Psychological Review* 79 (1972): 433–453.

Ornish, D. Dr. Dean Ornish's program for reversing heart disease: the only system scientifically proven to reverse heart disease without drugs or surgery. Ballantine Books N.Y. Random House, 1990.

Ornstein, R., and Sobel, D. *Healthy Pleasures.* Reading, MA: Addison-Wesley, 1989.

Patsch, J. "Exercise and Hardy Hearts." *Science Digest* 11 (July 1983): 87.

Pearson, D., and Shaw, S. *Life Extension.* New York: Warner Books, 1980.

Plomin, R. "Environment and Genes: Determinants of Behavior." *American Psychologist* 44: 105–111.

_____. "The Role of Inheritance in Behavior." *Science* 248: 183–188.

Plomin, R., and Rende, R. "Human Behavioral Genetics." *Annual Review of Psychology* 42: 161–190.

Quayle, D. "Why We Can't Prevent the Devastating Effect of Alcoholism and Drug Abuse." *American Psychologist* 38 (April 1983): 11–15.

Reichlin, S. "Relationships of the Pituitary Gland to Human Sexual Behavior." *Medical Aspects of Human Sexuality* 5 (February 1971): 157–162.

_____. "Prenatal Exposure to Synthetic Progestins Increases Potential for Aggression in Humans." *Science* 75 (March 13, 1981): 1171–1173.

Reinisch, J. M., and Sanders, S. A. "Effects of Prenatal Exposure to Diethylstilbestrol (DES) on Hemispheric Laterality and Spatial Ability in Human Males." *Hormone and Behavior* 26 (1) (1992): 62–75.

Riedal, S., and McKillip, J. "Friends, Lovers, and Physical Attractiveness." Paper presented at the meeting of the Midwestern Psychological Association, Chicago, May 1979.

Rosenhan, D. L. On being sane in insane places. *Science* (1990): 179, 250–259.

Rosenthal, D. *Genetic Theory and Abnormal Behavior.* New York: McGraw-Hill, 1970.

Ross, H. A., and Martin, C. L. "Children's Gender-based Inferences About Others' Activities, Emotions, and Occupations." Paper presented at the biennial meeting of the Society for Research in Child Development, New Orleans, LA, March 1993.

Rubinstein, C. "Wellness Is All: A Report on *Psychology Today's* Survey of Beliefs About Health." *Psychology Today* (June 1982): 28–37.

Rushton, J. P. "Is Altruism Innate?" *Psychological Inquiry* 2 (1991): 141–143.

Rushton, J. P., Fulker, D. W., Neale, M. C., Nias, D. K. B., and Eysenck, H. J. "Altruism and Aggression: The Heritability of Individual Differences." *Journal of Personality and Social Psychology* 50 (1986): 1192–1198.

Schulte, B. "A nation on a diet" *The Miami Herald* (June 6, 1994): 1A.

Schwibbe, G., and Schwibbe, M. "Judgment and Treatment of People of Varied Attractiveness." *Psychological Reports* 48 (February-June 1981): 11–15.

Shealey, T. "What Doctors Are Learning from Vegetarians." *Prevention* 38 (March 1986): 115–120.

Sizer, Frances S., and Whitney, Eleanor N. *Nutrition: Concepts and Controversies,* 6th ed. St. Paul, MN: West Publishing Company, 1994.

Skinner, B. F., and Vaughn, M. E. *Enjoy Old Age.* New York: W. W. Norton, 1983.

Snowden, D. A. "Adventists Are Rich Source of Data on Diet and Disease." *The Miami News* (November 20, 1986): 3D.

Tasker, F. "Doctors Program Promotes Change of Heart." *The Miami Herald* (February 1, 1991): E1.

Tellegen, A., Lykken, D. T. *Journal of Personality and Social Psychology,* (1988): 54, 1031–1039.

Valliant, E. G., and Valliant, C. O. "Natural History of Male Psychological Health, XII: A 45-year Study of Predictors of Successful Aging at Age 65. *American Journal of Psychiatry* 147 (1990): 31–37.

Walford, R. L. Quoted in "Beyond the Fountain of Youth: Life after Your 100th Birthday." *Miami Daily News* (July 27, 1983): 1C.

Wurtman, J. Eating sweets when depressed or tense. Harvard Medical School Mental Health Letter, (1987): 3, 8.

_____. *The 120-Year Health and Diet Plan.* New York: Simon and Schuster, 1987.

Whitney, E. N., and Hamilton, E. M. N. *Understanding Nutrition.* St. Paul, MN: West, 1977.

Wilson, E. O. *On Human Nature.* Cambridge, MA: Harvard University Press, 1978.

_____. *Sociobiology: The New Synthesis.* Cambridge, MA: Harvard University Press, 1975.

Wineberg, M. S. "The Problem of Midgets and Dwarfs and Organizational Remedies: A Study of the Little People of America." *Journal of Social Psychology* 74 (1968): 97–102.

Wolf, N. *The Beauty Myth: How Images of Beauty Are Used Against Women.* New York: William Morrow.

Wolman, B. B., and Money, J. (Eds.). *Handbook of Human Sexuality.* Englewood Cliffs, NJ: Prentice-Hall, 1980.

Yarasheski, K. E., and Zachwieja, J. J. "Growth Hormone Therapy for the Elderly: The Fountain of Youth Proves Toxic." *The Journal of the American Medical Association,* (Oct 1993), 270 r 14 p. 1694 (1).

■ *Answers to Review Questions*

Critical Review 1 1. T.   2. F.   3. F.
Critical Review 2 1. T.   2. T.   3. F.
Critical Review 3 1. T.   2. T.   3. F.   4. T.
Critical Review 4 1. T.   2. T.   3. T.
Critical Review 5 1. F.   2. T.   3. T.   4. T.
Critical Review 6 1. T.   2. F.   3. T.   4. T.

PERSONAL ACTION PLAN
Physical Self

Taking responsibility for our own physical selves is a new idea for many of us. We have trusted our lives first to our parents, then to our government, our food and drug companies, our doctors, or our spouses. A long and healthy life is something too important to be left to others. We must ensure it ourselves.

The way we eat and drink, work and play, worry and love have more to do with our life chances than such occurrences as accidents, epidemics, or wars. If we are aware of the risks associated with the way we now live, it may be that we will want to make changes that will increase our chances for a long and vigorous life.

I. *Taking stock.* Select the answer that applies to you at this time. Place the number associated with that answer in the space on the right.

Sex: Female (0), male (5). _____

Age/Sex: 35+ male (5), 50+ female (5), other (0) . . . . _____

Parents: No premature deaths due to heart attack, stroke, cancer, diabetes, and so on (0). One side of family (5) or both sides of family (10) contain at least one nonaccidental death before age 65 . . . . _____

Health: Excellent (0), fair (3), poor (5) . . . . _____

Smoking: Do not smoke (0), less than a pack a day (5), more than a pack a day or its equivalent (10). . . . . _____

Alcohol: Do not drink (0), less than one ounce a day (0), less than 2 ounces a day (3), three or more ounces a day (10) . . . . . . _____

Drugs: No drugs (0), infrequent light use (5), infrequent hard use (10), frequent hard use (20) . . . . _____

Weight: Slim (0), less than 10% under- or overweight (0), more than 10% under- or overweight (5) . . . . _____

Exercise: Regular, strenuous, prolonged (0), irregular, interrupted, less strenuous (5), little exercise (10) . . . . _____

Diet: Low in saturated fats, salt, and sugars (0), moderate in saturated fats, salt, and sugars (5), excessive in saturated fats, salt, and sugars (10). . . . . _____

Energy Input: Balanced with output (0), less/more than (calories) output (5), if obese with less, or underweight with more, (10) . . . . _____

Personality: Easygoing, relaxed (0), moderately competitive (5), very competitive and time conscious (10). . . . . _____

Moods: Usually positive (0), frequently anxious, angry, or depressed (5), usually anxious, angry, or depressed (10) . . . . _____

Coping: Usually feel in control (0), at times feel helpless and hopeless (5), frequently feel helpless and hopeless (10) . . . . _____

Job/Home/School: More support than demands (0), demands and support about equal (5), more demands than support (10) . . . . _____

Environment: Quiet; air, water, soil good (0), noisy; air, water, soil polluted (10) . . . . _____

Blood pressure: Normal or slightly below (0), do not know (5), high blood pressure (10) . . . . . _____

Blood Fats: Normal or slightly below (0), do not know (5), high blood fats (cholesterol) (10) . . . . _____

Blood Sugar: Normal or slightly below (0), do not know (5), high or low blood sugar (10). . . . . _____

Glucose Tolerance: Normal (0), do not know (5), low (10). . . . . _____

Total _____

Your total score is a general indicator of the amount of risk associated with your present living habits. A high score could imply a high risk. Highest possible score is 185 points. The lowest possible score that you can have is the sum of your scores on the Age/Sex and Parents

categories. (These are the only scores that you cannot modify by changing your lifestyle.) Only you can determine if your total score is too high. How much risk are you willing to live with? At risk are such premature physical disorders as heart attacks, strokes, and similar maladies.

Some Factors are undervalued—smoking, for example—and others may be overvalued, such as being overweight. The important fact is that you are now aware of the potential risks in your current adjustment pattern. Use this awareness to target certain areas for possible constructive change.

II. *Training for fitness.* If you are not satisfied with your results on the risk test or if you desire to maintain your low score, it is necessary to train. The exercise that is most efficient and effective for reducing the probability of premature physical disorders is aerobic training.

We have chosen a pulse-monitored exercise program that protects one from overexercising. However, we recommend that you receive a medical checkup prior to beginning an aerobic training program.

Steps to fitness are as follows:

1. Determine your training heart rate. In order to do this, first you need to determine your resting heart rate. You do this as follows:

   a. Locate your pulse by placing your fingers lightly on the thumb side of your wrist. You may wish to use the side of your neck rather than your wrist.

   b. Count your pulse for exactly six seconds. Use a sweep-second watch or clock to help you count.

   c. Multiply the number of beats you counted by ten. This figure is your resting heart rate.

   It is best to take this measurement on arising in the morning. An average resting heart rate taken over several mornings is the best figure to use in calculating your training heart rate. The resting heart rate is an indication of the efficiency of your heart. A low number of beats per minute is a sign of a well-conditioned cardiovascular system. Resting heartbeats for people of average fitness vary widely.

   d. Subtract your age in years from the number 220. This gives you your maximum heart rate. This is the fastest that your heart is predicted to beat under conditions of extreme stress. *Do not train at this rate.*

   e. Select a percentage of your maximum heart rate for training purposes. Aerobic fitness requires 50 percent, athletes training for competition select 90 percent. It is possible to train safely at 75 or 80 percent of your maximum heart rate. This will give you full benefit without risk.

   f. Compute your training heart rate. Your training heart rate is computed as follows:

      (1) Maximum heart rate minus resting heart rate multiplied by the selected training percentage.

      (2) Add your resting heart rate to the answer to step one. This is your training heart rate. For example:

You = 24 years old

(1)	Predicted maximum heart rate (220 − age) =	_____	196	(220 − 24)
(2)	Resting heart rate =	_____	65	
(3)	Result of (1) minus (2) =	_____	131	(196 − 65)
(4)	Selected training % =	× _____	0.75	
(5)	Product of (3) × (4) =	_____	98.25	(131 × 0.75)
(6)	Resting heart rate =	+ _____	65.00	
(7)	Training heart rate =	_____	163.25	(98.25 + 65)

2. Select an exercise that you believe you will enjoy or become accustomed to so that you will stay with it for some time. It is better if you select more than one exercise. This gives you variety and, also, better opportunity for stressed muscles to recover.

3. Begin the selected exercise slowly and continue for three minutes. Stop and *immediately count your pulse for six seconds*. Multiply your count by ten to obtain your pulse rate.

4. If your pulse rate is below your training heart rate, the intensity of your exercise was too light. Increase your activity level for three minutes, and count your pulse again. Compare it to your training heart rate. Continue this process until you have found the level of intensity that is required to produce your desired percentage of maximum heart rate. This is the pace at which you must work.

5. Continue the selected exercise at the optimum pace for twelve to twenty minutes. *Do not increase your pace during any training session.*

   Aerobic exercises are nonstop. Tennis, handball, weight lifting, ping pong and golf are not aerobic. Do them for fun, not for fitness.

High intensity (12 minutes)	*Moderate Intensity* (15 minutes)	*Low intensity* (20 minutes)
Chair Stepping	Jogging	Bicycling
Running in place	Running	Swimming
Jumping Rope	Dancing	Walking

6. If your intention is to maintain your level of fitness, do your exercises at the correct pace three days a week. If your intention is to improve your fitness, do your exercises at the correct pace six days a week.

7. After you have trained for a number of days, measure your resting heart rate. It will drop as you become increasingly fit. If it has dropped, you will need to calculate your training heart rate again to ensure an adequate level of intensity during training. Monitor your pulse during training to prevent overexertion and immediately after training to maintain proper intensity.

III. *Energy in/energy out.* Aerobic exercise is great for fitness. It can be but a part of any weight regulation plan. If you are under- or overweight and your physical self would improve by gaining or losing body fat, a plan to adjust the balance between energy in and energy out is called for. Energy out is produced by metabolism plus voluntary activity. Energy in is produced by food consumption. Both are measured in calories. To gain or lose one pound a week, you must increase or decrease your input/output balance by 500 calories each day. The following steps will allow you to adjust this balance while maintaining good health and learning habits of sound nutrition.

1. Check an appropriate weight for your sex, age, and body frame. If you are leading a sedentary life, choose the lower end of the range; if you are quite active, the higher range is appropriate as you will carry weight in lean muscle.

2. Set goals in terms of a target weight and a number of pounds per week (one or two) that you will gain or lose.

3. Complete a list of reasons why you over- or undereat. Example: I overeat when I am bored. I undereat when I am anxious.

   a. _____

   b. _____

   c. _____

   d. _____

   e. _____

   f. _____

4. Complete a list of reasons why gaining or losing weight would be desirable for you. Example: I would feel better.

   a. _____

   b. _____

   c. _____

   d. _____

   e. _____

   f. _____

5. Reflect on and directly observe your eating pattern for at least five days. Note situations and people that are associated with your under- or overeating. Example: I always remain at the table to talk and snack after supper.

   Situations: People:

   a.   a.

   b.   b.

   c.   c.

   d.   d.

6. Make a plan to avoid or alter the problem situations so that you can manage to stay with your diet. Example: A walking lunch break.

   _____

   _____

7. Make a plan to change your interactions with the problem people so that you can manage to stay with your diet. Example: Avoid them or ask for their assistance.

8. Construct a list of positive reinforcers, a series of activities or presents, or positive self-statements that will provide you with pleasure or satisfaction when you consume them. Be sure that they are under your control (that is, you can grant or withhold them from yourself) and that they are pleasures that you do not tire of easily. Examples: reading, shopping, watching TV.

   a. _____

   b. _____

   c. _____

   d. _____

   e. _____

   f. _____

9. Construct a list of steps that you can take to increase or decrease your energy input. Some suggestions are:

   (1) Shop for foods with good nutrition only. Avoid foods that contain excessive fats, sugars, or additives.

   (2) Shop when you are hungry/well fed.

   (3) Select/avoid prepackaged foods.

   (4) Snack/avoid snacking while preparing food.

   (5) Set up informal/formal place settings.

   (6) Serve large/small portions.

   (7) Serve/do not serve seconds.

   (8) Take large/small bites.

   (9) Chew quickly/slowly.

   (10) Linger/do not linger at the table.

   (11) Eat anywhere/only at one place.

   (12) Eat few large meals/many small meals.

   (13) Include high/low calorie servings.

10. Arrange the practices listed above in order of their difficulty. Start with the easiest practice for you to accomplish, and end with the practice that will be hardest for you to follow.

    a. _____ f. _____ k. _____

    b. _____ g. _____ l. _____

    c. _____ h. _____ m. _____

    d. _____ i. _____

    e. _____ j. _____

11. Make a pact with yourself (you may make a written contract with cosigners if you believe it will help) to grant yourself the right to have one or more of the positive reinforcers (from Step 8) each time you meet the criteria of a selected activity from Step 10. For example, grant yourself the luxury of reading a book for pleasure if your shopping bag contains no presweetened cereals. Withhold such pleasures from yourself if you do not meet the criteria you set for yourself.

12. Keep a written record of your activities, your consumption of the earned positive reinforcers, your physical activities (energy output), and your weekly weight gain or loss.

13. Make changes in your pact as needed. Do not blame yourself if you do not gain or lose as you had planned. Blame your activities and/or reinforcers

and change them. You can take larger or smaller steps, change goals, reinforcers, or activities, or consume the earned reinforcers more quickly.

14. When you have reached your desired weight, do not stop your weight program. This should become a lifetime approach to weight regulation. Change your reinforcers from presents to verbal praise and quiet satisfaction in your new physical self.

15. Write down a specific weight, approximately three pounds under or over your desired weight, depending on your problem.

6

THE THINKING SELF

Chapter Outline

FOCUS

As you read this, become aware of the amount of information bombarding your senses. From this page comes knowledge carried in the light that strikes your eyes. Additional visual data come to you from rays reflected from all of the other objects, including your own body, that are within your view. Look around. Be aware of the many colors, forms, textures, and perhaps patterns of motion that are converging on you.

As you handle this book, you receive information concerning its size, texture, weight, and configuration. Can you feel the information flowing to you from the table, chair, and floor? What is the temperature of the air around you? Is it still or in motion? What aromas are being brought to you in the air?

The real world outside us continuously supplies data for us. So does our inner world. Do your feet hurt? Are any muscles tense and uncomfortable? Can you hear gurgling from within? Is your heartbeat strong and regular? What about your breathing? Are your legs crossed, or is one hand in contact with your face? What information about yourself is being transmitted and received at the same time?

Have stray thoughts entered your consciousness during this reading? Information bombardment also comes from mental stimulation. Become aware of your feelings. Where does the information come from that lets us know how we feel? We are all engulfed in a sea of information all the time. More than one million messages make contact with us each second. What enables us to make sense of this buzzing confusion? How are we able to make use of it?

MAKING SENSE OF OUR WORLD

This chapter will focus on the psychological aspects of our attempts to make sense of our world and to bring regularity to its stream of information, which we must do as we constantly make adjustments to our changing world.

contemplation   thoughtful observation and conclusions

deliberation   thoughtfulness in decision or action

Aristotle wrote of two forms of thinking: **contemplation** or thinking about facts (what we believe is true or beautiful), and **deliberation** or the practical use of mental activity *in problem solving*. Both of these forms of thinking are required for successful adjustment. Thinking allows us to reconstruct a model of the past, reflect upon its meaning, and employ that knowledge in manipulating new information in anticipation of the future (Mayer, 1993). Thus *memory* is crucial to adjustment.

We are born with limited skill for processing information. A loud noise will produce a reflexive start in a newborn, but most complex stimuli simply pass by. On the other hand, there appears to be no limit to the capacity of a fully developed human brain to pick up information (Neisser, 1976). In addition, because we do not forget an old fact each time we learn a new one, the limits of human cognition on adjustment are not to be found in our ability to learn or remember but in our capacity to *control the flow of information* that we absorb.

DIRECTED THINKING

cognitive control   the act of choosing what to attend to and what response to formulate and act on so as to maintain a coherent path toward a goal

There are two avenues to **cognitive control.** The first is *the ability to focus on a single item of experience* out of the hundred million events of each moment. Our ability to learn is sharply limited by our ability to attend to or notice relevant cues. Robin Barr (1981) notes that we focus our attention by dividing incoming stimuli into two groupings, the *message* and the background *noise*. We use notions of what we think is important and what we predict will occur to help us distinguish the two groups. Divided attention destroys our concentration.

Max doesn't really like college. What he doesn't like most is having to conform to all the expectations associated with being a college student. He isn't happy here, and his poor attendance reflects his discontent. Max leaves the campus as quickly as possible after each class—no extracurricular activities for him.

His professors say he's bright enough, but he gets very little work done, and even less work done well. Following directions seems to be his academic Waterloo. Max never quite gets his assignments, never quite remembers deadlines or test days, and never quite gets the point of a lecture or discussion.

The first of his family to attend college, Max tells his dad that he didn't miss much. The mind of Max is always a million miles off campus, and it is embarrassing for him when he's called on in class and doesn't know the topic, much less the answer! Max can't or won't concentrate hard or long enough to get a sharp focus on the material he is expected to learn. His grades reflect this divided attention.

Cognitively, Max dropped out of college long ago. His friends don't expect him to finish this term.

Attention-Deficit Hyperactivity Disorder

Max's lack of attention is a product of his negative attitude. He is able to adjust well in other, nonacademic, situations. The central importance of attention in adjustment is dramatically illustrated by children who suffer from **attention-deficit hyperactivity disorder,** or ADHD. Such children display a general inability to attend to relevant clues; this deficit is accompanied by impulsive behavior and restless activity. Such children often fail in school and in social situations and are often labeled by parents or teachers as being willful or lazy. Although the specific cause of their adjustment disorder is not known, a metabolic dysfunction in the brain is suspected. Brain structure appears normal, but reduced cellular activity, as indicated by reduced blood flow, is reported in just those areas of the brain that control attention and movement (Zametkin, 1990). Because they have difficulty staying focused, ADHD individuals seem to be unable to benefit from the opportunity to observe others performing a difficult

attention-deficit hyperactivity disorder a developmental disorder that limits the scope and quality of academic achievement and may impair social functioning.

CRITICAL THINKING ISSUE
Infecting the Mind

The virus of sexual deviancy can be "caught" by children exposed to pornography.

Times have changed! Television, videocassettes, the internet, and even family magazines now display such previously taboo sights as full nudity and sexual intercourse. Obscene publications are now those that depict dismemberment, torture, and child rape. An entire generation of teenagers has had easy access to such eroticism, and the result we see around us is an explosion of premarital sexuality, sexually transmitted disease, unwanted pregnancies, and increased violence against women. Pornographic material should be eradicated and those producing and peddling it should be prosecuted!

Consenting adults have the right to see what they choose, regardless of whether their neighbors are offended by it.

Times have changed! These is no evidence demonstrating that sexually explicit materials cause sex crimes. We will no longer allow local, state, or federal agencies to engage in moral mob rule. They cannot suppress our individual freedom of expression in order to police "dirty pictures." Pornography can teach explicitly sexual techniques, encourage open communication about sex, and promote sexual growth that can perhaps help to preserve the very institution of marriage. We must keep pornography free if we are to use it wisely and not drive it underground.

I take the position that:

role, in other words, they are less able to learn from the successes and failures of others. This deficiency persists into adulthood (Zametkin, 1990).

Effective treatment includes the use of drugs such as *methylphenidate* (Retalin) that stimulate the control centers of the central nervous system or antidepressants such as *imipramine* that reduce their impulsive outbursts. There is no known cure, but we do know that punishment, shame, labels, and threats are not effective management tools. Good management, along with chemical therapy, includes counseling family and school members in the need for structuring the home and school so that ADHD children are able to:

1. avoid stressful situations
2. reduce overstimulation
3. avoid excessive fatigue
4. participate in a stable environment that includes regular routines
5. work and play within consistent, proper limits.

Poor attention can be a product of the situation, not the person. Stimulus factors, such as low intensity, small size, and slight motion can make it difficult for us to notice an important environmental clue. Dull colors, soft sounds, and endless repetition can also reduce our ability to pick out the relevant event from the noisy background. That is why aircraft traffic controllers are so highly stressed. For most of us, attention problems are not the result of stupidity, flawed thinking, or a malfunctioning mind—they are a result of how the mind actually works—*we see what we want to see and/or expect to see.*

The second avenue to cognitive control is *the ability to search meaningfully for connections* between (1) what we are attending to and (2) appropriate information that we have in memory from past experience. An infant can be expected *not* to notice a clear glass plate positioned in front of an attractive toy. He can be expected to react with surprise and rage when he crawls headlong into its hard surface. A toddler *will* notice the glass and effectively waddle around it to reach the toy. This increased capacity in attending to and receiving information, and in directing subsequent responses, represents quite a growth in directed thinking. This capacity can be measured as part of your **"experiential IQ,"** or the degree of insight you display by selectively (1) encoding critical information, (2) combining bits of information to "get the big picture," and (3) comparing the new information to old information you have in memory (Sternberg, 1986).

experiential IQ   the degree of insight you display in processing data, seeing the big picture, and comparing new information with old information

Adjustment as a Change in Thinking

The toddler is more able than the infant to cope with the real world. This is because good cognition is closely associated with good adjustment. Just as the toddler was able to reach his goal without frustration or emotional upset because he could see more selectively, interpret more accurately, and behave more flexibly, so many of our adult adjustment problems are grounded in faulty perceptions, irrational assumptions, and dysfunctional ideas.

Deliberation means problem solving, and is the very definition of adjustment. Listening, focusing attention, and remembering are the most important neurophysiological processes in deliberation. If we understand them, we can better understand adjustment.

We will begin with the theoretical. The process of thinking will be outlined first. We will then turn our attention to the practical—our rational and irrational thoughts. What specific thoughts occupy us during times of decision? What are the effects of certain patterns of thought on subsequent feelings and levels of adjustment?

Critical Review 1

1. Aristotle spoke of **contemplation** as thinking about what we believe is true or beautiful. T F

2. Listening, focusing attention, and remembering are the most important neurophysiological processes in **contemplation.** T F

3. Do you believe that the same person could have a very high **conventional IQ** and a very low **experiential IQ**? How?

4. Do you feel that clinical psychologists have any business attempting to change the way we think? Why or why not?

HOW WE SHOULD THINK: LOGICALLY

According to the Roman statesman Senaca, "Man is the animal who thinks." But how do we think? Deliberation should find expression in reason. We *should* adjust; make our decisions and solve our problems through the disciplined use of rational thought—through the application of deductive or inductive reasoning.

Deductive Reasoning

Deductive Reasoning is the *process of finding (deducting) a conclusion that is logically consistent with two or more premises.* (A premise is something presupposed to be true.) For example:

> Premise 1: A is B
> Premise 2: B is C
> Logical conclusion: A is C

deductive reasoning   the process of drawing inferences by reasoning from the general to the specific

This example is pure abstraction, and so is the process of deductive thinking. It is important to understand the distinction between deductive reasoning as an abstract thinking process and deductive reasoning as a means of adjusting to the real world. The *process of deductive reasoning is simply the correct use of the rules of logic applied to the premises under consideration.* Such a process may or may not yield a conclusion that is true in the physical world. *Deductive reasoning can lead to truth only when all relevant premises are true.* If one's premises are untrue, then one can "think logically" and still reach untrue conclusions. For example:

> Premise 1: If there is no penalty for guessing, higher scores are obtained if one answers all questions on a multiple-choice test. (True)
> Premise 2: Your first answer on a multiple-choice test is your best choice. (Untrue; Ramsey, Ramsey, and Barnes, 1987)
> Logical conclusion: Answer all questions on a multiple-choice test, even if you must guess. Never go back to change a first guess. (false conclusion).

Similarly, if we do not consider *all relevant premises* then we can deduce untrue conclusions regardless of the validity of the premises that we did consider. For example:

Premise 1: Tagamet is the brand name for a histamine antagonist. (True)
Premise 2: Hydrochloric acid in the stomach can be neutralized by Tagamet. (True)
Premise 3: *A stomach ulcer is an open sore associated with excess hydrochloric acid. (True)*
Logical conclusion: Taking Tagamet neutralizes stomach ulcers. (Untrue)

Tagamet does not neutralize ulcers. The needless dieting, recurrent pain, and billion dollar medical costs spawned from this logical but false conclusion resulted because another relevant premise was not considered: *Stomach ulcers are the result of a bacterial infection.*

Only if one's premises *are* true and *all* relevant facts are considered, and if one *applies* logic correctly, is *deductive reasoning an unerring path that leads to true conclusions.* One key to successful adjustment then is to examine all of one's assumptions, both for validity and completeness—and then to reach a conclusion using deductive reasoning. Although we *are* capable of such disciplined thinking in everyday life, we most often do not employ it because we are *not logic machines.*

HOW WE DO THINK: PSYCHOLOGICALLY

When psychologists study how we actually think while solving problems and making decisions they find that we seldom apply deductive reasoning properly. At the very least it takes an inordinate effort and length of time to actually validate all of the premises one needs to solve a real problem, and it is often literally impossible to know if those premises are complete. Consequently, we are compelled to make decisions with uncertain and/or incomplete premises. For practical reasons, we make decisions by *assuming* one or more premises to be true and then applying deductive reasoning to reach a conclusion. This shortcut process is called inductive reasoning. **Inductive reasoning** is the process of finding (inducing) a prediction by applying deductive reasoning to a set of assumed premises.

inductive reasoning   the process of deriving general principles from particular facts

To illustrate this process, predict the next symbol in this number series: 1, 3, 5, 7, ?. At first glance, it appears easy. Upon reflection, however, it can be seen that it is impossible to do with certainty, because *we don't know the **algorithm**, or step-by-step process, by which the numerals were produced; a crucial premise.* However, using inductive reasoning we can assume any number of premises and thus deduce various predictions—all *potentially* true.

algorithm   a mechanical process for testing all possible problem solutions

For example:

Assumed Premise 1: The series is composed of numbers that possess a mathematical relationship: $2 \times 1 - 1 = 1$; $2 \times 2 - 1 = 3$; $2 \times 3 - 1 = 5$; and $2 \times 4 - 1 = 7$.
Logical Conclusion 1: the next symbol in the series is the number given by $2 \times 5 - 1 = 9$.
Assumed Premise 2: The series is composed of consecutive prime numbers. (A number divisible only by one and itself).
Logical Conclusion 2: The next symbol in the series is the next prime number, 11.
Assumed Premise 3. The series is random.
Logical Conclusion 3: The next symbol could be any symbol.

Many other premises are possible, all leading logically to different predictions for the next symbol in the series. It is impossible to know, *at the outset,* which premise and therefore which prediction is correct. If this were a practical problem in which an adjustment had to be made, we would be compelled to choose a premise based on an assumed truth, induce a conclusion, and go with it! How and why one chooses one set of assumptions over another is of crucial importance to cognitive psychology. Research to date finds the following factors to be influential in our thinking process.

1. We make psychological errors in evaluating our deductive reasoning. At times *we believe a conclusion is valid simply because it conforms to what we believe is true.* We stop searching for a valid conclusion if the first conclusion we reach is highly believable (Oakhill and Johnson-Laird, 1985). This human tendency can be illustrated using the real-life example concerning Tagamet and stomach ulcers. The reason so many people believed Tagamet would "cure" their ulcers was because the medical and drug communities endorsed the idea. People simply believed what doctors told them and therefore accepted an incomplete and ultimately fallacious "logical conclusion." Furthermore, the doctors themselves believed it because it was what they were taught, and it seemed plausible because of their knowledge of basic chemistry. The medical world rejected the bacterium premise at first because it could not possibly follow from a premise that they "knew to be true," that is, that bacteria could not survive among the digestive juices of the stomach. (Wrong)

2. We learn different cultural norms relating to the use or nonuse of deductive reasoning. *Many cultures believe and teach that the laws of formal logic are less trustworthy or useful than are laws drawn from personal, sensory experience* (Solso, 1988). University of Moscow students were given the following problem.

> Premise 1: Ivan and Boris always eat together.
> Premise 2: Boris is eating.

When asked to draw a logical conclusion and answer the question, "What is Ivan doing?" most replied as follows: "How can I tell, I can't see him."

3. *We are more influenced by strong beliefs and/or strong emotions than we are by logic* (Forgas and Bower, 1988). Even though we may "know" something makes logical sense, we may act otherwise because of competing beliefs or emotions. We may not engage in fitness exercise because of our fatalistic beliefs concerning health or our reservations about body odor and our image of the ideal male or female, for example.

4. *We actively seek to confirm our initial views, a confirmation bias* (Klayman and Ha, 1987). We only reluctantly alter our existing pattern of thinking or behaving. We tend to close ourselves off psychologically from relevant information that disconfirms our existing beliefs. Never changing your first answer on a multiple-choice test is a good example of a false conclusion that is often slain, but never dies. We remember the times our first guess turned out to be correct. We forget the larger number of times that it turned out to be wrong. Teachers often hear, "I had it right, but changed it." They seldom hear, "Whew, I'm glad I reconsidered that question."

The No Rule Rule

We most often follow no fixed rules in deliberate thinking (Restak, 1988). Fortunately, most of our problems may be solved by application of a simple, direct

heuristic   a speculative formula to guide in the solution of a problem

solution that we have stored in memory. We just retrieve the necessary information and act on it. If the solution is not known, many possible solutions are generated and compared with information in long- and short-term memory. We attempt to structure our thinking so as to fill our need for a *rapid and efficient solution*. As we have seen, for practical reasons we reject the use of an *algorithm*—systematically exploring and evaluating *all* possible solutions until a correct one is found. Computer programs make use of this tactic, not humans. Instead, humans compromise between speed and certainty, and make use of a **heuristic**—an informal, *rule of thumb* method for generating and testing problem solutions. We make use of mental shortcuts that have worked for us in the past. For example, you may decide that because you did well on previous exams by reviewing only your lecture notes, you will review only your lecture notes prior to an upcoming exam. If we lose our car keys, we could search every room in the house. More likely, however, we would first search the one or two places where we usually keep our keys. Like inductive reasoning, a heuristic plan does not guarantee a solution, but it is usually less time-consuming and more sensible.

Heuristic Psychology

In choosing a general heuristic to guide our thinking, we also exhibit very human errors. The most common include:

availability heuristic   the rule of thumb that comes quickly to mind

1. The overuse of the **availability heuristic,** or the rule of thumb that comes most readily to mind. We tend to rely on examples that are easily remembered. This can be useful, but if not appropriate, its error is compounded by the fact that . . .

2. Our initial *mental set* is difficult to change, and this reluctance to change a way of seeing a problem may interfere with our finding a workable solution. This first estimate of the problem forms a starting point, or anchor, and often we do not move very far from our original judgment of the problem. This small adjustment of an earlier estimate is termed the **anchoring heuristic.**

anchoring heuristic   a first guess that serves to limit the range of possible solutions

representative heuristic   the most typical idea that fits the observed facts

3. The selection of a **representative heuristic.** We tend to think in terms of stereotypes, often ignoring the overall probabilities and focusing instead on what is typical of the facts we know. When feverish and coughing, for example, we might diagnose ourselves as having pneumonia (a rare disease) rather than the common cold. Finding the proper representation of a problem is THE stumbling block to finding a solution (Bourne et al., 1983).

framing   the context in which an idea is presented for consideration

4. The **framing** of a problem often determines how we will represent it in our minds. For example, would you be more likely to buy gas from a station that allowed you to save money by paying cash, or one that charged you more for using credit? How a problem is worded can make all the difference in how we see it (Levin, 1987).

DECISION MAKING SKILLS

How can we overcome these human barriers to logical thinking and problem solving? Psychology offers the following strategies that permit the problem solver to exercise some degree of control over the task at hand (Gagné, 1984).

1. Choose heuristics that have high *utility*. That is, choose a rule of thumb that, if correct, will solve your problem, not postpone it, or reduce it, or shift it to someone else.

2. Choose heuristics that have a high *probability* of being realized. Take steps to cure the common cold, not pneumonia, for example.

3. Choose a *hierarchy of subgoals*. Represent the problem as a series of smaller problems, and choose a workable heuristic for each subgoal.

4. Allow for *insight*. With preparation, a sudden representational change in how the problem is viewed can occur at odd places and times, and present a new and more appropriate heuristic for its solution. Allow it to happen. This restructuring, many believe, is central to the solution of all problems.

5. *Work backward*. If your problem is complex or ill-defined, first visualize the goal you are seeking, then work backward in small steps to form a model of the first subgoals that must be achieved if you are to make progress toward that final goal (Janis and Mann, 1977).

THE GROWTH OF THE MIND

Sigmund Freud gave us tremendous insight into the workings of the unconscious mind, and John B. Watson made us aware that our behaviors can be shaped by experiences we cannot recall. The writer of the twentieth century who has had the greatest impact on our understanding of cognition, however, is Jean Piaget (1896–1980), a Swiss psychologist. His notions on the nature of mental development and the effect of mental operations on adjusting to a changing environment are inspiring new avenues of research and application every day.

The Cognitive Theories of Jean Piaget

Piaget published observations, based on the development of cognitive processes in children, from 1927 until his death in 1980. Trained as a zoologist, Piaget was interested in logic and children. He was fascinated with the *wrong* answers children give to everyday questions, because he could learn from them how young minds work. After years of observing his own and other people's children, he concluded that intellectual development follows a definite pattern in all normal children.

To Piaget, *cognition is action* (Phillips, 1975). The mind is a dynamic system that constructs itself in order to take information from the environment. Each new input must filter through an existing knowledge structure, or scheme. At the same time, each new input will strengthen or produce changes in that **brain structure.**

brain structure   the arrangement of the various parts that comprise the brain

Our DNA codes for the building of a generalized brain—a structure that can learn almost anything. Experience determines the specific brain that each of us carries into adulthood. The sequence is as follows: The brain cells themselves are produced during the first half of the fetal period; connecting links (axons and dendrites) proliferate during the next year. From about ten months on, for the next twenty years, used links are strengthened and unused links wither away, making for an efficient but highly specialized brain. After age twenty, the rate of cell growth and cell link decay slows down and it becomes harder to acquire new habits or to alter old ones. In youth or old age, a high activity level seems to promote superior brain structure and mental performance.

Jean-Pierre Changeux, a neuroscientist, believes that "up to 80% of the early synaptic contacts between cells [in the brain] are eliminated during development, while a few are selected and strengthened. The changes occur only as a result of activity" (Pines, 1983, p. 51). Our brain is thus the property of *actions*. In childhood, these actions are largely physical interactions with real objects. Later the actions involve simple, mental representations of real objects encountered in the past. Finally, a complex network of mental representations can become free of specific experiences and form the logical-thinking structures of the adult. Prior to such mental growth, logical errors abound. No amount of training can get a bright three-year-old to make a distinction between appearance and reality, for example. If it looks like a Santa Claus, it must *be* Santa Claus (Flavell, Green, and Flavell, 1986). (See the box in this chapter entitled "Stages of Mental Growth.")

Surviving in a Changing World

Our minds have evolved to store generalizations rather than specifics as memories. Piaget believed that this helps us to survive in a changing world. It allows us to profit from experience even though no experience exactly repeats itself. We "both make sense and impose sense upon the world, simultaneously!" (Alloy and Tabachnik, 1984, p. 141). When we "impose sense," we **assimilate** new information into our existing thought patterns; when we "make sense," we **accommodate,** or modify, these patterns. Lower animals and you and I use the joint influence of prior expectations and current sensations to direct our thoughts, emotions, and actions.

Our cognitive adjustment also involves acting out **scripts.** Scripts involve "events in time," while **schemata** involve "objects in space." The two work together to give us a stage (schemata) to play on and a part (script) to perform. The college classroom is such a schemata, and the role of student or professor just such a script. Successful therapy often requires the painful restructuring of the script of life.

AUTOMATIZED THINKING

A simple example of adult schema formulation is to be found in learning to drive. At first we learn to apply previously mastered motor responses, such as grasping and pushing, to the steering wheel, brakes, and so on. Next we learn to make specific coordinated responses under limited driving conditions. Later we are able to drive a variety of automobiles under vastly different circumstances. Finally we are able to **automatize** driving and perform better when not thinking of the mechanics of driving. (Automatized thinking is the use of unconscious, automatic thought.) We are thus free to focus on the goals of driving, a more complex mental task. The more routines we have automated, the greater brain capacity we have free to focus on relevant, new information. Thus "becoming skillful involves a qualitative chance in how the task is performed" (Keele, 1982).

Automatized Thinking, Problem Solving, and Intuition

Blumenthal (1977) believes that "our ability to learn may thus be limited to the degree that our attention is free and to the degree that it can be directed to the events to be learned" (p. 150). In terms of adjustment, this suggests that if a problem occupies all our mental energy, it is most difficult for us to notice novel

assimilation   absorption of new data into existing mental structures; involves responding to something novel as if it were familiar

accommodation   adaptation of mental schemata to better fit incoming data

script   the perceived part that one plays in the drama of life. Scripts are learned in childhood and may be the root cause of adult maladjustment

schema   Piaget's term for a mental construct we generate to organize experience (the plural is *schemata*)

automatize   perceive and respond without conscious attention or deliberation

Stages of Mental Growth

Piaget's research on the thinking processes of children has led to changes in the way children are being taught at home and in school. He believed that the intellectual skills of all children progress through a series of distinct, orderly, and logical stages of development: the sensorimotor stage, preoperational stage, concrete operational stage, and formal operations stage.

The Sensorimotor Stage

From birth to approximately two years, a child progresses from reflex actions to the ability to form a mental construct, or model, of objects encountered during play. Until the child is about a year old, prior to the development of such constructs, an object that is out of sight is literally out of mind. It simply ceases to exist. A child will again and again respond with surprise as it reappears. At the end of the sensorimotor period a child will search for a missing object—a sign that an image is being retained to help direct the search. Such object permanence, said Piaget, allows the child to think in mental images and enter the world of symbols. Once children learn that their existing knowledge is imperfect—that it won't work for them—their *encoding* (the way they code and store new information for later use) plays a large role in their constructing more advanced knowledge (Siegler, 1983).

The Preoperational Stage

With language abilities, two- to seven-year-old children possess a new instrument with which to solve problems and come to terms with the environment. They will increasingly manipulate objects through mental acts rather than motor acts. Toward the end of the preoperational stage, a child will pause when presented a problem, think about it, and only then respond physically. This pause to reflect signals the emergence of intelligence. Preoperational children are quite egocentric—they can hold but one point of view, their own. This inability to grasp the perspective of the other accounts for much of the frustration for both child and caretaker that abounds during this period. The child's selfishness arises from limited awareness rather than from a character disorder.

The Concrete Operational Stage

The seven-to-eleven age span marks a dramatic unfolding of the child's intellectual capacities. In this stage the ability to

conserve—to understand that objects can be transformed and then changed back into their original shape—develops. Let's use as an example a ball of clay that can be stretched. A child of four will typically report that the stretched ball has more clay. A child of nine can reverse the stretching process in her mind and so is not fooled by the apparent increase in size. This concept of reversibility is the underlying mental operation that makes these giant intellectual strides possible. This stage also marks the emergence of the ability to classify objects in terms of their properties—to be able to discern that there are more yellow crayons than red crayons, for example. This is the beginning of abstract rational thought, the foundation of logic and science.

Interestingly, there is growing evidence that we act as scientists almost from birth. New research with children as young as two years old indicates that they have a remarkable understanding of cause-and-effect relationships, given their limited experience. Both physical and social causation (rather than magical causation) are explored by five- to eight-month-old babies as they turn on light switches, drop food, and watch for the reactions of both people and things around them. The search for cause-and-effect relationships appears to be built into our genetic code (Pines, 1983).

The Formal Operations Stage

Between the ages of twelve and fifteen, the final stage of mental growth occurs. **Formal operations** include conserving, reversing, and decentering (shifting focus on) abstract ideas. These operations allow adolescents to explore hypotheticals—problems that (may) exist only in the mind. Thus, they can reflect on possibilities, evaluate outcomes, and plan and direct future events. Adolescents and adults can explore alternative solutions prior to acting on one specific solution to any real-life problem of adjustment. Idealism flourishes as all things become possible. Piaget believes that giving challenging tasks that are appropriate to each child's stage of development will result in the construction of minds that are at the same time critical and creative. These minds are capable of leading us toward novel and improved responses to the world as it is. Such minds can change the world.

aspects of the situation that might provide useful cues in solving the problem. Rigid, compulsive behavior may result.

Intuition is essentially synonymous with pattern recognition. It grows out of experience that once called for a series of analytical steps (as in driving a car). As

formal operations   the fourth and last of Piaget's stages of cognitive development; characterized by manipulation of abstractions

Experiences with puzzles of varying size, color, and complexity will allow these young children to develop a wide range of specific motor responses to individual "pieces" of the future.

experience builds, the expert begins to chunk (automatize) the steps (and the information gained from each of them) into patterns and bypasses the steps. Experts see a pattern and feel a hunch (Benderly, 1989). "Automatism is not genius, but it is the hands and feet of genius," (Bryan and Harter, 1899) (See page 212 for four analytical techniques that allow us to store information like an expert).

Thinking More Effectively

If you equate poor adjustment with poor information processing, the work of Richard Feuerstein (1979) in helping train poor learners to improve their reasoning and problem-solving skills provides helpful suggestions for increasing effectiveness in adjusting. Feuerstein finds the thinking deficits of poor learners to include:

1. *A passive approach to the environment*. Poor learners readily say, "I don't know," rather than search for a plausible answer. This is like saying, "I can't cope." Adjustment, like learning, requires us to be active and persistent in seeking solutions.

2. *Impulsivity*. Good adjustment requires not acting impulsively but exercising patience and care in searching for meaningful connections.

3. *Failure to recognize problems or to notice that discrepancies are important*. These cognitive deficits in attending to relevant cues can cause poor adjustment in all areas of life.

4. *Failure to make comparisons*. The meaningful-search problem in cognitive control is concerned with making connections between old and new information. Failure to make such appropriate connections is associated frequently with failures to find workable solutions to problems of adjustment.

The importance of Feuerstein's work is that he has demonstrated that these deficits in cognitive skill can be identified in poor learners and remedial programs initiated with the expectation of good results.

MODELS OF REALITY

A single schema, in Piaget's theory, represents many things. It may be as simple as grasping reflex or as complex as a plan to obtain a university degree. The point to be emphasized is that schemata are formed via transactions with the real world. These schemata then direct the nature of future transactions. If we do not have an appropriate schema, we will have no pattern to recognize and will not be able to integrate information that is present in our environment. *This is the focusing-of-attention problem* in adjustment. If our schemata are not rich with relevant connections, we will not be able to make best use of the information that is received. *This is the meaningful-search problem in adjustment.* A schema is the knowledge we have, right or wrong, that leads to our expectations, our interpretations, and our behavior (Hamilton, 1989).

Individual, Schema, and Environment

Ulric Neisser (1976) beautifully illustrates the interaction among the environment, the person, and the schema by contrasting the ability of an infant, an amateur chess player, and a chess master to obtain information from a glance at a chessboard.

> This is the story of three wise men at play. The first wise man is very young, only an infant really. He is enthusiastic and impatient to begin. The second wise man is a novice at the game. However, he is fascinated by chess and eager to improve his performance. The third wise man is an expert. His years of top-level competition have honed his considerable skill to the level of a champion. And now for the performance.
>
> A large chess board is set up in the center of the room. A carefully conceived problem is presented by the exact arrangement of the chess pieces on the board. The audience leans forward as each player, in turn, approaches the problem in terms of his own unique cognitive style.
>
> The first wise man crawls onto the board, scattering the careful array. He quickly grasps the Bishop with both tiny hands and thrusts it into his mouth. The second wise man's eyes dance anxiously over the reassembled pieces. First one sector and then another comes under painful scrutiny. With a deep sigh, the second wise man moves a pawn. The third wise man glances intently at the whole board, turns away momentarily as if in deep thought, and then decisively makes his move.

All three of these "wise men" began on even terms. Each could see the board with its array of carved and colored pieces. They received exactly the same physical messages carried in the light (Gibson, 1966). However, the three differed in the anticipatory schemes each brought to that information and the way these schemes directed further search. The infant saw colors and shapes and was directed toward pieces that could be grasped and placed in his mouth. Such behavior is said to be "stimulus bound," because the external environment alone directs it.

The amateur player and the chess master possessed the capability to go beyond the data contained in the optic array. First of all, they held in memory the rules of chess. This enabled them to perceive the board and its pieces within a cultural system of roles, rules, and goals. This knowledge of the role of each piece, the rules that govern its movement, and the object of the game of chess *freed* both of them to look beyond the physical properties of each piece toward its relative position on the board. Here the amateur and the master parted company. A more limited perceptual schema directed the search of the amateur—the more limited the schema, the more likely a crucial aspect of a position was missed. Chase and Simon (1973) report that an expert player may have in memory as many schemata pertaining to chess positions as we have words in our vocabulary. The chess master is not necessarily brighter than the amateur, just richer in terms of perceptual schemata. Experts "see" in broad strategic concepts that allow them to look ahead and evaluate.

Units of Thought

The chess master has stored in his memory more chess-related information than the novice. But his mastery over the novice is not the result of superior information alone; it also results from the way the information has been stored. It has been stored for optimal retrieval from long-term memory. The ability to organize information in a way that makes it readily accessible for a variety of situations is the mark of a champion. Information must be encoded so that it is flexible and available for transfer to new problem situations.

The infant paid attention to the surface features of the chess pieces—their color, taste, weight, and texture. That is how he would code and store the elements of his chess experience. The amateur and the expert tended to pay attention to deeper, structural features of the chess problem as it was presented to them. The chess novice would tend to store the experience as a specific series of moves to make if the situation came up again. The chess master would tend to recognize the experience as an illustration of, or a variant of, a principle or rule that might be of use in several future situations. As you can see, it is the expert who would profit most from the experience.

The *units of thought* of the toddler consisted of *images* and *muscular responses,* images of things good to eat, and micro movements that allowed him to grasp a tasty chess piece. The novice and expert had two additional units of thought:

1. *concepts* concerning chess, including some with emotional or personal meaning, and

2. a system of symbols, or *language* of chess to help direct their thinking and acting.

These four elements—*images, movements, concepts, and language*—are what make up our thoughts.

THE PERCEPTUAL CYCLE

In terms of cognitive control, the game of chess is similar to the game of life. To be able to profit from experience is the key to good adjustment. Chess is a continuous series of moves and countermoves, an adjustment problem. Successful adjustment is determined by what Neisser terms the *perceptual cycle* (see Figure 6–1).

In this cycle, our original schema directs our sensory receptors (eyes, ears, and so on) and so influences what information we will pick up. This information modifies the original schema and so influences further search and subse-

CULTURAL CROSSCURRENTS
Culture, Language, and Cognition

Did the culture in which you grew up and the language of your childhood alter your brain and so shape its capacity for thought? An uncle of one of the authors of this text served in central Africa during World War II. The men with him spoke a remarkable number of languages, from Latin and Greek, through several Indo-European languages, to Swahili and additional native African tongues. They used to pass the long hours by trying to find what topics could best be conceptualized in which language. They agreed among themselves, at least, that each language gave the mind greater scope and flexibility in thinking of certain topics, *and limited one's ability to think* about others.

Linguist Benjamin Whorf argued that the language of our childhood *determines the structure of our thinking and shapes our basic ideas* (Whorf, 1956). Alaskan Indians can better think of snow, and Arabs can better think of camels,

for example, because they have many more words for those items in their vocabulary than does the average American.

One aspect of our mind—our ability to perceive two-dimensional figures in perspective and to interpret them as three dimensional—seems to be shaped by being brought up among rectangular rooms and buildings according to cross-cultural psychologists (Segall et al., 1990). The Zulu in isolated regions of southeastern Africa, live in a round world of homes and hills, and do not perceive two-dimensional rectangles as we do. On the other hand, Eleanor Rosch (1973) found that a limited vocabulary for colors does not limit one's ability to perceive shades of difference—the Dani in New Guinea just could not describe their perceptions with their two-word color vocabulary! It seems that, although language and culture do not determine thought, they certainly influence it.

quent responses. Our decisions (like moves in chess) can be no better than our information; our information can be no better than the schema that permits its reception. This complex relationship is known as the **encoding specificity principle.** We can retrieve only what has been stored, and how we retrieve that information depends on how it was encoded in the first place (Newby, 1987). All adaptive behavior, in life as in chess, is thus seen as beginning with a continuing set of thinking skills.

encoding specificity principle the relationship among perception, long-term memory, and recall of stored information

The Rules of Life

Piaget also viewed the rules of life as being much like the rules of chess—part natural, part arbitrary. The arbitrary rules are imposed by society. Other rules are laws of logic, or *logico-mathematical knowledge,* that accurately reflect the laws of nature. These can be learned only by individual **invention.** (An invention, in Piaget's formulations, is anything conceived of through insight from an experimental manipulation of objects.) He believed that teachers who tell young children something only to prevent them from inventing it themselves hinder their development. He preferred problems to solutions and structured play to formal instruction.

invent act on objects in order to uncover the properties of these objects, according to Piaget

Inventing Mental Abstractions Just as actions on physical objects, such as balls, can produce an abstract concept of *ball,* so actions on several objects can produce abstract concepts that relate these objects to one another. Piaget (1964) has told the story of a child playing with pebbles. He lays them in a row and counts them from left to right. Next he arranges them in a circle and counts them once more. His count is always the same—ten. This concept *ten* was not to be discovered in any one pebble; it existed only in the relations among the pebbles. It had to be *invented* by the young child. Such rules relating objects to each other are constructed by the mind. They are mental **operations,** or transformations of

operations internal transformations of information from one form to another, producing new structures that modify the object of knowledge

FIGURE 6–1
Our mental schema directs what objects we search for, and the nature of the objects we find influences both our future search and our mental schema.

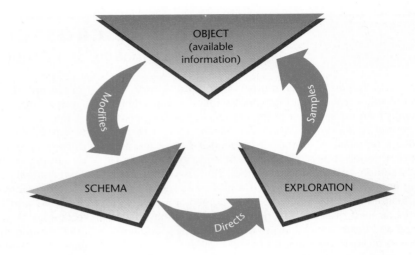

information received through action. To Piaget, such logico-mathematical experience is possible only because we live in an orderly universe.

At first, you remember, the child lives in a mystical, magical universe. Objects appear and disappear, events happen without cause, and time does not exist. As mental schemes develop through experience and maturation, a rich cognitive network becomes available for recall and association with each new experience. This creates more richness. Finally, by the time the child reaches puberty, his or her mind is capable of relating abstract concepts to other, equally abstract concepts. You may recall that Piaget termed this stage formal operations.

Young adults ponder the relationships between time and space, truth and beauty, and so forth. Such motivated inquiry, based on real-world experience but now free of its particularities, enables each of us to form conceptions of the laws of nature. Piaget believed that our collective cognitive structures can closely approximate the laws of nature as they exist because knowledge is cumulative. Long-term memory allows each generation to build on the past. Our very survival depends on our ability to discover properties of objects, to invent relationships among them, and to **accept** conventional wisdom.

accept demonstrate a willingness to receive something as true, right, or proper; to Piaget, a passive behavior

social information learned and shared ways of viewing the world that do not depend on the laws of nature

Social Information **Social information,** the conventional wisdom that makes up the other part of the rules of life, pertains to accepted ways of looking at or relating to objects or events. Such social information is learned in a less physically active manner. By telling or modeling a culture's collective folklore, older members transmit conventions to younger ones. This enhances the meaning and continuity of their lives. Examples of social information are: That is a TV (labeling objects); Polite boys open doors for their mothers (folkways); and Love America—it is the land of the free (accepted feelings and beliefs).

According to Piaget, discoveries and inventions reflect reality and are constantly being restructured to resemble it more closely. Social information also reshapes cognition, but it does not reflect the realities of the laws of nature. Such social realities are important to adjustment, however; we live in two worlds, one dictated by nature, the other dictated by custom and tradition.

Cognitive Influence on Attitudes

Much of our social information is composed of **attitudes.** These are social thoughts—acquired beliefs or opinions that can predispose us to act in certain ways. Ample evidence exists that changes in attitude *precede* changes in behavior (Kim and Hunter, 1993). It is comforting to know that attitudes are learned, and therefore can be changed. Using reason and **social comparison,** the process by which we evaluate our thoughts, feelings, and actions by relating them to other people, we can challenge our troublesome beliefs. If one attitude can be changed, other logically related beliefs will change as well (Reis, Gerrard, and Gibbons, 1993).

Such directed change in the content of our thoughts is known as **cognitive reappraisal,** and, in the words of George Kelly (1955), "No person need be a victim of his own autobiography" (p. 172). We can reinterpret the past, give it new meaning, and use it as a strength rather than a justification for bad feelings or inappropriate behavior. Such reappraisal of the significance of past events helps in adjustment because it:

1. distracts us from dwelling on threatening aspects of our past
2. evokes in us a positive emotional state, and
3. gives us a sense of control (Kim and Hunter, 1993).

See the Personal Action Plan at the end of this chapter for a way to use cognitive reappraisal in improving your own view of yourself and the world in which you live. A note of caution: Social comparison can lead to *groupthink*, a deterioration of "mental efficiency, reality testing, and moral judgment" that can come from giving in to in-group pressures (Janis, 1972).

attitude   a person's predisposition to evaluate other people and events positively or negatively

social comparison   the process of arriving at a self-evaluation by comparing those with attributes within oneself with those perceived in others

cognitive reappraisal   changing illogical or irrational thoughts or styles of thinking

Critical Review 2

1. Deductive reasoning is moving from the general to the specific. T F
2. "Rules of thumb" can never be as fast or efficient as systematic problem solving. T F
3. If a belief is changed, other beliefs that are logically connected to the first will also change. T F
4. How can "working backwards" help us overcome the errors of heuristic problem solving?
5. Do you believe that it is easier or harder for an older person to learn a new language? Use the ideas of neurobiology to support your position.
6. Do you agree with the statement that the amateur and champion chess players are more "free" than the infant? Back up your position with ideas drawn from the perceptual cycle.

TIME, MEMORY, AND REALITY

Cognition can be viewed as a movement away from confusion toward order and stability. To be stimulus bound, like the infant chess player, is to be controlled by the moment. Immediate experience must be integrated into large conceptual schemes if a meaningful, purposeful life is to be possible. Purpose implies desired movement toward a goal. Goal-directed behavior implies the cognition of time—in this case, future time.

The Time Factor in Thinking

Mental processes take time. A useful approach to understanding mental life is to separate short-term activity from long-term activity for purposes of study. Our senses receive information (are stimulated) in temporal order. This time-ordered sequence must be transformed into simultaneous happenings if we are to make sense of our sensations. If all input faded as quickly as it was received, we would be paralyzed or reduced to spasms of uncoordinated motion. Survival demands that we be able to hold information in store while we process it in order to respond in a resourceful manner.

The Psychological Present   Our psychological present is made up of impressions that we rapidly integrate into a single unit of attention. Stimuli bombard us, but we can attend to only one event at a time. Thus, many inputs produce but one impression (Blumenthal, 1977).

This rapid integration of experience takes place at intervals of approximately one-tenth of a second (White, 1963). Within each interval, all information, regardless of its source, is perceived as a unit. Sensations from our internal and external environments must compete with our recollections and new thoughts for attention. Stimuli not attended to disappear without a trace. *In a very real sense, memory is the mind* (Gray, 1991).

Sensory Memory

When two events happen together, they are fused into one, or one is masked from consciousness. At times this is a great advantage, as when the parts of a puzzle are seen as one and the solution appears as a flash of insight. At other times it is a great disadvantage, as when the light turns green just as another car enters the intersection.

Fortunately, we are capable of rapid shifts of attention. Our mind does not normally shut down when it is overloaded—that is, when it receives more information than it can process. It can briefly retain the surplus information it receives. This retention is known as **buffer delay**—a short (about one- to three-second) interval during which impressions are held as direct representations of the events of the past moment. These impressions are available for scanning if our perceptual schemata direct us to search them for additional information. Otherwise, they are displaced by new energy without our ever being aware of their existence.

We must first attend to something if we hope to retain it. In one study, if eight-week-old infants noticed the connection between moving their feet and the movement of a mobile hanging above their heads (it was attached to their feet), they gave evidence of remembering it two weeks later. If they didn't notice it at the time, they gave no indication of recalling it later (Davis and Rovee-Collier, 1983).

The brain stores the memory of each sense in a different part of the cortex. The limbic system has the job of binding these dispersed parts together as a single experience. The frontal lobes are the main site for *memory of source*, the time, place, or manner in which the memory originated (Goleman, 1994). We forget the source of our memories first. You know you have seen that face before, you remember it distinctly, but when—or where? Source memory is frail, and can lead to distortions of thinking and problems of adjustment. When we forget part

buffer delay   a brief absorption of sensory input. Information is held in its original form for 0.05 to 2.0 seconds

of something, we usually fill in the gaps with plausible events from related memories. Dangerous stuff.

Short-Term Memory

We also have the capacity to retain, for a longer period of time, information that was attended to but incompletely processed. This retention capacity, or buffer, is called **short-term memory.** We are able to hold information in our awareness for ten seconds or longer after we have focused on it. It is this capacity that makes us masters of our planet. Here is where intelligence, the ability to make adaptive choices, is to be found. Intentions may be recalled or generated, and information from our past may be combined with impressions of the moment and recent past. In these ten seconds, our past, present, and future are suspended in the same attentional *integration* (the same mental time and space) and can be scanned in order that we may give direction to our actions. This is where talent and experience help. Skill in any endeavor depends upon one's knowledge base

short-term memory   the part of memory that holds impressions for five to twenty seconds for monitoring or restructuring

Daydreaming is universal.

in that area. If you know a great deal, you can take in large critical chunks of information, recognize problem situations, and temporarily remember them longer than one who is less knowledgeable (Trotter, 1986). This gives the expert a greater chance of making a superior adjustment to the perceived problem.

Rehearsing Items in Short-Term Memory   This glorious opportunity rapidly fades. In ten seconds or less we are reduced to the lower primate level—perhaps capable of brilliant insight, but limited to immediate reactions. We can overcome this mental limitation by *rehearsing,* or repeating information to keep it in short-term memory. Look up a telephone number at random. Do not repeat the number to yourself or write it down. After thirty seconds try to dial it without error. It is difficult not to rehearse such information, because this cognitive strategy has become so much a part of our everyday adjustment pattern.

It is also very difficult to retain complex information in short-term memory and at the same time perform complex operations on it. For example, the really interesting parts of solving adjustment problems involve deciding what to do in the first place, monitoring our chosen response, and judging its progress and potential. These *metamemory* components of planning, monitoring, and evaluating compete for the limited space in our short-term memory. Both processes seem to occupy the same central psychological space. Perhaps it is difficult for you to retain specific statements you are reading while trying to relate them to cognition and adjustment. Stray thoughts having absolutely nothing to do with psychology may also intrude into your awareness, competing for the same mental time and space.

Long-Term Memory

Perhaps you also daydream while you study. Daydreaming is universal, and beneficial. Fantasy and daydreaming are associated with positive emotional adjustment, lower levels of aggression, and greater mental flexibility or creativity (Klinger, 1990). In daydreaming, we bring together, in short-term memory, separate impressions from events that happened at quite different times. This ability to reconstruct past events and fuse them with present integrations is included in what is termed **long-term memory,** or knowledge.

long-term memory   Knowledge. This part of memory involves persistent, organized, and often automatic ways of cognitive processing. Terms for mental structures related to long-term memory are *symbol, schema, concept,* and *attentional set*

Although impressions (rapid mental integrations) and immediate recall (short-term memory) are considered to be the product of electrochemical activities in the brain (Harter, 1968), long-term memory is considered to be a product of our own internal reconstruction (Neisser, 1967). The greater the time delay between exposure and recall, the greater the proportion of reconstruction found in the retrieved material (Singer, 1982). Konorski (1967) found the neural processes that produce mental images to be widely distributed across the entire brain. Such processes direct the formation of Piaget's schemata and your daydreams. Your dream fantasy may represent a close approximation of events of your past, or it may be an original composition. Combinations of fact and fancy are equally possible.

Cognition and Reality

From what has been said about human thinking, you may have concluded that our world is largely *of our own choosing* (through perceptual schemata) *and of our own making* (through internal construction). It follows that at times it is difficult

Thinking Styles and School Performance

In general, schools reward a particular cognitive style (Shade, 1983)—an **analytical** style that requires focusing on external stimuli and categorizing abstract events in terms of certain features. The typical high achiever tends to process information using the analytical, hypothesis-testing approach. He or she is self-motivated, self-directed, and task oriented.

Another style is displayed by the intuitive thinker. Students who trust their intuition more than they trust "scientific fact," who require more motivation and direction, who are more people centered and prefer global thinking, class discussions, student presentations, and "hands-on" class activities find college much more difficult because they do not profit as much from lectures, textbooks, and handouts.

If you are an intuitive thinker, you can master the analytical cognitive style once you know what professors and most professions expect. Alternatively, you can shop for that occasional professor who uses student presentations, review sessions, study questions, and other means of motivating students to give them a clear understanding of what they are to know. You can also profit from knowing that it is your right to obtain whatever structure and cues you need in order to learn. In short, you can either change your cognitive style or take the trouble to get the help your natural cognitive style demands. We strongly recommend the latter.

Study Aids

The findings of cognitive psychology support the notion that active study is most helpful. Encoding processes, such as the passive scanning of a text, are sufficient for immediate retrieval but are not usually sufficient for optimal long-term retention. Instead, you have to organize the information for future recognition or recall. Recognition and recall depend on similar information processing. In recognition, we quickly match our sensations with our perceptions by using cues from our past history, the environment, and the content of our problem. We use the same process in recall, with the difference that the matching takes longer. The term *search for associative meaning* (SAM) describes both recognition and recall (Gillund and Shiffrin, 1984).

Professors help you learn when they give you specific instructions to learn and inform you that you will be tested on the assigned material. In trying to anticipate what will be asked, you organize the information in a meaningful fashion; this encoding benefits long-term more than short-term retention. Without such organization, long-term recall is

poor (Masson and McDaniel, 1981; Halpin and Halpin, 1982). Recall is enhanced if we encode new information within a meaningful context and in a logical order (Wall et al., 1986). Students who study for and take a test have been found not only to achieve more but to retain their learning longer than students who "study to learn" rather than study for a test (Singer, 1982).

If speed of recall is your problem and you can't complete tests on time, night classes may be for you. Tilley and Warren (1983) found that information retrieval is faster at night because of generally increased levels of mental arousal. Errors also increase, though; so if you are "quick but sloppy," an early morning class seems in order.

Many college classes demand the mastery of a great number of vocabulary terms. If the word you are to learn refers to a concrete object, something that occurs in nature and can be seen, the use of vivid imagery as an encoding device improves retention and retrieval. The generation of similar images at both encoding and retrieval is a helpful strategy.

When encoding abstractions, words without concrete referents, the use of verbal coding produces significant improvement in retention. Memorizing definitions helps in these special cases. Finally, if you are mastering material that has a definite mood, such as a poem, painting, or period of history or culture, your retrieval will improve if you get yourself into a similar mood during both encoding and retrieval—while studying and again while being tested (Bower, 1981).

Cognitive psychology helps us adjust to the demands of learning by pointing to the importance of organizing new information into meaningful clusters while studying and connecting the new information with what is already known. The use of mnemonic devices is supported by research (Camp, Markley, and Kramer, 1983). When we use **mnemonic** memory aids, we tie new information to letters of the alphabet, vivid images from our past, familiar story lines, and the like. The new information is recalled as the familiar story unfolds, for example. Positive self-talk, as you will learn later, can be used to control your actions and improve your learning. You can use self-talk to inhibit extraneous motor behavior (such as pencil tapping or inappropriate talking) and better focus your attention on what is to be learned (Berk, 1986). The introduction to this text gives additional aids for learning and remembering the material from this textbook.

for us to be sure that what we are experiencing is really there. However, our original schemata are grounded in concrete actions on the real world, and our original mental constructions are immediately acted on or tested for reality. Thought and action in infancy are simultaneous events. Such stable, well-

analytical   pertaining to the separation of anything into its constituent parts

mnemonics   systems for improving memory

grounded knowledge forms a hard core of reality from which to distinguish fact from fancy. A part of this hard core of reality is our stable mental construction or schema for ourselves—our self-concept. Bower (1972) believes that we use self as a monitor of experience. Judgments of *self-not self and real-not real* flow from thoughts, actions, and images that have become automatized through constant attention and repetition. Our body image, for example, is based on such continuous observations and comparisons (see chapter 5 for more about body image). When impressions or mental constructs do not correspond to these stable mental models, we tend to reject their reality. We are even capable of training ourselves to monitor our dreams and alter the endings or awaken ourselves if they become disturbing.

Cognitive Dissonance Theory

cognitive dissonance theory
theory relating to the effects of perceived inconsistencies between beliefs or between beliefs and feelings or actions

Much interesting work is being done in investigating how our psyche works to bring its thoughts, feelings, and actions into harmony. **Cognitive dissonance theory** (Festinger, 1957) holds that we tend to reconstruct knowledge of our actions, beliefs, or feelings in order to balance them with each other. We seem to prefer a predictable world and a positive self-image. If, for example, we hear ourselves say one thing and then see ourselves do just the opposite, or if we discover that our best friend loves our worst enemy, we feel uneasy, guilty, or insecure. In order to reduce this psychological discomfort, or *cognitive dissonance*, we unconsciously reconstruct reality. We may manufacture a justification for our action or fail to notice obvious but disturbing facts. We may deny our thoughts, feelings, or actions and be surprised to find that our attitude toward both our friend and our enemy has subtly changed.

In 1979, Festinger and Carlsmith directed college students to complete about thirty minutes of very tedious and boring work. As they were about to leave, each student was asked to tell the next subject what an exciting and thrilling task it had been. Some students were given twenty dollars for telling this white lie; others were given one dollar. After the lie had been told and the fee collected, the subjects were asked to rate for themselves the interest level of the original task. Which group of students do you think rated the dull task most interesting?

Most people predict that the ones who received the twenty dollars would change their opinion on the basis that "money talks." Money does talk. In this

Living with Survival

On October 13, 1972, a Uruguayan Air Force plane crashed in the Chilean Andes. Sixteen people survived sixty-nine days of subzero temperatures and the constant threat of starvation. They were trapped in the wreckage with twenty-nine others who had died in the crash or shortly afterward. The survivors later revealed that they had stayed alive by eating the flesh of the dead.

They all held that cannibalism was horrible. In order to survive the awful knowledge of their actions, each survivor tried to reduce the gap between his beliefs and his behavior. One compared the cannibalism to a heart transplant, in which human organs are taken in by others so that they might live. Others found support in the tenets of their religious faith: They found a parallel between their actions and the ceremony of holy communion, in which each individual symbolically drinks the blood and eats the flesh of Christ so that he or she might live. (Reed, 1974)

instance, the students who were paid more said, "I lied for the twenty dollars." Somehow this sounds more acceptable than what the student who got less money said: "I'm an honest person, but I just lied to my fellow classmate for one dollar." The group members who received a dollar couldn't deny what they had told the next subjects, so they convinced themselves that the task was really interesting. They were the ones who rated it higher. The twenty-dollar group could justify their lie, so they didn't need to change their attitude.

Smoking provides us with a daily dose of cognitive dissonance. Those who smoke can see that negative consequences result from their behavior. They are in daily mental conflict and must add beliefs consonant with their actions to support their repeated smoking behavior that they can underestimate, but not deny: "The link between cigarettes and lung cancer is only statistical. My uncle smokes and he is seventy-five years old. Smoking keeps me slim; fat people die of heart attacks. Smoking relaxes me; stress kills." The wisdom of the addicted. Dissonance is reduced if they can say, "Everybody I know smokes."

Cognitive dissonance acts as a drive state. If we are hungry or thirsty, we take action to find food or drink. In the same way, if we sense an inconsistency between our behavior and our attitude, we do something to reduce the tension produced by that knowledge. Each time we make a decision, we feel such dissonance.

> Parents are a pain. If my parents knew I'd dropped biology, they'd probably tell me, "Get back into that lab or get yourself home!" I can't go back, either to the lab or home. I can't tell them.
>
> I'll have to tell them sometime. This is killing me. I know they can't afford for me to be dropping classes they've paid for. I also know I can't go back to that class. Maybe I'll write them a letter. No, I'll call Mom. She'll let me talk long enough to explain. On the other hand, Dad gets mad quickly but gets over it just as quickly. That's it; I'll call Dad and get it over with.
>
> The trouble is, no matter what I decide, I'll think I did something stupid. I'll feel bad no matter what I do.

Postdecisional Depression

Something like the preceding anecdote happens whenever we have to make a difficult choice. Immediately afterward we believe we've made the wrong choice and feel sad. Such *postdecisional depression* is quite common. We reevaluate the factors involved and elevate the importance of those that point toward the correctness of the choice we didn't take. The resulting anguish is usually short-lived. Because we cannot easily undo our choice, we quickly increase the importance of the factors that are consonant with out choice and thus reduce our pain. We avidly read brochures extolling the virtues of the automobile we have just purchased, for example.

Limits on Our Ability to Cope

Read the box entitled "Living with Survival." The process of cognitive dissonance reduction helped the Uruguayan survivors cope with stark reality. At times, however, the physical bases of our mental processes place limits on our ability to cope with complex human problems. For example, as you recall, we can retain in short-term memory only a limited number of impressions (about six to eight) at one time. This places a limit on the complexity of problems we can successfully attack. There are also limits on the complexity of an image that we can hold in our mind. Similarly, human adjustment problems are typically quite complex. They must be reconstructed into a series of simpler problems if they are to be resolved. Mental strategies provide for such restructuring by making it possible to:

1. Focus our attention on relevant cues.
2. Delay processing of overload information until later.
3. Bring together information from our past and present.
4. Transform impressions into long-term knowledge.
5. Scan these new constructions for meaningful cues.

These impressive capabilities enable us to select a potential solution and act on it or direct our actions toward further search.

Critical Review 3

1. Do you have an analytical or intuitive learning style?

2. Have you ever used a mnenomic such as HOMES to memorize a list of items? Can you still recite the list?

3. How do you handle postdecisional depression? How long does it usually last in your experience?

4. Why are each of these cognitive processes essential? A. Attention in sensory memory; B. Rehearsal in short-term memory; C. Connections in long-term memory.

5. How does cognitive dissonance theory help one to accept the mental gymnastics used by the surviving Uruguayan Air Force crash victims to rationalize their cannibalistic behavior?

SELF-TALK

The great contribution that cognitive theories have made to adjustment psychology is the notion that a great deal of what we feel and do is directed and controlled by what we think. Most clinical psychologists are practical. They tend to use what works in attempting to help their clients. There is growing evidence that a combination of interventions—that is, altering thoughts, feelings, and behaviors—is superior to a more pure form of insight, sensitivity, or behavioral therapy alone (Meichenbaum, 1977).

Our behavior does not seem to be determined by external events alone. Our thinking is also important. Albert Bandura observed that "If a child realizes that misbehavior will get him nowhere, he stops." The behavior of stopping is not merely a function of external punishment, but also of new cognitions. Even hyperactive children, who seem to overreact to the slightest stimulation, are chiefly directed by an interaction of sensations, perceptions, and emotions. If such children perceive that they are accepted and that the demands placed on them by others are reasonable, their episodes of hyperactivity are significantly reduced (Peter, Allan, and Horvath, 1983).

Internal Dialogue and Directed Thinking

internal dialogue   the soundless speech that makes up much of what goes on in our heads, our private verbal worlds

Internal dialogue, the flow of conscious events that goes on in our heads, is important in guiding all types of behavior. Donald Meichenbaum (1969) has

---

Bored? Just Pay Attention!

"In some cases, at least, people get bored because they're distracted from concentrating on whatever they're trying to do, not because the activity itself is boring. . . . It's not that boredom is the reason you can't concentrate, instead feeling bored lets you know that you're not concentrating the way you should be. It's the way one part of the mind tells the rest of the mind it's not doing a good job. . . . For everyone, there's a level of distraction which is too low to be noticed and identified as a distraction but high enough to interfere and make you feel bored."

—Dr. James Laird, Clark University, Worcester, Massachusetts

---

been successful in training hospitalized schizophrenic patients to emit "healthy talk" while being interviewed by teaching them to instruct themselves to do so during the course of an interview session. He believes that self-talk aids us in attending to the task at hand. It also prevents distracting stimuli from hurting our performance. A number of his trained subjects actually repeated aloud the verbal instruction "Give healthy talk; be coherent and relevant" while they were being interviewed. Vygotsky (1962) defines *intelligence* as the ability to benefit from instructions, including self-instructions.

As adults, we do not usually repeat out loud the speech that is directing our behavior. However, this was not always so. Luria (1961) proposed a three-stage process by which voluntary motor acts come under verbal self-control in humans. At first, the speech and gestures of significant others direct a child's behavior: "That's a good girl; put your toys in the toy box." The next step involves the child's talking out loud while regulating her own behavior: "Toys—box—good girl." Finally, the child will be governed by covert, or inner, speech while putting the toys away and feeling good about herself. Overt private speech seems to be stimulated by social experience (popular kids make greater use of it) and reaches its peak usage at age four among brighter children, one to three years earlier than the average age. All children stop overt private speech by age nine (Berk, 1986).

Inner speech is not always silent. When you are performing a task you have mastered, and all is well, you are not aware of your inner dialogue. It is unconscious. Under stress, however, speech fragments appear in consciousness or are actually uttered aloud (Gal'perin, 1969). You may be driving your car, performing all of the requisite motor tasks unconsciously and efficiently, when the image of a police car appears in your rearview mirror. At once you become painfully aware of your every driving act. You may well hear yourself saying aloud, "Slow down, left turn signal," and so on.

Inappropriate Self-Talk

People who have adjustment problems frequently engage in inappropriate self-talk. For example, both aggressive and impulsive children tend to emit immature verbalizations while engaged in problem-solving tasks (Camp, 1975; Meichenbaum, 1977).

In an interesting study of male university students who rarely dated and who had high anxiety concerning interpersonal relations, it was found that while they rated their own social performance as ineffective, an objective rating indicated that they actually had as many social skills as men who dated often

Handicapped Children

Billy and Lori are quiet children. They are well behaved but not really thoughtful. They do what they are told. In school, the teachers say that they are no trouble, but they seem to be slowly falling behind the other children in classroom performance. As schoolwork becomes more complicated and the children are asked to plan and complete increasingly complex tasks, Billy and Lori seem more and more lost.

Their parents use a "no-nonsense" approach to raising hard-working, God-fearing youngsters. Their father lays down the law and backs it up if he has to. Their mother says little; she just expects her children to mind. "Don't ask why, just do it—and don't try to talk me into anything, either."

Such authoritarian parental attitudes are often expressed in the liberal use of external punishments and the restricted use of verbal reasoning in producing home discipline. Children from such homes are handicapped because they have had little practice in using spontaneous speech to obtain help and little training in using internal speech to direct and control their own behavior. They enter school with this handicap, and it becomes more damaging as the years roll by. (Camp, Swift, and Swift, 1982)

(Glasgow and Arkowits, 1975). Their difficulty lay in their cognitive deficits, not their physical attractiveness or social skills. Twentyman, Boland, and McFall (1981) found infrequent daters to be victims of a low level of interaction with members of the opposite sex. They were less knowledgeable about social cues and less skillful in interpreting their effect on others. Added to these mental handicaps was a thinking style that labeled social setbacks, such as being turned down, as *catastrophic*. This caused them to avoid initiating interactions with attractive females.

"Apparently, a fear of failure is less of a problem to high frequency daters, some of whom reported making many unsuccessful overtures toward women for every instance of success—with little effect on their self-confidence" (Twentyman, Boland, and McFall, 1981, p. 544). Negative self-talk, rather than real success or failure, seems to have controlled the feelings and actions of the infrequent daters.

Noncreative people are also prone to engage in negative self-statements—verbal attacks on themselves (Patrick, 1937). They tend to label themselves as noncreative and to put down their own efforts and probability of success.

All of us have had some experience with negative self-talk. When we notice something unusual concerning our own behavior, some sign that our efforts are not working, we usually respond with an internal dialogue "comprised of negative self-statements and images, which likely have deleterious effects" (Meichenbaum, 1977, p. 217). Meichenbaum went on to say that we rarely consider the role our own thinking plays as a source of our poor performance.

Irrational Beliefs

The basic premise of cognitive therapists is that emotional suffering and inappropriate behavior are due to irrational mental constructions of events and faulty assumptions about the reactions demanded by these events. These assumptions lead to an internal dialogue that, in turn, gives rise to negative emotions and faulty behavior (Ellis, 1962). For example, if you enter a crowded

Negative self-talk may stand between this boy and his desire to interact in this social situation.

room thinking everyone is staring at you and making remarks about you, you may feel anxious, depressed, or infuriated and therefore walk with an air of bogus superiority, resignation, or animosity. Your feelings and actions are the direct result of your thinking process and the specific content of your thoughts.

Albert Ellis, the founder of **rational-emotive therapy,** lists the following as common sources of misconceptions about the true nature of everyday events (for a more complete list, see chapter 3):

1. I must be loved or approved of by everyone.
2. I must not make errors or ever do poorly on anything I undertake.
3. People and events should always be the way I want them to be.

rational-emotive therapy a technique for (1) determining the properties of upsetting events, (2) identifying specific beliefs that give rise to negative emotions, and (3) helping clients to alter these beliefs so as to improve behavior

Another, more fundamental irrational belief is that a person's worth as a human being is solely dependent on, and determined by, the opinions of other people. The specific cognitive beliefs just outlined lead to a rigid self-evaluation: "I must be perfect to be loved; I must be loved by all." They also lead to a rigid evaluation of others: "Everyone should think and act as I believe they should." To a person who has internalized such a belief system, the world is composed of people and events that are forever disillusioning, tragic, or threatening.

Our negative expectations, or irrational beliefs, can also become automatized. These beliefs then appear spontaneous and compelling. Such cognitions may lead to maladaptive actions that produce the very effect the irrational belief predicted, thus confirming and reinforcing the cognitive style. Although we all entertain irrational expectations at times, we usually manage to contain or repress such dysfunctional thoughts and act on more realistic assessments of the events that confront us (Meichenbaum, 1977).

Questionnaire

What Stands Between Myself and Professional Learning?

You are leaving the ranks of amateur competition and entering the arena of the professional learner. It is a different world. The professions require a cognitive style that allows for skillful, rapid processing of information. The following ideas, drawn from this chapter, can help you identify possible barriers that make it more difficult for you to take advantage of your opportunities to learn. Place a check next to those statements that seem to apply to you at this time.

_____ 1. I trust my own intuition more than scientific fact.

_____ 2. I say "I don't know" without searching for an answer.

_____ 3. I tend to be an impulsive, rather than a patient, learner.

_____ 4. I often fail to notice learning problems as they arise.

_____ 5. I require an outside reward or threat to get me to study.

_____ 6. I need very specific directions if I am to get my work done correctly and on time.

_____ 7. I am more people-centered than idea-centered.

_____ 8. I like to think in global terms, but find it hard to concentrate on the specific facts.

_____ 9. I learn most from class discussions, "hands-on" activities, and student presentations.

_____ 10. I seldom use positive "silent speech" to help me stay on a learning task.

_____ 11. I frequently dwell on negative images of myself as a learner.

_____ 12. I find myself thinking such irrational beliefs as "I must not make errors or do poorly on anything I undertake."

_____ 13. I learn very little from lectures or textbooks.

_____ 14. I find it easy to justify a personal conclusion that is not supported by the overall evidence, and to ignore important data that disconfirm something that I hold to be true.

_____ 15. I tend to exaggerate the negative meanings associated with learning activities.

_____ 16. I oversimplify events so as to find answers that are all good or bad, right or wrong.

_____ 17. I overgeneralize the importance of a single learning event, such as a poor test score.

_____ 18. I set short-term goals for my immediate satisfaction, rather than long-term goals for intellectual growth.

_____ 19. I become anxious about my anxiety about learning.

_____ 20. I become depressed about my lack of effective learning.

All of us check some of these barriers, none of us checks them all. Turn to the end of this chapter to see what these choices indicate.

---

cognitive-behavioral therapy
the branch of behavior therapy that deals directly with changing maladaptive thoughts

COGNITIVE-BEHAVIORAL INTERVENTIONS

Cognitive-behavioral therapy attempts to help people regain the ability to see the world as it is, to rationally assess the present, and to respond with greater

---

Destructive Beliefs

Each of us learns a system of verbal rules that we come to accept as true. This network of assumptions acts as the filter for our experiences. Automatically it guides our attention and directs our responses. Unfortunately, not all of these beliefs are literally true; not all will stand up to objective analysis and reflective reasoning. The untrue portion of our belief system accounts for many of our problems of adjustment.

Below you will find two listings of destructive beliefs. The first is associated with general emotional discomfort; the second is more specifically related to emotional depression.

- List 1. Beliefs associated with general emotional discomfort (Ellis, 1973, p. 37):
  - It is an absolute necessity for an adult human to be loved or approved of by virtually every significant other person.
  - One should be thoroughly competent, adequate, and achieving in all possible respects to consider oneself worthwhile.
  - Certain people are bad, wicked, or villainous, and they should be severely blamed and punished for their villainy.
  - It is catastrophic when things are not the way one would like them to be.
  - It is easier to avoid than to face life's difficulties and self-responsibilities.
  - Human unhappiness is externally caused, and people have little or no ability to control their terrors and disturbances.
  - One's past history is an all-important determiner of one's present behavior; and, if something once strongly affected one's life, it should definitely continue to do so.

- List 2. Four common misconceptions of the genuinely depressed (Raimy, 1975):
  - I will be depressed forever.
  - No one understands the depth of my misery.
  - If I get any more depressed, I will lose my mind.
  - If I recover at all, recovery will take a long time and will be incomplete.

---

flexibility to its demands. To do this, therapists attempt to help clients change both their style of thinking and some of their specific thoughts. Beck (1976), a cognitive-behavioral therapist, teaches his clients to recognize and monitor their own cognitions. Largely by keeping careful records, his clients learn to use specific examples of their own behavior to test the validity of their cognitions and to become aware of the negative effect of irrational beliefs on their emotions and subsequent actions. With the help of therapy, distortions in thinking and dysfunctional thinking styles are uncovered, examined, and made more realistic. For example, the statement "My whole week was a disaster" might be examined in terms of the assignments given and accepted for the week and in terms of any accomplishments made during the week and recorded on the mandatory activity record. Alternative and less-catastrophic interpretations are encouraged, and changed cognitions and behaviors are elicited and reinforced. Beck finds such an approach superior to nondirective and supportive procedures in the treatment of emotional disorders, especially depression.

Thinking Deficits of Clinical Patients

Larry, having failed a college algebra exam, is afraid that he is terrible in math, can never pass college algebra, and therefore must give up his dream of becoming an accountant. The situation appears hopeless.

In near desperation, Larry meets with his algebra professor. He learns from her that his mathematical reasoning, as demonstrated in class discussions, is excellent. The professor asks a few questions and then tells Larry there are several glaring gaps in his high school training in algebra. She offers Larry the use of a programmed text in algebra, a self-paced book that will allow Larry to catch up on his preparation for college work. She notes that Larry views math as an endless series of steps to memorize, and she emphasizes that math is instead a language, a tool for precise thought.

Larry begins to reconceptualize his problem. He is weak in math skills but thinks well in mathematical terms. He now knows that math is a tool for thought. His deficits are not overwhelming, and he has access to both text and teacher to help him overcome them. He wants to be an accountant, and an extra semester of study, or the use of a math tutor, does not seem too high a price to pay for a chance at a lifelong career.

Nothing, and everything, has changed. Larry has still failed his college algebra exam, but somehow now that does not seem to be so terrifying.

Beck (1970) finds that his clinical populations, like Larry, tend to:

1. Make faulty inferences (draw conclusions inconsistent with available evidence).
2. Exaggerate the negative meaning of events.
3. Ignore important data that disconfirm a belief.
4. Oversimplify events as being all good or bad, right or wrong.
5. Overgeneralize the importance of a single event—for example, view a poor test score as a sign of a worthless life.

Imagine, for example, that you find yourself playing golf in a foursome with three strangers. They know each other and, after giving you a courtesy greeting, stick pretty much to themselves. If you (1) inferred that their lack of involvement with you signified that they did not respect you, you could (2) feel insulted and resentful, and (3) not be aware of the little courtesies of the course that were being extended to you during the round, and (4) conclude that they were deliberately insulting you. If you saw this as confirmation that you lacked worth as a person, you could (5) view the entire round as a catastrophe.

Posttreatment Changes in Thinking Style

After successful therapy, Beck's clients are reportedly more aware of what they fail to say to themselves that would help (cognitive deficiencies) and what thoughts or thought patterns interfere with adaptive responses (cognitive excesses). Such clients become more capable of viewing negative events as *disappointing* rather than tragic and *unfortunate* rather than catastrophic.

Cognitive-behavioral therapists also teach new beliefs, such as: (1) that it is irrational to expect others to act as you think they should act; (2) that it is not necessary to be loved or approved by everyone; and (3) that the disapproval of others is not proof of inadequacy. As a result of such rethinking, clients' assessments of themselves and others become more positive and supportive. In their work "Mistakes That Can Ruin Your Life, and How to Avoid Them," Lazarus and Fay (1975) list the most common mistaken beliefs, explain them, and give instructions on how to rethink and change to avoid making them in the future.

When we learn to view cognitions as behaviors that can be modified, *learned helplessness* (the belief that we are powerless to change life's circumstances) can be restructured to become *learned resourcefulness* (the belief that we can systematically improve existing conditions). Goldfried and Goldfried (1975) train their clients to generate a series of statements that instruct them to:

1. Identify problems.
2. Produce alternative solutions.
3. Subject each to logical and/or empirical tests.
4. Repeat this sequence until a satisfactory adjustment is made.

Recently, a comprehensive cognitive-social learning model for social skill training was tested and found to be effective (Ladd and Mize, 1983). The model featured three basic training objectives:

1. Enhancing social skill concepts. This means building concrete images of what skillful behavior looks like.

2. Promoting skillful performance. This means giving opportunities for the practice of correct mental and behavioral responses.

3. Fostering skill maintenance and generalization. This means providing opportunities for follow-up training and for appropriate application of the new skills in a variety of social situations. "This requires training in self-evaluation and self-adjustment" (p. 156).

Barriers to Changing Our Style of Thinking

Successful cognitive therapist Albert Ellis (1987) noted that his clients are intelligent enough to understand and want to change, but often fail to do so. Those who fail:

1. Set only short-term goals for their own immediate gratification rather than long-term goals for their growth.
2. Berate themselves.
3. Become anxious about their own anxiety.
4. Fall into depression about their perceived lack of efficacy.
5. Become depressed because they are depressed, thus beginning a downward spiral.

We began this chapter with Piaget saying that "cognition is action"; we end it with Ellis saying that "cognition without action is crazy." He instructs such "talented screwballs" (his term for those who are talented in maintaining resistance to needed change) as follows: "Don't just understand the problem, but start acting so as to remedy it" (see chapter 11 for a discussion of goal setting and decision making).

MASTERY OF THE THINKING SELF

In summary, by modifying our understanding of our thinking selves, we can learn to:

1. Attend to important events.
2. Focus on relevant cues within each event.
3. Rationally reappraise problem situations.
4. Flexibly scan long-term memory stores for appropriate meanings and associations.
5. Modulate excessive, deficient, or inappropriate thoughts.

6. Initiate a problem-solving series of behaviors leading to an increased probability that we will arrive at an adaptive response and act on it.

By becoming aware of our directed thinking, we can learn to reconstruct our self-talk so that it becomes an automatized pattern of resourceful thinking rather than a considerable part of our adjustment problems.

Critical Review 4

1. Boredom is an emotion we feel when we are not paying attention to information we believe is important. T F

2. Identify a belief that you hold that might prevent you from getting as much out of college as is possible.

3. Use self-talk to help you construct a three-sentence explanation of how strict, "no-nonsense" parents can hinder their children's ability to get the most out of college.

4. Recall a problem or stressful situation that seems to happen again and again to you. Write any irrational beliefs you hold that make the event more difficult for you to change or accept.

5. Do you identify with any of the cognitive deficits or barriers to change that are mentioned by Beck and Ellis? If so, what can you say to yourself to overcome these barriers to your own growth?

6. Do you believe that it is ethical for a cognitive-behavioral therapist to attempt to change the way you think? Why or why not?

SUMMARY

■ It is possible to treat aspects of mental operations with scientific precision and formulate laws describing the basic nature of thought.

■ Contemplation is thinking about facts, deliberation is the practical use of mental activity in problem solving.

■ Our control of cognition is limited by our ability to focus on important events and search our memory for meaningful connections to apply to adjustment problems or to direct further search.

■ Logical thinking includes the use of deductive and inductive reasoning. Humans make many systematic errors in reasoning.

■ Heuristic thinking, or using "rules of thumb" to guide behavior is quicker and more sensible than trying out all possible solutions to an adjustment problem. Humans also make errors in the use of heuristics.

■ The process of thinking includes attending to, organizing, storing, and retrieving information.

■ Jean Piaget believed cognition to be a product of action that grows from interactions between the mind and the environment.

■ A *schema* is a mental outline or diagram as simple as a grasping reflex or as complicated as a plan for college graduation.

Schemata allow us to move away from confusion and rigidity and toward order and flexibility.

■ Mental processes, such as those used in buffer delays and short-term memory, allow us to perceive life as a stream of information and to hold information in store long enough to process it further.

■ Long-term memory, or knowledge, is a product of internal mental reconstruction. It represents choice and is not an exact replica of past events. Our cognitive world is grounded in reality but is largely of our own choosing and our own making.

■ Images, movements, concepts, and language make up our units of thought.

■ Attitudes can be modified by changing beliefs regarding the meaning of past events. We need not be victims of our personal history.

■ Our mental processes place a limit on our ability to cope with the demands of reality. Human adjustment problems typically must be recast into a series of simpler problems.

■ A great deal of what we feel and do is directed by what we think—our internal dialogue.

■ Irrational beliefs form the content of inappropriate thought. Such beliefs, when automatized, appear spontaneous and compelling, but are in fact learned dysfunctional behaviors.

■ Irrational beliefs can be a barrier to efficient learning.

■ Faulty cognitive beliefs and styles of thinking are considered behaviors that can be modified via cognitive reappraisal.

■ Learned resourcefulness can replace learned helplessness when we use functional self-talk to cope with problems of adjustment.

SELECTED READINGS

Beck, A. T. *Love Is Never Enough*. New York: Harper & Row, 1989. A clearly written presentation of cognitive therapy in marital problems.

Gardner, H. *The Mind's New Science: A History of the Cognitive Revolution*. New York: Basic Books, 1987. An account of cognitive science, an empirically based effort to explain human knowledge.

Goleman, D. *Vital Lies, Simple Truths: The Psychology of Self-Deception*. New York: Simon and Schuster, 1986. An exploration of how cognitive psychologists' growing ability to track the flow of information through the brain can give us a better understanding of how we deceive ourselves.

Helmstetter, S. *What to Say When You Talk to Yourself*. New York: Pocket Books, 1988. Shad Helmstetter spells out the details of what to say to yourself to improve your life. He guides you in the development of your own self tape.

Levenkron, S. *Obsessive-Compulsive Disorders*. New York: Warner Books, 1991. Levenkron helps you overcome this thought disorder with the help of family, talking therapy, and anxiety reduction.

Meichenbaum, D. *Cognitive-Behavior Modification: An Integrative Approach*. New York: Plenum Press, 1977. A book that beautifully describes cognitive change through client-therapist interaction.

Scarf, M. "Images That Heal." *Psychology Today* (September 1980): 32–46. An exploration of the growing faith in the mind's powers to heal.

Schiffman, H. R. *Sensation and Perception: An Integrated Approach*, 3rd ed. New York: John Wiley and Sons, 1990. An introduction to the study of our active conversion of selected sensations into personal perceptions.

Wallace, B., and Fisher, L. E. *Consciousness and Behavior*, 2d ed. Boston: Allyn and Bacon, 1991. A very readable summary of current information about hypnosis, sleep, dreams, and mind-altering drugs.

REFERENCES

Alloy, L. B., and Tabachnik, N. "Assessment of Covariation of Humans and Animals: The Joint Influence of Prior Expectations and Current Situational Information." *Psychological Review* 91 (1984): 112–149.

Barr, R. A. "How Do We Focus Our Attention?" *American Journal of Psychology* 94 (December 1981): 591–603.

Beck, A. *Cognitive Therapy and Emotional Disorders*. New York: International University Press, 1976.

_____. "Nature and Relation to Behavior Therapy." *Behavior Therapy* 1 (1970): 184–200.

Benderly, B. L. "Everyday Intuition." *Psychology Today* (September 1989): 35–40.

Berk, L. E. "Private Speech: Learning Out Loud." *Psychology Today* (May 1986): 20, 34–42.

Blumenthal, A. L. *The Process of Cognition*. Englewood Cliffs, NJ: Prentice-Hall, 1977.

Bourne, L. E. Dominowski, R. L., and Loftus, E. F. *Cognitive Process*. Englewood Cliffs, NJ: Prentice-Hall, 1983.

Bower, G. H. *Cognitive Perspectives on Emotion and Motivation*. Boston: Kluwer Academic Publishers, 1981.

_____. "A Selective Review of Organizational Factors in Memory." In *Organization of Memory*, edited by E. Tulving and W. Donaldson (pp. 323–343). New York: Academic Press, 1972.

Bryan, W. L., and Harter, N. "Studies on the Telegraphic Language: The Acquisition of a Hierarchy of Habits." *Psychological Review* 4 (1899): 27–53.

Camp, B. "Verbal Mediation in Young Aggressive Boys." Unpublished manuscript, University of Colorado School of Medicine, 1975.

Camp, B. W., Swift, W. J., and Swift, E. W. "Authoritarian Parental Attitudes and Cognitive Functioning in Preschool Children." *Psychological Reports* 50 (1982): 1023–1026.

Camp, C. J., Markley, R. P., and Kramer, J. J. "Naive Mnemonics: What the 'Do-Nothing' Control Group Does." *American Journal of Psychology* 96 (Winter 1983): 503–507.

Chase, W. C., and Simon, H. A. "The Mind's Eye in Chess." In *Visual Information Processing*, edited by W. G. Chase, New York: Academic Press, 1973: 193–214.

Davis, J., and Rovee-Collier, C. K. "Alleviated Forgetting of a Learned Contingency in 8 Week Old Infants." *Developmental Psychology* 19 (October 1983): 353–365.

Ellis, A. *Humanistic Psychotherapy*. New York: McGraw-Hill, 1973.

_____. "The Impossibility of Achieving Consistently Good Mental Health." Address given to the American Psychological Association and reported in *Psychology Today* (February 1987): 8, 21.

_____. *The Practice of Rational Emotive Therapy*. New York: Spring Publishing Company, 1987.

_____. *Reason and Emotion in Psychotherapy*. New York: Lyle Stuart Press, 1962.

Festinger, L. A. *A Theory of Cognitive Dissonance*. Stanford, CA: Stanford University Press, 1957.

Festinger, L. A., and Carlsmith, M. Conflict, Decision and Dissonance, *Journal of Psychology* (March 1961), Vol 98 (2), pp. 267–275.

Feuerstein, R. *Instrumental Enrichment: An Intervention Program for Cognitive Modifiability.* Baltimore, MD: University Park Press, 1979.

Flavell, J. H., Green, F. L., and Flavell, E. R. "Development of Knowledge about the Appearance-Reality Distinction." *Monographs of the Society for Research in Child Development,*" Serial No. 212 (1986): 51.

Forgas, J. P., and Bower, G. H. Affect in social and personal judgments. In Fiedler, K., and J. P. Forgas (Eds.). *Affect, Cognition, and Social Behavior.* Toronto: Hogrefe, 1988.

Gagné, R. M. "Learning Outcomes and Their Effects: Useful Categories of Human Performance." *American Psychologist* 39 (1984): 377–386.

Gal'perin, P. "Stages in the Development of Mental Acts." In *A Handbook of Contemporary Soviet Psychology,* edited by M. Cole and I. Maltzman (pp. 84–97). New York: Basic Books, 1969.

Gibson, J. J. *The Senses Considered as Perceptual System.* Boston: Houghton Mifflin, 1966.

Gillund, G., and Shiffrin, R. M. "A Retrieval Model for Both Recognition and Recall." *Psychological Review* 91 (January 1984): 1–67.

Glasgow, R. E., and Arkowits, H. "The Behavioral Assessment of Male and Female Social Competence in Dyadic Heterosexual Interactions." *Behavior Therapy* 6 (1975): 488–498.

Goldfried, M., and Goldfried, A. "Cognitive Change Methods." In *Helping People Change,* edited by F. Kanfer and A. Goldfried. New York: Pergamon Press, 1975.

Goleman, D. "How Reliable Is Your Memory? Coding Process May Hold Answer. *The Miami Herald* (June 2, 1994): G1.

Gray, P. *Psychology.* New York: Worth Publishers, 1991.

Halpin, G., and Halpin, G. "Experimental Investigation of the Effects of Study and Testing on Student Learning, Retention, and Ratings of Instruction." *Journal of Educational Psychology* 74 (February 1982): 32–37.

Hamilton, D. I. *Cognitive Processes in Stereotyping and Intergroup Behavior.* Hillsdale, NJ: Erlbaum, 1989.

Harter, M. R. "Excitability Cycles and Cortical Scanning: A Review of Two Hypotheses of Central Intermittency in Perception." *Psychological Bulletin* 70 (1968): 47–58.

Janis, I. L. *Victims of Groupthink: A Psychological Study of Foreign Policy Decisions and Fiascoes.* Boston: Houghton Mifflin, 1972.

Janis, I. L. and Mann, L. *Decision Making.* New York: Free Press, 1977.

Johnson-Laird, P. N. *Deduction.* Hillsdale, NJ: Erlbaum Associates, 1991.

Keele, S. W. "Learning and Control of Coordinated Motor Patterns: The Programming Perspective. In *Human Motor Behavior,* edited by J. A. S. Kelso, (pp. 177–182). Hillsdale, NJ: Erlbaum.

Kelly, G. A. *The Psychology of Personal Constructs.* New York: Norton, 1955.

Kim, M., and Hunter, J. E. *Relationship Among Attitudes, Behavioral Intentions, and Behavior. Communications Research* 20 (1993): 331–364.

Klayman, J., and Ha, Y. W. "Confirmation, Disconfirmation, and Information in Hypothesis Testing." *Psychological Review* 94 (1987): 211–228.

Klinger, E. *Daydreaming.* Los Angeles, CA: J. P. Tarcher, 1990.

Konorski, J. *Integrative Activity of the Brain: An Interdisciplinary Approach.* Chicago: University of Chicago Press, 1967.

Ladd, W., and Mize, J. "A Cognitive—Social Learning Model of Social Skill Training." Psychological Review 90 (April 1983): 127–157.

Lazarus, A., and Fay, A. "Mistakes That Can Ruin Your Life, and How to Avoid Them." *Good Housekeeping* (October 1975): 64–76.

Levin, I. "Associative Effects of Information Framing." *Bulletin of the Psychonomic Society* 25 (1987): 85–86.

Luria, A. *The Role of Speech in the Regulation of Normal and Abnormal Behaviors.* New York: Liveright, 1961.

Masson, M. E. J., and McDaniel, M. A. "The Role of Organizational Processes in Long-Term Retention." *Journal of Experimental Psychology* 7 (Summer 1981): 100–101.

Mayer, R. E. *Thinking, Problem solving, and Cognition.* New York: Freeman, 1993.

Meichenbaum, D. Cognitive-Behavior Modification: An Integrative Approach. New York: Plenum Press, 1977.

_____. "The Effects of Instructions and Reinforcement on Thinking and Language Behaviors of Schizophrenics." *Behavior Research and Therapy* 7 (1969): 101–114.

Melton, G. B. "Toward 'Personhood' for Adolescents: Autonomy and Privacy as Values in Public Policy." *American Psychologist* 36 (January 1983): 99–103.

Neisser, U. *Cognition and Reality: Principles and Implications of Cognitive Psychology.* San Francisco: W. H. Freeman, 1976.

_____. *Cognitive Psychology.* New York: Appleton-Century-Crofts, 1967.

Newby, R. W. "Contextual Areas in Item Recognition Following Verbal Discrimination Learning." *Journal of General Psychology* 114 (1987): 281–287.

Orton, R., and Phillips, D. C. "The New Causal Principle of Cognitive Learning Theory: Perspectives on Bandura's Reciprocal Determinism." *Psychological Review* 90 (April 1983): 158–165.

Patrick, C. "Creative Thought in Artists." *Journal of Psychology* 4 (1937): 35–73.

Peter, D., Allan, J., and Horvath, A. "Hyperactive Children's Perceptions of Teachers' Classroom Behavior." *Psychology in the Schools* 20 (April 1983): 234–240.

Phillips, J. L., Jr., *The Origins of Intellect: Piaget's Theory,* 2nd ed. San Francisco: W. H. Freeman, 1975.

Piaget, J. "Development and Learning." *Journal of Research in Science Teaching* 2 (1964): 176–186.

Pines, M. "Baby, You're Incredible." *Psychology Today* (February 1982): 51.

_____. "Can a Rock Walk?" *Psychology Today* (November 1983): 46–54.

Raimy, V. *Misunderstandings of the Self.* San Francisco: Jossey-Bass, 1975.

Ramsey, P. H., Ramsey, P. P., and Barnes, M. J. "Effects of Student Confidence and Item Difficulty on Test Score Gains Due to Answer Changing." *Teaching of Psychology* 14 (4) (1987): 206–209.

Reed, P. P. *Alive.* New York: Lippincott, 1974.

Reis, T. J., Gerrard, M., and Gibbons, F. X. "Social Comparison and the Pill: Reactions to Upward and Downward Comparison of Contraceptive Behavior." *Personality and Social Psychology Bulletin* 19 (1993): 13–21.

Restak, R. M. *The Mind.* New York: Bantam, 1988.

Rosch, E. H. "On the Internal Structure of Perceptual and Semantic Categories." In *Cognition and the Acquisition of Language,* edited by T. E. Moore (pp. 582–586). New York: Academic Press, 1973.

Schwartz, R., and Gottman, J. "A Task Analysis Approach to Clinical Problems: A Study of Assertive Behavior." Unpublished manuscript, Indiana University, 1974.

Segall, M. H., Dasen, P. R., Berry, J. W. and Poortinga, Y. H. *Human Behavior in Global Perspective.* New York: Pergamon, 1990.

Shade, B. J. "Cognitive Strategies as Determinants of School Achievement." *Psychology in the Schools* 20 (October 1983): 488–493.

Siegler, R. S. "Five Generalizations about Cognitive Development." *American Psychologist* 38 (March 1983): 263–277.

Singer, M. "Comparing Memory for Natural and Laboratory Reading." *Journal of Experimental Psychology* 3 (September 1982): 331–346.

Solso, R. L. *Cognitive Psychology.* 2nd ed. Boston: Allyn and Bacon, 1988.

Sternberg, R. J. *Intelligence Applied.* New York: Harcourt Brace Jovanovich, 1986.

Tilley, A., and Warren, P. "Retrieval from Semantic Memory at Different Times of Day." *Journal of Abnormal Psychology* 92 (August 1983): 718–723.

Trotter, R. J. "The Mystery of Mastery." *Psychology Today* (July, 1986): 20, 32–36.

Twentyman, C., Boland, T., and McFall, R. M. "Heterosocial Avoidance in College Males." *Behavior Modification* 5 (October 1981): 523–552.

Vygotsky, L. S. *Thought and Language.* Cambridge, MA: MIT Press, 1962.

Wall, H., Karl, K., and Smigiel, J. "Use of Contextual Information in the Formation of Cognitive Maps." *American Journal of Psychology* 99 (Winter 1986): 547–558.

White, C. T. "Temporal Numerosity and the Psychological Unit of Duration." *Psychological Monographs* 77 (1963): 12.

Whorf, B. L. "Science and Linguistics." In J. B. Carroll (Ed.), *Language, Thought, and Reality: Selected Writings of Benjamin Whorf* (pp. 192–213). Cambridge, MA: MIT Press.

Zametkin, A. J. "Cerebral Glucose Metabolism in Adults With Hyperactivity of Childhood Onset." *The New England Journal of Medicine* 323 (1990): 1361–1366.

■ *Questionnaire Scoring Key*

Analytical Thinker

"One who uses the self-motivating, self-directing, rational cognitive style associated with high college achievement."

Your responses should give you a greater understanding of the degree to which you are an *analytical thinker.* Checked items represent learning deficits that you identify with at this time. Look up the context in which the idea associated with each of your checked responses is discussed. It is important for you to notice the cognitive process that this barrier makes less effective.

What I Can Do to Overcome These Barriers to Learning

Review the suggestions for change that appear toward the end of the chapter. Then *rewrite each checked negative as a positive self-statement.* For example, "I become depressed about my lack of effective learning" can be rewritten as "I feel good about the progress I am making in becoming a professional learner." Use these affirmations to direct your learning efforts.

■ *Answers to Critical Review Questions*

Critical Review 1 1. T.   **2.** F.
Critical Review 2 1. T.   **2.** F.   **3.** T.
Critical Review 4 1. T.

PERSONAL ACTION PLAN
Cognitive Assessment

In this activity, the cognitive component of difficult situations will be explored. When an individual's cognitive world is poorly organized, the tendency is to respond to the clutter rather than to the meaningful information. This experience will allow you to: (1) appraise your cognitive style, (2) find out if your characteristic beliefs and assumptions are adaptive, and (3) make a beginning alteration in your thinking style and content so as to become more resourceful.

Step IA.

Cognitive Content: What to Look For. The following statements are examples of immature beliefs that can be at the base of emotional and behavioral adjustment problems (Ellis, 1987). Read each statement carefully and check the degree to which you act as if each were literally true. A = all of the time, M = most of the time, S = some of the time, L = little of the time, and N = none of the time.

1. I must be loved by everyone and everyone must approve of everything I do. _____

2. I must be thoroughly competent, adequate, intelligent, and achieving in all possible respects. _____

3. Certain acts are wrong or wicked or villainous, and people who perform them should be severely punished. _____

4. It is a terrible catastrophe when things are not as I would like them to be. _____

5. My unhappiness is the result of external events and happenings that are forced on me and over which I have no control. _____

6. I should be greatly concerned about dangerous and fearful things and I must center my thinking on them until the danger has passed. _____

7. I find it easier to avoid difficulties and responsibilities in life than to face them. _____

8. I need someone or something stronger than myself to rely on. _____

9. Because something greatly influenced me in the past it must determine my present behavior. The influence of the past cannot be overcome. _____

10. What other people do is vitally important to me, and I should make every effort to change them to be the way I think they should be. _____

11. There is one perfect solution to every problem, and if it is not found, the result will be terrible. _____

12. I have virtually no control over my emotions. I am their victim and cannot help how I feel. _____

Step IB.

Cognitive Restructuring. Go back to each statement above that was lettered A or M (all or most of the time) and rewrite it so that it would read true for an individual who does not expect perfection. For example, you might change #4 from "It is a terrible catastrophe when things are not as I would like them to be" to "It is unfortunate and disappointing when things are not as I would like them to be."

Step IIA.

Cognitive Style: What to Look For. The following statements reflect a consistent style of thinking that is irrational and associated with adjustment difficulties. Read each statement carefully and check the ones that correspond to your present cognitive style. (These statements reflect the findings of Beck, 1976.)

1. I *exaggerate* the negative meaning contained in an event. _____

2. I *oversimplify* events, rigidly labeling them as being all good or all bad. _____

3. I *draw faulty inferences* from the available evidence. My conclusions often contradict those of others. _____

4. I *ignore important aspects* of events if they do not support my preconceptions. _____

5. I *magnify the importance of single events* and tend to *overgeneralize* the future impact of such events. _____

6. I tend to *act on impulse,* without pause for reflection. _____

7. I tend to view unpleasant events as being *catastrophic.* _____

8. I tend to *center my thoughts on negative possibilities* more than on positive realities. _____

9. My *mood* is typically irritable or depressed. _____

10. I tend to *create negative images* of myself and my actions. _____

11. I tend to *respond more to my inner thoughts* than to actual events as they occur. _____

12. When I make a mistake, I tend to *say hurtful, uncharitable things* about myself. _____

13. When in a difficult situation, I tend to think *helpless and hopeless* thoughts. _____

Step IIB.

Positive Affirmations. For each statement above that you checked, rewrite the same idea as a positive affirmation. A positive affirmation is a statement that describes a condition that you desire as if it were a fact.

Example: #10. I now create positive images of myself and my actions.

Select some action that you do several times each day, such as looking at your watch. Use this action as a signal to repeat to yourself one of these positive affirmations. Affirm on cue.

Step IIIA.

Selecting a Difficult Situation. Your list of rewritten statements represents cognitive processes and content that you view as being dysfunctional in their original form. In question 3 of this step, use this list as a reference to help you assess your style of thinking and your specific thoughts in a difficult real-life situation. For this step, select a situation that has been difficult for you in the past.

Rather than trying to avoid the situation, try to be on the lookout for it. Allow yourself to behave in a manner that is typical of your past performance under similar circumstances. As soon as possible after the event, record the event itself, then answer the following questions about your activities during its occurrence. Use your list of rewritten statements as a guide.

Description of a difficult event

Step IIIB.

Beliefs, Assumptions, and Emotions.

1. What did I fail to say to myself that would have helped me through this situation?

2. What irrational beliefs or assumptions did I find myself falling back on while in the situation?

3. What negative emotions and/or actions did I emit as a result of these immature beliefs, images, or assumptions?

Step IV.

Cognitive Processes. In addition to the thinking style and content observed as part of your difficult situation, what cognitive processes, if any, do you believe formed a part of your difficulties in adjusting to the demands of the situation?

1. What goal(s) or intention(s) did you have when the situation occurred? Do you believe that your motivation altered the meaning that you gave to it?

2. Were more events happening at once than you could comfortably handle? If yes, list them:

3. Was your mind free to pay attention to the critical aspects of the situation? List aspects that were, on reflection, critical or novel:

4. Were you able to delay making your assessment and conclusions of the situation so as to respond reflectively?
   If not, what tactics could you employ that would give you time to respond reflectively?

5. While in the situation, were you able to retain the critical aspects of it in *short-term memory* while you searched for rational interpretations of the meaning and demands of the situation? If not, what was your

immediate interpretation? What was your reflective interpretation?

6. While keeping the critical events in memory, were you able to recall one or more rational alternative responses to the demands as you perceived them? If yes, list the alternatives that came to mind:

7. Were you able, at the time, to select one or more of your alternatives and mentally test the likely consequences of acting it out? If possible, list a rejected alternative.

8. Do you believe that you will be able to profit from the experience by transferring the situation, your responses to it, and the subsequent consequences into your *long-term memory*? If yes, what have you learned from this activity?

Step V. *Thoughts about Cognitions.*

1. After your assessment of the situation, are you now less confused by its dynamics?
   Yes _____ No _____

2. What "healthy talk" would help you respond better if a similar situation again presented itself?

3. Do you believe that you benefit from breaking a problem into smaller, more manageable parts: If so,

list aspects of the situation that could be broken into smaller parts.

4. Were your actual responses in conformity with your present self-image? Were your actual emotional responses in conformity with your affective disposition?

5. Do you believe an improved self-image would help you to respond more reflectively in similar situations?

6. Did anything occur during this activity to encourage you to approach difficult situations with the idea of trying to alter your habitual ways of responding with new, rational alternatives? If so, list the occurrence(s):

7. Did anything about this activity support the notion that your cognitive world is largely of your own making? If yes, what supported this notion?

8. Did anything connected with this activity support the notion that your cognitions are learned and can be modified? If yes, list the evidence that supports this contention:

9. Finally, do you believe that, by modifying certain of your beliefs, you can improve your human potential?

CHAPTER

7

EMOTIONAL INFLUENCES

Chapter Outline

How do you feel? Close your eyes and relive a moment when you were keenly alive. Allow the memory to fill your consciousness. Do not rush, but experience again the special occasion.

What dominated your recollection? Was it vivid images? Did smells, sensations, or actions come to mind most clearly? For most of us, our richest memories bring forth a rush of emotion. The joy, anger, fear, or embarrassment associated with the occasion never fades, even though other details recede from memory.

In all its many forms, emotion constitutes a necessary and precious part of our lives. It is emotion that makes liv-

ing worthwhile, for without the richness and even the disruptions of our emotions, our lives would be barren and robotlike. Most Americans who attempt suicide suffer from depression, an emotional disorder that can rob us of hope and make life itself unbearable. Joy, empathy, love, and happiness are the wellsprings of optimism and hope. Even grief, fear, and anger, when they are not overwhelming, add texture and fullness to human existence. Positive emotions can spur and direct our growth, and negative ones can alert us to the need for change in our lives.

EMOTION AND SURVIVAL

Emotions contain the wisdom of the ages, warning us of danger, guiding us toward what is good and satisfying, signaling our intentions and our reactions to others. (Goode, Schrof, and Burke, 1991).

This view of the central importance of emotion to survival is new to psychology, but old to Charles Darwin. Earlier theory held that emotions disturbed the otherwise rational human who psychologists were trying to understand; and while emotion always formed part of every serious thought disorder that counseling psychologists were trying to correct, it was the thinking human, not the feeling human, who was to define the discipline. The very concept of emotion becomes fuzzy when psychologists try to define it for study. Sometimes emotions are treated as a motive for behavior: "He hit me because he was angry." At other times, they are viewed as a result of behavior: "He was angry at himself for hitting me." Whether cause or effect, emotions need definition.

Defining Emotion

emotion   feelings, internal changes, and overt acts that have a survival function

An **emotion** is an intense, relatively uncontrollable feeling that affects, and is affected by, our thoughts and actions. Emotions have been defined in terms of motivational states, subjective feelings, internal changes, facial expressions, and overt acts. Emotions can involve all of these, but only one is always a component of any aroused state. *Emotions always involve internal bodily changes.* We may cry in sadness, frustration, or joy. Our faces may remain placid while we fume. We are even capable of being completely unaware of the rage or hurt being expressed in our voices. No matter how we fool ourselves or others, we cannot experience an emotion without having changes take place in our nervous system, internal organs, muscles, and glands. It is emotion defined as *an internal bodily change* that has received the greatest attention in modern times.

The Seat of Emotion

If Elizabeth Barrett Browning had been writing in the time of William Shakespeare, her famous question "How do I love thee? Let me count the ways," might have been answered: "With all my liver." In biblical times in the Near East, the answer might have been: "With all my genitals." In ancient Rome and in our own time, it is answered: "With all my heart." For the last three hundred years, however, scientists, if not the general public, have known that the brain is the source of our emotional behavior. (In ancient Greece, Aristotle thought the brain could not be the center of emotion because the brain was insensitive to pain. He believed the brain was the radiator of the blood.) Only within the last ninety years have scientists begun the process of tracing the complex neural pathways involved in the cognitive, skeletal, and **visceral** (internal organ) activity necessary for us to feel and express emotion. It is now known that the *two hemispheres of our frontal lobes play distinctly different emotional roles.* The right hemisphere is dominant when we feel sad, when we express fear or disgust, and when we perceive the emotional signals of others. The left hemisphere dominates when we are happy or amused. A set of neurons, next to facial recognition neurons in the temporal lobe, helps recognize which emotion a face displays. Very primitive emotions, such as fear, can travel along a direct pathway from sensory receptors in the eye or ear, for example, to the thalamus and on to the amygdala (an ancient emotional center deep within our midbrain), never passing through higher centers of thought. It seems we have a separate and unconscious neural network for basic emotions (Goode, Schrof, and Burke, 1991).

viscera the internal organs of the body, such as the heart

Thus, a modern, scientific answer to the question "How do I love thee?" might be as follows:

> How do I love thee?
> Let me count the ways:
> I love thee with my left frontal lobe
> I love thee with my dopamine and saratonin secretions
> I love thee with my thalamus and amygdala
> I love thee with my basal ganglia
> But most of all,
> I love thee with all the outpourings of my pituitary.

CRITICAL THINKING ISSUE
Self-Slaughter: A Time To Die

The timing of my death should be honored as my personal right.

"Pay me now or pay me later." The grim reaper demands payment—the terms and conditions of that payment should be my last, most personal choice. Suicide is a rational, sane way of escaping my life when I consider it painful and no longer worth living.

When I am in helpless physical or mental decline, or the people and events that make my life meaningful and worthwhile are removed, I demand of my church and state the moral and legal right to do the proper thing—to plan my death and carry it out (or have it carried out for me) at my discretion.

The timing of my death should properly be left in hands far more competent than my own.

A prayer: If ever I begin to demand that my life is livable only on my terms; if ever I begin to use the possibility of self-inflicted death to make my life more bearable; if ever I begin to threaten suicide in order to entertain the fantasy of being rescued from all my troubles—then grant me life until times are more favorable. Protect me from an irrevocable act in a time of ambivalence and uncertainty.

Because I know that life cannot be captured in pluses and minuses, because I know that suicide attempts are cries for help, if ever I try self-slaughter and fail; grant that those who respond in my time of need do not refuse me treatment so as to honor my right to die.

I take the position that:

Evolution and Emotion

Of Frogs and Men Darwin observed that facial expressions, gestures, and reflexive acts such as elimination are associated with fear in a continuous series of higher forms of life. If you pick up a frightened frog, you run the risk of a wet hand. Have you noticed that you frequently go to the bathroom just before an exam? These emotional responses are similar, although millions of years of evolution separate you from the frog. If an animal meets a dangerous predator and does not feel fear, it may not flee and may not live to reproduce. Sociobiologists propose that every emotion has some survival value (Chance, 1980).

EMOTION AND SOCIAL SURVIVAL

To Darwin, basic emotions are universal among humans because they have *survival value*. Emotions represent a successful adjustment, or adaptation, to specific environmental demands—an example of the survival of the fittest. Humans are social creatures, and emotions may be classified as either prosocial or antisocial.

ANTISOCIAL EMOTIONS

antisocial emotion a feeling state that has the effect of impairing social relationships

The bared fangs and claws of a threatened cat are recognizable expressions of **antisocial emotions**. They ready the cat for defense or attack. This mobilization of energy either to fight or to flee is one of the chief products of emotion (Cannon, 1929).

anger one of the primary emotions; in its mildest form, it is termed *annoyance*. Very strong anger is termed *rage*

Anger

basic emotions eight that augment the fundamental behaviors of all living organisms

In addition to direct survival value, Darwin saw *signal value* in the physical expression of **anger**. Antisocial postures, sounds, and gestures signal to a foe an impression of the sender's size, strength, and willingness to fight. Such displays

---

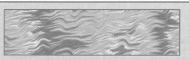

CULTURAL CROSSCURRENTS
One Species

Charles Darwin published *The Expression of the Emotions in Man and Animals* in 1872. He held that emotions are the products of evolutionary history and are therefore *innate* and *universal*. Darwin reported that **basic emotions** are the same across all human racial groupings, and that neither age nor culture seriously distorts emotional expression. Plutchik's research (1980) also supports the contention that emotions are innate. He believes there are but eight basic emotions: fear, anger, disgust, sadness, acceptance, anticipation, surprise, and joy (see Figure 7–1).

Moreover, Izard (1977) found that most students from nine cultures agreed about the basic emotion depicted in posed photographs presented to them. Natives of Borneo and New Guinea agreed also.

Although this section, "Cultural Crosscurrents," is built into each chapter specifically to highlight the richness of cultural diversity and the uniqueness of each individual, it is also important to remind ourselves of the fundamental idea that *we are all one species.*

Ask a friend from another culture to identify each of the eight basic emotions of Plutchik's emotion "wheel" (Figure 7–1) *as you model them.* Alternately, have your friend "make a face," for each, and you try to "Name that Emotion." Both the social expression and recognition of basic emotions are innate and largely independent of culture.

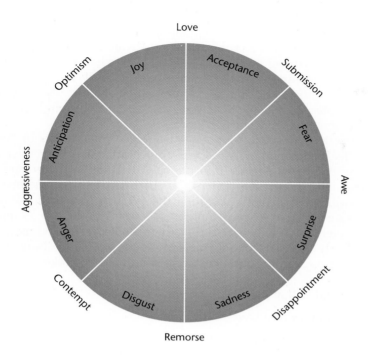

FIGURE 7–1
Plutchik's emotion "wheel" represents the eight primary emotions and "dyads" resulting from mixtures of adjacent primaries. The wheel plots the similarities among emotions—and what they produce when mixed—as described by lab subjects. Thus, the primaries of fear and surprise, when combined, yield the dyad awe, and joy mixed with acceptance leads to love.

(From R. Plutchik, 1980b. Reprinted from *Psychology Today*. Copyright © 1980. Ziff-Davis Publishing Company).

have indirect survival value because they lead to the dominance within a species of certain individuals and reduce actual combat. In today's "jungle," anger is less functional.

Why Do We Get Angry?

"The usual cause of anger is the *thwarting of some goal-directed behavior or a threat from a nonfeared source*" (Bankart and Bankard, 1991). For example, not being treated fairly makes us angry. Watching a loved one or a close friend perform a misdeed makes us angry (Lazarus, 1991). What makes us really angry (enraged) is seeing the other's misdeed as being *unjustified, avoidable, and willful* (Averill, 1983). Being cornered and in extreme pain can also cause animals and humans to explode in anger as can unrelieved boredom.

Being angry has a strong impact on ourselves and on our social relationships. An angry emotional style creates several problems of adjustment. For example, an angry person:

1. tends to overinterpret the slightest negative action of others as being personally demeaning.

2. displays a "chip on the shoulder" attitude that alienates others.

3. tends to become more and more bitter.

4. increasingly engages in verbal and physical abuse, all too often ending as in the case of O. J. Simpson, with

5. an inability to inhibit the expression of anger and

6. unrestrained and recurrent violence (Tavris, 1989).

In 1989 Tavris described this escalating dance of anger in words that foretold the sequence of events fearfully reported by Nicole Simpson during her 911 phone call of October 25, 1993.

"Expressions of anger . . . getting angrier . . . a precipitating event . . . an angry outburst . . . shouted recriminations . . . screaming or crying . . . a furious peak (often accompanied by physical assault) . . . exhaustion . . . and a sullen apology or just sullenness. Anger is much more difficult to control than other dysfunctional emotions—sadness, for example. The *Personal Action Plan* of this chapter is devoted exclusively to helping you gain new insight into your anger and to learn new ways to control it.

In the 1960s, counselors routinely encouraged their clients to "vent their anger," to "let it all hang out" so as to produce **catharsis**—the release of anger or aggressive energy by directly or vicariously engaging in anger or aggression. In psychoanalytic theory, the catharsis hypothesis states that *behaving angrily reduces subsequent anger.* Social learning theory, in contrast, states that *angry engagements are reinforced.* Angry people are rewarded for their anger, and watching anger on television only makes them more skilled at exploding into anger. Research clearly supports the social learning theory. There is no long-term cathartic effect, and angry outbursts stimulate domestic violence (Archer and Gartner, 1976).

The Personal Action Plan can help you to:

1. lower your arousal level
2. cope in ways that involve neither anger or sulking
3. break out of habits of finding everything annoying
4. find routes to increased empathy
5. engage others in both giving and gaining help.

catharsis   the release of anger or aggressive energy by engaging in angry or aggressive acts

PROSOCIAL EMOTIONS

Emotional signals that represent submission also facilitate survival; the successful attacker will seldom kill the submissive rival. These submissive signals may be considered expressions of **prosocial emotions**. In aggressive animals the prosocial emotions of courtship (acceptance, anticipation, surprise, joy, **love**, passion, affection) also have survival and signal value. Courtship rituals suppress aggression, ready the organism for mating, and signal a willingness to mate (and to protect, the sociobiologists would add).

prosocial emotion   a feeling state that has the effect of facilitating social relations

love   a complex, undefinable, prosocial emotion

Happiness

Happiness is a socially attractive emotion. It is infectious—and others want to catch it. When happy, we are less defensive, less contained, more eager, more generous, more expansive, and more effective. When happy, we allow our best thoughts and warmest feelings to flow (Lazarus, 1993).

Again, psychology is late in making happiness a respected area of investigation. The 1991 edition of *The Encyclopedic Dictionary of Psychology* did not even contain the word! The emergence of health psychology and the recurring positive correlation between happiness on the one hand, and health and long life on the other hand, has made this prosocial emotion an area of major research interest. Although anger is both functional and dysfunctional, there does not seem to be any downside to happiness, *if it is appropriate* (see the section titled "Failed Emotional Expression: Aggression").

happiness   a feeling state marked by pleasure or joy

Characteristics of Happy People

The four main characteristics of happy people are (1) high self-esteem, (2) optimism, (3) extroversion, and (4) personal control (Myers, 1992). With the possible exception of extroversion, each of these personal attributes can be learned! (see *Seligman's Learned Optimism* in the "Selected Readings" section at the end of this chapter).

What Makes Us Happy?

Any positive way in which we experience our lives can make us happy. We do not have to have or do extraordinary things to find happiness, nor is there but one happy path. Diener (1984) found that high self-esteem, a good marriage or love relationship, positive social contacts, regular exercise, the ability to sleep well, and a meaningful religious faith each produce happiness in varying intensities. Apparently it is *the frequency of positive emotions compared to the frequency of negative emotions* that spells happiness or despair. Frequency, not intensity, is the key. (An extremely positive experience can reduce the positive affect of future, less exquisite but more frequent events).

What Does Not Make Us Happy?

Common sense would seem to lead us to many of the factors influencing happiness. Often social science is at its best when it disconfirms ideas that we "all know to be true." Many of the "common sense" factors that create happiness do not stand the test of psychological investigation. Consider the following:

1. The young are not happier than the old.
2. Men are not happier than women.
3. White people are not happier than people of color.
4. Intelligent people are not happier than less intelligent people.
5. Educated people are not happier than less educated people.
6. Parents are not happier than childless couples.
7. Drunk, spaced-out, smoke-filled people are not happier than sober, sane, smoke-free people.
8. Finally, lottery winners are not happier than the rest of us. (Diener, 1984)

Making Ourselves Happy

We do not seem to be able to make ourselves happy by simply making money. *Once we have enough money to buy life's necessities,* additional wealth does not buy happiness. However, there is much that we *can do* to increase the frequency of positive experiences and reduce the frequency of negative experiences in our lives. For example, psychologist Mihaly Csikszentmihalyi (1990) finds that optimal experiences occur during both the best and the worst of times. In fact, he does not find people more happy during passive, relaxing times. Happiness or **flow** as he terms it, is to be found *when a person's body or mind is stretched to the limits in a voluntary effort to achieve something difficult and worthwhile.* We can make ourselves happy if we:

flow a deep happiness that comes when people feel they have a sense of mastering something

1. adopt an optimistic outlook on life (Scheier and Carver, 1992). (Choose to be optimistic, not realistic.)

2. actively seek out opportunities and challenges to expand our lives. Although these challenges may not necessarily be pleasant at the time, they give us

3. a sense of participation in determining the content of our lives that

4. allows us to become fully absorbed while engaging in an activity that is both difficult and of value to us.

It is this committed, absorbed, productive consciousness that we come to value as "the happiest time of my life."

Happiness should not be left to chance! It is something we make happen!

Critical Review 1

1. "Emotions contain the wisdom of the ages, warning us of danger, guiding us toward what is good and satisfying, signaling our intentions and our reactions to others." This view supports the theory of the central importance of emotion in human survival. T F

2. We have a separate, unconscious neural network for emotion in our brain. T F

3. The usual cause of anger is the thwarting of some goal-directed behavior or a threat from a feared source. T F

4. What are the silent, emotionally charged "signals" that often pass between yourself and your A. Parents; B. Friends of the same sex; and C. Date or mate?

5. Are they easily recognized or often confused by one or both?

6. Are your signals usually prosocial or antisocial? If antisocial, how can you leave negativism behind?

7. Recall a time when your body or mind was stretched to its limits in an effort to achieve something both difficult and worthwhile. Do you remember it as a happy time? Are you happy thinking of that moment? How can you create happiness for yourself and those around you?

EMOTIONS IN INFANCY

It is the greatest challenge of parenthood to provide the infant and toddler with the warmth, acceptance, stimulation, patience, firmness, and freedom necessary for innate emotional potentialities to unfold.

Newborn infants display few emotions. They are either asleep, quiet and alert, mildly distressed, or very upset. With great sensitivity to their environment they shift in and out of these few moods quickly. It is not unusual to find a newborn irritable one moment and contented the next. However, Izard (1987) tells us that "an infant's reaction to a stimulus that has emotional significance . . . [something that will produce sadness or distress, for example] . . . tells us something about the infant's emotional traits, about the infant's personality, if you please" (p. 44).

The Smile

The first smile is a response to random firing of neurons in primitive areas of the brain and not an adjustment to any outside stimulation (including hugs and kisses). The intriguing fact is that the infant's facial muscles are, at birth, capable of giving expression to any emotion. Infant facial muscles must contract in a very precise manner to produce a genuine smile; this implies that a central neural mechanism (most likely the basal ganglia of the brain) of great coordination is functional at birth (Konner, 1987). A smile, however caused, is the most easily recognized emotional expression and has the effect of building an attachment with the caregiver. In childhood a smile facilitates play and reduces conflict by acting as a sign of friendship, a submissive signal, or a sign of benign dominance. A ready smile is thus an important survival tool and remains a social asset throughout life.

Intellectual Growth and Emotion

The development of emotional responses is linked to the infant's intellectual growth. In a four-month-old child, a gentle tickle may produce a laugh. This was not possible earlier. It is evidence of the first appearance of a sense of self, an awareness of a selfhood distinct and apart from others. Have you ever tried to tickle yourself? You cannot do it, nor can you successfully tickle an infant who has not gained a sense of independent existence. Growing independence and ample opportunity to express it seem to be necessary parts of the development of **emotional maturity**, the appropriate and effective use of emotion.

emotional maturity   a developed capacity for the full and appropriate expression of feelings

By three months, smiling is a common response in a healthy baby. Smiling behavior keeps loving caretakers close at hand.

stranger anxiety   an infant's fear response to unfamiliar people

A growing memory gives the baby the ability to differentiate between friends and strangers, and the generous social smile becomes restricted to friends. **Stranger anxiety**, a protective antisocial emotion, appears in the seven-month-old child. Fretting, crying, and clinging may be produced at the sight of people who are not total strangers. However, the fact that the seven-month-old toddler may swing from grief to contentment in a matter of seconds indicates that his or her memory is still primitive. Mood swings typically lengthen as we age. The normal teenager comes down from extreme happiness or up from deep sadness within forty-five minutes; in contrast, adults' happy or sad moods usually extend for several hours (Csikszentmihalyi and Larson, 1984).

By eighteen months, a developing sense of self allows the toddler to evaluate his or her image and behavior against learned social standards. Lipsitt (1987) reports that self-conscious emotions such as empathy, jealousy, shame, guilt, and pride, which could not exist earlier, now emerge.

Because of their physical and cognitive growth, toddlers daily come into direct and vicarious contact with frustration, grief, anger, and anxiety, as well as pride, joy, and love. Their lives become emotionally enriched. Children also hear the names associated with these subjective feelings, names they will later use to label their own emotional sensations (see chapter 2 for a discussion of conditioning).

Temperament

By the end of the first year infants display emotional traits that are strong and consistent. Some are wary, timid, vigilant, shy, and fearful; others are outgoing, bold, and sociable. This basic temperament is preserved throughout life and appears likely to be genetic (Kagan, 1984). Although genetics may give impetus to and place limits on emotional development, nurture (the environment) interacts with nature in sculpturing the development of our feelings throughout life.

The Frown

At about two and a half years of age another stage of emotional development arrives. A two-year-old who causes damage, heartache, or anxiety does it in innocence. Two-year-olds are absorbed in exploring and manipulating. If things get broken, it is the result of a friendly accident, not planned malevolence. At two and a half, however, this may not be the case. By this time, children have learned to say no.

negativism   defiant behavior, common in early childhood, but present in all age groups

Negativism is a sign of a developing sense of self. That you have a choice, that you *can* say no and act in defiance of rules, is a powerful discovery to a child not yet three years old. A sense of mastery, of control, is awakened in this blossoming mind. However, if these early assertions are completely indulged, temper tantrums and prolonged emotional infancy will likely result. Such children can become immature adults, forever crying, yelling, or moping in order to get their own way. It is important to know that temper tantrums are primarily the result of inborn genetic patterns, not indulgent parents.

PHYSICAL PUNISHMENT AND EMOTION

If, at the other extreme, these assertions are physically crushed in the toddler, especially if rejection and coldness accompany the punitive countermeasures, repression, excessive shyness, and an inability to respond emotionally can become part of the child's personality. Severe punishment, especially physical spanking, reaches its peak against the two-and-a-half-year-old. Those spanked often and harshly are found, on the average, to be "quieter, less articulate, and more sullen" later in life (Gilmartin, 1979). In our culture boys receive three times as much physical punishment as girls. This may be one factor responsible for the fact that men in our society cannot express their feelings as well as women. Many suffer social and physical problems because of this reduced emotional capacity (see chapter 4, on "Stress and Health.")

The Importance of Negative Feelings

Burton White, in *The First Three Years of Life* (1975), stresses the importance of negative feelings in the development of emotional stability. At three, the child's vocabulary includes the phrase "I hate you." This is usually said in frank honesty and, if taken as a valid expression of the moment, is quickly replaced by other emotions. Such honesty is too often intolerable to parents, however, and the children are taught to deny or repress their own feelings: "You don't really feel that way. Only bad children hate their mommies!"

> "I hate you! I hate you, Mommy!"
> No one told Cindy that being a mother would always be fun. But no one told her that the little bundle she nursed and rocked so lovingly would, just three years later, scream and yell and kick at her, either. And all because Cindy wouldn't let her little girl pour the milk for Daddy at dinner.

The expression of negative feelings may include a predisposition to kick, swing, or bite. Refusing to accept this antisocial behavior will not blunt the child emotionally. With firmness, gentleness, and a sense of humor, parents can teach the child to distinguish among feelings, the acknowledgment of them, and the hurtful expression of them. In general, it is best if parents allow their toddler the greatest freedom of negative expression that the parents can tolerate. In any case, children have a right to be taught not to deny or reject their feelings, but rather to accept and express them in ways that are within the bounds of group living. *Thus, spontaneity and openness and consideration and thoughtfulness may be combined in healthful ways in our children.*

If the toddler is treated with gentle firmness and allowed to win at times, an emotionally strong, assertive, and affectionate young child will emerge. Only when you know that you can choose to say no and survive, only when you know that you have the right of opposition, can you freely express the right to say yes, to cooperate by choice. By the age of three, the emotionally healthy child has developed his or her range of emotional responding and has learned to leave negativism largely behind (White, 1975; see chapter 3, on self-esteem, for related topics).

The ability to feel deeply and to appropriately express pleasures and pains to loved ones, work mates, and friends constitutes a hallmark of emotional health. The biological expression of emotion, necessary for survival in animals, finds its greatest expression in humans if, during their first years, they learn self-acceptance and the ability to get along with others.

Critical Review 2

1. An infant's reaction to a stimulus that will produce sadness or distress tells us something about the infant's emotional traits, about the infant's personality. T F

2. The normal teenager comes down from extreme happiness or up from deep sadness within several hours. An adult's happy or sad moods often extend for days on end. T F

3. The basic temperament of an infant is preserved throughout life and appears likely to be largely genetic. T F

4. Explain why the smile is so important to survival throughout life.

5. Why must we develop a "sense of self" before we can feel such emotions as guilt, jealousy, pity, regret, or shame?

6. Why does the use of punishment often result in children who are inarticulate, sullen, or hostile?

7. How can parents interpret and respond to their children's negative outbursts in a manner that will help them grow?

A GENERAL THEORY OF EMOTION

The infant is delightful because his or her emotional expression is quick, complete, and honest. You know just where you stand with an infant. This is not so with an adult; we mask our feelings. To understand emotions, then, we must examine internal sensations as well as external expressions.

> Cristy, the airline flight attendant, was tired. Her feet were tired. Her shoulders were tired. But most of all, her face was tired. As she worked in the rear of the plane, cleaning up after the in-flight meal, Cristy heard the dreaded words, "Why aren't you smiling?" "You smile first," she answered, without looking up and with no emotion. The traveler broke into a big grin. "Fine," said Cristy, "Now freeze, and hold that expression until we land in Miami."
>
> Contrast the tyranny of the frozen professional smile with the exultation of an infant's quick, spontaneous smile. What effect do you believe forced smiling has on our emotions?

THREE DIMENSIONS OF EMOTION

motivation   internal states that activate and direct behavior

Internal sensations are often used in explanations of **motivation,** the purpose behind our actions. Common sense says that emotions initiate action. "You see a bear, feel afraid, and run." This vivid example, cited more than a century ago (James, 1884), can be used to illustrate the three dimensions of an emotion that must be addressed by any comprehensive theory—the *cognitive, motor, and visceral responses* associated with the emotion (see Plutchik, 1980 for an example of such a theory).

Today, an emotion is often thought of as an "action set" (Lang et al., 1983) or as "a patterned bodily reaction" (Plutchik, 1980) brought about by a stimulus. This complex state of arousal is assumed to have a survival potential. In modern humans this affective state is thought to be the product of both biology and social learning (Averill, 1983; Izard, 1987).

Emotion as Cognitive Construction

To analyze an emotion, let us start with the bear in "You see a bear." First there must be an appropriate stimulus event, the bear. Second, it must receive our attention.[1] Next, this stimulus must be seen as a bear. We must discriminate the

---

1. However, we do not have to be consciously aware that we are attending to the bear (Lazarus, 1982), nor must the bear really be there.

bear from a tree trunk, for example. At the same time, a cognitive appraisal of the meaning or significance of the presence of a bear must be made. (We do not have to complete information to react emotionally to this meaning; remember that we have primitive circuits for fear and anger that bypass cognition.) We are stimulated to gain access from long-term memory to our conceptual information about bears, the danger of bears, and the social norms pertaining to expected responses to the presence of a bear in the context in which we find ourselves (Schachter and Singer, 1962; Lang et al., 1983; Averill, 1983). Every society has such norms—**"feeling rules"**—about how people should feel and act in various situations (Hochschild, 1979); see chapter 6 for more on thinking).

feeling rules social norms relating to preferred or enforced emotional expression

Emotion as Physical Action

Now we come to the next phase of our story. You feel afraid and run. The cognitive process just mentioned releases a *response set* that involves at least three patterns of *behavior:* (1) affective language behavior to describe the event and our feelings toward it (our subjective state of feeling fear); (2) overt motor behavior to act out the reactions expected of us under the perceived circumstances (our running); and (3) visceral behavioral support for these motor responses (our heart pounding).

Finally, our description of emotion as a set of patterned bodily reactions would not be complete without repeating that current theory holds that the cognitive, motor and visceral responses stimulated by the bear *have survival value.* In this case, we run to protect our life.

The Social Purpose of Emotion

Remember that our whole body and mind respond as one to an emotion-provoking event. Also remember that humans respond within a set of learned social rules that organize the emotion, and that these rules serve a social purpose, what sociobiologists would call the inclusive fitness of the group (Averill, 1983). For example, if you saw a bear and were in charge of young children, you might organize your emotion as anger and find a means of attacking the bear or at least keeping it at bay. An antisocial emotion may be prosocial, particularly with respect to the protection of one's own family.

Table 7–1 shows Plutchik's formulation of the complex events involved in the development of an emotion. It is interesting to note that Plutchik believes that the effects in the table represent universal patterns of behavior that are emitted by all complex organisms. The emotions associated with each of the eight effects are the basic emotions (see Figure 7–1), and all of our other emotional sensations are combinations of these eight.

THE PHYSIOLOGY OF EMOTION

When we are in the grip of a strong emotion, we are aware that changes are taking place within our bodies. Psychologists who view emotion as primarily a biological event tend to focus on these agitated or depressed bodily states (Cannon, 1929).

The Nervous System

Understanding the physiology of emotion requires some understanding of the nervous system. When you see a bear, it is represented in your brain, your

TABLE 7–1

Sequence of Events Involved in the Development of an Emotion

STIMULUS EVENT	INFERRED COGNITION	FEELING	BEHAVIOR	EFFECT
Threat	Danger	Fear, terror	Running	Protection
Obstacle	Enemy	Anger, rage	Hitting	Destruction
Potential mate	Possess	Joy, ecstasy	Courting, mating	Reproduction
Loss of object	Isolation	Sadness, grief	Crying for help	Reintegration
Group member	Friend	Acceptance, trust	Grooming, sharing	Affiliation
Gruesome object	Poison	Disgust, loathing	Vomiting, pushing away	Rejection
New territory	What's out there?	Anticipation	Examining, mapping	Exploration
Novel object	What is it?	Surprise	Stopping	Orientation

SOURCE: Adapted from R. Plutchik, "A General Psychoevolutionary Theory of Emotion." In *Emotion: Theory, Research, and Experience,* vol. I. Edited by R. Plutchik and H. Kellerman (New York: Academic Press, 1980), Table I–2, p. 16.

central nervous system (CNS) the brain and spinal cord

peripheral nervous system that part of the nervous system outside the brain and the spinal cord

sympathetic nervous system (SNS) the neural subsystem that mobilizes the body for action during times of stress

parasympathetic nervous system (PNS) a neural subsystem that conserves bodily energy during times of rest and security

central nervous system (CNS). But the CNS by itself is senseless and helpless. It cannot feel or act. It requires that information be brought to it by neural subsystems, and it must direct neural subsystems to initiate and coordinate action (see *Opponent Process* in chapter 4. These information-action subsystems comprise our **peripheral nervous system**. (Study Figures 7–2 and 7–3 as you read on.)

The peripheral nervous system is divided into two parts, the *somatic nervous system* and the *autonomic nervous system*. The somatic nervous system enervates the muscles attached to our bones and so enables us to move (to run, for example). The autonomic nervous system (ANS) enervates the muscles of our internal organs and glands, our viscera.

The autonomic nervous system is itself divided into the **sympathetic nervous system (SNS)** and the **parasympathetic nervous system (PNS)**. The SNS and the PNS have evolved to mobilize and conserve energy for survival. The heart, lungs, pancreas, kidneys, stomach, intestines, genitalia, and adrenals are examples of visceral organs and glands enervated by the ANS (see Figure 7–3).

FIGURE 7–2
The Nervous System.

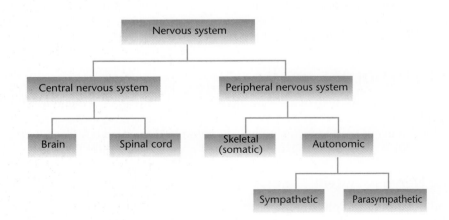

The Nervous System's Emotional Signals

Let's return to the bear. If you see a bear and wish to run, it is apparent that first the ANS must become activated. Your muscles need energy to work, and so the heart must beat faster, the lungs expand more rapidly, and so on. Your brain (CNS) receives impulses from these glands as they change, and it is these internal sensations of visceral changes that help us perceive an emotion. Have you ever "whistled in the dark" to divert your attention from your visceral changes and so not to feel afraid?

Notice in Figure 7–3 that the SNS mobilizes energy and the PNS conserves energy. Both functions are necessary for adequate adjustment. It is the SNS that accelerates heartbeat and prepares us to run. The PNS comes into play when the danger is past. Increased activity in the PNS is associated with a slower heartbeat, lower blood pressure, and so on. We conserve or restore our energy after the emergency has passed. *The two systems work cooperatively and jointly* to maintain an appropriate response to the demands of life. From the biological viewpoint, emotion is adaptive. It helps us survive. As we discussed in chapter 4, emotion can also constitute a danger to our health. For example, you or I might well die from "a broken heart" (Bishop, 1994). This is possible because of our seemingly regular heart rate is actually highly variable—shifting back and forth between the signals from the SNS and the PNS. These signals, in turn, are gov-

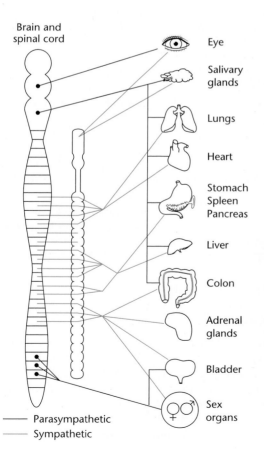

PARASYMPATHETIC SYSTEM
Constriction of pupil
Secretion of tear glands
Salivation
Inhibition of heart action
Constriction of respiratory passages
Stomach contraction: secretion of digestive fluids
Intestinal peristalsis
Contraction of bladder
Erection

SYMPATHETIC SYSTEM
Dilation of pupil
Inhibition of tear glands
Inhibition of salivation
Acceleration of heart action
Opens respiratory passages
Inhibits stomach contractions and digestive secretions
Inhibits intestinal peristalsis
Relaxes bladder
Inhibits Erection

FIGURE 7–3
The autonomic nervous system. Observe how the two systems complement one another.

Shut Your Mouth—You'll Feel Much Better!

We've known from infancy that sucking our thumbs makes us feel better. In childhood we are surprised to find out that chewing gum gives us satisfaction long after the flavor is gone. Most of us later learn that kissing is an even better way to elevate our mood. Robert Zajonc (1990) of the University of Michigan notes that all of these "feel good" activities force us to close our mouth and breathe through our nose. This forces air along our nasal passages, which lowers the temperature of the arterial blood, which cools the hypothalamus, the emotional center of our brain. Such increased cooling is sensed as pleasurable by the brain and has a positive effect on our mood. A "hothead" is one who contorts his or her face and breath into a pattern that heats the arterial blood, which is sensed as a discomfort by the brain and produces a negative effect on that person's mood.

insular cortex   a dense, isolated nugget of nerve fibers at the base of the cerebrum that helps regulate the autonomic nervous system

erned by signals from the **insular cortex** of our CNS. If it fails to govern, our heart can flutter, and fail to pump life-giving oxygen. The insular cortex seems to be quite vulnerable to stress and has been recently linked to cardiac deaths, voodoo deaths, and deaths from broken hearts.

Critical Review 3

1. Every society has the same norms or "feeling rules" about how people should feel and act in various situations. T F

2. Describe how you attempt to control yourself when you wish to mask your true feelings:
  A. Your language (what you say to yourself and to others)
  B. Your motor responses muscles of face and body)
  C. Your visceral responses (heartbeat, etc.)

3. What honest emotions are impossible for you to express while staying within the "feeling rules" of your peer group:
  A. At home
  B. At work
  C. At college

4. Using Table 7–1, trace the feeling of disgust from its stimulus source to its intended effect.

5. Our seemingly regular heartbeat is actually highly variable, shifting back and forth between the signals from the SNS and the PNS under the control of the insular cortex. How can this fact be used to understand voodoo death?

DIMENSIONS OF EMOTIONAL FAILURE

Dysfunctional Emotional Reactions

As mentioned earlier, emotions can be seen as adaptive reactions used by living organisms in their quest for survival. However, not all aspects of emotion are positive for humans. The evolutionary notion that emotions work for us, derived from animal studies, seems to ignore the fact that for millions of humans, emotion constitutes a problem in living, not a successful adaptation to life. Antisocial emotions, mentioned earlier in this chapter, include fear, anger, jealousy, and depression. These "negative" emotions can be functional, as when we feel fear when endangered, anger when frustrated, and anxiety when in conflict. But they can also be dysfunctional. Emotions become dysfunctional when they incapacitate us, rob us of personal fulfillment or the good company of our friends, or impel us to impulsive and hurtful acts.

Emotions may have been a survival mechanism for our species, but they can also be the cause of severe problems of adjustment, even suicide, if they fail in one or more of three dimensions: (1) appropriateness, (2) level of intensity, or (3) effectiveness of expression.

Suicide: Myth and Reality

It is likely that you have heard many of these statements concerning suicide. All appear to be reasonable; some are false. Mark a T for the ones you think are true and an F for the ones you think are false.

True/False

1. _____ When severely depressed people begin to feel better, the risk of their suicide decreases.

2. _____ More women that men attempt suicide.

3. _____ If people talk about suicide, they seldom do it.

4. _____ Not all people who kill themselves are depressed.

5. _____ If you think about it, you are likely to try to kill yourself.

6. _____ People have to be psychotic to kill themselves.

7. _____ Young Americans (ages 15 to 24) are killing themselves at an increasing rate.

8. _____ Suicide is inherited.

9. _____ More men than women kill themselves.

10. _____ Suicides occur much more frequently at certain times of the year, such as at Christmas.

11. _____ People may kill themselves for altruistic reasons.

12. _____ Many deaths listed as "accidents" by doctors and coroners are really suicides.

13. _____ Strong, silent types who have few significant social contacts and keep to themselves seldom take their own life.

14. _____ Substance abuse is the major problem for suicides under thirty years old.

15. _____ Because of "suicide pacts," there are more suicides among married couples than among single individuals.

16. _____ Certain learned professions, such as medical, dental, legal, and psychological, have much lower than average suicide rates among their members.

17. _____ People who are suicidal have many more negative life events happen to them before their suicide attempts.

18. _____ Suicidal teenagers report more problems with friends and sexual relationships than problems within their family

To see how well your "facts" match with statistical reality, look on page 280. The average number of correct responses in our college sample was 12.5.

APPROPRIATENESS

The first dimension of emotion is *appropriateness*. Is the emotion felt and expressed suitably in terms of the psychological situation? This is a matter of judgment. Others (including our conscience, acting as an internalized other) judge the appropriateness of our emotions.

Cognitive Appraisal

Richard Lazarus (1982) speaks of *cognitive appraisal*, the sometimes rational and sometimes irrational assessment of emotionally arousing stimuli. (For example, is the bear dangerous?) Spiesman (1965) investigated cognitive appraisal by giving subjects different appraisals of the meaning of a very gory film and then monitoring their emotional reactions while they viewed it. A control group saw the film without sound. One experimental group heard a factual description of the filmed events. Another heard a distant, overly intellectualized account, and still another was presented with a dialogue that tended to deny or gloss over the bloody incidents being shown on the screen. All groups were tested for emotional levels during and after the movie. Those who were led to deny or intellectualize what they were seeing were significantly less affected than the controls or those watching the straightforward presentation. Clearly, our emotional responses are affected by the way we interpret a situation.

The *power of positive thinking* (believing that the future holds good things in store for us) gains its appraisal power from the fact that it allows us to plan better, to take direct action to solve our problems, and to be more focused (Scheier and Carver, 1993).

If your cognitive appraisal (optimistic or pessimistic) agrees with that of people around you, your emotion is likely to be deemed appropriate. If their assessment calls for laughter and you feel terror, you may have a problem. Even if your assessment agrees with others' appraisals, your response may be deemed inappropriate if it is not the one expected under the circumstances. You may place different emphasis or different meanings on the same sensations. Your social class or cultural background may influence you to conclude that a different emotional response is called for (Douvan and Adeson, 1966). For whatever reason, if your emotional expression is judged inappropriate, an adjustment becomes necessary, because the other people serve as jury and executioner as well as judge.

Social Pressure

You may well ask what business it is of others how you feel. In truth, others make it their business because all of us depend on the emotional expressions of others to serve as cues to help us judge what a situation means and what response is called for. If you are unreliable or habitually respond in a unique way, the security and togetherness of those around you are undermined. Their world becomes less ordered and less sane. Pressure is typically applied to bring the errant member into line—hence, the adjustment problem.

> George loves to please: He loves to entertain. If he wants something from someone, he will appeal to pity or to debt for past favors. George loves affection and is uncomfortable around people who are angry or aggressive. He loves those who help and hates those who hurt.

According to Richard Wallen (1972), George's emotional style is that of a "friendly helper" who embraces the tender emotions and will attempt to use them even when they are inappropriate—that is, when stronger emotions are clearly called for.

This does not mean we can never use our own values to judge the appropriateness of an emotion or its expression. We have a perfect right to do so. It does mean, however, that we should be ready to take responsibility for the consequences of such judgments. To feel and express outrage at an injustice that is tolerated by those around you, for example, may reflect personal growth and mark the beginning of social progress for your school, town or nation.

Accepting Our Feelings

A common failure related to emotional appropriateness occurs when our emotional reaction does not fit our self-image. To others, our appraisal and reaction may seem perfectly justified, even necessary. We become furious or grief stricken when our home is broken into, for example. But to us, public displays of such strong emotion may be totally unacceptable. Such self-talk as "Anger is for the weak" or "Never cry over spilled milk" can cause us to reject our own feelings and their honest expression (Ellis, 1973). The irrational but common belief that we *must always be perfect* rules out negative emotions and forces us into inappropriate emotional assessments or expressions.

Although we do not have to be perfect, it is interesting to note that research has shown that expressing anger can (1) make us angrier, (2) solidify an angry attitude, and (3) establish an angry habit (Tavris, 1982). People who display such actions, attitudes, and habits find it difficult to maintain close, warm personal relationships (see the discussion of assertiveness, page 267, for suggestions on appropriate expression of negative emotions).

INTENSITY

The second dimension of emotion involves *emotional intensity*. Remember that many hold that the only thing that differentiates emotions from one another is their level of intensity (Duffy, 1941; Lindsley, 1951). Consider this example: While you are walking alone through a dark alley, the silence is broken by a sudden noise! Your reaction may be apprehension, fear, or terror. Except for their intensity, these emotions are indistinguishable. If you were feeling powerful at that moment, but not fearful, the noise might have made you annoyed, angered, or outraged. Again, these emotions fall along a continuous line of increasing intensity; Plutchik (1980) looks at them as being separated only by intensity.

Intensity becomes an adjustment problem when it is either so deficient or so excessive that it interferes with our ability to meet the demands of the situation.

Kurt is tough as nails! He walks tough, talks tough, looks tough, and loves it. You can get mad around Kurt, and you can fight. Kurt's comfortable around a fight. It's when you get warm and affectionate that Kurt shies away. He doesn't like losers. If he wants something from you, he'll tell you just what you'll get if you don't comply. Kurt can take as good as he gives, too.

Richard Wallen (1972) says Kurt is a "sturdy battler" whose explosive emotional style is always excessively intense.

Being a "sturdy battler" restricts our range of emotional expression.

Excessive Emotionality

We typically associate emotional-adjustment problems with excessive intensities of emotion—rage rather than annoyance, terror rather than apprehension. These states involve a loss of control, a disintegration of the capacity to respond appropriately. Brain mechanisms control the intensity of emotional states. The wide range and rapid changes in infant emotion are largely due to the immaturity of these structures at birth. Neurochemical imbalances in these areas due to genetic deficiency, alcohol, drug abuse, injury or disease can provoke intense rage and terror reactions. A familiar example is the drunken rage, an alcohol-abuse reaction. "The cocaine explosion" is the term used to identify a modern drug-induced rage. Both illustrate failures to regulate emotional intensity due to brain dysfunction.

Surprisingly, behavioral disorders characterized by apathy, withdrawal, and unresponsiveness are examples of excessive emotional arousal. Forbes and Chaney (1978) monitored the heart rate, blood pressure, and other skeletal and visceral activity of neurotic patients undergoing group therapy. They reported that arousal is just as high in depressed patients as in those recognizably tense, angry, or anxious. Extremes of depression are associated with excesses of emotional intensity.

Optimal Arousal

The Yerkes-Dodson Law "Test anxiety" illustrates a relationship between emotional intensity and task complexity known as the Yerkes-Dodson law (Morris, 1979). Simply stated, the law says that *the more complex a task, the lower the level of emotion that can be tolerated without impairment of performance.* The typical college exam is a complex task. "Aceing it" requires a low level of arousal. The skill of cultivating low levels of arousal can be learned and used to improve test performance (as discussed in chapter 4).

Mild levels of emotional arousal appear to be both functional and fun. When mildly aroused, we are more alert and more attentive and feel more alive. We learn and remember better. That is why good teachers are forever trying to stimulate their students.

The relationship between mood and memory is now well established (Bower, 1981; Laird et al., 1982). In general, if we can match the mood of the material we are learning, or if we can recapture the mood we were in at the time we learned it, we can recall more. The facts of a melancholy tale can be recalled better if we are melancholy while hearing it and while retelling it. Events are coded for emotion, and the activation of similar emotions aids in information retrieval (see the discussion of memory in chapter 6).

Do you frequent amusement parks or football stadiums? Those who do are seeking mild levels of *aversive stimuli* (such as danger, injustice, or the threat of loss) so that they may feel and express negative emotions, such as fear and anger, for the pleasure such emotions bring when they are experienced under conditions of security and social acceptance.

Do you like watching plays or movies? "As if" emotions are clearly present among actors and audiences in good theater. In order to experience these uniquely human emotions, you must balance belief (needed to become involved in the plot) and disbelief (needed to maintain sanity). Three-year-old children experience real emotion at the theater, but they cannot yet experience theater.

Strong Emotion and Good Adjustment

Even high emotional intensity is not always associated with an adjustment problem. Sexual pleasure, for example, is associated with intense levels of arousal and strong emotional expression. (But even here, performance suffers under conditions of overstimulation). We are, at other times, called upon to produce extreme bursts of energy. Fleeing from danger or attacking a foe demands excessive energy mobilization and release. Herculean feats of strength and endurance seem impossible without the accompaniment of intense emotion. For example, a mother who lifts the front end of an automobile to free her trapped child will later find the feat impossible.

EXPRESSION

The third dimension of emotion involves *emotional expression.* We can also fail in this social dimension.

> I never see him laugh. I never see him cry. Looking at Tom, you never know if he is winning or losing. He is the coolest man I've ever seen. That's okay by me, but his poor wife and kids seem kind of forlorn. Tom takes great pride in his knowledge and

always tries to get what he wants by overwhelming you with facts and quotes. He always makes me feel uncomfortably stupid and awkward.

Richard Wallen (1972) terms Tom a "logical thinker." People with this emotional style are reluctant to express any emotion.

The Language of Emotion: Facial Expression

Facial expressions constitute the basic vocabulary of our emotional language (Ekman and Friesen, 1975). The eighty muscles in the face can create more than 7,000 expressions (Levenson, 1986). These are "internal states that take form on the face." As an emotion is formed in the brain, signals "feed forward" to the face, which assumes an expression. By providing feedback to the brain, facial movements may also be tied to the production of an emotion. The facial muscles work together to produce the smiling, frowning, laughing, or crying face that gives others insight into our inner lives.

Levenson, (1986) analyzed the effect particular facial expressions have on automatic bodily responses, such as our heart rate, finger temperature, and skin conductivity. They found that angry, fearful, or sad faces produce elevations in heart rates. In contrast, a disgusted look is associated with a slower heart rate. Finger temperature rises with an angry face, but decreases with a frightened one. "The easiest explanation for this is a sociobiological one," Levenson reports. Emotions are often associated with a need to act on short notice. An elevated heart rate is functional in a time of danger. If we intend to fight, blood to the hands is essential; not so if we intend to flee.

The ability to interpret correctly the emotion contained in a facial expression increases with age (Izard, 1977). This means that maturation and experience, as well as physical evolution, play a part in this survival skill. Facial expressions may be misinterpreted, however. We rarely depend on the face alone to carry our emotional messages. The meaning that is carried by how we say something is to be found in the volume, pitch, rate, and fluidity of our speech (Rosenthal et al., 1974). An angry message is usually high in volume, pitch, and rate. Depres-

---

Let Him Talk. He'll Hang Himself.

The ancients used the mouth to determine the guilt or innocence of an accused person. If seeds, forced into the mouth, came out dry, the accused was guilty. If the accused could not spit on command, she was guilty. Saliva, under the control of our autonomic nervous system, stops when we are under stress. An innocent person who has nothing to fear should be able to let the saliva flow while being interrogated; at least this was the assumption behind the tests.

A lie detector that uses the voice has been developed on the principle that all muscles, when in use, have a slight tremor or vibration. This tremor is dampened by the autonomic nervous system when the person is under stress. When we are innocent or truthful (relaxed), our voices should include this tremor. When we are guilty or lying (tense), our voices should not include the tremor.

A machine, the voice stress analyzer, can detect and record the presence or absence of our tremors and convict us "out of our own mouths." It can be attached to a telephone. No connections to the person are needed. It can be used without the knowledge or consent of the accused, who may not even know he is being accused or suspected of anything.

The validity of the technique (many variables other than guilt can cause tremor reduction) and the ethics of using it (because of violation of privacy and so on) are under question. (This technique is discussed in more detail in B. Rice "The New Truth Machine." *Psychology Today* 12 (1978): 67–78.

sion is reflected in low volume, rate, and pitch. Lack of fluidity—broken-up speech—is associated with both repressed anger and depression. We also reveal anxiety by a break in the flow of our speech (see the boxed feature "Let Him Talk. He'll Hang Himself").

The Language of Emotion: Body Expression

Our bodies as well as our faces and voices help us communicate emotion. Specific acts, like slamming doors, are expressive. More subtly, we use *body language*. You may not be able to describe a silent sexual "come-on," but after experiencing one, you can never forget it. Birdwhistell (1952) has developed a science of **kinesics** to explore the human body as a language system. Posture and gesture combine to produce body language. Body language gives a dimension to our emotional expression that facial and vocal muscles are incapable of communicating.

kinesics the science of body language

Our posture usually indicates our emotional state quite clearly. The forward-thrusting, assertive stance of anger can hardly be confused with the apathetic slump of depression or the recoiled cringe of terror. When depressed patients improve, they spend increased time in motion, they initiate and terminate motion more quickly, and they make more complex bodily motions than when they were deeply depressed (Fisch, Frey, and Hirsbrunner, 1983). Even distance can be expressive. The amount of distance we establish and maintain between ourselves and those with whom we communicate reveals the degree of trust, warmth, and intimacy we are prepared to extend. Using his Profile of Nonverbal Sensitivity Scale (PONS), Rosenthal et al. (1974) concluded that women are more sensitive and accurate than men in reading body language.

Our posture usually indicates our emotional state quite clearly.

The Cultural Basis of Poor Emotional Expression

We often suffer problems in adjustment because we have been carefully taught not to trust our own emotions. The muscles that contract to form our posture, gestures, facial expressions, and vocal patterns are voluntary muscles. Even our visceral muscles can come under a degree of voluntary control. Muscles can contract automatically, as in an infant's smile; but they can also be directed to contract, as in the smile of the used-car salesperson. Our culture values the strong, undemonstrative type who places reason above emotion. The sensitive, expressive person is often seen as handicapped in this business-oriented civilization. The poker face is prized in a game in which deception counts. Children learn to manipulate their emotional expressions in order to keep their parent's love and support. Under these conditions, spontaneity is lost and certain emotions become taboo. According to Fritz Perls (1969), the open and honest expression of emotion is essential to mental health. Much of his therapy was devoted to helping clients relearn this lost skill.

The difficulty for many of us in expressing negative emotions without guilt or anxiety pinpoints a unique problem of human adaptation: We can *feel about how we feel*. We can be taught to feel guilty for feeling anger toward one we love, or ashamed at feeling grief over the loss of a prized possession. "Don't cry. It's only a toy," translates into, "You're silly or selfish for having such feelings. Don't allow yourself to have them. Never express them."

As honest feelings become associated with negative outcomes, children learn to mistrust feelings and restrict their expression. Izard (1977) finds that our facial muscles trigger an automatic reaction within our brain. He believes that this reaction tells us which emotion we are feeling. If your face is formed into a smile, for example, you should feel happiness. (Try it yourself). This may mean that to learn not to *show* feelings may actually lessen our capacity to *have* feelings. A failure in expression becomes a failure in intensity and appropriateness as well.

We conclude this chapter by examining two powerful antisocial emotions in some detail. These two feeling states, anger and depression, represent opposite extremes of *emotional intensity*. A complex prosocial emotion, love, is explored in chapter 9, on intimacy.

FAILED EMOTIONAL EXPRESSION: AGGRESSION

Losing the capacity to feel deeply is the greatest personal failure in emotional expression. On an interpersonal level, the greatest failure in emotional expression occurs when we express anger, hostility or rage through **aggression**-behavior intended to injure another person or to destroy property. Hostile aggression, rather than instrumental aggression, represents a failure in emotional expression. *Instrumental aggression*, the calculated use of violence to achieve some desired end, can be devoid of emotion. "For many of the worst offenders (wife beaters), violence in not impulsive, and their fury is paired with a cool control (Goleman, 1994). The end (noble or ignoble) is thought to justify the means. We may show cold-hearted aggression to protect ourselves, for example. *Hostile aggression* is the venting of anger on a victim. It is violence carried out for the sole purpose of inflicting injury.

aggression   instrumental or hostile action intended to injure people or property or to gain specific outcomes

Instinctive Aggression

Freud believed that aggression was instinctive, an expression of the *death wish* that could be directed against others or against oneself. Prosocial emotions (such as love), substitute victims (such as bowling pins), and vicarious forms of aggression (such as watching sports contests) were seen by Freud as the only way humans could reduce the carnage of aggressive behavior (see chapter 2, on personality, for an explanation of Freudian theory).

Frustration Aggression

In the 1930s the idea that aggression was an emotional response to frustration was introduced (Dollard et al., 1939). This **frustration-aggression hypothesis** offered another avenue toward reducing aggression—the reduction of frustration. Aggression was seen as an instinctive release of pent-up pain, psychological or physical. The idea that this release of aggression had a biological basis was buttressed by the finding that humans, as well as lower animals, had neurological mechanisms in the brain that released aggressive behavior (Papez, 1937). Chemical imbalances within these mechanisms, increasing or inhibiting the flow of excitement within the brain, have been associated with abnormal childhood aggression and impulsive violence (Rogers, 1983). "Unpleasant events tend to evoke aggression in humans, as in other animals" (Berkowitz, 1983, p. 1135). For normal people, however, neither brain structure nor brain chemistry alone is believed to be the *cause* of aggression.

frustration-aggression hypothesis a theory in which aggressive responses are said to be the direct result of painful personal experiences

Learned Aggression

Human aggression is considered by many today to be a product of our social lives. The frequency, the form, and the function of aggression are determined by learning and the influence of others (Bandura, 1977). In other words, we learn the when, how, and what for of aggression. We also learn when not to be aggressive and which people are appropriate or inappropriate victims of aggression. See chapter 5 for a discussion of prejudice and discrimination, so often the advanced guard of aggression.

Gang Violence

Gang violence in America is exploding. Gang leaders now routinely recruit children as young as eleven for their most aggressive acts. Both they and the police report that young offenders are often back on the street only hours after being arrested for a violent crime.

What are the factors that influence such behavior? As you might guess, there are individual, social, and cultural factors that interact in complex ways to create this explosive reality. You are asked to consider the following factors and then suggest the intervention that you believe might bring the level of gang violence within reasonable bounds.

Group Factors

A human group is defined as two or more people who interact and influence each other (Shaw, 1981). Two contradictory effects are observed in group interaction. On the one hand, individuals are more aware of being observed and

evaluated by other members of their group. On the other hand, individuals lose their sense of individuality while participating as part of a group.

The effect of our increased awareness of being watched from within is termed *evaluation apprehension*. The effect of this fear of group censure is to *increase the strength of our dominant responses*. If we are shy, we become increasingly shy, for example.

The effect of our becoming lost within the group is termed *anonymity* and makes one less self-conscious and more responsive to cues present in the situation (Spivey and Prentice-Dunn, 1990). Be very aware that the findings report that we become more responsive to *both pro-social and anti-social cues;* for example, we can become more loving while in the embrace of a loving group. Another term associated with group submersion is **deindividuation**.

—*Continued*

Gang Violence—*Continued*

This invisibility to those outside the group acts to diffuse responsibility and diminish normal inhibition. When the situational cues are anti-social, this lessening of restraint increases the probability and the intensity of antisocial acts. We throw and scream more, we engage in vandalism, orgies, and thefts in order to gratify ourselves more, we even explode into brutality, rioting, and lynching more (Spivey and Prentice-Dunn, 1990).

Let us repeat, however, that what was formally thought to be a *risky shift*, a tendency for groups to always gravitate toward greater risk, is now seen as a tendency for group involvement to act to enhance the individuals' initial leanings, either *prosocial or antisocial*.

Such within-group sensitivity and between-group insensitivity often leads to *polarization*, an increase in the initial gap that might have existed between groups. Polarization increases between-group competition and reduces between-group cooperation. The resulting sense of being surrounded by "hostile others" increases our sense of personal threat.

Outside threat, real or imagined, influences individuals to ignore within-group differences that might weaken them, and also to ignore between-group similarities that might lesson their hostile resolve. One result of this "circling of the wagons" is to encourage *group think,* which reduces dissent in the face of threat (Turner, Pratkanis, Probasco, and Leve, 1992). We control free thought and free speech within the group so as to share the illusion of being invulnerable, moral, and united. The result is often a reduction in *deliberation* that ends in tragic mistakes of judgment (Turner et al., 1992).

Cultural Factors

America is a culture of violence. We won our freedom with the musket ball; we won the West with the rifle and the ax; we won World War II with the atomic bomb—all acts of orchestrated aggression. Our mass culture reflects our increasing submersion in violent themes. MTV is more violent than was radio in its infancy; professional football, basketball, and hockey are more violent than the older national pastime, baseball. Pulp magazines, soap operas, and talk shows attempt to package sexuality in a cloak of violence in order to meet the ever increasing demands of the American viewing public.

Subcultures of Violence

In gangs violence is valued. As this value is learned and shared, *many situations are interpreted as menacing* and *demanding of an aggressive response*. High status in a gang is earned primarily through displays of violence, first appearing in gang play. People in the gang are expected to follow these aggressive norms. If they do not, they may be ostracized, made a victim of internal aggression, or offered as a sacrificial lamb. Importantly, social learning theorists have shown how important *imitation* is to both the acquisition and the performance of aggressive behavior (Bankart and Bankart, 1991).

Individual Factors

Genetics as well as social learning and frustration plays a role in aggression. A twenty-year study of aggressive children reflects the stability of this personality trait. Children who were rated highest in aggression in the third grade received more than three times the number of criminal convictions by the time they were 30 (Huesmann, 1984). They were also found to be more likely to drive while drunk and to severely punish their children.

As adults, most violent men use *instrumental aggression* to bolster their egos and/or to meet the demands of their violent role. A smaller number are motivated by excessive self-interest. They appraise a situation only in terms of their self-needs with no regard for the needs or rights of the victim or of society. A very small percentage of violent men report that they resort to aggression to relieve personal tension *(catharsis)* (Toch, 1969).

Releasing and Restraining Factors

Violence does not simply explode. There are always cues in the situation that serve to release or restrain violent acts. On chillingly live television, Americans recently watched in horror as Haitian military men, armed with billy clubs, brutally and senselessly attacked their own people while fully armed and armored American soldiers watched—emotionally anguished—but physically frozen.

What are forces that "freeze the hand of action"? Restraining factors reduce themselves to empathy, fear, and guilt. American military men were acting "under orders," and they feared the negative consequences for themselves, their unit, and their country if they broke military discipline. Holding ranks while observing each other remain uninvolved allowed our soldiers to detach themselves somewhat from the victims, reduce their empathy, and lessen their moral need to act.

For the Haitian soldiers, there was a reduction of restraining forces. Frustrated and threatened by recent events, they banded together and acted out their aggressive impulses in the manner that their selection, training, and experience suggested. The situation seemed out of control, and their personal safety as well as their sworn duty to maintain order mandated violence. They were free of fear or guilt as long as they held a monopoly of force; that is, as long as they acted as a unit and as long as the American units were pas-

Gang Violence—*Continued*

sive. On the following day, the empathy, fear, and guilt relationships were reversed. American troops were released from their constraining orders, and the Haitian troops were restrained by their commanders and by the certain knowledge that the well-trained, well-armed, and morally outraged American soldiers were free to act. The systematic violence stopped.

Chemical-releasing Factors

Naturally occurring biochemicals, such as high insulin and testosterone levels, are associated with increased irritability and aggression. *Chemical additives* can be much more explosive. Many a victim of violence has had to endure the added insult of hearing the aggressor rationalize his or her brutality by saying, "I was drunk" or "I was high." It reduces shame, guilt, and fear if one believes that alcohol or drugs are the devils that "make me do it."

In small doses, alcohol, like marijuana, influences us to be *less aggressive when provoked.* No aggression is produced by large amounts of alcohol *if there are no provoking circumstances.* However, in large doses alcohol causes **cognitive disruption,** a lessening of our thinking capacity that makes us less able to notice and respond to reduced situational cues that often serve to diffuse anger or to offer nonviolent means of expressing it (Leonard, 1989). In recent years cognitive psychologists have demonstrated that it is our learned and shared *expectations about whether alcohol will stimulate aggressive behavior,* rather than the alcohol level itself, that is the release mechanism for violence (Lang and Sibrell, 1989).

Phencyclidine (PCP or Angel Dust) is directly connected with violence, and barbiturates have been shown to be capable of eliciting irritability, hostility, and overt aggression among their users (Medicine, Police, Volvo, and Gabrielle, 1982). Cocaine use can produce paranoia and aggressiveness, and those who use steroids to "build up" the ancient tools of aggression, the muscles, often find themselves irritable and socially explosive. Much of the violence surrounding the use of alcohol and other drugs is multiplied by the social fact that their illegality and expense force users to operate within a criminal, and violent, subculture.

What Direction for the War on Childhood Crime?

Taking into consideration what we know about individuals, groups, and the forces that control them, which of the following policies do you believe holds the greatest promise for a long-term reduction in gang violence in America?

1. **We should construct a realistic deterrent to gang violence.** We should get tough on criminal children.

2. **We should work to prevent the need for childhood violence.** We should attack crime at its social and cultural roots.

3. **We should isolate the violent models.** We should work to identify, select, and incapacitate those few violent children who can create an aggressive norm within the gang.

The War on Criminal Children
What Doesn't work.

1. **Creating catharsis.** Feeding American children a diet of vicarious aggression will not make them less likely to aggress. Providing them with controlled aggressive outlets might make them feel better, but not less likely to respond to violence.

2. **Providing punishment.** This most favored tactic has very limited utility. Although, it might deter a specific act of aggression, it models and reinforces the very aggression it seeks to curtail (Baron, 1987).

What works but appears difficult to accomplish.

1. **Modifying social conditions that encourage aggression.** Providing every child with good health, good parents, a good home, a good neighborhood, a good school, and the good income needed to sustain them all is proving to be a gargantuan social undertaking.

2. **Modifying social responses that reinforce childhood aggression.** If we could get our mothers and fathers to socialize their sons in the identical ways that they now socialize their daughters, the explosive "macho" mentality could be brought within reasonable bounds.

What possibly could work.

Because of the fact that human violence is largely a learned and shared response, the following seems feasible:

1. **Intervene to reduce the potential of the violent child.** Concentrate on those few who are likely to construct or maintain a tradition of violence.

2. **Modify children's TV programming** to reduce its violent and pornographic content.

3. **Model and reward assertive responses** to frustration that work and that are incompatible with violence (e.g., empathy, humor, and negotiating skills).

4. **Make alcohol, drugs, and weapons less glamorous and less accessible** to children, at home or on the street.

Professional boxers display aggression. The murder rate in the United States rises after major televised fights. See "TV Violence and Aggression".

We learn to be aggressive in the same manner we learn other social skills—by direct instruction, by imitating others, and by receiving incentives or rewards for being aggressive. Parental admonitions such as "to be strong, you have to fight for what you get" can be overlearned. Observing models acting aggressively (as on television) teaches aggression. Learning (directly or indirectly) that "violence pays" also increases aggressive behavior (see chapter 8, dealing with socialization, for more about social learning).

Social learning theorists believe that two conditions must be present for aggressive responses to occur in adults. There must be an arousing stimulus—such as frustration, sexual attraction, or competition, that causes our heart to pound and our blood pressure to rise. And there must be a stimulus that elicits an aggressive response—previous pain, a vulnerable person, something to be gained or avoided. If someone annoys you and you are later aroused—*by whatever means*—and given a chance to act aggressively against the annoying party, you are more likely to show an intense aggressive response. However, simple arousal, including sexual arousal, without prior aversive exposure does not produce increased aggression (Zillmann and and Sapolsky, 1977).

Curbing Violence

Because of our increased awareness and knowledge of the causes of aggression, it may now be possible to keep violence within bounds. Indeed, in these days of weapon proliferation—from automatic weapons to atomic bombs—it is mandatory.

Reducing frustration, competition, and alcohol consumption can help. Teaching nonaggressive ways of responding, and being careful never to reinforce aggression when it occurs, can reduce the stimuli that trigger aggression. Would Nicole Simpson have been repeatedly battered if the Los Angeles police and judicial systems were more responsive to earlier abusive incidents involving O. J. Simpson? Beta blockers are drugs that can be used in conjunction with psychotherapy to reduce aggression in brain or drug/alcohol-damaged people. Such strong psychobiological interventions were being advocated for cynical hostility marked by suspiciousness, resentment, frequent anger, distrust, and antagonism as early as 1991 (Friedman, 1991).

SUCCESSFUL EMOTIONAL EXPRESSION: ASSERTIVENESS

Cooperation, negotiation, problem solving, and **assertiveness** are all social skills that have been found to reduce the need for violence. A behavioral approach that helps reduce both anxiety and hostility is **assertiveness training**. The training occurs in small support groups in which shy or hostile people practice firm but controlled assertive responses under the direction of a therapist. They then are encouraged to try them in real life.

Those in training practice insisting on their rights *without abusing the other person*. Real-life situations are drawn from the group members and presented to the support group. The members act out assigned roles in which they behave shyly, assertively, or aggressively. Postures, gestures, voice levels, and specific dialogues are enacted and constructively criticized. Assertive alternatives are suggested. Group members act together and help one another. The effective expression of negative emotions, such as fear or anger, is often the objective of a group session. In addition to development of specific skills, another desired outcome is increased awareness of freedom and social responsibility (see chapter 9 for more about various styles of communication).

assertiveness a style of responding in which individual rights are protected without abusing others

assertiveness training the formal teaching and modeling of assertive behavior

Betty and her family are eating out at a nice restaurant. Always mindful of her diet, she orders a salad and requests that the dressing be delivered "on the side." A short while later the waiter presents the salad, with the dressing on top.

Shy Betty: Says nothing to the waiter but grumbles to her husband and vows never to eat there again. Her husband, Jim, feels bad because he didn't take action for his wife. The kids just feel bad.

Aggressive Betty: Loudly calls the waiter back and gives him hell for not having brains enough to remember a simple order. Betty demands, and gets, another salad. She also gets embarrassed looks and a prolonged silence from her family. The meal is ruined.

Assertive Betty: Motions the waiter to her table and notes that she had ordered her dressing on the side. Betty asks politely but firmly that the salad be returned and her original request be honored. The waiter soon returns with the order corrected.

Television Violence and Aggression

There is a growing body of evidence that television violence increases the number of Americans who use violence as an adjustment alternative. However, television violence does not affect all of us the same way. Children who believe television reflects real life and who identify with aggressive characters (heroes or villains) display more aggressive actions at home and school. Such children are less popular at school and watch more and more violent television (Eron, 1982). Unpopularity is painful, and pain stimulates aggression. Such children become caught in a cycle of aggression, rejection, and more aggression. Adults also are influenced by real violence on television. After a highly publicized prized fight, the number of murders committed increases. *The victim is likely to be of the same race as the loser of the televised fight* (Phillips, 1983).

Critical Review 4

1. Strong, silent types who have few significant social contacts and keep to themselves seldom take their own life. T F

2. Cognitive appraisal is sometimes a rational and sometimes an irrational assessment of the meaning of arousing stimuli. T F

3. We associate emotional adjustment problems with excessive intensities of emotion—rage rather than anger, terror rather than apprehension. T F

4. Recall an example from your own life when you were painfully aware of each of these dimensions of emotional failure:

I. **Appropriateness**
A. Cognitive appraisal (when you misinterpreted a situation)
B. Social pressure (when your group influenced how you felt)
C. Self-concept (when you couldn't accept your own feelings)

II. **Intensity**
A. Excessive (when you lost control)
B. Deficient (when you didn't respond)

III. **Expression**
A. Facial (when your face gave you away)
B. Posture (when your pose gave you away)
C. Gesture (when your hands gave you away)

5. Recall a social situation in which you were able to insist on protecting your own rights *without abusing the other person.* How did it turn out? How do you feel about it now?

DEPRESSION

As we mentioned, a useful scheme for classifying human emotions is to divide them into high and low intensity. Under this system, for example, fear and anger are high intensity and disgust is low intensity. In this last section we explore an emotion that is not an emergency reaction like fear or aggression. Rather, it represents a low-intensity emotion that exacts a huge toll from all of us, a toll in suicides, missed workdays, and wasted days on the job. The staggering cost of depression each year in America is estimated at $43.7 billion (Miller, 1993).

Characteristics of Depressed People

depression a feeling of personal worthlessness, apathy, and hopelessness

Termed the "common cold of psychopathology" by Martin Seligman, **depression** has replaced anxiety as the disease of the decade. The profile of depression as seen in alcoholic men (Steer et al., 1982) is, in many ways, a typical profile of depression. Such men exhibit the following characteristics:

1. Negative attitudes (pessimism, a sense of failure, self-accusation, and self-dislike).
2. Physiological disorders (anorexia, weight loss, sleep loss).
3. Performance deficiencies (work impairment, general fatigue).

Serious depression thus illustrates a failure in the three dimensions of emotion. Physiologically, depressives maintain high levels of internal arousal. Behaviorally, they emit inappropriate and excessively low levels of expression and outward activity. The dejected mood, sad face, and slumped posture of depressed persons stand in stark contrast to their high-energy mobilization. Prosocial emotions and pleasurable activities such as sexual activities, sleeping, and eating are maintained at low levels, while antisocial emotions and painful activities such as worrying, complaining, crying, and withdrawing are more consistently exhibited. With high-energy mobilization accompanied by only low-energy activities, it might be reasonable to expect depressed people to be agitated. On the contrary, fatigue is the most common ailment they report.

> Susan appears tired and strangely quiet, not at all like the energetic and articulate "young aspiring professional" image she wants to project. The problem is that Susan's part-time job just doesn't seem to be leading anywhere. The income is poor and the opportunity not much better. There aren't many attractive men at work, either. Susan often regrets that her formal education was interrupted by an early and brief marriage.
>
> Susan wants to appear bright and enthusiastic so that she can get full-time work. A full-time job will pay enough for the university and professional training she dreams of. But it's so hard to pretend, and so hard to fight fatigue.

Atypical Depression

It is hard for "atypical depressives," that is, people who have chronic, mild depression, to like themselves, or to see how anyone else could possibly like them. After all, they prefer to eat and sleep most of the time. They tend to be moody and irritable as well. Seldom diagnosed as being ill, and rarely hospitalized, their illness is nonetheless painfully real.

> Barbara is sad, but not your typical sad person. Her "blue" periods are seldom severe, but she never feels really good either. She often wonders if those around her, those who seem energetic or buoyant, are being honest. Unlike classic depressives, Barbara sleeps well—to well—up to fifteen hours a day! She usually wakes in a decent mood, but by evening she is exhausted and down. While most depressed people lose their appetite, Barbara spends her entire waking day eating. What most people quickly learn about Barbara is how sensitive to criticism she is; the slightest hint that something about her is less than perfect sends her into long bouts of anger and sadness. Sincere compliments, on the other hand, can only briefly raise her spirits.

SELF-TREATMENT

Until now, because of individual ignorance, the inability of health professionals to recognize and diagnose depression, the lack of health insurance for preventative treatment, and the stigmatization of "being emotionally ill," most people who suffered from depression would *self treat* by the use of alcohol, drugs, and "feel good" foods! The result has been prolonged suffering, suicide, and lost dollars and days (Leshner, 1992).

Fortunately for Barbara, and thousands of others like her, her disorder is being recognized for the physical illness that it is, and professional treatment with therapy and antidepressant drugs is proving to be quick and effective. She was treated on an outpatient basis and now leads a normal and highly productive life. The return of Barbara's "social skills" within a matter of weeks is a dramatic illustration of the chemical nature of her illness, for social skill training is impossible to accomplish in so short a time.

Organic View of Depression

The organic view of depression explains the origins of this disorder in physiological terms and the outcomes of it in behavioral terms (Akiskal and McKinney, 1973). A malfunctioning thyroid gland causes sluggishness, for example, and certain cortical mechanisms of reinforcement (pleasure centers in the brain) may not receive appropriate stimulation because of a shortage of various neurotransmitters (substances that carry messages between nerve cells). "Clinical depression has been experimentally assessed and dramatically confirmed to be highly dependent on active serotonergic transmission" (Guze and Freedman, 1991).

Less severe depressive episodes can also be the result of chemistry. Dr. Judith J. Wurtman (1987), a nutritional biochemist at the Massachusetts Institute of Technology, reports that "What you eat and when you eat it can make you irritable or calm, energetic or lethargic, sleepy or alert." The diet of the depressive might be low in protein-rich food, resulting in less of the amino acid tyrosine, which leads to lower levels of catacholamines (dopamine and norepinephrine) in the brain and a decrease in energy.

Some depression is seasonal. It intensifies in late fall when days are shorter and there is less sunlight and diminishes with the coming of spring. Such seasonal affective disorders can be treated by bright, artificial light, or by a trip south during winter.

Chemical or radiant imbalances can make us incapable of receiving pleasure from ordinary stimuli, so normal rewards are not adequate to shape and maintain prosocial responding. A smile, a pat, and an admonition to cheer up will not suffice.

Coppen (1967) found depression to be associated with potassium and high sodium levels. He theorized that this state results in reduced neurological activity. The use of enzymes to regulate the amount of this brain activity resulted in the first antidepressant drug—**lithium**, a carbonated salt solution that is often dramatically effective in the treatment of depression.

lithium   simple, inorganic salts used to decrease the severity of both manic and depressive episodes in some bipolar depressives

At this time more than twenty antidepressants are available by prescription. *Tricyclic antidepressants* are effective in helping reduce the apathy, loss of appetite, and disturbed sleep characteristic of melancholic depression. *Monoamine oxidase inhibitors* work well for those who are depressed but eat and sleep *more*, not less, than normal. *Prozac* relieves depression and energizes rather than sedates. It seems to have a few adverse side effects. (Prozac appears to be the doctor's drug of choice for suicidal females, for it is less deadly when taken as an overdose in combination with alcohol.) Although therapy alone is often effective in curing mild depression, medication alone is seldom sufficient to successfully treat severe depression.

CHEMICAL TREATMENT OF DEPRESSION

The organic view of depression leads directly to the chemical treatment of the disorder. A three-year study has recently been completed that is encouraging medical doctors to radically change the way they treat depression. This 1991 study (Guze and Freedman) reported that:

1. The usual procedure in which an initial high dosage of a tricyclic antidepressant is given for three or four months, followed, after remission or stabilization, with a lower dosage for up to four months *is a failure*, because:

2. Fifty to sixty percent of major depressive disorders are recurrent. They again become depressed under this treatment plan.

3. A new treatment plan was found to be *eighty percent effective*. This plan included three departures from standard practice:

   a. The useful general principle of "the less drug the better" was abandoned when treating recurrent depression.

   b. The high dosage of the drug used in the acute phase was sustained for up to twelve months after remission or stabilization had been achieved. (Such high dosages were found to be well tolerated.)

   c. The patient, family, and physician were trained to notice the earliest signs of recurring depression, and to reinstitute the high dosage treatment immediately. This saved the patient and family from four to five months of suffering compared to the control group patient and family, who waited, hoping for the best.

Psychotherapeutic View of Depression

The psychotherapeutic approach to depression (Arieti and Bemporad, 1979) defines depression as "an unresolved state of sorrow or sadness." It appears that the chief risk factor for depression in both men and women is the early loss of a parent (Roy, 1981). A person who learns to ease the pain of such early losses by denying them rather than working them through may not be prepared later to respond to other severe losses by the usual process of grief work, or mourning.

In young children the pain of losing something or someone they love is often made worse by the pain of guilt. Before the age of seven, children are egocentric and prelogical (magical). Because they believe that wishes can make things happen and are involved in all natural events, children are vulnerable to the belief that their wishes "caused" their parents to die, for example. Adults often exploit this vulnerability. Parents at times engage in *moralistic blaming* ("Don't lie to me. Only bad people lie!") and in *threats of abandonment* ("If you lie again, I am going to go off and just leave you"). They do this to control their children. Children so abused can come to accept the chilling "fact" that they are evil or bad. Blaming themselves for a loss and being too young to bear the double pain of guilt and loss, they short-circuit their agony by the use of denial.

This unresolved guilt and loss can be successfully repressed as long as such people can depend on a strong person or a strong goal to provide them with constant reassurance that they are worthy of existing. When the person or the goal is removed (by death, separation, or repeated failure), the guilt returns and depression is precipitated.

Steps in Normal Grieving Parkes (1972) traces the following steps in normal grieving: an initial shock followed by denial of the loss; severe pangs of bereavement coupled with hopes of recovery of the loss; an acceptance of the permanence of the loss; and finally, the slow beginnings of readjustment. Kubler-Ross (1969) identifies similar steps in people who are grieving in anticipation of the loss of their own lives. First, there is *denial:* Not me! This is followed by *anger.* Why me! The third stage is *bargaining with God* for more time. *Depression* follows, finally to be replaced by *acceptance.*

Not everyone goes through all five stages (Kastenbaum, 1977). Notice, however, that the knowledge of a significant loss generally produces anger, which is followed by depression. In psychoanalytic theory, depression is related to loss by way of *introjected anger*. Remember a time when you were frustrated or provoked but did not feel capable of directly expressing your rising anger in aggression. You may have coped with this emotional tension by turning it inward, on yourself. This is introjection. "Anger turned inward" is one definition of depression. Newman and Hirt (1983) find that those who typically cope by introjecting are typically swayed by external influences, rather than trusting their internal sensations; these people display more depression.

Behavioral View of Depression

The behaviorists' view of depression (Lazarus, 1982; Lewinsohn and Hoberman, 1982) centers on the effects of insufficient rates of positive reinforcement. It holds that a deficiency in reinforcing stimuli extinguishes prosocial responses in the depressed. For example, when the neglected infant's cries or coos for attention are ignored, the child may give up, slip into depression, and die (Spitz, 1945).

A lack of social skills can result in a person receiving low levels of positive reinforcement. Depressed responses can also elicit certain kinds of reinforcement from others and so be strengthened. Consider the businessman whose depression acts both as an excuse for failure (his work problems are due to sickness, not incompetence; this involves negative reinforcement) and acts as a releaser of help (anyone would help a sick man; this involves positive reinforcement). These reinforcing *side effects* are known as *secondary gain* and alternative sources of reinforcement must be established if therapy for depression is to be successful. The long-term problem with depressive responses is that the depressed persons low frequency of prosocial behavior is aversive, not reinforcing, to others. People tend to avoid those who habitually are sad and withdrawn. This, of course, only reduces further the level of positive reinforcement received by depressed people and extinguishes the social skills they still employ. Thus, they drive away the very reinforcement they need to end this downward cycle.

Cognitive View of Depression

Although telling a depressed client, "Cheer up! Think positively" is seldom effective, cognitive-behaviorists view depression as primarily a thought disorder. A particular style of thinking, *negative overgeneralization*, is an excellent predictor of depression (Carver and Ganellen, 1983). Depressed people generally:

1. Set standards for themselves that are too high.
2. Are intolerant of their failure to meet the standards.
3. Interpret a single failure as an indication that they have little self-worth.

Depression in University Students

Do you always wait until the last minute to begin your college assignments? Saddler and Sacks (1993) find *academic procrastination* to be both a good predictor of perfectionism and of depression in college students. They report that *attitudes of stringent self-evaluation, attaining perfection, and avoiding failure* seem to be instrumental in student's mood problems.

This tendency to be critical and punitive becomes a morbid preoccupation. The gloom of the depressed accurately reflects their morbid thoughts. They tend to have a rigid self-image that is distorted downward. This gives rise to negative expectations and hopeless projections for themselves and often for those they love. Beck (1967) reports three important irrational thoughts of the depressed.

1. They believe that they are responsible for their misfortunes and that they are worthless, inferior, and bad.

2. They see their lives as a continuous encounter with tragic misfortunes and failures.

3. They believe that the future will be much like the past and present, that there is little hope for improvement. Suicide becomes a possibility.

Lewinsohn and Hoberman (1982) believe that depressing thoughts and feelings are responses to reduced rates of positive reinforcement caused by actual deficiencies in social skills.

Learned Helplessness

Martin Seligman (1977) was able to produce behavior similar to human depression in laboratory animals by placing them in situations in which they suffered pain and could not escape or reduce the pain. Such animals experienced *learned helplessness*. Later they responded helplessly in situations in which it was possible to escape or to reduce pain. For example, a dog trained in helplessness failed to learn to leap a barrier to avoid an electric shock, while untrained fellow dogs learned without difficulty.

Feelings of being helpless and without hope are expressed frequently by humans who are depressed and suicidal. In an attempt to demonstrate learned helplessness in humans, Miller and Seligman (1975) subjected groups of student subjects to loud, unpleasant noises through earphones. One group was able to escape the noise; another was not. Later the groups were tested with simple problems and puzzles. The "no-escape" subjects, like their canine counterparts, performed poorly. Perhaps they had temporarily learned helplessness. Already-depressed subjects in both groups also performed poorly. They had long ago mastered helplessness.

Seligman (1987) has revised his theory to account for the fact that depressed people typically have poor self-esteem. He now believes that it is our **explanatory style**, how we explain to ourselves why bad events happened to us, that determines the extent to which we will be helpless or depressed. If we "explain the bad things in *stable, global, and internal* terms (It's going to last forever, it's going to affect everything I do, and it's all my fault) [we are] most at risk for depression when bad events occur" (p. 32).

Not all agree with Beck and Seligman. Alloy and Abramson (1987) believe that "depressed people have a more accurate view of reality than non-depressed people" (p. 5G). Depressed and nondepressed college students were asked questions about their emotional reaction to midterm exams. "The depressed students were very accurate in judging their degree of control over events," Alloy stated. "It was the non-depressed students who made the systematic errors in grossly overestimating their control when the event had a good outcome and underestimating their control when the event had a negative outcome" (p. 5G). Depressed people might be suffering from an absence of this positive bias and illusion. Alloy believes that depressives "have lost the capacity for distorting reality in a positive direction" (p. 5G).

explanatory style a cognitive style for explaining why an event happened when the cause was ambiguous. A stable, global, and internal style is associated with helplessness and depression

Depression and Alcohol Addiction: A Potentially Deadly Combination

Older Americans who commit suicide are not usually alone, poor, or in pain, nor are they suffering from a degenerative or disfiguring disease. Often their self-destruction arises from a loss of control brought on by depression and, perhaps as self-medication, a chronic abuse of alcohol. Younger Americans who commit suicide often have a history of impulsive behavior and the abuse of drugs (including alcohol) prior to any emotional disorder that may accompany their suicide.

Answer the following questions about your parents. Then, substituting the words *friends* and *drugs* for *parents* and *alcohol*, answer the questions again for yourself or your friends.

Agree/Disagree

1. I think one or both of my parents abuse alcohol.
2. I feel strange having to do things that are really my parent's job because he or she has an alcohol problem.
3. I often fight with my parent when he or she is drinking.
4. I worry about my parent's health because of his or her abuse of alcohol.
5. Frequently I hear my parents fight when one or both of them are drunk.
6. I sometimes hide or empty my parent's liquor bottles.
7. I have a hard time believing that my drinking parent really loves me.
8. At times I lose sleep because of my parent's drinking.
9. I sometimes just stay away from home to avoid my drinking parent.
10. I am jealous of the home life of my friends who do not have parents who abuse alcohol.
11. I hate it when my parents break promises to me because of their use of alcohol.
12. I am so embarrassed and ashamed of my parent's drinking that I avoid situations (people and events) that otherwise I would enjoy.

***If you agree with any one of these statements, it indicates that alcohol or drug use is an adjustment problem for you at this time and perhaps a serious problem for those you love. If you agree with several or all of these statements, you would be well advised to take some positive steps to help yourself and those close to you. For a good place to start, contact Alcoholics Addiction Hotline any hour of the day or night. Their toll-free number is 1-800-777-2721.

At times, the ability to positively deceive ourselves may be helpful. Cognitive therapy, in which subjects are encouraged to locate and reshape depressing thought patterns, has proven to be as effective as drug therapy in the treatment of depression. Unlike drugs, cognitive therapy has no bad side effects (Bechtel, 1985).

Learned helplessness can be reversed through reeducation (Fowler and Peterson, 1981). Children with a history of failure in reading were given direct attribution retraining. They were taught new ways to look at failure and were given partial reinforcement for persistence in the face of frustration. Their reading improvement was attributed to a new respect for effort and an improved sense of self-esteem.

THINKING OF SUICIDE WHILE IN COLLEGE

In the early part of this chapter we presented an ethical dilemma: Should suicide be considered in law and custom to be an acceptable personal choice? In order to face this dilemma, you were forced to think of the unthinkable—taking your own life. For many college students, such thoughts dominate their college careers. We will end this chapter by looking at the factors that contribute to such suicidal ideation.

Suicidologists (those who study suicide and how to prevent it) find that three factors, in combination with the stress of life's events, make suicide more

Effective Self-Treatment

What if you believe yourself to be mildly anxious and at times blue, but certainly not clinically depressed? Are there any self-help strategies that work? Daniel Coleman (1992) reports that successful and nonsuccessful strategies for lifting spirits are emerging from studies in health psychology. He reports:

Successful Adjustment Strategies for Lifting Sadness

The most direct adjustment is to try to change whatever or whoever is causing your bad mood. If this is impossible or impractical:

1. *Turn to the company of others.* However, don't just rehearse your sadness by repeating what has already been said, this can make things worse.

2. *Exercise.* This increases your arousal state *if you are typically* **sedentary**, and makes you feel better.

3. *Accept a small challenge.* Find something to work hard at and to take pleasure in accomplishing.

4. *Indulge in nondestructive, sensual pleasures.* Take a hot bath, make love, listen to energizing or relaxing music.

5. *Direct your thoughts.* Remind yourself of past successes, resolve to do better, think of someone worse off.

Successful Adjustment Strategies for Reducing Anxiety

Again, while attempting to change whatever it is that is causing your anxiety, try:

1. Learning specific relaxation skills (see chapter 4).

2. Talking it over with others.

3. Lending a helping hand to someone in need.

4. Distracting yourself by becoming immersed in TV, movies, or magazines. This is a common response, but offers temporary relief at best.

Partly Successful Adjustment Strategies

Three popular antidotes to anxiety and depression offer immediate success but soon wear off, and the bad moods often swing back and are worse than before: (see the Opponent Process, described in chapter 4). The most used "feel good" self-medications are (1) desserts, (2) alcohol, and (3) drugs.

Unsuccessful Adjustment Strategies

We've all done these, but now we know better.

1. *Yelling or crying.* Venting bad feelings offers little relief and often reinforces bad feelings.

2. *Blaming others.* This reduces your opportunity to make needed changes.

3. *Being alone.* Alone you can neither get nor give help.

4. *Being fatalistic.* Learned helplessness perpetuates mood disorders.

There is much we can do to make our emotions work for us. The process outlined in the Personal Action Plan for this chapter can be applied, with slight modifications, to other problem moods as well. Give it a try.

---

likely to happen to college students (Dixon, Heppner, and Anderson, 1991). The first of these factors is a *predisposition to suicide* caused by genetics or by cultural or individual experiences. The second factor is whether such vulnerable individuals *see themselves as poor problem solvers*. If this factor is present, then an overload of stressful events can lead to factor three, a sense of *profound hopelessness*. It is this condition of despair that leads to suicidal thoughts and, at times, to actual suicide by the young, bright, and healthy among us. Perhaps problem-solving training and stress-management training should be included in college curricula.

Critical Review 5

1. Depression exacts a toll in suicides, missed workdays, and wasted days on the job estimated at more than $43 billion a year. T F

2. The use of alcohol, drugs and "feel good foods" as self-medication for depression is an example of a successful adjustment strategy for lifting sadness. T F

sedentary   accustomed to sitting and/or taking little exercise

3. Academic procrastination has proven to be a good predictor of depression in college students. T F

4. List at least three characteristics of depressed people you have actually known, at least briefly.

5. What do you find in each of the following theories of depression?
   A. The organic view:
   B. The therapeutic view:
   C. The behavioral view:
   D. The cognitive view:

6. Think of a situation in which *your explanation of the event,* rather than the event itself, caused you to feel depressed. Did you make any of the type of thinking errors described in this text? If so, list them.

7. Why do you think the atypical depressive is seldom treated for depression? Do you think there is a real health danger in keeping a patient on high dosages of antidepressive drugs for long periods of time? If so, how might one get the benefits without the risks of such a program?

SUMMARY

■ In all its forms, emotion is a necessary and precious part of human existence.

■ Emotion is a subjective feeling state accompanied by internal changes and a predisposition to act so as to enhance survival.

■ Charles Darwin held that emotions are innate and universal, a product of evolution that has signal and survival value.

■ Prosocial emotions, such as happiness, facilitate human interaction. Prosocial emotions can be learned.

■ Antisocial emotions, such as anger, hinder such interaction and can lead to abusive violence. Antisocial emotions can be controlled.

■ The hypothesis that behaving angrily reduces subsequent anger has not been supported by research findings.

■ Children are born with a potential for full, deep emotional sensation and expression. They require opportunities to be expressive and a degree of freedom to express negative emotions if they are to reach their full potential.

■ Cognitive growth affects emotional development in the infant. The social smile, negativism, stranger anxiety, and fear of the dark illustrate the connection between growing thinking skills and emotional responses.

■ Basic emotional temperament is preserved throughout life and appears likely to be genetic.

■ Physical growth affects emotional development. Increased size and strength makes possible a wide range of behaviors that bring forth strong emotional reactions from both the toddler and others.

■ Those spanked often and harshly are found, on the average, to be "quieter, less articulate, and more sullen" later in life.

■ Contemporary theories of emotion stress an associational network among thoughts, action impulses, and somatic disturbances.

■ The Yerkes-Dodson law states that the more complex a task, the lower the level of arousal that can be tolerated without impairing performance.

■ Emotions become dysfunctional when they are: (1) inappropriate, (2) deficient or excessive, and/or (3) expressed in nonconventional or aggressive ways.

■ Every society has "feeling rules" governing how people should feel and act under specific circumstances.

■ The complex network of neural systems must work cooperatively and jointly to maintain an appropriate emotional response to the demands of life.

■ Aggression is seen as the result of (1) instincts, (2) frustrations, and (3) social learning experiences. Abusive violence must be controlled in civil society.

■ Negotiation, compromise, and assertive behavior are seen as healthy and helpful alternatives to the aggressive response.

■ Emotional expression is communicated by (1) facial expressions, (2) verbal and vocal language, and (3) body language.

■ Appropriateness of emotional expression is determined by both self and others.

■ Believing that the future holds good things in store for us gains power for us because it allows us to take direct action to solve our problems, to plan better, and to be more focused.

■ Emotional adjustment is complicated by the fact that we pass judgment on our own feelings.

■ Our bodies as well as our faces and voices help us communicate emotion.

■ The sensitive, emotionally expressive person is often seen as handicapped in this business-oriented civilization.

■ The greatest failure in emotional expression occurs when we express anger, hostility, or rage through aggression—behavior intended to injure another person.

■ In humans, the frequency, the form, and the function of aggression are determined by learning and the influence of others.

■ Reducing frustration, competition, the reinforcement of aggression, and alcohol consumption can reduce the stimuli that trigger aggression. Teaching nonaggressive (assertive) ways of responding can do more.

■ Depression is seen as an unresolved state of sorrow or sadness that is accompanied by low self-esteem, a low rate of prosocial responding, feelings of helplessness, negative self-talk, and perhaps malfunctioning pleasure centers in the brain.

■ For many reasons, most people who suffer from depression self-medicate by the use of alcohol, drugs, and "feel good" foods! The result has been prolonged suffering and lost dollars and days.

■ The useful general principle "the less drug the better," has to be abandoned when treating recurrent depression.

■ Doctors, family, and patient should be trained to notice the earliest signs of recurring depression, and to reinstitute the high dosage treatment plan immediately.

■ The diverse psychological views concerning the cause of depression offer several useful forms of counseling that have proven beneficial in the treatment of depression, without negative side effects.

■ Explanatory style, rather than misfortune, is seen as the basis of learned helplessness.

■ Although immediate professional help is advised for clinical depression, there are several effective strategies for reducing anxiety and lifting spirits. These do not include yelling, crying, or use of alcohol, drugs, or excessive sweets.

■ Guilt and anger, often repressed, are associated with depression and help account for its resistance to change.

SELECTED READINGS

Csikszentmihalyi, M. *Flow: The Psychology of Optimal Experience.* New York: Harper & Row, 1990. Flow, a deep happiness that comes when people feel they have a sense of mastering something, is put forward as the antidote for boredom and anxiety.

Csikszentmihalyi, M., and Larson, R. *Being Adolescent: Conflict and Growth in the Teenage Years.* New York: Basic Books, 1984. A sensitive and thoughtful treatment of these turbulent years.

Klein, D. F., and Wender, P. H. *Do You Have a Depressive Illness?* New York: New American Library, 1988. This work gives the warning signs of depression and tells where to go for help.

Lewinsohn, P., Munoz, R., Youngren, M., and Zeiss, A. *Control Your Depression,* rev. ed. New York, NY: Fireside, 1992. Easy-to-follow, step-by-step methods take you through a number of strategies for controlling depression. Excellent examples are given throughout.

Montagu, A. *Learning Non-Aggression: The Experience of Non-Literate Societies.* New York: Academic Press, 1980. An explanation of how our very survival seems to depend on our rapid understanding and control of aggression.

Myers, D. *The Pursuit of Happiness.* New York: William Morrow, 1992. The four main characteristics of happy people—self-esteem, optimism, extroversion, and personal control—are woven into what makes a happy marriage, sound friendships, and meaningful work.

Plutchik, R., and Kellerman, H. *Emotion: Theory, Research, and Experience.* New York: Academic Press, 1980. A very careful consideration of the sociobiological, physiological, and cognitive-behavioral approaches to emotion.

Seligman, M. E. P. *Learned Optimism.* New York: Knopf, 1991.

Tavris, C. *Anger: The Misunderstood Emotion,* 2nd ed. New York: Simon and Schuster. A challenge to "letting it all hang out"; this timely book explains how expressing anger makes you angrier and establishes a hostile habit. You are helped to rethink anger and to make more adaptive choices.

Wood, J. *How Do You Feel?* Englewood Cliffs, NJ: Prentice-Hall, 1974. A short paperback test that presents an excellent overview of emotions.

REFERENCES

Ainsworth, M. D. *Infancy in Uganda: Infant Care and the Growth of Attachment.* Baltimore: Johns Hopkins University Press, 1967.

Akiskal, H. S., and McKinney, W. T., Jr. "Depressive Disorders: Toward a Uniform Hypothesis." *Science* 182 (1973): 20–29.

Alloy, Lauren, B., and Abramson, Lyn. "A Distorted View of Life is Healthy, Study Finds." The *Miami Herald* (April 12, 1987): 5G.

Archer, D., & Gartner, R. "Violent Acts and Violent Times: A Comparative Approach in Postwar Homicide." *American Sociological Review* 41 (1976): 937–963.

Arieti, S., and Bemporad, J. *Severe and Mild Depression.* New York: Basic Books, 1979.

Averill, J. R. "Studies on Anger and Aggression: Implications for Theories of Emotion." *American Psychologist* 38 (November 1983): 1145–1160.

Bandura, A. Social Learning Theory. Englewood Cliffs, N.J.: Prentice-Hall, 1977.

Bankard B. B., and Bankard, P. C. "Anger." In *The Encyclopedic Dictionary of Psychology* 4, edited by Terryl F. Pettijohn, (pp. 15–16). Guilford, CT: Dushkin, 1991.

Bankart, B. B., and Bankart, P. B. "Aggression." In Terry F. Pettijohn (Ed.) *The Encyclopedia Dictionary of Psychology*. 4th ed., Guilford, CT: The Dushkin Publishing Group, Inc., (pp. 7–9), 1991.

Baron, R. A. "The Control of Human Aggression: A Strategy Based on Incompatible Responses." In R. G. Green and E. I. Donnerstein (Eds.), *Aggression: Theoretical and Empirical Reviews*, Vol. 2 (pp. 173–190). New York: Academic Press, 1987.

Bechtel, S. "Self-Talk: New Ways to Beat the Blues." *Prevention* (March 1985): 37, 140–147.

Beck, A. T. *Depression*. New York: Harper & Row, 1967.

Beier, E. G. "Nonverbal Communication: How We Send Emotional Messages." *Psychology Today* (October 1974): 53–56.

Berkowitz, L. "Aversively Stimulated Aggression." *American Psychologist* 38 (November 1983): 1135–1144.

Birdwhistell, R. L. *Introduction to Kinesics*. Louisville, KY: University of Louisville Press, 1952.

Bishop, J. E. "Secrets of the Heart: Can It Be 'Broken'?" *The Wall Street Journal* (February 14, 1994): B1, B5.

Bloomberg, M. L. "Depression in Abused and Neglected Children." *American Journal of Psychotherapy* 35 (July 1981): 342.

Bower, G. H. "Mood and Memory." *American Psychologist* 36 (February 1981): 129–148.

Cannon, W. B., "Bodily Changes in Pain, Hunger, Fear, and Rage, 2nd ed. New York: Appleton-Century-Crofts, 1929.

Carver, C. S., and Ganellen, R. J. "Depression and Components of Self-Punitiveness." *Journal of Abnormal Psychology* 92 (August 1983): 330–337.

Chance, M. R. A. "An Ethological Assessment of Emotion." In *Emotion: Theory, Research, and Experience*, vol. 1, edited by R. Plutchik and H. Kellerman, (pp. 73–81) New York: Academic Press, 1980

Coleman, D. "Strategies for Lifting Spirits Are Emerging From Studies." *New York Times*, Health (December 30, 1992): 8–9.

Condon, W. S., and Sander. L. "Neonate Movement Is Synchronized with Adult Speech: International Participation and Language Acquisition. *Science* 183 (1974): 99–101.

Coppen, A. "The Biochemistry of Affective Disorders." *British Journal of Psychiatry* 113 (1967): 1237–1264.

Csikszentmihalyi, M. *Flow*. New York: Harper & Row, 1990.

Csikszentmihalyi, M., and Larson, R. *Being Adolescent: Conflict and Growth in the Teenage Years*. New York: Basic Books, 1984.

Darwin, C. *The Expression of the Emotions in Man and Animals*. London: Murray, 1872.

Diener, E. "Subjective Well-being." *Psychological Bulletin* 95 (1984): 542–575.

Dixon, W. A., Heppner, P. P., and Anderson, W. P. "Problem-Solving Appraisal, Stress, Hopelessness, and Suicide Ideation in a College Population." *Journal of Counseling Psychology* 38 (February 1991): 51–56.

Dollard, J., Doob, L. W., Miller, N. E., Mowrer, O. H., and Sears, R. R. *Frustration and Aggression*. New Haven, CT: Yale University Press, 1939.

Douvan, E., and Adeson, J. *The Adolescent Experience*. New York: Wiley, 1966.

Duffy, E. "An Explanation of 'Emotional' Phenomena without the Use of the Concept 'Emotion'." *Journal of General Psychology* 25 (1941): 283–293.

Ekman, P., and Friesen, W. V. *Unmasking the Face*. New York: Prentice-Hall, 1975.

Ellis, A. *Humanistic Psychotherapy: The Rational Emotive Approach*. New York: Julian Press, 1973.

Eron, L. D. "Parent-Child Interaction, Television Violence, and Aggression of Children." *American Psychologist* 37 (February 1982): 197–211.

Fisch, H., Frey, S., and Hirsbrunner, H. "Analyzing Nonverbal Behavior in Depression." *Journal of Abnormal Psychology* 92 (August 1983): 307–318.

Forbes, L. M., and Chaney, R. H. "Physical Arousal Concealed during Emotional Stress." *Psychological Reports* (1978): 35.

Fowler, J., and Peterson, P. "Increasing Reading Persistance and Altering Attributional Style of Learned Helpless Children." *Journal of Educational Psychology* 73 (1981): 251–260.

Friedman, H. S. (Ed.). "Psychobiological Interventions." *Hostility, Coping, and Health*. Washington, DC: American Psychological Association, 1991, pp. 243–247.

Friedman, M., and Rosenman, R.F. *Type A Behavior and Your Heart*. New York: Knopf, 1974.

Gilmartin, B. G. "The Case against Spanking." *Human Behavior* 8 (February 1979): 17.

Goleman, D. "Therapy May Not Change Most-Vicious Batterers." *The Miami Herald* (June 28, 1994); 1E.

_____. "Who Are You Kidding?" *Psychology Today* (March 1987): 21, 24–30.

Goode, E. E., Schrof, J. M. and Burke, S. "Where Emotion Comes From." *U.S. News & World Report* (June 24, 1991); 54–60, 62.

Guze, B. H., and Freedman, D. X. "Psychiatry." *JAMA* 265 (June 19, 1991): 914–918.

Hochschild, A. R. "Emotion Work, Feeling Rules, and Social Structure." *American Journal of Sociology* 85 (1979): 551–575.

Huesmann, L. R. "Stability of Aggression over Time and Generations." *Developmental Psychology* 20 (1984): 1120–1134.

Izard, C. E. *Human Emotions*. New York: Plenum Press, 1977.

_____. Quoted in Trotter, R. "You've Come a Long Way Baby." *Psychology Today* (May 1987): 21, 34–45.

James, W. "What Is an Emotion?" *Mind* 9 (1884): 188–205.

Kagan, J. *The Nature of the Child*. New York: Basic Books, 1984.

Kastenbaum, R. *Death, Society, and Human Behavior*. St. Louis: Mosby, 1977.

Konner, M. "The Enigmatic Smile." *Psychology Today* (March 1987): 21, 42–47.

Kubler-Ross, E. *On Death and Dying*. New York: Macmillan, 1969.

Laird, J. D., Wagner, J. J., Halal, M., and Szegda, M. "Remembering What You Feel: Effects of Emotion on Memory." *Journal of Personality and Social Psychology* 42 (1982): 646–657.

Lang, A. R., and Sibrell, P. A. "Psychological Perspectives on Alcohol Consumption and Interpersonal Aggression." *Criminal Justice and Behavior* 16 (1989): 300–325.

Lang, P. J., Levin, D. N., Miller, G. A., and Kozak, M. J. "Fear Behavior, Fear Imagery, and the Psychophysiology of Emotion: The Problem of Affective Response Integration." *Journal of Abnormal Psychology* 92 (August 1983): 276–306.

Lazarus, R. "Thoughts on the Relations between Emotion and Cognition." *American Psychologist* 37 (September 1982): 1019–1024.

Lazarus, R. S. *Emotion and Adaptation.* New York: Oxford University Press, 1991.

———. "From Psychological Stress to the Emotions: A History of a Changing Outlook." *Annual Review of Psychology* 44 (1993): 1–21.

Leonard, K. E. "The Impact of Explicit Aggressive and Implicit Nonaggressive Cues on Aggression in Intoxicated and Sober Males. *Personality and Social Psychology Bulletin* 15 (1989): 383–394.

Leshner, A. I. "Winning the War Against Clinical Depression" *USA Today* (July 1992): 86–87.

Levenson, R. Quoted in "Emotion: The Face of Feeling." *Psychology Today* 2 (January 1986): 20.

Lewinsohn, P. M., and Hoberman, H. M. "Depression." In *International Handbook of Behavior Modification and Therapy,* edited by A. S. Bellak, M. Hersen, and A. E. Kazdin, (pp. 74–81). New York: Plenum Press, 1982.

Lipsitt, L. Quoted in Trotter, R. "You've Come a Long Way, Baby." *Psychology Today* (May 1987): 21, 34–45.

Medicine, S. A., Police, V., Volvo, J., and Gabrielle, W. F., Jr. "Biology and Violence." In M. E. Wolfing and N. A. Wiener (Eds.), *Criminal Violence* (pp. 523–545). Beverly Hills, CA: Sage.

Miller, M. W. "Dark Days: The Staggering Cost of Depression." *The Wall Street Journal* (December 2, 1993): p. B1.

Miller, W. R., and Seligman, M. E. P. "Depression and Learned Helplessness in Man." *Journal of Abnormal Psychology* 84 (1975): 228–238.

Morris, C. G. *Psychology: An Introduction.* Englewood Cliffs, NJ: Prentice-Hall, 1979.

Mowrer, O. H., and Sears, R. R. *Frustration and Aggression.* New Haven, CT: Yale University Press, 1939.

Newman, R. S., and Hirt, M. "The Psychoanalytic Theory of Depression: Symptoms as a Function of Aggressive Wishes and Level of Field Articulation." *Journal of Abnormal Psychology* 92 (January 1983): 42–47.

Papez, J. W. "A Proposed Mechanism of Emotion." *Archives of Neurology and Psychiatry* 38 (1937): 725–743.

Parkes, C. M. *Bereavement: Studies of Grief in Adult Life.* New York: International University Press, 1972.

Perls, F. S. *Gestalt Therapy Verbatim.* Lafayette, CA: Real People Press, 1969.

Peterson, C., Seligman, M. E. P., and Luborsky, L. "Attributions and Depressive Mood Shifts: A Case Study Using the Symptom-Context Method." *Journal of Abnormal Psychology* 92 (1983): 96–103.

Phillips, D. P. "The Impact of Mass Media Violence on U.S. Homicides." *American Sociological Review* 48 (August 1983): 560–568.

Plutchik, R. *Emotion: A Psychoevolutionary Synthesis.* New York: Harper & Row, 1980a.

Plutchik, R., and Kellerman, H. *Emotion: Theory, Research, and Experience.* New York: Academic Press, 1980b.

Rice, B. "The New Truth Machine." *Psychology Today* 12 (June 1978): 61–78.

Rogers, J. E. "Brain Triggers: Biochemistry and Behavior." *Science Digest* 1 (1983): 60–65.

Rosenthal, R., Archer, D., DiMatteo, M. R., Koivumaki, J. H., and Rogers, P. L. "Body Talk and Tone of Voice: The Language without Words." *Psychology Today* (September 1974): 64–68.

Roy, A. "Specificity of Risk Factors for Depression." *American Journal of Psychiatry* 138 (July 1981): 959–961.

Saddler, C., and Sacks, L. A. "Multidimensional Perfectionism and Academic Procrastination: Relationship with Depression in University Students." *Psychological Reports* 73 (3) (December 1993): 863–871.

Schachter, S., and Singer, J. E. "Cognitive, Social and Physiological Determinants of Emotional State." *Psychological Review* 69 (1962): 379–399.

Scheier, M. F., and Carver, C. S. "Effects of Optimism on Psychological and Physical Well-being: Theoretical Overview and Empirical Update." *Cognitive Therapy and Research* 16 (1992): 201–228.

———. "On the Powers of Positive Thinking." In *Psychology: Annual Editions 94/95* (pp. 210–214) (Guilford, CT: Dushkin, 1993.

Seligman, M. E. P. *Helplessness.* San Francisco: W. H. Freeman, 1975.

———. Reversing Depression and Learned Helplessness." In *Psychology and Life,* edited by P. G. Zimbardo and F. L. Ruch, (pp. 506–511). Glenview, IL: Scott, Foresman, 1977.

———. In "Stop Blaming Yourself" by Robert J. Trotter, *Psychology Today* 21 (February 1987): 30–32.

Spiesman, J. C. "Autonomic Monitoring of Ego Defense Process." In *Psychoanalysis and Current Biological Thought,* edited by N. S. Greenfield and W. C. Lewis. Madison: University of Wisconsin Press, 1965.

Spitz, R. A. "Hospitalism: An Inquiry into the Genesis of Psychiatric Conditions in Early Childhood." In *The Psychoanalytic Study of the Child,* edited by A. Freud (pp. 126–138). New York: International University Press, 1945.

Spivey, C. B., and Prentice-Dunn, S. "Assessing the Directionality of Deindividuated Behavior: Effects of Deindividuation, Modeling, and Private Self-consciousness on Aggressive and Pro-social Responses. *Basic and Applied Social Psychology* 11 (1990): 387–403.

Steer, R. A., McElroy, M. E., and Beck, A. T. "Structure of Depression in Alcoholic Men." *Psychological Reports* 50 (February–June 1982): 724–731.

Tavris, C. "Anger Defused." *Psychology Today* 18 (November 1982): 25–35.

_____. *Anger: The Misunderstood Emotion.* 2nd ed. New York: Touchstone, 1989.

Toch, H. *Violent Men: An Inquiry into the Psychology of Violence.* Chicago: Aldine Press, 1969.

Turner, M. E., Pratkanis, A. R., Probasco, P. and Leve, C. "Threat, Cohesion, and Group Effectiveness: Testing a Collective Dissonance Reduction Perspective on Groupthink." *Journal of Personality and Social Psychology* 63 (1992): 781–796.

Wallen, R. "Emotional Styles Typology." In *An Expanding Repertoire of Behavior*, edited by C. Mill and L. Porter (pp. 222–229). Washington, DC: NTL Institute for Applied Behavioral Science, 1972.

White, B. L. *The First Three Years of Life.* Englewood Cliffs, NJ: Prentice-Hall, 1975.

Wurtman, J. J. "To Change Your Mood, Change Your Food." *The Miami Herald* (February 8, 1987): 4G.

Zajonc, R. "The Face as Window and Machine for the Emotions." *LSA Magazine* (University of Michigan) 14 (1) (Fall 1990): 17–21.

Zillmann, D., and Sapolsky, B. S. "What Mediates the Effect of Mild Erotica on Annoyance and Hostile Behavior in Males?" *Journal of Personality and Social Psychology* 35 (1977): 587–595.

■ *Questionnaire Scoring Key*

Suicide: Myth and Reality

1. False: The opposite is true! A person who is coming out of a severe depression now may have the energy needed to carry out the act. Many become more relaxed and feel in better spirits after they have finalized the specifics of their suicide attempt.

2. True: More women do try.

3. False: Most people who kill themselves do talk about it. It may well be a cry for help.

4. True: Many are emotionally calm or actually euphoric.

5. False: As many as one in ten of us has entertained thoughts or fantasies concerning self-destruction. Many of us, especially during adolescence, feel unloved and misunderstood. We do not act during our age of discontent, but rather grow and mature and find our lives to be worthwhile.

6. False: Most suicides are in good contact with reality and are not beset with delusions or hallucinations.

7. True: However, the elderly are still the largest suicidal group.

8. False: Most suicides have family that do not kill themselves, but a recent study of suicide among the Amish in southern Pennsylvania established a genetic link across several generations of suicides, and this information has led to the location of an abnormal gene on chromosome 11 that is thought to have made them vulnerable. Other research has failed to duplicate this finding, or has pointed to other genetic markers.

9. True: Men use cars, knives, and guns. Women prefer overdosing on drugs (alcohol, sleeping pills, and tranquilizers).

10. False: Neither the time of year (Christmas) nor the weather (stormy night) nor lunar cycle (a full moon) are consistently related to suicide rates.

11. True: We are capable of sacrificing ourselves for ideas, objects, or people we hold dear.

12. True: For religious, family, and/or insurance reasons, many suicides are not reported as such in America.

13. False: People with few human contacts and diminished communication skills are among those at higher risk for suicide.

14. True: More than half of all suicides under thirty are related directly to substance abuse. More than half had drug-related problems prior to any problem with depression, for example.

15. False: Marriage may be a source of stress, but married people die less often from all causes, including self-inflicted ones.

16. False: The professions named, including clinical psychologists, are at increased risk of suicide.

17. True: They are reported to have four times as many. But most people who are under great stress do not attempt suicide.

18. False: The family comes first, friends second, and sexual relationships third on their problem lists. Injury, incapacity, deformity, illness, or physical pain rank well below human relationships.

***If you or anyone you know appears to be at risk, call the National Suicide Hotline, 1-800-621-4000, for immediate help.

■ Answers to Critical Review Questions

Critical Review 1 1. T. 2. T. 3. T.
Critical Review 2 1. T. 2. T. 3. T.
Critical Review 3 1. F.
Critical Review 4 1. F. 2. T. 3. T.
Critical Review 5 1. T. 2. F. 3. T.

PERSONAL ACTION PLAN
Anger Assessment

The purpose of this plan is to give you an opportunity to explore an antisocial emotion, anger, that constitutes a problem in living for many of us, and to develop a plan that will enable you to respond more constructively to frustration or pain.

At this time, anger is a problem to you. If you wish to change the way you view and express anger, follow the steps outlined below. You may thereby gain a greater awareness of your emotional patterns, greater understanding of the functions that anger plays in your life, and a greater possibility of successfully modifying your response when in situations that provoke anger.

Step 1. *Accepting My Anger as a Legitimate Part of Me*

Relax and take a few deep breaths. Assume a very comfortable position. Now repeat at least five times the following statement: "I accept the fact that at the present time many situations provoke me to anger. Anger is a legitimate part of me and I accept myself."

Saying this sincerely to yourself in a calm voice helps in bringing your concern into the open and making it manageable. Note how the statement is worded. First, "at the present time" implies that it need not be for all time. It opens the possibility for change. Second, "many situations" implies that not all situations provoke anger. Your response is situational. These two basic beliefs—that situations control behavior and that

change is possible—are essential to your success in bringing anger under your control. Have you been led to believe that this feeling style is part of your genetic makeup? "You're just like your father (or mother)" and so on. Accepting that your emotion is not a genetic flaw but a *part of the self that is learned* will help you to complete Step II.

Step II. *My Assessment Log*

Keep a written log of your daily angry outbursts for a period of not less than five days. Include the following information for each entry:

A. The date and time your anger was provoked.
B. The place and the people present.
C. The events that were going on.
D. An indication of the intensity of your outburst (1 = little intensity; 10 = uncontrolled intensity).
E. The physiological sensations accompanying your anger (pulse rate, muscle tension, heart rate, and so on).
F. Your behavior (facial expressions, verbalizations, violent acts, and so on).
G. The immediate consequences of your angry behavior on yourself and on those around you.

This log must be complete and accurate. Do not rely on memory, but record the information as soon as possible. It is a great deal of work, but it is worth its weight in gold. After completion, use your daily log to complete Step III.

Step III.   *My Record of Anger*

Study your log entries and search for specific patterns. Using concrete examples drawn from your log, complete the following form. Do not attempt to do this from memory before beginning your log. Misinformation is much worse than no information at all. (Note from your entries that your feeling was not associated with everyone, all the time, under all circumstances.)

A. Based on my written observations, I frequently display anger when:
   1. I am with:

   (Name the specific persons involved)

   2. I am at:

   (Name the specific places involved)

   3. I am engaged in:

   (Name the specific activities involved)

B. When I am provoked:
   1. My sensations include:

   (Describe your pulse rate, muscle tension, and so on.)

   2. My actions include:

   (Describe what you do or say after being provoked.)

C. As a result of my display of anger:
   1. I feel:

   (Describe your feelings, such as shame, enjoyment, control, power, and so on.)

   2. Other patterned responses include:

(Record any other insights that came from a study of your log.)

Step IV.   *An Accurate Description of My Profile of Anger*

Study and reflect on your anger profile as outlined above. Then answer the following questions:

A. I most frequently respond with anger when I feel (check one or more) afraid _____, embarrassed _____, disappointed _____, anxious _____, helpless _____, threatened _____, uncertain _____, and other _____.

B. By responding this way, I feel (check one or more) in control _____, powerful _____, active _____, justified _____, and other _____.

C. My anger is accompanied by such self-talk as:

(Recall and record what you said to yourself during each episode.)

D. Other possible causes for my angry display include:

(Describe other internal events that trigger your anger.)

Remember, no one and no circumstance can make you feel angry; *you have to choose to respond that way.* This perception of personal choice is essential to control anger.

Step V.   *The Costs of My Anger*

Now that you know the situations that provoke you to anger and some of the benefits you derive from expressing it, such as getting what you want, feeling better, and looking stronger or more threatening, you are ready to focus realistically on the *price you pay* for these benefits. Review this immediate consequences of your angry outbursts on yourself and others and answer the following questions:

A. Did my anger disrupt completion of the task at hand?

B. Did my angry display disrupt my thinking and reasoning?

C. Did my anger lead to impulsive behavior?

D. Did I use unfortunate, hurtful words?

E. Did I use direct, personal attacks that hurt my self-esteem or that of others?

F. Did my display of anger invite others to be antagonistic toward me?

G. Did my display of anger invite others to take advantage of me?

H. Did my display of anger lead me or others to act defensively? (passively sulking, for example)

I. Did my display of anger lead others to seek to avoid me?

J. Did my display of anger leave me or others weak, exhausted, or in physical discomfort or pain?

K. Did my anger produce any other problems?

(List any other negative results that you observed.)

Now that you are aware of the costs and benefits associated with your present angry habit, as well as the conditions that trigger or release this antisocial feeling, are you ready to consider some practical alternative responses when frustrated or in pain? If you are ready, these alternative response suggestions are located in the Personal Action Plan section of chapter 4.

THE SOCIAL SELF

Chapter Outline

GROUPS

group   people working or playing together toward common goals

A **Group** may be defined as people working or playing together to achieve common goals. All of us are members of several groups. Some groups, such as our family or ethnic group, are involuntary in nature; we are born into them. Others, such as our sorority, bowling club, or peer group, are voluntary; we choose to join them. Understanding groups and our relationship to them is important for two reasons. First, it helps us see the importance of groups to each of us in terms of our adjustment and growth. Second, it helps us function better as group members.

Group Membership

We join groups for many reasons, including fulfilling the need to belong; developing, enhancing, or confirming a sense of identity; maintaining self-esteem; establishing and testing reality; and, increasing security and a sense of power. Some of us join simply because our friends belong. We enjoy interacting with those we like or find attractive. Many students, for instance, attend a particular college to be with their friends.

Often, people meet with others who have similar interests in order to learn and to share ideas. People also form groups to share stress. During times of disaster (hurricanes, floods, fires, and so on), people often band together for emotional and physical support. They work together to find shelter and to rescue victims. When people are under stress, it quickly becomes apparent that the best way to survive is to work with others so there can be collective support. Study groups to help you prepare for a final exam offer such support.

Throughout our lives each of us joins at least one support group of close friends with whom we can share our problems, our concerns, and our happiness. For many, a particular support group may serve as a source of encouragement and nurturance for their entire lives. The cohesiveness of such groups is often stronger and more long lasting than the cohesiveness of the family to which each support-group member belongs. This is perhaps because we are able to choose the members of our support groups but not the members of our families.

Another reason people join particular groups may have little to do with the group's goals. Instead, the motivation may involve external rewards not always apparent to other group members. An insurance salesperson moves to a new community and immediately joins a church or civic club to establish contacts for future business. A college man joins a fraternity because he believes it will afford him the necessary status to meet women.

Group Pressure

As we have seen, group membership has advantages. However, it may also have disadvantages. Group pressure may negatively influence our need for independence in choosing our beliefs, values, and life goals. Sometimes, for example, "going along with the crowd" seems so much easier than making up our own minds about an issue. Also, we may rely excessively on a group to help us make important life decisions. Consequently, our need to belong to groups may impede the realization of our potential as human beings. As individuals, it is important to recognize the difference between our responsibility to the group and our responsibility to ourselves.

When our initial motivation for joining a particular group is not fulfilled, we may lose interest and drop out. Have you ever noticed in some of your classes that the attendance at the beginning of the term is much better than at the end?

> Richard had met Carla two months before they were to begin their freshman year at the community college. He was fascinated by her for several reasons, especially by the fact that she spoke both English and Spanish. Hoping to get her to care more for him, he enrolled in a beginning Spanish course. Two months into the term, Carla decided to renew a relationship with someone she had dated previously, and Richard dropped his Spanish course.

Subgroups

In groups larger than eighteen to twenty members, **subgroups** often form to allow the warm and intimate contact that is possible in groups of five or less (Theodorson, 1953). These groups are usually formed in the same way as the larger group. Subgroups may make the larger group more functional for its members by helping them achieve their common goals. To increase our chances for contact and perhaps remedy our discomfort, we tend to arrange ourselves

subgroups   small groups within a larger group, formed to allow the warmth and intimate contact possible in groups of five or less

---

CRITICAL THINKING ISSUE
Group Membership and Personal Growth

Membership in groups fosters personal growth in the individual.

Membership in groups helps us to meet our needs for love and belongingness. It helps us to enhance our self-esteem by confirming a sense of identity for us. It increases our security by providing a web of support, thus encouraging us to set high goals for ourselves. Without membership in groups, we could never become all that we are capable of becoming.

Membership in groups inhibits personal growth in the individual.

Membership in groups leads to conformity and obedience. It leads invariably to giving in to group pressure and obeying rules or authorities that restrict the free movement and direction of our creative spirits. This restriction prevents personal growth. As long as we belong to groups, we can never become all that we are capable of becoming.

I take the position that:

These neighbors and national guard workers piling sandbags during a flood show how people join together in times of need.

into smaller, more manageable, subgroups. It is interesting to observe the subgrouping phenomenon when attending large parties, for example.

Group Structure

Perhaps you have observed that in certain groups a variety of behaviors differentiate members from each other. Some talk more, some have more respect or influence, and all perform different tasks. This differentiation usually is determined by the *roles, status, norms,* and *cohesiveness* within each group. These factors determine **group structure,** which is commonly defined as the observable pattern of relationships among the members within a group.

group structure differentiation among group members, influenced by roles, status, norms, and cohesiveness

Roles   Each member of a group is expected to behave in certain ways during group interaction. Consider the college classroom, for example. The instructor has the expected role of preparing adequately each day to teach the class. For the most part, this person directs the activities and topics and controls the interaction between the members of the class. In a highly structured class the instructor controls the interaction among all the class members.

Students also have an expected role in the class. They are to ask questions, answer questions, do assignments, prepare for class discussions, and show evidence that learning has occurred. Certain members begin to emerge early in the life of the class as individuals who interact more often with the instructor by answering and asking questions. These individuals often become the focus of attention, both of the instructor and of other class members. It is not long before they have the expected role of major responders in class activities and discussions.

Status and Power   Each expected role is evaluated by the members of the group according to its importance and prestige. This evaluation results in each member having some degree of social status within the group. The degree of social status a person enjoys usually corresponds to the amount of influence or power the person has in the group (see Figure 8–1).

Influence and power are also the key factors in determining who becomes the leader (or leaders) of any group. **Influence** is the capacity to have an impact on the course of events in a group or on the behavior of a group or person. **Power** is the ability to require specified behavior of other group members. The presence of power implies the ability to apply sanctions in case of noncompliance.

We all have some form of power at various times in our lives. All of us have the potential to use our power effectively as members of various groups. In most situations the person holding a position of authority, such as the president or supervisor of a business, does appear to have the power to do as he or she sees fit. However, other forms of power, such as expertise or personal charm, are also very important.

> Eric is the most knowledgeable person in the computer center of a large corporation. He is instrumental in creating programs and systems that are helping his company become very competitive in the marketplace. On several occasions he has been offered the position of manager, but he enjoys his present work so much that he always turns the promotion down. He is admired by his peers, his supervisor, and the president of the company, and can do nearly anything he wants. In addition, he does not have the responsibility and the "headaches" that usually go with being the manager. Eric has expert power.

Norms   Norms are rules of behavior that usually emerge to increase the successful functioning of the group. All members are expected to obey the norms, and any deviations from them may result in punishment from other group members. Some examples of group norms are being on time, waiting to be acknowledged by the chairperson before speaking at meetings, and respecting the dignity of other group members. Of course, it is also possible for an indi-

influence   the capacity to have an impact on the course of events in a group or on the behavior of other group members

power   the ability to require specified behavior of group members

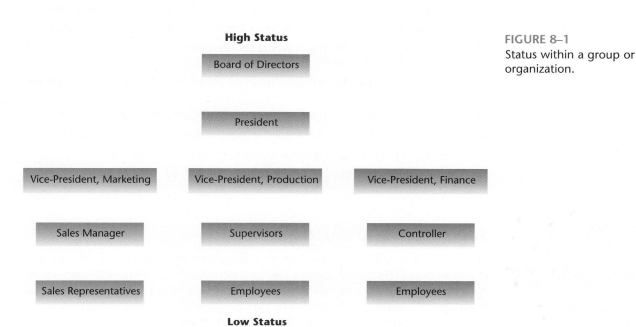

High Status

Board of Directors

President

Vice-President, Marketing	Vice-President, Production	Vice-President, Finance
Sales Manager	Supervisors	Controller
Sales Representatives	Employees	Employees

Low Status

FIGURE 8–1
Status within a group or organization.

vidual to become socialized into a deviant group whose norms could include smoking dope, participating in group sex, or stealing.

Cohesiveness   Group cohesiveness is the attraction the members feel toward the group. Members of a cohesive group usually are deeply involved with group's goals, feel very close to one another, and are loyal to the group. Groups vary in their degree of cohesiveness.

Group cohesiveness is influenced by the same variables that initially determine the formation of the group. Each member's attraction to other individuals in the group, enjoyment of group activities, and belief that membership in the group will be beneficial in attaining his or her goals all contribute to the cohesiveness of a group. Relatively small group size, the presence of outside threats, competition, and cooperative and friendly communication are other influences.

Critical Review 1

1. The term *group* is defined as people working or playing together to achieve the goal of happiness. T F

2. Membership in groups often helps individuals provide for their affiliation needs of friendship, support, love, and affection. T F

3. Group membership also provides for a sense of identity, helps us maintain our self-esteem, and may offer some status. T F

4. "United we stand, divided we fall" implies that a group may provide social status for its members. T F

5. When a group becomes too large to satisfy some of its members' needs, subgroups may be formed to provide for these needs. T F

6. The observable pattern of relationships among the members in a group is referred to as the interactive pattern. T F

7. Four variables that determine group structure are roles, norms, status, and goals. T F

8. The importance and prestige a member enjoys in a group are called social status. T F

9. The capacity to have an impact on the course of events in a group or on members of a group is called impact ability. T F

10. A person with the ability to require specified behavior of other group members has power. T F

11. Norms are rules that emerge to govern the functioning of a group. T F

12. The attraction members have toward a group is called the attraction factor. T F

13. How does membership in a group contribute to personal growth?

14. Describe the factors that contribute to group structure.

society   a self-sufficient and self-perpetuating group that includes persons of both sexes and all ages

culture   a way of life that is transmitted from one generation to the next

socialization   the process by which culture is transmitted

SOCIETY AND SOCIALIZATION

One group that is likely to exert great influence on our adjustment and growth is our **society.** This self-sufficient and self-perpetuating group with persons of both sexes and all ages has elaborated a **culture,** a way of life that is transmitted from one generation to the next. The process by which culture is transmitted is called **socialization.** It is a critically important process that involves the interplay of hereditary and environmental factors in the physical, cognitive, emotional, and social development of the person.

The Importance of Culture

Without culture, the human species would perish. Like all other living species, we survive because of our ability to adapt to the environment. But our adaptation is significantly different from that of other life forms in at least two major respects. First, we have not evolved specific physical adaptive characteristics equal to those of other species. The polar bear, for example, can thrive in an extremely cold environment because of its heavy fur, but human skin alone will not permit survival in such frigid temperatures. Second, we do not exhibit forms of complex, unlearned activity comparable to those of other species. Experimentation has shown, for instance, that South African weaver birds completely isolated from their natural environment and from others of their species for a period of six generations can build nests in the typical pattern of their wild ancestors when supplied with appropriate materials (Williams, 1972). We, on the other hand, must learn to build our shelters. Indeed, as a species, we must learn our social heritage, or culture, to survive, for culture is our unique adaptive mechanism.

Heredity Versus Environment

No one really knows whether heredity or environment has a stronger influence on our development. Some of our characteristics are obviously products of genetic inheritance. A female, for example, can conceive and give birth to a child; a male cannot. Just as certainly, other characteristics are produced by environmental factors. You could not speak English if you had never been exposed to the English language. Still other characteristics such as intelligence seem to be products of the interaction of hereditary and environmental factors. Thus, both heredity and environment are important factors in our development, and the debate concerning their respective influence will, no doubt, continue for some time.

Human Nature and Human Contact

Socialization involves not only the unfolding of our physical and mental capacities but also the existence of an ongoing society and significant interaction among the people of that society. It is through our interaction with others that we acquire *human nature,* a critical prerequisite to our developing human potential.

Human nature means different things to different people. Freud viewed it as our tendency to seek pleasure while at the same time avoiding punishment and guilt; Skinner viewed it as our innate ability to respond to differential stimuli; and Rogers viewed it as our drive to actualize our potentialities. Here, however, we are using the term *human nature* in the sense that Frederick Elkin and Gerald Handel (1984) use it: "The ability to establish emotional relationships with others and to experience such sentiments as love, sympathy, shame, envy, pity, and pride" (p. 11).

According to Elkin and Handel, human nature is not part of our biological inheritance; it is learned. It develops in **primary groups** such as the family, in which we have close, intimate, and intense face-to-face contacts frequently. It is through interaction in primary groups that we begin to empathize—to under-

primary groups groups of people, such as a family, in which close, intimate, and intense face-to-face contacts are frequently shared

stand and share the feelings of others. Only when this happens are we prepared to become human within the context of our culture and society.

Hypothetically, children deprived of human contact cannot develop human nature. Although there are no known cases in which children have been totally deprived of human contact and have survived, there are some cases in which children have been reared in isolation or have suffered a severe lack of attention and affection as infants. In all cases, the children displayed a distinctive lack of human nature.

Two well-documented instances in which children were reared in isolation are the cases of Anna and Isabelle (Davis, 1949). Anna was an illegitimate child who was confined to an isolated existence in a single room. She had only minimal social contact and scarcely any instruction. Even her bedding and clothing were rarely changed. When, at age six, she was found and taken from the room, she could neither walk nor display any behavior that reflected human intelligence. She was emaciated, expressionless, and apparently indifferent to herself and her surroundings. She made no attempt to feed, dress, or care for herself. For the next four years Anna was provided with human contact and the care and attention usually extended to a child, first in a county home and later in a foster home and a school for retarded children. By the time she died from hemorrhagic jaundice at age ten and a half, she had learned to follow verbal instructions, talk in phrases, wash her hands before and after meals, brush her teeth, walk, and run without falling. Generally, she had a pleasant disposition. At the time of her death, her social behavior approximated that of a normal two-and-a-half to three-year-old child. Anna probably was somewhat mentally deficient, but it is unclear whether her lack of social development was due primarily to mental deficiency, lack of human contacts in early life, or a combination of the two.

Isabelle was also illegitimate and was found at age six in circumstances similar to Anna's. Perhaps the most significant difference between Anna and Isabelle was the human contact provided Isabelle by her deaf-mute mother. Although their communication was restricted to gestures, Isabelle and her mother spent considerable time with each other in a darkened room. When found, Isabelle could make only a few croaking sounds. Because of the inadequate diet and a lack of sunlight, she suffered from rickets, and she responded to strangers with apparent fear and hostility. Initial testing revealed that her social development approximated that of a normal nineteen-month-old infant. Unlike Anna, Isabelle was given a systematic program of training by a variety of specialists. At first she responded slowly, but after a few months her development accelerated rapidly. Within two years she achieved a social and cultural level typical of an American six-year-old, and by age fourteen her sixth-grade school teachers rated her as a well-adjusted and competent student. She was described as energetic, cheerful, and bright.

Although the cases of Anna and Isabelle cannot be considered definitive, they do lend support to the argument that children deprived of primary relationships will not develop their human potential fully.

Amount of Human Contact

No one knows exactly how much human contact is required for the normal development of a person, but it seems clear that some is necessary. Perhaps the meager contact between Isabelle and her mother was enough; perhaps it was not. Maybe Isabelle had potentialities she was unable to fulfill because of her isolation.

Eric Berne (1964) maintains that all people need to be touched and to be recognized by others. Our hunger for touch and recognition are satisfied by strokes, which Berne defines as "any act implying recognition of another's presence" (p. 15). Physical strokes involve physical contact such as touching or holding. Psychological strokes are symbolic acts such as words, gestures, or looks that imply recognition. According to Berne, physical stroking is absolutely essential to physical and mental growth. Infants who do not receive sufficient stroking suffer physical and mental deterioration. As children mature, they also develop a hunger for psychological strokes. They seek and need recognition that stimulates their growth and verifies their presence. Berne notes that although even negative strokes such as hitting or scolding may serve as recognition of a child's presence, only positive strokes such as hugs or smiles lead to healthy emotional development. A lack of sufficient strokes always produces a negative effect on development. If Berne is correct, it certainly makes sense to give infants and children a great deal of positive stroking so that their needs for touch and recognition will be fulfilled and they will develop to their fullest potential. Of course, the same holds true for adults.

> Angela did not receive much recognition from her parents when she was a child. It's not that they treated her badly, but they almost never showed affection in a physical way through hugs or kisses. Also, they—and others—rarely complimented her achievements.
>
> A young woman now, Angela tends to keep to herself. She has no great ambitions and lacks confidence in her ability to accomplish anything beyond the ordinary. Underassertive and lonely, she seems to have committed herself to an uneventful, unfulfilling, and sad life.

Critical Review 2

1. The fundamental survival mechanism of human beings is culture. T F

2. Heredity has a much stronger influence on the socialization process than does environment. T F

3. Socialization is the process of transmitting human culture. T F

4. According to Elkin and Handel, human nature is learned. T F

5. Primary groups are those in which we have close, intimate, and intense face-to-face contacts frequently. T F

6. Hypothetically, children who are deprived of human contact will not become human. T F

7. It has been established beyond doubt that children who suffer extreme social and cultural isolation must receive adequate human contact and treatment by the time they are six years old or they will never become fully socialized. T F

8. According to Berne, lack of sufficient strokes always produces a negative effect on development. T F

9. Why is culture important to humans?

10. What is the relationship between human contact and our development as human beings?

Agencies of Socialization

At any given time, every society is only one generation removed from extinction. If the culture is not transmitted to the young, the society will no longer exist. Because socialization is such a critical process, societies are unwilling to allow people to act randomly to control it. Rather, to ensure that important beliefs, values, customs, and social norms are transmitted, societies channel their transmission through particular social structures, often referred to as **agencies of socialization.** In virtually all societies the family is the first agency to socialize the child, and its influence on the person's development tends to be powerful.

agencies of socialization   social structures such as the family or school that are extremely important in the transmission of culture

Family   The family's influence is powerful primarily for three reasons: (1) our initial conceptions of ourselves, other people, and the external environment are formed within the context of the family; (2) we have a tendency to maintain family contacts throughout our lives; and (3) our family places us in our society (that is, our initial placement on the social stratification scale is that of the family into which we are born), and we reflect that placement.

In most instances the dominant cultural beliefs and values are transmitted through the family, although other particular beliefs and values peculiar to the individuals within the family may also be transmitted. Many societies have distinctive subcultures, and their general approaches to life may be different from one another. One would expect, for example, that the lifestyle of African-Americans, Italian Americans, Mexican Americans, and Anglo-Americans would be different from one another. Families that are part of a strong subcultural tradition may teach beliefs and values that vary somewhat from those of the dominant culture. Therefore, although the family's influence on a person's development tends to be powerful, societies that contain a variety of subcultures cannot rely too heavily on the family to transmit the dominant culture.

Neighborhood and Peer Group   Closely related to the family and the subculture are the neighborhood and the peer group. In some instances the neighborhood itself may have a strong subcultural flavor. Children who grow up in such a neighborhood will, no doubt, gain a wider exposure to the traditions they learn in their own homes. Even in mixed neighborhoods in which no particular subcultural tradition dominates, the influence of socioeconomic class tends to produce a sameness in many of the beliefs and values expressed by the people. Children who live in a poor neighborhood are likely to learn to view the world differently from children who live in an affluent neighborhood.

The childhood peer group comprises people of approximately the same age who share similar social statuses. It becomes increasingly significant as an agency of socialization as the child moves away from his or her early dependence on family members and toward more independent behavior.

The neighborhood and the peer group, then, are important agencies of socialization. However, like the family and the subculture, they may not transmit the dominant culture as completely and efficiently as the society demands. Clearly, a more reliable agency of socialization is needed. This more reliable agency is the school.

School   Some small, primitive societies do not have schools (Mendoza and Napoli, 1995), but in these societies other social structures such as the family and the religious bodies are sufficiently strong to transmit the culture. In societies such as ours, schools are definitely needed. In fact, the major societal function of the school in modern societies is to transmit the dominant culture. Notice that in the public school system in the United States, for example, classes are taught in the English language, American history is emphasized, all students are exposed to the value of cleanliness, the virtues of a democratically based political system are extolled, and virtually everyone learns about George Washington's tree-cutting escapade. It is not very likely that these are aspects of the typical curricula in French, Italian, Russian, or Chinese schools. It is also unlikely that you would be the person you are today if you had attended school in the former Soviet Union rather than in the United States. Thus, the school affords us the opportunity to become a relatively complete social product.

Of course, the school cannot transmit *all* aspects of a culture. Indeed, it is virtually impossible for any one person to know the entire content of a given culture (Davis, 1949), and no one is expected to have this knowledge. But everyone is expected to know the essentials—the language; the basic social, political, economic, and moral beliefs and values; the social norms; and the customary behaviors. Going to school ensures that we will be exposed to these aspects of culture, regardless of the provincialism of our family, subculture, neighborhood, or peer group.

Occupation   Beliefs, values, and behavior patterns acquired from occupation tend to be transmitted from parents to children through child-rearing practices. Kohn (1969), for example, argues that middle-class occupations stress the value of self-direction and tend to deal with the manipulation of interpersonal relations, ideas, and symbols. Conversely, working-class occupations stress the value of conformity to rules established by authority and tend to deal with the manipulation of material objects. Through their child-rearing practices, middle-class and working-class parents tend to transmit their own values to their children. In turn, the children grow up with a tendency to move into occupational statuses similar to those of their parents. Thus, occupation plays a role not only in the transmission of culture but in the perpetuation of the social class structure from one generation to the next.

Mass Media   Elements of the **mass media** may also serve as transmitters of culture. Although they do not offer the direct, person-to-person contact found within the other agencies of socialization, radio, television, newspapers, magazines, movies, and so on may teach aspects of the culture to vast audiences. For example, a televised speech by the president of the United States may expose millions of viewers to democratic values as well as to the English language. Advertising may convince us of the values of bathing regularly, eating moderately, dressing appropriately, and keeping our breath fresh and our teeth clean. Because we are exposed to the mass media at an early age and because this exposure tends to continue indefinitely, components of the mass media are potentially significant agencies of socialization throughout our lives.

> **mass media**   channels of communication such as television, newspapers, radio, and magazines that may reach and influence very large audiences

Critical Review 3

1. The family is the first agency of socialization for human beings. T F

2. The childhood peer group comprises people of approximately the same age who have about the same amount of wealth. T F

The mass media, such as television, may be a powerful transmitter of cultural beliefs and values.

3. The major function of the school in modern societies is to teach people to be functional literates. T F

4. No one is expected to know the entire content of his or her culture. T F

5. The peer group, although impersonal, may teach aspects of the culture to vast audiences.

6. Identify the major agencies of socialization and describe their influence on the person's development.

LIFE CYCLE

The *life cycle* is the general sequence of events in our physical, psychological, and social development as we progress from infancy through old age. Many scholars have dealt with the life cycle. As we saw in chapter 2, for example, both Freud and Erikson have commented extensively on it. Two other scholars worth noting here are Daniel J. Levinson and Roger L. Gould. Both have concentrated on adult development—Levinson on men's, Gould on both men's and women's.

Levinson's Seasons of Life

Levinson (1978), who studied male subjects, believes women pass through approximately the same stages as men do, but in a slightly different fashion. He identifies three adult "eras": *early adulthood* (ages seventeen to forty-five), *middle adulthood* (ages forty to sixty-five), and *late adulthood* (starting at about age sixty). Note that there is an area of overlap as one era ends and the next begins. This overlap is a transition between eras.

Each era consists of an alternating series of stable (structure-building) periods and transitional (structure-changing) periods. The primary task of a stable period is to build a *life structure*—that is, to make choices and commitments to particular beliefs and values and to a particular lifestyle. In addition, each stable period has other unique tasks that reflect its place in the life cycle. The primary tasks of a transitional period are "to question and reappraise the existing structure, to explore various possibilities for change in self and world, and to move toward commitment to the crucial choices that form the basis for a new life structure in the ensuing stable period" (Levinson, 1978, p. 49). Like stable periods, each transitional period has additional unique tasks that reflect its place in the life cycle.

Early Adult Transition

Adult development begins with the *early adult transition* (ages seventeen to twenty-two).[1] One of the two tasks here is to move out of the pre-adult world. This requires modification or even termination of existing relationships with important persons, groups, and institutions. The second task is to move into the adult world. This involves the creation and consolidation of an initial identity. By the end of the early adult transition the young person has begun to create a life within the adult world.

Entering the Adult World

The period from about age twenty-two to about age twenty-eight is called *entering the adult world.* Within this period a variety of initial choices are made and tested with regard to occupation, love relationships (often including marriage and family), peer relationships, values, and lifestyle. There are two primary, yet antithetical, tasks: exploring the possibilities for adult living and creating a stable life structure. In order to complete these tasks, the young person must keep his options open while at the same time making something of his life.

Age-Thirty Transition

During the *age-thirty transition* (from about age twenty-eight to about age thirty-three) there is a critical examination of the choices and commitments made in the preceding period. Adjustments made as a result of this examination may be used as the basis for the formation of a more satisfactory life structure in the next stable period. There is a sense of urgency connected with the age-thirty transition as a man becomes more serious, more "for real." He senses that if there are things he would like to change about his life, he had better get started, for soon it will be too late. For some people, the age-thirty transition is smooth, without great disruption or crisis. They make modifications but not fundamental changes in life structure. For most men, however, this transition takes a more severe and stressful form, the *age-thirty crisis.* A man may find, for example, that his present life structure is intolerable, but may have great difficulty forming a better one. Thus, considerable pain may be experienced during this period.

---

1. The ages given for this and other periods are not to be taken as absolutes; however, most periods do not vary by more than a couple of years in either direction. Thus, the early adult transition could begin anywhere between fifteen and nineteen and could end anywhere between twenty and twenty-four.

Charles will celebrate his thirtieth birthday in two weeks. From his point of view, however, there will be little to celebrate. He has been working for the same company since he graduated from college at twenty-two. Although his first couple of promotions came relatively soon, he has not been promoted in almost four years, and he feels stuck in his current position. Charles believes that at this rate he will never reach the upper level of management to which he has long aspired. Thus, he is not happy with his present work situation. He has been thinking of looking for a position with another company.

On the other hand, in just two more years Charles will be fully vested in the company's retirement plan. Furthermore, he likes the company and feels relatively comfortable working there. The company likes him, too, and it appears that the security of a long career with the company is most likely if Charles desires it. When he thinks of these factors, he becomes reluctant to begin the search for a position with another company.

Charles is in the midst of a personal crisis.

Tasks of the Novice Phase

Levinson refers to the first three periods of adulthood (the early adult transition, entering the adult world, and the age-thirty transition) as the *novice phase* of adulthood (ages seventeen to thirty-three). During this time, a young person emerges from adolescence, finds his place in adult society, and commits himself to a more stable life.

Although each of the periods in the novice phase has its own particular tasks, several tasks are common to all three periods and characteristics of the entire novice phase. Among these common tasks are relating to authorities, gaining greater authority oneself, and forming adult values with regard to community, ethnicity, politics, and religion. However, the most prominent of the common tasks in the novice phase are: (1) forming a "Dream" and giving it a place in the life structure; (2) forming mentor relationships; (3) forming an occupation; and (4) forming love relationships, marriage, and family.

The Dream   During the novice phase each man conceives a *Dream*, a vision, "an imagined possibility that generates excitement and vitality" (Levinson, 1978, p. 91). The Dream is initially vague and only loosely connected to reality, although it may include concrete images such as being a highly respected community member, a great artist, or an athletic superstar. The developmental task of the young person is to give the Dream greater definition and find ways to live it out. So the Dream takes shape in the early adult transition and is gradually integrated within an emerging adult life structure in the novice phase. Failure to achieve this integration may lead to the death of the Dream, and with it the young person's sense of purpose in life.

The Mentor   At some point during the novice phase the young man forms a relationship with a *mentor*, a person who is usually about eight to fifteen years older than his protege. The mentor serves a variety of functions, teacher, sponsor, host and guide, exemplar, and counselor. The mentoring relationship is often found within a work setting, with the mentoring functions being performed by a boss, senior colleague, or teacher. Sometimes the relationship evolves informally, with the mentor being a friend, neighbor, or relative.

The most crucial developmental function of the mentor is to support and facilitate the realization of the Dream. He accomplishes this by believing in his

Advice, acceptance and emotional support from a mentor at some time in the novice phase is critical to the social and psychological development of a young person.

protegé, by giving the Dream his blessing, and by helping to define and accepting his protegé's newly emerging adult self.

Over time this relationship between apprentice and expert evolves into a relationship in which the balance of giving and receiving is more equal. This critical shift is part of an ongoing process by which the young man will ultimately transcend the father-son, man-boy division of his childhood, a process that continues throughout the novice phase.

The mentoring relationship is relatively short-lived, usually lasting two to three years and never more than ten. It may end completely, perhaps with a gradual loss of involvement, or may end with the formation of a modest friendship; it may end when one man dies, changes jobs, or moves. Often, intense mentor relationships become embroiled in strong conflicts and end with bad feelings on both sides. Still, however, the young man has learned and will continue to learn from the mentor as he incorporates the mentor's admired qualities into himself. This internalization of the qualities of significant people is a primary source of adult development.

Occupation   The process of forming an occupation takes place throughout and often beyond the novice phase. The first serious occupational choice is usually made sometime between ages seventeen and twenty-nine, during the early adult transition or the entering the adult world stage. Having made an initial choice, the young man must then acquire skills, values, and credentials as he attempts to establish himself within the occupational world. Some men commit themselves to a particular occupation relatively soon, while others may struggle for years to sort out their interests and to discover what occupations may help them to live out those interests. By the end of the age-thirty transition, when the novice phase has been completed, the early phase of occupational choice has been concluded. The formation of an occupation continues throughout early adulthood, but usually within the pattern already established by the end of the novice phase.

Love Relationships   Like his occupation, a man's marriage and family life are formed and continue to develop throughout the novice phase and often beyond. Developmental tasks include forming the capability of having adult peer relationships with women and accepting the responsibilities of marriage and parenthood. Approximately 80 percent of the men in Levinson's study entered into first marriage by age twenty-eight. Unfortunately, according to Levinson, "Most men in their twenties are not ready to make an enduring inner commitment to wife and family, and they are not capable of a highly loving, sexually free and emotionally intimate relationship" (p. 107). Men who marry for the first time between twenty-eight and thirty-three, during the age-thirty transition (as did approximately 20 percent of Levinson's sample), have the advantages of having gained greater self-knowledge and of having resolved some of the conflicts that might have prevented them from making an appropriate commitment to marriage and family. However, they may also have the disadvantage of marrying under pressure. The sense of urgency typically experienced during the age-thirty transition may motivate them to marry more to "normalize" their lives than to fulfill deep love relationships.

A love relationship that has particularly great impact on a young man during the novice phase is his relationship with the *special woman*, who may or may not be his wife. It is a unique relationship that goes beyond loving, tender, romantic, and sexual feelings. The unique quality of the special woman is found in her connection to the man's Dream. Like his mentor, she "helps him to shape and live out the Dream: she shares it, believes in him as its hero, gives it her blessing, joins him on the journey and creates a 'boundary space' within which his aspirations can be imagined and his hopes nourished" (Levinson, 1978, p. 109).

Also like the mentor, the special woman is the transitional figure. Early, as he struggles to become an autonomous adult, she fosters the young man's adult aspirations while accepting his dependency. Later, he will develop into a more complete adult and will have less need of her sometimes actual and sometimes illusory contributions.

By end of the age-thirty transition, a man's life is remarkably different from what it was when he entered the novice phase at seventeen. Adolescence has long since past, and he is well on his way to becoming a member of the adult world. Now, he will move toward major new choices or recommit himself to those already made as he attempts to work out a relatively satisfactory life structure. Choices consistent with his Dream, values, and talents will provide the basis for satisfactions; choices inconsistent with these factors will lead to considerable pain in the second structure-building period.

Settling Down

The second life structure, which is the vehicle for the culmination of early adulthood, takes shape at the end of the age-thirty transition and lasts until age forty; it is called *settling down*. This period involves two major developmental tasks: establishing a niche in society (anchoring oneself more firmly in one's occupation and in society generally) and "making it" (striving to advance, to build a better life, and to be affirmed by others). In short, this period is characterized by attempts to advance in virtually all areas of life: social rank, power, fame, creativity, quality of family life, and so on.

Progress in the settling down period brings new rewards but also produces greater responsibilities and pressures. As each man becomes "more his own man," he must give up even more of the little boy within himself, an internal figure he never completely outgrows.

Midlife Transition

Early adulthood ends in the late thirties, and middle adulthood begins at about age forty-five. The *midlife transition* (ages forty to forty-five) is a bridge between these two eras. This structure-changing period brings a new set of developmental tasks as the life structure again comes into question. Men ask themselves: "What have I really accomplished? What do I really want for myself and others? What do I really get from and give to my family, my work, my community, and myself?"

Although some men are relatively untroubled by these questions, most experience the midlife transition as a period of moderate or severe crisis. They believe they cannot go on as before. They need at least a few years to form new directions or to modify old ones.

Entering Middle Adulthood

By about age forty-five, the time for reappraisal and exploration is over and the process of forming a new life structure begins. The life structure that emerges in the first middle adulthood period, *entering middle adulthood* (ages forty-five to fifty), varies greatly in satisfactoriness from one man to the next. Some men seem unable to overcome their failure to handle the developmental tasks of earlier periods. For these men, middle adulthood will be an era of frustration and decline. Others form life structures that appear workable in the world but are poor reflections of their true selves. For them, life lacks inner excitement and meaning. Still other men form life structures that build on the successes and self-knowledge gained in the past. For them, middle adulthood is often the most creative and fulfilling era of the life cycle.

Other Periods

Levinson's study does not focus on men beyond forty-five or fifty; however, he suggests that there is evidence that the sequence of alternating structure-building and structure-changing periods continues throughout the life cycle. The age-fifty transition (ages fifty to fifty-five), for example, is the time in which changes can be made so that a man can settle into middle adulthood. The *culmination of middle adulthood* (ages fifty-five to sixty) is the structure-building period that completes middle adulthood, and the *late adult transition* (ages sixty to sixty-five) ends middle adulthood and establishes the basis for entering late adulthood. Figure 8–2 summarizes Levinson's stages of development.

Gould's Transformations

Roger L. Gould (1978), who studied both men and women, presents a view of the life cycle that is strikingly similar to Levinson's in several respects but, of course, different in others. According to Gould, four major phases of adulthood occur between the ages of sixteen and fifty. The developmental task in each of these phases is to challenge and resolve one of four false assumptions, formed during childhood, that tend to keep us in a state of dependency. Each of these assumptions is related to our childhood desire to obtain absolute safety from harm by following the dictates of our parents. The resolution of each false assumption signifies a change in consciousness from more childlike to more adult ways of interpreting life events. Over time, we relinquish our childish desire for absolute safety and with it, our reliance on our parents to protect us from harm. Ultimately, we become our own persons.

Ages Sixteen to Twenty-Two   The first phase lasts from about sixteen to about twenty-two. The false assumption to be challenged and resolved is "I'll always belong to my parents and believe in their world." Even before completing high school, we begin to challenge this belief in minor ways. The challenge becomes stronger between the ages of eighteen and twenty-two, when events such as living away from home foster a questioning of the assumption. Leaving our parents' world is a critical first step in building an independent, adult identity.

Ages Twenty-Two to Twenty-Eight   The second phase takes place between ages twenty-two and twenty-eight, when we make decisions on major issues such as marriage, pregnancy, and careers. The false assumption here is "Doing things my parents way, with willpower and perseverance, will bring results. But if I become too frustrated, confused or tired or am simply unable to cope, they will step in and show me the right way." During this period we begin to realize that willpower and perseverance alone do not always bring positive results and that we must live our own lives. We become more self-confident as we prove our competence by dealing effectively with major life issues.

Ages Twenty-Eight to Thirty-Four   By the end of the second phase, most of us have become self-reliant adults. Indeed, by this time "our adult consciousness is developed enough so that we feel able to turn inward and reexamine ourselves for something other than the narrow limits of independence and competence that seemed so all-important a few years earlier" (Gould, 1978, pp. 153–54). Thus, the major false assumption related to the third phase (ages twenty-eight to thirty-four) is "Life is simple and controllable. There are no significant coexisting contradictory forces within me." As we open up to what is inside us, we begin to understand the complexity of living and to realize that many of our simple rules about life do not work in the complicated real world. We begin to accept our limitations and the fact that life is not fair. With this acceptance, both our competence in the world and our adult consciousness are increased.

FIGURE 8–2
Standard and comparison lines

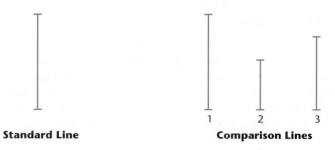

Standard Line   **Comparison Lines**

Ages Thirty-Five to Forty-Five   During the midlife decade (ages thirty-five to forty-five), we become aware of the pressure of time in our lives: "Whatever we do must be done now" (Gould, 1978, p. 217). The major false assumption of this fourth phase is "There is no evil or death in the world. The sinister has been destroyed." As we come to terms with our own mortality, we dig deep inside ourselves and begin to accept the ugly, demonic side of life, a part of us and of the world from which the immature mind tries to protect itself by creating the false illusion that absolute safety is possible. "Eventually we work our way deeper into our core, to form a new understanding of the meaning of our life uncontaminated by the need for magical solutions or protective devices (Gould, 1978), p. 218). By about age fifty we resolve the last major false assumption, and with its resolution, we complete the passage from childhood to adult consciousness, from "I am theirs" to "I own myself."

Levinson and Gould have extended and enhanced the work of Freud and Erikson on the life cycle. They have provided us with insights into adult development and a general understanding of how the process of socialization continues after childhood and adolescence.

Critical Review 4

1. Levinson defines three adult eras: early adulthood, middle adulthood, and late adulthood. T F

2. The two developmental tasks of the early adult transition are to move into the adult world and to create a secure identity. T F

3. Two people who are especially important to a young man in the novice phase because they support and facilitate the realization of his Dream are the mentor and the special woman. T F

4. A man's first serious occupational choice is usually made some time between the ages twenty-five and thirty-five. T F

5. Early adulthood ends in the late thirties; middle adulthood begins at about age forty-five. The bridge between these two eras is called the early adulthood transition. T F

6. Gould identifies four major phases of adulthood that occur between the ages of sixteen and fifty. T F

7. The false assumption "Life is simple and controllable; there are no significant contradictory forces within me" is related to Gould's third phase (ages twenty-eight to thirty-four).

8. According to Gould, we resolve the last major false assumption by about age forty. T F

9. What are the major similarities and differences between Levinson's and Gould's conceptions of the life cycle?

PERSONAL COSTS AND EFFECTS OF GROUP MEMBERSHIP

As we have seen, group membership has both advantages and disadvantages. By being good group members we can partially fulfill our needs for affiliation, security, positive self-esteem, and a sense of personal power. On the other hand, group pressure may encourage us to take actions and even to think thoughts and experience feelings that impede our personal growth. In this section we examine three results of group membership that may thwart the development of individual potential: *deindividuation, conformity,* and *obedience.*

Deindividuation

Deindividuation is the process in which the person gives up individual identity and assumes the group's identity. For example, upon induction into military service, a person stops using the individual name (Ms. Smith) in favor of using the group name (Private Smith) and stops wearing personal attire in favor of wearing a military uniform. Upon marriage a wife may drop her maiden name in favor of accepting her husband's name (Ms. Susan Smith becomes Mrs. Susan Jones, or Mrs. John Jones). Deindividuation can occur in small groups such as a family as well as in large groups such as the military. Zimbardo (1970), however, indicated that deindividuation is more likely to occur in large groups than in small groups. He also stated that people are more likely to become deindividuated in groups in which they remain relatively anonymous, dress in similar manner to other group members, and do not feel personally responsible for their actions. In addition to anonymity and lack of personal responsibility, Diener (1980) identified arousal due to noise and crowding and focus of attention on group process as factors that lead to deindividuation.

Once deindividuated, individuals tend to feel little fear, guilt, or shame about their behavior, and they are more likely to behave in a socially unacceptable manner. Notice, for instance, the tendency for individuals to be more aggressive when behaving as crowd members than when alone. In an attempt to study the process and effects of deindividuation, Zimbardo (1975) set up a mock prison at Stanford University. It contained several barred cells, each with sufficient room for three bare beds. It also had a guardroom from which "guards" could observe the "inmates." Twenty-four male students were selected for the experiment. Twelve were arbitrarily assigned as inmates; the other twelve became guards. Zimbardo's description of these students is as follows: "mature, emotionally stable, normal, intelligent college students from middle-class homes throughout the United States and Canada."

In order to facilitate deindividuation, the inmates were given a uniform to wear: a white, dresslike garment. They were referred to by numbers instead of their names and were required to sleep at night with a chain around one leg. Guards also were given uniforms: khaki pants and shirts and sunglasses dark enough to hide their eyes. The guards were told that they had complete control of the prison and inmates; Zimbardo played the role of prison warden. The experiment was to last for two weeks.

The effects of deindividuation on the students were astounding. Many of the guards seemed to lose their sense of personal restraint and even brutalized the inmates, who, obsessed with their own survival, became "servile, dehumanized robots" who hated the guards. In Zimbardo's words, deindividuation "undid (temporarily) a lifetime of learning; human values were suspended, self-concepts were challenged, and the ugliest, most base, pathological side of human nature surfaced." Because of these effects, the experiment was terminated six days later, instead of at two weeks.

The Zimbardo prison experiment is extreme in the sense that most of us will never belong to a group that deindividuates its members to such an extent. The experiment is critically instructive, however, in focusing our attention on the process of deindividuation and its potential effects. In order for the members of any group to grow, each must strike a comfortable balance between individual freedom and social control. By understanding the process of deindividuation and its effects, we are better prepared to strike such a balance.

Conformity

Conformity is behavior that is in accordance with group norms. All groups demand conformity of their members because, without a reasonable degree of conformity, the activities of members would not be coordinated enough to achieve group goals and fulfill the members' needs. Would you, for instance, want to belong to a group in which people rarely followed the rules?

Generally, there are two types of conforming behavior: *public compliance* and *private acceptance.* Public compliance occurs when the individual conforms while being observed by others but not when alone. The person may conform in public because he or she needs the acceptance of group members but may refuse to conform in private because he or she dislikes or personally rejects the required behavior. Private acceptance occurs when the individual conforms both in public and in private. This usually requires a change in attitude to justify the behavior.

> Sam and Charley are two of the newest members of a college fraternity. They share several things in common. Both joined the fraternity in an attempt to fulfill personal needs for security, affiliation, and acceptance. Both also had a relatively low tolerance for and liking of alcohol when they joined. But all of this fraternity's members drink alcohol on social occasions, which occur frequently. As you might expect, both Sam and Charley now drink alcohol at fraternity socials, but Sam never drinks when alone; he still cannot stand alcohol. Charley, however, not only drinks in public *and* private, he has convinced himself that drinking is a sign of sophistication and that alcohol actually tastes good.

Why We Conform   As the preceding anecdote indicates, people will often conform even when the conformity challenges their personal beliefs and values. Think about some of the times you have given in to group pressure and done something that you really did not want to do. What causes this to happen? Why do we conform?

Two forms of influence seem to be responsible for the group's ability to demand and get conformity: **informational influence** and **normative influence.** Informational influence is the impact on a person's behavior when he or she relies on other group members to provide information about reality. Sometimes individuals are unsure what to think or how to behave. They look to the group for direction. If the majority of the group's members have adopted a particular position, the individual does, too. In this manner individuals accept and support the group's position because of informational influence.

Normative influence is the impact on a person's behavior when he or she responds to real or potential rewards and punishments that may be bestowed by the group for following or not following group norms. Generally, groups reward loyalty and punish deviance by means of acceptance or rejection: Loyal members are accepted; deviants are rejected. Because the need for acceptance tends to be strong, members are usually loyal. Thus, groups demand and usually get conformity because of their ability to accept or reject members who have a relatively strong need for acceptance. The normative influence is usually more potent than the informational influence in ensuring the conformity of group members.

Studies of Conformity   Perhaps the most famous series of experiments dealing with conformity was conducted by Asch (1951, 1955, 1956, 1957). He want-

conformity   behavior that is in accordance with group norms

informational influence   the impact on a person's behavior when he or she relies on other group members to provide information about reality

normative influence   the impact on a person's behavior when he or she responds to real or potential rewards bestowed by the group for following or not following group norms

ed to know if group pressure could cause an individual to abandon his or her own correct judgment in favor of conforming with the group's erroneous judgment. His studies reveal that groups can influence individuals to conform with incorrect positions taken by the group.

In a typical Asch experiment a group of eight persons look at a large card that displays a standard line and three comparison lines (see Figure 8–3). Their task is to determine which of the comparison lines (1, 2, or 3) is the same length as the standard line. The group repeats this task eighteen times, each time using a different set of lines. In every instance the standard line is the same length as only one of the comparison lines.

At first glance the task appears to be very simple for all eight of the "subjects." However, it turns out to be difficult for one of them, because only one is the true subject of the experiment. The other seven are confederates working for the experimenter. During each trial, the confederates, acting one after another, say aloud their answers. The subject then says his or her answer. The confederates respond truthfully in only six of the eighteen trials; in the other twelve they give incorrect responses. The experimenter observes the subject's responses during the twelve trials in which the confederates give incorrect answers. Because he or she must respond last, the subject is placed in a difficult position: knowing the correct response but hearing all of the others give a different and unanimous answer. How would this affect the subject's behavior? (How would this affect your behavior?) In the experiments nearly one-third of the subject's responses were incorrect (Asch, 1957). The subjects reported being confused, feeling self-conscious and under pressure, trying to figure out what was happening, wondering if they had misunderstood the instructions, and questioning their eyesight. Even those who refused to conform reported feeling some apprehension. It is perhaps significant that only approximately 25 percent of the subjects refused to conform on all of the critical trials. About 75 percent did conform to a greater or lesser extent. Interviews after the experiments revealed that most of the conformity consisted of public compliance without private acceptance; the subjects conformed publicly but rejected the group's judgment privately.

Factors Influencing Conformity   The foregoing discussion of the Asch experiments indicates that groups can influence conformity, but it does not address the factors that affect the *amount* of conformity in groups.

One factor that affects the amount of conformity is *size of the majority*. If the majority is unanimous, the pressure for conformity increases with the size of the unanimous majority (Asch, 1955; Rosenberg, 1961). For example, subjects confronted by only one other person in an Asch-type experimental situation rarely respond incorrectly. However, when confronted by two persons, the subjects' number of incorrect responses increases. The subject conforms at an even higher rate when confronted by three persons. The exact size at which the effect of a unanimous majority begins to level off is in question (Gerard, Wilhelmy, and Conolley, 1968), but increases beyond three or four persons appear insignificant. When the group's majority is not unanimous, a subject is less likely to conform. For example, when Asch (1956) instructed one of his confederates to respond differently from the other six, subjects responded incorrectly only about 8 percent of the time (as opposed to almost 33 percent of the time in the unanimous condition). Thus, a lack of unanimity has a liberating effect on behavior.

Questionnaire

Social Approval

When asked a question on a psychological test or during an interview, are you likely to respond with what you think is the answer other people approve of, whether or not that is what you really believe? Would you distort the truth in order to obtain social approval?

Taking the following test may help you to understand the strength of your need for social approval. After reading each statement, put a T in the true column if you think the statement is true for you, and put an F in the false column if you think the statement is false for you. The scoring key on page 328 will help you to score and interpret your responses.

True   False

1. I am always a good listener.
2. I have never deliberately hurt someone's feelings.
3. I always wear seat belts when in a car.
4. I sometimes like to gossip.
5. I always go out of my way to help someone in trouble.
6. I always admit my mistakes.
7. I have sometimes been jealous of the good fortune of others.
8. I sometimes find it difficult to continue working if I am not encouraged.
9. I am always careful about my physical appearance.
10. I have taken advantage of some individuals in the past.
11. I am always courteous.
12. I have never felt like telling someone off.
13. I always admit when I do not know something.
14. I often resent being asked to return a favor.
15. I always practice what I preach.
16. I am as well mannered at home as when I am in public.
17. I sometimes doubt my ability to succeed in life.
18. I have sometimes felt like rebelling against authorities even though I knew they were right.
19. I sometimes resent it when I do not get my way.
20. I have never intensely disliked someone.

A second factor affecting the amount of conformity is *attraction to the group.* Those more highly attracted to a group tend to conform more than those less highly attracted (Mehrabian and Ksionzky, 1970). A third factor is *commitment to future interaction.* Individuals are more likely to conform when they believe their relationship with the group will be long term, as opposed to short term (Lewis, Langan, and Hollander, 1972). A fourth factor is *level of competence.* Group members who believe themselves to be more competent than other group members with regard to the task at hand are more likely to resist group pressure (Stang, 1972).

Critical Review 5

1. Once deindividuated, individuals tend to feel very guilty and shameful about their behavior. T F

2. Some of the effects of deindividuation on the students in Zimbardo's prison experiment were unanticipated. T F

3. Public compliance occurs when the individual conforms while being observed by others but not when alone. T F

4. Groups can demand and usually get conformity because of their ability to accept or reject members who have a relatively strong need for acceptance. T F

5. In the Asch studies only about 25 percent of the subjects conformed to a greater or lesser extent. T F

6. Individuals are less likely to conform when they believe their relationship with the group will be long term rather than short term. T F

7. How may deindividuation and conformity thwart the development of individual potential?

Obedience

obedience the act of following the orders of a more powerful person

authority power that emanates from rights vested in a social role

Obedience is the act of following the orders of a more powerful person. As we have seen, some group members exercise more influence and power within the group than do others. One form of power is **authority,** power that emanates from rights vested in a social role. For example, the president of the United States is a more politically powerful person than an ordinary citizen because the role of president confers important political rights that the role of ordinary citizen does not.

In most instances we obey someone because he or she holds a position of authority, and not because of threats or promises. Obedience to authority occurs every day and in virtually all groups: Children obey parents, students obey teachers, and workers obey bosses. But how often? To what extent will we obey? Put another way, what are the limits of authority?

Milgram's Study of Obedience to Authority The most famous experiments dealing with obedience to authority were the series conducted by Milgram (1963, 1965a, 1974). He wanted to know the degree to which one person (the subject) would obey the directions of another person (the authority) to carry out actions that would hurt a third person (the victim). Milgram used hundreds of subjects in several variations of the research design that we are about to describe. His studies reveal that most people have a strong tendency to obey authority.

The subjects in Milgram's experiments were men and women aged twenty to fifty years old in a range of occupations, from laborers to professionals. They were recruited primarily through newspaper advertisements and were paid a small monetary fee for their participation. Upon arrival for the experiment, the subject met a gentle, forty-seven-year-old accountant who had also answered the newspaper ad. When the experimenter appeared on the scene, he told the volunteers that the research was designed to study the effects of punishment (in the form of electric shocks) on learning. One subject was to play the role of teacher, with the other being the learner. Based on a random drawing, the accountant was selected as the learner. As he was taken to an adjacent room and strapped into an "electric chair," the accountant revealed that he had heart trouble and was concerned that the shock might be dangerous to him. The experimenter indicated that although the shock would be painful, it would not cause permanent damage.

The teacher was then taken to a separate room and seated at an electric-shock generator equipped with thirty levers labeled from 15 to 450 volts. The words *slight shock* appeared over the lower levers, and the words *danger: severe shock* appeared over the upper levers. The highest lever was marked *XXX*. To demonstrate how the generator worked, the experimenter gave the teacher a sample shock of 45 volts. The shock, although only 45 volts, was painful.

The teacher's task was to ask the learner a series of questions and administer a shock whenever the learner answered incorrectly. The first shock was to be 15 volts, and with each ensuing incorrect answer, the shock was to be increased by one level (from 15 volts to 30 volts to 45 volts, and so on, up to the 450-volt maximum). The experiment began.

The learner grunted loudly at the 75-volt level. At 120 volts he shouted a cry of pain. At 150 he begged to be let out of the experiment. By 180 volts he banged on the wall and cried out that he could not stand the pain, and at 270 volts he let out an agonizing scream. When the teacher questioned the procedure in any way, the experimenter looked at him calmly and said, "You have no other choice; you must go on."

At the 300-volt level, the learner refused to answer any more questions and begged to be released from the chair. The teacher, however, was told by the experimenter to treat a refusal to answer as an incorrect response. At 315 volts the learner screamed violently, and at 330 volts, he fell silent. The experimenter told the learner to continue administering shocks at increasingly higher levels even though the learner failed to respond.

As you already know, the purpose of this research was not to study the effects of punishment on learning but to study obedience to authority. And as you probably guessed, the learner receiving the shocks was not really an accountant but an actor hired by the experimenter. He did not, in fact, receive shocks, but his performance was realistic enough to convince the subjects that they were administering real shocks. And administer shocks they did, even to what they believed to be dangerously high levels. How high?

The victims' anguish notwithstanding, approximately 65 percent of the subjects were completely obedient; they continued to administer shocks all the way to the 450-volt level! This, incidentally, does not indicate a complete lack of concern for the victims. The experimental situation was very stressful for the subjects. A majority expressed concern about the victim's welfare. They became increasingly worried as the shock level increased. Many asked the experimenter to check and make sure that the victim was all right. Some were so distressed that they refused to follow the experimenter's orders. However, as already indicated, the general level of compliance was very high.

Thus, we may conclude that most people have a strong tendency to obey authority. Why? Milgram (1974) stated that the "essence of obedience consists in the fact that a person comes to view himself as the instrument for carrying out another person's wishes, and he therefore no longer regards himself as responsible for his actions" (p. xii).

Factors Affecting Obedience to Authority   Milgram's study indicates that although obedience to authority is more common, defiance sometimes occurs. Other studies support this finding (French, Morrison, and Levinger, 1960; Michener and Burt, 1975). This leads to a consideration of factors that affect obedience to authority. What are the conditions under which people will obey, and what are the conditions under which they will disobey?

One factor that affects obedience is the *extent to which the person is under surveillance by the authority.* In altered versions of his basic research design, Milgram (1965a, 1974) varied the degree of surveillance maintained by the experimenter. In one version the experimenter stayed with the subject, sitting only a few feet away from him. Another version had the experimenter leaving the laboratory and issuing orders by telephone. Obedience was almost three times greater in the face-to-face research design. It is interesting to note that some subjects in the telephone version told the experimenter that they were raising the shock level when they actually were administering only the lowest shock. In this manner they could feel less guilt about administering shocks while at the same time avoiding a complete break with authority.

A second factor affecting obedience is the *role a person plays within the chain of command.* Kilham and Mann (1974) conducted a Milgram-like study in which one subject conveyed the orders from the experimenter to another subject who actually administered the shock. The rate of obedience was approximately twice as high among subjects who simply conveyed orders as among those who administered shocks. It appears that we are more likely to obey when positioned closer to the authority but farther from the ordered task.

Peer-group pressure is a third factor that affects obedience. Results of some of Milgram's experiments (1965b, 1974) indicate that when peers obey the authority, the subject experiences increased pressure to conform, and the subject has a greater tendency to obey. Conversely, when peers resist, peer-group pressure produces a tendency to disobey.

Critical Review 6

1. Power that emanates from rights vested in one's role is called authority. T F

2. Milgram's experiments dealing with obedience to authority reveal that most people have a strong tendency to obey authority. T F

3. One factor that affects obedience is the extent to which the person is under surveillance by the authority. T F

4. Generally, why do people obey authority?

5. Under what conditions will a person disobey authority?

TECHNIQUES OF SOCIAL INFLUENCE

social influence an interaction process in which one person (the source) behaves in a way that causes another person (the target) to change an opinion or act in a manner different from what he or she normally would do

source in social influence, the person who attempts to change the behavior or opinion of another person

target in social influence, the person whose behavior or opinion someone is attempting to change

Social influence is an interaction process in which one person (the **source**) behaves in a way that causes another person (the **target**) to change an opinion or act in a manner that is different from what he or she would normally do. For example, Ed uses good arguments to convince Rita to quit smoking. By promising to pay him ten dollars, Ms. Hill gets her son, Jim, to cut the grass.

Attempts at social influence can be either *open* or *manipulative* (Tedeschi, Schlenker, and Lindskold, 1972). Open attempts are apparent to the target: he or she knows that the source is trying to induce a change in opinion or behavior. Manipulative attempts are hidden from the target. Techniques such as flattery, playing dumb, or exaggeration are examples of manipulation. In this section we focus on open attempts at social influence.

Persuasion

Persuasion is a technique of open influence in which the source uses information or argument in an attempt to change the opinion of the target. Four factors determine whether or not the attempt to persuade will be successful: the communicator, the message, the target audience, and the medium through which the message is sent.

The Communicator Suppose two people—your next-door neighbor and a world-famous economist—tell you why you will make a fortune if you invest money in a particular stock. Why would you be more likely to believe the economist? Because the economist has more credibility than your next-door neighbor does. **Communicator credibility** is the extent to which the target audience perceives the communicator as a believable source of information.

One factor that contributes to high communicator credibility is *expertise*. Generally, people are more persuaded by a message from a source with more expertise than by one from a source with less expertise (Maddux and Rogers, 1980). That is why the economist would be more persuasive than your neighbor. But would this always be the case? Suppose you are an expert investor in the

persuasion a technique of open influence in which the source uses information or arguments in an attempt to change the opinion of the target communicator credibility

communicator credibility the extent to which a target audience perceives a communicator as a believable source of information

Lobbyists often use persuasion in their attempts to influence legislation.

stock market who is thoroughly familiar with the particular stock that has been mentioned. Would the economist's tip be more believable than your neighbor's? Not necessarily. Research suggests that the more the target is involved with or knowledgeable about an issue, the less likely that communicator expertise will affect persuasion (Rhine and Severance, 1970). If involvement or knowledge is high, the content of the message is more likely to change opinion than the expertise of the communicator.

Sometimes, a communicator with high expertise is still not credible. Suppose you do not know much about the stock market, and the world-famous economist gives you a tip on a stock. Suppose further that this world-famous economist owns a controlling interest in the company. Under these conditions, would you believe her? *Trustworthiness*, then, is another factor that contributes to high communicator credibility. The more trustworthy we perceive the communicator to be, the more likely that he or she will persuade us. We tend to distrust and to discount the message of a communicator whose message is very self-serving. You might be reluctant to believe that you are better off buying a used car than a new one if the individual trying to persuade you to accept that idea is a used-car salesperson. Conversely, a communicator who argues against his or her vested interests appears to be very trustworthy; therefore, he or she is very persuasive (Walster, Aronson, and Abrahams, 1966). Thus, you would be likely to believe a used-car salesperson who tries to persuade you to buy a new car rather than a used one.

Attractiveness is a third factor that contributes to high communicator credibility. Generally, we like attractive communicators more than unattractive ones; therefore, they are more likely to persuade us to change opinions (Chaiken, 1979). Notice the large number of attractive models in television and magazine advertisements. Notice also the large number of attractive candidates for political office.

The Message   Persuasive messages may differ from one another in many ways. For example, the arguments they contain may be simple or complex, strong or weak, one-sided or two-sided, or rational or emotional. Thus, the message itself can affect the communicator's relative success at persuasion.

An important consideration with regard to any persuasive message is its degree of *discrepancy*, the degree to which it is different from what the target believes. A message must have some degree of discrepancy in order to persuade, for a message without discrepancy can only reaffirm the target's current opinions. What is the optimum degree of discrepancy? Generally, a more discrepant message is more likely to change the target's opinion than a less discrepant message (Jaccard, 1981). There is, however, a point beyond which the degree of discrepancy becomes so large that the message becomes completely unbelievable. Can you imagine trying to persuade one of your classmates that the earth is flat?

A slightly discrepant message may be persuasive even if it comes from a low-credibility source, but a highly discrepant message will persuade only if it comes from a high-credibility source (Rhine and Severance, 1970). You might believe your physics professor if he or she told you that new information suggests that sound travels faster than light, but you probably would not believe a friend who told you the same thing.

Some persuasive messages appeal to rationality and, therefore, tend to be factual in nature. Suppose you are trying to persuade your spouse that the family needs a new car. You have already determined that an emotional appeal is unlikely to work in this case, so you are going to appeal to reason through solid and specific arguments. One approach is to use a *one-sided message,* one that presents only those arguments that you, the source, are advocating. Thus, you try to persuade by listing all of the reasons why the family needs a new car. Another approach is to use a *two-sided message,* one that recognizes opposing arguments and then rebuts them. In this instance, you would list reasons for buying and for not buying the new car but emphasize only the reasons for buying and downplay those for not buying. Which approach is more likely to get you the car? It depends on your spouse. One-sided messages tend to work better when the target audience already agrees with the source or is not knowledgeable about the issue. Two-sided messages work better when the target audience initially disagrees with the source or is knowledgeable about the issue (Karlins and Abelson, 1970; Sawyer, 1973).

> Todd wanted to convince Marleen that they should spend a little more money than usual on their upcoming summer vacation. He knew that Marleen was also interested in the idea but that she hadn't had time recently to keep up with how much of their money was being allocated to each item in their budget.
>
> Being a stickler for detail, Todd decided to present his case by identifying and discussing all of the reasons, both pro and con, why they should spend more on their vacation. Unfortunately, he chose the wrong strategy.
>
> As Marleen listened to Todd's arguments, she became more knowledgeable, not only about why they should spend more but why they shouldn't. Within a short time, she changed her position from supporting to opposing the proposal. After a long discussion, Todd reluctantly accepted Marleen's argument that a more expensive vacation was out of the question.
>
> Todd should have used a one-sided message.

Although some persuasive messages appeal to the target's rationality, others appeal to emotion. *Fear arousal* is often used in emotional messages that attempt to motivate the target to act. Generally, messages that arouse high levels of fear are more likely to produce change than those that arouse low levels of fear. Imagine how you would respond if your doctor told you that if you do not quit smoking immediately, you will suffer a heart attack within six months.

However, fear arousal tends to be effective only when certain conditions prevail (Michener, DeLamater, and Schwartz, 1986). First, the message must indicate that unless the target's behavior changes, serious negative consequences will follow. Second, the message must indicate that the negative consequences are highly probable. Third, the message must suggest that the target can avoid the negative consequences by carrying out a particular behavior. It is significant to note that the target is unlikely to change if the third condition is unmet. Would you quit smoking if you thought that you were going to have a heart attack within six months, *whether or not* you quit smoking?

The Target Audience   Like the communicator and the message, the target audience is an important factor in persuasion. As you are well aware, some individuals are easier to persuade than others. One reason for this is related to the target's *level of intelligence.* Research indicates that high intelligence may increase one's understanding of a message and, as a result, lead to greater change in the target. However, greater understanding may also lead to resistance and little or no change in the target (McGuire, 1972). Who, then, is more likely to be persuaded by a particular message—a person of high intelligence or a person of low intelligence? If we presume that both perceive the message to be valid, the answer depends on the message itself. Complex messages tend to be more persuasive for persons of higher intelligence, while simple messages tend to be more persuasive for persons of lower intelligence (Eagly and Warren, 1976).

Another factor in the degree to which persons can be persuaded is the extent of their *involvement with the issue*. Persons who are highly involved with an issue tend to study the message carefully. Strong arguments are more likely to change their thinking about the issue. Conversely, persons with less involvement do not study the message as carefully. Arguments are less likely to change their thinking. If their thinking does change, it is more likely that the change is caused by other factors such as communicator credibility rather than by the message itself (Petty, Cacioppo, and Goldman, 1981).

The Medium   There are two basic channels of communication: face-to-face and mass media. Face-to-face communications involve relatively small audiences, while mass media such as television, newspapers, and radio may reach and influence very large audiences. But how influential will these mass-media messages be?

Persuasive messages transmitted through mass media tend to produce change in the thinking of only a small percentage of the target audience (Bauer, 1964). Research suggests, for instance, that only about 7 to 10 percent of the voters in a presidential election are likely to change their voter preferences during a campaign, despite the fact that political parties spend millions of dollars on advertising (Benham, 1965). On the other hand, a shift of 7 to 10 percent of the votes might easily change the election's outcome. Thus, even a relatively small change in attitudes might justify spending such large sums of money (Mendelsohn, 1973).

Generally, there are three reasons why mass-media campaigns tend to produce such relatively small changes in public opinion. The first is *selective exposure*. Often, messages do not reach their intended target audiences. Remember, if the message is received by persons who already agree with it, the message tends to reinforce and not to change views. Sears and Freedman (1967) have found that, in general, mass-media messages tend to support rather than challenge preexisting audience attitudes. Thus, we may conclude that many advertising dollars are spent to hold on to or protect the advertiser's share of the market.

Resistance is a second reason mass-media campaigns tend to produce only small changes in public opinion. In the same manner that he or she might reject a face-to-face message, the target might reject the message outright or attribute little credibility to the communicator.

Third, *counterpressure* may block a change in opinion, even when the message appeals to the target (Atkin, 1981). You may become convinced that Miller Lite™ beer "tastes great and is less filling," but your family's long-standing taboo that rejects alcoholic beverages might stop you from buying a six-pack. Or your inclination to buy a six-pack of Miller Lite™ might be thwarted by a television commercial for Bud Light™.

Critical Review 7

1. Attempts at social influence can be either open or closed. T F

2. High communicator credibility contributes to effective persuasion. T F

3. There may be times when even a communicator with a high degree of expertise is not credible. T F

4. A highly discrepant message will persuade only if it comes from a low-credibility source. T F

5. Generally, messages that arouse low levels of fear are more likely to produce change than those that arouse high levels of fear. T F

6. A strong argument is highly likely to change the opinion of a person who has little involvement with an issue. T F

7. Persuasive messages transmitted through mass media tend to produce change in the thinking of only a small percentage of the target audience. T F

8. Identify and discuss four factors that determine whether an attempt to persuade will be successful.

Threats and Promises

Threats and **promises** are two more techniques of open influence. A *threat* is a message that involves contingent punishments. It asserts that if some action is not carried out, then the person who failed to act will be punished. The parent, for instance, might tell the child, "If you don't clean up your room, then I'm going to take away your allowance this week." A *promise* is a message that involves contingent rewards. It asserts that if some action is carried out, then the person who acted will be rewarded: "If you clean up your room, then I'll give you an extra five dollars this week."

Notice that threats and promises attempt to elicit compliant behavior from the target, as opposed to persuasion, which is more concerned with changing the target's opinion. Also, you may note that threats and promises restructure a situation by adding a new contingency to it, whereas persuasion merely attempts to change the way a situation is viewed.

Although threats and promises seek compliance from the target, they create a range of alternative responses. If you issue a threat to me, I can (1) comply, (2) refuse to comply, or (3) issue a counterthreat (Boulding, 1981). If you issue a promise, I can (1) comply, (2) refuse to comply, or (3) issue a counterpromise (counteroffer). What, then, determines whether or not I will comply?

Two characteristics of threats and promises are primary determinants of the probability of target compliance: their *magnitude* and their *credibility*. Generally, the greater the punishment threatened or the reward promised, the greater the level of compliance. You would be more inclined to comply with a threat that included a fine of ten thousand dollars as a punishment for noncompliance than you would with a threat that included a fine of only ten dollars. Similarly, you would be more inclined to comply with a request if you were promised ten thousand dollars as a reward for compliance than you would with a request having a promised reward of only ten dollars.

Credibility also affects the probability of compliance. If the threatened punishment or promised reward is believable, then the target is more likely to comply. Of course, if *both* the magnitude and credibility of a threat are high, even greater pressure is exerted on the target and compliance is even more likely than when only one of these two variables is present (Faley and Tedeschi, 1971). The same principle holds true for promises.

Although threats and promises may be effective techniques of open influence, they pose several problems for the source. First, the target must perceive the source as being *credible;* otherwise, compliance may be low. Generally, the source's identity is crucial to his or her credibility. A promise to reward a partic-

threats messages that involve contingent punishments (i.e., if some action is not carried out, then the person who failed to act will be punished)

promises messages that involve contingent rewards (i.e., if some action is carried out, then the person who acted will be rewarded)

ular behavior with one thousand dollars is more believable when coming from a successful businessperson than from a vagrant. A second problem for the source is *surveillance.* The source must watch over or monitor the target's behavior to verify compliance. Such surveillance may cost the source in money as well as in time and energy. A third problem for the source relates more to threats than to promises: Threats may arouse resentment or hostility toward the source or may produce other secondary consequences that are undesirable (see the discussion of Skinnerian ideas in chapter 2).

Bargaining and Bilateral Threat

Although there many situations in which one person tries to influence another to change an opinion or a behavior, there are other situations in which both persons may exercise influence. The potential for **bargaining** exists when each person controls rewards that the other values. The potential for **bilateral threat** exists when each controls punishments that the other fears.

Bargaining is a process in which two or more persons with different preferences seek a mutually acceptable agreement by making a series of concessions. When completed, the agreement specifies future behavior for each person (Morley and Stephenson, 1977). People often bargain over the price of something, but sometimes other factors such as better working conditions are more important than price. In a typical bargaining situation each person seeks to gain more than he or she will concede. It is important to realize, however, that a bargaining agreement can be obtained only through compromise by each of the bargainers. It is therefore unlikely that any bargainer will be completely satisfied with the agreement. A bargainer may be more or less satisfied, but an agreement that all bargainers can accept as at least "something I can live with" is necessary for a true resolution.

Because each bargainer attempts to get more than he or she will give, a consideration of specific bargaining moves is necessary to understand how to obtain a favorable agreement. Suppose, for example, you are looking for an apartment to rent. After considering several factors such as location, type of neighborhood, size and layout of apartment, and so on, you conclude that one particular apartment comes closer than the others in meeting your personal needs. The only factor left to deal with is price.

Suppose the landlord is asking $350 per month in rent. This is his *level of aspiration,* the highest price he believes someone might currently pay. But you are aware that there are several unrented apartments, not only in this building but in others in the same neighborhood. This leads you to believe that the landlord will accept less than $350. But how much less? In other words, what is his *limit,* the lowest price he is willing to accept? Let's say his limit is $300 (although, of course, you cannot be sure what his limit is).

Now, you also have a level of aspiration and a limit. Suppose you have noticed that similar apartments in other neighborhoods have recently rented for as little as $275. You would like to rent this apartment for $275, which is your level of aspiration. On the other hand, you like the apartment very much and would be willing to pay more for it—all the way up to $340, which is your limit, the highest price you are willing to pay (which, of course, is unknown to the landlord). Thus, neither you nor the landlord knows the limit of the other. However, the ultimate price is likely to fall somewhere between the limits ($300 and $340). The distance between limits ($40 in this case) is called the *bargaining range.*

bargaining a process in which two or more persons with different preferences seek a mutually acceptable agreement by making a series of concessions

bilateral threat a condition in which two bargainers have the capacity to make threats and inflict punishments

Even though the level of aspiration of each of you is unrealistic, and an agreement may not be reached, there is room for bargaining. When bargaining begins, should your initial offer be high (say, $340), low (say, $275), or somewhere in between (say, $310)? Research suggests that you are more likely to obtain a more favorable (for you) agreement if your initial offer is low, provided that it is not so low that it causes bargaining to cease (Bartos, 1974). This is so because a low initial offer tends to reduce the other party's level of aspiration (Yukl, 1974), which sometimes leads to larger concessions on his or her part.

Concessions are the stuff of which bargaining is made. Successful bargaining often includes a series of concessions by each party so that an agreement can be obtained. A usual pattern consists of *matching* concessions in which each concession by one bargainer is matched by a concession by the other bargainer. The landlord asks $350 a month for the apartment, and you offer $275. The landlord responds by asking $340; you offer $285, and so on. Sometimes *mismatching* can occur: One bargainer refuses to make a concession in response to a concession by the other bargainer. After hearing your offer of $285, the landlord responds by asking $330; but, sensing weakness on his part, you hold firm at $285. You have refused to match his last concession.

Sometimes, bargainers may mismatch in terms of the size of the concessions rather than in terms of the number of concessions. Suppose the landlord responds to your initial offer of $275 by dropping his asking price from $350 to $340. You respond with an offer of $280. He drops from $340 to $330, and you increase from $280 to $285, and so on. One can easily see that although you are matching him concession for concession, his concessions are larger than yours. You are taking advantage of his perceived weakness. If you had perceived him as operating from a position of strength, you would be more likely to match the size of his concessions. This is so because *any* concessions from a bargainer operating from a position of strength are usually interpreted as conciliatory in nature and are likely to elicit concessions of similar size (Wall, 1977).

Often, bargaining culminates in the acceptance of a strict compromise that is the best possible result. Sometimes, however, bargaining produces better results when it is approached as a problem-solving process in which considerable effort is extended to meet the needs and interests of all bargainers. The basic objective of such "win-win" bargaining is to create *integrative proposals*: alternatives that provide important benefits to all bargainers (Pruitt, 1981). Filley (1975) provides the example of a couple who have bought an air conditioner for their family room, the only room in the house with air conditioning. A conflict arises because the husband wants to watch television in the air-conditioned room, but the wife, who wants to read there, complains that the TV distracts her from reading. Notice that it would be possible to resolve this conflict by a strict compromise in which room use is alternated between husband and wife. This, however, is far from satisfactory because the husband will invariably miss some of his favorite shows, and the wife will invariably be unable to read at times when she most feels like reading.

By focusing on needs and interests rather than acceding to a strict compromise, the couple discovers that the wife wants a quiet as well as a cool place to read; the husband is not opposed to her reading, but he wants to hear the TV. Further exploration results in an integrative proposal: Put an earplug adapter on the TV so that the husband can use a headset whenever the wife wants to read. Now he can watch (and hear) the TV whenever he wants, and she can read in a quiet place whenever she wants. In addition to providing a more satisfactory resolution, this problem-solving approach has provided the couple with the shared experience of working together to solve a problem. Thus, it brings them closer together and provides the basis for future cooperative behavior.

Often the process of bargaining is not so smooth. There may be times, for instance, when one of the bargainers attempts to gain leverage by making threats. Even worse is the condition of *bilateral threat* in which both bargainers have the capacity to make threats and inflict punishments. If an initial threat is made, it might provoke a counterthreat that, in turn, leads to another, larger threat, and so on. This threat-counterthreat spiral makes it difficult to resolve the conflict (Smith and Anderson, 1975). Bargaining may break down completely. Research indicates that even in situations in which bargaining does not break down completely, bilateral threat produces more undesirable results than either unilateral threat or no-threat conditions (Deutsch and Krauss, 1960, 1962).

Critical Review 8

1. Threats and promises are usually more concerned with changing the target's opinion than with eliciting compliant behavior. T F

2. Threats may arouse resentment or hostility toward the source. T F

3. The potential for bargaining exists when each person controls rewards that the other(s) value. T F

4. You are more likely to obtain an outcome favorable to yourself if your initial bargaining offer is relatively high. T F

5. Bargainers may mismatch in terms of the size of concessions or the number of concessions. T F

6. The problem-solving approach to bargaining encourages cooperative behavior. T F

7. Bilateral threat produces more desirable results than unilateral threat. T F

8. Discuss the problems associated with threats and promises as effective techniques of open influence.

9. When is it unlikely that a strict compromise will be the best possible result of bargaining? Explain.

PHYSICAL ENVIRONMENTAL INFLUENCES

This chapter has focused thus far on factors related to the social environment that influence our thoughts, feelings, and actions. Now, in this final section, we consider the effects of several factors that stem from the physical environment. Our discussion begins with a consideration of physical space and how it may influence us.

Physical Space and Human Adjustment

You may have noticed that you and the other students in your psychology class tend to take the same seats each class meeting. Moreover, if you have had the experience of coming to class a little later than usual and finding someone else in "your" seat, you probably also have had the experience of feeling upset about it. You may be relieved to find that your emotional response is a common one. It is an expression of **territoriality**.

territoriality the process of claiming exclusive use of areas and objects

Territoriality

Territoriality is the process of claiming exclusive use of areas or objects (Porteous, 1977). Many animals display territoriality and even will resort to aggression to defend what they have claimed. Usually, the claim is restricted to only one area. Humans, however, often lay claim to many areas and objects (for example, your home and your seat in your psychology class as well as your car, your clothes, and so on).

Unlike animals, humans have different types of territories. Altman (1975), for instance, has identified three types: *primary, secondary,* and *public*. Primary territories such as our homes are those to which we are most attracted and protective. They are owned and controlled by us exclusively. We may also become emotionally attached to and protective of secondary territories such as our usual seats in our psychology class. Although we do not own them, we treat them as ours and attempt to control them. Public territories are those that we clearly do not own but attempt to control when occupying them. For example, you would probably protect your place while standing in line to buy concert tickets by not allowing someone to cut in line ahead of you, and, having left your place in line, you would realize that you have relinquished any prior claim on it. Generally, the response to an uninvited invasion of one's territory becomes less intense from primary to secondary to public territories. You would no doubt be a lot less upset to discover someone sitting in your usual seat in your psychology class than to discover someone sleeping in your bed at home.

Although no one knows precisely why we respond as we do when our territory has been invaded, it seems clear that having control over territory presents advantages. One advantage is that it promotes social order. Misunderstanding and social conflict tend to be reduced when people have recognized a division of property among them. Another advantage is greater protection. Perhaps because they are on more familiar ground, people are usually better able to protect themselves on their own territory than on someone else's. A third advantage is psychological. Being on home territory tends to increase the sense of security and motivation to take charge (Edney, 1975). This "home-field advantage" is a well-recognized phenomenon in athletic contests.

Personal Space   While territoriality deals with fixed areas such as your home, office, or usual seat at the dinner table, **personal space** is the area immediately surrounding you that moves with you whenever interaction with another person takes place. While studying people from a variety of cultures, anthropologist Edward Hall (1959, 1966) noticed that people tend to treat the physical space immediately surrounding them as their personal property and that, generally, others do not invade this personal space. He also discovered that an acceptable distance between people is determined by cultural factors, personality factors, and the social situation.

According to Hall (1966), there are four *body-buffer zones* (degrees of personal distance) that we maintain in our interactions with other people: intimate, personal, social, and public. Each zone has a close phase and a far phase. The *intimate* zone extends from the body to eighteen inches away from the body. Physical contact often takes place between people when in the close phase (zero to six inches) of the intimate zone, and even when in the far phase (six to eighteen inches), people often sense one another in terms of odors, body heat, and so on. Generally, people feel uncomfortable when their intimate zone has been

personal space   area immediately surrounding a person that moves with him or her whenever interaction with another person takes place

penetrated. We invite in only those with whom we share a close relationship, and even they are invited in only under certain conditions.

The *personal* zone is from one and a half to four feet from the body. Comfortable interaction with close friends is common in the close phase (one and a half to two and a half feet) but uncommon with strangers. We keep others at arm's length when maintaining the far phase (two and a half to four feet) of the personal zone, although personal topics are often discussed at this range.

The *social* range extends from four to twelve feet from the body. The close phase (four to seven feet) is usual for interaction at social events and for interaction with co-workers. We relegate social encounters of relatively little importance to the far phase (seven to twelve feet) of the social zone. We tend to speak louder when maintaining the far phase, and social interaction tends to be maintained primarily through visual contact.

The *public* zone extends from twelve to beyond twenty-five feet from the body. Interaction when in the close phase (twelve to twenty-five feet) tends to be limited and verbal. Feedback between a college lecturer and his or her audience exemplifies interaction at the close phase of the public zone. Interaction in the far phase (beyond twenty-five feet) tends to be very formal in nature and typically involves important public figures.

As previously mentioned, several factors may influence what people consider to be acceptable distances between them when interacting. For example, Hall (1959, 1966) indicates that Latin American cultures allow for closer comfortable interaction between people than do North American cultures. When interacting with each other, the Latin American might move relatively close to the North American, while the North American might step back a little in order to maintain an appropriate distance. Thus, culture may affect the way we treat space.

Another factor that influences our use of personal space is sex. Generally, males prefer to sit across from friends when interacting, whereas females prefer to sit next to friends when interacting (Byrne, Baskett, and Hodges, 1971). Apparently, males are more sensitive to frontal space, and females are more sensitive to side space. Also, males have larger space zones than females, and the typical distance maintained between same-sex pairs is greater than that between male-female pairs (Heckel and Hiers, 1977). Worchel and Cooper (1979) suggest that this may be related to the strong taboo against homosexuality in Western culture, particularly male homosexuality. They argue that we teach youngsters that it is inappropriate for males to interact at close distances, but close interaction between females or members of the opposite sex is acceptable.

> Benjamin has just received a phone call telling him that his mother has suddenly died of a heart attack. Benjamin loved his mother dearly and his feeling of sadness is overwhelming. His friend Phil, who is visiting, literally offers Benjamin a shoulder to cry on. Benjamin desperately needs comforting now, but something in him won't allow him to accept physical support from Phil. After all, Phil is a man, and men are not supposed to be physically expressive with one another. Benjamin chooses to go it alone in this moment of deep emotional need.

Density and Crowding   The amount of physical space available to each of us is shrinking. This is because the size of the earth remains constant, while the world's population continues to grow. Does this shrinking availability of space affect our adjustment and growth patterns? If so, how?

In order to answer these questions, we must clearly understand two concepts—**density** and **crowding.** *Density* is an expression of the amount of physical space available to an individual. If there were 2,500 people living within an area of five square miles, the density would be 500 people per square mile. In contrast, *crowding* is having more social contact than one desires. It is an expression of the psychological reaction of the individual to his or her physical environment. A person living in a small house with ten other people might feel crowded; another person in the same situation might not. Thus, crowding is a subjective concept, whereas density is objective. One feels crowdedness, but one does not feel density.

Animal studies conducted prior to and during the 1960s focused attention on the potential effects of high density. The most famous of these was Calhoun's (1962) study of rats confined to restricted living quarters. The rats were given enough food and water to live comfortably, and their population increased rapidly. As density increased, the normal behavior patterns of the rats began to break down, resulting in abnormal sexual behavior, disruptions in nest building, improper care of the young, and enormously increased aggressive behavior. In addition, females had unusually high rates of miscarriage and cancer of the sex organs and mammary glands.

Studies on the effects of density on humans have not yielded such clear-cut results. On the contrary, it appears that density alone does not contribute to faulty adjustment. (Epstein, 1981). This realization has led some researchers to examine more closely the relationship between density and behavior. For example, Jonathan Freedman (1975), who has conducted an extensive examination of the literature on density and crowding as well as conducted research on the topic, argues that density simply intensifies a person's normal reaction so that a positive experience becomes more pleasant and a negative experience becomes more unpleasant.

Crowding, on the other hand, often produces maladjustive responses. Responses to crowding are influenced by the desire for privacy (Altman, 1975). One of the reasons we desire privacy is because it allows us to maintain control over environmental stimuli. A loss of control over environmental stimuli (stimulus overload) adversely affects our ability to adjust, so we often behave in a maladjusted way when we suffer a loss of privacy (Rodin and Baum, 1978). Another reason we desire privacy is because it allows us to maintain freedom of choice. A loss of the freedom to choose leads to a feeling of being threatened, which, in turn, may lead to maladjustive behavior (Rodin, 1976). Thus, when we lose privacy, we feel crowded.

Crowding is associated with uncomfortable and anxious feelings (Sundstrom, 1978). In fact, just the experience of anticipating crowding resulted in a negative mood for the subjects of one study (Baum and Greenberg, 1975). Crowding is also associated with breakdowns in interpersonal relationships. Individuals who feel crowded in their living quarters like each other less than do those who do not feel crowded (Baron, Mandel, Adams, and Griffin, 1976). Crowded people also display more aggressive behavior than uncrowded people (Hutt and Vaizey, 1966). In addition, crowding has been associated with health problems such as high blood pressure and with poor performance on tasks (particularly complex tasks). Males appear to be more affected by crowding than females (Stokols, Rall, Pinner, and Schopler, 1973).

density   an expression of the amount of physical space available to an individual

crowding   having more social contact than one desires

CULTURAL CROSSCURRENTS
Maintaining a Proper Distance

During the 1960s, a group of recent Cuban-American immigrants in New York City had applied for and received a permit to conduct a peaceful demonstration in front of the United Nations building. On the day of the demonstration, one of the leaders approached a New York City policeman to ask where the demonstrators needed to confine themselves. As the two men were talking, the police officer was becoming increasingly uncomfortable because the demonstrator kept getting too close to him. The officer told the demonstrator to "get out of my face," but owing to language differences, the demonstrator didn't understand what the policeman wanted. The Cuban-American just continued talking to the policeman while standing closer to the officer than the officer felt was appropriate. Within minutes, the Cuban-American was arrested for threatening the safety of a law enforcement officer.

This scenario, which ended unhappily, illustrates a cross-cultural misunderstanding of a very subtle aspect of culture. According to Edward T. Hall (1966), people adhere to predictable spacial distances when communicating. In other words, how close an individual will get to another while talking is, to a large extent, dictated by one's culture. To illustrate, Hall has found that most middle-class North Americans choose a normal conversational distance of no closer than twenty-two inches from each other's mouth. However, for certain South American and Caribbean cultures (such as Cubans), the distance is approximately fifteen inches, while still other cultures (in the Middle East) maintain a distance of nine to ten inches. These culturally produced spacial patterns are extremely important when communication, or trying to communicate, with culturally different people because they are so subtle, and thus, so frequently overlooked.

The problem that occurred between the Cuban-American and the New York City policeman was that their respective cultures had different ideas about spacial distancing. The Cuban-American was attempting to establish what for him was a comfortable conversational distance of approximately fifteen inches. Unfortunately, the policeman felt threatened because his personal space, as defined by his culture, was being violated. Had either the patrolman or the Cuban-American demonstrator understood this aspect of cultural behavior, the breakdown in communication—and the arrest—could have been avoided.

SOURCE: Taken from G. Ferraro. *Cultural Anthropology: An Applied Perspective.* St. Paul, MN: West, 1992, p. 87.

Critical Review 9

1. Territoriality is the process of claiming exclusive use of areas or objects. T F

2. Public territories such as our homes are those to which we are most attached and protective. T F

3. The second zone of personal space extends from the body to eighteen inches away from the body. T F

4. Feedback between a college lecturer and his or her audience exemplifies interaction at the close phase of the public zone of personal space. T F

5. Crowding is an expression of the amount of physical space available to an individual. T F

6. Crowding is influenced by the desire for privacy. T F

7. Females appear to be more affected by crowding than males. T F

8. What is the difference between territoriality and personal space, and how is each related to human adjustment?

9. How do density and crowding affect human beings?

City Life

Few Americans live in the countryside; most live in or near cities. In fact, many of us have lived our whole lives in an urban environment. Does living in cities influence our thoughts, feelings, and actions? If so, how? In order to answer these questions, we must briefly consider the nature of city life—its characteristics, including advantages and disadvantages.

Freedom and Variety   Two words that immediately come to mind when considering the positive characteristics of cities are *freedom* and *variety*. City dwellers have an enormous amount of personal freedom: freedom in the choice of friends, living and work situations, attire, opinions, schedules, and so on (assuming, of course, that the exercise of such freedoms does not involve transgressing others' rights). Generally, this great latitude in matters of personal choice stems from the fact that cities are large enough to provide substantial anonymity. We can get lost in the crowd, something that is virtually impossible in small towns and villages. Thus, the sheer size of cities provides the basis for great personal freedom.

Variety is also found in abundance in cities—variety in people, jobs, entertainment, architecture, health, educational and social services, and almost every other aspect of human experience. The opportunities for social and cultural stimulation abound.

Stimulation Overload and Lack of Privacy   Cities have drawbacks, too. Perhaps most important among these is the stimulus overload and relative lack of privacy associated with it. When social or psychological stimulation becomes too great, the individual's tendency is to construct filtering devices to reduce its intensity (Milgram, 1970). For example, people may engage in superficial forms of contact or simply ignore others, as when people riding an elevator or subway train stare ahead in silence or read their newspapers rather than interact with one another. Or people may look the other way when they see someone on the sidewalk in need of help.

Factors other than stimulus overload and lack of privacy may also contribute to the cold and unfriendly behavior observed in city dwellers from time to time. For example, one factor that plays a role in situations involving a person in need of help is knowledge of the distressed individual. People tend to help a person in distress only if they know that person (Latané and Darley, 1976). Three other factors are (1) not knowing exactly how to help; (2) assuming that because others are not helping, the distressed person does not have a serious problem; and (3) assuming that because others are present, someone else will provide the required assistance (Latané and Darley, 1976).

Chemical Pollution   Another drawback or disadvantage of city life is increased chemical pollution. Poisonous substances in city water and air have reached levels that are sufficiently high to threaten the health of virtually all city dwellers. For instance, studies reveal a positive correlation between chemical pollutants found in water and heart disease (Evans, 1981). The most common air pollutant, carbon monoxide, is part of industrial smog, auto emissions, and even cigarette smoke. It is a health hazard because it prevents vital organs from receiving an adequate supply of oxygen. High concentrations of carbon monoxide are positively correlated with decreased information-processing skills (Lewis, Baddeley, Bonham, and Lovett, 1970) as well as fatigue, headaches, and epilepsy. Even small doses impair learning ability (Beard and Wertheim, 1967). Another air pollutant, lead, is found in auto fumes. It can lead to hyperactivity and retardation in children (Evans, 1981). Fortunately, recent regulations requiring the use of unleaded gasolines and more stringent auto-emissions standards represent an attempt to deal more effectively with chemical pollution.

Noise Pollution   Unfortunately, there have been few successful attempts to deal with noise pollution, a third disadvantage of city life. City dwellers are exposed to a tremendous array of everyday noises, from the sounds of traffic to sounds made by construction crews, airplanes, and their neighbors' stereo systems. Hardly any of the usual sounds of the city are caused by nature; they are produced by humans and human technology. The noise can be loud; in fact, it can be deafening.

Noise volume is measured in terms of the *decibel* (dB). The point that separates hearing from nonhearing in normal humans is 0 dB. A whisper registers about 30 dB; normal conversation, about 60 dB; very heavy traffic, about 80 dB; and loud thunder, about 120 dB. Close-up listening to typical amplified rock music exposes you to a painful 140 dB level and, if exposed to 150 dB, you might suffer ruptured eardrums. Using a "real-life" example, eight hours of consistent exposure to the 90 dB level (the level of a ride on a New York City subway train) could impair your hearing (Raloff, 1982). However, eight hours of consistent exposure at any level is not necessary to produce hearing loss. All that is necessary is repeated exposure to high decibel levels over time. Thus, prudence dictates that we turn down the volume on our stereo systems and wear earplugs when attending loud concerts.

Noise pollution may contribute to stress, particularly when people experience stimulus overload or a loss of control over environmental stimuli. Research indicates that individuals adjust better when they can control noise or at least predict when it will occur (Glass and Singer, 1972). On the other hand, noise that is uncontrollable or unpredictable leads to a variety of maladjustive behaviors, including an inability to concentrate and reduced tolerance for frustration (Cohen and Weinstein, 1981), learning deficiencies in children (Cohen, Glass, and Singer, 1973), and even a reduced tendency to assist someone in need of help (Matthews and Canon, 1975).

Critical Review 10

1. One way to reduce stimulus overload is to ignore other people. T F

2. City dwellers tend to help a person in distress only if they know him or her. T F

3. High concentrations of carbon monoxide are positively correlated with hyperactivity in children. T F

4. Exposure over time to high decibel levels may lead to hearing loss. T F

5. Uncontrollable noise is positively correlated with the incidence of learning deficiencies in children. T F

6. Discuss the advantages and disadvantages of city life.

SUMMARY

■ All of us belong to several groups. We are born into some groups (e.g., our family); we join others (e.g., a college sorority).

■ We join groups and maintain our membership in them for many reasons, including fulfilling the need for affiliation, confirming a sense of identity, maintaining self-esteem, testing reality, increasing security and a sense of power, and accomplishing tasks.

■ In groups larger than eighteen to twenty members, subgroups often form to allow the warm and intimate contact that is possible in groups of five or less.

■ Group structure, the observable pattern of relationships among group members, is determined by roles, status, norms, and cohesiveness within the group.

■ Society is a self-sufficient and self-perpetuating group that includes persons of both sexes and all ages. Each society has a culture, a way of life that is transmitted from one generation to the next through the process called socialization.

■ Socialization involves not only the unfolding of our physical and mental capacities but significant interaction between us and other members of our society. It is through this interaction that we acquire human nature, a critical prerequisite to developing our human potential.

■ To ensure that important beliefs, values, customs, and social norms are transmitted from one generation to the next, societies channel their transmission through particular social structures called agencies of socialization. Among the important agencies of socialization are the family, subculture, neighborhood, peer group, school, occupational group, and mass media.

■ The life cycle is the general sequence of events in our physical, psychological, and social development as we progress from infancy through old age. Daniel J. Levinson, who has concentrated on adult male development, has identified a life cycle that consists of alternating series of stable (structure-building) periods and transitional (structure-changing) periods. Roger L. Gould, who has focused on the development of both male and female adults, believes there are four major phases of adulthood between ages sixteen and fifty, each with the developmental task of challenging and resolving one of four major false assumptions formed during childhood.

■ Group membership has both advantages and disadvantages. Group pressure may encourage us to take actions, think thoughts, or experience feelings that impede our personal growth. Three results of group membership that may thwart the development of individual potential are deindividuation (giving up individual identity and assuming the group's identity), conformity (behaving in accordance with group norms), and obedience (following the orders of a more powerful person).

■ Social influence is an interaction process in which one person (the source) behaves in a way that causes another person (the target) to change an opinion or act in a manner that is different from what he or she would normally do.

■ Persuasion is a technique of open influence in which the source uses information or argument in an attempt to change the opinion of the target. Four factors determine whether or not the attempt to persuade will be successful: the communicator, the message, the target audience, and the medium through which the message is sent.

■ Threats and promises are two more techniques in which one person tries to influence another to change either opinion or behavior. Bargaining and bilateral threat are techniques used in situations in which both persons may exercise influence.

■ One aspect of the physical environment that exerts a potentially powerful influence on human adjustment is physical space. Of particular concern here are the concepts of territoriality, personal space, density, and crowding.

■ Another important factor of the physical environment for people who live in societies such as ours is city life. Important concepts to consider in this regard are freedom, variety, stimulus overload, lack of privacy, chemical pollution, and noise pollution.

SELECTED READINGS

Aronson, E. *The Social Animal*, 5th ed. New York: Freeman, 1988. An excellent overview of social psychology.

Cialdini, R. B. *Influence: Science and Practice*, 3rd ed. New York: Harper Collins, 1993. A survey of techniques of social influence.

Milgram, S. *Obedience to Authority: An Experimental View*. New York: Harper & Row, 1974. Milgram's classic study of the extent to which people obey authority.

Pratkanis, A. R., and Aronson, E. *Age of Propaganda: The Everyday Use and Abuse of Persuasion*. New York: Freeman, 1991. An examination of how techniques of persuasion are used to manipulate thoughts and attitudes.

Ross, L., and Nisbett, R. E. *The Person and the Situation: Perspectives of Social Psychology*. New York: McGraw-Hill, 1991. An excellent overview of the social self.

Turner, J. C. *Social Influence*. Pacific Grove, CA: Brooks/Cole, 1991. A review of research on social influence and conformity.

REFERENCES

Altman, I. *The Environment and Social Behavior: Privacy, Personal Space, Territory, and Crowding*. Monterey, CA: Brooks/Cole, 1975.

Asch, S. E. "Effects of Group Pressure upon the Modification and Distortion of Judgments." In *Groups, Leadership, and Men*, edited by H. Guetzkow, p. 243–277. Pittsburgh: Carnegie Press, 1951.

_____. "Opinions and Social Pressure." *Scientific American* 193 (1955): 31–35.

_____. "Studies of Independence and Conformity: A Minority of One Against a Unanimous Majority." *Psychological Monographs* 70, p. 1–82, no. 416 (1956).

_____. "An Experimental Investigation of Group Influence." Symposium on Preventive and Social Psychiatry. Walter Reed Army Institute of Research, Washington, DC: U.S. Government Printing Office, 1957.

Atkin, C. K. "Mass Media Information Campaign Effectiveness." In *Public Communication Campaigns*, edited by R. E. Rice and W. J. Paisley, p. 128–141. Beverly Hills, CA: Sage, 1981.

Baron, R. A., Mandel, D., Adams, C., and Griffin, L. "Effects of Social Density in University Residential Environments." *Journal of Personality and Social Psychology* 33 (1976): 434–446.

Bartos, O. J. *Process and Outcome in Negotiation*. New York: Columbia University Press, 1974.

Bauer, R. "The Obstinate Audience: The Influence Process from the Point of View of Social Communication." *American Psychologist* 19 (1964): 319–328.

Baum, A., and Greenberg, C. "Waiting for a Crowd: The Behavioral and Perceptual Effects of Anticipated Crowding." *Journal of Personality and Social Psychology* 32 (1975): 667–671.

Beard, R. R., and Wertheim, C. A. "Behavioral Impairment Associated with Small Doses of Carbon Monoxide." *American Journal of Public Health* 57 (1967): 2012–2022.

Benham, T. W. "Polling for a Presidential Candidate: Some Observations of the 1964 Campaign." *Public Opinion Quarterly* 29 (1965): 185–199.

Berne, E. *Games People Play*. New York: Grove Press, 1964.

Boulding, K. E. *Ecodynamics: A New Theory of Societal Evolution*. Beverly Hills, CA: Sage, 1981.

Byrne, D., Baskett, C. D., and Hodges, L. "Behavioral Indicators of Interpersonal Attraction." *Journal of Abnormal and Social Psychology* 81 (1971): 137–149.

Calhoun, J. B. "Population Density and Social Pathology." *Scientific American* 206 (1962): 139–148.

Chaiken, S. "Communicator Physical Attractiveness and Persuasion." *Journal of Personality and Social Psychology* 37 (1979): 1387–1397.

Cohen, S., Glass, D. C., and Singer, J. E. "Apartment Noise, Auditory Discrimination, and Reading Ability in Children." *Journal of Experimental Social Psychology* 9 (1973): 407–422.

Cohen, S., and Weinstein, N. "Nonauditory Effects of Noise on Behavior and Health." *Journal of Social Issues* 37–1 (1981): 36–70.

Davis, K. *Human Society*. New York: Macmillan, 1949.

Deutsch, M., and Krauss, R. M. "The Effect of Threats upon Interpersonal Bargaining." *Journal of Abnormal and Social Psychology* 61 (1960): 181–189.

_____. "Studies in Interpersonal Bargaining." *Journal of Conflict Resolution* 6 (1962): 52–76.

Diener, E. "Deindividuation: The Absence of Self-Awareness and Self-Regulation in Group Members." In *The Psychology of Group Influence*, edited by P. B. Paulus. Hillsdale, NJ: Erlbaum, 1980.

Eagly, A. H., and Warren, R. "Intelligence, Comprehension, and Opinion Change." *Journal of Personality* 44 (1976): 226–242.

Edney, J. J. "Territoriality and Control: A Field Experiment." *Journal of Personality and Social Psychology* 31 (1975): 1108–1115.

Elkin, F., and Handel, G. *The Child and Society: The Process of Socialization*, 4th ed. New York: Random House, 1984.

Epstein, Y. M. "Crowding Stress and Human Behavior." *Journal of Social Issues* 37–1 (1981): 126–144.

Evans, G. W. "Environmental Stress." *Journal of Social Issues* 37–1 (1981): 201–223.

Faley, T., and Tedeschi, J. T. "Status and Reactions to Threats." *Journal of Personality and Social Psychology* 17 (1971): 192–199.

Filley, A. C. *Interpersonal Conflict Resolution*. Glenview, IL: Scott, Foresman, 1975.

Freedman, J. L. *Crowding and Behavior*. San Francisco: Freeman, 1975.

French, J. R. P., Jr., Morrison, H. W., and Levinger, G. "Coercive Power and Forces Affecting Conformity." *Journal of Abnormal and Social Psychology* 61 (1960): 93–101.

Gerard, H. B., Wilhelmy, R. A., and Conolley, E. S. "Conformity and Group Size." *Journal of Personality and Social Psychology* 8 (1968): 79–82.

Glass, D. C., and Singer, J. E. *Urban Stress: Experiments on Noise and Social Stressors*. New York: Academic Press, 1972.

Gould, R. L. *The Hidden Dimension*. New york: Doubleday, 1966.

_____. *Transformations: Growth and Change in Adult Life*. New York: Simon and Schuster, 1978.

Hall, E. T. *The Silent Language*. New York: Fawcett, 1959.

Heckel, R. V., and Hiers, J. M. "Social Distance and Locus of Control." *Journal of Clinical Psychology* 33 (1977): 469–471.

Hutt, C., and Vaizey, M. J. "Differential Effects of Group Density on Social Behavior." *Nature* 209 (1966): 1371–1372.

Jaccard, J. "Toward Theories of Persuasion and Belief Change." *Journal of Personality and Social Psychology* 40 (1981): 260–269.

Karlins, M., and Abelson, H. I. *How Opinions and Attitudes Are Changed*, 2nd ed. New York: Springer, 1970.

Kilham, W., and Mann, L. "Level of Destructive Obedience as a Function of Transmitter and Executant Roles in the Milgram Obedience Paradigm." *Journal of Personality and Social Psychology* 29 (1974): 696–702.

Kohn, M. L. *Class and Conformity*. Homewood, IL: Dorsey, 1969.

Latané, B., and Darley, J. M. "Help in a Crisis: Bystander Response to an Emergency." In *Contemporary Topics in Social Psychology*, edited by J. W. Thibaut, J. T. Spence, and R. C. Carson, pp. 328–344. Morristown, NJ: General Learning Press, 1976.

Levinson, D. J. *The Seasons of a Man's Life.* New York: Ballantine, 1978.

Lewis, J., Baddeley, A. D., Bonham, K. G., and Lovett, D. "Traffic Pollution and Mental Efficiency." *Nature* 225 (1970): 96.

Lewis, S. A., Langan, C. J., and Hollander, E. P. "Expectation of Future Interaction and the Choice of Less Desirable Alternatives in Conformity." *Sociometry* 35 (1972): 440–447.

Maddux, J. E., and Rogers, R. W. "Effects of Source Expertness, Physical Attractiveness, and Supporting Arguments on Persuasion: A Case of Brains over Beauty." *Journal of Personality and Social Psychology* 39 (1980): 234–244.

Matthews, K. E., and Canon, L. K. "Environmental Noise Level as a Determinant of Helping Behavior." *Journal of Personality and Social Psychology* 32 (1975): 571–577.

McGuire, W. J. "Attitude Change: The Information-Processing Paradigm." In *Experimental Social Psychology,* edited by C. G. McClintock. New York: Holt, Rinehart and Winston, 1972.

Mehrabian, A., and Ksionzky, S. "Models for Affiliative and Conformity Behavior." *Psychological Bulletin* 74 (1970): 110–126.

Mendelsohn, H. "Some Reasons Why Information Campaigns Can Succeed." *Public Opinion Quarterly* 37 (1973): 50–61.

Mendoza, M. G., and Napoli, V. *Systems of Society: An Introduction to Social Science,* 6th ed. Lexington, MA: D.C. Heath, 1995.

Michener, H. A., and Burt, M. R. "Use of Social Influence under Varying Conditions of Legitimacy." *Journal of Personality and Social Psychology* 32 (1975): 398–407.

Michener, H. A., DeLamater, J., and Schwartz, S. H. *Social Psychology.* New York: Harcourt Brace Jovanovich, 1986.

Milgram, S. "Behavioral Study of Obedience." *Journal of Abnormal and Social Psychology* 67 (1963): 371–378.

_____. "The Experience of Living in Cities." *Science* 167 (1970): 1461–1468.

_____. "Liberating Effects of Group Pressure." *Journal of Personality and Social Psychology* 1 (1965b): 127–134.

_____. *Obedience to Authority: An Experimental View.* New York: Harper & Row, 1974.

_____. "Some Conditions of Obedience and Disobedience to Authority." *Human Relations* 18 (1965a): 57–76.

Morley, I. E., and Stephenson, G. M. *The Social Psychology of Bargaining.* London: Allen and Unwin, 1977.

Pepitone, A., and Kleiner, R., "The Effects of Threat and Frustration on Group Cohesiveness." *Journal of Abnormal and Social Psychology* 54 (1957): 192–199.

Petty, R. E., Cacioppo, J. T., and Goldman, R. "Personal Involvement as a Determinant of Argument-Based Persuasion." *Journal of Personality and Social Psychology* 41 (1981): 847–855.

Plunkett, W. R. *Supervision: The Direction of People at Work.* Dubuque, IA: William C. Brown, 1975.

Porteous, J. D. *Environment and Behavior.* Reading, MA: Addison-Wesley, 1977.

Pruitt, D. G. *Negotiation Behavior.* New York: Academic Press, 1981.

Raloff, J. "Occupational Noise—The Subtle Pollutant." *Science News* 121–21 (1982): 347–350.

Rhine, R. J., and Severance, L. J. "Ego-Involvement, Discrepancy, Source Credibility, and Attitude Change." *Journal of Personality and Social Psychology* 16 (1970): 175–190.

Rodin, J. "Density, Perceived Choice, and Response to Controllable and Uncontrollable Outcomes." *Journal of Experimental Social Psychology* 12 (1976): 564–578.

Rodin, J., and Baum, A. "Crowding and Helplessness: Potential Consequences of Density and Loss of Control." In *Human Response to Crowding,* edited by A. Baum and Y. Epstein, pp. 176–192. Hillsdale, NJ: Erlbaum, 1978.

Roethlisberger, F. J. "The Administrator's Skill." *Harvard Business Review* 91 (December 1953): 61.

Rosenberg, L. A. "Group Size, Prior Experience, and Conformity." *Journal of Abnormal and Social Psychology* 63 (1961): 436–437.

Sawyer, A. "The Effects of Repetition of Refutational and Supportive Advertising Appeals." *Journal of Marketing Research* 10 (1973): 23–33.

_____. Organizational Psychology, 2nd ed. Englewood Cliffs, NJ: Prentice-Hall, 1970.

Sears, D. O., and Freedman, J. L. "Selective Exposure to Information: A Critical Review." *Public Opinion Quarterly* 31 (1967): 194–213.

Smith, W. P., and Anderson, A. "Threats, Communication, and Bargaining." *Journal of Personality and Social Psychology* 32 (1975): 76–82.

Stang, D. J. "Conformity, Ability, and Self-Esteem." *Representative Research in Social Psychology* 3 (1972): 97–103.

Stokols, D., Rall, M., Pinner, B., and Schopler, J. "Physical, Social and Personal Determinants of the Perception of Crowding." *Environment and Behavior* 5 (1973): 87–110.

Sundstrom, E. "Crowding as a Sequential Process: Review of Research on the Effects of Population Density on Humans." In *Human Response to Crowding,* edited by A. Baum and Y. Epstein, p. 53–91. Hillsdale, NJ: Erlbaum, 1978.

Tedeschi, J. T., Schlenker, B. R., and Lindskold, S. "The Exercise of Power and Influence: The Source of Influence." In *The Social Influence Process,* edited by J. Tedeschi, p. 182–209. Chicago: Aldine-Atherton, 1972.

Theodorson, G. "Elements in the Progressive Development of Small Groups." *Social Forces* 31 (1953): 311–320.

Wall, J. A., Jr. "Intergroup Bargaining: Effects of Opposing Constituent's Stance, Opposing Representative's Bargaining, and Representatives' Locus of Control." *Journal of Conflict Resolution* 21 (1977): 459–474.

Walster, E., Aronson, E., and Abrahams, D. "On Increasing the Persuasiveness of a Low-Prestige Communicator." *Journal of Experimental Social Psychology* 2 (1966): 325–342.

Williams, T. R. *Introduction to Socialization: Human Culture Transmitted.* St. Louis: Mosby, 1972.

Worchel, S., and Cooper, J. *Understanding Social Psychology.* Homewood, IL: Dorsey, 1979.

Yukl, G. A. "Effects of Situational Variables and Opponent Concessions on a Bargainer's Perception, Aspirations, and Concessions." *Journal of Personality and Social Psychology* 30 (1974): 323–335.

Zimbardo, P. G. "The Human Choice: Individuation, Reason and Order versus Deindividuation, Impulse and Chaos." In *Nebraska Symposium on Motivation, 1969*, edited by W. J. Arnold and D. Levine, pp. 135–164. Lincoln, NE: University of Nebraska Press, 1970.

_____. "On Transforming Experimental Research into Advocacy for Social Change." In *Applying Social Psychology: Implications for Research, Practice and Training*, edited by M. Deutsch and H. Hornstein, pp. 46–60. Hillsdale, NJ: Erlbaum, 1975.

■ *Questionnaire Scoring Key*

Social Approval

To figure your score: Circle all the answers in the scoring key that agree with your responses. Add the number of circled answers and place the total on the following line.

1. T.   **2.** T.   **3.** T.   **4.** F.   **5.** T.   **6.** T.   **7.** F.   **8.** F.   **9.** T.   **10.** F.   **11.** T.   **12.** T.   **13.** T.   **14.** F.   **15.** T.   **16.** T.   **17.** F.   **18.** F.   **19.** F.   **20.** T.

Interpretation: If your score is 15 or higher, you probably have a strong need for social approval.

■ *Answers to Review Questions*

Critical Review 1   **1.** F.   **2.** T.   **3.** T.   **4.** F.   **5.** T.   **6.** F.   **7.** F.   **8.** T.   **9.** F.   **10.** T.   **11.** T.   **12.** F.

Critical Review 2   **1.** T.   **2.** F.   **3.** T.   **4.** T.   **5.** T.   **6.** T.   **7.** F.   **8.** T.

Critical Review 3   **1.** T.   **2.** F.   **3.** F.   **4.** T.   **5.** F.

Critical Review 4   **1.** T.   **2.** F.   **3.** T.   **4.** F.   **5.** F.   **6.** T.   **7.** T.   **8.** F.

Critical Review 5   **1.** F.   **2.** T.   **3.** T.   **4.** T.   **5.** F.   **6.** F.

Critical Review 6   **1.** T.   **2.** T.   **3.** T.

Critical Review 7   **1.** F.   **2.** T.   **3.** T.   **4.** F.   **5.** F.   **6.** F.   **7.** T.

Critical Review 8   **1.** F.   **2.** T.   **3.** T.   **4.** F.   **5.** T.   **6.** T.   **7.** F.

Critical Review 9   **1.** T.   **2.** F.   **3.** F.   **4.** T.   **5.** F.   **6.** T.   **7.** F.

Critical Review 10   **1.** T.   **2.** T.   **3.** F.   **4.** T.   **5.** T.

PERSONAL ACTION PLAN
Understanding Yourself

The exercises in the Personal Action Plan on personality description in chapter 2 helped you to become more aware of your personality. The exercises in this Personal Action Plan are designed to provide a more complete description of who you are so that you can begin to make some judgments about yourself.

Both the past and the present play significant roles in the emerging future. In order to gain greater understanding of your emerging self, it is important to focus both on aspects of your personal past and on your present functioning. The first few exercises, dealing with beliefs and values, focus on both.

I. Directions.

Below are five areas within which you hold a number of beliefs. For each area there are two incomplete sentences. Think about your most fundamental beliefs in each area. Then complete the sentences by filling in your beliefs.

Example: A person who has learned to value equality might write:

Political

1. I believe that democracy is *the best form of government*.

Belief Area

Anesthetic

1. I believe that people are creative because

2. I believe that the purpose of art is

Economic

1. I believe that economic competition is

2. I believe that government regulation of the economy is

Political

1. I believe that power should reside in

2. I believe that the best way to resolve conflict is

Religious

1. I believe that God is

2. I believe the greatest sin is

Social

1. I believe you can identify a person's social class by

2. I believe the easiest way to achieve social status is by

II. Directions.

Now that you have clearly identified some of your fundamental beliefs, let's see where they came from. Below is a matrix designed to help you. Consider each belief and the social structure from which it came. Then, place an X in the appropriate cell.

	Home	Peers	School	Occupation	Mass Media	Other
Aesthetic 1.						
Aesthetic 2.						
Economic 1.						
Economic 2.						
Political 1.						
Political 2.						
Religious 1.						
Religious 2.						
Social 1.						
Social 2.						

Study the matrix carefully. Then write short answers to the following questions

a. Are there any patterns you can identify?

b. Do any particular social structures seem to be more influential than others in the formation of your fundamental beliefs? Why or why not?

c. Who were the significant people who taught you these beliefs?

III. Directions.

Concentrate on your values. Each time a value comes clearly into focus, write that value in one of the following spaces. Example: Honesty.

Scan your list of values and determine which is most important to you. Then write that value in space 1 below. Determine which of the remaining values on your list is most important to you and write that value in space 2 below. Continue this process until you have rank-ordered all the values on your list.

1.	5.	9.	13.	17.
2.	6.	10.	14.	18.
3.	7.	11.	15.	19.
4.	8.	12.	16.	20.

Consider each value and the social structure from which it came. Then fill in the matrix below by writing each value, together with its rank-order number, in the appropriate cell.

Home	Peers	School	Occupation	Mass Media	Other

Study the matrix carefully. Then write short answers to the following questions:

a. Are there any patterns you can identify?

b. Do any particular social structures seem to be more influential than others in the formation of your values? Why or why not?

c. Who were the significant people who taught you these values?

The exercises so far in the Personal Action Plan have helped you to identify some of your fundamental beliefs and values, and to identify where they came from. Now it will be most useful for you to focus on your self-concept.

IV. Directions.

Consider the way you think about yourself with regard to each area listed. Then complete the sentences for each area by filling in your thoughts about yourself.

Physical: I am _____
            I am _____
            I am _____
Social: I am _____
            I am _____
            I am _____
Emotional: I am _____
            I am _____
            I am _____
Intellectual: I am _____
            I am _____
            I am _____
Spiritual: I am _____
            I am _____
            I am _____

Ethical: I am _____
            I am _____
            I am _____

Below are duplicates of the exercise you have just completed. Ask two people who know you at least fairly well to provide their thoughts about you by completing the exercise and discussing their responses with you (Do not allow them to see each other's answers.) Then compare their responses with your own.

Person 1

Physical: I am _____
             I am _____
             I am _____
Social: I am _____
             I am _____
             I am _____
Emotional: I am _____
             I am _____
             I am _____
Intellectual: I am _____
             I am _____
             I am _____
Spiritual: I am _____
             I am _____
             I am _____
Ethical: I am _____
             I am _____
             I am _____

Person 2

Physical: I am _____
             I am _____
             I am _____
Social: I am _____
             I am _____
             I am _____
Emotional: I am _____
             I am _____
             I am _____
Intellectual: I am _____
             I am _____
             I am _____
Spiritual: I am _____
             I am _____
             I am _____
Ethical: I am _____
             I am _____
             I am _____

Having completed this Personal Action Plan, you should be developing a greater awareness of who you are and of the significant people, situations, and experiences that have helped mold you into who you are.

PART THREE

ADJUSTMENT AND GROWTH IN INTERPERSONAL RELATIONSHIPS

P art III explores two of the most important factors affecting the adjustment and growth of nearly everyone—intimacy and communication.

Chapter 9 focuses on our need for intimacy and on how we can successfully meet this important need. It explores ways in which we can increase our capacity for finding satisfying intimacy. It also discusses the effects of role conflicts, value conflicts, social pressures, loneliness, and romantic ideals on our success in establishing intimate relationships.

Chapter 10 explores the processes of communicating and understanding through verbal and nonverbal means. It discusses skills (sending and receiving messages) and styles of communication, as well as barriers to communicating effectively. Many people believe that ineffective communication is the major cause of interpersonal problems within relationships, within the family, at work, at school, and between nations.

Chapter Outline

FOCUS

The need for intimacy is one of our strongest needs. Maslow (1968) indicates that achieving deep intimacy is essential for us to become self-actualizing and fulfilled. Yet, our confusion about love and intimacy often result in feelings of alienation, which psychotherapists believe is the most prevalent problem of our time.

The need for intimacy is recognized by TV, radio, magazine, and billboard advertisers. We are supposed to buy the toothpaste with "sex appeal." Our deodorant should make us smell like a "real" woman or a "real" man and should hold up under the stresses of everyday life. Perfumes and colognes are supposed to contain secret formulas intended to make us irresistible to potential romantic partners. Some of us even find ourselves taking ocean cruises or flying to exotic places where we hope to find, at last, that special person awaiting us with open arms.

The pursuit of intimacy is clearly one of our most important human undertakings. Because we place such great importance on intimacy, we may often experience fear of failure when attempting to achieve it.

SOURCES FOR INTIMACY

Our need for intimacy would go unmet were it not for other people. We are often the recipients of their expressions of intimacy, and we learn to model the behavior they use to find intimacy with others. Throughout life our major sources of intimacy are family, friends, pets, and marriage or cohabitation.

Family Intimacy

Intimate contact ideally is found within the family unit. Newborn infants are totally dependent on adults (usually parents) for physical and emotional survival. Their physical needs are usually met with great care. Most children in our society grow up with proper nutrition and exercise. Monitoring the quality of this care is relatively easy for parents and others. Less obvious is the quality of care focused on emotional growth. Children need a warm, loving, touching, and stable environment. This means that the healthy, successful family provides opportunities for physical and emotional closeness for the infant.

There seems to be an increasing awareness of the importance of intimacy in the rearing of children. Organizations such as the Parent Effectiveness Training Program offer valuable assistance for parents and prospective parents. Throughout the country, various schools, YMCAs and YWCAs, and other agencies teach parents and children together how to make their relationships more effective and fulfilling.

The maintenance of close social bonds, the formation of gender identification, and the acceptance and adoption of sex roles are important provisions of the family. Our experiences in the family are extremely important to our future success with significant intimate relationships.

Single-Parent Families   Many people think of the term *family* to mean a mother, father, and at least one child. However, the *single-parent* family is on the increase. Single-parent families headed by women increased by 25 percent from 1980 to 1988 (U.S. Census Bureau, 1990). A study by census analyst Amara Bachu examined women between the ages of 18 and 44 who had never married (see Figure 9–1). By 1992, 24 percent had become mothers, up from 15 percent a decade ago (DeParle, 1994). A group called Parents Without Partners has been formed for those who have become single parents either through divorce or the

The family is our greatest potential source of love and intimacy.

death of a spouse. The practice of single parenting among women has become so popular that such mothers have formed a national group called Single Mothers By Choice (American Broadcasting Corporation, 1987). The group is for single women with children and single women who are hoping to have children. According to the U.S. Census Bureau, three out of five children in the last half of the 1980s spent at least part of their lives in a single-parent home. With financial security and a support group it appears that the most significant problem these children may face is uncertainty about the missing parent. If given a choice between a single parent who provides love and intimacy and two parents without love and intimacy, a child fares better in a single-parent family. However, most social science research indicates that children in single-parent families do tend to have more educational, financial, and emotional problems than those

CRITICAL THINKING ISSUE
Romance and Intimacy

Romance, intimacy, and marriage are the keys to achieving the ultimately satisfying love relationship.

Romance, intimacy, and long-term love relationships are more myths than realities.

Many believe a satisfying love relationship is one of the greatest achievements of life. More energy is expended in the pursuit of romance, intimacy, and marriage than in any of life's other goals. Most people experience, at least partly, the joys that accompany the process of meeting our needs for love and belonging.

Although a desirable and necessary achievement, intimacy is severely hampered by the other pursuits of life. The daily responsibilities of work and survival leave little energy or time for developing truly satisfying relationships. The news of broken relationships outweighs the news of harmonious ones. It appears life has some trade-offs. Lasting intimacy may be one of them.

I take the position that:

raised by two parents (DeParle, 1994). These tendencies seem to be supported by the Census Bureau data contained in Figure 9–1. Women with the least amount of education are the ones most likely to be single-parents.

Another type of single-parent family is on the increase as a result of dramatic changes in rates of teenage pregnancies. The consequences of teenage pregnancy are discussed later in the section "Sexual Responsibility."

Friendships

We have numerous opportunities to establish satisfying, need-fulfilling friendships. We would be overlooking a great source of interpersonal stimulation if we restricted our contact to our parents and siblings, our spouse, or the person with whom we are living. Friendships offer us the opportunity to grow and share in the experiences and lifestyles of others. Friendships provide us with variety that may improve the quality of our lives in many respects. They also help us meet some of the needs that our families or partners may be unable or unwilling to fulfill.

Some people have little need for friends either as a result of their personality or as a result of their needs being met by family or nonsocial interests. On the other hand, some people may choose to have all of their needs for intimacy met by friends. Many people neither marry nor cohabit; they are satisfied to live alone and interact daily with their friends. This may be a satisfying alternative for meeting needs for intimacy.

Attraction   Psychologists have identified some general factors that influence most people's attraction to others. People tend to like others who:

■ Are likable, are physically attractive, have pleasant personalities, and are competent.

FIGURE 9–1
Never Married, With Children Percentage of Never-Married Women Age 18–44 Who Have Children

SOURCE: Census Bureau; Reported in The New York Times, July 14, 1993.

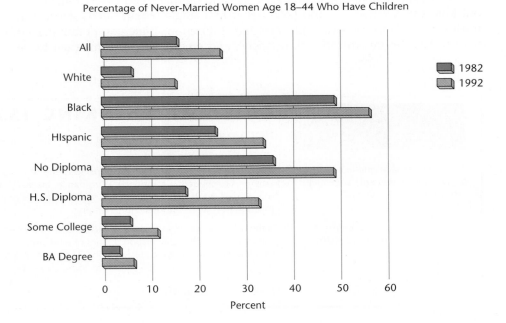

Percentage of Never-Married Women Age 18–44 Who Have Children

- Live close to them and are available.
- Like them, do favors for them, and praise them.
- Are similar in attitudes, interests, and personality.
- In many cases, are "complementary"—possess characteristics that seem to go nicely with theirs.

Living in the same neighborhood, enrolling in the same classes in college, working for the same company, participating in the same community project, and attending the same church are examples of the numerous conditions under which individuals come in contact. The friendships formed under such conditions illustrate the principle of **propinquity,** which holds that social ties tend to form among those who share a common physical location and who have had the opportunity to interact with each other over an extended period of time.

propinquity the principle that social ties tend to form among those who share a common physical location and who have had the opportunity to interact with each other over an extended period of time

Characteristics of Friendship   In addition to the factors that cause people to be attracted to each other, other factors are involved in friendship. According to Steven Duck (1983), "Friendships do not just happen; they have to be made—made to start, made to work, made to develop, kept in good working order, and preserved from going sour" (p. 9). *Psychology Today* surveyed people to determine what they believed were the qualities of their friends that helped the friendships develop and grow (Rubenstein and Shaver, 1982). The findings revealed that people value the following qualities in their friends: the ability to keep confidences, loyalty, warmth and affection, supportiveness, and frankness. "In the few weeks prior to the survey, each of the respondents had an intimate talk with a friend, asked for a favor, or were asked to do one, and had shared a meal with a friend" (p. 109).

Pets

Many consider pets as substitutes for intimacy not received from other human beings; however, surveys and studies seem to indicate that pets are more than substitutes. The claim that a dog is a person's best friend may not be far from the truth. Cain (1985) reports that in a survey of 896 families, 68 percent thought that pets were full family members; 30 percent said they were close friends, and 96 percent described the pet's role in the family as important.

Pets provide us with unconditional love; they ask no questions and tell us no lies. Morris (1971) sees our loving attachment to animals as encouraging. Our tenderness toward animals reveals that we are capable of such behavior. It also serves as a constant reminder that the human animal, when not warped by what must paradoxically be called the savageries of civilization, is fundamentally endowed with great potential for tenderness and intimacy. The importance of a pet has been documented further by Carmack (1985), who found that the death of a pet was equal to the death of a family member. This event disrupts the family function and may establish a similar need for counseling to deal effectively with the loss.

A study of the interaction between children and dogs revealed that such interaction can play a significant role in the development of the child by enhancing social and emotional development (Filiatre, Millot, and Montagne, 1986). In his book, *Pet-Oriented Child Psychotherapy,* Boris Levinson (1969) documents case after case in which having a pet in the room enhanced the therapeutic process and helped the young client to see him as more trustworthy. Isaacs and Soares

(1987) state that people who had pets as children seem to have higher self-esteem as adults, a conclusion based on a limited sample's responses when asked to express feelings about themselves on the Minnesota Multiphasic Personality Inventory.

In their book *Between Pets and People: The Importance of Animal Companionship*, researchers Aaron Katcher and Alan Beck (1984) reported that 80 percent of the people interviewed said they believed their dogs were sensitive to their feelings. A third of those interviewed said that they confided in their dogs, showing an unconscious belief that the animals could understand them. The authors found also that this relationship has a calming effect on the nervous system of the owner and reduces blood pressure. This "seems to help people live longer and apparently can reduce the number of deaths from heart attacks" (Pothier, 1984). Further, regularly walking a dog provides exercise for the owner and also aids in the management of stress (Friedman and Thomas, 1985). The results of these studies have prompted some operators of animal shelters to provide animals to homes for the elderly.

Marital Intimacy

Marriage ideally can provide most of our needs for intimacy. It has many untapped potentialities for those who are willing to learn and grow together toward the fulfillment of their individual and mutual needs. Each of us has a powerful longing for a meaningful relationship with at least one other person. This longing, either conscious or unconscious, is often felt as loneliness, which can only be relieved by the interpersonal satisfaction derived from an intimate relationship. Marriage is intended to be an intimate relationship in which we have the opportunity to share our entire life with another person.

The permanency of marriage to one mate or the reliance on one mate for a lifetime, a belief inherited from Judeo-Christian tradition, appears for some to be rapidly becoming a thing of the past. To believe that one person can provide us with all we need for the development of self-esteem, intimacy, and personal growth may seem quite unrealistic to some. Further, to believe that every individual should stay attached emotionally and physically to another for a lifetime regardless of needs and growth may suggest that people are static and do not change. On the contrary, we know that people do change and have the capacity to do so throughout their lives. We also know that two people can choose to grow and change together for a lifetime and continue to meet each other's needs. Success in marriage greatly depends on the value we place on ourselves, our partners, and the concept of marriage. Those of us who do not value marriage highly will tend to discard it and our partners, as we do many other things that lose their appeal or develop problems. Those of us who view marriage as one of our highest-priority values will expend great effort in finding suitable marital partners and in maintaining a satisfying union with those partners.

In our culture, we are fortunate that we are free to choose mates that we believe to be emotionally compatible with us. In some other cultures, people do not have this freedom and often must learn to adjust to partners in *arranged marriages*, marriages that are arranged by other family members (see "Cultural Crosscurrents: Arranged Marriages").

cohabitation an arrangement in which people who are emotionally and physically involved live together without being married

Alternatives to Marriage

There are some alternatives to marriage. **Cohabitation** (living together as mates without being legally married) is quite common in our society among all age

CULTURAL CROSSCURRENTS
Arranged Marriages

In Western societies, with their strong value on individualism, mate selection is largely a decision made jointly by the prospective bride and groom. Aimed at satisfying the emotional and sexual needs of the individual, the choice of mates in Western society is based on such factors as physical attractiveness, emotional compatibility, and romantic love. Even though absolute freedom of choice is constrained by such factors as social class, ethnicity, religion and race, individuals in most contemporary Western societies are relatively free to marry whomever they please.

In many societies, however, the interests of the families are so strong that marriages are arranged. Negotiations are handled by family members of the prospective bride and groom, and for all practical purposes, the decision of whom one will marry is made by one's parents or other influential family members. In certain cultures, such as parts of traditional Japan, India, and China, future marriage partners are betrothed while they are still children. In one extreme example—the Tiwi of North Australia—females are betrothed or promised as future wives *before* they are born (Hart and Pilling, 1960: 14). Since the Tiwi believe that females are liable to become impregnated by spirits at any time, the only sensible precaution against unmarried mothers is to betroth female babies before birth or as soon as they are born.

All such cases of arranged marriages, wherever they may be found, are based on the cultural assumption that since marriage is a union of two kin groups rather than merely two individuals, it is far too significant an institution to be based on something as frivolous as physical attractiveness or romantic love.

SOURCE: G. Ferrard, *Cultural Anthropology: An Applied Perspective.* St. Paul, MN: West Publishing Co., 1992.

groups (see Figure 9–2). The acceptance of cohabitation has no doubt been aided by Robert H. Rimmer's novel *The Harrad Experiment* (1966). When it was published, this novel was the talk of sociologists, psychologists, and educators and a cause of concern for many parents. Rimmer advocated experimental cohabitation as part of the curriculum of higher education. He suggested that men and women could best learn about intimacy by experimentally living together. The U.S. Census Bureau (1990) reported that as of 1988 there were approximately 2,600,000 unmarried couples living together, five times the number estimated in 1970. The largest increase was in the group between age twenty-five and forty-four. This group increased nearly sixteen times during the same period.

Jennifer and Scott had been dating since their senior year in high school. Upon graduation, they applied for admission to the same colleges, hoping that at least one college would accept both of them. Their hopes were realized and they went away to college together. The college they attended required all freshman students to live on campus in dormitories. After the first year, students were permitted to live off campus and were even encouraged to do so because of limited campus housing. Scott and Jennifer often discussed their future living arrangements, and increasingly so as the freshman year came to a close. Many freshman couples had decided to live together the following year, a decision that Jennifer began to favor. Scott wanted to live with Jennifer but was afraid of what his parents might say. Jennifer thought her parents would understand, as she and Scott had been dating for more than two years. The decision became a source of conflict between them.

Finally, Scott agreed to the living arrangement but only if neither of their parents were told about it. Jennifer wanted to tell her parents, but Scott was afraid they might tell his parents. Before they left for summer break, Jennifer and Scott arranged to rent a small, one-bedroom apartment near campus. Scott decided he would tell his parents that he was going to live off campus in an apartment with other men, and Jennifer agreed to tell her parents she was going to live off campus with women friends.

In the fall, Scott and Jennifer moved into the apartment, arriving a week before school to buy the necessary items to set up housekeeping. They found living

FIGURE 9–2

Unmarried Couples Living Together

SOURCE: U.S. Census Bureau, *Statistical Abstract of the United States, 1990.*

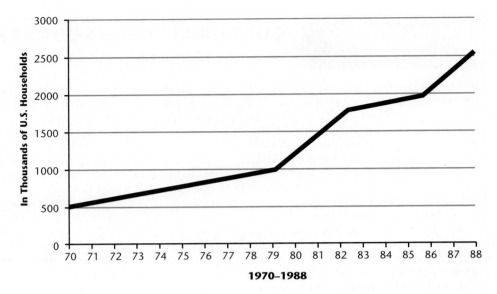

together even better than they had imagined it would be. In fact, it was so satisfying, they had to remind themselves constantly that they were still students and had to force themselves to study.

One afternoon in November, while on a business trip, Scott's father made an unplanned four-hour stop in the city where Scott and Jennifer went to college. He decided to surprise Scott by dropping in unannounced and inviting him to dinner. Stunned at the sight of his father at his apartment door, Scott blurted out his secret. Fortunately, to the surprise of both Jennifer and Scott, his father intimated that he had wondered for some time why they had not decided to live together. In fact, it had been a topic of conversation at least once between him and Scott's mother. As they discussed it further, it became apparent to Scott that the thought of living with Jennifer without being married was more uncomfortable for him than for his parents.

Living together seldom is permanent. Most couples either break up or get married (Bower and Christopherson, 1977). Indeed, some couples view cohabitating as a trial marriage. If it works out for a specified time, they get married. However, when referring to couples who lived together before getting married, people often remark, "Now that they are married, they hate each other." It may appear that these couples should have continued to cohabit instead of ruining a good thing by getting married. But this dissatisfaction with marriage may not be the result of living together, say sociologists Alfred Demaris and Gerald Leslie (1984). It may be that the type of people who decide to live together before marriage are poorly suited for marriage in the first place. Demaris and Leslie interviewed 309 recently married couples about their marital satisfaction and found that those who had lived together were less likely than others to be satisfied with their marriages. The researchers believe that this may be the case for several reasons, among them the following: (1) because the couples lived together before marrying, they may expect more from the marriage from the beginning; (2) they may adapt less readily to the role expectations of marriage; and (3) they are probably the least likely to conform to traditional marriage conventions.

Some couples, though, see cohabitating as a permanent alternative to marriage. They are extremely critical of the traditional and constraining laws regarding marriage. These couples plan to remain unmarried, yet they often write their own unique contracts to ensure an equal relationship.

Responsibility in Intimate Relationships For years it appeared that the only responsibility cohabiting people had toward each other was responsibility based on personal agreement. In the mid-1970s a few court cases broke with tradition and awarded **meretricious spouses** (intentionally unmarried persons living together as if married) property at the termination of their relationship. One famous case in April 1979 involved the actor Lee Marvin, who was sued for *palimony* (alimony granted to people not legally married) by Michelle Triola, the woman he had lived with for six and a half years. The court ruled that Triola should be paid $100,000 in alimony. Since that time, several other such suits have been brought with similar results. It would appear that although cohabitation does not have all the legal complexities of marriage, it does have some.

meretricious spouses intentionally unmarried persons living together as if married

Even though cohabitation is a viable alternative for some couples, many believe that when a couple wants to have children, marriage is the best alternative. A survey of 1,191 college students showed that only 12 believed children should be reared outside of marriage (Bower and Christopherson, 1977).

Some couples may want to stay married and still have physically and emotionally intimate relationships with others outside the marriage. Whether this sort of relationship can be functional, however, depends on the couple choosing it. Two anthropologists, Nena and George O'Neill (1972), suggest in their book *Open Marriage: A New Life for Couples* that each member of a married couple can have relationships—even sexual relationships—with persons outside the marriage. Such relationships can be accepted and even encouraged as a normal part of a stable marriage. Unlike the traditional "closed marriage," the open marriage replaces "ownership of the mate with independent living, denial of self with personal growth, possessiveness with individual freedom, rigid role behavior with flexible roles, absolute fidelity with mutual trust, and total exclusivity with expansion through openness" (p. 46). Contrary to the belief that love, sex, and jealousy go hand in hand, there is no place for the learned response of jealousy in the open marriage. Although the O'Neills have put forth an intriguing concept of marriage, there is presently no evidence to substantiate the success of such marriages.

Of all the relationship options discussed here, it appears that marriage is still a viable choice. In the survey by Campbell (1975), married people reported greater life satisfaction than single, divorced, or widowed people. From this we can infer that marriage is still a strong institution in our society.

Critical Review 1

1. Friends, initially, are the major sources of intimate contact. T F

2. The practice of single parenting among women is on the increase, both by choice and by necessity. T F

3. The principle of propinquity holds that we tend to form friendships among those who share our immediate environment. T or F

4. Although thought to be substitutes for intimacy by some, pets have been used by psychotherapists to build trust with children who are in counseling. T F

5. Marriage can fulfill our needs for intimacy when we are willing to learn and grow together with another person. T F

6. Sociologists claim that practicing cohabitation guarantees couples success later in marriage. T F

7. The term meretricious spouse refers to intentionally unmarried persons living together as if married. T F

8. Identify the sources of intimacy available to us.

9. Describe how each source influences our needs for love and belonging.

EMOTIONAL INTIMACY

Romance

Two years to the day have passed since Sandra and Jerry were married. As they sit in the waiting area of the marriage counselor's office, both are thinking about what went wrong in their relationship. The thoughts are not new. They are often the topic of conversation, conversation that frequently ends in their blaming each other. The wedding seems like yesterday, and yet, so long ago. Both are wondering how the romance, the wonder, and the warmth of the first few months of their marriage could have disappeared from their lives. What should they have done to ensure that their intimacy remained more satisfying and more lasting?

People often use the terms *romance* and *intimacy* interchangeably. This could explain some of the confusion that exists about the role of romance in intimacy. Many love songs of the past several decades have perpetuated some of the myths we have learned about love and intimacy. They portray the ecstacy, possessiveness, pain, and loneliness many of us associate with the search for love and provide opportunities for us to sit for hours dreaming in our fantasies or wallowing in our self-pity. Novelists and songwriters have grown wealthy writing about the ecstasy and agony of **romantic love.** Unfortunately, the expectations associated with romantic love often contribute to our disappointment in relationships, disappointment that often leads to breaking up, estrangement, and divorce.

romantic love   a set of idealized standards by which we judge the quality of a relationship

Characteristics of Romantic Love   Romantic love involves a set of idealized images by which we judge the other person and the quality of our relationship. The images of romantic love result in role expectations for each partner. Among the forces that shape romantic desire in both men and women are the depictions of relationships and sexual expressions in popular fiction. Two "scripts" are represented. A *romantic script* based on fairy tales and romance novels is aimed at females, and an *adventure script* incorporated in action comic books, adventure novels, and pornography is directed at males ((Rose, 1985). The man is to be strong, confident, protective, and masterful at all times; the woman is to be always charming, loving, fragile, and dependent. We may hope to transform each other into the unreal heroes or heroines (princes or princesses) these images portray. Studies show that people who measure the quality of love relationships against romantic ideals tend to be more jealous and irrational in their thinking and behavior (Lester, Deluca, Hellinghausen, and Scribner, 1985).

In addition to promoting unrealistic role expectations, romantic love requires that each partner become the complete center of the universe for the other. The result is the belief that love, possessiveness, and jealousy are synonymous. However, such romanticized standards bear little relationship to satisfying intimacy in the real world. In fact, we must hesitate when we refer to romantic love as love at all, for it is based on selfishness. This may be difficult for many

Judging a relationship only on the ideals of romance can result in disappointment and frustration.

of us to grasp, for romance is usually expressed by generous promises—"My love for you will last forever" or "I'll make you the best wife a man ever had." When we rationally analyze such guarantees of instant and enduring happiness, we can readily see how unrealistic they are for human beings, implying as they do that human beings are unchanging. The selfishness of romantic love becomes more obvious when we think about romantic lovers' misery when the two are separated. This misery is caused by selfishness of the most egocentric type; each lover is sorry for himself or herself and is grieving over his or her personal loss of pleasure and intimacy. Unfortunately, the romantic adventure scripts of romance encompass primarily the courtship phase of relationships but provide little guidance in maintaining long-term relationships.

The Value of Romantic Love   Romantic love does have some value in a relationship. It is important to entertain our romantic fantasies from time to time to stimulate and add enjoyment to our lives. Romantic ceremony and ritual can provide much happiness in our relationships. However, attempting to build a fulfilling and lasting intimate relationship on the unrealistic ideals of romance seldom results in our meeting our needs and encourages disappointment and frustration when our expectations are not met.

The Disappointment of Romantic Love   People often fall in love with their romanticized expectations rather than with their mates. This tends to produce one of two actions. Either the spouse is rejected in search of the ideal partner, or an attempt is made to change the spouse to fit the romantic ideal. The following is how John Clark (1961) describes the process of loving when it is based on romantic ideals:

In learning how to love a plain human being today, what we usually want unconsciously is a fancy human being with no flaws. When the mental picture we have of someone we love is colored by wishes of childhood, we may love the picture rather than the real person behind it. Naturally, we are disappointed in the person we love if he [she] does not conform to our picture. Since this kind of disappointment has no doubt happened to us before, one might suppose we would tear up the picture and start over. On the contrary, we keep the picture and tear up the person. Small wonder that divorce courts are full of couples who never gave themselves a chance to know the real person behind the pictures in their lives. (p. 18)

Divorce and Romantic Ideals   The high rate of divorce may be due, in part, to various ideals associated with marriage:

1. As we just discussed, people often get married with unrealistic expectations both for their mate and the marriage. They expect that the marriage will provide sexual fulfillment, intellectual stimulation, congeniality, shared recreation, mutual security, companionship, and numerous material satisfactions.

2. A majority of divorced people remarry and many do so quickly, suggesting that people are frantically searching for more satisfying intimacy. This implies that people see marriage as the major source for emotional satisfaction and cannot endure a relationship that does not provide this.

3. People often get married because they believe it is expected of them. We are raised to believe that marriage is the normal and approved status of adulthood. This means that people will marry even if they are temperamentally unsuited to each other or to marriage. For some, the appearance of marriage is perhaps more important than the success of it.

Intimacy

intimacy   the meaningful intellectual, emotional, and physical interaction between two or more individuals

The need and desire for **intimacy** has been for centuries the central theme in much of our poetry and literature. Movies and television programs nearly always portray some struggle to achieve intimacy. Wars have been fought as a result of it. Without intimacy, it is doubtful that anyone can achieve a satisfying level of happiness. The potential each person has for achieving the rewards of intimacy is enormous. However, although essential for healthy adjustment, intimacy is extremely difficult to achieve.

There are many definitions of intimacy. Some people think exclusively of the word *sex* when they hear the word *intimacy*. Others think that it is any significant interaction between two or more people. We like the definition proposed by Carolynne Kieffer (1977): "Intimacy is the experiencing of the essence of one's self in intense intellectual, physical, and/or emotional communion with another human being."

Achieving this degree of intimacy may seem quite difficult for many; we hope this chapter will be of help. The most important thing to remember is that intimacy is a process that requires constant attention (Dahms, 1976); this means the expenditure of time and energy directed toward growth in the areas of *emotional intimacy* and *physical intimacy*. Emotional intimacy is never attained once and for all, just as we do not eat once and for all. Can you imagine what would happen to many of us if we ate food only as often as we are intimate with someone, or if the quality of food were only as good as the quality of our intimate relationships? We would either starve or die of malnutrition. The fact is that many are starving emotionally and some are literally dying (by suicide) because of a lack of intimacy.

Emotional intimacy is the highest level of intimacy and focuses on our feelings. It evolves and is maintained and enhanced by constant evaluation and growth. Unless it is maintained by this process, it soon disappears. After emotional intimacy has been lost, physical intimacy will soon disappear as well.

emotional intimacy the highest level of intimacy, characterized by accessibility, naturalness, and nonpossessiveness, and focused on feelings

Finding, Developing, and Maintaining Intimacy

Finding the "Right" Mate   Ultimately, for most people the process of dating and falling in love is part of the search for the "right person" to marry. According to Goldberg (1983), finding a mate begins with an *intrinsic attraction* to the other person. This attraction is the most essential ingredient in finding an intimate partner, and it is motivated by the other person's presence. The other person is important as an individual, not as a means to an end. What we do together is not important as long as we do it together. The ideals of romantic love, unfortunately, play an important part in this search. A man and woman meet, fall in love, and decide they cannot live without each other, no matter how impractical the match. In the face of often incredible odds, they get married with the idea that they will live "happily ever after."

Factors that are important to the process of finding a mate include complementarity, proximity, and similarity. Other things being equal, people tend to date those whom they see most often and whose needs and characteristics seem to mesh with or *complement* their own or whose strengths match their weaknesses (Rubin, 1973). As we discussed earlier, the principle of propinquity, or *proximity*, plays an important part in finding a mate. Work relationships, for example, have the potential for developing into intimate relationships (see chapter 10). Perhaps the most important variable in mate selection is *similarity*. A study by Murstein and Brust (1985) showed that one of the best ways to determine similarity is through shared humor. If two people view similar events or circumstances as being humorous, they are more likely to have similar values, needs, and views of the world. The researchers believe that not only is humor significantly associated with attraction, it actually precedes attraction. In other words, we seem to be attracted to those with whom we share a sense of humor.

Healthy emotional relationships are characterized by accessibility, naturalness, and nonpossessiveness. In order to find, develop, and maintain an intimate relationship, we must be available for daily contact with another person. Although it is important to maintain our capacity for privacy (Weiss, 1987), if we make ourselves unavailable (through excessive privacy), we will experience difficulty developing an emotionally intimate relationship with anyone. Partners in satisfying intimate relationships are mutually accessible. Songs such as "I'll Be There" and "You've Got a Friend" describe this accessibility. Finding the right person may seem difficult. The question is often asked, "How can we meet people who can and will help us fulfill our needs for intimacy?" The answer is that we may have to discard many of our beliefs about intimacy—the games we play; restrictive "shoulds" and "oughts"; and a superficial, one-line communication style—and risk the natural, honest expression of our desire for intimate contact with the other person (see chapter 10 for more about communication).

Many believe it is quite risky to be honest with others, especially where intimate feelings are concerned. However, communicating naturally and honestly with a stranger is probably more frightening than risky. It may appear to be risky, though, because occasionally we have been rejected when we were natural and honest. From those experiences we learn to be careful in risking honesty. Unfortunately, many of us tend to generalize our relatively few experiences of rejection to every new encounter. Consequently, we go through life concealing ourselves—a process that is ultimately self-defeating. Jourard and Whitman (1976) state,

> We not only conceal ourselves; we also usually assume that the other person is in hiding. We are wary of him because we take for granted that he too will frequently misrepresent his real feelings, his intentions or his past, since we so often are guilty of doing those very things ourselves. (p. 105)

Because we believe the other person is also playing the game of "guess who I really am," we choose to be dishonest. It is no wonder that after a lifetime of hiding, many of us no longer know who we are.

Mutual Self-Disclosure   We must be *mutually known* to each other. Jourard (1974) believes that people can best come to know each other through *mutual self-disclosure*. It is through the freedom to share our hopes, fears, joys, plans for the future, and memories of the past that we come to know each other intimately. Although privacy is seen as an obstacle to intimacy, privacy and intimacy have an interdependent relationship (Weiss, 1987). Franzoi, Davis, and Young (1985) found in one study that men and women who pay more attention to their own thoughts and feelings through constructive privacy (Fisher, 1975) are more likely to disclose private aspects of themselves to others when doing so is appropriate to the development of intimacy. "Intimacy is, in part, interpersonal privacy, the coming together of two or more people each with a secure sense of their

It is through the freedom of sharing our hopes, fears, joys, plans for the future, and memories of the past that we come to know each other intimately.

own privacy" (Weiss, 1987). Consequently, this interaction results in a more satisfying relationship.

When we are genuine, other people love us for being who we are instead of for matching some contrived image. It is sad when we realize that we have allowed someone to love the person we would like to be rather than the person we are. As much as we might like to, we cannot maintain a facade indefinitely. Eventually, deception takes its toll on us, our partner, and our potentially intimate relationship. We must take the perceived risk of practicing honest and accurate self-disclosure with our potentially intimate partner. Taking this risk may ultimately invite our significant other to take a similar risk. In this way, we each let our needs be known to the other.

Overcoming the Fear of Self-Disclosure   The fear of not being loved is the main reason many of us are afraid of letting our "real selves" be known. It is here where one of the problems with intimacy—fear of making contact—is connected with self-esteem. If our self-esteem is positive, we can realize that if someone knows who we really are and does not choose to become intimate with us, we would have been starved for intimacy in a relationship with that person anyway; the relationship would not have satisfied our needs. Thus, letting ourselves be known, even though it may result in rejection, is worth the apparent risk. Our efforts are not wasted but rather are essential to finding a significant someone with whom we can grow naturally.

Growing Together

In his book *The New Male-Female Relationship,* Goldberg (1983) says we must grow together in several ways by becoming playmates, friends and companions, and lovers. Growing together means that:

1. *We must engage in mutual acceptance* without the need to judge or change each other. This is possible when we are able to accept ourselves without needing to be perfect. Acceptance involves accepting all that we have become and all that the other person has become. This is essential to a relationship because no one can change anything that has already happened.

Experiencing Mutual Self-Disclosure

It is easier for some people to talk about mutual self-disclosure than to experience it. To experience it may involve some risk. We often overcome our uncomfortableness when we practice doing what we fear. So, let's practice some self-disclosure.

Find someone you care about and with whom you desire a closer relationship and invite him or her to participate in the following mutual self-disclosure experience. Each of you should begin the experience by alternately sharing with each other your responses to the following:

Some of my greatest joys have been . . .

My saddest moment was . . .

My hopes are . . .

The most confusing time of my life was . . .

The happiest moment was . . .

My greatest fear is . . .

I need . . .

I want . . .

I feel . . .

If you'd like, continue sharing more of yourself with your partner. Let your feelings take you where they want to go. Take the risk and enjoy yourself!

When we accept the sum of our combined life experience as having meaning and value together, we have life experience from which to grow and to become intimate with each other. Acceptance does not mean being attracted to another only until we find out that there are differences between our religion, family, status, goals, educational training, and so on. It means that we have unconditional positive regard for each other by accepting, supporting, and respecting the worth of the other without reservation. Our caring and concern do not change because the other person is not what we would like him or her to be.

2. *We must engage in free expression* of our thoughts and feelings. This process is enhanced by personal warmth, which conveys our acceptance of others in a way that encourages them to feel comfortable enough to express their innermost feelings. In natural relationships, feelings are of ultimate importance and are highly respected. Feelings represent conscious, current, yet changing sensations that are responses to what has happened, is happening, and will happen in our lives. They usually represent more accurate and personalized pieces of information about oneself than do thoughts. Failure to express our feelings in a potentially intimate relationship usually means we cannot achieve intimacy. We must trust our understanding of ourselves, our urges, desires, needs, wants, and so on and trust the humanness of the other person.

3. *We must be able to transcend gender defensiveness.* No behavior or response should be repressed because of its reflection on the masculinity of the male for the femininity of the female. Interaction is gender free, person to person. Protecting the other by withholding behavior or responses may deprive the other of the opportunity to grow and change with respect to sex-role stereotype.

4. *We must base our attraction and interaction on want* rather than need. The decision to come together and be together is based on the pleasure of being together rather than defensive need. For example, sexual expression becomes spontaneous—free of feelings of responsibility, defensive proving, and the need for affirmation that one is loved. Without this freedom, sex would become work and eventually a source of fear and distress.

5. *We must be able to maintain separate identities.* Caring on the highest level brings delight in the independence of others, not in the possession of them (Dahms, 1976). To want to possess another person usually means that we want to own, direct, and control another person for our needs and insecure purposes. Our insecurity results in the fear of losing our hold on the other. No healthy individual can stand to be suffocated, suppressed, and held back by possessiveness. The irony is that in attempting to possess the other, we can drive the other away, losing what we hoped to keep through our possessive behavior. As one person put it, "I want to be loved and I want to be free. Give me the freedom to breathe and grow and I probably will be with you for a long time, even forever. Try to possess and control me and I will be gone." Buscaglia (1982) states, "Love can only be given, expressed freely. It can't be captured or held, for it's neither there to tie nor to hold. Love is trusting, accepting, and believing, without guarantee" (p. 107). To grow naturally in an intimate relationship, then, the individuals involved must accept all of what they have been, what they are, and what they have the potential to become, both separately and together. As you may see, there is

no room for possessiveness in an intimate relationship. Emotional intimacy can only exist when we are nonpossessive. To share our lives with another significant person without possessiveness may be a big order for many of us. However, unless we can be secure enough in our own self-esteem to avoid attempting to possess other persons, we may destroy many potentially intimate relationships.

6. *We must have the objective love and admiration* of our partner. This means enjoying, respecting, and appreciating our partners—being able to say that we would like each other even if we were not each other's mate.

Using your knowledge of the previous characteristics of a healthy and growing relationship, read the following example and try to diagnose what you believe are the problems existing in the relationship.

> Rick believed his relationship with Monique was a dream come true. Many times he wondered what she saw in him. She was popular, attractive, and a straight-A student. Rick considered himself lucky indeed. He felt proud when he was seen walking with her across the campus. Unfortunately, as time passed, when Monique wanted to spend time with some of her other friends, Rick would become angry and resentful. Even though he felt bad about his behavior, he did not seem able to deal with his feelings and discuss them with her. Monique, realizing that her freedom was severely restricted by Rick's behavior, decided to end their relationship.

Critical Review 2

1. The expectations of romantic love can add more to our relationships than any other factors. T F

2. For most of us, intimacy is essential if we are to achieve a satisfying level of happiness. T F

3. Sexual intercourse represents the highest level of intimacy. T F

4. Intrinsic attraction is the most essential ingredient in finding a mate. T F

5. Complementarity, proximity, and similarity are factors that contribute greatly to the process of finding a mate. T F

6. In the process of developing emotional intimacy, we come to know ourselves and each other through mutual self-disclosure. T F

7. A major factor in maintaining and growing in a relationship is mutual acceptance without the need to judge or change the other person. T F

8. How does the concept of romance influence our search for intimacy?

9. What are the important ingredients to building an emotionally intimate relationship?

PHYSICAL INTIMACY

The need for **physical intimacy** is basic to all human beings: to be close, to be touched, and to feel the warmth and life of another human being bring vibrant sensations into our awareness from deep inside. An organization concerned with parental effectiveness and child development distributes a bumper sticker that asks, Have you hugged your kid today? No one seems to object to hugging children. Perhaps we need bumper stickers that ask, Have you hugged your mate, your fellow worker, your boss, or anyone today?

physical intimacy the expression of emotion through touch and sexual fulfillment

The Need to Touch

Touch Taboos We have been taught verbally and through observation that touching, if it is to be done at all, is reserved for a select few and only under special circumstances such as greetings, good-byes, and comforting of the bereaved. Americans are known the world over as a reserved, no-touch society (Hartman, 1970). This is perhaps due in part to the taboos on touching that grew out of a fear closely associated with the various denominations of the Christian tradition—the fear of bodily pleasures. The anthropologist Ashley Montagu (1978) believes that "two of the negative achievements of Christianity have been to make a sin of tactual pleasures, and by the repression of sex, to make it an obsession" (p. 249).

Physical intimacy draws strong reactions from some people. It is ladened with taboos, guilt feelings, distortions of fact, myths, and so on. These impediments to intimacy, combined with fears concerning body image and rejection, cause some people to become so physically rigid that if someone touches them, they shudder in fear or embarrassment.

A college professor decided to use a touching exercise with his class in human relations. After having discussed the importance of touching in interpersonal relationships, he explained that the exercise would be conducted in the classroom and that students who felt too uncomfortable to participate could move to the periphery of the room. To his surprise, more than half the class moved to the outside of the room, giggling and embarrassed at the thought of touching some of their classmates.

Many people are reluctant to touch others because of fear of rejection for doing so. Sometimes you may feel awkward when touching another person, especially if you really care about him or her. Most of us have experienced this awkwardness. Perhaps you are not sure of the other person's response. Comfort usually comes from knowing the other person feels the same as you. One of the ways to test this is to risk disclosing your fear and awkwardness to your partner or potential partner. You may discover that your fear and awkwardness will soon diminish. It is important to begin overcoming fear and awkwardness by slowly exposing yourself to the things you fear.

Sometimes our touching may be misinterpreted as an indication that we seek sexual contact. If that happens, we should let the other person know that physical intimacy and touching have benefits in addition to those related to sexual encounter. There is much to be experienced and learned about ourselves and others by touching, stroking, caressing, massaging, hugging, and holding without the contact necessarily ending in sexual intercourse. When attempting to avoid sending erroneous messages, consider the appropriateness of the type of touch to the situation. For example, if our intention is to communicate that we have missed someone and are glad to see him or her, it would be inappropriate to demonstrate our intention by touching the other person on an erogenous zone, or area of the body that brings about sexual pleasure. It may be equally inappropriate when engaged in the process of sexual arousal with another person to avoid touching the erogenous zones and to instead continually pat the person on the arm (see chapter 10 for more about communication and mixed messages).

The Mutual Experience of Touch Walter Ong (1967) wrote that "touch involves my own subjectivity more than any other sense. When I feel this objective something 'out there,' beyond the bounds of my body, I also at the same instant experience my own self. I feel other and self simultaneously" (p. 169). To demonstrate this phenomenon, place one of your hands in an open position in front of you. Do you feel your hand? Now touch the hand you are holding in front of you with your other hand. You feel both hands. In the same way, when you touch another person you also feel yourself.

The importance of physical intimacy (touching) begins before conscious memory, when the fetus is nestled in the mother's womb and the developing nervous system begins recording sensations of touch and movement.

These then, are our first real experiences of life—floating in a warm fluid, curling inside a total embrace, swaying to the undulations of the moving body, and hearing the beat of the pulsing heart. Our prolonged exposure to these sensations in the absence of other competing stimuli leaves a lasting impression on our brains, an impression that spells security, comfort, and passivity. (Morris, 1971, p. 15).

These beginnings of intimacy are eventually interrupted by the moment of birth, as we experience for the first time a loss of intimate body contact. What happens from this point on in our lives determines many things, including our attitudes, behaviors, feelings, and capacity for experiencing physical intimacy. According to Montagu (1978), the newborn looks forward to "a continuation of that life in the womb—to a womb with a view—before it was so catastrophically interrupted by the birth process" (p. 60). For most of us, the physical contact so important before birth continues to be important throughout our lives.

Sexual Intimacy

Sexual activity is an emotional necessity for some individuals, but not for all; it is associated with emotional meanings that may be different for some human beings. In one person's formula sex equals the ultimate expression of love, and, in this way, is an emotional necessity. For others, it seems to be more a biological function that is expressed without emotional involvement. A lifetime of sexual abstinence may be the choice of others.

True sexual intimacy is the physical parallel of emotional intimacy. It is body conversation in which two people become part of each other, in a sense, both physically and psychologically. Their thinking, emotional expression, and sexual behavior are unified. Sexual intimacy can often give us the courage to disclose ourselves emotionally on an even more intimate level to the other person. In this way, our emotionally intimate relationship continued to grow and have meaning for each of us.

Sexual Attitudes It did not take long for our society, founded primarily on commercial values, to discover the usefulness of a powerful motivator like sex for advertising. Advertisers equate sex appeal with personal success, happiness, and affluence. Countless films, magazine stories, and television programs associate love, particularly romantic love, with sexual attraction. Whereas the Victorian morality treated sexual relations as sinful and nearly subhuman, the new fashionable sexual ideology creates taboos at the other extreme by focusing on the horrors of sexual abstinence and sexual inadequacy. Marin (1983) wrote that the "commercialization of sex now destroys true feelings as badly as traditional taboos did."

One of the unfortunate by-products of the new sexual ideology is the creation of unrealistic standards governing sexual functioning. With this new set of standards, we are often unduly concerned about whether we are long enough, big enough, deep enough, tight enough, fast enough, slow enough, attractive enough, tall enough, or good enough. "For many people, sex has become a labor rather than an adventure: the immense cultural pressure to do—whether spontaneously or not—the 'right' thing can be exhausting and destructive" (Marin, 1983). Realizing our needs and our confusion, writers have offered sex manual after sex manual to teach "accurate" techniques. Often the need for orgasm is made the priority in intimate relationships and the achievement of simultaneous, mutual orgasm "the crowning glory." The other intimate aspects of a relationship frequently are omitted. Sexual expression may become a drudgery focused on achievement rather than on joyful pleasure. Some of us certainly need to know something about how to have sexual intercourse with another person. However, the overemphasis on technique in sexual intimacy can foster a mechanistic attitude toward lovemaking. It can also support feelings of alienation, feelings of loneliness, and depersonalization—the feeling of being inadequate as a person—which is one of the fundamental problems of our time.

Sexual Decision Making   The decisions about when and with whom to have a sexual relationship are important ones. The current sexual freedom has made these decisions more difficult than in the past. Adolescents and young adults are often under pressure to engage in sexual relations even though they may not be ready. The sexual revolution has moved from the college campus to the high school to the junior high school and into the grade school. Peter H. Patterson, M.D., (1994) reports that 88 percent of black males, 60 percent of black females, 56 percent of white males, and 47 percent of white females he surveyed have had intercourse between the ages of 15 and 19. Unfortunately, only 10–20 percent of the individuals in this age group use condoms consistently when having sexual intercourse. It appears that there is considerable pressure, both from peers and the media, for adolescents to be sexually active.

Individuals face conflicting choices of how and when to include sex in their lives. Even though some believe sex is a way to obtain approval and achieve an identity, Wrightsman (1977) believes that people most often resolve the conflict over divergent sexual choices in favor of having sexual relations but within the context of a loving relationship. Most people continue to believe that genuine affection must be present for sex to be enjoyed. After sex without affection, the participants often feel cheapened and disgusted with themselves and their partners.

The questions of whether to have sexual relations and with whom involve very personal decisions. Each person must make his or her own decisions about sex and assume responsibility for the consequences. Of greatest consequence to all concerned is a possible pregnancy and the transmission of sexually transmitted diseases.

> Kim, an eighteen-year-old college freshman, has not experienced sexual intercourse. Although she has not lacked opportunities, she has chosen to wait to have sex until she feels an emotional attachment to the other person. She has dated many males of varying degrees of maturity, but none has inspired her to want to pursue a physically intimate relationship. Unfortunately, most of the males she has dated appear by their actions to want a physical relationship as a prerequisite to an emotional relationship. This has resulted in her dating an individual one or two times at most, certainly not enough times to get to know anyone on an emotional level. Although disappointed with her experiences and at times uncertain about her own standards for intimacy, Kim still intends to wait until her feelings for someone can justify a sexual relationship.

Sexual Orientation   Sexual decision making is not just about when and with whom to have a heterosexual relationship. For some, it means the choice of practicing either a *homosexual* or a *bisexual* lifestyle. Prior to the 1900s, it was generally believed that people were either heterosexual or homosexual (Byer and Shainberg, 1991). Today, as a result of the work of Kinsey (1948) and his associates, it is believed that sexual orientation is a continuum on a six-point scale, with 0 signifying exclusive heterosexuality, 6 signifying exclusive homosexuality, and points in between representing varying degrees of bisexual preference.

Homosexuality is having a physical attraction and an emotional attachment to someone of the same sex. Homosexuals are often referred to as "gays" and may be either men or women. The term *homosexual* is used by most people when referring to men who have an attraction for each other. Women who have an attraction for each other are referred to as **lesbians.** People are seldom entirely homosexual or heterosexual. Gay people represent all facets of society. For this reason, they are not easily recognized. For example, some effeminate men are homosexuals, while others are not. Conversely, a 280-pound football player may be gay.

For decades, people have argued the causes of homosexuality. Some argue that it results from genetic factors. Others believe that it is a choice and the result of environmental influences. Some studies suggest that genetic factors may have something to do with the preference for homosexuality. Hamer, Hu, Magnuson, Hu, and Pattatucci (1993) found a link between male homosexuality and genetic material on the X chromosome. Bailey and Benishay (1993) discovered that lesbianism tends to run in families. And, LeVay (1991) found size differences in an area of the hypothalmus governing sexual behavior between homosexual and heterosexual men. Research in this area is relatively new and much is yet to be discovered. Regardless of discoveries in this area, many researchers and experts still believe that our sexual orientation is not just the cause of any one factor, but a combination of factors (Whitman, Diamond, and Martin, 1993).

Although there is still a cultural bias against homosexuality, over the past few decades homosexuals have gained greater acceptance in many areas. However, in 1986, a Gallup poll began to notice a change in attitudes toward gays as a result of Acquired Immune Deficiency Syndrome (AIDS). More than 40 percent of Americans, in 1985, believed that homosexual relations between consenting adults should be legalized. One year later, the figure had dropped to 30 percent (Gallup Report, 1987). Since that time, acceptance of gays has been on the increase. This increase in support may be due, in part, to the realization that AIDS is no longer just a gay disease but affects all segments of the population. A 1993 *New York Times*/CBS News Poll indicated that 78 percent of Americans believe gays should have equal rights on the job. This compares to a similar study in the later 1970s that indicated that only 56 percent supported gay rights (Schmalz, 1994).

Some people may have an attraction to members of both sexes. Physical attraction and emotional attachment to either sex is termed **bisexuality.** These individuals may feel a considerable degree of tension and stress attempting to divide their sexual needs between the lesbian and gay community on one hand and the heterosexual community on the other. Both heterosexual and homosexuals may find bisexual behavior difficult to understand; each group is offended by the lack of commitment to its kind of lifestyle (Paul, 1984). Freud first suggested that the human being is bisexual at birth. He proposed that the homosexual component is blocked during our psychosexual development and by socialization. Others believe that some people go through a bisexual stage as they attempt to

homosexuality   a physical attraction and an emotional attachment to someone of the same sex

lesbian   a woman who has an attraction to another woman

bisexuality   sexual attraction to members of both sexes

make the transition from heterosexuality to homosexuality. McDonald (1981) suggests that bisexuals may be individuals who are primarily homosexual but, because of the guilt or uneasiness they feel, engage in some heterosexual activity.

Sexual Responsibility

Forced Sexual Behavior   People most often engage willingly in sexual activity with others. Unfortunately, some people force sexual behavior on others who are not willing. Forcing sexual behavior on another person who does not give consent is called *rape*. Rape can ensue from strangers, acquaintances, friends, people we are dating, and family members. In recent years, their has been an alarming increase in what has been called *date rape* on college and university campuses. Koss, Gidycz, and Wisniewski (1987) reported the results of a survey conducted with nearly 7,000 college students about their sexual experiences since age 14. Fifteen percent of the women reported that they had actually been raped while 12 percent reported they had experienced attempted rape. Perhaps because of sexual expectations often learned by both men and women, only 27 percent of the women in this study labeled the forced sex as "rape" and 8 percent of the men interviewed admitted to forcing sex on a woman, or trying to do so, yet did not view themselves as rapists. Koss (1990) believes that between 38 to 67 percent of women are subjected to some kind of sexual abuse by the time they are 18 years of age.

Confusion may exist for many of us regarding what constitutes rape. If it comes from a stranger, it is thought of as rape. If it comes from someone we know, it is not. Some believe that nearly two million incidences of rape occur each year inside marriages although this cannot not accurately be confirmed as many women do not define forced sex by husbands as rape. Many men and women in marriages still believe that sex is the duty of each partner whether or not the partner wants to engage in sex.

Rape seems quite extensive today. Many believe that is is because some men are socialized to be sexually aggressive, regarding women as inferior objects to be used at their discretion. Browne and Williams (1993) suggest that rapists seem to use aggression to amplify their sense of masculinity. They also act out of a hatred for women. According to Bohmer and Parrot (1993), men who forced sexual activity on women often reported that they did it because of the traditional myths that women wanted to be raped and that they as men were unable to control their sexual desires.

Contrary to what some may think, rape is an extremely traumatic experience for the victim. Rape victims experience a wide spectrum of feelings from initial shock to sadness, anger, fear, and depression, and some even respond with suicide (Allen and Santrock, 1993). Recovering from rape depends often on the person's ability to deal rationally with the incident. Support from parents and friends and professional counseling are important factors to consider in helping the person make a satisfying recovery.

Sexual responsibility means not only being responsible for the decision to engage in sexual relations but also taking the responsibility for protection from unwanted pregnancy and sexually transmitted diseases. Abstinence, abortion, contraception, sterilization, and bearing children constitute the range of choices available to those sexually active during their fertile years. Birth and birth control are the vital concerns of many individuals, religious and racial communities, and nation states. On the one hand, the issue of birth control is a subject of controversy with religious groups; on the other hand, it is viewed as the salvation for overpopulated Third World countries. The People's Republic of China, for example, demands that couples have no more than one child. Before the 1960s in the United States, religion and the state stood together to restrict the practice of birth control, limiting even the dissemination of information under obscenity laws. Some advocate providing free information, contraception, and abortion on request. Others condemn the active role of religion or the state in such activity and work for the restriction or abolition of such practices.

Teenage Pregnancy The prevalence of teenage pregnancy among white and black Americans was revealed in 1985 by the Alan Guttmacher Institute. The results from the thirty-seven-country study indicated that the United States leads nearly all other developed nations in its incidence of pregnancy among girls between the ages of fifteen and nineteen (Wallis, 1985). Each year in the United States, more than one million young women under age twenty, or one out of every ten teenage girls, becomes pregnant (Stevens-Simon and White, 1991).

Teenage pregnancy in the United States is nearly twice that of France, Britain, and Canada, three times greater than Sweden, and seven times that of the Netherlands, one of the most liberal countries regarding sexual behavior. In these countries, teenagers are equally as active as those in the United States but have greater access to sex education and contraceptives (Hyde, 1990). Of the more than one million American teenagers who become pregnant annually, 41 percent choose to have an abortion, 46 percent choose to have the baby, and the rest either miscarry or bear a stillborn fetus. The pregnancy rate among non-whites is twice that of whites (Henshaw and Van Vort, 1989). Ninety-five percent of the births to nonwhite teenagers were unplanned as compared to 75 percent for white teenagers (Hardy, Dugan, Masnyk, and Pearson, 1989).

> Before the baby came, her bedroom walls were decorated with posters of her favorite rock stars. Now the walls in Angie's room are painted white. Her room has become the nursery for three-week-old Rachel Ann. Angie, who just turned fifteen, finds it difficult to think of herself as a mother. She is still the typical teenager, seeking permission to stay out late and asking for a pet dog for her birthday. The weight of her responsibilities is just beginning to sink in. "Last night I couldn't get my homework done, and she cried nearly all night. I kept feeding her and feeding her, and she still wouldn't go to sleep. Having a baby is so much work. Maybe I should have given it more thought."

Many teenage girls see pregnancy as a route to acceptance and self-worth. "As long as adolescents look in the mirror and see nobody there [low self-esteem], they are likely to seek identity by becoming—ready or not—somebody's mother" (Wallis, 1985, p. 90). "With the stigma of illegitimacy largely removed, girls are less inclined to surrender their babies for adoption" (p. 80). Unwed motherhood has even become glamorous to some teenagers. It is common to see Hollywood stars on TV talking about the children they have had out of wedlock and describing how "wonderful life is." Other reasons for teenage pregnancy include a lack of goals, low educational and occupational achievement, a valuing of fertility and desire for pregnancy, poor communication skills about sex, lack of information about contraception, membership in a society that does not encourage the use of contraceptives, and escape from an unhappy home life (Butler and Burton, 1990; Chilman, 1990).

The consequences for the infant seem to be great. Teen mothers are many times more likely than other women with young children to live below the poverty level. As infants, the offspring are often the victims of child abuse at the hands of their immature parents. As a result, they have higher rates of illness and mortality, and later in life they often experience educational and emotional problems. Eventually, these infants often become teenage parents themselves. Wallis (1985) reports on one study in which 82 percent of girls who gave birth at age fifteen or younger were daughters of teenage mothers.

Studies suggest that the highest teenage pregnancy rates are in countries with the least open attitudes toward sex. In the United States, emphasis on sexual abstinence as opposed to sexual information on contraceptives does not seem to be effective. In one study, 191 teenagers who participated in six program sessions focusing on the importance of saving sex until married were compared to 121 teenagers who did not participate in the session. The only change observed by the researchers was an increase in sexual activity among those who participated in the programs (Christopher and Roosa, 1990).

Sexually Transmitted Diseases   Protection from *sexually transmitted diseases* has become a major concern in the United States and many other countries, with the biggest focus centered on **AIDS.** AIDS is an acronym for *acquired immune deficiency syndrome.* The AIDS virus attacks the immune system of the body, rendering the body incapable of defending itself against a variety of diseases. These diseases include numerous infections and malignancies. Originally AIDS was thought to be transmitted predominantly among homosexual and bisexual males with numerous partners, hemophiliacs, Haitian immigrants to the United States, and intravenous drug users. Homosexual males, bisexual males, and intravenous drug users who share needles with others are still the predominate victims. However, AIDS is now becoming a major concern of heterosexuals as well, with AIDS cases among heterosexuals growing faster than any other group. From 1988 to 1989, the Centers for Disease Control reported an increase of 36 percent in AIDS cases resulting from heterosexual transmission (Hilt, 1990). Overall, it is estimated that there will be nearly 100,000 new cases of AIDS diagnosed each year through the 1990s. It was estimated, in 1993, that 98,000 people would die from AIDS but, as it turned out, there were 103,500 deaths (Centers for Disease Control, 1994). So far, in the United States, nearly half a million people have died from AIDS (see Figure 9–3). The disease presently is growing the fastest among the teenage population. Unfortunately, the teenage population—the group having sex the most—is using condoms the least (Centers for Disease Control, 1994).

One of the most frightening aspects of AIDS is in not knowing who has the disease. Sex partners may not know they have been infected, and it may take as long as three years before the virus is detected in the bloodstream (Chase, 1989). Then it can take from five to ten years from the time of infection until the onset of the disease (Centers for Disease Control, 1989). Consequently, concern for safe sex has become the focus of both sexually active homosexuals and heterosexuals. The condom, once viewed by many as the most uncomfortable method of contraception, is rapidly becoming the method of choice. According to public health officials, condoms, the source of protection from sexually transmitted diseases for decades, continue to offer the best form of protection, if properly used, from the transmission of AIDS among the sexually active. A 1993 survey at the University of Virginia revealed that 37 percent of the students *always* use a condom, 22 percent *usually* use a condom, 10 percent *sometimes* use a condom, 10 percent *seldom* use a condom, and 20 percent *never* use a condom when having

AIDS   an acronym for acquired immune deficiency syndrome, a virus that attacks the immune system of the body and renders the body defenseless to all kinds of disease-producing organisms

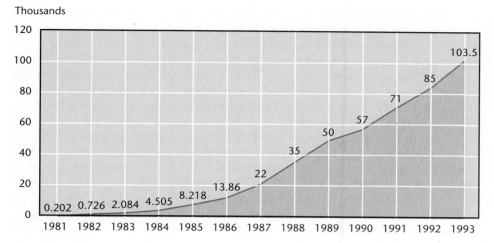

Thousands

FIGURE 9–3
Growth of AIDS in the United States

SOURCE: Centers for Disease Control, 1994.

sexual intercourse (Patterson, 1994). These statistics indicate that nearly 40 percent of the students surveyed are at risk of contacting AIDS.

American sexual attitudes have played a role in the treatment of sexually related problems. Many religious fundamentalists believe that AIDS is God's way of eliminating homosexuals and promiscuous heterosexuals from the earth. Other people believe that if we are meant to suffer from sexually transmitted diseases, there is nothing we can do to prevent such suffering. Still others see premarital sexual abstinence and sexual fidelity in monogamous marriages as the only ways to halt the spread of AIDS.

As with many such epidemics, panic results from the spread of erroneous information, myths, and half-truths. Such is the case with AIDS. AIDS is not spread by casual contact. It spreads mainly through anal and vaginal intercourse and especially among those who have numerous sex partners. One of the biggest problems with the disease is the task of contacting the numerous sex partners of those who are found to have acquired the disease.

In addition to AIDS, other sexually transmitted diseases such as *gonorrhea, chlamydia, syphilis,* and *herpes* are still a problem. Gonorrhea and chlamydia are the most common of the sexually transmitted diseases especially among college students. The gonorrhea (Neisseria gonorrheo) bacterium is spread through genital, oral-genital, or anal-genital contact. In women, a green or light yellow discharge may be present, but in many cases goes undetected until a later stage that can cause pelvic inflammatory disease. In men, however, the disease is more readily detected. Common symptoms are a cloudy discharge from the penis accompanied with a burning sensation when urinating. Chlamydia (Chlamydia trichomatis), like gonorrhea, is transmitted through any sexual contact. It can also be transmitted by the fingers from one body site to another. Chlamydia is detected in women by disrupted menstrual periods, abdominal pain, an increase in body temperature, headache, nausea, and vomiting. These symptoms are usually a result of pelvic inflammatory disease caused by the presence of the bacterium. Men may experience a discharge and burning sensation while urinating. In addition, they also may experience an inflammation of the scrotal skin or a painful swelling at the bottom of the scrotum (Crooks and Bauer, 1990).

Syphilis and herpes, although not as common as gonorrhea and chlamydia, are still a threat and considered to be quite dangerous. Syphilis (Treponema pallidium) is a bacterium that is transmitted from an open lesion during genital, oral-genital, or anal-genital contact. During the *first stage* of the disease, a painless chancre may appear at the site where the organism entered the body. The *second stage* develops when the chancre disappears and is replaced by a rash. In the *third stage,* called the latent stage, the victim may believe that the worst has passed as there may be no observable symptoms. In the *final stage,* blindness, mental disruption, heart failure, or other symptoms may occur. For some, even death may result.

Two kinds of herpes can be transmitted from physical contact with others. HSV-1 (oral herpes) is transmitted primarily through kissing. HSV-2 (genital herpes) is transmitted through sexual contact. Red bumps (papules) appear in the area around the mouth or genitals. These papules develop into painful blisters that eventually rupture into wet, open sores.

It is important to remember that any contact with semen, vaginal secretions, saliva, blood, urine, or feces of another person may expose you to one or more of the many sexually transmitted diseases. Unless you and your partner are in an exclusive relationship, you are constantly subjected to infection (Reinisch, 1990).

Sexual responsibility with respect to sexually transmitted diseases appears to have at least three concerns: the responsibility to protect yourself, the responsibility to protect your partner or partners, and the responsibility to contact all those you may have infected.

Critical Review 3

1. Taboos about touching may impede our satisfying the need for physical intimacy. T F

2. Sexual attitudes are beliefs that can either facilitate or hinder the attainment of our satisfaction from physical intimacy. T F

3. Current attitudes about sexual freedom have made the decision about whether or not to have sex an easy one. T F

4. Sexual responsibility means being responsible for the decision to have sexual relations as well as the responsibility for protection from unwanted pregnancy and sexually transmitted diseases for both you and your partner. T F

5. The lack of open attitudes about sex coupled with a lack of information about contraception has resulted in the fact that the United States leads the developed nations of the world in the number of sexually transmitted disease cases.

6. First believed to be a health problem only for gay men, AIDS is now becoming a major concern of heterosexuals as well. T F

7. The discovery of AIDS has made all other sexually transmitted diseases insignificant. T F

8. Research now confirms that homosexuality is entirely the result of choice rather than genetics. T F

9. Describe why physical intimacy is or is not important in an intimate relationship.

10. In what ways has sexual responsibility become an important issue in satisfying our needs for physical intimacy?

BARRIERS TO INTIMACY

Terri and Phil had one important thing in common when they met. Neither had dated anyone longer than a year. The magic both felt when they first met led them to believe that they had finally met the "right" person. After they had dated just over a year, they decided to marry. They appeared to have similar values and goals. Each had a professional career; Terri was a physical therapist at a large metropolitan hospital, and Phil was an attorney with a prestigious law firm. They had good incomes and could afford nearly anything they wanted. They were the envy of their friends, who believed them to be an ideal couple in an ideal relationship. To their friends' surprise and dismay, however, Terri and Phil filed for a divorce just eighteen months after their wedding. What had happened?

As you read the following section, see if you can determine some reasons why this relationship deteriorated.

Opportunities to develop a variety of significant intimate relationships seem nearly limitless. There are more people in the world than ever before. Through modern methods of travel our chances of meeting others who are capable of meeting our needs for intimacy are greatly increased. Yet many of us are unable to develop a satisfying, fulfilling, and lasting relationship with anyone. Goldberg (1983) asks, "How often has the tragedy been played out? Two people who believe they have achieved a deep and meaningful relationship see it dissolve into feelings of alienation and hatred" (p. 46).

A variety of factors affect our ability to find and sustain satisfying intimate relationships. The demands of our rapidly growing, complex technological society leave little time for intimacy. These demands have greatly affected the quality of one of our greatest sources of intimacy, the family. Our search for intimacy is also hampered by certain social norms and stereotypes that have developed from societal beliefs and early religious teachings as well as romantic ideals (discussed earlier) by which we judge our mates and the quality of our relationships.

Social Norms and Role Stereotypes

Deeply felt needs for intimacy draw us together, yet carefully taught inhibitions drive us apart. Norms constitute a host of shoulds and should nots that greatly affect the roles of women and men in our society. *Role stereotypes* are assumed differences between, say, women and men that a social group believes to be universally applicable. Fortunately, many of the traditional sex-role stereotypes that have been allowed to govern our behavior are gradually changing for the better. Our purpose in this chapter is to explore the effects of such stereotyping on our capacity for intimacy.

Norms, though intended to ease social interaction, often conflict with our needs. Consider the beliefs described in the box entitled "The Male Image." Such beliefs have serious and far-reaching consequences for intimacy. The male must suppress an important part of his humanness; in effect, he must bottle up the very feelings that are essential to tenderness and the development of a satis-

The Male Image

Many American males believe that to be considered masculine (strong, aggressive, in control, and so on) they must suppress their tears when in public regardless of their feelings. Any suggestion of an emotional display reinforces the fear that they may lose control and demonstrate "weakness," as females are expected to do. If crying is a sign of weakness in men, and many men and women believe it is, then a man, when he feels the need to cry, must cry alone or not at all. In this way he retains his masculine self-image.

fying intimate relationship. He must always be on guard, and he becomes disabled by the stress of hiding his feelings. Norms, particularly those that define rigid role behaviors, may create barriers to the fulfillment of intimacy.

Similarly, the role stereotype based on the traditional belief that the woman is inferior and must depend on the man is one that some believe greatly affects our search for intimacy, even though this role limitation appears to be gradually diminishing.

Constantina Safilios-Rothschild (1977) states:

When men and women are drastically unequal and women occupy a clearly inferior, disadvantaged sociological position, they necessarily become psychologically unequal; then men and women are unable to understand each other and to relate to each other as human beings. Within this context, the development of a mature, fulfilling love has been almost impossible. This has led not only to separation of love from marriage, but also to the separation of love from sexuality and to a profound alienation of men and women from their feelings and emotions. (p. 3)

There is strong evidence that the traditional role stereotypes that have limited both sexes is changing, especially for the American man. In a survey conducted by *American Health* magazine and Gallup (Segell, 1989), both men and women were in close agreement as to what characteristics make up the "ideal man." From the old role models portrayed by John Wayne, Sylvester Stallone, and others is emerging a new set of qualities. Men and women agreed that it is most important for the "ideal man" to be a good husband and father, to be intelligent, and have a good sense of humor (Figure 9–4). This perception is a far cry from the tough, strong, and aggressive male of the past. The survey also provides an interesting comparison between college graduates and noncollege graduates. Forty-five percent of the college graduates surveyed think it is good for a man to be emotionally sensitive, compared to only 23 percent of the noncollege graduates.

A Traditional or Liberal Marital Role?

Role conflicts in a marriage or relationship can cause discord. Such conflicts do not mean that the people in the relationship are incompatible. It may mean, however, that some compromise and understanding of the other person's point of view may be necessary in order to establish harmony.

The following ten items may help you determine to what degree you support traditional or liberal roles for couples in a marriage or relationship. Answer each item by circling the letter combination (SA, MA, MD, SD) that best describes your opinion. The numbers under each letter combination will be used later to score your responses. (The scoring directions are found at the end of this chapter.) This questionnaire is most useful when each member of a relationship responds to it separately. Then each person should share and discuss the results.

SA = Strongly Agree
MA = Mildly Agree
MD = Mildly Disagree
SD = Strongly Disagree

1. A wife should respond to her husband's sexual advances even when she is not interested.

SA	MA	MD	SD
4	3	2	1

2. In general, the father should have greater authority than the mother in the raising of children.

SA	MA	MD	SD
4	3	2	1

3. Only when the wife works should the husband agree to help with housework.

SA	MA	MD	SD
4	3	2	1

4. The husband and wife should share equally in planning the family budget.

SA	MA	MD	SD
1	2	3	4

5. In marriage matters (money management, assignment of household chores, where the family lives, etc.), the husband should make the major decisions.

SA	MA	MD	SD
4	3	2	1

6. If a couple agrees that sexual fidelity is not important, there is no reason why both should not have extramarital affairs if they want to.

SA	MA	MD	SD
1	2	3	4

7. If a child becomes ill and the wife works, the husband should be just as willing to stay home from work and take care of the child.

SA	MA	MD	SD
1	2	3	4

8. In general, women should be responsible for the housework.

SA	MA	MD	SD
4	3	2	1

9. After sharing in the household expenses, wives should be able to use their money in any way that they please.

SA	MA	MD	SD
1	2	3	4

10. In family matters, both spouses should have equal say on important issues.

SA	MA	MD	SD
1	2	3	4

Below each of your responses (SA, MA, MD, and SD), there is a number. Add together the numbers under each of your responses to obtain your total score: _____.

Adapted from a survey conducted by Karen Oppenheim Mason, with assistance of Daniel R. Denison and Anita J. Schacht. *Sex-Role Attitude Items and Scales from U.S. Sample Surveys.* Rockville, MD: National Institute of Mental Health, 1975, pp. 16–19.

Demands of Society

The demands and diversions of life often take precedence over our need for intimacy. These demands and diversions come from numerous involvements, leaving little time or energy for intimacy. We may find it easy to get caught up in the rush of life only to realize at some point in our lives that we are lonely. We may work many hours to buy things we believe will improve the quality of our lives. Many of us, in search of the "good" life, sacrifice our need for love and belonging.

Work   Work is an acceptable substitute for intimacy in our society. Few people question the motives of someone who continually works long hours and

---

Another View

Not everyone believes sex-role stereotypes restrict intimacy. Rubin, Peplau, and Hill (1976) studied attitudes toward sex roles by interviewing 231 couples who were college students. Ninety-five percent of the women and 87 percent of the men stated that they believed men and women should have "exactly equal say about their relationship." A follow-up study of these same couples indicated that even though they had liberal ideas about sex roles, very few of them managed to stay together in a lasting relationship. The reviewers

concluded that if couples have similar values and beliefs, the sharing of these values and beliefs is more significant to their happiness than the content of the beliefs. For example, couples who share the belief that the wife should stay at home, raise the children, and maintain the house are just as happy as couples who believe that each individual should be free to pursue a career in addition to the mutual obligations of caring for children and for the home.

---

appears to be productive. After all, the desire to "get ahead" is considered an admirable personal quality. Unfortunately, some people become workaholics in order to feel worthwhile and to provide a substitute for intimate personal relationships.

Greed Many people believe greed is a motivating force in our society. Bernikow (1986) says that "American life has become 'privatized.' People are wrapped up in selfish, individual pursuits of material goods" (p. 60). For some, the quest for material wealth provides a replacement for intimacy. Horn (1976) points out that there is little relationship between a child's family income and how much he or she values money as an adult; regardless of the level of affluence, however, people who grow up in love-poor families seem to value money more than those who receive ample love as children. Horn further states that adults who are not receiving much love usually value material possessions very highly and that persons who place a high value on money and goods tend to avoid intimacy.

FIGURE 9–4

Qualities of an "Ideal Man" (American Health/Gallup Poll Survey)

SOURCE: American Health, January–February, 1989, pp. 59–61.

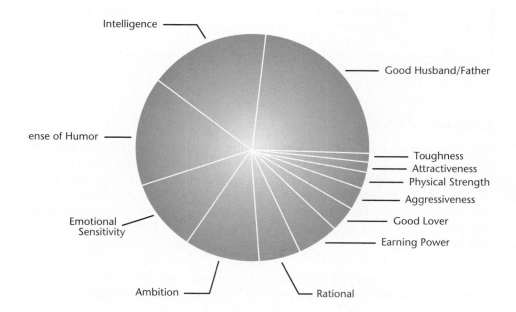

Intelligence

Good Husband/Father

ense of Humor

Toughness
Attractiveness
Physical Strength
Aggressiveness
Good Lover
Earning Power

Emotional Sensitivity

Ambition

Rational

CULTURAL CROSSCURRENTS
Just How Involved Is Daddy?

It's no secret that mothers do most of the child-rearing duties in the average family. Fathers do not bathe, dress, or feed their children very much. Mother predominates, even in such activities as playing, reading stories, and helping children with schoolwork. This is disheartening, because studies show that paternal involvement in child-rearing is related to a child's academic competence as well as to a number of other desirable outcomes.

Just what keeps fathers from being more involved with their children? Could it be that fathers view diapering, feeding, and comforting as feminine activities that are not appropriate for a male?

This was the question that Graeme Russle (1978) sought to answer. To understand his research the term **androgyny** must be introduced. Russell defines androgyny as the state of possessing the best characteristics of masculinity and femininity. For instance, many people think of being objective, competitive, aggressive, and not expressing one's feelings easily as masculine traits and being tactful, gentle, not being very aggressive and being sensitive to other people's feelings as feminine characteristics (Broverman et al., 1972). Whether these characteristics are adaptive or maladaptive depends on the situation. Emotionality and subjectivity may be adaptive in some situations but not in others. Both extremely high masculinity and very high femininity are associated with a narrowness of sex role. The individual who has the best of both worlds is in the most flexible position to react, being capable of both showing emotions and not showing them, being subjective or objective as the situation warrants. People who are androgynous have the flexibility to combine the best characteristics of both males and females. Russell reasoned that fathers who score high on a scale that

measures androgyny would be more likely to perform such child-rearing tasks as diapering and feeding and would interact more frequently with their children than men who score low on the androgyny dimension. Because the role of mother is so well stereotyped, whether or not a woman is androgynous probably would not matter as much.

To test this hypothesis, Russell interviewed forty-three couples living in the Sydney, Australia, area. He asked questions relating to the amount of time each parent spent at home or at work, the amount of time father and mother spent in child-rearing activities, and the kinds of activities that parents and children participated in together. Each parent was also given the Bem Sex Role Inventory, which measures androgyny.

Russell noticed that the father diapered the child only 19 percent of the time and fed the child only 14 percent of the time. One reason often advanced for this dismal record is lack of time. If father works all day and comes home late at night, he simply doesn't have the time to interact with his children. But this explanation does not fit the facts. Although all the fathers in Russell's sample had full-time positions, almost half the women were also employed either full- or part-time. In addition, duties performed mostly at night, such as helping children with schoolwork, playing with them, attending to their needs before bed, and reading them stories, are also heavily weighted toward the mother, even though most of the fathers were at home and available. These percentages are very close to those found in studies done in the United States.

SOURCE: Kaplan, P. S. *The Human Odyssey: Life-Span Development.* St. Paul, MN: West Publishing Co., 1988.

Grinker (1977) suggests that in some ways the children of the rich resemble the children of the poor. Their awareness of themselves and others is limited, and they lack the capacity for tenderness. Their interaction with others is limited by their compulsiveness and their desire to exclude others who are unlike them. They are often left with feelings of being bored, depressed, and, most of all, unloved. It appears there is a high price to be paid for wealth.

androgyny the state of possessing a high degree of both masculine and feminine qualities

Stress   The capacity for experiencing intimacy is more greatly affected by excessive stress than most people are aware. Our response to stress is often characterized by intellectual, emotional, and physical withdrawal. When our physiological and security needs are threatened by an overcrowded, technological, and highly mobile society and our primary concerns are related to such mundane matters as whether we have enough fuel in our cars, we necessarily become preoccupied with satisfying those more basic survival needs at the expense of intimacy.

Effect on the Family   The family unit has perhaps suffered most of all from the demands of society. Social critics have had a field day speculating on the future of the family. Some believe it is near extinction, and others believe it is already dead, having outlived its usefulness. Still others, however, believe that, having survived this long, the family will continue to exist, though modified, and will continue to serve an important function.

The family has been called the "giant shock absorber" of society—the place to which the bruised and battered individual returns daily after having faced the everyday battles of life. But as Alvin Toffler (1971) put it, "As the superindustrial revolution unfolds, this 'shock absorber' will come in for some shocks of its own" (p. 238). Psychologist Perry London (1978) notes that at one time the family was the basic structural unit within the community; it implied intimacy because it was supposed to represent people's most significant aspirations. The basic unit today is the individual, who is able financially to live alone and also is able to find amiable companionship, sex, and other recreation without having to provide anything in return. He points out, though, that the individual may pay a price—the loss of dependability and familiarity in his or her personal life, the dependability and familiarity that can exist in the family unit.

The Effects of Separation and Divorce   Separation and divorce often mean the end of a relationship. In a sense, it is often accompanied by the same feelings of loss as one experiences following the death of a loved one. It can also be viewed as a rebirth for the individual, which can be almost as difficult as the experience of death or loss. Once the mourning, grief, and anger subside, the separated or divorced individual is faced with important choices about his or her life's direction. The major dangers facing the newly separated and divorced are living with the hope that the loved one will return, remaining in prolonged seclusion, focusing on hostility and getting back at the former mate, and jumping too quickly into another relationship. Separation and divorce also are usually complicated by the presence of children or property. Counseling before or after separation and divorce can help couples learn from their mistakes and make satisfactory adjustments to the change in their lives.

FAILURE AT INTIMACY

Restrictive social norms, a demanding lifestyle, separation from intimacy, and other hindrances to intimacy can produce numerous psychological problems (alienation, low self-esteem, etc.). These problems create even more severe difficulties—lack of trust, **loneliness,** fear, and even suicide.

loneliness   a painful wish for meaningful human contact or intimacy

Lack of Trust

We place our trust in government, corporations, organizations, businesses, doctors, lawyers, neighbors, and friends. Unfortunately, they often disappoint us. We hear people say, "You can't trust anyone anymore," or "I will never trust that person again." However, these are irrational statements and irrational beliefs. In the interest of our personal happiness, we must risk trusting again, for without trust we can have no satisfying relationships. We doom ourselves to what one psychologist, Robert Weiss (1973), calls social loneliness and emotional loneliness—both resulting from the absence of self-esteem and intimacy.

Loneliness

Nearly everyone goes through a period of loneliness, but "now too many people are lonely too much of the time," says Bernikow (1986). Commercial advertisers have taken advantage of our loneliness with such scenes as beer advertisements showing people drinking together. They are not selling beer as much as they are selling friendship. Loneliness is a fact of life for many people in the world today and is at its most desperate level in our crowded cities (Dauw, Watts, and Watts, 1979). Paranoia from the fear that others may be seeking to do us injustice results in a lack of involvement with people. The alienation from lack of involvement filters into our personal lives. Family units are not as close, and our friendships become mechanized into calculations of how much each person has done for the other. This depersonalization in American life has contributed to our feelings of loneliness (Skoglund, 1980).

The fear of intimacy results in loneliness.

social loneliness   the absence of a supportive social network

emotional loneliness   the lack of an intimate relationship

Social loneliness is the lack of a social network of people with whom to enjoy things. When we change jobs, move to a new neighborhood, or begin a new term in a new class and do not know anyone, we often experience this loneliness. The obvious cure is to use our creativity to establish contact with others. **Emotional loneliness** is the lack of an intimate relationship. It cannot necessarily be remedied by just making contact, although that is certainly the first step. The cure for this painful loneliness is risking emotional intimacy with a significant other, as discussed previously.

Many of us become lonely for some of the same reasons we seek excessive privacy: the fear of being known, the fear of exposure, and the fear of rejection. As in the progression of an undetected disease, the comfort and security of privacy may lead to the isolation of social loneliness and the anguish of emotional loneliness. Burns (1984) suggests that although everyone seeks intimate connections, finding someone to love is not necessarily the solution to loneliness. Because lonely people suffer from low self-esteem, loneliness is overcome by learning to love and value oneself. Only when people have developed loving relationships with themselves can they relate successfully to others.

Fear

Many of us are held back by our own fears. As a result of our fears of getting involved, being known, suffering rejection, and sharing intimacy, we cut ourselves off from contact with others. We hide in a crowd; we sit alone; we ride alone. We use our automobiles to insulate ourselves not only from the environment but from human contact as well. They permit only the most limited types of interaction, usually competitive, aggressive, and destructive.

> Patty lived in a suburb of Chicago nearly twenty miles from her workplace. Every day she drove for an hour or more each way. Even though it was expensive, she said, she was happy to have the freedom of owning her own car and not depending on anyone or anything. Then one day she received a notice that her apartment had been sold and the new owners were going to live in the apartment. She had six months to find a new home.
>
> Frantically, Patty searched every possible area, only to discover that the only apartment she could afford was more than sixty miles from her workplace, a much longer drive by car. A friend suggested that she give up driving to work and take the commuter train from her apartment to her workplace. Reluctantly, she decided to try it. The first few days seemed strange, but she noticed that the ride was less than an hour long and that everyone seemed to be having a good time. It was not long before Patty met other commuters, and soon she was thoroughly enjoying the trip. She began to look forward to seeing her new acquaintances each day. One day she phoned her friend to thank her for the suggestion. She had not known how lonely she had been driving to and from work until she began riding the train.

Our fears of being known and of being rejected often compel us to disguise our loneliness and our need for intimacy from ourselves and from others. We are desperate to come together, to really know each other, yet we communicate in ways that guarantee we will stay apart. We deliver mixed messages—love me and leave me alone. Our concern for our emotional security has prompted Alan Dahms (1976) to write, "People exchange ideas in ways that tend to protect rather than expose their inner selves. Everyone stays safe in their emotional aloneness. They strive to be 'cool,' to appear unruffled, attractive, and invulnerable" (p. 86). Such interactions are common in discotheques and nightclubs—two of society's answers to our need for contact.

Larry and Becky met at the beginning of their sophomore year in college. They believed there was a "certain chemistry" between them almost from their first meeting. They seemed to get along perfectly—at times, it seemed, too perfectly. As their relationship grew, they wished to communicate more of their needs to each other but were reluctant to do so, afraid to disturb the harmony they thought was the basis for the relationship. Ironically, protecting what they thought they had and avoiding the risk of growing together resulted in their eventual breakup.

Suicide

Loneliness is a major reason for suicides. Several researchers (Achte and Karha, 1986; Kleist, 1986) have demonstrated a correlation between loneliness and psychological problems such as depression and suicide. Suicide may result when prolonged loneliness pushes people to the point where no alternative seems to provide hope. Shneidman (1987) views this loneliness as an alienation from both self and others. He believes there is potential for suicide when the needs for security, achievement, trust, worth, and friendship go unmet. "Suicide is both a movement away from pain and a movement away from consciousness. Underlying all these is a sense of powerlessness and impotence and the feelings that no one can help with this pain and that there is nothing to do except commit suicide" (p. 57).

Statistics show that suicide is the twelfth leading cause of death in the United States (*World Almanac and Book of Facts*, 1991). Victims come from all walks of life and from all economic and educational backgrounds; physicians, lawyers, and even psychologists have an unusually high rate of suicide. An alarming fact is that in 1988 there were 22,200 murders in the United States and nearly 30,300 suicides (U.S. Census Bureau, 1990). Johnson (1987) reports that "from 1950–1980, there was a 278 percent increase in teen suicide, moving it from fifth to second as a cause of death." From these statistics it appears that we encounter a greater risk from ourselves than we do from each other.

Historically, depression has been a major cause of the alarming increase in suicides among the under-thirty age group. However, it appears that the rate of increase in this group is beginning to lessen slightly. Achte and Karha (1986), on the other hand, believe the risk of suicide is increasing in older people as a result of isolation and feelings of hopelessness and helplessness. Kleist (1986) notes that the highest risk of suicide is among white men over fifty-five and between twenty and thirty-five. He links these findings to depression and alcohol abuse in both groups and, in addition, drug abuse in the younger group. Alcohol and drug abuse implies that these individuals are undergoing excessive stress and are looking to substances to relieve them of the pressures of adjusting to the problems of life.

Stressful events such as the loss of a family member or friend, the loss of a lifestyle, or the threat of terminal illness are possible causes of suicide. It appears that people who attempt suicide after stressful events have less capability of solving their problems than do those who do not attempt suicide (Schotte and Clum, 1982). Alcohol and barbiturates are perhaps the two drugs that have been most studied as far as abuse is concerned. Their excessive use can cause confusion and depression, states of mind conducive to suicide. Another stressor thought by some to be relieved by alcohol and drugs is boredom. Boredom seems to be more of a problem for women with suicidal tendencies than for nonsuicidal women. They also often feel more anxious, angry, guilt ridden, helpless, and inadequate than other women (Neuringer, 1982).

Loneliness and Aloneness

existential loneliness   the experience of loneliness from which we personally and creatively learn and grow; temporary aloneness that is used creatively

The effect of *prolonged aloneness* often takes its toll on us. "Loneliness is such an omnipotent and painful threat to many persons that they have little conception of the positive values of solitude, and even at times are frightened at the prospect of being alone" (May, 1953, p. 26). Being alone can have beneficial effects, however. Moustakas (1961) refers to solitude as **existential loneliness.** Solitude is essential to creativity; out of the depths of grief and despair spring the urges to create new forms and images and to discover unique ways of being aware and of expressing experience. Songwriters and poets often create their best works as the result of experiencing solitude. Winnicott (1958), in his paper "The Capacity to Be Alone," draws the distinction between enjoying a sense of privacy and feeling isolated or lonely. He also speaks of the capacity to be alone as "one of the most important signs of maturity in emotional development" (p. 418). Thus, the aloneness of solitude can lead to fulfillment, creativity, growth, and satisfaction.

THE FUTURE FOR LOVE AND INTIMACY

Love, in its most loving sense, is appreciation and respect for another person for all that he or she has been in the past, is now, and has the potential to become. It is appreciation of the other person as someone with whom we can learn and grow. It is the belief that the other person complements us. As Leo Buscaglia defines it, it is "a process not of my wanting to make you over in my image as I would desire you, but my wanting to lead you back to yourself, to what you are, to your uniqueness, to your original beauty" (1982, p. 41).

> *I should have told you*
> *that love is more than being warm*
> *in bed.*
> *More than individuals seeking*
> *an accomplice.*
> *Even more than wanting to share.*
> *I could have said*
> *that love at best is giving what*
> *you need to get.*
> *But it was raining*
> *and we had no place to go*
> *and riding through the streets*
> *in a cab*
> *I remembered that words are only*
> *necessary after love has gone.*
>
> (Rod McKuen, Stanyan Street and Other Sorrows. New York: Random House, 1970, p. 33.)

In our search for intimacy we may head in as many directions as the mind can conceive. Old patterns of intimacy in friendships, love affairs, and marriage seem to have been undone in barely one generation (London, 1978). New ones are not yet well enough developed to be entirely clear. For both young and old, sexual values, housekeeping arrangements, and coping patterns are in transition. People of all ages are baffled by vague new demands and possibilities. Many seem to be using whatever means they can to find intimacy. They are living by new standards, defying the norms under which they were reared.

It may seem that a miracle is necessary for intimacy to survive as the beginning of the twenty-first century approaches. We must remember, though, that we are flexible, capable of flowing with change and adjusting to nearly any situation to meet our needs. Even though our modern society appears to discourage intimacy in many ways, we are searching for it more fervently than ever. Carl Rogers (1970) has contended that we are now probably much more aware of our inner loneliness than at any other time in history. As a result, we are more intensely seeking relationships that provide a higher quality of intimacy. Further, Buscaglia (1982) believes that our ability to form these meaningful and lasting intimate relationships is directly related to the condition of our mental health. Intimacy is more difficult to achieve when we are in a state of poor mental health.

Finally, we must unlearn much of what we have been taught in the past about love and intimacy and learn new attitudes that best fit each of our own sets of needs. By establishing our own norms for intimacy, we can grow toward becoming the healthy individuals we have the potential to become.

Critical Review 4

1. Horn suggests that the accumulation of money and the high value placed on it may hamper our chances to achieve intimacy. T F

2. Existential loneliness is the experience of alienation from ourselves and from others. T F

3. The lack of a social network may cause people to experience social loneliness. T F

4. The most important deficiency from lacking an intimate relationship is sexual deprivation. T F

5. Suicide is more common among black men over the age of fifty-five and those between twenty and thirty-five. T F

6. The experience of solitude is referred to as existential loneliness.

7. Describe how each barrier to intimacy may influence our fulfillment from love relationships.

8. What can we do to combat loneliness in our lives?

SUMMARY

■ Intimacy is one of our strongest needs. It is an intense and meaningful communion between two people. It is focused on the interpersonal expression of intellectual, physical, and emotional aspects of selfhood.

■ Our major sources of intimacy are family, friends, pets, and marriage or cohabitation. The successful family provides opportunities for physical and emotional closeness. Friends provide us with acceptance and nurturance outside the family unit. Pets provide unconditional love and seem to facilitate a healthy emotional development in children. Marriage is a source of intimacy chosen by many people. It has the potential of fulfilling most of our needs for intimacy. Cohabitation, or living together outside of marriage, is becoming a choice of many couples. However, there is some question as to whether this arrangement prepares a couple for success in marriage.

■ People often confuse romance and intimacy. They may have a limited and unrealistic concept of love. The definition of romantic love is based on selfishness, possessiveness, and idealism. These standards cause us to have unrealistic expectations of ourselves and our partners.

■ Emotional intimacy, the highest level of intimacy, is achieved and maintained by continual evaluation and growth. It is achieved through mutual self-awareness and self-disclosure of our innermost feelings.

■ We find a mate when we are able to have an "intrinsic attraction" for another person. This is when the other person is important as an individual and not just as a means to our satisfaction. Complementarity, propinquity, and similarity are the essential ingredients of the initial stage of finding a mate.

■ We are able to grow together when we are mutually acceptable to each other, are able to express ourselves freely, are able to transcend gender defensiveness, are able to base our attraction and interaction on want rather than need, are able to maintain separate identities, and can objectively love and admire our partner.

■ Physical intimacy is the physical expression of emotional intimacy through touch and sexual communion. Our intimate relationships can be greatly enhanced by allowing ourselves to act on our need to touch.

■ Sexual responsibility means being responsible for the decision to engage in sex, for protection from unwanted pregnancy, and for protection from sexually transmitted diseases.

■ Social norms, role stereotypes, and the stresses of society often inhibit our achievement of a satisfying intimacy. This often results in loneliness. Although being alone at times can be beneficial, emotional loneliness and social loneliness may lead to depression and eventually suicide.

SELECTED READINGS

Burns, D. D. *Intimate Connections.* New York: Signet Books, 1985. The principles of cognitive therapy are applied to help eliminate the negative thinking and low self-esteem that cause loneliness and shyness. The author provides a step-by-step process to help you assert yourself in everyday situations and loving relationships.

Gorski, T. T. *Getting Love Right: Learning the Choices of Healthy Intimacy.* New York: Simon & Schuster, 1994. This book explains how to become a healthy partner, how to choose a healthy partner, and how to develop and maintain a healthy intimate relationship.

Gottman, J. *Why Marriages Succeed or Fail.* New York: Simon & Schuster, 1994. Psychologist John Gottman has used his experience of more than a decade of working with more than 2,000 couples to write this practical guide to repairing the way wives and husbands relate to each other. He also helps the reader discover destructive patterns that often lead to divorce.

Johnson, J. *Why Suicide?* New York: Oliver Nelson, 1987. An authoritative expose of the teenage culture and the personal problems that lead to self-inflicted death among teenagers. It presents clues that alert others to suicidal intentions and what can be done to help prevent suicide.

McCoy, K. *Coping with Teenage Depression.* New York: Signet Books, 1982. A practical guide to ways parents can communicate and listen more effectively to troubled young adults. Special advice is given on how to handle such problems as eating disorders, sexual promiscuity, pregnancy, and truancy, as well as information on how these acting-out behaviors are triggered.

Rubin, L. B. *Just Friends: The Role of Friendship in Our Lives.* New York: Harper & Row, 1985. A discussion of the full range of friendships both prior to and outside and inside marriage. Rubin describes the importance of friendship in our personal growth and development.

Smith, A. D., and Reid, W. J. *Role-Sharing Marriage.* New York: Columbia University Press, 1986. A book based on indepth personal interviews with married couples who equally share bread-winning, home-care, and child-care responsibilities, with the goal of achieving family cohesion.

REFERENCES

Achte, K., and Karha, E. "Some Psycho-Dynamic Aspects of the Presuicidal Syndrome with Special Reference to Older Persons." *Crisis* (March 1986): 24–32.

Allen, L. and Santrock, J. W. *Psychology: the Context of Behavior.* Dubuque, IA: Wm. C. Brown, 1993.

American Broadcasting Company. Report on "20/20" (January 15, 1987).

Bailey, J. M. and Benishay, D. S. "Familial Aggregation of Female Sexual Orientation." *American Journal of Psychiatry,* 150, (1993): 272–277.

Bernikow, L. "Loneliness as an American Epidemic." *U.S. News and World Report* (July 21, 1986): 60.

Bohmer, C. and Parrot, A. *Sexual Assault on Campus.* New York: Lexington Books, 1993.

Bower, D. W., and Christopherson, V. A. "University Student Cohabitation: A Regional Comparison of Selected Attitudes and Behaviors." *Journal of Marriage and the Family* 39 (August 1977): 447–452.

Browne, A. and Williams, K. R. "Gender, Intimacy, and Lethal Violence: Trends from 1976 Through 1987." *Gender and Society,* 7, (1993): 78–98.

Burns, D. D. *Intimate Connections: The New Loneliness Therapy.* New York: Morrow, 1984.

Buscaglia, L. F. *Living, Loving, and Learning.* New York: Ballantine Books, 1982.

Butler, J. R., and Burton, L. M. "Rethinking Teenage Childbearing: Is Sexual Abuse a Teenage Link?" *Family Relations* 39 (1990): 73–80.

Byer, C. O., and Shainberg, L. W. *Dimensions of Human Sexuality,* 3rd ed. Dubuque, IA: W. C. Brown, 1991.

Cain, A. O. "Pets as Family Members." *Marriage and Family Review* 8 (Summer 1985): 5–10.

Campbell, A. "The American Way of Mating: Marriage Si, Children Only Maybe." *Psychology Today* (August 1975): 37–43.

Carmack, B. J. "The Effects on Family Members and Functioning after the Death of a Pet." *Marriage and Family Review* 8 (Summer 1985): 149–161.

Centers for Disease Control. "AIDS in the United States." 1988 Update, MMWR 1989: 38 Suppl. No. 5–4.

_____. *Sexually Transmitted Disease Surveillance (1993)*. Atlanta, GA: CDC, 1994.

Chase, M. "Many Who Risk AIDS Now Weigh Carefully Whether to be Tested." *The Wall Street Journal* (June 13, 1989): 1.

Chilman, C. S. "Promoting Healthy Adolescent Sexuality." *Family Relations* 39 (1990): 123–131.

Christopher, F. S., and Roosa, M. W. "An Evaluation of an Adolescent Pregnancy Prevention Program: Is Just Say No Enough?" *Family Relations* 39 (1990): 68–72.

Clark, J. R. *The Importance of Being Imperfect*. New York: McKay, 1961.

Crooks, R. and Baur, K. *Our Sexuality*, 4th ed. Menlo Park, CA: The Benjamin/Cummings Publishing Co., 1990.

Dahms, A. M. "Intimacy Hierarchy." In *Process in Relationship: Marriage and Family*, edited by E. A. Powers and M. W. Lees, pp. 36–43. St. Paul, MN: West, 1976.

Dauw, D. C., Watts, T., and Watts, J. *The Stranger in Your Bed: A Guide to Emotional Intimacy*. Chicago: Nelson-Hall, 1979.

Demaris, A., and Leslie, G. "Cohabitation with Future Spouse: Its Influence on Marital Satisfaction and Communication." *Journal of Marriage and the Family* 46 (February 1984): 77–83.

DeParle, J. "Big Rise in Births Outside Wedlock." In *The New York Times: Themes of the Times-Sociology*, edited by S. Veale and W. T. Ethridge, pp. 1, 5, 11. New York: The New York Times, 1994 (Spring).

Duck, S. *Friends for Life: The Psychology of Close Relationships*. New York: St. Martin's Press, 1983.

Filiatre, J. C., Millot, J. L., and Montagne, H. "New Data on Communication Behavior between the Young Child and His Pet Dog." *Behavioral Processes* (January 1986): 33–44.

Fisher, C. "Privacy as a Profile of Authentic Consciousness." *Humanitas* 11 (1975): 27–43.

Franzoi, S. L., Davis, M. H., and Young, R. D. "The Effects of Private Self-Consciousness and Perspective Taking on Satisfaction in Close Relationships." *Journal of Personality and Social Psychology* (June 1985): 1584–1594.

Friedman, E., and Thomas, S. A. "Health Benefits of Pets for Families." *Marriage and Family Review* 8 (Summer 1985): 191–203.

Gallup Report. *Legalized Gay Relations*. Gallup Report, No. 254, p. 25), 1987.

Goldberg, H. *The New Male-Female Relationship*. New York: Morrow, 1983.

Grinker, R. R., Jr. "The Poor Rich." *Psychology Today* (October 1977): 74–81.

Hamer, D. H., Hu, S., Magnuson, V. L., Hu, N., and Pattatucci, A. M. L. "A Link Between DNA Markers on the X Chromosome and Male Sexual Orientation." *Science,* 261, (1993): 321–327.

Hardy, J. B., Dugan, A. K., Masnyk, K., and Pearson, C. "Fathers of Children Born to Young Urban Mothers." *Family Planning Perspectives* 21 (1989): 159–163.

Hartman, W. E., Fithian, M., and Johnson, D. *Nudist Society*. New York: Crown, 1970.

Henshaw, S. K., and Van Vort, J. "Teenage Abortion, Birth, and Pregnancy Statistics: An Update." *Family Planning Perspectives* 21 (1989): 85–88.

Hilt, P. J. "AIDS Advancing Among Heterosexuals." *The News and Observer* (Raleigh, NC) May 1, 1990): 4A.

Horn, J. "Love: The Most Important Ingredient in Happiness." *Psychology Today* (July 1976): 98, 102.

Hyde, J. S. *Understanding Human Sexuality*, 4th ed. New York: McGraw-Hill, 1990.

Information Please Almanac—1987. Boston: Houghton Mifflin, 1987.

Isaacs, S., and Soares, C. "Animal Magnetism." *Parents Magazine* (March 1987): 92–97.

Johnson, J. *Why Suicide?* New York: Oliver Nelson, 1987.

Jourard, S. M. *Healthy Personality*. New York: Macmillan, 1974.

Jourard, S. M., and Whitman, A. "The Fear That Cheats Us of Love." In *Process in Relationship*, edited by E. A. Powers and M. W. Lees, pp. 88–96. St. Paul, MN: West, 1976.

Katcher, A., and Beck, A. *Between Pets and People: The Importance of Animal Companionship*. New York: Perigee Books, 1984.

Kieffer, C. "New Depths in Intimacy." In *Marriage and Alternatives: Exploring Intimate Relationships*, edited by R. Libby and R. White Hurst, pp. 57–63. Glenview, IL: Scott Foresman, 1977.

Kinsey, A. C., Pomeroy, W. B., and Martin, E. E. *Sexual Behavior in the Human Male*. Philadelphia: W. B. Saunders, 1948.

Kleist, T. "Age, Depression, Drugs Linked to Suicide." *Science News* (October 11, 1986).

Koss, M. P., Gidycz, C. A., and Wisniewski, N. "The Scope of Rape: Incidence and Prevalence of Sexual Aggression and Victimization in a National Sample of Higher Education Students." *Journal of Consulting and Clinical Psychology*, 55 (1987): 162–170.

Koss, M. P. "The Women's Mental Health Research Agenda: Violence Against Women." *American Psychologist*, 45 (1990): 374–381.

Leishman, K. "Heterosexuals and AIDS." *Atlantic Monthly* (February 1987): 39–58.

Lester, D., Deluca, G., Hellinghausen, W., and Scribner, D. "Jealousy and Irrationality in Love." *Psycholgical Reports* (February 1985): 210.

Levinson, B. *Pet-Oriented Child Psychotherapy*. Springfield, IL: Thomas, 1969.

LeVay, S. "A Difference in Hypothalmic Structure Between Heterosexual and Homosexual Men." *Science,* 253, (1991): 1034–1037.

London, P. "The Intimate Gap." *Psychology Today* (May 1978): 40–45.

Marin, P. "A Revolution's Broken Promises." *Psychology Today* (July 1983): 50–57.

May, R. *Man's Search for Himself*. New York: Dell, 1953.

McDonald, A. "Bisexuality: Some Comments on Research and Theory." *Journal of Homosexuality* 6 (1981): 21–35.

Montagu, A. *Touching: The Human Significance of the Skin,* 2nd ed. New York: Harper & Row, 1978.

Morris, D. *Intimate Behavior.* New York: Random House, 1971.

Moustakas, C. E. *Loneliness.* Englewood Cliffs, NJ: Prentice-Hall, 1961.

Moslow, A. H. *Towards a Psychology of Being,* 2nd ed. Princeton, NJ: Van Nostrand, 1968.

Murstein, B. I., and Brust, R. G. "Humor and Interpersonal Attraction." *Journal of Personality Assessment* (December 1985): 637–640.

Neuringer, C. "Affect Configurations and Changes in Women Who Threaten Suicide Following a Crisis." *Journal of Consulting Clinical Psychology* 50 (1982): 182–186.

O'Neill, N., and O'Neill, G. *Open Marriage: A New Life Style for Couples.* New York: Avon Books, 1972.

Ong, W. *The Presence of the Word.* New Haven, CT: Yale University Press, 1967.

Patterson, P. H. "Substance Abuse and Sexual Behavior." Paper presented at the 72nd Annual Meeting of the American College Health Association, The University of West Virginia, June, 1994.

Paul, J. "The Bisexual Identity: An Idea Without Social Recognition." *The Journal of Homosexuality* 9 (1984): 45–63.

Pothier, D. "Pets Good for the Heart." Knight-Ridder News Service, *The Miami Herald* (January 19, 1984): pp. D–1, 5.

Rimmer, R. H. *The Harrad Experiment.* Los Angeles: Sherbourne, 1966.

Rogers, C. R. *Carl Rogers on Encounter Groups.* New York: Harper & Row, 1970.

Rose, S. "Is Romance Dysfunctional?" *International Journal of Women's Studies* (May-June 1985): 250–265.

Rubenstein, C., and Shaver, P. *In Search of Intimacy: Surprising Conclusions From a Nationwide Survey on Loneliness and What to Do About It.* New York: Delacorte Press, 1982.

Rubin, Z. *Liking and Loving.* New York: Holt, Rinehart and Winston, 1973.

Reinisch, J. M. *The Kinsey Institute New Report on Sex: What You Must Know to be Sexually Literate.* New York: St. Martin's Press, 1990.

Rubin, Z., Peplau, L. A., and Hill, C. T. "Loving and Leaving: Sex Differences in Romantic Attachments." *Sex Roles,* 7 (8): 1981, pp. 821–835.

Russell, G. "The Father's Role and Its Relation to Masculinity, Femininity, and Androgyny." *Child Development* 49 (1978): 1174–1181.

Safilios-Rothschild, C. *Love, Sex, and Sex Roles.* Englewood Cliffs, NJ: Prentice Hall, 1977.

Schmalz, J. "Poll Finds an Even Split on Homosexuality's Cause." In *The New York Times: Themes of the Times-Sociology,* edited by S. Veale and W. T. Ethridge, New York: The New York Times, 1994 (Spring).

Schotte, D. E., and Clum, G. A. "Suicide Ideation in a College Population: A Test of a Model." *Journal of Consulting and Clinical Psychology* 50 (1982): 690–696.

Skoglund, E. *Beyond Loneliness.* Garden City, NJ: Doubleday, 1980.

Segell, M. "The American Man in Transition." *American Health* (January-February 1989): 59–61.

Shneidman, E. "At the Point of No Return." *Psychology Today* 21 (March 1987): 54–58.

Stevens-Simon, C., and White, M. "Adolescent Pregnancy." *Pediatric Annals* 20 (6) (1991): 322–331.

Toffler, A. *Future Shock.* New York: Bantam Books, 1971.

U. S. Census Bureau. *Statistical Abstract of the United States, 1984.*
———. *Statistical Abstract of the United States, 1990.*

Wallis, C. "Children Having Children." *Time* 9 (December 1985): 78–90.

Weiss, A. G. "Privacy and Intimacy: Apart and a Part." *Journal of Humanistic Psychology* 27 (Winter 1987): 118–125.

Weiss, R. *Loneliness: The Experience of Emotional and Social Isolation.* Cambridge, MA: M.I.T. Press, 1973.

Whitman, F. L., Diamond, M. and Martin, J. "Homosexual Orientation in Twins: A Report of 61 Pairs and Three Triplet Sets." *Archives of Sexual Behavior,* 22, (1993): 187–198.

Winnicott, D. "The Capacity to Be Alone." *International Journal of Psychoanalysis* 39 (1958): 416–420.

World Almanac and Book of Facts. Mawak, NJ: Funk and Wagnalls, 1991.

Wrightsman, L. S. *Social Psychology,* 2nd ed. Monterey, CA: Brooks/Cole, 1977.

■ *Questionnaire Scoring Key*

A Traditional or Liberal Marital Role?

To figure your score: The score can range from 10 to 40. A score of 10–20 shows moderate to *high liberalism,* while a score of 30–40 shows moderate to *high traditionalism.* A score of 20–30 indicates that you are neither traditional nor liberal in your views.

Remember, your results are neither right nor wrong. However, compared with your mate or potential mate, they may indicate whether you have some areas of difference that may cause conflict. Discussing your differences is vitally important to developing and maintaining a satisfying relationship.

■ *Answers to Review Questions*

Critical Review 1 1. F.   2. T.   3. T.   4. T.   5. T.   6. F.   7. T.
Critical Review 2 1. F.   2. T.   3. F.   4. T.   5. T.   6. T.   7. T.
Critical Review 3 1. T.   2. T.   3. F.   4. T.   5. F.   6. T.   7. F.   8. F.
Critical Review 4 1. T.   2. F.   3. T.   4. F.   5. F.   6. T.

PERSONAL ACTION PLAN
Attitudes Toward Intimacy

The exercises in this section are designed to help you assess your present attitudes, feelings, and behaviors concerning intimacy and begin to improve the quality of your expression of intimacy with significant others.

I. This Personal Action Plan consists of several statements focusing on the intimate interaction between you and a significant other in your life. If there is presently no intimate relationship in your life, focus on one that you had in the past or one you hope for in the future. Rate each statement as accurately as possible first in terms of how you would rate the statement and then in terms of how you think your significant other would rate each statement. Draw a circle around both ratings for each statement.

Your Rating	Statement	Other's Rating
1. frequently occasionally never	The other feels free to personally disclose anything to you.	frequently occasionally never
2. frequently occasionally never	You feel free to personally disclose anything to your significant other.	frequently occasionally never
3. frequently occasionally never	The other trusts you completely.	frequently occasionally never
4. frequently occasionally never	You trust your significant other completely.	frequently occasionally never
5. frequently occasionally never	The other is completely himself or herself with you.	frequently occasionally never
6. frequently occasionally never	You are completely yourself with your significant other.	frequently occasionally never
7. frequently occasionally never	The other has warm, positive feelings when with you.	frequently occasionally never

Your Rating	Statement	Other's Rating
8. frequently occasionally never	You have warm, positive feelings when with your significant other.	frequently occasionally never
9. frequently occasionally never	The other feels happy, optimistic, and confident when in your presence.	frequently occasionally never
10. frequently occasionally never	You feel happy, optimistic, and confident when in your significant other's presence.	frequently occasionally never
11. frequently occasionally never	The other feels important and worthwhile when in your presence.	frequently occasionally never
12. frequently occasionally never	You feel important and worthwhile when in your significant other's presence.	frequently occasionally never
13. frequently occasionally never	The other helps you build your self-esteem.	frequently occasionally never
14. frequently occasionally never	You help build the self-esteem of your significant other.	frequently occasionally never
15. frequently occasionally never	The other feels free to discuss any topic with you.	frequently occasionally never
16. frequently occasionally never	You feel free to discuss any topic with your significant other.	frequently occasionally never
17. frequently occasionally never	The other shares his or her joys, pressures, or strain concerning work or school with you.	frequently occasionally never
18. frequently occasionally never	You share your joys, pressures, or strain concerning work or school with your significant other.	frequently occasionally never
19. frequently occasionally never	The other shares with you his or her ambitions and concerns about the future.	frequently occasionally never
20. frequently occasionally never	You share your ambitions and concerns about the future with your significant other.	frequently occasionally never

Your Rating	Statement	Other's Rating
21. frequently occasionally never	The other shares his or her sensitivities with you.	frequently occasionally never
22. frequently occasionally never	You share your sensitivities with your significant other.	frequently occasionally never
23. frequently occasionally never	The other feels free to express what is most gratifying sexually with you.	frequently occasionally never
24. frequently occasionally never	You feel free to express what is most gratifying sexually with your significant other.	frequently occasionally never
25. frequently occasionally never	The other feels free to share that which he or she feels guiltiest about or most ashamed of from his or her past.	frequently occasionally never
26. frequently occasionally never	You feel free to share with your significant other what you feel guiltiest about or most ashamed of from your past.	frequently occasionally never
27. frequently occasionally never	The other feels free to discuss differences between him or her and you without fear of disrupting the relationship.	frequently occasionally never
28. frequently occasionally never	You feel free to discuss differences with your significant other without fear of disrupting the relationship.	frequently occasionally never
29. frequently occasionally never	The other listens with interest when you talk.	frequently occasionally never
30. frequently occasionally never	You listen with interest when your significant other talks.	frequently occasionally never
31. frequently occasionally never	The other shows an interest in you and your activities (work, school, hobbies, organizations, interests, and so on).	frequently occasionally never
32. frequently occasionally never	You show an interest in your significant other and his or her activities.	frequently occasionally never
33. frequently occasionally never	The other is respectful and courteous toward you in private and in public.	frequently occasionally never

Your Rating	Statement	Other's Rating
34. frequently occasionally never	You are respectful and courteous toward your significant other in private and in public.	frequently occasionally never
35. frequently occasionally never	The other believes that your relationship has improved in quality since you first met.	frequently occasionally never
36. frequently occasionally never	You believe your relationship has improved in quality since you first met.	frequently occasionally never

One of the best ways to use this exercise is to go back through the statements one by one and identify areas where you and your significant other can realize more potential growth together. This may be a risk, but it is well worth your effort.

The following pages contain another copy of the exercise you have just completed. If your significant other is willing, ask him or her to rate each statement in the same way you have. It might be quite revealing to compare your perceptions of how your partner would rate each statement with your partner's actual rating. This comparison may result in a valuable growth experience for both of you. Take the risk to honestly disclose yourselves to each other. Now is always the beginning.

Your Rating	Statement	Other's Rating
1. frequently occasionally never	The other feels free to personally disclose anything to you.	frequently occasionally never
2. frequently occasionally never	You feel free to personally disclose anything to your significant other.	frequently occasionally never
3. frequently occasionally never	The other trusts you completely.	frequently occasionally never
4. frequently occasionally never	You trust your significant other completely.	frequently occasionally never
5. frequently occasionally never	The other is completely himself or herself with you.	frequently occasionally never
6. frequently occasionally never	You are completely yourself with your significant other.	frequently occasionally never
7. frequently occasionally never	The other has warm, positive feelings when with you.	frequently occasionally never

Your Rating	Statement	Other's Rating
8. frequently occasionally never	You have warm, positive feelings when with your significant other.	frequently occasionally never
9. frequently occasionally never	The other feels happy, optimistic, and confident when in your presence.	frequently occasionally never
10. frequently occasionally never	You feel happy, optimistic, and confident when in your significant other's presence.	frequently occasionally never
11. frequently occasionally never	The other feels important and worthwhile when in your presence.	frequently occasionally never
12. frequently occasionally never	You feel important and worthwhile when in your significant other's presence.	frequently occasionally never
13. frequently occasionally never	The other helps you build your self-esteem.	frequently occasionally never
14. frequently occasionally never	You help build the self-esteem of your significant other.	frequently occasionally never
15. frequently occasionally never	The other feels free to discuss any topic with you.	frequently occasionally never
16. frequently occasionally never	You feel free to discuss any topic with your significant other.	frequently occasionally never
17. frequently occasionally never	The other shares his or her joys, pressures, or strain concerning work or school with you.	frequently occasionally never
18. frequently occasionally never	You share your joys, pressures, or strain concerning work or school with your significant other.	frequently occasionally never
19. frequently occasionally never	The other shares with you his or her ambitions and concerns about the future.	frequently occasionally never
20. frequently occasionally never	You share your ambitions and concerns about the future with your significant other.	frequently occasionally never

Your Rating	Statement	Other's Rating
21. frequently occasionally never	The other shares his or her sensitivities with you.	frequently occasionally never
22. frequently occasionally never	You share your sensitivities with your significant other.	frequently occasionally never
23. frequently occasionally never	The other feels free to express what is most gratifying sexually with you.	frequently occasionally never
24. frequently occasionally never	You feel free to express what is most gratifying sexually with your significant other.	frequently occasionally never
25. frequently occasionally never	The other feels free to share that which he or she feels guiltiest about or most ashamed of from his or her past.	frequently occasionally never
26. frequently occasionally never	You feel free to share with your significant other what you feel guiltiest about or most ashamed of from your past.	frequently occasionally never
27. frequently occasionally never	The other feels free to discuss differences between him or her and you without fear of disrupting the relationship.	frequently occasionally never
28. frequently occasionally never	You feel free to discuss differences with your significant other without fear of disrupting the relationship.	frequently occasionally never
29. frequently occasionally never	The other listens with interest when you talk.	frequently occasionally never
30. frequently occasionally never	You listen with interest when your significant other talks.	frequently occasionally never
31. frequently occasionally never	The other shows an interest in you and your activities (work, school, hobbies, organizations, interests, and so on).	frequently occasionally never
32. frequently occasionally never	You show an interest in your significant other and his or her activities.	frequently occasionally never
33. frequently occasionally never	The other is respectful and courteous toward you in private and in public.	frequently occasionally never

Your Rating	Statement	Other's Rating
34. frequently occasionally never	You are respectful and courteous toward your significant other in private and in public.	frequently occasionally never
35. frequently occasionally never	The other believes that your relationship has improved in quality since you first met.	frequently occasionally never
36. frequently occasionally never	You believe your relationship has improved in quality since you first met.	frequently occasionally never

II. List some personal concerns that you now may have regarding your attitudes, feelings, and behaviors about intimacy in the space below. Create an action plan that will help you begin working on a desired change for the most important (or all, if you wish) of the concerns listed above. Refer to chapter 12 for a guide to aid you in designing your action plan(s).

Chapter Outline

It can help you make or break a relationship. It can help you get a job and also lose it. It can help you get what you want and need from others, and it is essential for your survival. Of all living beings, human beings have the most sophisticated and complex communication system. Since the beginning of time, more effort has gone into the development of this system than, perhaps, any other human undertaking.

One of our greatest needs is to be understood. Even when imprisoned and isolated, human beings use their genius to find ways to communicate with others. Many of us assume that if we have mastered language, we have all the necessary tools to communicate effectively. However, language is only the beginning. The process of communication is one that requires understanding, diligence, and skill.

EFFECTIVE COMMUNICATION

Communicating effectively can reduce the misunderstandings and unresolved conflicts that often result in the termination of intimate and working relationships. Each of us has some skills in communication. However, the results we hope to achieve from our communications often are not realized.

Defining Communication

communication the process of sending and receiving messages through which we and others are known and understand

encoding the process of sending a message

decoding the process of receiving and understanding a message

Communication is the process of **encoding,** the act of sending messages and **decoding,** the act of receiving messages through which we and others are known and understood. Encoding may involve words (oral, signed, or written), symbols, or nonverbal language. Decoding involves careful receiving and analysis of the words (oral, signed, or written), symbols, and nonverbal language by the person to whom the message is directed (DeVito, 1992). That sounds like a simple process. However, a number of overt and subtle skills are essential for the communication process to be effective.

Effective communication entails an *interchange,* a two-way contact in which information, ideas, and/or perspectives are exchanged with understanding as the primary goal. This means we need to know, first, what it is we want to communicate, and second, how to communicate it so that the person or persons receiving our message can understand it as accurately as possible.

Let's consider the communication process in Figure 10–1. The sender transmits a message to the receiver through a selected medium. The receiver acknowledges the message by responding through feedback to the sender, indicating that the message is understood. Ideally, this is how effective communication takes place. However, problems may exist at each point in the process.

Sending a Message

First, the sender must know what his or her intentions are in sending the message. In other words, what is the desired outcome? Second, the sender must decide what information about himself or herself (feelings or thoughts) or about the topic (concepts or ideas) is most important. Third, the sender must have as much information as possible about the receiver or receivers, needs, background information, knowledge, and abilities (Samovar and Mills, 1992). Fourth, the sender must decide how to convey the message clearly and accurately and choose the best medium to do this.

The sender needs to be competent in expressing thoughts and feelings in words and behavior with accuracy and clarity so that the listener can fully understand the message (Wahlstrom, 1992). To help us understand the sender's responsibility, Miller, Nunnally, and Wackman (1975) have developed a model for effective communication called the awareness wheel. The awareness wheel has five parts, as shown in Figure 10–2. The five parts, or dimensions, are designed to help the sender gather the information necessary to send the message accurately and effectively. Let's take a closer look at how it can help us communicate more effectively.

> Chris looks up from his magazine and says, "Gloria, let's take a break now. We could ride our bikes over to Dino's for a pizza. Do you want to?" Without looking up from her accounting work, Gloria responds, "Just a moment," and continues working. After a few minutes pass, Chris asks again, "Come on, Gloria, are you ready to go now?" Gloria mumbles and continues to work on her figures. Chris waits a few more minutes, then abruptly leaves the room, slamming the door on the way out. Gloria looks up in shock and amazement at Chris's behavior. She runs to the door only to see Chris riding his bike out onto the street.

Let's analyze the interchange between Gloria and Chris to discover how this breakdown in communication could have been avoided. Chris and Gloria might have been able to convey their messages more effectively had they used the concepts in the awareness wheel. Chris could have used at least four of the five dimensions of the wheel to communicate more clearly his needs or wishes. Suppose he had chosen to use the *feeling* dimension. He could have said, "I'm feeling left out," or "I'm feeling bored," or "I'm feeling lonely," or "I'm feeling angry." Sharing his feelings would have let Gloria understand more accurately the basis for his wishes. He might have added statements from the *thinking* dimension, such as "I'm thinking you've been very busy with your work lately and we haven't done much together," or "It's such a beautiful day—I think it would be fun to go for a bike ride together." The message could have been further clarified by statements from the *wanting* dimension, such as "I want us to pack a picnic lunch and ride our bikes to the beach for the afternoon" or "I want us to ride our bikes to Dino's for a pizza." He might have clarified his message even more by stating, "I'm going to ride my bike over to Dino's for a pizza. Would you like to come with me?" This statement represents the *doing*, or action, dimension of the awareness wheel.

The more dimensions used, the clearer the message. The more information we can convey, the fewer the chances that we will be misunderstood. The more we are understood, the greater the satisfaction we will experience in our rela-

---

CRITICAL THINKING ISSUE
Communication Problems

Communication is a problem because people don't say what they mean.

Communication problems exist because people don't listen.

People are often accused of not thinking before they speak. They give confusing messages and assume that others understand them. Therefore, they don't communicate effectively.

People are too busy thinking about their own thoughts, opinions, ideas, and problems. Therefore, they cannot concentrate on what others are saying.

I take the position that:

FIGURE 10–1
Communication is a complex two-way process.

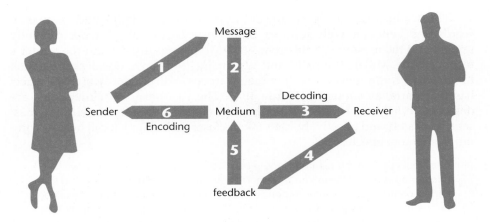

tionships. By speaking for himself, Chris could have let Gloria know what he was feeling, thinking, wanting, and doing.

Now let's explore the ways Gloria could have used the awareness wheel to speak for herself and respond to Chris. Suppose Gloria had begun with the *sensing* dimension. Our senses help us tune in to what is going on around us. Using this dimension, Gloria might have said, "You've had a sad look on your face lately. I've seen you sit around the house, and nothing seems to interest you. I've even heard you sigh while I do my accounting." Sensing data only relay what has been observed with the senses. Gloria could have added interpretive meaning to her sense data by using the *thinking* dimension. Her interpretation would have stemmed from her own past learning experiences in connecting sensory information with meaning. She might have said, "I think you are bored," or "I think you are lonely," or "I think you are annoyed." By using these two dimensions, she could have let Chris know that she was aware of him through his behavior.

By using the other three dimensions, she could have given Chris her response to his statements. She might have begun by saying, "I'm feeling pressured to complete this project I've been working on the past two weeks. I'm beginning to feel bored with it, and I'm quite annoyed with myself for agreeing to work at home to complete it. When I agreed to do it, I thought we could use the extra money, but I didn't know it would involve this much time. I, too, want to spend time with you right now. I'm going to try to finish this within the next

FIGURE 10–2
The awareness wheel helps us remember to send a message more accurately and effectively by communicating what we are sensing, thinking, feeling, wanting, and doing.

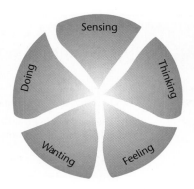

We spend much of our lives trying to make other people understand us.

hour, and even if I don't, we'll go for a bike ride to the beach or to Dino's, whichever you prefer."

Chris might well have responded, "That's great! I'll make the picnic lunch to take to the beach, and I'll make sure there's enough air in the bike tires."

With more information about their sensings, feelings, thoughts, wants, and actions, and more understanding of each other's needs, Gloria and Chris may have achieved a satisfying solution to a situation that otherwise could result in a serious misunderstanding.

Male and Female Communication

Men and Women seem to view the communication process differently. Deborah Tannen (1990), in her book *You Just Don't Understand: Males and Females in Conversation,* analyzed how women and men communicate. She describes two distinct types of talk, *rapport talk* (or private talk) and *report talk* (public talk). Women seem to be more inclined to be comfortable using rapport talk as a way to establish connections and build relationships. Women generally are more comfortable talking when they feel close to others. Men are more inclined to be comfortable using report talk as a way of getting and holding center stage and confirming their status among others. Women enjoy conversations that center on discussing similar events or experiences. Men often find this type of conversation uninteresting and prefer to communicate by joking, storytelling, or giving information. These differences of style and emphasis are often quite annoying to the opposite sex. Tannen believes that if each of us understood more about the conversational styles of the other gender, there would be fewer harmful and unjustified misinterpretations.

John Gray (1993), in his book, *Men are from Mars, Women are from Venus,* believes that men and women have different communication styles because they have different values. These differences in values often get each gender in trouble with the other. Men often mistakenly offer solutions and invalidate feelings while women offer unsolicited advice and direction. When experiencing stress, men usually pull back and think about what is bothering them while women talk about what is bothering them. Men are motivated when they feel needed whereas women are motivated when they feel cherished. Men primarily need a kind of love that is characterized by trust, acceptance, and appreciation. Women need a kind of love that is caring, understanding, and respectful. When attempting to please, men are concerned with the big gift while women are concerned with the little expressions of love. When women talk about problems with their mates, they often want to feel close and secure and have their mates just listen to them. Instead, men often believe they must offer solutions to the problems as a way of showing their love. In situations like these, neither of them get what they need.

Gray believes that men and women in a relationship need to take more time to understand the values and needs that motivate the other person. They can do this by learning to communicate their feelings and thoughts more accurately and by becoming more careful and concerned listeners.

Communicating Feelings and Thoughts   Feeling and thinking are both essential to effective communication; however, saying "I feel" when we mean "I think" often muddles our messages. In general, *thinking* (head talk) involves an explanation of an interactive situation, while *feeling* (gut talk) leads to an understanding of it. Head talk is the prose of communication; gut talk is the poetry (Banet, 1973).

Most of us have learned to use *think* statements correctly—that is, we do not say "I think" when we mean "I feel." We are taught that *think* statements are important, as they represent attempts to define, opine, observe, infer, rationalize, categorize, generalize, and summarize, all of which are certainly important for survival in our interpersonal environment. *Think* statements are bound by the rules of logic and scientific inquiry, and they require words or symbols to be communicated. They may be true or untrue and may also be proven or disproven. Perhaps it is because the validity of our *think* statements can be tested that many of us hedge our statements by erroneously using "I feel" instead of "I think."

Feel statements report our affective, immediate, nonrational, emotional, gut responses to people and events. They are usually personal and idiosyncratic in that they refer to our inner states—that is, to what is happening inside of us. *Feel statements are not true or false, good or bad, but are only communicated honestly or dishonestly.* Unlike *think* statements, *feel* statements may not require words. In fact, sometimes they are best communicated nonverbally, a process we will discuss later in this chapter.

To communicate our messages more effectively, we need to practice using "I feel" and "I think" accurately. For example, "I feel that Jane is responding irrationally" is not an expression of feeling but a statement of opinion based on an observation of Jane's behavior. If your intention is to share your feeling about Jane's behavior, it is more accurate to say, "I am uncomfortable (annoyed, angry, hurt, sad, frightened) with Jane's response." "I feel that all people are created equal" expresses adherence to an abstract principle that cannot really be felt. This is a statement of belief that may be more accurately stated, "I believe all people are created equal." Often, the presence of the words *that* or *like* after the words *I feel* is a clue that we are inaccurately using the word *feel* to make a *think* statement.

Following is a partial list of words that convey feeling and that may help us identify feeling statements.

angry	glad
anxious	grieved
apathetic	hesitant
bored	jubilant
calm	lonely
cautious	loved
comfortable	proud
confident	sad
confused	satisfied
content	silly
daring	surprised
elated	uncomfortable
excited	uneasy
fearful	weary

Sharing our feelings with others is important to effective communication. Many of us share our feelings so seldom that we may condition ourselves to screen out awareness of our internal reactions to people and events. By getting in touch with our innermost feelings and by communicating them along with our thoughts, we greatly enhance our communication and enrich our interpersonal relationships.

Responsible Communication *Effective communication occurs when we take responsibility for our thoughts, feelings, and behaviors.* We do this by speaking only for ourselves and by letting others speak for themselves. How many times have you heard yourself or someone else say something like "We all feel great." "She will be angry if you do that." "This would make most people happy, don't you think?" "It might be good for us to be more understanding with each other." You might ask, What is wrong with these statements? I use them all the time. Perhaps you do, and so do many of us. This is one of the many reasons we may be ineffective as communicators. When you speak for anyone other than yourself, you make a glaring assumption—the assumption that you are either a mind reader or such an expert on the inner experience of others that you know what they think, feel, and want.

We can avoid this error by remembering to speak only for ourselves. Statements that include *I, me, my,* or *mine* help us communicate our feelings, thoughts, needs, and desires more clearly. Instead of the speaking-for-others statements used in the previous paragraph, we could say, "I feel great." "I would be angry if you did that to me." "This would make me happy." "I am going to be more understanding of your ideas." When we speak for others, we are behaving irresponsibly. Only when we speak for ourselves and let others speak for themselves can we respond authentically to each other.

Assertive Communication When we speak for ourselves, we are more likely to demonstrate **assertive communication**. We also demonstrate that we are acting in our own best interest by being fully responsible for our intentions,

assertive communication
responsible communication that does not decrease our self-esteem or the self-esteem of others

We communicate more effectively when we use all of our personal resources (thoughts, feelings, and wants).

thoughts, and feelings, and thus enhancing our personal power and self-esteem (Bower and Bower, 1991).

Perhaps we can best define assertive communication by describing what it is not. First, it is not making passive statements, such as "Uh, excuse me, but I was wondering if you would be willing to tell me again how to do this." This need would be better expressed in an assertive way by simply saying, "I want you to explain again how you want me to do this." Second, it is not making aggressive statements, such as "I am sick and tired of the way you tell me what to do." An assertive statement is, "I feel put down when you tell me what to do." Assertive communication, then, is communicating in such a way that we make our needs, feelings, thoughts, and desires known without decreasing our self-esteem and the self-esteem of others.

Self-Esteem and Assertiveness   People who employ passive statements convey their timidity by asking permission to be heard ("If anyone is interested, I may have a solution to the problem" or "This may not be important to any of you, but . . ." or "This is probably not a good idea, but . . ."). They seem to assume that no one is interested in hearing what they have to say. Bower and Bower (1976) describe them as *silent martyrs*. They often use martyr statements in an attempt to manipulate others into giving them what they want, hoping others will feel sorry for them. The use of passive statements results in a continual eroding of their self-confidence, self-respect, and self-esteem.

The self-esteem of people who use aggressive statements also suffers. These people attempt to get what they want by verbally attacking others, forcing a win/lose confrontation. They usually "have the last word" and walk away from a confrontation as "the winner." However, they make few friends, and their self-esteem suffers from feelings of guilt at having mistreated others. Among the benefits of assertive communication are the following:

1. Assertive persons realize that they can and will defend themselves. In this way, they become increasingly self-confident and less fearful in their dealings with others. They know they can be strong when necessary and thus do not have to approach others fearing control and domination.

2. Assertiveness frees positive energy toward others. Being less preoccupied with self-protection, they can see, hear, and love others more easily.

3. Assertive people are free from the need to control and dominate others. They can allow themselves and others to choose freely, following their own desires.

4. Assertive people have knowledge of themselves. They know what they feel and what they need. Therefore, they are able to determine when someone else is attempting to take advantage of them.

5. Assertive people are able to maintain a clear conscience in terms of their relationships with others. Their actions affirm the values of self-worth and integrity for themselves and for others.

Conflict Resolution   Conflict, the tension that results from the clash of opposing values, attitudes, beliefs, needs, and desires, is inevitable. Conflict management becomes the testing ground for our skill at assertive communication. When confronted with a conflict situation such as a disagreement with a mate or a confrontation with a boss, most people give in to their fear or anger and either do nothing or hostilely confront the other person. Either behavior usually results in the person feeling poorly about how the situation was handled. Through practicing the art of assertive communication, we can successfully manage conflict situations as they arise. In this way, we can develop more confidence in ourselves and ultimately improve our self-esteem. In addition, we may lessen the possibility of damaging the self-esteem of others. The following is a list of suggestions that may assist you in constructively dealing with conflict:

1. Be specific when you state what you believe to be the problem.

2. Avoid just complaining. Offer a reasonable suggestion that you believe will relieve the problem.

3. Ask for feedback on your major points. This gives you evidence that you are heard and understood.

4. Confine your remarks to one issue at a time. When you skip from one point to another, it causes confusion in your mind and the mind of the other person.

5. Avoid being glib or intolerant. Be open to your feelings as well as the feelings of the other person.

6. Always consider a compromise. The other person's view of reality may be just as valid as yours. There are not many totally objective realities.

7. Avoid counterdemands until the original demands are understood and there has been a clear response to them.

8. Avoid assuming that you know what the other person is thinking and avoid predicting his or her reactions.

9. Avoid correcting the other person's statement of feelings. Speak only for your own feelings.

Practicing Assertive Communication

Each day we find ourselves attempting to deal with conflicts with others. Many of us often wish we had handled these conflicts differently, as is evidenced by the frequency of such statements as, "I wish I had said this . . ." or "I wish I had another chance to. . . ." Becoming assertive takes practice. Sometimes we need to rehearse our assertive communication ahead of time so that when situations arise that call for assertiveness, we are prepared. Practice writing several assertive statements for each of the following situations. Discuss your statements with classmates and encourage them to discuss their statements with you. You can learn from each other.

1. You are in a restaurant and have ordered a steak, medium. When the steak arrives you discover that it is very rare. The waiter leaves and does not return for quite some time. Finally the waiter arrives and asks if you are enjoying your meal. You respond . . .

   _____

   _____

   _____

2. You have been working for a company for one year. Because you have wanted to be accepted and liked by your new boss, you have worked overtime on many occasions. Today, you have made plans to go out with a friend immediately after work. Just as it is time to leave, you boss asks you if you will stay and work two more hours. You respond . . .

   _____

   _____

   _____

3. Your doctor prescribes medication for a current ailment. When you ask him for more information about the ailment, he responds by telling you not to worry because it is nothing major. You respond . . .

   _____

   _____

   _____

4. A salesperson approaches you and asks if she can be of assistance. You respond, "No thank you. I am just looking right now." The salesperson continues to follow you as you walk, telling you that you would look nice in nearly everything you see. You begin to be annoyed and respond by saying . . .

   _____

   _____

   _____

5. You are the parent of three children ranging in age from five to eleven. One day you discover that you are yelling at them because they do not seem to be listening to you. The more you yell, the less they seem to listen. Deciding on another approach, you say to them . . .

   _____

   _____

   _____

6. You have been married to your mate for nearly eight years. In the beginning of your relationship, sex with each other was more frequent. The last time you attempted to discuss the infrequency of sex with your mate, he/she got angry and refused to talk about it. Realizing that the problem is continuing, you decide to make an attempt at open communication again. You say . . .

   _____

   _____

   _____

7. Your family meets for dinner, without exception, every Friday night at home. After dinner, the family shares the events of the week. Your parents expect you and your brothers and sisters to be there. Last Friday night, they made a rare exception and allowed you to go out on a special date. All week long, you have been thinking about the wonderful time you had. The date calls and asks you to go out again this Friday night. When you explain about your family tradition, you are told that Friday evening is the only time that he/she is available because of work requirements. You want to go out. You meet with your parents and say . . .

   _____

   _____

   _____

8. A friend invites you to a large party so you can meet some "influential people." When you arrive, everyone seems to be in small groups or paired off with someone. You begin to feel lonely and uncomfortable. As you gaze around the room, you notice a person of the opposite sex standing by the punch bowl. You walk up and say . . .

   _____

   _____

   _____

10. Avoid labeling your partner by calling him or her names such as coward, neurotic, or childish. These sweeping judgments do little to influence the resolution of conflict.

11. Avoid using sarcasm. It is abusive and only reinforces antagonism.

12. Avoid talking about the past. Stay in the present. It is difficult to remember our feelings or what was said in the past. Deal with all conflict situations as soon as possible. Using past events to reinforce the present may look like unfair weaponry.

13. Avoid overloading the other person with grievances. To do so makes the other person feel hopeless and suggests that you may have been storing complaints. It may also imply that you have not thoroughly thought about what is troubling you.

14. Meditate. Take time to consult your thoughts and feelings before speaking. Your surface reactions may mask some very important information.

15. Express your feelings. Say, "I feel angry when . . ." instead of "You make me angry." By stating our feelings, we can avoid creating defensiveness in the other person.

16. Avoid naming a winner or loser. If you have been successful at conflict resolution, both of you are winners.

Critical Review 1

1. The process of sending and receiving messages, with understanding as the goal, is called communication. T F

2. If the sender of the message is certain about the information to be sent, knowledge about the receiver's needs is unimportant. T F

3. The awareness wheel is designed to help the sender gather important information to aid in effective communication. T F

4. "I feel that the United States is the best country in the world" is an accurate statement from one dimension of the awareness wheel. T F

5. It is important to differentiate between feeling statements and thinking statements when communicating. T F

6. Feeling statements are neither good nor bad, true nor false, but are either honest or dishonest. T F

7. Sharing our feelings as well as our thoughts is crucial to effective communication. T F

8. When we assume that we know what the other person is thinking, feeling, sensing, wanting, or doing, and speak for them, we are behaving irresponsibly. T F

9. Using words effectively to "put others in their place" is called assertive communication. T F

10. Conflict management requires aggressive communication so that the other person will see our point of view. T F

11. What are the components of responsible communication? In what ways does responsible communication contribute to our effectiveness and to our self-esteem?

12. In what ways does assertive communication help us resolve everyday problems and conflicts?

OBSTACLES TO COMMUNICATION

Aggressive Communication

Many people erroneously assume that being assertive means being aggressive. Manipulating and controlling others in an overpowering manner is not what it means to be assertive. We demonstrate aggressive communication by:

■ *directing, ordering,* or *commanding* another person to do something. We are telling others that their feelings and needs are not important and that they must conform to our feelings and needs. "I don't care what you want. You do what I told you to do and do it now!" We produce fear of our power and communicate unacceptance of the other person. These messages usually engender feelings of resentment and anger, frequently causing the other person to express hostility.

■ *warning, admonishing,* or *threatening* another person into realizing what the consequences are going to be if he or she does other than what we want. This communicates that you do not have any respect for the other person's needs or wishes. "If you do that again, I will see to it that you never get a promotion!"

■ *moralizing, preaching,* or *obliging.* We tell another person what he or she ought to do. "You shouldn't act that way." Such messages attempt to force, through external authority or obligation, the other person to change. The result is that people frequently respond to such "shoulds," and "oughts" by resisting and defending their own positions more strongly.

■ *judging, criticizing, disagreeing,* or *blaming.* We make negative judgments or evaluations of others. "It's all your fault!" These messages, perhaps more than any other, make people feel inadequate, inferior, stupid, and unworthy, through such messages, self-concepts develop in negative ways, causing people to respond in defensive ways.

■ *name-calling, ridiculing,* or *shaming.* We make others feel foolish, unworthy, and unloved, by stereotyping or classifying them. Such messages have a devastating effect on the self-image of the other person, who usually focuses on the unfair label rather than any constructive message.

■ *withdrawing, distracting,* or *humoring.* We deny the other person's expression of feelings by distracting them or by humoring them. These messages communicate that we are not concerned about the well-being of the other person. "Boy, I wish I had your problems." By responding with such messages, we cause the other person to feel hurt, rejected, and belittled. Putting people off or diverting their feelings for the moment may appear to be a remedy to a problem or unpleasant situation, but a person's feelings do not go away so easily. Problems put off are problems unsolved. When we continually brush aside the problems of others, we may lose our friendships, because others will take their important feelings and problems elsewhere.

When we communicate in aggressive and unfeeling ways, we communicate a lack of understanding and empathy to others. Aggressive communication is usually interpreted by others as communicating nonacceptance. To communicate in this way means that we will eventually alienate ourselves from others.

Indirect Communication

The Question   The question is perhaps the most frequently used form of **indirect communication** (communication that approaches the issue in an ambiguous way). In fact, many questions are *pseudoquestions* (Pfeiffer and Jones, 1974). Here, the questions may not be seeking information or even an answer from the receiver. Instead, the questioner is offering an opinion and hoping to force the other person to agree.

Our communication would be more effective if we eliminated many kinds of questions entirely. By replacing many questions with statements, we could come closer to honest communication with each other. Before we can achieve this goal, however, we must be able to identify the various pseudoquestions that people use.

According to Pfeiffer and Jones (1974), there are eight basic types of pseudoquestions: co-optive questions, punitive questions, hypothetical questions, imperative questions, screened questions, set-up questions, rhetorical questions, and "got 'cha" questions (see Table 10–1). *Co-optive questions* ("Don't you think . . . ?" "Isn't it true that . . . ?" "Wouldn't you rather . . . ?" "Don't you want to . . . ?" "You wouldn't want that, would you?") attempt to limit the response of the other person by building into them certain restrictions.

Questions such as "What proof do you have for those statements?" are *punitive questions* used when the questioner wants to expose or punish the other person without appearing to do so. The goal of punitive questioning is to put the other person on the spot. The *hypothetical question* is often used by the sender to criticize or to probe for an answer he or she is reluctant or afraid to ask for directly. Hypothetical questions often begin with "If," "What if," of "How about."

A type of pseudoquestion that actually makes a demand is the *imperative question*. Questions such as "Have you done anything about . . . ?" or "When are you going to . . . ?" are examples. This type of question implies a command: "Do what you said you were going to do." Like the punitive question, it is often used to put someone on the spot; it implies that he or she has been negligent.

The *screened question* is a very common variety of pseudoquestion. Its use is most often to blame for misunderstandings in attempts to communicate. The sender, afraid of simply stating a choice or preference, asks the other person what he or she likes or what he or she wants to do, hoping the choice will be what the sender secretly wants. For example, suppose you and your partner decide to go out to dinner together. Afraid to take the risk of making a suggestion that you are not sure will be accepted, you resort to the use of a screened question by asking your partner, "What kind of food do you prefer?" You secretly hope the other person will name your favorite food, say, Mexican. To your concealed disappointment, your partner names Chinese food, which you do not like. However, because you gave your partner the choice of naming the food of the evening, you suffer through a Chinese meal. Screened questions may also greatly frustrate your partner. Questions such as "What are you doing Friday night?" and "What do you think about our relationship?" ask the other person to reveal himself or herself at no expense to the sender. If the sender is intent on being responsible and communicating effectively, he or she might say, "I would like to go out for dinner and a movie Friday night, and I would like you to join me." "I think our relationship is a good one, but I think we can improve it by improving our communication."

indirect communication   communication that involves ambiguous messages

TABLE 10–1
Pseudoquestions as
Communication

PSEUDOQUESTION	TYPICAL USE	EXAMPLE	ALTERNATIVE
Co-optive question	To limit the receiver's responses by building in restrictions	Wouldn't you rather go to the art museum than to the beach?	I would like to go to the art museum.
Punitive question	To expose or punish	What right do you have to be in this room?	I want you to leave this room.
Hypothetical question	To criticize or probe	What would you do if that happened to you?	I would be shocked if that happened to me.
Imperative question	To put someone on the spot by implying that they have been negligent.	When are you going to turn in your project?	I would like you to turn in your project soon.
Screened question	To get the other person to assume responsibility for your preference	Where would you like to go for our vacation?	I would like to go to Canada for our vacation.
Set-up question	To maneuver the other person into a vulnerable position	May I assume that you were not prepared for this exam?	I feel sorry that you failed this exam.
Rhetorical question	To seek agreement	Isn't that right?	I think that is correct.
Got'cha question	To trap	Aren't you the person I saw him with last night?	I believe I saw you with him last night.

"Would you agree that . . . ?" and "Is it fair to say that you . . . ?" are examples of the *set-up question.* This pseudoquestion attempts to maneuver the other person into a vulnerable position—to "lead the witness" as a skillful attorney might do in the courtroom. One of the simplest types of pseudoquestions is the *rhetorical question.* The sender may make a statement and immediately follow it with a phrase that assumes approval in advance: "Right?" or "OK?" or "You see?" or "You know?" The sender is not asking for a response and, in fact, hopes not to get one. When people are feeling insecure, they often use "Right?" as an attempted guarantee that their statements will meet agreement. The eighth type of pseudoquestion, the *"got'cha" question,* is a more trapping form of the set-up question: "Didn't I see you . . . ?" "Didn't you say that . . . ?" "Weren't you the one who . . . ?" are examples. Here, the sender tries to trap the other person by digging a pit for the respondent to fall into.

A good rule to remember is that behind every pseudoquestion is a responsible and direct statement that will contribute to effective communication. By beginning our statements with "I want . . . ," "I feel . . . ," "I think . . . ," "I heard . . . ," "I will . . . ," and so on, we can achieve greater accuracy and less chance for misunderstanding.

Of course, we may legitimately use questions to gather information about various things we need or want to know. Questions such as "Do you have an interest in this project?" or "Would you like to join the organization?" are examples of questions that do not disguise our motives. Other legitimate questions ask for feedback ("How am I doing?") or request information about another person's needs ("How may I help you?"). Questions that are used to enhance effective communication are certainly permissible and are indeed necessary.

Cliches   When we use cliches, we do not communicate much of ourselves but use pat, standardized, and stylized ways of communicating. Examples of cliches are plentiful: "She's as cute as a button." (How many times have you thought of a button as being cute?) "Her mind is as sharp as a tack." "Better safe than sorry." "Better late than never." "It's an open and shut case." "He has us over a barrel." "She left no stone unturned." "The early bird catches the worm." "If you've seen one, you've seen them all." "He's beating around the bush."

   We all have been taught numerous cliches, which we often use, and it may be difficult to avoid using them occasionally. But the frequent use of worn-out phrases greatly diminishes the effectiveness of our communication.

The Effects of Indirect Communication   Indirect communication has several negative effects:

1. Indirect communication encourages people to make guesses about each other's intentions. Without direct, open communication, people cannot get to know each other successfully; and what they do not know, they will make guesses about. Guessing games inhibit and obstruct communication.

2. Indirect communication fosters inaccurate assumptions. If we are forced to guess about others, we may often be wrong. Yet we attempt to communicate with others based on our assumptions, even though we are unable to check their accuracy.

3. Indirect communication increases the probability that we will be forced to infer the motives of others. In other words, we try to psych each other out: Why is she doing that? What does he hope to gain by that?

4. Indirect communication encourages game playing, which is usually dishonest or deceptive. To deliberately choose not to be open and straightforward leads us away from the goal of understanding. Game playing is often contagious; one person starts, and others, for their own survival, join in. Game playing often includes sending **mixed messages.** Mixed messages are the result of incongruent communication (changing the message, speaking inconsistently, or behaving in ways not aligned with our words), and they often cause misunderstanding and hurt feelings: "Thanks for not coming to my birthday party," or "You're a nice jerk."

5. One of the surest effects of indirect communication is defensiveness. People tend to become defensive because there is often an implied threat behind indirect communication. Their need to defend themselves makes effective communication even less likely. Defensiveness can be recognized by such postures as denial and projection.

mixed messages   the result of incongruent communication

Deceitful Communication

Many people believe that **deceitful communication** is becoming more of a norm in our society than honesty. From Watergate to Wall Street, in the boardrooms of

deceitful communication   cruel and altruistic lying

Many times we send mixed messages to hide our feelings.

major corporations, in the divorce courts, and in our personal relationships, deceit seems to be evident. The statement, "You can't trust anyone anymore," is heard often. Sadly, lying seems to have become a way of life for some of us. Paul Ekman (1985), in his book *Telling Lies: Clues to Deceit in the Marketplace, Politics, and Marriage*, describes the results of his research on how to improve our ability to tell whether someone is attempting to deceive us. Before we point the finger at others, it is important to remember that all of us have lied at one time or another.

> Lying is such a central characteristic of life that better understanding of it is relevant to almost all human affairs. Some might shudder at that statement, because they view lying as reprehensible. It is too simple to hold that no one in any relationship must ever lie; nor would I prescribe that every lie be unmasked. (p. 23)

Lies can be of two types, cruel and altruistic. Most people rationalize the use of altruistic lies by calling them "white lies," implying that this type of lie is harmless, even humane. Whether right or wrong, some family members may decide to withhold the truth from a terminally ill member of the family. Revealing certain lies may humiliate others or even cost them their lives. Jody Powell (1984), formerly President Jimmy Carter's press secretary, justifies certain kinds of lies in his book *The Other Side of the Story*: "From the first day the first reporter asked the first tough question of a government official, there has been a debate about whether government has the right to lie. It does. In certain circumstances, government not only has the right but a positive obligation to lie" (p. 63). He goes on to describe an incident where he spared "great pain and embarrassment for a number of perfectly innocent people, and admits that he lied to help cover up the military plans to rescue the American hostages from Iran.

Most liars can choose not to lie. Ekman (1985) suggests that "the person who lies could choose to lie or to be truthful, and knows the difference between the two." On the other hand, there are **pathological liars** who know they are lying but cannot control their behavior. There also are those who, through self-deceit, may not know that they are lying. They have lied for so long that they believe they are telling the truth.

The success of lying depends on the liar's ability to conceal the lie and the recipient's inability to keep from being misled. Sometimes the recipient agrees to be misled, wanting to believe a lie. Natural liars know their ability and have been getting away with lying since childhood, fooling their parents, teachers, and friends. They feel no *detection apprehension* about being deceitful. In fact, just the opposite is true. They are confident in their ability to deceive. Natural liars often capitalize on their talent through careers as actors, salespeople, trial lawyers, negotiators, spies, and diplomats (Ekman, 1985).

Sometimes the liar believes that the target will benefit more from the telling of the lie than the deceiver. Worried about whether a young crash victim can withstand the shock, a medical team withholds the truth about the child's parents: "Your mother and father are just fine." The extreme circumstances of such a situation may relieve the deceiver of any *deception guilt* (guilt that refers to the feeling about lying). If a boy lies to his father about going someplace he is forbidden to go, he feels guilty about lying to his father. However, if his father is cruel and abuses his mother, he may lie to his father about his mother's whereabouts and not feel guilty. A summary of detection apprehension and deception guilt follows:

Detection apprehension is greatest when:

- the receiver has a reputation for being tough to fool;
- the receiver starts out being suspicious;
- the liar has had little practice and no record of success;
- the liar is vulnerable to the fear of being caught;
- both rewards and punishments are at stake; or, if it is only one or the other, punishment is at stake;
- the punishment for being caught lying is great, or the punishment for what the lie is about is so great that there is no incentive to confess;
- the target in no way benefits from the lie.

Deception guilt is greatest when:

- the receiver is unwilling;
- the deceit is totally selfish, and the receiver derives no benefit from being misled and loses as much as or more than the liar gains;
- the deceit is unauthorized, and the situation is one in which honesty is authorized;
- the liar has not been practicing the deceit for a long time;
- the liar and receiver share social values;
- the liar is personally acquainted with the receiver;
- the receiver cannot easily be faulted as mean or gullible;
- there is reason for the receiver to expect to be misled; or the liar has acted to win the receiver's confidence and trustworthiness.

Source: Adapted from P. Ekman, *Telling Lies: Clues to Deceit in the Marketplace, Politics, and Marriage* (New York: Norton, 1985).

We can improve our ability to detect deceit by learning how to observe the speaker's words, voice, facial expressions, and body language. Nonverbal communication is a topic we discuss at length later in this chapter.

Self-Concept and Communication

The question may be asked, Why would anyone choose to communicate deceitfully, indirectly, and irresponsibly? One of the most important single factors affecting people's communication with others is their self-concept—how they see themselves and their situations (Chartier, 1974). People have thousands of concepts about themselves: who they are, what they stand for, where they live, what they do and do not do, what they value, and what they believe. Perceptions of self vary in clarity and importance from person to person. We can think of our self-concepts as filters through which we see, hear, evaluate, and understand the world around us.

A weak or negative self-concept often distorts our perception of how others see us and generates feelings of insecurity and sometimes fear as we attempt to relate to others. Our negative view of ourselves causes us to have difficulty conversing with others (for example, difficulties in admitting we are wrong, expressing our feelings or wants, accepting constructive criticism from others, or voicing ideas or thoughts different from the ideas and thoughts of others). Our concern is that others may not like us if we are different or if we disagree with them. However, we soon realize that we are lying to others and deceiving ourselves. The result is that our self-esteem suffers; we feel devalued, unworthy, inadequate, and inferior. This lack of confidence causes us to believe that our ideas are uninteresting to others and not worthy of communicating. We may become even more seclusive and guarded in our communication.

Even as our self-concepts affect our ability to communicate, so our communication with others shapes our self-concepts. Most of our perceptions of ourselves are derived from our experiences with others. We learn who we are from the ways we are treated by significant others in our lives. From verbal and nonverbal communication with those important people we learn whether or not we are liked, accepted, worthy of respect, and successful as human beings. If we are to have strong self-concepts, we need love, respect, and acceptance from the significant others in our lives. We also need authentic and effective communication with others. Through *self-disclosure* and *feedback*, we can begin to improve our self-concepts and build significant relationships (see the discussion on self-disclosure in Chapter 9, "Intimacy and Sexuality").

Psychologists Joe Luft and Harry Ingham developed a classic model of self-disclosure and feedback in the 1960s. It is called the Johari Window, of Self-Disclosure and Feedback, and it is still appropriate for use today (see Figure 10–3). The model can be viewed as a *communication window* through which you can give and receive information about yourself to and from others.

The first pane, the *open self*, represents the information that you know about yourself and that is also known by others. Luft and Ingham called this the *arena*, as it is characterized by free and open exchange between you and others. Common information such as the fact that you are a student, a male or female, single or married is represented in this pane. The second pane, the *blind self*, or *blind spot*, as Luft and Ingham called it, represents that information that is known about you to others of which you are not aware. Other people are aware of

	Known to Self	Not Known to Self
Known to Others	Open Self	Blind Self
Not Known to Others	Hidden Self	Unknown Self

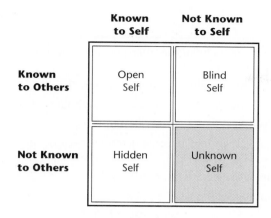

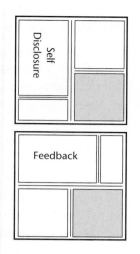

FIGURE 10–3

The Johari Window of Self-Disclosure and Feedback can assist us in building our self-concepts and our relationships.

SOURCE: Luft, J. *Group Processes,* Mountain View, CA: Mayfield Publishing, 1984.

things about us that they observe such as mannerisms, the way we say things, the way we communicate to others, personality traits, and other types of information. Perhaps the fact that you always interrupt other people when they are talking or finish your statements with the question, "you know?" are examples of information that others are aware of that is not obvious to you. This area has also been referred to as the "bad breath" area. The third pane, the *hidden self*, was referred to as the *facade* by Luft and Ingham. This pane contains information you know about yourself that others do not know. It may be embarrassing or humiliating information about which you believe others would judge you negatively if they did know. Therefore, to share your thoughts, feelings, opinions, or perceptions with others may seem quite risky to you. For example, your carelessness may have been the cause of someone else's injury. Or, you have been the brunt of others' badgering because of a stand you took on an issue in the past. Or, you may have been arrested for shoplifting when you were a teenager. The last pane, the *unknown self*, represents those things that are neither known to you nor to others. This pane contains that information, such as detestable childhood traumas, that may be deeply hidden in what Freud called our unconscious. The unconscious could also be the realm wherein lies untrapped potential or resources that still are unknown to you. Hidden within you may be a singer, a sculptor, or a poet (Luft, 1984).

When you engage in *self-disclosure* with significant others, you let them know more about what was heretofore hidden in your private world. In taking this risk, you deepen the level of trust between you and the other person and also increase your self-acceptance by owning your experience in a shared way. As a result, your open self grows as your hidden self gets smaller. When you open yourself to *feedback* from significant others, you gather valuable information about yourself that can allow you to grow and overcome some of the deficiencies that others see. One of the greatest measures of self-concept and self-esteem is the ability to ask for, accept, and use feedback from others as a way to grow and realize your potential. In this way, your open self continues to grow as your blind self gets smaller.

Critical Review 2

1. When we are directing, ordering, or commanding another person to do something, we are using aggressive communication. T F

2. People often purposely use indirect communication to confuse others. T F

3. Asking a question is always one of the most direct methods of communicating. T F

4. Effective communication should never include the use of questions. T F

5. When we use indirect communication, others may become defensive because they feel threatened. T F

6. Indirect communication often results in inaccurate assumptions. T F

7. Pathological liars know when it is appropriate to lie. T F

8. *Deception guilt* is greatest when the liar is fearful of being caught. T F

9. *Detection apprehension* is greatest when the liar is personally acquainted with the target of the lie. T F

10. Risking self-disclosure has little to do with our self-concepts. T F

11. How does the use of questions hamper our ability to communicate?

12. Deceit seems to be becoming a norm in our society. If this is true, how can we deal with this?

LISTENING

Imagine the futility of a radio station's broadcasting of programs to a community that has its radios either tuned to another station or turned off. The same futility exists when someone is attempting to communicate with you and you are either tuned in to something else or turned off.

A Society of Poor Listeners

listening the process of integrating our past experience to help us interpret messages with meaning and understanding

In communication, careful **listening** is at least as important as careful sending. In fact, DeVito (1992) believes it is our most important communication activity. In a study conducted with college students, it was found that 53 percent of their time is spent in listening activities (Barker, Edwards, Gaines, Gladney, and Holley, 1981). Listening is more difficult than many people think. Unfortunately, it is the one aspect of communication that many overlook when attempting to become better communicators (Chiasson and Hayes, 1993). This may be why many of us are poor listeners.

Listening experiments conducted with college students indicate that they listen with only 20 to 25 percent efficiency. We are poor listeners for several, interrelated reasons. First, much of our training in communicating focuses on the essential skills of expressing ourselves and persuading others to adopt our views. Until quite recently, little attention has been paid to the skill of listening. Although most of us agree that listening is important, the overemphasis on sending skills and the underemphasis on receiving skills cause many of us to devalue the importance of effective listening. A related problem is the assumption that if we can hear, we are listening. Listening involves much more than the physical process of hearing. Listening is an emotional and intellectual process integrating our past physical, emotional, and intellectual experiences, which help us interpret the message as we search for meaning and understanding.

The second reason we are poor listeners stems from the fact that the act of listening is less obvious to the observer than the act of sending a message. For example, someone is speaking to you about something of utmost importance to him or her. By all appearances you are listening: Your head is nodding, your posture appears accepting, and your eyes are fixed on the sender's face. Unfortunately, for the sender and possibly for you, you are actually thinking about your activities for the upcoming weekend. This *deceptive listening* is one of the cruelest ways we demonstrate our lack of positive regard and even our contempt for the sender. Occasionally, we are exposed by being so far removed from listening that we interrupt the sender with our own unrelated messages. We are also exposed when the sender asks us for a response, and our response is quite unassociated with the sender's message. Our apparent lack of interest and concern most often leaves the sender with feelings of not being important enough to be heard and understood. Think of a recent incident during which you were sharing something important to you and the person to whom you were speaking interrupted you in the middle of your message to interject an unrelated comment. Try to remember how you felt at that moment.

How Well Do You Listen?

Questionnaire

The following is a list of behaviors that describe the shoulds and should nots of listening. Using the scale that follows each behavior, objectively rate how you typically behave by checking the appropriate response. The scoring of this scale is described on page 417. Don't feel badly if your score is not what you want it to be. Most people are not good listeners. This questionnaire may help you identify some listening behaviors you can begin working on to improve your listening ability.

1. Making eye contact with the person who is speaking.

Never	Seldom	Sometimes	Often	Always
1	2	3	4	5

2. Judging the subject as uninteresting.

Never	Seldom	Sometimes	Often	Always
5	4	3	2	1

3. Letting personal feelings and thoughts of prejudice interfere.

Never	Seldom	Sometimes	Often	Always
5	4	3	2	1

4. Keeping an open mind about the speaker's ideas.

Never	Seldom	Sometimes	Often	Always
1	2	3	4	5

5. Faking attention.

Never	Seldom	Sometimes	Often	Always
5	4	3	2	1

6. Listening just for the facts.

Never	Seldom	Sometimes	Often	Always
5	4	3	2	1

Questionnaire
—continued

7. Resisting external and internal distractions.

Never	Seldom	Sometimes	Often	Always
1	2	3	4	5

8. Judging the speaker's delivery.

Never	Seldom	Sometimes	Often	Always
5	4	3	2	1

9. Using your thinking speed to reflect on the message.

Never	Seldom	Sometimes	Often	Always
1	2	3	4	5

10. Interrupting the speaker or jumping to conclusions.

Never	Seldom	Sometimes	Often	Always
5	4	3	2	1

Such behavior on the part of the intended receiver leads us to the third reason we are poor listeners: We are often more concerned with what is important to us than with what is important to others. We would actually be more honest if we put our fingers in our ears when we stopped listening to alert others that we are no longer interested in what they are saying and are ready to interrupt them with tales of our own.

A fourth reason we are poor listeners is similar to the second reason, except for intent. Rather than acting on the assumption that what we have to say is more important than what others have to say, we continually interrupt their messages to demonstrate to them how much we understand their problem by citing numerous examples from our repertoire of similar experiences. The result is that we often demonstrate just the opposite of our intent. Although we attempt to show understanding, we do not allow others to communicate their thoughts or feelings.

A fifth reason for being poor listeners is that we often do not want to hear what others are saying, because their message may pertain to some behavior or statement from us that is disturbing to them. For example, a husband may often remind his wife that he feels put down by her remarks, and she may continue to ignore his message. We often selectively listen by tuning in and tuning out as we choose.

Effective Listening

The effective listener must be able to discern and understand the sender's message—the goal of communication. Reik (1972) refers to the process of effective listening as "listening with the third ear." This means that we not only listen to the words but to the meanings behind the words—to what the speaker is feeling and thinking. Contrary to what many people think, effective listening is not a passive activity but an active one. The effective listener interacts with the sender to develop meaning and reach understanding.

Chartier (1974) suggests several principles that help us increase the effectiveness of our listening skills. A few follow:

1. The listener should have a purpose for listening: What can I learn from this information? How can it improve my life?

2. It is important that the listener withhold any judgment until the sender has completed the message. The information that we want or need may be coming later.

3. The listener should resist distractions (such as noises, views of others, extraneous thoughts, and so on).

4. The listener should digest what the sender has said before responding: How does this apply to me? How do I feel about this?

5. The listener should seek the important themes of what the sender says by listening through the words for additional meaning. We should listen to the tone of the voice and notice the nonverbal expressions.

We can increase our listening effectiveness by developing competency in the following skills:

1. Establish *eye contact* with the speaker. You are less likely to succumb to distractions when you keep your eyes on the person who is talking.

2. Use your *thinking speed* wisely. Your thinking speed is approximately ten times faster than you speaking speed. Speaking speed is between 125 to 250 words per minute. That gives you ample time to either daydream or think about what the speaker is saying and connect that information with previously learned information.

3. Learn to be an *observer*. This is more effectively accomplished when you keep quiet and observe how the speaker is communicating the message both verbally and nonverbally.

4. Keep an *open mind*. Even though you may disagree with what the speaker is saying, make that judgment after you have openly listened to what has been said. You can always learn more when you are open to new possibilities.

5. *Resist prejudice.* Do not let your biases about members of the opposite sex, other ethnic groups, other age groups, or differences in education get in the way of effective listening. As with keeping an open mind, you may be surprised at what you can learn.

6. Never *jump to conclusions*. When we jump to conclusions, we are refusing to listen to all of what another person is trying to say. We are communicating that we already know what the other person is going to say. The result is that we keep the other person from fully expressing his or her point of view.

Empathic Listening Empathic listening is vital to the communication process. Frequently, people mistake hearing for listening. Hearing can be defined as receiving sounds to gain information for our own purposes. Listening refers to caring for and trying to exhibit understanding toward the other person. Good listening requires you to really focus on others (Phipps, 1987).

Empathic listening requires that you put the needs of the other person, at least temporarily, ahead of your own. This means that you cannot be thinking about what you are going to say when the other person stops talking. The response, "Let me think about what you have said before I respond," is the type of response that lets you know that the other person is listening. Empathic lis-

empathic listening understanding what the other person is experiencing and feeling

tening requires that we listen to the other person's feelings as well as to the words. Sharon says, "My parents have been fighting and it really hurts me to watch it." Rob responds, "That's too bad. Why don't you leave home?" Rob's response indicates that he may have listened to the words, but it does not indicate that he is aware of Sharon's feelings. A more empathic response may be, "I hear you saying you are hurt, but I get the impression that you're also frustrated." This type of listening helps the other person realize that he or she has been not only heard, but understood.

Many people confuse empathy with sympathy. A listener who conveys to the speaker that he or she feels sorry is not necessarily communicating empathy. The response, "Aw, that's too bad," to Jane's remark, "I didn't get asked to the dance by my boyfriend," is more a response of sorrow than understanding. A more empathic response may be, "I hear you being really angry, but it also appears that you're hurt." We learn to listen with empathy by:

1. Imagining ourselves in the speaker's shoes and trying to understand what he or she might be feeling;

2. Trying to get a picture of what the person is describing and then attaching feeling words to what we believe he or she might be experiencing;

3. Paying attention to nonverbal clues and putting labels on those emotions the speaker is showing but not talking about.

Listening for Meaning   Groder (1987) suggests that we can learn more about what people are saying if we pay attention to the speaker's choices of similes and metaphors. Similes and metaphors are figures of speech that use comparisons or storytelling to make a point. A simile includes the words *like* or *as* (She is as quick as lightning); a metaphor only suggests a likeness (He's a bull in a china shop).

Metaphors and similes often reveal what a person is thinking and feeling. A young man who feels trapped by his girlfriend, who is insisting that they get married, may say, "Sometimes I feel like escaping to a deserted island in the South Pacific." His message is that he is feeling pushed by her demands and wants her to stop pressuring him. If someone asks you when you will finish a project about which you are experiencing fear of failure, you may respond, "Well, it is going to be tight, but I think I will have it done on time." This response may convey a feeling of constriction and incompetence.

Listening for Understanding   The assumption that others understand us is one of the major barriers to successful communication. When we are in doubt, however, we can ask the receiver for feedback to help us gauge his or her degree of understanding. Miller, Nunnally, and Wackman (1975) suggest an excellent method to evaluate the listener's degree of understanding. They call it the shared meaning process, and it unfolds in the following manner (see Figure 10–4). First, the sender prefaces the message by saying, "I would like to share an important meaning with you. It is so important to me that I am going to ask you to reflect (send back) what you think I mean." After stating the message, the sender asks, "What do you hear me saying?" The receiver then reflects as accurately as possible his or her understanding of the message. The sender then either acknowledges that the receiver has understood the message or restates the message, asking again for a reflective response. This process continues until

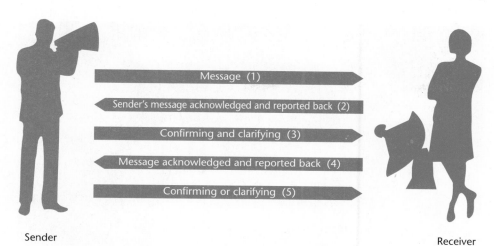

FIGURE 10–4
Shared meaning process.

the sender is satisfied that the receiver has understood the meaning of the message. Let's use a dialogue to illustrate the use of the shared meaning process.

> Colleen: Bruce, I'd like to share something with you that is very important to me.
> Bruce: OK.
> Colleen: Lately, when we've been with Don and Connie, I've felt put down by the way you talk to me and about me. For example, last night you said that I wouldn't have the good job I have if it weren't for your pushing me. I think I got this job through my own efforts. I do appreciate your support, but I do not believe you pushed me to find this job. Sometimes I think you exaggerate your part in some of my accomplishments. So I'd appreciate it if you would be more considerate of me by being more accurate in what you say about me. What do you hear me saying?
> Bruce: I hear you saying you always feel put down by me and I exaggerate when I talk about you.
> Colleen: No—that's not quite what I'm saying. I'm saying that I feel put down by you lately, when we're with Don and Connie, and sometimes I think you exaggerate your influence on my decisions and successes. What do you hear me saying?
> Bruce: I hear you saying that lately, when we've been with Don and Connie, you've felt put down by some of the things I say about you and me. I also hear you saying that, at times, I exaggerate the influence I have on your decisions and accomplishments.
> Colleen: Yes. That's right.

Bruce may not want to respond by sharing a meaning of his own. Colleen will then reflect her understanding of Bruce's message before she makes another response, if another response seems necessary, and so on until Bruce is satisfied that Colleen understands his message.

Reflecting   It is certainly not necessary to use the shared meaning process every time you talk. The process is most useful when you have an important message for which a clear meaning is essential, or when you believe you are being misunderstood.

However, the process is useful for other reasons as well, for example, if we want to use someone as a sounding board to clarify a personal concern. In this way, we may use another person to help us get in touch with our thoughts, feelings, and intentions. Another way in which the process is useful and necessary is when certain procedural steps to a situation need to be conveyed accurately.

Resolving conflicts requires careful listening and honest responses.

In cases where accurate communication is important, the use of the shared meaning process is essential.

If either the sender's or the receiver's intention is not to understand, the shared meaning process certainly will not work. For example, if the sender's intention is to prove to the receiver that he or she is not a good listener—if the sender is seeking to trap the receiver—the process is being used ineffectively and will not work. The process will not work when the receiver succumbs to the temptation to respond to the message by agreeing or disagreeing instead of reflecting the message to clarify understanding. This may be especially true if the issue is an emotional one. The process also may not work if the sender's message is too long and complicated. If the message is long, it may be better to break it into several small parts and several shared meanings. Finally, the process will not work if the sender forgets his or her original message and intent or changes the message when resending it.

In order for the process to work, it is important for the sender to remember (1) to keep to the intent of the message, (2) to make brief statements, (3) to send the message clearly and directly, (4) to acknowledge the receiver's accurate reflection, and (5) not to change the original message. The receiver should remember (1) to report back the message heard in his or her own words, (2) to refrain from responding to the message without first reflecting on it, and (3) to keep reporting back the message received until the sender confirms that it is correct.

Critical Review 3

1. A listener who uses his or her thinking speed wisely is less likely to succumb to daydreaming. T F

2. When we are able to convey to the speaker that we are sorry for what has happened, we are always demonstrating empathic listening. T F

3. Listening is the complex process of searching for meaning and understanding in a message. T F

4. When we appear to be listening but actually are thinking about something other than what the speaker is saying, we are engaged in deceptive listening. T F

5. Reik's reference to "listening with the third ear" refers to the importance of listening to the words of the speaker. T F

6. The shared meaning process is one of the best ways to check on the listener's understanding of the message. T F

7. What are the reasons some of us are poor listeners?

8. How does the shared meaning process assist us in the experience of listening?

NONVERBAL COMMUNICATION

No discussion of effective communication would be complete without including **nonverbal communication** (Fast, 1970). Nonverbal communication has fascinated writers, sculptors, and painters for centuries as they have attempted to describe the human condition. Often we communicate more of our messages nonverbally than verbally. An understanding of nonverbal communication may help us express ourselves more fully, and it certainly will help us become more effective listeners, as Reik suggests when he encourages us to seek greater understanding of the sender by "listening with the third ear." Julius Fast (1977) makes the following observation:

nonverbal communication   any means we use to communicate other than the spoken word

> We all, in one way or another, send our little messages out to the world. . . . And rarely do we send our messages consciously. We act out our state of being with nonverbal body language. We lift one eyebrow for disbelief. We rub our noses for puzzlement. We clasp our arms to isolate ourselves or to protect ourselves. We shrug our shoulders for indifference, wink one eye for intimacy, tap our fingers for impatience, slap our foreheads for forgetfulness. The gestures are numerous, and while some are deliberate . . . there are some, such as rubbing our noses for puzzlement or clasping our arms to protect ourselves, that are mostly unconscious (p. 97).

Defining Nonverbal Communication

Nonverbal communication includes any means we may use to communicate other than spoken words. It is characterized by facial expressions, gestures, body position and movement, space, tone of voice, and general appearance. At times, nonverbal communication may be more effective than words—for example, in expressing despair at losing a loved one or the ecstasy of being in love. At these moments, the touch of a hand or an embrace may communicate what words cannot. Perhaps we have heard people say, "Words cannot describe the feelings I have at this moment." We know by the expression on their faces and the look in their eyes the genuineness of their feelings.

As infants we effectively use nonverbal communication to convey our desire for food, affection, warmth, and so on. It does not take parents long to learn to interpret this nonverbal behavior. As adults, we all use nonverbal means to let others know what we want and do not want. These nonverbal messages are often referred to as "good vibrations" or "bad vibrations." Strangers often become acquainted by nonverbal communication.

A man and a woman are among the guests at a large party. Both are experiencing the loneliness of being in a crowd of strangers. As they look around the room for a familiar face, their eyes meet momentarily, then quickly move away. After a short time, their eyes meet again for a more prolonged look, then turn away again. She notices his neat appearance and the way he walks and stands. He notices the expressiveness of her eyes and her welcoming smile. As the evening progresses, they find it easier to establish eye contact. Having assigned meaning to each other's nonverbal messages, by evening's end, they make verbal contact.

Nonverbal Meaning   We learn the meaning of nonverbal communication from years of observing and modeling the behavior of others. Some nonverbal cues are quite obvious; others are subtle and go unnoticed by our conscious minds. Throughout our lives we learn to attach verbal meaning to nonverbal behavior.

Kinesics

kinesics   the study of nonverbal communication

Kinesics, the study of nonverbal communication (personal space, eye contact, facial expressions, hand gestures, body language, and voice intonation), was nearly nonexistent until early in this century. From 1914 to 1940 there was considerable interest in how people communicate by their facial expressions. Psychologists ran dozens of experiments. Similar interest was shown by anthropologists, who studied body movement. Edward Sapir (quoted in Davis, 1973, p. 2) wrote that, "We respond to gestures with an extreme alertness, and one might almost say, in accordance with an elaborate code that is written nowhere, known by one, and understood by all." Beginning in the 1950s, social scientists such as anthropologist Edward T. Hall (1959, 1968, 1990) began to tackle the nonverbal phenomenon in a systematic way. The study of *kinesics* (see chapter 5) has since become a popular topic for research among anthropologists, psychologists, sociologists, and psychiatrists.

proxemics   the study of the use of interpersonal space

Interpersonal Space   Interpersonal space has a dramatic effect on the communication process. The study of how people use their interpersonal space is termed **proxemics**. Hall (1968, 1990) describes four interpersonal distance zones that seem to be appropriate for certain kinds of interactions that reflect communication in American culture; *intimate distance, personal distance, social distance,* and *public distance.* Intimate distance is reserved for interaction between family members and between lovers. Personal distance is the distance usually maintained between friends. Social distance governs our interactions with acquaintances at school, in business affairs, and with co-workers. Public distance is the distance usually maintained with strangers (for a more detailed explanation of personal space, see chapter 8, "Social and Physical Environmental Influences.")

Hall believes that the distance between people is governed by social norms, the nature of our relationships, and the situation. As is true with other forms of nonverbal communication, interpersonal distance conveys information about our personality, age, sex, social status, and cultural background.

Communicating with the Eyes   The eyes have often been referred to as "the window to the soul" because they are easily observed and often are very revealing. Consequently, some people are uncomfortable looking another person in the eye. Much can be revealed, for example, from the pupillary dilation of the eyes. Physiologically, the eyes dilate in darkness to open their lenses and receive more light. They also dilate in response to psychological factors. Hess (1965) contends that pupillary behavior accurately reflects differences in interests, emotions, and attitudes. His classic study reported that male homosexuals showed greater pupillary dilation when viewing male pinups than to female pinups, with heterosexual males exhibiting the opposite result. Females showed pupillary dilation when looking at male pinups and even greater dilation when looking at pictures of mothers with babies. It was further found that heterosexual males showed much greater pupillary dilation when looking at female pinups who had dilated eyes. It is interesting to note that for centuries women used the ancient drug belladonna to dilate their eyes, thus enhancing their attractiveness to members of the opposite sex.

Communicating with Facial Expressions Harper, Weins, and Matarazzo (1978) believe that in many respects the face may be the single most important body area in the channeling of nonverbal communication. Other researchers have made the following comments about facial expression:

> The face is rich in communicative potential. It is the primary site for communicating emotional states; it reflects interpersonal attitudes; it provides nonverbal feedback on the comments of others; and some say that, next to human speech, it is the primary source of giving information. For these reasons and because of its visibility, we pay a great deal of attention to what we see in the faces of others. (Knapp, 1972, pp. 68–69)
>
> Although there are only a few words to describe different facial behaviors (smile, frown, furrow, squint, and so on), man's facial muscles are sufficiently complex to allow more than a thousand different facial appearances; and the action of these muscles is so rapid, that these could all be shown in less than a few hours' time. (Ekman, Friesen, and Ellsworth, 1972, p. 1)
>
> Facial expression is perhaps the area in nonverbal communication research that comes closest to the more traditional concerns of psychology. The question of nature versus nurture as the origin of behavior is very much present here as is the issue of the components of human emotionality. (Weitz, 1974, p. 11)

Well-documented research (Blurton-Jones, 1972; Eibl-Eibesfeldt, 1971) suggests that facial expressions may be an innate characteristic of humans that cuts across cultures, unlike most other aspects of human behavior, which are largely cultural. Ekman and Friesen have identified six primary emotions that have distinctive facial expressions: anger, disgust, fear, happiness, sadness, and surprise (Ekman, 1992; Ekman and Friesen, 1984). To ethologists these are examples of **fixed action patterns**, or preset sequences of muscle activity often triggered by specific cues in the environment. They serve the function of **social display**, acts of communication that have evolved by virtue of their contribution to survival and reproduction and are apparently under marked genetic control (Konner, 1987). If there is one human social display that qualifies as a fixed action pattern, it is the tendency of people in certain well-defined situations to draw back the corners of their mouths and expose their teeth. Smiling, it appears, is something we are born to do. It appears that these facial expressions, and the meaning attached to each, are universal, and that people from different cultures can identify them correctly (Ekman and Friesen, 1984).

Researchers have proposed several categories to describe the wide range of facial expressions. Plutchik (1962) has suggested the following categories: (1) coyness, happiness, joy; (2) surprise, amazement, astonishment; (3) apprehension, fear, terror; (4) pensiveness, sorrow, grief; (5) annoyance, anger, rage;

fixed action patterns   innate nonverbal behavior that responds to certain environmental cues

social display   certain genetic acts of communication that seem to contribute to survival and reproduction

Understanding Nonverbal Expression

Using Plutchik's (1962) categories, match the corresponding facial expression to each category from the following pictures:

Category _____   Category _____   Category _____

(6) tiresomeness, disgust, loathing; (7) attentiveness, expectancy, anticipation; (8) acceptance, incorporation. Take a few moments to look over this list of emotions. Make facial expressions that you believe communicate each emotion. Do your facial expressions accurately convey your feelings?

Ekman (1985) has stated that next to words, people most often check facial expressions of others to determine the honesty of the speaker's message. The face is the symbol of oneself. Sergent and Bindra (1981) say that a part of the brain is reserved for recognizing faces: "I may not remember a name, but I never forget a face." The face is the primary site for the display of emotion, more so than the body and the tone of the voice. Facial expressions are most difficult to conceal, because they are connected to areas of the brain reserved for emotion. For the most part, facial expressions are involuntary, except when someone is deliberately trying to conceal a message by controlling the muscles of the face.

Hand Gestures   In our society, certain gestures have agreed-upon meanings—the hand wave (greeting), the hitchhiking thumb (I want a ride), the thumb up (It looks good), the thumb down (It looks bad), the salute (Yes, sir/ma'am), the index finger and the thumb held to form an *O* (It's OK), the clenched fist (power or determination), and the open hand (welcoming acceptance). However, not all body signals are easy to interpret nor do they mean the same thing throughout the world (see this chapter's "Cultural Crosscurrents").

Body Language   Fast (1970) suggests that when a woman sits with her legs parallel and slightly crossed at the ankles, it may indicate that she is an orderly

CULTURAL CROSSCURRENTS
Different Meanings in Different Places

If we stop to consider it, we must realize that we use a number of hand gestures every day. We cup our hand behind the ear as a nonverbal way of communicating that we cannot hear. We thumb our noses at those we don't like. We can thumb a ride on the side of the highway. We can wave hello or goodbye. We tell people to be quiet by holding our forefinger vertically against our lips. We give the peace sign by holding up our forefinger and middle finger. And we send a very different message when we flash half the peace sign. Some of these hand gestures used widely in the United States are also used and understood in Europe, which should come as no surprise, given our strong European heritage. Nevertheless, as Morris, Collett, Marsh, and O'Shaughnessy (1979) reminds us, there are a number of other nonverbal hand gestures used in Western Europe that have not been diffused across the Atlantic. For example,

stroking the face between the cheek bones and the chin with the thumb and forefinger is a nonverbal way of saying "You look ill or thin" in the southern Mediterranean; pulling down on the lower eyelid with the forefinger means "Be alert" in parts of Spain, Italy, France, and Greece; and in Italy, pulling or flicking one's own ear lobe is a way of calling into question a man's masculinity ("You are so effeminate that you should be wearing an earring.") The hand gesture of making a circle with the thumb and forefinger, which means OK, in the United States, signifies "money" in Japan, "worthless" or "zero" in France, and is a sexual insult in parts of South America.

SOURCE: From Ferraro, G. *Cultural Anthropology: An Applied Perspective.* St. Paul, MN: West Publishing Company, 1992.

person; but it is far more likely to be an affected positioning or the result of charm-school training. Many believe that crossed legs or arms folded across the chest indicate rejection, discomfort, insecurity, or lack of trust. However, they may also mean that a person has simply changed position for the sake of comfort. According to Ekman (1985), the body is a good source for clues to deception. Unlike the face or the voice, most body movements are not directly tied to the areas of the brain involved in emotion. As a result, manipulation of body movements is quite easy. However, most people do not concern themselves with body movements because they believe that others do not notice them or recognize their meanings, if any. Rarely are people held accountable for what they reveal in their body movements.

Paralanguage   **Paralanguage** is the term given to *how* something is said rather than *what* is said: tone of voice, loudness or softness, speed, rhythm, and quality of speech. Even though most people are less aware of vocal cues than they are of facial expressions, these vocalizations can affect the message being sent. Like facial expressions, they are tied to areas of the brain involved with emotion. It is very difficult to conceal some of the changes in the voice that occur when emotion is aroused. According to Ekman (1985) in 70 percent of the people studied, the voice pitch becomes higher when they are stressed, especially from anger or fear. On the other hand, some evidence indicates that the pitch of the voice drops when people are sad or sorrowful. When a person is attempting to conceal something, his or her voice may take on the pitch of fear. Responding to studies on the pitch of the voice, several manufacturers have developed machines (voice-stress analyzers) that they claim can detect deceit by evaluating the pitch of a person's voice. However, as Ekman points out, they can only detect stress, not necessarily lying.

paralanguage the vocal cues used to send a verbal message

Congruence   In chapter 2 we used the term *congruence*, which also applies here. People often use *incongruent* body language, both consciously and unconsciously, when this happens, their appearance is different from what they are thinking or feeling at the moment. How many times have you attempted to smile when you felt like crying, or stood rigid and erect to stop your knees from shaking, or frowned and shook your fist when you were actually frightened and felt like running away? If you are like most of us, you have probably exhibited incongruent behavior many times as a way of surviving situations in which you believed you could not allow your actual feelings or thoughts to be known.

Body language can be incongruent in other ways as well. Many politicians adopt various body language generalities to achieve what we call *charisma*. John Kennedy had such charisma; no matter what he said, a few gestures or a correct posture captivated his audience. Lyndon Johnson and Richard Nixon took lessons in effective body language to manipulate their audiences (Fast, 1970). Mimics such as David Frye and Rich Little have used the body language of many politicians and celebrities to entertain their audiences, who recognize each individual's specific mannerisms.

The real value of nonverbal communication is in the blending of all forms of communication—spoken words, tone of voice, eyes, facial expressions, hand movements, and body position. The message someone is conveying can most often be trusted when observations indicate that all methods of communications being used are congruent.

Critical Review 4

1. Some facial expressions may be innate human characteristics that are examples of fixed action patterns which are often triggered by specific cues in the environment. T F

2. Social display refers to genetic acts of nonverbal communication that have evolved because of their contribution to humor and entertainment. T F

3. Any means used to communicate other than the spoken word is called silent communication. T F

4. Words may not be sufficient to describe our thoughts and feelings. T F

5. Much of our nonverbal communication is learned through observing and modeling the behaviors of others. T F

6. The ear is often referred to as the "window to the soul."

7. Pupillary dilation may result from both physiological and psychological factors. T F

8. The arms are thought to be the single most important body area for nonverbal communication. T F

9. Some people believe that crossed legs and folded arms are signs of uncomfortableness. T F

10. Like the face, the voice is tied to areas of the brain involved in emotion. T F

11. Studies indicate that voice pitch becomes lower when people are stressed and higher when people are sad or sorrowful. T F

12. Communication is most effective when all levels are congruent. T F

13. In what ways does understanding nonverbal communication contribute to the communication process?

14. How can nonverbal communication detract from the communication process?

SUMMARY

■ The process of sending and receiving messages is termed *communication*. Ineffective communication is the source of most misunderstandings and unresolved conflicts.

■ Effective communication is an interchange of information, ideas, and perceptions with understanding as the goal.

■ The awareness wheel is a five-dimensional communication aid that helps people send messages more accurately. The sender can focus on what he or she is doing, sensing, wanting, thinking, and/or feeling.

■ It is important when communicating, to differentiate between "I think" and "I feel" statements. Thinking statements refer to rational thoughts (head talk), while feeling statements refer to emotional sensations (gut talk).

■ Assertive communication is more likely to take place when we take responsibility for our thoughts, feelings, and behaviors and speak only for ourselves. When we speak for ourselves, we are usually communicating more directly.

■ Conflict resolution becomes the testing ground for assertive communication. Through self-confidence and practice, we can learn to trust ourselves to handle most conflict situations when they arise.

■ Aggressive communication is often mistaken for assertive communication. Aggressive communication is usually interpreted by others as communicating nonacceptance, a lack of understanding, and a lack of empathy. Alienation usually results.

■ Questions are often a form of indirect communication designed to expose, punish, criticize, probe, set up, trap, or disarm the other person.

■ Cliches are another form of indirect communication that greatly diminish effective communication.

■ Indirect and irresponsible communication is often used by people with weak or negative self-concepts. These people are afraid to own their thoughts or feelings for fear of being rejected or ridiculed by others. They also believe that what they have to say is of little value to others.

■ Deceitful communication appears to be an evolving norm in our society. Deceit has been labeled as either cruel or altruistic. Understanding more about lying can help us more readily perceive when someone is being untruthful.

■ The *Johari Window* is a model that helps us use the process of self-disclosure and feedback to both share more of ourselves with others and gather more information about ourselves from others. This model is designed to help us improve our self-esteem by taking the risk of disclosing ourselves to others and opening ourselves to feedback from others.

■ Careful listening is as important as careful sending. Unfortunately, many of us are poor listeners because little attention has been given to the skill of listening. Pretending to listen when we are actually thinking about something else is often one of the cruelest ways we demonstrate our lack of respect for others.

■ Empathic listening, being able to understand what another is feeling, is vital to effective communication. Empathy is not to be confused with sympathy. Sympathy is feeling sorry for another person, not necessarily understanding what he or she is feeling.

■ Effective listening is an active process. It includes not only carefully listening to the words but "listening with the third ear"—that is, for the meaning behind the words or for what the sender is thinking and feeling.

■ The shared meaning process is a reflective process designed to aid in the accurate understanding of important messages. It is especially useful in resolving relationship issues.

■ Nonverbal communication often effectively communicates what words cannot. Facial expressions are believed by many to be the single most important body area for channeling nonverbal communication. We also use eyes, hands, and body positions to communicate many nonverbal signals to others.

■ Communication is effective when all levels of communication—words and nonverbal behavior—are congruent. Understanding through congruence is the goal of communication.

SELECTED READINGS

Bower, S. A., and Bower, G. H. *Asserting Yourself: A Practical Guide for Positive Change (2nd ed)*. Reading, MA: Addison-Wesley, 1991. The Bowers have written a book that helps the reader deal with the problem of nonassertiveness by looking at how it relates to self-esteem and anxiety. They help the reader develop a systematic plan for becoming more assertive.

Ekman, P. *Telling Lies: Clues to Deceit in the Marketplace, Politics, and Marriage*. New York: Norton, 1985. A presentation of the author's research and the research of others on the phenomenon of lying. The author includes ways that we can learn more about detecting deceit through words, facial expressions, paralanguage, and body language.

Gabor, D. *How to Start a Conversation and Make Friends*. New York: Simon & Schuster, 1983. A presentation of information that, if applied, will help the reader be more confident and successful in social encounters. The author discusses how to start and maintain conversations. This is a good book for those who characterize themselves as shy but want to become more outgoing.

Gray, J. *Men are from Mars, Women are from Venus*. New York: Harper Collins Publishers, 1993. A practical guide for improving communication and getting what you want from relationships. Gray has determined that their are distinct differences in the communication styles of men and women. He describes how these differences often get in the way of satisfying and fulfilling love relationships and how to overcome them.

Tannen, D. *You Just Don't Understand: Women and Men in Conversation.* New York: Ballantine Books, 1990. Deborah Tannen describes the different conversation styles used by men and women that result from having grown up in two different cultures. She believes that men and women can communicate more effectively by understanding each others different styles.

Tannen, D. *That's Not What I Meant.* New York: Ballantine Books, 1986. A discussion of how conversation style can make or break a relationship. How we say what we say is often most important. Signals like voice level, pitch and intonation, and rhythm and timing are important and give clues to feelings behind the words. Strategies are offered for success in job interviews, business negotiations, and social encounters.

Weisinger, H., and Lobsenz, N. M. *Nobody's Perfect: How to Give Criticism, and Get Results.* New York: Warner Books, 1981. A book to help you learn how to give and take criticism in a way that does not diminish your self-esteem or the self-esteem of others.

REFERENCES

Banet, A. G. "Thinking and Feeling." In *The 1973 Annual Handbook for Group Facilitators.* Edited by J. E. Jones and J. W. Pfeiffer, pp. 139–141. Iowa City, IA: University Associates, 1973.

Barker, L., Edwards, R., Gaines, C., Gladney, K., and Holley, F. "An Investigation of Proportional Time Spent in Various Communication Activities by College Students." *Journal of Applied Communication Research* 8 (1981): 101–109.

Blurton–Jones, N. E. (Ed.). *Ethological Studies of Child Behavior.* Cambridge, UK: Cambridge University Press, 1972.

Bower, S. A., and Bower G. H. *Asserting Yourself: A Practical Guide for Positive Change.* Reading, MA: Addison-Wesley, 1976.

_____. *Asserting Yourself: A Practical Guide for Positive Change (2nd ed.).* Reading, MA: Addison-Wesley, 1991.

Chartier, M. R. "Five Components Contributing to Effective Interpersonal Communication." In *The 1974 Annual Handbook for Group Facilitators* edited by J. E. Jones and J. W. Pfeiffer, pp. 125–128. Iowa City, IA: University Associates, 1974.

Chiasson, C., and Hayes, L. "The Effects of Subtle Differences Between Listeners and Speakers on the Referential Speech of College Freshmen." *The Psychological Record* 43 (1993): 13–24.

Davis, F. *Inside Intuition: What We Know about Nonverbal Communication.* New York: McGraw-Hill, 1973.

DeVito, J. *The Interpersonal Communication Book* (5th ed.). New York: HarperCollins, 1992.

Eibl-Eibesfeldt, I. "Transcultural Patterns of Ritualized Contact Behavior." In *Behavior and Environment: The Use of Space by Animals and Men,* Edited by A. H. Esser, pp. 126–141. New York: Plenum, 1971.

Ekman, P. "Facial Expressions of Emotion: New Findings, New Questions." *Psychological Science* 3 (1) (1992): 34–38.

_____. *Telling Lies: Clues to Deceit in the Marketplace, Politics, and Marriage.* New York: Norton, 1985.

Ekman, P., and Friesen, W. V. *Unmasking the Face.* Palo Alto, CA: Consulting Psychologists Press, 1984.

Ekman, P., Friesen, W. V., and Ellsworth P. *Emotion in the Human Face: Guidelines for Research and an Integration of the Findings.* New York: Pergamon, 1972.

Fast, J. *Body Language.* New York: M. Evans and Co., 1970.

_____. *The Body Language of Sex, Power, and Aggression.* New York: Lippincott, 1977.

Gray, J. *Men Are From Mars, Women Are From Venus.* New York: Harper Collins Publishers, 1993.

Groder, M. G. "How to Read People by What They Say." *Bottom Line* (May 30, 1987): 9–10.

Hall, E. T. *The Hidden Dimension.* Garden City, NY: Doubleday, 1990.

_____. "Proxemics." *Current Anthropology* 9 (1968): 83–107.

_____. *The Silent Language.* Greenwich, CT: Fawcett, 1959.

Harper, R. G., Wiens, A. N., and Matarazzo, J. D. *Nonverbal Communication: The State of the Art.* New York: Wiley, 1978.

Hess, E. H. "Attitude and Pupil Size." *Scientific American* (April 1965): 46–54.

Konner, M. "The Enigmatic Smile." *Psychology Today* (March 1987): 42–44.

Knapp, M. L. "The Field of Nonverbal Communication: An Overview." In *On Speech Communication: An Anthropology of Contemporary Writings and Messages,* edited by C. J. Steward and B. Kendall, pp. 212–220. New York: Holt, Rinehart and Winston, 1972.

Luft, J. *Group Processes.* Mountain View, CA: Mayfield Publishing, 1984.

Miller, S., Nunnally, E. W., and Wackman, D. B. *Alive and Aware: Improving Communication in Relationships.* Minneapolis: Interpersonal Communication Programs, 1975.

Morris, D., Collett, P., Marsh, P., and O'Shaughnessy, M. *Gestures: Their Origins and Distribution.* New York: Stein and Day, 1979.

Pfeiffer, J. W., and Jones, J. E. "Don't You Think That . . . ? An Experiential Lecture on Indirect and Direct Communication." In *The 1974 Annual Handbook for Group Facilitators,* Edited by J. E. Jones and J. W. Pfeiffer, pp. 203–208. Iowa City, IA: University Associates Publishers, 1974.

Phipps, K. "Communication in the Family." *Malone Messenger* (Winter 1987): 2–4.

Plutchik, R. *The Emotions: Facts, Theories, and a New Model*. New York: Random House, 1962.

Powell, J. *The Other Side of the Story*. New York: Morrow, 1984.

Reik, T. *Listening with the Third Ear*. New York: Pyramid, 1972.

Samovar, L., and Mills, J. *Oral Communication: Message and Response*. Dubuque, IA: William C. Brown, 1992.

Sergent, J., and Bindra, D. "Differential Hemispheric Processing of Faces: Methodological Considerations and Reinterpretation. *Psychological Bulletin* 89 (1981): 554.

Tannen, D. *You Just Don't Understand: Women and Men in Conversation*. New York: Ballentine Books, 1990.

Wahlstrom, B. *Perspectives in Human Communication*. Dubuque, IA: William C. Brown, 1992.

Weitz, S. (Ed.). *Nonverbal Communication: Readings with Commentary*. New York: Oxford University Press, 1974.

■ Questionnaire Scoring Key

How Well Do You Listen?

Add the numbers that appear under the response you checked for each item. Your score is _____.

Your score is interpreted as follows:

25 or below:

You may need listening training. Your deficiency may be causing you some learning difficulties as well as interpersonal problems.

26 to 35:

You are an average listener. With more attention to some of the listening behaviors described in the questionnaire, you should be able to become a good or excellent listener.

36 to 45:

You are a good listener. With a little effort, you should be able to become an excellent listener. You are well above the average person.

46 to 50:

You are an excellent listener. Keep it up. You certainly are benefitting from this important skill, especially in the realm of interpersonal relationships.

■ Answers to Critical Review Questions

Critical Review 1 1. T. 2. F. 3. T. 4. F. 5. T. 6. T. 7. T. 8. T. 9. F. 10. F.

Critical Review 2 1. T. 2. T. 3. F. 4. F. 5. T. 6. T. 7. F. 8. F. 9. F. 10. F.

Critical Review 3 1. T. 2. F. 3. T. 4. T. 5. F. 6. T.

Critical Review 4 1. T. 2. F. 3. F. 4. T. 5. T. 6. F. 7. T. 8. F. 9. T. 10. T. 11. F. 12. T.

PERSONAL ACTION PLAN
Effective Communication

The exercises in this section are designed to help you determine the effectiveness of your communication style and improve your skills as a sender and a listener.

I. *Directions:* Complete the following feeling statements (remember that feelings are different from thoughts):

1. When I speak before a group I feel

2. When I am introduced to someone for the first time I feel

3. When I am late for an appointment I feel

4. When I am called on in a group I feel

5. When someone does all the talking I feel

Share your feeling statements with your classmates to check for clarity. You may also want to help them clarify their statements.

II. *Directions:* Change the following indirect statements or pseudoquestions into two possible direct statements:

1. What are you doing Friday night?

2. What do you think of a professor who does not care if people come late to his class?

3. I wish someone would clean up this room.

4. Doesn't your beard bother you?

5. Don't you think he/she is good looking?

6. Aren't you the person I saw on the beach last Saturday?

III. *Directions:* Complete the following statements:

1. My effectiveness as a sender of messages could be improved by

2. My effectiveness as a listener could be improved by

3. My nonverbal communication could be improved by

4. My communication could be more congruent by

IV. *Directions:* Write a statement or statements relative to each of the following situations using at least three dimensions of the Awareness Wheel.

1. Your best friend is telling you how disappointed he/she is in your behavior and is smiling.

2. You are trying to tell your friend that he/she is very important to you. While you are talking, your friend looks out the window and informs you that it is raining.

3. For several days your mate has been very quiet and has only spoken to you when you initiate conversation. His/her responses have been brief and unfeeling.

4. The play that you have been wanting to see is closing tonight. You know that your friend wants to see a movie that has won an Academy Award.

5. You and your friend have been enthusiastic about taking a vacation trip together. One day while you are both talking about your plans, you suggest that it would be fun to take a tent and do some camping. Your friend's facial expression changes from a smile to a frown, then back to a smile again.

V. *Directions:* The following exercises are intended to help you discover how you use nonverbal behavior to enhance your communication.

1. Choose a day when you will have numerous encounters with other individuals or groups. During these encounters, imagine that you are seeing yourself as others see you. Try to let yourself be as

you usually are, yet make mental notes about your facial expression, movements, and body positions. After each encounter, record your observations of yourself on paper or tape.

2. Select at least two people you see often and whom you trust. Ask them to share with you the nonverbal behavior that they associate with you. You may even ask them to dramatize your behavior. (This may seem like a hilarious exercise, but do not worry.

We can all use a little more humor in our lives. Besides, a sign of growth is being able to laugh at yourself.)

3. Compare the observations of others with your own observations of yourself in the space below. What meaning do you find from this information?

ADJUSTMENT AND GROWTH THROUGH LIFE MANAGEMENT AND THE WORLD OF WORK

Part IV focuses on adjustment and growth by discussing life management and the world of work.

Chapter 11 is concerned with personal growth. It explores the ways in which we set goals and make decisions and, in so doing, examines the processes that may be used to guide and direct our personal growth.

Chapter 12 discusses types of work, motivations to work, and employment patterns. It also assists you in the personal process of selecting a suitable career. The section on career adjustment discusses the aspects of job satisfaction and how the individual can be more in control in the work environment.

CHAPTER

11

LIFE MANAGEMENT: GOALS AND DECISIONS

Chapter Outline

FOCUS

By reading, understanding, and reflecting on the material in this book, you are, no doubt, increasing your understanding of yourself. You are gaining insights into your own adjustment and growth patterns, into factors that have influenced your personality development, and into other factors that build up and tear down your self-esteem. You are considering the physical, cognitive, and emotional aspects of yourself and the impact of stress on your life. You are contemplating your own socialization and your relationships with others, as they relate to communication, intimacy, and in the next chapter, the world of work. You are also identifying some of your dysfunctional behavior patterns and some of the general approaches that may be used to change them. Now, you will focus on the processes that may be used to put your self-knowledge to some practical use: goal setting and decision making.

GOAL SETTING

- What are you going to be when you grow up?
- How are you spending your summer vacation?
- What is your major in college?
- What courses are you planning to take next semester?
- Where are you going after you graduate?
- When are you getting married?
- How many children are you going to have?
- Where do you want to live?
- When do you plan to retire?
- What are you going to do after retirement?
- Who is included in your will?

These questions are commonly asked of most of us at some point in our lives. The implied question in each is, What are your goals or what decisions have you made?

Life decisions and life goals are dependent on each other. Without a clear understanding of our goals, we may make capricious decisions that we later regret (see the discussion on single-parenting and teenage pregnancy in chapter 9, "Intimacy and Sexuality." We may discover later in life that some of our decisions made apart from our goals were the most important decisions we ever made.

Importance of Goal Setting

Goals give our lives direction and purpose. They let us know where we have been, where we are now, and where we hope to be in the future. Furthermore, life goals help us make personal adjustments. We should have goals in several areas: personal goals (say, to develop a healthier body), educational goals (to earn a master's degree), professional goals (to become a manager), and social goals (to develop skills in interpersonal interaction). By setting a variety of goals, we can avoid becoming too occupied with any one aspect of our lives.

Goal setting is analogous to the planning that goes into taking a trip in an automobile. Let's imagine that we are preparing to embark on a summer camping trip from Boston to Los Angeles. There are several considerations we must address before we begin. We must consider first, the total *time* we have allotted; second, the places of *interest* we want to visit (Mt. Rushmore, Yellowstone National Park, Grand Canyon); third, the *preparation* necessary to do all the things we want to do (locate maps, determine campground locations, assemble camping and backpacking equipment, pack warm clothing, save enough money); and fourth, an assessment of the *personal abilities* necessary to successfully complete such an adventure (physical stamina, knowledge of places, driving skill).

Without such planning we may discover to our dismay that we do not have the proper clothing for the cold nights we encounter in the mountains; we are not physically strong enough to climb the mountains; the tent leaks; the car is not capable of ascending the steep, winding roads without overheating; we do not have enough food and water for our backpacking expedition; and we must be rescued from a mountaintop. Furthermore, we have lost so much time because of our lack of preparation that we are able to go only a third of the way to our hoped-for destination.

In short, what we thought would be an enjoyable experience turned out to be very disappointing in many respects. Perhaps if we had spent more time planning and more time thinking about where we were going and what we needed, we could have ensured a more successful and satisfying adventure. The same is true about the way we live our lives.

Although goal setting is essential to healthy adjustment, we should not become so obsessed with our goals that we fail to enjoy the present. Some people are so preoccupied with the future that they fail to adjust to the present. College students who believe they cannot spend time in extracurricular activities because they must constantly prepare for a profession are not demonstrating healthy adjustment. Future goals are important, but they should facilitate rather than hinder our adjustment to and enjoyment of the present.

Goal-Setting Criteria

Before we can effectively formulate life goals, we need as much information about ourselves as possible. We must seek information about our strengths and values. An assessment of our strengths helps us determine our capabilities; an assessment of our values helps us determine what is more important to us. This information will enable us to set goal priorities. We must bear in mind, however, that our goals must be realistic. Therefore, we must choose them carefully. Goals

---

CRITICAL THINKING ISSUE
Success

Success ultimately comes from luck.	Being in the right place at the right time, knowing the right people, living one day at a time, waiting for your big chance, or winning a lottery makes you successful. No matter how hard you work, these elements are what help you get ahead in life.
Planning for success is the greatest factor in achieving it.	Personal assessment, values clarification, goal setting, careful decision making, and taking risks are the greatest contributors to one's success in life.

I take the position that:

that are beyond our capabilities may cause us frustration and disillusionment. On the other hand, if our goals are set too low, we will suffer boredom. The first step in setting goals, then, is to learn as much about ourselves as we can. You have begun this process with your involvement in the previous chapters.

If you have determined that one of your most important values is developing interpersonal relationships, you may be quite disappointed to discover that one of your life goals, to become a laboratory technician, provides limited interaction with others. A more satisfying and value-oriented occupational goal could be one that provides you with an opportunity to develop relationships.

An awareness of our *strengths* helps us determine the feasibility of achieving our goals. A goal must be realistic when measured against our personal qualities and capabilities. For instance, if an assessment of your capabilities indicates a lack of ability in math and the sciences, the goal of becoming a physician or an engineer would be quite unrealistic. To pursue a goal that is not aligned with your strengths increases the possibility of frustration, disappointment, and failure.

We can test a goal to see if it is realistic by determining if we are motivated enough to want to expend the energy necessary to achieve it. Another criterion to consider is whether we have the time to achieve a particular goal. Often our expectations of ourselves are unrealistic in terms of the amount of time available.

> Ann, realizing that her summer vacation at the beach is just two weeks away, decides she should lose ten pounds so she will look more attractive in her swimsuit. The day before her vacation is to begin, she realizes that she is five pounds short of her goal. Feeling disappointed, she blames herself for her inability to reach her goal. With better planning, Ann would have started her diet earlier and increased the possibility of successfully reaching her goal.

A goal must be *measurable*. Thus, it should be stated as concretely and specifically as possible. To say that you are going to study harder in biology is vague and not measurable. It becomes measurable when you state, "I will read chapter 8 in my biology book and answer all of the study questions at the end of the chapter." When our goals are vague and not measurable, it is unlikely that we will ever achieve them to our satisfaction.

Knowing that procrastination is a common trait, we might go a step further and state, "I will read chapter 8 and answer all of the study questions at the end of the chapter by Tuesday, October 18." The goal stated this way provides a deadline for completion. Without deadlines, most of us would seldom achieve our goals.

Finally, a goal should be stated *without an alternative*. Either/or goals divert our attention and energy away from what we really want to do. Rather than say, "I will either go to the library tonight or read chapters 3 and 4 in my history book," it is better to decide on the one goal that is most important and plan to achieve it.

Long-Range and Short-Term Goals

long-range goals   goals to be accomplished in the distant future

From a time perspective, there are two basic types of goals. *Long-range goals* represent accomplishments we hope to achieve some time in the distant future—for example, I hope to be a forest ranger in the Rocky Mountains; I hope to live in a beautiful house overlooking the Pacific Ocean; I hope to win a gold medal in the Olympics; or I hope to live to be a hundred years old and do it in good health. Long-range goals such as these certainly are attainable. However, just hoping for

This couple has just reached their long-term goal of owning their own home.

them will not make them happen. Our long-range goals are relatively few in number and may take years or a lifetime to achieve. We usually achieve them by setting and accomplishing many related *short-term goals*. Short-term goals help us to move steadily toward the achievement of our long-range goals. Our short-term goals are usually more immediate and may be achieved within hours, days, weeks, or months.

short-term goals   goals that are achieved within hours, days, weeks, or months

Stephanie Culp (1991) suggests that we can stay on track and keep our goals organized if we write them down. She recommends creating a separate page for each long-range goal, listing the steps (short-term goals) for each, and setting a deadline. She also suggests that we set one-year, five-year, and lifetime goals and try to accomplish something each month toward reaching those goals.

Let us demonstrate the relationship between long-range and short-term goals. Suppose your long-range goal is to become a forest ranger in the Rocky Mountains. To attain this goal, you will have to achieve several short-term goals. The first short-term goal may be to complete successfully the botany course in which you are currently enrolled. The second short-term goal might be to visit the library or a career resource center to gather as much information as you can about what it takes and what it is like to be a forest ranger. If you are still convinced that being a forest ranger is for you, a third short-term goal would be to visit a counselor or academic adviser to find out what courses are required and

Goal Profile

List five long-range goals you are currently working toward. For each long-range goal, list three short-term goals that will lead you toward its achievement.

Long-Range Goals

1. _____

2. _____

3. _____

4. _____

5. _____

Short-Term Goals

A. _____
B. _____
C. _____
A. _____
B. _____
C. _____
A. _____
B. _____
C. _____
A. _____
B. _____
C. _____
A. _____
B. _____
C. _____

what extracurricular activities might be helpful in order for you to attain your long-range goal. A fourth short-term goal might be to interview a person who is a forest ranger. (The next three goals may be either short-term or long-range goals, depending on how close we may be to achieving them.) A fifth goal could be to spend a summer working in a national park. The sixth goal would be to complete your baccalaureate studies successfully by satisfying all of the requirements for a bachelor's degree in forestry. Finally, the seventh goal would be to submit applications to prospective employers. With regular short-term goal setting we develop a sense of autonomy, self-motivation, and self-determination directed toward the accomplishment of our long-range goals. The Goal Profile in the following box will help you identify some long-range and short-term goals.

Critical Review 1

1. It is unnecessary to consider life goals when making most of our life decisions. T F

2. Some major decisions are final and there is little we can do later to change them. T F

3. When formulating life goals, we need to consider our values and strengths. T F

4. Values and strengths are the only criteria necessary in establishing goals. T F

5. A goal should be stated in such a way that we know specifically when we have achieved it. T F

6. Deadlines are unnecessary when setting goals. The important thing is to achieve them whenever possible. T F

7. Goals should be stated with alternatives in case we change our minds at the last minute. T F

8. The only important goal is a long-range goal. T F

9. Short-term goals are the day-to-day goals that help us achieve our long-range goals. T F

10. Why is it important to set goals?

11. How does measuring our goals against certain criteria help us set the right goals?

12. What is the relationship between short-term and long-range goals?

Goal Priorities

Roger and Carolyn met while they were both sophomores in college. Excited about the thought of spending the remainder of their lives together, they often sit and share their goals with each other. They have made a partial list of their goals:

- To each have a profession
- To travel
- To write a book together
- To get married
- To have four children
- To give their children a college education
- To graduate from college with honors
- To acquire at least a master's degree or Ph.D.
- To have a large house with a pool on a beach
- To own an airplane
- To save money
- To own a large sailboat
- To own several investment properties
- To sail around the world

Before long, Roger's and Carolyn's views of the future become cluttered with so many goals that they feel overwhelmed. Even after much discussion, it is difficult to decide what goals they should begin working toward first.

It is important to establish some *goal priorities* for both long-range and short-term goals so we can determine which goals we should begin working toward first. We will need to achieve some goals earlier as a prerequisite for achieving later goals. Some earlier goals will be those we have the capability of completing successfully very soon. Goal setting for success is a very important consideration in establishing goal priorities. Success is our greatest motivator. For this reason it is important to plan to complete some of our goals soon; we may lose our determination if many of our goals seem too far in the future.

Our goal priorities most often consist of a combination of short-term and long-range goals. Let us demonstrate the process of setting goal priorities by using Roger and Carolyn as examples. In order to begin this process, the *first* thing they should do is identify their most important values and match these values to their list of goals. After a lengthy discussion, they discover that their

goal priorities planning step-by-step goal achievement

Achievement of the ultimate goal is more likely when we set goal priorities.

five most important values in order of priority are (1) a full and rewarding life, (2) freedom and spontaneity, (3) peace and harmony, (4) a satisfying love relationship, and (5) recognition for their accomplishments. A comparison of their value priorities and their list of goals reveals that each goal fits their values except the goal of having children. A discussion reveals that both Roger and Carolyn always believed their parents expected them to have children. However, an assessment of their values indicates that neither of them seems to need or value having children. The goal of having children is removed from the list.

The *second* step is to determine which goal or goals will take the longest time to achieve and will also depend on the completion of other goals. Roger and Carolyn discover that writing a book together and sailing around the world will probably take the longest time to complete. With some discussion, they discover that their ultimate goal is to write a book about their venture of sailing around the world.

The process continues until they have either deleted or added goals and listed all of their goals in order from most immediate to years in the future. Roger and Carolyn eventually arrive at this goal priority list:

1. To graduate from college
2. To have a profession
3. To rent an apartment together
4. To get married
5. To enter graduate school on a part-time basis
6. To save enough money for a down payment on a house
7. To continue saving money for investments
8. To graduate with a master's degree

9. To invest in some real estate
10. To travel
11. To learn to sail
12. To buy a house on or near the ocean
13. To buy a small, used sailboat
14. To buy a large cruising ketch
15. To sail around the world
16. To coauthor a book about their sailing adventures.

Goal Setting for Success

Nowell (1960) writes that novelist Thomas Wolfe dreamed of some day becoming a great novelist and socializing with the elite of New York City. Finally, after achieving his dream and meeting the members of the elite group, he was greatly disappointed in the qualities of the people he met. There are no guarantees that we are going to attain our goals or that they will meet our expectations. However, keeping in mind the following points may help us increase our goal satisfaction (Lee, 1978):

1. Be careful not to invest too much of your life focusing on long-range ambitions. Seek satisfaction in the achievement of numerous short-term, day-to-day goals.

2. Choose long-range goals you can enjoy working toward as much as reaching. Even if you fail to reach a goal, you have the satisfaction and enjoyment of trying. Many of us have discovered that the journey is often more enjoyable than the destination. Having reached our goals, we may look back and realize that we have lived through the happiest moments of our lives without fully appreciating them.

3. If you have a goal that involves helping others, make sure your satisfaction comes from the act of helping, doing, or giving rather than from the appreciation, recognition, or respect you expect to receive from the recipients. When the accomplishment of a goal is to be measured by recognition and appreciation from others, we often set ourselves up for disappointment.

4. Your goals should be chosen on the basis of your enjoyment or your feeling of accomplishment rather than on the basis of impressing or pleasing others. People often go to college or enter a profession because they give in to parental pressure or because they want to impress others. The result is that they end up unhappy about their choices. It is important to remember that our first priority is to please ourselves and be happy. If then we impress or please others, we have an added reward.

5. Be flexible after choosing your long-term goals. You may discover that your primary goal is not realistically achievable. A goal to enter medical school should have some backup goal, such as pharmacy or biological or chemical research. Although initially it is important to set a goal without an alternative, we are less likely to be disappointed with the failure to reach a primary goal if we use the time and energy spent in a related way.

6. It is important to remember that failure in achieving a goal need not be devastating, for failure sometimes forces us to seek alternatives that may be more desirable for us. We may discover that by changing our goals we

afford ourselves an opportunity to explore many paths we might otherwise have overlooked.

Harrison (1976) relates the story of the world-renowned psychologist Hans Eysenck, who emigrated from Germany to England to pursue his education in physics. A particular regulation delayed him from pursuing his goal. As a result, he became interested in a topic he knew little about, psychology. He was able to turn his misfortune into a goal more interesting to him than physics. When doors close in lives, we may discover that we have the opportunity to explore literally hundreds of unlocked doors we may otherwise have overlooked.

Critical Review 2

1. It is desirable to establish priorities as you formulate goals. T F

2. Success is a key factor in early goal setting. T F

3. Goal priorities provide us with a tentative timetable to help us begin working toward the achievement of our goals. T F

4. Most of our time and energy must be spent attempting to achieve our primary goals. T F

5. Enjoyment is not a primary factor in achieving our goals. T F

6. The goal of achieving recognition and appreciation from others for helpful deeds may cause us some disappointment. T F

7. The failure to achieve a particular goal may result in an opportunity to achieve other worthwhile goals. T F

8. One of the most important priorities to remember when setting goals is to please yourself. T F

9. How do goal priorities help us attain success?

10. How can we keep from being overcome by the drudgery that sometimes is associated with goal achievement?

Goal Setting as a Lifelong Process

In our rapidly changing, mobile world, the opportunities for everyone to continue to grow and live a long, productive life are limitless. Once it would have seemed odd to encounter a middle-aged or older person as a student in college. Increasingly, we discover older people, both men and women, enrolled in part-time and full-time college programs. These people are taking advantage of their right to change their minds about their previously chosen goals (work, interests, and so on) or to set new goals to improve the quality of their lives.

Frieda Laufgraben (1978) writes about beginning nurse's training at age fifty-four. Seven weeks before her graduation, her husband died. In spite of this setback, she graduated, earning a 93 percent score on her state board exams. She worked for the next ten years as a nurse in a hospital. In addition, she states, "I have worked for six summers as a nurse in children's camps—worked four days each year on the Board of Elections—taken a thirty-one-day trip abroad, occasional shorter trips, weekends with family and friends, their homes or mine, and manage to squeeze in a luncheon, book review, a bit of reading and knitting, and a weekly game of Canasta." At age seventy she is the president of the Friendship Club, which has more than three hundred members, and is a member of the NRA (Neighborhood Resources for the Aging).

Neugarten (1986), an expert on life-span development, believes we have become an age-irrelevant society. We are increasingly aware of the 26-year-old mayor, the 62-year-old father of a newborn, and the 75-year-old college student.

No matter how active they are during their lives, most people retire sooner or later. The fact is that **retirement** is becoming a middle-aged phenomenon (Schlossberg and Entine, 1977). It is more common to find people retiring in their mid- to late forties instead of sixty-five or seventy. Robert C. Atchley (1972) defines *retirement* as "the institutional separation of an individual from his occupational position." Retirement is a long-range goal for many people. We often hear people say, "I can hardly wait until I retire." Many people seem to be in a hurry to retire. The hope for some is that they will have more time to fish, more time to loaf, and more time to do the challenging things that they always wanted to do but could not do because of the alarm clock and rigid time schedule of their professions. Unfortunately, many people arrive at retirement only to discover that they are unprepared for this lifestyle change. They often lose their sense of purpose and their self-esteem suffers.

retirement   the institutional separation of an individual from his or her occupational position

Atchley (1972) believes our retirement goals should be focused on at least three areas; economic goals, health maintenance goals, and interest goals. First, it is imperative that we provide for ourselves economically. Most retired people regret that they did not save and invest more money. Many say that retirement always seemed so far away. We can prepare for the future by learning more about such investments as stocks, bonds, annuities, mutual funds, and retirement funds. Financial planning for retirement should begin soon. Retirement may be thirty or forty years away, but the effect of continuous investment and compound growth depends on time. Table 11–1 shows how capital grows over time for various rates of return. It makes little sense to wait until ten years before retirement to begin saving and investing. The capital necessary to continue your quality of life will be much greater than you can accumulate in such a short time.

Lifelong goal setting. We are all responsible for our own happiness.

TABLE 11–1
Retirement Investment Projections

Annual %*	5.50%	10.00%	15.00%	20.00%
	MONTHLY SAVINGS $300.00			
Years				
1	$3,798	$3,960	$4,140	$4,320
2	$7,805	$8,316	$8,901	$9,504
3	$12,032	$13,108	$14,376	$15,725
4	$16,492	$18,378	$20,673	$23,190
5	$21,197	$24,176	$27,913	$32,148
6	$26,161	$30,554	$36,240	$42,897
7	$31,398	$37,569	$45,817	$55,797
8	$36,923	$45,286	$56,829	$71,276
9	$42,751	$53,775	$69,493	$89,851
10	$48,901	$63,112	$84,057	$112,142
11	$55,388	$73,383	$100,806	$138,890
12	$62,232	$84,682	$120,067	$170,988
13	$69,453	$97,110	$142,217	$209,505
14	$77,071	$110,781	$167,689	$255,726
15	$85,108	$125,819	$196,983	$311,192
16	$93,587	$142,361	$230,670	$377,750
17	$102,532	$160,557	$269,411	$457,620
18	$111,970	$180,573	$313,963	$553,464
19	$121,926	$202,590	$365,197	$668,477
20	$132,430	$226,809	$424,116	$806,492
21	$143,512	$253,450	$491,874	$972,111
22	$155,203	$282,755	$569,795	$1,170,853
23	$167,537	$314,990	$659,404	$1,409,343
24	$180,549	$350,449	$762,455	$1,695,532
25	$194,278	$389,454	$880,963	$2,038,958
26	$208,761	$432,360	$1,017,248	$2,451,070
27	$224,041	$479,556	$1,173,975	$2,945,604
28	$240,161	$531,471	$1,354,211	$3,539,045
29	$257,168	$588,578	$1,561,483	$4,251,174
30	$275,110	$651,396	$1,799,845	$5,105,728
31	$294,039	$720,496	$2,073,962	$6,131,194
32	$314,009	$796,506	$2,389,196	$7,361,753
33	$335,078	$880,116	$2,751,715	$8,838,423
34	$357,305	$972,088	$3,168,613	$10,610,428
35	$380,755	$1,073,256	$3,648,044	$12,736,834
36	$405,494	$1,184,542	$4,199,391	$15,288,520
37	$431,594	$1,306,956	$4,833,440	$18,350,545
38	$459,130	$1,441,612	$5,562,596	$22,024,974
39	$488,180	$1,589,733	$6,401,125	$26,434,288
40	$518,828	$1,752,667	$7,365,434	$31,725,466

*Earnings are based on annual simple interest. Earnings would be greater if compounded monthly.

You can determine what you will need at retirement by considering the following. Begin by estimating what you expect your earnings to be after you have been working in your career for fifteen years. At that point in your life, you will be established and your quality of life will reflect the achievement of numerous worthwhile goals. Let us suppose you will be earning $50,000 a year. If you plan to retire at sixty-two years of age, you will work an additional twenty-five years. Assuming that your earnings will increase at least 5 percent per year, you will need approximately $125,000 a year to continue your quality of life at retirement. This means that your retirement nest egg must be at least $1.25 million so that you can live on a 10 percent return on your capital.

We can also prepare economically for retirement by developing skills that may someday help us earn money after we retire. Many people, having gained much knowledge and experience, offer their services as consultants. Some pursue other career goals they may have only thought about earlier in their lives.

Second, we need to make decisions today about our potential health needs. It is one thing to plan to live a long life, but that life may not be very pleasant unless we are in good health. We have more knowledge today than ever before about how to maintain healthy bodies. We know that the decisions we make today about nutrition, exercise, and medical care have either far-reaching rewards or consequences.

Third, it is essential that we develop a variety of interests that will provide us with opportunities to grow emotionally, intellectually, and physically. These interests will contribute to our self-esteem. Many people talk about how they are going to use their precious retirement time. Then, when retirement finally comes, they cannot seem to discover what they want to do. Having unlimited time to pursue your interests is one of the greatest benefits of retirement.

We should also consider a fourth retirement goal: the development of relationships with others. Friendship during retirement age is at least as important as it is earlier in life. Having friends with similar interests can greatly add to the quality of life and help to increase self-esteem during retirement (Antonnuci, 1990). Some might believe that our happiness and life satisfaction decrease as we get older. In fact, older people report just as much happiness and life satisfaction as younger people (Ingelhart and Rabier, 1986).Talking, playing, and traveling together can make the retirement years the greatest years one can experience.

Referring to retirement goals, Julietta K. Arthur (1969) states:

> Those who count on spending their remaining days just in "enjoying life" or achieving a more adequate income, or attempt to wrap their lives around their children or their grandchildren, will have considerable success in encountering frustration. No one can expect happiness in retirement as a right to which he is entitled; nearly always it has to be earned, sometimes painfully. (p. 22)

Siegmund May (1978) believes that many of our previously held assumptions about aging have to be discarded. Increasingly, attention is being focused on the study of the inner resources that lead people to long years of usefulness and enjoyment. Many believe that aging means adjusting to a new set of circumstances. However, each of us has learned to adjust continually to many new situations from birth to the present. Perhaps the successful goals we set and the successful decisions we make throughout our lives are the best training and preparation for a continued life of happiness and fulfillment.

Every day we live affords us the opportunity to discover more about ourselves, our lives, our environment, our relationships to others, and our opportunities. This new information allows us to revise our goals and establish new ones. In short, life should be a never-ending process of goal setting.

Critical Review 3

1. If our goal-setting process is completed carefully, we should never need to revise our goals. T F

2. People who revise their career goals midway through their lives probably did not know what they wanted to do in the first place. T F

3. When changing our goals, it is important to consider how much time we will have wasted thus far in our lives. T F

4. When one considers the accrued benefits of being in a career for twenty years or longer, it is foolish to entertain the possibility of changing a career. T F

5. People should retire only when they are forced to do so. It is more acceptable and respectable to work as long as possible. T F

6. When preparing for retirement, there are only two points we need to consider: what we are going to do to keep our minds occupied, and how we are going to survive financially. T F

7. Why must goal setting be a lifelong process?

8. How and at what point in our lives should we begin planning for retirement?

DECISION MAKING

decision making   the choices we make throughout our lives

To have a fulfilling and satisfying life, we need to make decisions that relate to our life goals. A thorough understanding of the process of formulating and achieving goals is the basis for effective **decision making.** A decision is a choice that usually affects a future course of action. In other words, the choice we make from among available alternatives most often results in our making additional related choices in the future. These choices move us toward the achievement of our goals. Miller (1978) says that critical decisions are characterized by their impact on the future, their impact on the lives of others, their degree of importance to you, and the amount of time required to reach them.

We make decisions every day that range from "What shall I wear?" to "Should I get married?" Decisions of lesser importance usually are made without much thought. However, decisions of greater importance demand more

CULTURAL CROSSCURRENTS
The Freedom to Choose: Another Point of View

For most college students, the decisions that accompany the goals relating to college majors, careers, places of employment, and retirement are important ones. However, these decisions are not necessarily universal. In China, which is becoming one of America's greatest trading partners, students do not have to be concerned about these decisions. The Communist Party, in the People's Republic of China, assumes the responsibility for selecting a career for each citizen; The selection is based on what the Party believes to be the abilities of each citizen. In this way, they believe that each person will be best suited for what he or she does for an occupation and the country and the individual will be served best by this process. When questioned about this process, a young Chinese tour guide responded this way:

In America, college students have to worry about what they are going to do when they graduate from college and whether or not there will be jobs for them. This concern distracts them from their studies. In China, the government decides who is going to go to college, what will be studied, and where each person will work upon graduation. Therefore, we can concentrate all our attention on studying and not worry about what we are going to do when we graduate.

When asked if he would have elected what the Party chose for him if he had the chance, he responded, "I probably would have chosen to be a teacher, but I am honored to use my ability to do what is best for my country. Perhaps later on, when I retire, I will be able to teach."

time and thought, for we want to be sure we make the right choice; we want to guarantee success. Because we fear that we will make a mistake, we often procrastinate, fret, worry, and even avoid making these decisions. Our decision then is not to make a decision. Ironically, in avoiding a decision, we make a decision anyway.

What Steps Do You Take When Making Major Decisions?

Questionnaire

Identify two major decisions you have had to make in the past. One should be a decision in which the outcome affected only you. The other should be a decision in which the outcome affected you and others. List the steps you took to arrive at each decision in the spaces provided.

Decision affecting only me:

Decisions affecting me and others:

Steps I used in the decision-making process:

1. _____
2. _____
3. _____
4. _____
5. _____

Steps I used in the decision-making process:

1. _____
2. _____
3. _____
4. _____
5. _____

Whose advice did you seek?
_____

Whose advice did you seek?
_____

How helpful was this advice?
_____
_____

How helpful was this advice?
_____
_____

What were the results of your decision?
_____
_____

What were the results of your decision?
_____
_____

Describe your satisfaction with the choice:

Describe your satisfaction with the choice:

Even though we can procrastinate with some life decisions, many decisions are thrust on us by external events beyond our control. Being fired from a job forces us to make decisions such as where to find another job or whether we should move to another city. Bills must be paid, food purchased, and perhaps a

Wise decisions are made by gathering all of the pertinent information before making a choice.

home sold or bought. Decisions about such matters cannot be avoided for long. We must act as quickly and as carefully as possible. Miller (1978, p. 7) states that people often make decisions in the following ways:

1. They take the safe way.
2. They let somebody else decide.
3. They use intuition by choosing what they feel is right.
4. They do what others expect.
5. They take the first thing that comes along.
6. They select the most difficult choice, believing that the payoff might be greater.
7. They delay deciding until something happens and other possibilities are gone.

It never hurts to ask the advice of others when clarifying the important factors necessary in making a decision. However, the actual decision is a personal choice that we must make by ourselves. The importance that each of us places on various decisions is a very personal matter. We all have our own special needs, values, desires, and goals. The way that we each measure success may differ greatly from how our friends measure success. Our friends may be quite proficient at making decisions in some areas, while we may be proficient in other areas. For example, a decision that may be matter-of-fact to you may be quite stressful to someone else. Your friend may break out in a cold sweat trying to decide which shirt to wear on a date but decide how to invest thousands of dollars without any qualms whatsoever. Some of us may have great difficulty deciding whom to go out with, whom to go to bed with, and whom to develop a lasting relationship with. Many of us seem to be quite interested in the opinions of others when it comes to our choices about a mate. We seek support for our decisions by asking, "What do you think about my boyfriend (girlfriend)?"

Some of us, consciously or unconsciously, seek advice from others so we have someone to blame if the decision does not turn out as we hope it will. Sometimes we ask advice *only* to receive support and approval for what we have already decided we want to do. The best advice anyone can give us, then, results from first finding out what we want to do and then telling us to do it.

Sometimes your decisions may not be acceptable to others, such as parents, relatives, or peers. Even though it is important to consider the effect your decisions may have on significant others, it may take some courage to make a decision and stand by the results. Even though others may not support you in your decisions, only your well-thought-out assessment of the situation will result in a decision that is satisfying to you.

The Decision-Making Process

An important decision usually results from a *systematic process* much more complex than the flipping of a coin or the drawing of an option from a hat. A coin toss may be an effective way to begin sports events or to decide which of two favorite restaurants you will visit, but the decision of whether to have children, for example, requires a more thoughtful and systematic decision-making process.

Most people tend to treat decision making as though it were an either/or proposition—for example, I can *either* move out of my parents' house *or* stay and put up with their rules. This either/or belief about decisions severely limits many of us and keeps us from reaching the best available alternative to an identified personal circumstance. A search for other alternatives may reveal that in addition to either moving out of our parents' house or staying and tolerating their rules, we may negotiate some new rules acceptable to both us and our parents. We may also negotiate to move out on a temporary basis to give us and our parents a chance to experience a change in the living arrangement.

Decisions that greatly affect our lives require much thought and planning. They become easier, however, when we follow a step-by-step process. Just as there are several *steps* to consider in the scientific process, there are several steps to consider in the *decision-making process* (see Table 11–2). First, we must *identify* the particular *circumstance* we are trying to manage and *state it clearly and specifically.* Let's use as an example a circumstance that you may have to consider in the future: which graduate school you should attend. To explore this circumstance further, let's assume that you have applied to several graduate schools and have been accepted by five. Now the decision is yours. The identified circumstance is to choose a graduate school that is best suited to you.

After the circumstance has been clearly identified, the *second step* is to *gather all the information available* that relates to the circumstance. The *most important information* is *information about you*—your value priorities, interests, aptitudes, goals, obstacles, and so on. Additionally, you need information about *significant others* who will be affected by your decision: family, boyfriend or girlfriend, friends, and relatives. People who make up your support system of close relationships must be included in your information gathering, as their continued support and nurturance are usually important.

You also need *information* about the available *alternatives.* Using the example of choosing the graduate school that best suits you, imagine that you are actually going through the process of gathering information about the various graduate schools available. What information is important to you? Location, reputa-

TABLE 11–2
Steps to Effective Decision Making

1. Identify the problem you want to manage, and state it clearly and specifically.
2. Gather personal information that relates to the problem.
3. Gather pertinent information about possible alternatives.
4. Weigh the evidence.
5. Choose among the alternatives.
6. Take action.
7. Review the decision.

tion, programs, and desirability of the degree may be information essential to your choice.

Once you have identified the possible alternatives, it is now time to *weigh the evidence.* In other words, you use the information you have gathered so far and weigh the pros and cons of choosing each alternative. You might ask yourself the question, Which graduate school meets most of my needs and/or requirements? Which graduate school has the best reputation in my chosen field? After having listed the pros and cons for each school, you should have a clearer picture of which graduate program(s) *would not* be suited to you.

The *fifth step* is to *choose from among the remaining alternatives* to determine the program you will attend. If you have followed the decision-making process carefully and honestly, the choice should be quite simple. There should be little doubt in your mind that you are making the *best choice*.

You are now ready for the *sixth step, taking action.* Send in your letter of acceptance, set a date for departure, pack your bags, and go. Trust that you have made the best decision possible at the moment, and with this positive attitude and faith and confidence in your choice, you are on your way to potential success.

After you have arrived, registered, and settled into the academic and social environment, and after you have experienced a term or two, another part of the decision-making process is about to take place, the process of *reviewing your decision.* You may discover that your choice was even better than your expectations; you may have discovered that some of the information you had gathered earlier was not completely accurate; or you may have changed. This review may indicate that you should continue to pursue your educational goals at this institution or leave and go elsewhere.

Making a Choice

As an example of this process, let us look at how one person used it to make an important decision in her life.

The college Joanne attended required only freshman students to live on campus. Near the end of her freshman year, she felt the need to make a decision about where she would live during her sophomore year. Several of her friends had already decided to live off campus in college-approved housing; however, a few of her friends, including her roommate, had decided to stay in the college dormitories at least another year. Influenced by both sets of friends, Joanne vacillated between the two alternatives. She realized that the only way to approach this dilemma was to use a logical decision-making process.

Joanne began by identifying pertinent personal information such as value priorities, goals, interests, and obstacles. To help review the information carefully, she decided to write out the personal information on a sheet of paper, as shown.

PERSONAL INFORMATION

Value Priorities	Goals	Interests	Obstacles
Personal growth	Education	Tennis	Lack of money
Honesty	Career	Backgammon	Parents' wants
Independence	Marriage	Acting	Loyalty to friends
Love relationship	Travel		
Family			
Friendship			

Joanne's next step was to identify the alternatives available to her. There appeared to be at least three alternatives: (1) live on campus in the dormitory with a roommate, (2) live off campus in an apartment with four friends, or (3) live off campus in a private room by herself. She recorded the pertinent information for each alternative on a sheet of paper, as shown.

IDENTIFICATION OF ALTERNATIVES

Alternatives	On Campus	Off-Campus Apartment	Off-Campus Room
Studying	Some quiet time	More distractions	Ample quiet time
Privacy	Some	Minimal	Ample
Interaction	Ample	Ample	Minimal
Freedom	Moderate	Ample	Ample
Parents' Wants	Yes	No	Maybe
Proximity	Close to everything	6 miles from campus	Walking distance
Cost	$100 per month	$185 per month	$135 per month

Next, Joanne weighed the pros and cons of each of the alternatives by listing each alternative and its pros and cons on a separate sheet of paper, as shown.

PROS AND CONS OF LIVING ON CAMPUS

Pros	Cons
1. I have become good friends with my roommate, and we respect each other's privacy and needs (friendship).	1. I feel restricted by some of the dormitory rules (freedom).
2. There are designated times for studying, and most people seem to respect this use of time (growth).	2. During social time, people in the dormitory seem to impose and often borrow things (privacy, independence).
3. The dormitory is close to the building where I have most of my classes, near the cafeteria, and near the tennis courts (proximity).	3. The dormitory environment seems monotonous at times (freedom, personal growth).
4. My parents prefer that I live on campus (parents' wants).	4. I may be keeping myself from developing more responsibility and independence (independence, personal growth).
5. I have adjusted to living on campus (comfort, security).	
6. It is cheaper to live on campus (costs).	

PROS AND CONS OF LIVING OFF CAMPUS IN AN APARTMENT

Pros	Cons
1. It will be a new experience and seems challenging and exciting (personal growth, freedom).	1. The adjustment may get in the way of my homework (studying).
2. It seems like the adult and mature thing to do (personal growth).	2. It may require more self-discipline than I want (freedom).
3. I will be able to spend more time with my boyfriend (love relationship).	3. The additional time spent with my boyfriend may get in the way of my homework (studying).
4. I will get to know my new roommates (friendship, interaction).	4. Adjusting to three new roommates may take a lot of time and energy (studying, privacy).
	5. It may be far from the campus, and I do not have my own transportation (proximity).
	6. My parents do not believe it is the best choice (parents' wants).
	7. My share of the rent, utilities, and other expenses may be more than I can afford, and I will have to get a part-time job (cost, studying).

PROS AND CONS OF LIVING OFF CAMPUS IN A ROOMING HOUSE

Pros	Cons
1. Complete privacy and freedom to come and go as I please (freedom, privacy).	1. I may feel lonely and alienated at times (interaction).
2. Complete freedom to spend intimate time with my boyfriend (love relationship).	2. My boyfriend and I may have more freedom together than either of us is prepared to handle (studying, parents' wants).
3. Optimal opportunity to study in peace and quiet (studying).	3. The rooming house is within walking distance of campus but is far enough to require my getting up earlier in the morning. It would also require trips back and forth to campus for tennis and meals at the cafeteria (proximity, cost).
4. Less expensive than the apartment (cost).	4. More expensive than the dormitory (cost).
	5. Parents are reluctant (parents' wants).

After weighing the pros and cons for each alternative and reviewing her value priorities and goals, Joanne was ready to choose what she believed to be the best alternative. Joanne chose to spend her sophomore year on campus in the dormitory.

This step-by-step decision-making process is designed to help you organize the essential information necessary to make good decisions. As you improve your decision-making skills, you gain greater control of your own life and your own destiny. It is to the realization of that end that this book has been written.

Critical Review 4

1. Most important decisions can usually be narrowed to an either/or choice. T F

2. The best approach to effective decision making is to solicit the advice of your friends and acquaintances. T F

3. Ironically, putting off a decision is a decision. T F

4. An assessment of our needs, values, desires, and goals is essential to making satisfying decisions. T F

5. The first step in effective decision making is to list all available alternatives. T F

6. The most important information that we need to make a decision is information about ourselves: needs, value priorities, desires, and goals. T F

7. When making an important decision, it is best not to consider the opinions or desires of our significant others. T F

8. The second step in effective decision making is to list alternatives that relate to the essential information gathered. T F

9. Weighing the evidence is a step in the process that consists of listing the pros and cons of each alternative. T F

10. After we have made a decision, it is important to evaluate our decision by reviewing it in light of any new information. T F

11. Why is it important to follow a prescribed decision-making process rather than to rely on feelings or intuition?

12. What are the dangers of relying on advice from others in making important life decisions?

SUMMARY

■ Life decisions and life goals are interdependent. Without a clear understanding of our goals, our decisions have little focus. Without good decisions, chances of reaching our goals are limited.

■ Life goals provide us with milestones that let us know where we are and where we have been. They also give us a destination for the future. Without goals, our lives have little purpose and direction.

■ In order to set meaningful and achievable life goals, we need to identify some important personal information. This information consists of two categories: our *personal value priorities* and our *personal strengths*. Goals should directly relate to our top values and our realistic capabilities. Goals set without consideration of this information are often the goals of others, goals we have little interest or desire in achieving.

■ In addition to relating to our values and strengths, goals should be *motivating* to us. We should want to accomplish them. Goals should be realistic in terms of the amount of *time* we have to achieve them and in terms of *available resources*. A goal must be *measurable*. It should be stated in concrete and specific terms. Stating a goal in measurable terms helps us know clearly when we have achieved it. If possible, the goal should be set with a *deadline* for completion. Without deadlines, many goals become "someday goals." Unfortunately, for many, someday never comes. Finally, a goal should be stated *without an alternative*. Either/or goals tend to divide our attention and our energy, keeping us from achieving either goal.

■ Goals are divided into two categories, *long-range goals* and *short-term goals*. Long-range goals are in the distant future. These goals may take years or a lifetime to achieve. Short-term goals are more immediate goals that can be achieved within days, weeks, or months. A series of short-term goals may lead us to the achievement of our long-range goals.

■ In the same way that we set value priorities, we set *goal priorities*. The first consideration is to set goals that offer some degree of *success*. Nothing is more encouraging when setting new goals than the successful completion of earlier goals. When setting goal priorities, it is also important to set some goals that can be achieved within a relatively short period of time. Our goal priorities should also consist of goals that can effect an improvement in the quality of our lives.

■ When we work toward the achievement of our goals, it is important to realize that very few life goals turn out to match our idealized expectations. Expectations built on perfectionistic fantasies may leave us feeling disappointed, as often our goal achievement does not turn out as we hope. When setting goals, it is important to realize that goals give us direction and help us achieve a more satisfying lifestyle.

■ Goal setting is a *lifelong process*. Goals should be periodically reviewed throughout our lives. We may discover that our value priorities have changed, or our environment has changed. These changes may result in new career and lifestyle goal changes. We achieve our goals through *effective decision making*. A decision is a choice we make from alternatives that usually result in other choices in the future. We make thousands of decisions in a lifetime, from the insignificant to the very important.

■ Although we may want to seek advice from others, we each must make our own decisions. The best and most effective way to make important decisions is through a *systematic process*. This process helps us gather all of the information necessary to make a decision: *information about ourselves, information about significant others,* and *information about possible alternatives.* The process also includes *weighing the evidence* from the pertinent information—in other words, weighing the pros and cons. Finally, the process requires that we choose *from among the identified alternatives* the alternative that seems to best suit our particular circumstance.

■ Having followed a step-by-step decision-making process with confidence, we *act* on the decision and *assume full responsibility for the outcomes* of our decision. Effective decision-making places each of us in control of our own lives and our own destiny.

SELECTED READINGS

Becker, B. *Decision: Getting What You Want.* New York: Grossett and Dunlap, 1978. A description of a clear and easy-to-follow program that helps the reader eliminate the stress and worry surrounding important life decisions. The discussion centers on your knowledge, your intelligence, and your experience, all tools that you can employ to help you make better decisions.

Culp, S. *Streamlining Your Life: A Five-Point Plan for Uncomplicated Living.* Cincinnati, OH: Writer's Digest Books, 1991. This book suggests several steps for streamlining specific areas of your life. It covers topics that include adjusting your attitude, prioritizing and planning goals, and creating simple systems for managing your life.

Fries, J. F. *Aging Well: The Life Plan for Health and Vitality in Your Later Years.* Reading, MA: Addison-Wesley, 1989. This book represents a positive view on aging. With understanding and planning, we can discover some of the richest years of our lives.

Jorgensen, J. D., and Fautsko, T. F. *Quid: How You Can Make the Best Decisions of Your Life.* New York: Walker, 1978. A logical, systematic approach to making personal decisions that many of us face daily, decisions such as Shall I buy that new sports car? or Should I change my job? *Quid* is an easily understood guide to effective decision making.

Keyes, R. *Chancing It: Why We Take Risks.* Boston: Little, Brown, 1985. A consideration of why risk is one of the things that people fear when making decisions. Keyes discusses the elements of risk in nearly every decision we make in life and the benefits of taking risks.

Lee, W. *Formulating and Reaching Goals.* Champaign, IL: Research Press, 1978. A comprehensive guide to effective goal setting. Readers are introduced to numerous exercises and discussions designed to help them become more effective self-managers.

Swenson, A. *Starting Over.* New York: A & W Publishers, 1978. An encouraging book for anyone who is struggling with the possibility of changing career goals. It is well documented with case studies about the successes of people who have dared to make a major change in their livelihoods. It is a highly recommended reference.

Wheeler, D. D., and Janis, I. L. *A Practical Guide for Making Decisions.* New York: The Free Press, 1980. A description of five stages of decision making that help readers approach decision making forcefully. The steps are accepting the challenge, searching for alternatives, evaluating alternatives, becoming committed, and adhering to the decision.

REFERENCES

Antonnuci, T. C. "Social Support and Relationships." In *Handbook of Aging and the Social Sciences,* edited by R. H. Binstock and L. K. George, p. 181–191. San Diego: Academic Press, 1990.

Arthur, J. K. *Retire to Action: A Guide to Voluntary Service.* New York: Abingdon Press, 1969.

Atchley, R. C. *The Social Process in Later Life: An Introduction to Social Gerontology.* Belmont, CA: Wadsworth, 1972.

Culp, S. *Streamline Your Life: A Five-Point Plan for Uncomplicated Living.* Cincinnati, OH: Writer's Digest Books, 1991.

Harrison, P. "The Eysenck Personality." *Human Behavior* 5 (2) (February 1976): 38–46.

Ingelhart, R., and Rabier, J. "Aspirations Adapt to Situations—But Why Are Belgians So Much Happier Than French? A Cross-Cultural Analysis of the Subjective Quality of Life," In *Research on the Quality of Life,* edited by F. M. Andrews, p. 66–71. Ann Arbor, MI: Institute of Social Research, University of Michigan, 1986.

Laufgraben, F. "My Advancing Years." In *The New Old: Struggling for Decent Aging,* edited by R. Gross, B. Gross, and S. Seidman, p. 104–119. Garden City, NY: Anchor Books, 1978.

Lee, W. *Formulating and Reaching Goals.* Champaign, IL: Research Press, 1978.

May, S., "The Crowning Years." In *The New Old: Struggling for Decent Aging,* edited by R. Gross, B. Gross, and S. Seidman, p. 133–146. Garden City, NY: Anchor Books, 1978.

Miller, G. P. *Life Choices: How to Make the Critical Decision about Your Education.* New York: Crowell, 1978.

Neugarten, B. L. "The Aging Society." In *Our Aging Society: Paradox and Promise,* edited by H. Pifer and L. Bronte, p. 52–63. New York: W. W. Norton, 1986.

Nowell, E. *Thomas Wolfe: A Biography.* Garden City, NY: Doubleday, 1960.

Schlossberg, N. K., and Entine, A. D. *Counseling Adults.* Monterey, CA: Brooks/Cole, 1977.

■ *Answers to Critical Review Questions*

Critical Review 1 1. F. 2. T. 3. T. 4. F. 5. T. 6. F. 7. F. 8. F. 9. T.
Critical Review 2 1. T. 2. T. 3. T. 4. F. 5. F. 6. T. 7. T. 8. T.
Critical Review 3 1. F. 2. F. 3. F. 4. F. 5. F. 6. F.
Critical Review 4 1. F. 2. F. 3. T. 4. T. 5. F. 6. T. 7. F. 8. F. 9. T.
10. T.

PERSONAL ACTION PLAN
Life Management

The exercises in this Personal Action Plan are designed to give you practice in managing your life. By establishing goal priorities, setting long-range and short-term goals, and experiencing the process of making decisions, you will be better prepared to handle the tough choices that may lie ahead.

I. **Establishing goal priorities.**

1. Many of our goals result from the ability to fantasize our hopes for the future. This exercise calls for you to allow your mind to fantasize as many possibilities (do not be restricted by your present reality) as you can. As you think of a possibility, write it down in the space below (use a separate sheet if necessary), no matter how out of reach it may seem. Go to it and have fun.

2. Now that you have identified the list of possible goals, it is important to check them against the reality of your value priorities (see the Personal Action Plan in chapter 7). Using your value priority list, look at each goal (stated in Step 1) and write the value priority that you believe fits the goal in front of each goal. When you have finished, you will have a list of goals that you believe in, at least in terms of your val-

ues. What are your thoughts about the goals that do not fit your values?

Count the goals that fit your values. Starting with the numeral that represents the total number in your list, prepare a reverse-ordered numerical list in the space provided below (34, 33, 32, . . . 3, 2, 1). Now, determine which goal will probably take the longest to attain in terms of time, money needed, and the completion of shorter-range goals. Place this goal at the top of your list. Then, identify the goal that will take the next longest to attain and place it next on the list. Continue this process until you have all your goals listed in a priority from furthest to most immediate (see the example of Roger and Carolyn in this chapter).

II. **The process of achieving your goals.**

Having a list of goals is good, but unless we begin the process of achieving them, they remain only a list. The following exercises are designed to help you begin the process of achieving your life goals.

1. In the spaces provided, indicate at least five long-range goals from the list in Exercise I, Step 2, that you hope to achieve before your life ends. List the

values, strengths, and interests you have that will help you achieve each of these goals. Remember the following goal-setting criteria: (1) You must be motivated enough by the goal that you want to achieve it; (2) the goal must be realistic in terms of its feasibility (time and resources); (3) the goal must be measurable; and (4) the goal should be stated without an alternative.

Long-range Goals	Values	Strengths	Interests

2. This step of the goal-setting exercise is designed to give you the experience of setting and achieving short-term goals over the next several weeks and months. When you have finished the exercise, you will be ready to begin achieving some short-term goals. These goals should meet the goal-setting criteria and if possible relate to your long-range goals listed above.

a. List five goals that you will be able to achieve within the next six months. List your values, strengths, and interests for each goal. Also indicate the specific deadline date by which you plan to complete the goal. On reaching the deadline date, indicate the degree of satisfaction you feel in having completed or not completed the goal in the column under "Outcome."

Goals	Values	Strengths	Interests	Date	Outcome

b. List five goals you hope to achieve within one month from today. Follow the instructions given in section a.

Goals	Values	Strengths	Interests	Date	Outcome

c. List three short-term goals that you will be able to achieve within one week from today.

Goals	Values	Strengths	Interests	Date	Outcome

III. Decision-making.

This exercise will give you the opportunity to experience two different approaches to the process of decision making. You may find each very useful in making future decisions from the simple to the very complex.

1. This decision-making process involves gathering as much information as possible. You may want to use an actual decision that you are facing or one that we suggest in order to help you practice using the process. If you choose to use our example (you just made a decision), imagine that you are considering the possibility of enrolling somewhere in a graduate school program. In the spaces provided below, indicate the information that you have gathered that would help you best prepare to make this decision.

a. *Information about yourself.*

Values in the order of priority:

Interests:

Aptitudes:

Goals:

Obstacles (if any):

b. *Information pertaining to significant others* (feelings, opinions, hopes, and so on).

Family:

Boyfriend or girlfriend:

Friends:

Relatives (grandparents, uncles, aunts, and so on):

c. *Information about available alternatives.*
Types of graduate schools available:

Programs offered:

Entrance requirements:

Size of graduate school:

Opportunities for social activities:

Other pertinent information:

d. The next step in this process of decision making is to list the *alternatives* that seem to comply with the information you previously gathered.

The graduate schools that now meet my requirements are:
(1)
(2)
(3)
The next step is to make application to each of the alternative schools you are considering.
The final step is to pack your belongings and go.

2. The following decision-making process is slightly different from the one used above in that it helps look at the obstacles that we often allow to prevent us from making a timely decision. This process is useful for those especially tough decisions we may face in the future. Using the hypothetical circumstance in section a, respond to each section of the process as accurately and concisely as possible.

a. Identify a real or hypothetical circumstance you may have to face in the future that will result in your having to make a decision. Describe the circumstance in the space provided. (Example for use in this process: You are thirty-five years of age, have no children, and believe the time has come to make a decision about having children.)

b. Specifically state the goal you hope to reach by having managed this circumstance effectively.

c. Identify the value that supports the above goal.

d. Identify any obstacle or obstacles that may get in the way of your managing this circumstance.

e. Identify the value priorities that are contained in the obstacle(s).

f. Considering the value in the goal and the value(s) in the obstacle(s), which value is a higher priority to you?

g. Based on your value priority, is your goal for managing this circumstance the same now as in section b? If not, what is the new goal?

i. Considering your analysis of the circumstance as indicated in sections b–g, which alternative represents the best decision that you can make at this time?

h. List below three possible alternative decisions that you could use to manage this circumstance. List the strengths you possess that may help you employ each alternative. List the most likely outcome of each alternative.

j. If you were actually using this process to make a decision now, the next step is to act.

Alternatives	Strengths	Most Likely Outcome

Chapter Outline

FOCUS

Many Americans believe that the *work* we do is the greatest indicator of success. Many also believe that success is synonymous with the accumulation of money and material possessions. Owning a house, a car, a boat, and a vacation cottage is indicative of this success. However, to obtain success from our work will require greater personal adjustment than at any other time in history. Futurists say that we are entering an era in which the degree of change will be similar to that which occurred during the Industrial Revolution, but the rate of change will be even more rapid.

Technology has become the byword of the last part of the twentieth century. Sophisticated technology has taken routine jobs away from millions of workers. People currently employed by factories in semiskilled and unskilled jobs will find themselves unemployed unless they are willing to seek training or retraining to do the jobs that require more technical skills. In progress is a long-term shift from a goods-producing economy to a service-producing economy. By the year 2000, four out of five jobs will be in services such as health care, education,

insurance, banking, data processing and management consulting (U.S. Bureau of Labor Statistics, *Occupational Outlook Handbook, 1992–1993*).

Even though millions of jobs are being taken away by new demands and technology, millions more are being created. The Bureau of Labor Statistics forecasts that the high-technology industries alone will generate 1.7 million new jobs by 1995 and continue until the end of the century—slightly more than the 1.6 million manufacturing jobs lost from 1979 to 1984. Engineers and other highly skilled technicians will benefit from these new demands. "Jobs in the future will be more demanding. Tomorrow's workers will constantly have to learn new techniques to maintain their marketability. Life-long learning will become a necessity" (Enzer, 1986 p. 37). Today, people entering the world of work must be prepared to understand and adjust to change. Each new generation will sweep through the marketplace, bringing its own set of values, and the workplace will continue to change (Deutsch, 1985).

MOTIVATION TO WORK

Work has become a major part of our personal identity and worth, both to ourselves and in the eyes of others. This point is illustrated in the following conversation:

David: So, Bob, what do you do?

Bob: Well, right now I am the assistant manager for a small company that assembles monitors for computers. I like my work, but the pay isn't as good as I think I can make and there doesn't appear to be much opportunity for advancement. So I am looking for work someplace else. What do you do, David?

David: I'm currently working for a restaurant chain, managing one of the restaurants. It really isn't what my degree is in, but the pay is good as are the fringe benefits and opportunities for advancement.

Bob: Do you like what you do?

David: Not really. I'd rather be teaching biology courses in high school. My father said he thought I was crazy wasting my time teaching for so little money. So, Dad knew a guy who does the hiring for the restaurant, and he hired me. I've been there three years, and I'm one of the senior managers. I don't think it would be a good idea to change now.

Bob: It doesn't seem right that people can't find jobs that they really like and still make ample money.

David: Well, it hasn't turned out the way I hoped it would. Sometimes I really wonder if I am doing the right thing.

Most of us spend the greater part of our existence working. We give the best hours, days, weeks, months, and years of our lives to this activity we call work.

Some of us enjoy our work and believe that what we do brings us ongoing satisfaction and pleasure. Some of us may admit that even though we once liked our jobs, now we are bored. Others of us believe that work is drudgery and only serves as a means to an end. Most of us rarely take the time to think about what our work means to us and about the effect work has on our psychological adjustment and growth.

Traditional Work Values

Economics   When you ask people why they work, they often say, "For the money." For centuries *economic* needs have been one of the major reasons people have worked. Work gives us the means for paying our bills and for buying necessities. It is easy to understand why we often are preoccupied with how much money we earn for the work we do. Many of us also believe there is a correlation between our ability to earn money and provide for ourselves and the *status* we enjoy in the community. For these and other reasons, many people work more than one job. The average American, from the lowly paid to the highly paid professional, is working one extra month a year to afford all of the things money can buy. The result is less time available for family and leisure activities (Schor, 1993).

Security   People also work for the feeling of *security.* The belief that our needs must always be met is a major concern of most of us. Knowing that a regular paycheck, health insurance, and other protection will remain constant throughout our lives becomes increasingly important. Uncertainty about the future always causes some concern. A secure job in a secure field can relieve some of this apprehension. We also feel the security of being a part of the work force by the strength of the belief that "united we stand, divided we fall."

Work Ethic   Some of us have learned from an early age that work is a *moral obligation.* This **work ethic** suggests that it is our moral responsibility to society to contribute to the good of all. We should do something that benefits humanity and repays society for all that has been provided for us. Even people who are

work ethic   the moral obligation that people feel toward work

CRITICAL THINKING ISSUE
Career Decision Time

The most important things to consider when choosing a career are job availability and earning potential.

Job availability and earning potential are important, but of much greater importance is how the career suits your personal needs, values, capabilities, and goals.

The fact that over 20 percent of today's college graduates do not find jobs in the careers for which they have studied means that they have not done enough investigation before choosing a major program. Considering the cost of a college degree in both time and money, it makes no sense to seek a career that cannot reward you with numerous fringe benefits and high earning potential.

Many people find themselves unhappy with their career choices even though they make high salaries and have numerous job opportunities. Students should choose a career that will satisfy their personal needs and goals.

I take the position that:

financially independent feel some of this responsibility and often volunteer their time or their money to repay society.

Contemporary Work Values

Personal Identity   In addition to the traditional work values, there appears to be a growing need for work to enhance our identity, self-worth, personal growth, and social contact. Our society, and many others, connect what we do for a living to our *social identity*. The conversation between Bob and David at the beginning of the chapter speaks to this identity. It seems that the natural question to be asked after What's your name? is What do you do? We describe ourselves by the work we do. This social identity then transfers to our *personal identity*—I am an accountant, or I am a social worker. It is part of how we are known to ourselves as well as to others. For many of us, work becomes part of our psychological development. Our membership in a work group provides for developing, enhancing, and confirming our sense of identity and self-esteem.

Enhancement of Self-Worth   As we discussed in chapter 3, an important part of our psychological development is the development of our *self-esteem*. Our self-worth, for better or worse, often is connected to what we do as a career. If we are recognized for our accomplishments and appreciated for what we do, we

For many of us, work becomes part of our psychological development.

have some status in the eyes of others and a personal feeling of worth. If we fail at our work or lose our jobs, our self-worth may plummet rapidly. If we become bored at what we do, we may begin to feel stagnant.

Personal Growth and Fulfillment   Contemporary work values demand that careers replace boredom and stagnation with long-term *personal growth* and *fulfillment*. Most of us would admit that we are stimulated and happy when we are growing and learning and feeling that what we do seems worthwhile and important. Perhaps you can recall a job you once held (or the one you currently hold) and the excitement you felt in the beginning when you were acquiring new skills. Later, when you had learned most of what there was to know, you became bored and could hardly wait for each workday to end. Perhaps when you first began working, what you did seemed to provide a worthwhile service to others; but later people seemed to take for granted what you did, and your personal needs were no longer fulfilled.

Social Contact   Our need for *social contact* and *affiliation* is also an important aspect of a satisfying career. To associate with others whom we respect and with whom we find comradeship is quite important to our long-term satisfaction. This involvement has the potential to provide for friendships, support, love, and affection (see the discussion in chapter 9 on propinquity). The old adage, "Never mix work with pleasure" no longer applies to the contemporary worker. Some of the best friendships result from our interaction with others in the workplace.

One-Career Families

Many families with children still function as *one-career families* with one parent working outside the home and the other staying at home to take care of the children and the domestic tasks. Traditionally, the husband, if able, was the one employed outside the home, and the wife stayed home, raised the children, and performed domestic tasks. Though for some families this is still true, it is less so than in the past. Concern for the husband's dignity, which depended on his role as the sole provider, is of less importance today. In fact, many families now have reversed the roles of husband and wife. The wife is the major provider of income, and the man has become the **househusband,** responsible for the domestic chores.

househusband   a man who is a homemaker and whose wife is the sole or primary breadwinner

Two-Career Families

Economics and a change in our thinking about traditional marital and sex roles have brought about an increase in the number of *two-career families* in which both the husband and wife are employed outside the home. A 1986 survey of college students indicated that 92 percent of the women and 77 percent of the men said they wanted a dual-career marriage (Casale, 1986). This arrangement calls for extra planning and organization so that the rearing of children and the performance of household tasks do not suffer. It requires that both workers share in the responsibilities that before may have been determined by the roles each expected to play and expected the other to play. Two-thirds of all married women were working outside the home in 1988, and it is projected that more than three-fourths of all married women will be working outside the home by the mid-1990s (U.S. Census Bureau, 1990).

Single-Parent Families

Single-parent families are also on the increase. As was noted in chapter 9, between 1980 and 1988 the number of single-parent families increased dramatically (U.S. Census Bureau, 1990). The Bureau of Labor Statistics reports that 45 percent of mothers with children under three have jobs. The result has been that each year more women are joining the work force outside the home. Later, we will consider some of the problems women face in the workplace and what is being done to resolve some of these problems.

Men who head single-parent families face responsibilities and challenges similar to those that female single parents face. As was discussed in chapter 9, the U.S. Census Bureau reported that three out of five children born in the last half of the 1980s spent at least part of their childhood in a single-parent home. This suggests that learning how to cope with being single and simultaneously raise children, take care of a home, and work will be a concern of more people each year.

Single-parent workers usually have greater difficulty managing their responsibilities and suffer more stress, according to a study by Boston University's Center on Work and Family (Shellenbarger, 1994). The single-parent worker makes up a "forgotten and stigmatized" group in the workplace and has more problems balancing work and family than other employees. Single parents often experience more anxiety, more career setbacks, and a sense of being viewed by the boss with mistrust. Single parents are twice as likely to feel that their children's problems hamper them at work. The study also reported that only 9 percent of the single workers had supervisory jobs as compared to 22 percent of married workers.

Careers and Children

According to the Bureau of Labor Statistics, nearly half of the work force is made up of two-career couples and single parents. An important consideration in two-worker families and single-parent families is providing for the care of children when the adults are working. Most children of two-provider families and of single-parent families are cared for by day-care centers, nursery schools, baby-sitters, or relatives. Fern Chapman (1987) states, "More and more parents are asking whether the higher salary, bigger title, or extra professional recognition can make up for leaving a toddler in tears each morning, or returning to a teen who is hurt and angry each night." This concern is nearly equal for both fathers and mothers. The results of a nationwide survey of 400 working parents conducted by *Fortune* magazine revealed that 55.4 percent of the men and 58.2 percent of the women believe that the children of working parents suffer by not being given enough time and attention. The University of Michigan Institute for Social Research (1987) reports that working fathers spend an average of only ten minutes a day reading, talking, or playing with their children. Working mothers spend an average of only sixteen minutes per day interacting with their children (*Bottom Line/Personal*, 1987, p. 15). Some companies are providing on-site day-care facilities for workers so they can spend time during breaks or at lunch with their children. Some even provide infirmary facilities that would allow parents to be near their children when they are ill. The result is that many children are beginning to look forward to "going to work" with their parents.

Although "quality time" may be more important than "quantity time," the long-term effects that such child-care arrangements will have on our children and our society remain to be seen. Chapman (1987) reports on two studies that deal with the effects of day-care centers on children. A 1985 study of kindergarten and first-grade children who had spent their first year of life at the University of North Carolina's highly regarded day-care center found that these children were more likely than their home-reared counterparts to show antisocial behavior such as hitting, kicking, pushing, threatening, swearing, and arguing. A 1983 study in Detroit showed that babies who regularly attended day-care facilities were more apathetic, less attentive, and less responsive and verbal than infants who were cared for at home.

Arlene Cordoza (1986), in her book *Sequencing,* describes how some women are coping with the problem of working and raising a family by separating their lives into four basic phases. During the first phase, the woman, either single or married, focuses on establishing herself in a career. This phase may last for several years. The second phase begins when the woman finds a man with whom she believes she can successfully raise a family. During this phase, the woman concentrates her attention fully on her family. When her children are old enough to go to school, she begins the third phase by gradually returning to her career on a part-time basis. Finally, when the children are grown, she enters the fourth phase by returning full-time to her career.

The dilemma of child care versus work affects people's work lives in many ways. In his book *Childcare and Corporate Productivity,* John P. Fernandez (1986) reported that 77 percent of the women and 73 percent of the men he surveyed take time away from work attending to their children with such activities as making phone calls and taking long lunch breaks to attend a school play. This translates into hundreds of millions of dollars of lost output for U.S. corporations, according to Fernandez. In the *Fortune* survey, 41 percent of the parents lost at least one day's work in a three-month period to care for a sick child or attend a special function; nearly 10 percent of those parents took three to five days off during the three-month period.

Some possible solutions to the problems facing parents may include the use of computers with modems at home to network with their place of employment. In this way, they can take care of their ill children and be productive at the same time. Some companies are now permitting workers, both with and without children, to do more work at home through computer networks. In addition, more companies are allowing workers to work flexible hours that suit their personal needs (Chapman, 1987).

Single Workers

Many young people are choosing to remain single longer than in previous years. The rush to find a permanent mate and start a family is not as prevalent as it once was. According to the Census Bureau, more young people each year are deciding to remain single (see Figure 12–1). This trend may mean that single workers may become more attractive to employers because of their flexibility to move from place to place without the restraints of a family.

Women in the Workplace

In 1970 half of all women between the ages of twenty-five and fifty-four had jobs. Today, 70 percent of the women in this age range, or 49 million, are employed (Hellwig, 1986). The Department of Labor reports that by 2005

FIGURE 12–1

Unmarried 20- to 24-Year-Olds

SOURCE: U.S. Census Bureau and Statistical Abstract of the United States, 1990.

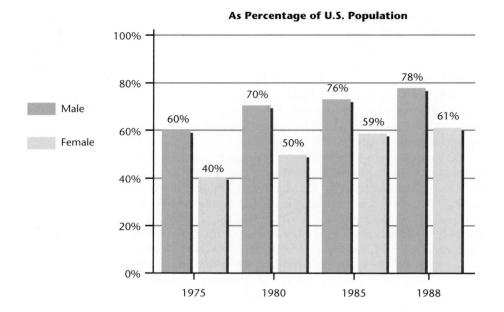

women will hold nearly half of all jobs in the United States (*Occupational Outlook Handbook, 1992–1993*).

The Contributions of Women   For women, work outside the home has meant more independence and more self-confidence. Women are represented in nearly every facet of the employment world. Basia Hellwig (1986), in her article "How Working Women Have Changed America," says that women hold power in the workplace from Wall Street to Smokestack America, and in 1985, 9.2 percent of all working women were executives. Hellwig goes on to list seven ways in which she believes women have had a dramatic effect not only in the workplace but in changing the way we do things in America.

1. The needs of career women with children have helped *create* whole *new businesses* (child-care facilities such as KinderCare had two centers in 1969; today they number over 1,000).

2. Women have continued to *hold more government jobs* (more than 1,000 legislators are women, 3 times the number 15 years ago, and there are more than 1,300 female judges).

3. The *American family has been reshaped* (equality in the home with regard to household responsibilities and more independence for each family member).

4. *Increased family purchasing power* has resulted in new communities and new designs for housing (more purchases of big-ticket items and low-maintenance, care-free homes).

5. Relationship-centered values are *humanizing the workplace* (the workplace is becoming a more comfortable place in which to work).

6. The new *needs of women* have *revolutionized marketing*. How, where, when we shop, and what we shop for have changed (e.g., Chrysler and Ford have internal marketing committees that study the automotive needs of women; frozen foods have become more creative and of better quality).

7. Women's skills and energy as business owners are fueling an unprecedented boom in *entrepreneurship*. Women are creating new companies with new jobs that boost the economy (Elizabeth Claiborne Ortenberg cracked the Fortune 500 companies by building her own company, Liz Claiborne, Inc.).

Women in Management   Earlier in this chapter we discussed the effect that dual-career couples have on the raising of children and vice versa. F. Milene Henley (1986), author and onetime manufacturing manager for IBM (International Business Machines), contends that motherhood can contribute to, rather than detract from, a woman's success as a manager. She says that motherhood and management neither clash nor coexist; instead, "they complement each other by giving the woman who practices both arts new insights into herself and others" (p. 271). She adds, "Motherhood taught me patience. It forced me to delegate more, to organize better and to clarify my objectives. Most important, perhaps, it gave me confidence in myself rather than in my education" (p. 268). Manager Deborah Steven (1991) states that the secret of success as an accomplished manager is to trust what you have learned from your experience and your knowledge. She believes a good manager should possess:

- *ambition:* or you will give up the struggle.
- *judgment:* or you will go off on a tangent.
- *stamina:* or you won't keep plugging.
- *organization or administrative skill:* or there will be chaos.
- *planning ability:* or you won't know where you are going.
- *communication:* or you won't be able to sell your plans or persuade anyone to follow you.
- *job knowledge:* or you will fail to win the respect of your subordinates.
- *courage and integrity:* or you will fade when things get rough.

A growing number of women are successfully achieving positions in management. "Companies have discovered that selecting only male candidates means ignoring about half of the best talent available, and many are now actively recruiting women managers," says Janice Castro (1986). In fact, she believes that "women executives are on the move and taking over *top* jobs in corporations." Some firms have been quicker than others to regard women as executives. Management expert Peter Drucker, in his book *Innovation and Entrepreneurship* (1986), reports that New York's Citibank was among the first major companies to go after female M.B.A.s in the 1970s. Recruiters who were sent out after the best male graduates in finance and marketing began reporting back to headquarters that many of the best graduates were women, not men. The bank's response was simply to hire the best. Even though there are reports indicating that some men resent working for a female manager, Castro (1986) reports that a *Harvard Business Review* survey indicated that men forty years of age and younger were more likely than older men to say they would be comfortable working for a woman supervisor. It appears, then, that as each generation enters the workplace, the resentment toward female managers will lessen.

Even though women are making great strides as managers, men still have a firm hold on the top managerial jobs. Results from the more than 38,000 companies reporting to the U.S. Equal Employment Opportunity Commission in 1992 indicate that women still hold less than a third of the managerial jobs.

However, women have gained considerably during the decade from 1982 to 1992. U.S. Bureau of Labor Statistics data show that women held 30.5 percent of the managerial jobs in 1992, up from 21.7 percent in 1982 (Sharpe, 1994).

Sex Discrimination in the Workplace   Although sex discrimination is diminishing in the workplace, it still exists. In the United States women account for 99 percent of all secretaries, 95 percent of the registered nurses, 91 percent of the bank tellers, 90 percent of the telephone operators, and 84 percent of the elementary school teachers, yet only 22 percent of the lawyers, 18 percent of the physicians and 3 percent of the airplane pilots (U.S. Census Bureau, 1990). Women are still paid less than men for comparable work. The Census Bureau (1990) reported that in 1987 women earned 79 percent as much as men with the same experience. The traditional stereotypes of men and women, although more damaging to women, also may be damaging to men. These stereotypes certainly have a negative effect on our nation's productivity. Our society and our employers need to recognize equally the competency of both men and women in all aspects of the workplace. A study conducted by the Center for Creative Leadership found that executive women and men were equally able to lead, influence, and motivate other group members; able to analyze problems; able to be task-oriented; and able to be verbally effective (Morrison, Randall, White, Velsor, 1987).

Although women and men are judged equal in actual ability, sex stereotypes have greatly affected the ability of women to climb the corporate ladder. Another study done at the Center for Creative Leadership indicated that women have to overcome barriers typically nonexistent for men and, in fact, must outperform men. The stereotype of women as both aspiring hard-nosed executives and delicate females has forced women to display toughness and independence while at the same time demonstrate dependence on others. Using such logic, women should take steps to ensure that they are seen by their bosses as "better than women" as a group, but should not forfeit all traces of femininity at the risk of making them too alien to their superiors and colleagues. They are to do what is not expected of them, while doing enough of what is expected in order to gain acceptance (Morrison, Randall, White, and Velsor, 1987).

Resolving Inequality   Barrett (1979) recommends several ways to lessen the inequality that exists between men and women in the workplace:

1. *Education and training* in areas other than those traditionally dominated by females should be pursued. Also, women should plan for a career that may last a lifetime.

2. *Accurate information should be provided for employers* about the competencies and potential long-term employment of women.

3. *The importance of the woman's career in dual-career marriages* should be stressed. (Chapmen [1987] reported that husbands and wives share almost equally in child care.)

4. *Employment continuity and stability* for the wives should be the concern of both husbands and wives. Either childbearing should be postponed or child care should be shared equally so that both the husband and wife can show commitment to their jobs (see Cordoza's *Sequencing* [1986], described earlier).

5. *Flexible hours and child-care facilities should be provided* as benefits by the employer. Some 150 companies, such as Campbell Soup, IBM, and Merck & Co. (Chapman, 1987), are taking steps in this direction.

6. *Recruitment of qualified women* in areas that were traditionally held by men must be encouraged by the government, educational institutions, and employers alike.

Women Working with Women

Some women not only have to overcome discrimination in the workplace from men but ironically must endure discrimination from each other. Companies owned or run by women can be antediluvian when hiring or promoting women (Mulholland, 1994). Women, when asked whether they would prefer working with men or other women, often indicate that they would prefer working with men. Briles (1989) reports the results of a survey where women were asked to respond to the question: "In your opinion, have you been treated unethically by a man or woman in a business situation?" Fifty-three percent of the women said other women had treated them unethically. This may be the case because women are more apt to "sabotage each other simply because women are likely to work together and because they are viewed as weaker due to their lack of experience, not knowing the rules, or being naive" (p. 137). She further indicates that this sabotage is more likely to occur as women move up the occupational ladder: "As women move up, they have more power to do something unethical. And when the woman moving up is working with other women, the victim of her unethical behavior is most likely to be another woman" (p. 137). This may be due to the competitive pressures that some women feel. From early in their lives, women have been competing with each other for male attention; this competition seems to carry over into the workplace. "Women may easily fall into the trap of victimizing other women out of anger or a desire to impress those in the higher-status male group" (p. 137). For this reason, they may see other women as a threat.

As women become more educated and confident in the positions they hold, this tendency may diminish. Their attitudes about work as well as the attitudes of men about women working are changing in favor of women. The lessening of male dominance in the workplace will also have an effect on the way women work with each other. The trend for women appears to be moving toward supportive networks that will help them realize their deserved place in the world of work.

Critical Review 1

1. Futurists believe that the degree of change in the workplace will be similar to that of the Industrial Revolution. T F

2. Concern exclusively for the work ethic and economic and security needs is characteristic of contemporary work values. T F

3. The concern for the development of self-esteem, social contact, personal growth, and fulfillment is characteristic of traditional work values. T F

4. Single-parent families have grown ten times faster in the past decade than two-parent families. T F

5. The care of children has become a major concern in families where all the adults work outside the home. T F

6. By 2005, over fifty percent of all jobs in the United States will be held by women. T F

7. Contrary to traditional belief, a *Fortune* survey indicated that in dual-career families, the husbands and wives share almost equal concern for the care of the children. T F

8. Working outside the home has meant more independence and more self-confidence for women. T F

9. The relationship-centered values of working women in general, have resulted in more humanity in the workplace. T F

10. Women still account for forty percent of the secretaries. T F

11. Women account for only eighteen percent of the physicians. T F

12. Increased provisions for flexible hours and child-care facilities may be an indication that companies are giving more recognition to the needs of employed parents. T F

13. How do values affect the degree of satisfaction we may feel about the career we choose?

14. How would you describe the impact women have made on the workplace?

CHOOSING A CAREER

fantasy period   refers to the first of three phases of development in choosing a career. During this childhood phase, we often dream about unrealistic and glamorous careers

tentative period   the second phase of career development in which the teenager begins to blend dreams with the reality of abilities, interests, etc.

realistic period   the final phase of career development in which the person blends personal information with information about various careers in a realistic manner

One of the most important and most difficult decisions facing college students today is what career they will choose to pursue. Our thoughts about careers probably began in early childhood. We were always being asked, What are you going to be when you grow up? The responses we gave to this question usually were as limited as our awareness of the possibilities. Our responses may have included an airplane pilot, a nurse, a doctor, a police officer, an actress or actor, a rock star, or a football player. These responses reflect what Ginzberg (1972) calls the **fantasy period,** the first of three phases of development in choosing a career. The fantasy period usually lasts from early childhood until age eleven. During this period, the child usually dreams about having a glamorous career that would fulfill the needs to feel important and powerful. The second phase of development is called the **tentative period.** This period lasts from about eleven years of age to near the end of high school. During this period, young people begin to realize what they like and what they do not like as a result of knowledge gained through experience. This awareness allows them to consider tentative career choices that may still include glamour yet are appropriate to their interests, abilities, and limitations. From seventeen on, students enter the **realistic period,** and their thoughts about a career begin to become narrower and more realistic. They attempt to blend information about themselves with certain job requirements, the potential for rewards, and the future of certain careers. The realistic period includes three stages. The first stage, *exploration,* is when the young adults find a job after school or get further education in an attempt to explore what it is like to enter a particular occupation. The second stage is *crystallization,* when the individuals begin to fix their attention on a fairly clear vocation. The third is the *specification* stage, when they definitely choose a particular career or occupation. To many, making a career choice is a frightening decision. When we must make a decision with such far-reaching implications and consequences, it stands to reason that we would be intimidated and fearful. If we make accurate career choices, we will find satisfaction in the work we do and perhaps remain in our jobs for a long time. However, the realization that many people are unhappy with their career choices and feel locked into the decisions they made years ago adds to the anxiety of such a choice. This is perhaps why many of us seek advice from others and procrastinate about such decisions. We want to be sure. Like so many decisions we must make in life, the choice of a career offers no guarantee. We realize that if the choice proves unwise, we will have no one to blame but ourselves. However, with careful planning and the right information, we can increase the likelihood that our career decision will be the best that we can possibly make.

Career Goals

Many people believe that much of what happens to them is the result of fate or luck, with each person's work determined largely by accident. A young woman graduates from high school and learns from a friend that they are hiring sales-clerks at a local department store. If the young woman gets the job, she may believe this turn of events is directly related to her luck in having a friend who told her about the job. Many of us have long believed that selecting a job is a matter of being in the right place at the right time or knowing someone who can "pull the right strings." Although opportunities are sometimes beyond our control, those of us who want to manage our lives will rely more on planning than on luck. When we manage our own lives, we are more likely to achieve satisfaction now and in the future.

Goals are the foundation for planning and successful decision making, especially when it comes to a career choice (for more information on goal setting and decision making, see chapter 11). We have set and achieved numerous goals from the time we were children to the present, from earning our way to a position on the school volleyball team to learning to drive a car to graduating from high school. We know that without goals we tend to wander from one idea to another, never knowing which direction we should pursue. Traditionally, more people set their career goals when they were young. Many times they were guided by their parents, teachers, or society to fit into a particular career. Many today still approach the world of work in this way. Well-meaning adults may want us to achieve in areas where they believe they never could or in areas where they believe we will be more likely to succeed. When asked what their children are going to do someday, parents often reply, "Oh, he's going to follow in his father's footsteps." The assumption is that if it is good for Father or Mother, it is good for the children, too. Of course, this is not always true. Career goals usually result from two major considerations: our desired **quality of life,** and our desired **quality of work.**

The Quality of Life   Before we can begin thinking about which career is best for us, we must first determine the *quality of life* we are seeking in the future. Many things come to mind when we think about our future, such as where we want to live, what kind of activities we would enjoy, how much stress we can endure, and the kinds of relationships we want to develop.

Certainly, where we live has a dramatic effect on our quality of life. As we see in "Living and Working in San Francisco," where we live becomes the center for most of the activities we enjoy and the center for the development of our interpersonal relationships at home, in our neighborhoods, and at work (Haddock, 1986). Casale (1986) reports in *USA Today: Tracking Tomorrow's Trends* that 53 percent of the people surveyed for the book said they would not move from their present community for a better job. Of course, if we do not have particular preferences about where we live, we can be more open to future work possibilities.

The Quality of Work   The quality of work is also an important ingredient that directly or indirectly affects our quality of life. The satisfaction we gain from the

quality of life   our view of life with respect to where we live, how we live, who we live with, the kinds of activities we enjoy, and the work we do

quality of work   all of the things we desire that we believe will bring us job satisfaction

Living and Working in San Francisco

Patricia Haddock describes the lifestyle in San Francisco. "It's been called the Baghdad-by-the-Bay, Wall Street of the West, City of Golden Hills, The City That Knows How. But those who live here usually call it 'the City,' never ever Frisco.

San Francisco thrives on contrasts. Century-old cable cars carry workers to high-rise office buildings that look down on the pagodas of Chinatown.

San Franciscans are friendly and conversations are easy to start. You can join noon-time joggers along the water-

front, trotting past cruise liners and cargo vessels. Or explore the city's unique shops and sample its restaurants with coworkers."

San Francisco is known for its ". . . public gardens and parks . . . free tennis courts and golf courses. . . . Golden Gate Park lures joggers, bicyclists, rollerskaters, skateboarders, walkers, and outdoor enthusiasts of all kinds . . ."

SOURCE: Condensed from "Living and Working in San Francisco." *Business Week Careers* (October–November 1986): 42–46.

work we do and the career relationships we enjoy greatly enhances our perception of our quality of life. We find ourselves talking about our work at home and about our home lives at work. As hard as we may try, it is quite difficult to separate the two major parts of our lives. The satisfaction we gain from the quality of the work we do is dependent upon the extent to which we find sufficient outlets for the expression of our personalities, interests, and abilities.

Critical Review 2

1. The realistic period is a time in our lives where we dream about a glamorous career, such as a rock star or an astronaut. T F

2. The tentative period lasts from about eleven years of age to high school. We are more knowledgeable about our interests and abilities at this time. T F

3. During the fantasy period we begin to blend the information we know about ourselves with certain job requirements and the future opportunities in certain careers. T F

4. The exploration stage of the realistic period is when we find a job or get further education in order to discover what it is like to work in a particular occupation. T F

5. We begin the process of fixing our attention on a fairly clear vocation during the crystallization stage. T F

6. We definitely choose a particular career or occupation during the specification stage. T F

7. When we think about our desired lifestyle, where we live, our hobbies and recreational activities, we are thinking about our quality of life. T F

8. The perception we have regarding our quality of work, depends upon the extent to which we find outlets for the expression of our personalities, interests, and abilities. T F

9. Describe the stages we go through in search of a satisfying career choice.

10. What connection exists between our career choice and our desired quality of life?

Fantasy and Reality

Dreams   Earlier we discussed the *fantasy period*. The *dreams* that we originally had in childhood often prevail and to some extent determine the degree of satisfaction we experience from the jobs we obtain later in our lives. However, without these dreams we may never aspire to achieve the level of work that is equal to our potential. In fact, many people settle for much less in their lives only to regret later that they had not chosen something that was more challenging and rewarding. They choose safety over growth. Our dreams can facilitate our choices of a career when they are blended with the reality of our *personality* characteristics, *interests, abilities,* and the *constraints* of *time* and *money.*

Personality   When most people think about *personality*, they think about either having a "good" personality or a "bad" personality. However, when exploring career possibilities, we should not be concerned with whether our personalities are good or bad. Instead, we should be concerned with which careers are right for the kinds of personalities we have. Our personalities give us self-portraits we can view when considering our careers.

Psychologist John Holland (1973) theorizes that people select occupations through which they can express their personalities and that will provide them with experiences appropriate to their personalities. He further believes that people who choose the same vocation have similar personalities and react to many situations and problems in similar ways. From his theory, he has identified six personality types, which he matches to certain occupations. Holland also suggests that people who have similar personalities tend to create home and work environments that are like them.

Career satisfaction is achieved when people are able to blend their personalities with their work.

Holland's Job-Related Personality Traits

Realistic

PERSONALITY

These types tend to deal with the environment in objective and concrete ways. They avoid tasks that require subjectivity or intellectual and artistic abilities. They are nonsocial, emotionally stable, and materialistic. They prefer occupations in areas such as agriculture, the technical and skilled trades, and engineering.

ENVIRONMENT

This environment is one where the tasks are clear, physical, and concrete. Problems are solved usually by mechanical skill, persistence, and moving from place to place. Work is often performed outdoors. Social skill is unnecessary because most interaction is businesslike, brief, or casual. Gas stations, military bases, machine shops, farms, and barber shops are typical of this type.

Investigative

PERSONALITY

These types usually prefer to use their intelligence to deal with the environment. They like to work with ideas, words, and symbols. They are more suited to such fields as biology, chemistry, and physics. They often enjoy activities such as art and music. Like the realistic types, they are usually nonsocial. In addition, they tend to be scholarly, persistent, and introverted.

ENVIRONMENT

These people work with ideas rather than with things. Relationships with others usually are not close. The work environment may be characterized by a research lab, a library, or offices with science equipment.

Social

PERSONALITY

Social types usually interact well with people. They prefer activities such as education, religion, and the helping professions. They are characterized as social, cheerful, responsible, and self-accepting. They usually think of themselves as leaders who are popular with others and are often described by others as aggressive. They usually have higher verbal than mathematical ability.

ENVIRONMENT

The social environment is one where people work with others to solve problems. These people seem to care for others. The appropriate environment for these types are schools, hospitals, colleges, churches, and recreational facilities.

Conventional

PERSONALITY

These types prefer to deal with the environment by selecting goals and activities that are socially approved. They create a favorable impression by being clean, neat, sociable, and conservative. They prefer occupations in the business world such as clerical and computational jobs. They view themselves as shrewd, controlled, and stable. They usually have a higher math than verbal ability.

ENVIRONMENT

The environment most desired by conventional types is one that is predictable and systematic. The work usually involves dealing with written and computational materials. Business offices, banks, accounting firms, and post offices are typical places for employment.

Enterprising

PERSONALITY

These types are characterized as coping with the environment by being expressive, adventuresome, enthusiastic, and engaged in leadership. They are confident, persuasive, verbal, outgoing, and aggressive. They usually aspire toward careers that allow them to assert themselves, such as sales and supervision. They like athletics, dramatics, and public speaking. They are characterized as cheerful, emotionally stable, impulsive, adventurous, and strong.

ENVIRONMENT

The tasks in this environment usually include verbal ability required to direct or persuade others. Typical settings include real estate offices, auto dealerships, advertising agencies, and political organizations.

Artistic

PERSONALITY

Artistic people deal with the environment in aesthetic and artistic ways. They prefer to deal with subjective impressions and feelings in solving life problems. They seek careers in music, art, literature, and drama. They are often nonsocial, sensitive, impulsive, introspective, and flexible. Their abilities are usually higher in verbal skills than in mathematical skills.

ENVIRONMENT

This environment centers around tasks that require interpretation and creativity. This person manipulates the environment through feeling and imagination. Typical work settings include the stage, galleries, concert halls, studios, and libraries.

Holland believes that career satisfaction is greater when individuals are able to blend their personalities with their work environments. Failure to understand their personality characteristics and match them carefully to the characteristics of the work environment accounts for much of the dissatisfaction that people experience today. The search is for environments and careers that can best complement our interests, abilities, attitudes, and values, which are the major contributors to our personality.

Interests   Interests are defined as those things we like, those activities we like to do, or those things about which we are curious. When we become aware of our concerns, feelings, or curiosity about certain things, we begin to understand our **interests.** Awareness of our interests is important before we decide on a career, because people in particular careers seem to have similar likes and dislikes. Thus, if we can determine our interests and compare those interests to people who like what they do and are successful at what they do, we will have part of the information necessary in making a wise career choice. Although certain interests will come and go, others are likely to last throughout our lives. If we can discover our more permanent interests, we are better able to link these interests to a career decision. The U.S. Employment Service publication *Guide for Occupational Exploration* (1979) defines twelve interest patterns of occupational groups. Of course, everyone does not fit into these interest patterns; however, they are worth contemplating:

interests   things that we like or about which we are curious

1. *Artistic.* Interest in creative expression of feelings and ideas.

2. *Scientific.* Interest in discovering, collecting, and analyzing information about the natural world and in applying scientific research findings to problems in medicine, life sciences, and natural sciences.

3. *Plants and animals.* Interest in activities involving plants and animals, usually outdoors.

4. *Protective.* Interest in the use of authority and power to protect people and things.

5. *Mechanical.* Interest in using mechanical principles in practical situations, using machine tools, hand tools, or techniques.

6. *Industrial.* Interest in repetitive, concrete, organized activities in a factory.

7. *Business detail.* Interest in organized and clearly defined activities that require accuracy and attention to detail, usually in an office environment.

8. *Selling.* Interest in influencing others to accept your point of view through persuasion by using sales techniques.

9. *Accommodating.* Interest in catering to the wishes of others, usually in a service-type relationship.

10. *Humanitarian.* Interest in helping others with their mental, spiritual, social, physical, or vocational needs.

11. *Leading-influencing.* Interest in leading and influencing others through verbal activities.

12. *Physical performing.* Interest in physical activities usually performed before an audience.

Several measurements of vocational interest have been developed and used over the years that attempt to show a relationship between our values, goals, and interests and various occupations. One such inventory is the *Strong-Campbell Interest Inventory.* This inventory asks the participant to choose from among numerous activities and then from these choices attempts to determine not only the participant's interests but how these interests compare with those of individuals who have already entered particular fields. This inventory and others may assist students in making wiser career choices. However, we cannot accept the results of these inventories as infallible. Interest inventories are not crystal balls; they do not attempt to predict success in a particular occupation.

Many people assume that if they have an interest in a particular area, they will be successful at working in that area. You may have a score that indicates that you have some interest in becoming a lawyer. However, you may not have the emotional or intellectual capabilities to actually endure the rigorous training to become a lawyer. Even if you do, you may discover later on that you do not have the personality or skill to continue to find satisfaction in such a career. Interests should not be confused with abilities. Interests are important in helping us determine what choices may provide us with enjoyment, but they may not indicate how successful we might be at performing a particular task.

Abilities Throughout our lives we have been acquiring all kinds of skills. Some things we do extremely well, and other things we do adequately. We may even notice a pattern in our skills. This pattern is known as our **aptitude.** An aptitude is a talent we have for completing a number of tasks that require a similar kind of skill. You may never have repaired a carburetor on your car, but you have done tune-ups and repaired the brakes. Therefore, you probably have enough mechanical aptitude to repair the carburetor. If you also have an aptitude for mathematics, you may want to pursue a career in engineering. Our aptitudes suggest the areas of skill we have the potential for developing.

By the time we get to college, most of us have some idea about our aptitudes. In college we have the opportunity to take introductory courses in various preprofessional fields, and our success in these courses usually tells us something about our abilities. For example, many students discover their ability in the business profession by taking courses in accounting, economics, marketing, or management. Most college counseling centers offer several standardized aptitude tests that can assist you further in determining your aptitudes or abilities. These tests may differ, but most include measurements of the following:

aptitude a talent we have for doing a number of tasks that require a similar kind of skill

- *Verbal ability.* The ability to use written or spoken language easily and effectively.

- *Numerical ability.* The ability to understand and use mathematical reasoning.

- *Abstract reasoning.* The ability to think about and analyze ideas that have little or no connection with concrete or tangible objects.

- *Spatial relationships.* The ability to visualize how things fit together and relate to each other.

- *Mechanical reasoning.* The ability to figure out how tools or machinery work or could be used.

- *Clerical speed and accuracy.* The ability to be organized and see detail in written material such as proofreading words and numbers and identifying errors.

The U.S. Employment Service General Aptitude Test Battery (GATB) includes most of the areas just listed and goes further by including measurements in the following:

- *Form perception.* The ability to see pertinent detail in objects, pictures, and graphs. The ability to make comparisons and see differences in shapes and shadings of figures and widths and lengths of lines.

■ *Motor coordination.* The ability to coordinate eyes and hands rapidly and accurately in making precise movements with speed.

■ *Manual dexterity.* The ability to move the hands easily and skillfully.

■ *Finger dexterity.* The ability to move the fingers and manipulate small objects with the fingers rapidly and accurately.

Linda and Barry Gale (1990) in their book *Discover What You Are Best At* assist the reader in discovering possible abilities in more general areas such as business aptitude and social aptitude. They indicate that the typical occupation often requires more than a single aptitude. For example, to be competent in the nursing career may require that you have aptitudes in the social and clerical areas, science and math, and manual dexterity.

Time and Money   The balance between the amount of *time* and *money* you must invest in the preparation to enter a career and the long-term payoffs is also an important consideration. Having enough money or getting the necessary financial backing through financial aid, loans, scholarships, or part-time work is essential to pursuing a career goal. Also, can you realistically spend up to ten years acquiring the necessary learning and credentials to enter a certain professional career? Do you have the patience and endurance? In ten or twenty years will the investment of time and money reward you adequately for your efforts? These constraints are important items to consider as part of the information-gathering process.

Critical Review 3

1. The theory that people select occupations through which they can express their personalities was developed by psychologist John Holland. T F

2. People who prefer occupations in the areas of agriculture and engineering are said to have enterprising personalities. T F

3. Those who like to work in the investigative environment prefer working in research laboratories and using scientific equipment. T F

4. Preference for working in schools, hospitals, and recreational facilities indicates that a person prefers the conventional environment. T F

5. People with realistic personalities prefer working in clerical and computational type jobs. T F

6. If you are persuasive, outgoing, and aggressive, you may have an artistic type personality. T F

7. Work settings such as art galleries, concert halls, and studios are characteristic of those who enjoy the enterprising environment. T F

8. Interests are defined as our likes or preferences. T F

9. Your aptitude is the talent you have for doing a number of tasks that require a similar kind of skill. T F

10. The ability to think about and analyze ideas that have little or no connection with concrete or tangible objects is called abstract reasoning. T F

11. An aptitude in spatial relationships is the ability to visualize how things fit together and relate to each other. T F

12. The ability to coordinate eyes and hands rapidly and accurately in making precise movements with speed is called motor coordination. T F

13. What role do interests play in our search for career satisfaction?

14. Describe the importance of personality in choosing a career.

Making a Career Choice

Making a career choice requires having preliminary information from a variety of sources. First, we must consider pertinent information about ourselves. Second, we must consider information about the various careers that may fit our interests. Finally, we must consider the availability of jobs in these various careers.

Gathering Personal Information   So far we have discussed various kinds of *personal information* that are very important to consider when entering the *realistic stage* of career decision making. We have discussed dreams, values, goals, personality characteristics, interests, and abilities. Now it is time to bring all of this information together and begin applying it to a career choice. The questionnaire "Personal Career Data" will help you do this.

Questionnaire

Personal Career Data

Our dreams and fantasies play a part in career decision making in the sense that they give us an opportunity to use our imagination and creativity. Human-potential specialists suggest that many of us reach only a fraction of our potential because we fail to think about what could be if we really tried to accomplish something. Think about some of the career dreams and fantasies that you have had in the past. If you were functioning at your best ability, which of these fantasies could become a reality? In the spaces that follow, list a few of your dreams and fantasies that you believe may be possible for you.

My Career Dreams and Fantasies

_____   _____

_____   _____

_____

Next, we will look at our *work values*. Values often reflect deeply held beliefs about how we should live. They may also be a response to needs that we want to satisfy. Earlier in this chapter we discussed *traditional work values* and *contemporary work values*. Look over that section again to see if you can more accurately fix in your mind the work values that are most important to you. Then, in the following list of spaces write what you think are your *five* most important work values in order of the *most important* to *least important*. (A more extensive work-value assessment is contained in the Study Guide that accompanies this text.) Some examples of work values are helping others, working alone, and being creative.

My Five Most Important Work Values

1. _____

2. _____

3. _____

4. _____
5. _____

Now that you have determined your five most important work values, think about some of the *career goals* that you have. Begin by describing the type of *lifestyle* you hope to have in the future. Consider where you want to live, your ideal living arrangement (with a roommate or a spouse, or by yourself, etc.), the kind of activities (recreational, etc.) you expect to continue or develop, the kind of relationships you hope to develop, the amount of stress you believe is healthy for you, and any other ingredients you believe are important. Use the spaces provided to describe your desired lifestyle.

My Desired Lifestyle

Where I hope to live: _____
_____

My preferred living arrangement: _____

I expect to continue these activities: _____
_____

I expect to form these kinds of relationships: _____
_____

My family life will include: _____
_____

With regard to stress: _____
_____

My other considerations are: _____
_____

When thinking about the *quality of work* we hope to enjoy, it is important to determine exactly what our *motivation* is for working. We can discover more about our desired quality of work if we can find out what we want from the work environment. In the spaces provided, *brainstorm* as many "wants" as you can think of that represent the expectations you have for the career you will eventually choose. Do not be limited by what you think most careers provide. Use your imagination and creativity to develop a list of wants that you believe would provide you with the most satisfaction. For example, some possible considerations might be flexible hours, recognition, responsibility, good leadership, adequate wages, and friendship. Try to brainstorm a list of at least *twenty* wants.

My Career Wants

_____	_____	_____
_____	_____	_____
_____	_____	_____
_____	_____	_____
_____	_____	_____
_____	_____	_____
_____	_____	_____

To be realistic, we must admit that there are probably few occupations that would provide you with all of your wants. If you could narrow your wants down to the five you believe would bring the greatest satisfaction over a long period of time, which five would you choose? Place a *1* in front of the *most important* want, a *2* in front of the second most important, and so on until you have identified the five most important motivators for your quality of work. This is an indication of what you believe a career optimally should provide.

Questionnaire
—continued

Next, let us consider our *personality characteristics*. As we mentioned earlier, our long-term satisfaction with our work is dependent on our ability to express our personalities in the work that we do. To begin thinking about how personality affects career choice, you may want to answer the following questions.

My Personality Characteristics
- Do I like to meet new people?   Yes   No
- Am I an outgoing person?   Yes   No
- Do I like to work alone rather than with others?   Yes   No
- Am I a leader?   Yes   No
- Am I a follower?   Yes   No
- Do I like to supervise others?   Yes   No
- Am I neat and careful?   Yes   No
- Am I flexible?   Yes   No
- Do I like change?   Yes   No
- Do I enjoy competition?   Yes   No
- Do I need a lot of encouragement?   Yes   No
- Do I work well under pressure?   Yes   No

These questions have no right or wrong answers. If you felt uncomfortable saying no to "Am I an outgoing person?" it is important to realize that being outgoing is not necessarily better than being shy. However, if a particular job that you are interested in requires that you meet new people, then perhaps it would be a better job for someone who is more outgoing. If you are a shy person, you may fit into other types of jobs much better than those who are outgoing and thrive on meeting new people. This does not mean that your personality cannot change; however, it may be better to begin a career where you are most comfortable rather than a career where you must make dramatic changes. You can always change gradually at a rate that is comfortable for you.

As we mentioned earlier, our interests can tell us about the kinds of occupations that we may be more likely to enjoy over a long period of time. Perhaps your answers to the following questions can provide more insight into your appropriate career interests:

My Interests
- What kinds of things do I like to do around the house?

_____

_____

- What kinds of books do I like to read?

_____

_____

- What kinds of entertainment do I enjoy?

_____

_____

- What kinds of people do I enjoy?

_____

_____

- What kinds of school subjects do I enjoy?

_____

_____

- What have I enjoyed on jobs I have had?

_____

_____

■ What kinds of television programs do I enjoy?

_____

_____

    Abilities are the ingredients that permit us to be successful at doing the kinds of things for which we may have some interest. The fact that many of us may not know our full potential suggests that we develop our potential over our entire lifetime. However, by the time most students arrive in college, they do have some idea about what abilities come easy for them and what abilities take great effort. Using the following scale of abilities, rate each ability as it describes you at this time in your life. If you are not sure about some of your abilities in these areas, you may want to ask a friend or someone who knows you well to help you.

	Very High	High	Aver-age	Low	Very Low
Verbal. Able to understand and use words and ideas in speaking and writing	___	___	___	___	___
Numerical. Able to work with numbers accurately and quickly	___	___	___	___	___
Reasoning. Able to think through complicated problems and carry out logical processes	___	___	___	___	___
Perception. Able to see similarities and differences in the things around you	___	___	___	___	___
Coordination. Able to use feet, hands, and fingers easily and skillfully	___	___	___	___	___
Clerical. Able to type, file, copy, keep accurate records, and do other clerical work	___	___	___	___	___
Social. Able to relate well to others and talk easily	___	___	___	___	___
Leadership. Able to infuence, lead, and supervise others effectively	___	___	___	___	___
Mechanical. Able to work with, understand, and fix machines, appliances, and tools	___	___	___	___	___
Musical. Able to sing, play an instrument, and read music	___	___	___	___	___
Artistic. Able to work with light, color, composition, and design to produce art objects	___	___	___	___	___
Athletic. Able to perform in a variety of sports	___	___	___	___	___
Entertainment. Able to perform for others in drama, dance, comedy, and similar activities	___	___	___	___	___

Gathering Career Information   Now that we have acquired some of the necessary personal information, it is important to begin combining it with pertinent *career information.* Before beginning to gather career information, you should select at least three occupations that you think may appeal to you. Most students tend to be too narrow in their considerations of careers, and this may keep them from discovering a career that would be most suitable. It is important to explore all options before we begin to narrow down our choices. The *Dictionary of Occupational Titles* can help you discover a variety of occupations to consider. Reading is one important way to find valuable information.

    There are literally hundreds of books, journal articles, and magazine articles that have been written about occupations. Occupational information is gathered and published by numerous governmental and private agencies. Your college library or counseling and placement center most likely has a large collection of these materials. The U.S. Government Printing Office publishes the *Occupational Outlook Handbook* every two years. Governmental departments such as the Departments of Agriculture, Commerce, Defense, Education, Health and Human Services, and Labor also publish occupational information. Journals published by numerous professional organizations such as the American Institute of Certified Public Accountants, American Psychological Association, American Institute of Architects, and the American Culinary Federation often offer literature on careers in their professions. Magazines such as *Business Week Careers, Ebony, Working Woman, Mademoiselle,* and *Seventeen* offer many articles describing what it is like to work in certain careers.

Occupational literature usually describes the work itself, how it is organized, the necessary qualifications, the training required, the future outlook, the monetary rewards, and the benefits. When reading literature about various occupations, you sould keep in mind several important questions. First, is the information current? Most literature about occupations becomes dated quickly. Therefore, it is important to note the date of publication. Many occupations are rapidly changing as the supply and demand and technology change. One of the best publications to anticipate change is the U.S. government's Bureau of Labor Statistics *Occupational Outlook Handbook.* Second, does the work in this occupation *interest* you? It is important to consider the things you will have to do and whether you can see yourself enjoying doing those things over a period of time. Third, *where* is the work done? The environmental conditions of an occupation have much to do with our degree of job satisfaction. The setting and conditions in which we would work are important. Fourth, what is the future *outlook* for this career? The expected employment trends over the next several years are important. Fifth, what are the *requirements* to enter or succeed in this career? The amount of education and training as well as abilities and interests should be addressed in answering this question. Sixth, what are the opportunities for *advancement* in this career? Answers to this question should include how you can advance (through more education, experience, examinations, etc.) and what level of advancement you might expect. Finally, what are the earnings? This should include beginning and optimal earnings, as well as fringe benefits such as insurance, vacations, and retirement plans.

Written career information alone is not going to answer each of your questions. It is important also to gather information by *talking to people* who work in a particular field or who employ those who do. This can be accomplished either by setting up a formal interview or by attending a career conference (held on most college campuses each year) and asking pertinent questions. When interviewing someone, it is important to think of questions such as the following:

- How did you decide to choose this career?
- How is your work different from your original expectations?
- What are your major duties or responsibilities?
- What do you like about your work?
- What do you not like about your work?
- What do you find most difficult?
- How would you describe the place where you work?
- How would you describe your typical workday?
- Where in the country do you think a person could find the most opportunity to succeed in this career?

- What changes have you seen since you began working in this career?
- What changes do you foresee in the future?
- What are the average earnings where you work?
- What are the fringe benefits where you work?
- How do the average salary and fringe benefits compare to other areas of the country?
- If you were to choose a career again, what would you choose?
- What advice would you give someone who is considering choosing your occupation?

By asking some of these questions, you can determine how similar your interests are to the person you are interviewing and perhaps determine whether you might also like to do what that person is doing.

Perhaps the *best* way to gather career information is to acquire *part-time work* in a job that is related to what you are considering. For example, someone interested in teaching could work as a teacher's aide to see if the duties and responsibilities were compatible with his or her skills, personality, and interests. Someone interested in a medical career could seek a job as an orderly or nurse's aide. Finding part-time work allows you to gather information in two ways. You not only get firsthand experience, but you also have the opportunity to talk to those who work in this occupation as well as observe the numerous things that they do.

Data Analysis   Now it is time to analyze the information you have acquired and begin thinking about a career decision. It is important, though, to realize that career development is an ongoing process in which each decision leads to others later on. Earlier, we discussed the importance of considering several career possibilities. We also gathered information about our work values, our wants in terms of lifestyle and quality of work, our personality characteristics, our interests, and our abilities. This information, combined with the information we have gathered about the careers we are considering, will give us a more accurate picture about the reality of our career considerations.

Now, let us see how we might use this information to analyze three career possibilities. The three careers we will consider are business manager, psychologist, and computer-science professional. The following example may serve as a guide for your career profile. On the left side of the profile, list your *personal data*. Then, match your data with the data you gathered about each of the careers you are considering. This will help you see which career most closely fits your personal requirements. Based on the value you place on each of the personal datum used to consider a career decision, you should be able to make a more logical and rational career choice and eventually find the job most suited to you.

Assessing Job Availability   Although it is true that college graduates have an edge over high-school graduates in finding better jobs and higher pay, gone are the days when those who completed college had unlimited employment opportunities. Competition among college-educated workers is increasing. The Bureau of Labor Statistics reports that more students are attending and graduating from college each year, increasing the competition among college graduates (*Occupational Outlook Handbook, 1992–1993,* see Figure 12–2) Although there is still a demand for students with degrees in fields that are critically short handed, most students must undertake a rigorous job-hunting campaign (see Figure

FIGURE 12–2

Workers, 25 to 64 Years of Age, With a College Background

SOURCE: Bureau of Labor Statistics, U.S. Department of Labor, Occupational Outlook Handbook, 1992–1993.

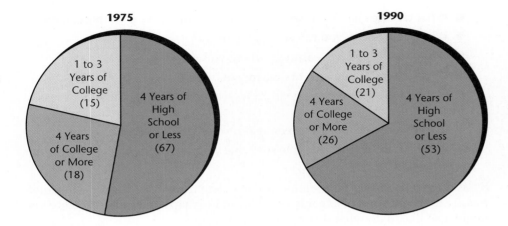

1975

1 to 3 Years of College (15)

4 Years of High School or Less (67)

4 Years of College or More (18)

1990

1 to 3 Years of College (21)

4 Years of College or More (26)

4 Years of High School or Less (53)

entrepreneur   a person who takes the risk of organizing and managing a new business

12–3). The Bureau of Labor Statistics reports that by the year 2005, most jobs will be in the technological and related fields. But the fastest growing sector will be in the service industries, especially health services and business services (*Occupational Outlook Handbook*, 1992–1993).

College graduates often respond to their immediate needs for money, status, and security by leaping into jobs that meet those needs but ignore the needs for ongoing growth and creativity. The result is often unrewarding and leads to job dissatisfaction.

Successful job hunting requires *planning, energy, imagination*, and *endurance*. Information about *job availability* can help in the search. For example, according to an article in *USA Today* (1986, p. 10), "In recent years, small businesses have created more than 70% of this country's new civilian jobs. Employment in the 500 largest industrial corporations has declined." Because change will occur more suddenly as products and services become obsolete, and because most large corporations have difficulty responding to sudden change, the future will belong to the **entrepreneurs** and owner-managed firms of fewer than 100 employees. Steven Jobs, the founder of Apple Computers, is one such example of an entrepreneur who carved a niche for himself in a field that had been dominated by such corporate giants as IBM. He hired young, creative, and innovative college graduates who were able to develop a product that met the needs of millions of people.

Life will be dramatically different when comparing the small company to the large corporation. "The work environment will be much more stressful, but less attention will be paid to bureaucratic detail. Employees will be under pressure to make innovative and creative attempts to help the company grow and succeed" (*USA Today*, 1986, p. 10). Such information is crucial to understanding the process of finding the right job.

Many of us, perhaps resistant to change, look for jobs only in traditional places and consequently are unsuccessful at finding appropriate career-related work. This prevents many college graduates from finding jobs that are related to their college degrees. It may further be an indication that some college students do not adequately investigate the availability of jobs in their chosen major.

International Employers   Perhaps one of the biggest challenges some American workers will continue to face is working for corporations not owned and managed by Americans. It is anticipated that the People's Republic of China will

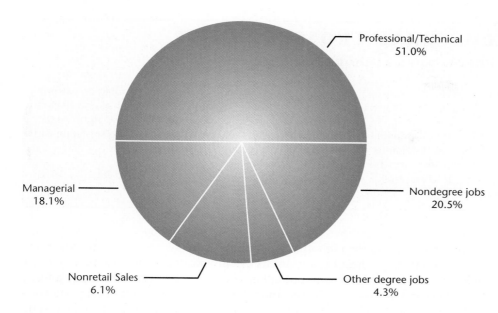

FIGURE 12–3
Types of Jobs College Graduates
Will Enter, through 1995

SOURCE: Occupational Outlook Handbook,
1992–1993.

Professional/Technical
51.0%

Managerial
18.1%

Nondegree jobs
20.5%

Nonretail Sales
6.1%

Other degree jobs
4.3%

become the world's greatest economy, beyond that of the United States and Japan, by the year 2000 (Naisbitt, 1994). This reality almost ensures that Americans will be dealing with, if not working for, numerous Chinese companies. According to Powell (1987), nearly 250,000 Americans already work for the Japanese. Tokyo's Ministry of International Trade and Industry predicts Japanese investment will spawn an additional 840,000 American jobs in the next decade. Such changes will require adjustment in work attitudes on the part of Americans. For example, Japanese companies are different from many American companies in that they place less emphasis on worker competition and more emphasis on teamwork. The attitude that "we're all in this together" forms the basis for the Japanese style of management, which may be the most successful management style in history. The Japanese, in turn, are having some difficulties adjusting to American trade unions and assertive women in the workplace, two aspects of American work life not common in Japan. However, their influence on the American economic structure has been dramatic and will no doubt continue to be as will the influence of other countries. Perhaps it is to our advantage to become more familiar with the cultures and customs of other nations with whom we associate in the world of business and work (see the "Cultural Crosscurrents" feature in this chapter).

Getting Help   We can gather information about job possibilities and seek help in finding a job in a variety of ways. Most colleges and universities have *career-resource centers* and/or *job placement centers*. These centers can provide you with pertinent information on job openings and the conditions of supply and demand for your particular field. Additional help is often provided in securing and filling out applications, preparing for the job interview, and following up on job advertisements.

It is also important to register with your local *state employment agency*. These offices provide referral services for those who register. State employment agencies attempt to match the qualifications of the registrant with the requests of local employers. They also are able to offer information about the labor market

CULTURAL CROSSCURRENTS
International Customs and Business Relations

Sometimes our best intentions can lead to breakdowns in cross-cultural communication. Among middle-class North American men, it is customary to shake hands as a gesture of friendship. When wanting to communicate extra friendliness, a male in the United States may, while shaking hands, grasp with his left hand his friend's right arm. However, if a North American businessman should attempt to emphasize the sincerity of his friendship in this manner to his Saudi Arabian business partner, he would be sending an extremely offensive message, because in Saudi Arabia, and generally throughout the Muslim world where the right hand is sacred and the left hand is profane, touching someone with the hand is considered highly offensive.

SOURCE: Ferraro, G. *Cultural Anthropology: An Applied Perspective.* St. Paul, MN: West Publishing Company, 1992.

within the state and throughout the nation. You can also register with a *commercial placement office.* These organizations usually provide services similar to those of state employment agencies, but either you or the employer must pay a fee.

Counselors, instructors, friends, and *relatives* are also sources of job information. Keeping in touch with these resources can be quite beneficial. Make certain they know what kind of job you are looking for. More jobs are obtained this way than probably any other. You can also get an idea about the kinds of jobs available in a certain location and field by reading the employment-opportunities section of the *newspaper.*

The Job Interview   Once you have discovered a job possibility and attracted a potential employer, you will embark on one of the most important aspects of finding the right job: the job interview. Job interviews are usually somewhat stressful for the applicant. The fear is that you may not present a favorable first impression. When entering the interview session, you should be prepared for anything. It is a good idea to prepare for the kinds of questions you think may be asked (see the box entitled "Questions for the Job Interview"). The interviewer's demeanor may range anywhere from warm and cordial to cold and calculating. You may be asked to answer several open-ended questions in an attempt to get you to reveal yourself. It is important to be as honest as possible yet present a positive image. Knowing your personal strengths can assist you in this preparation.

Dorothy Leeds (1991), author of the book *Marketing Yourself,* describes what she believes are the ten most marketable skills:

- adaptability (ability to adjust and change)
- commitment (to self and others)
- communication (ability to express your ideas and be a good listener)
- creativity (ability to think of new ways of doing things)
- decision making (ability to make the tough choices)
- evaluation (ability to make good judgments)
- foresight (ability to see beyond the present)
- independence (ability to rely on yourself)
- being a team player (ability to work well with others)
- value added skills (ability to offer that little something extra)

Questions for the Job Interview

- Why did you choose your academic major or field?
- Describe any previous employment you have had in this field.
- What did you learn from your previous work experience?
- Were you ever fired from a previous job? Why?
- Did you ever quit a previous job? Why?
- What courses did you take that you think helped you prepare for this field? How did you do in them?
- What are your long-range goals five years from now? Ten years from now?
- What do you want most from your job?
- Do you have any geographical preferences for where you work?
- How do you spend your leisure time?
- What are your greatest personal strengths? Weaknesses?
- What do you know about our company?
- Why have you decided to interview with our company?
- How much money do you expect to be making five years from now?
- What do you think you can contribute to this company?
- Imagine that you are working with our company. What would you do if . . .?

She believes it is important to communicate these marketable skills to potential employers in the job interview.

There are several things to remember when considering the job interview.

1. *Be on time* for the appointment. If you are going to be even a few minutes late, call ahead. These kinds of first impressions are important.

2. *Go alone.* Never take a friend or parent with you. Doing so may create the impression that you are not mature enough to handle the job.

3. *Dress appropriately.* Your dress and physical appearance make a lasting impression.

4. *Listen carefully.* Often when we are under stress we become preoccupied with our own discomfort. Concentration and active listening are important for you to respond accurately to the interviewer's questions.

5. *Answer questions concisely.* By getting to the point quickly, you will impress the interviewer with your ability to be efficient in the communication process.

6. *Learn about the potential employer before you go.* You may find good source material in your college library. Demonstrating that you have knowledge about the employer will indicate to the interviewer that you are interested in that particular company.

If you think the interview went poorly, it is important to analyze what you think went wrong and try to plan for improvement the next time. If you do not get the job, do not assume that you made a poor impression in the interview. It is important to realize that there are often many qualified individuals applying for the same position, and it would be nearly impossible to guess why you did not get the job. Remind yourself of your personal strengths and your educational training and go on to the next interview with confidence.

Critical Review 4

1. The *Dictionary of Occupational Titles* describes a variety of occupations that we can explore. T F

2. We can gather career information by reading and talking to people, and working on a part-time basis in a career-related job. T F

3. Vocational reference books such as the *Occupational Outlook Handbook,* published every two years, offer information on job requirements, salaries, and projected availability for most occupations. T F

4. In recent years, only 20 percent of the country's jobs were available in small businesses. T F

5. Someone who organizes, manages, and assumes the risk of a new enterprise is called an entrepreneur. T F

6. Many colleges and universities have job placement centers that assist students in gathering career information and finding jobs. T F

7. The U.S. Department of Labor's Bureau of Labor Statistics reports that by the year 2005 the greatest number of jobs will be in the technical fields, but the greatest increase will be in the service industries. T F

8. The most important aspect of finding a job is the job application. T F

9. Describe the process of making a career choice.

10. Once we have made a career choice, what steps should we take to find a career-related job?

CAREER ADJUSTMENT

John works as an operating-room nurse. Each day is different from the day before, even though he uses most of the same skills every day. His job demands that he be alert and use the best possible judgment in all situations. He is able to keep his skills up-to-date by attending training sessions held both within his department and at monthly professional nursing organization meetings. He is highly respected for his work. In fact, many of his colleagues have requested that he be the officiating nurse on occasions when they or their family members require surgery. Even after eleven years, John finds great satisfaction in what he has chosen for a career.

Robin is a junior partner in a law firm. She is required to research the law in preparation for cases that the firm is handling. This sometimes means long hours in the law library or at times traveling to another city to gather information. She likes the importance of her work, knowing that what she does may directly affect the lives of others. She also has several legal assistants who help her. As a result, she is developing some managerial skills. Even though her work is often routine, she finds it challenging and rewarding.

Jessica and Bradley met when they were in college. They both majored in education and are now teaching high school math and junior high school science, respectively. They both find their jobs very rewarding. The children they teach all seem to like them, as is evidenced by attendance at the after-school clubs Jessica and Bradley have organized. Even though they each have a supervisor, they are usually left alone to be responsible for what they do in the classrooms. Their only requirement is to have weekly lesson plans so that if they should be absent, someone could substitute and know the current plan for teaching. Occasionally they are required to attend faculty meetings and bimonthly PTA (Parent-Teacher Association) meetings. Their salaries are not as high as some of their classmates in college, but one of the major fringe benefits is the two-month vacation they enjoy in the summer. One summer they both worked at other interests: Jessica as a tax preparer and Bradley as a researcher on an oil-exploration ship. Last summer they traveled to China.

Job Satisfaction

The previous examples may help us discover some of the factors that lead toward **job satisfaction.** One of the most important concerns of workers today is the attainment of job satisfaction over a long period of time. Job satisfaction can be defined as the degree to which our needs are satisfied by the work we do, the conditions under which we perform what we do, and the rewards we receive for what we do. Certainly, this assessment of job satisfaction depends on how the worker *perceives* the job as meeting his or her needs. We tend to weigh the pros against the cons. If the pros outweigh the cons, then we are more likely to be satisfied with our jobs; if the cons outweigh the pros, we are more likely to be dissatisfied with our jobs.

When we hear news reports of low worker productivity, high turnover, absenteeism, union walkouts, sickouts, low morale, and so on, we may conclude that most people do not like what they do. For these reasons we know that job dissatisfaction is quite costly and that there is a direct connection between the quality of our work life and productivity. Phrases like "Blue Monday," "Wednesday is over-the-hump day," and "Thank God it's Friday" attest to the degree of job dissatisfaction that some people experience.

However, several surveys report that most people *do* like their jobs (Jahoda, 1981). In fact, a large-scale government survey shows that Americans are strongly attached to their jobs and that many of them want to work more rather than less (Trost, 1986). Janet Norwood, commissioner of the Bureau of Labor Statistics, who conducted the government survey, says that "commitment to work is stronger than we thought" and that "women in the labor force are here to stay."

The elements of job satisfaction have been the focus of many behavioral scientists since the 1930s. The underlying principle of surveys about job satisfaction is that workers are human beings with a great many needs, many of which must be satisfied on the job if workers are to be happy and productive. Herzberg (1966, 1968), of the University of Utah, collected data about job satisfaction by interviewing some 200 engineers and accountants from eleven industries in the Pittsburgh area. The participants were asked to identify what made them happy/satisfied and unhappy/dissatisfied with their jobs. From the results, Herzberg concluded that meeting some of the needs of workers may reduce dissatisfaction yet not increase satisfaction. He also concluded that people have two different categories of needs that are essentially independent of each other and affect behavior in different ways.

When people are dissatisfied with their jobs, they tend to be more concerned about their lower-level needs (see Maslow's list of needs in chapter 2); factors such as the working environment, salary, and safety meet these needs. Herzberg calls the objectives related to meeting these needs the *hygiene* or *maintenance* factors. Providing fringe benefits, status, and job security may prevent dissatisfaction and thus are hygienic, but they do not ensure long-term job satisfaction. Tough hygiene factors produce little growth in worker output, they do prevent losses in work performance. In other words, when the hygiene factors are not adequate, workers are unhappy; when the hygiene factors are adequate, workers tend to be more satisfied but not necessarily happy. Workers are happier and more productive only when the *motivating* factors such as enjoyment from what they do, recognition, opportunity for growth and advancement, and job autonomy (authority and responsibility to make decisions) are present (see Figure 12–4).

job satisfaction the degree to which our needs are satisfied by the work we do, the conditions under which we perform the work, and the rewards we receive from what we do

FIGURE 12–4
Herzberg's Hygiene-Motivation
Theory

SOURCE: Herzberg, F. *Work and the Nature of Man.* London: Staples, 1968.

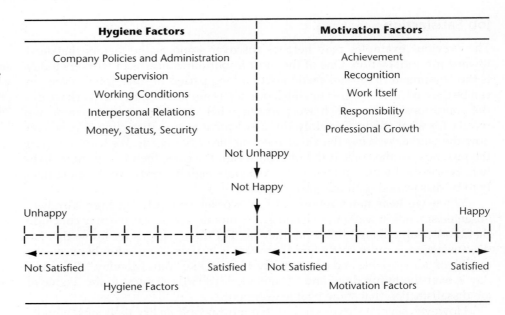

Human Relations The stimulus, in part, for Herzberg's work may have come from the earlier work of others surrounding the concepts of human relations in the workplace and the motivation to produce.

One of the first major human relations theories grew out of a study that began in 1924 at a Western Electric Company plant in Hawthorne, Illinois. Some efficiency experts wanted to study the effect of illumination on productivity. They assumed that increases in illumination would result in higher productivity from the workers. An experimental and a control group were selected, and illumination was increased for the experimental group and kept the same for the control group. As expected, the work output of the experimental group went up as the lighting power was increased. Unexpectedly, however, the output of the control group also went up—without any increase in light. Surprised by these results, the experimenters called in Elton Mayo of the Harvard Graduate School of Business Administration and his associates to see if they could determine why this had happened.

Mayo's research began with improving the working conditions of a group of women who assembled telephone relays. Such innovations as scheduled rest periods and shorter work weeks were implemented. As expected, productivity increased. Then the researchers took the innovations away and the workers returned to the working conditions that had existed before the experiment. This radical change was expected to have an extremely negative impact on productivity. Instead, the output jumped to a new high. Baffled by these results, the reseachers set out to discover why.

They finally concluded that the workers' increase in productivity had come not from a change in working conditions, but from a change in the amount of human interaction! As a result of the attention lavished on them by the researchers, the women came to feel that they were an important part of the company. They no longer viewed themselves as isolated individuals, but as members of a congenial, cohesive work group. The relationships that developed as a result of the study elicited feelings of affiliation, competence, and achievement. The workers' needs for these feelings, which had previously gone unsatisfied, were now being fulfilled. As a result, the women worked harder and more effectively than they had before. This unexpected outcome became known as the *Hawthorne effect*.

From these Hawthorne studies, researchers learned that it was necessary for leaders and managers to understand the importance of relationships among people. The most significant factor affecting organizational productivity, they said, was the interpersonal relationships developed on the job, not just the pay and working conditions, as had been previously thought.

Mayo (1933) viewed his findings as an indictment of industrial society, which treated human beings as insensitive machines. According to Mayo, too many managers assumed that society consisted of a horde of unorganized people whose only concern was self-interest and self-preservation. Management's basic assumption was that workers, on the whole, were a contemptible lot who wanted as much money as they could get for as little work as possible. Mayo called this assumption the *rabble hypothesis*. This assumption resulted in workers' being taught to look at work only as money in exchange for labor, a view that still robs many of us of the joy and satisfaction that come with accomplishment.

Some scholars believe that Mayo's work paved the way for Douglas McGregor's (1960) classic theories. McGregor believed that the traditional organization, with its centralized decision making, superior-subordinate pyramid, and external control of work, is based on false assumptions about human nature and human motivation. He calls these assumptions *Theory X.* Theory X is quite similar to Mayo's rabble hypothesis. It assumes that most people prefer to be told what to do, are not interested in assuming responsibility, and want security above all. This philosophy is accompanied by the belief that people are motivated only by money, other financial benefits, and threat of punishment.

McGregor believed that people in a democratic society, with their increasing level of education and standard of living, are capable of more mature behavior than they are credited with. Influenced by Maslow's hierarchy of needs, McGregor concluded that Theory X assumptions about human nature, when applied universally, are often inaccurate, and that management approaches based on these asumptions often fail to motivate individuals to work toward the organization's goals. People whose physiological and security needs have been met are seldom motivated by managers and leaders who use direction and control strategies.

As a result of his belief, McGregor developed an alternative theory of human behavior called *Theory Y.* This theory assumes that people are not, by nature, lazy and unreliable. They can be self-directed and creative at work when positively motivated. Properly motivated people can achieve their goals best by directing their own efforts toward the accomplishment of the organization's goals. This is encouraged by **integrative leadership,** which assumes that all the major kinds of human needs can be somewhat satisfied at work and that the very activity of contributing to organizational success can be highly rewarding to the worker. Thus, it is believed that the employee's needs can be tied to those of the organization (Torgersen and Weinstock, 1972). Table 12–1 compares McGregor's Theory X and Theory Y assumptions.

In Theory X organizations, people are unable to satisfy social, esteem, and self-actualization needs. When a job does not provide need satisfaction at every level, today's employee will be forced to look elsewhere for significant need satisfaction. We often hear someone say, "Thank God it's Friday!" Many people work to live, but live for the weekends. This lack of need fulfillment on the job perhaps explains some of the current problems organizations are facing with

integrative leadership a leadership or management style that assumes that the needs of human beings can be integrated with the needs of organizations

TABLE 12–1

McGregor's Theory X and Theory Y
Assumptions

THEORY X	THEORY Y
1. Work is inherently distasteful to most people.	1. Work is as natural as play, if the conditions are favorable.
2. Most people are not ambitious, have little desire for responsibility, and prefer to be directed.	2. Self-direction is often indispensable in the achievement of organizational goals.
3. Most people have little capacity for creativity in solving organizational problems.	3. The capacity for creative problem solving is widely distributed in the population.
4. Motivation occurs only at the physiological and security levels.	4. Motivation occurs at the social, esteem, and self-actualization levels, as well as the physiological and security levels.
5. Most people must be closely controlled and often coerced to achieve organizational objectives.	5. People can be self-directed and creative at work if properly motivated.

high turnover and increasing absenteeism. McGregor argued that this does not have to be the case; Theory Y organizations can provide for greater need fulfillment.

From our discussion of Theory X and Theory Y, you may get the impression that Theory X is bad and Theory Y is good. We must offer a word of caution, though, about drawing these conclusions. Theory X and Theory Y are attitudes about human nature, and people sometimes behave in the immature ways suggested by Theory X.

Torgersen and Weinstock (1972) report that many people are not psychologically prepared for the higher levels of individual responsibility and freedom associated with integrative leadership. Some people are stuck at the security need level or the social need level. They neither desire nor feel ready to cope with a Theory Y system. Some feel generally inadequate or inferior. Such people, it is held, want strong leadership and routine, stable jobs. Their performance might suffer, as would their satisfaction levels, should they be expected to assume more responsibility. Other workers are so accustomed to autocratic leadership that they would question the sincerity, indeed the sanity, of a participative democratic approach. Thus, we can understand the difficulty a Theory Y manager might have with a group of Theory X workers.

The knowledge and skills we learned in the previous chapters on self-esteem, intimacy, and communication apply, in part, to human relations in the work setting.

Enjoyment   The *enjoyment* we experience from the work that we do seems to be one of the most important ingredients of job satisfaction. To feel that what we do is worthwhile and to get satisfaction from the performance of the task allow us to enjoy the feeling of wanting to go to work. In the examples with John, Robin, Jessica, and Bradley, each seems to enjoy his or her work. They see how what they do contributes to a larger goal and to the good of society. Anyone—from a sewage-plant worker to an astronaut—can feel this satisfaction.

Rewards   The *rewards* we receive for what we do stimulate ongoing satisfaction. Typically, people think of money when they think about rewards from work. But there are other important rewards such as recognition and promotion. As Herzberg and other surveyors have discovered, workers asked to rank pay along with other factors in job satisfaction often rank it low, and very few rank it first.

The amount of money we receive for what we do should be equal to the training, skill, and effort that are required to perform our occupational tasks. The income usually is commensurate with the degree to which the job we perform is highly valued or in demand. For example, a physician or an airline pilot usually commands more pay than a teacher or nurse. However, the people who find satisfaction in each of these occupations may value what they do for reasons more important than the pay.

Next to enjoying what we do, receiving *recognition* is one of the most important factors in job satisfaction. Appreciation for what we do in the form of verbal acclaim from our supervisors and fellow workers, perhaps for finding a better way of doing a certain task, is highly motivating. In addition to verbal recognition, recognition through increases in pay and promotions is also highly motivating. It is quite demoralizing when those who perform poorly and are unproductive receive the same pay and promotions as those who perform well. Recognition helps build self-esteem and rewards those who are productive, making the workplace a more enjoyable environment.

Timely *promotions* are also important to job satisfaction. Promotions allow us to continue to grow and contribute to the organization. A common complaint about many jobs is that they are dead-end positions. Journalist David Halbertsam (1986) believes that some workers, especially salesclerks, delivery-truck drivers, and service workers, are unmotivated not only because of low pay but because they lack a **career path;** their current job does not provide for advancement. Jobs that offer promotions may provide us with opportunities to grow and develop our potential and further enhance our self-esteem. Promotions do not always mean that you will be "in charge" of other people. A promotion may mean more autonomy or a new title, such as the promotion from assistant professor to associate professor at a college or university.

career path the opportunity for advancement in your career

Knowing whether to accept a promotion is also an important decision. Many workers in the pursuit of "success" have accepted promotions only to find that they were promoted from a position that was more rewarding and satisfying to one that was less enjoyable.

> Roberta had worked for three years as a nurse in a hospital. The patients were her most important consideration. Her supervisor even received letters from her patients applauding her for her tenderness, understanding, and care. It was apparent that she was a highly valued employee. When her supervisor left the hospital, she was encouraged to accept the position of head nurse. Feeling the pressure from the chief administrator of the hospital, coupled with her own need for achievement, she accepted the position. Unfortunately, the responsibilities of the job required her to spend most of her time writing reports, filling out payroll forms, making floor assignments, and finding replacements for those who called in sick. In fact, many times she had to fill in for those who could not work during the night shift because she could not find replacements. It was not long before she discovered that she no longer had the time to do the thing she enjoyed the most about her profession— applying her nursing skills with patients.

Personal and Professional Growth   Employers who are aware that self-esteem is essential to job satisfaction and productivity provide opportunities for personal and professional growth. They do this by supporting further education and training with both time and money, again, creating a *career path* for the worker. Additional training and education are the most commonly reported methods for improving performance and productivity (Katzell and Guzzo, 1983). Nevertheless, writes Stephen Koepp (1987), associate editor of *Time*, "Businesses in general spend too little time training and motivating their front-line employees, whom they treat as the lowest workers on the ladder" (p. 51).

Relationships   Relationships that we develop on the job become a source of enjoyment and satisfaction. We look forward to going to work to share what we do with our friends. The feeling of being part of a production team provides us with feelings of identity and belonging. These team relationships exist with our supervisors and peers alike. The need for teamwork, even in small organizations, has never been greater. In almost all situations, team effort is superior to individual effort. However, team effort requires good human relations skills that allow managers to assign work responsibilities among team members for optimal performance, satisfaction, and productivity (Katzenbach and Smith, 1993). We also need our supervisors to tell us how we are doing by acknowledging our achievements and by offering helpful suggestions as to how we might improve. In turn, it is important for us to share appreciation and constructive assistance to help the manager feel significant and competent. Granted, we are always going to run into intolerable supervisors who are know-it-alls, dictators, or incompetents and who have no business supervising anyone. Actually, intolerable managers often aid those they supervise in the sense that employees learn what boss behaviors to avoid when they become managers (Lombardo and McCall, 1984).

We also need positive interaction with our peers. Little is more rewarding than when a colleague praises us for something we have done well. Also, suggestions from peers, especially those with more experience, on how we might improve our skills can only serve to enhance our professional growth. An important thing to remember when discussing human relations at work and elsewhere is that we should learn to give what we need to get from others. Sometimes we need to be the model for growth-promoting behavior even for our supervisors, who we often think should know how to motivate and lead us to greater productivity. Relationships with our fellow workers are probably the most important factor in determining job satisfaction.

job autonomy   freedom to assume responsibility for what you do on the job

Responsibility   **Job autonomy** is another souce of motivation and satisfaction. To be hired to do the job and then to be given the freedom to do it to the best of your ability is often a rewarding experience. When workers are allowed to make decisions about what they do within the limits of their jobs and are supported in those decisions, they become more confident and more productive (Herzberg, 1966, 1968).

Job Security   Job security, though not essential to our happiness and motivation (another of Herzberg's hygiene factors), is important in determining our feeling about the work we do. To be concerned every day about whether you are going to lose your job reduces morale to such an extent that your productivity may be affected even though you fear losing the job if you do not do better. Job security is so important to some that even if they received a lower salary over a long period of time versus a high salary over a shorter period of time, they would choose a lower salary.

Physical Environment Comfort within the physical environment is also an important contributor to long-term satisfaction on the job. A major environmental consideration when choosing a career is whether we want to work indoors or outdoors or a combination of the two. We often take this consideration for granted when we are comfortable where we work. As Herzberg (1966, 1968) discovered in his studies on motivation, for many, good working conditions become a focus of importance only when they are absent. Our working environment does not necessarily motivate us to be happier with our work, but in the absence of a comfortable environment, we can become quite unhappy. We take for granted the fact that every day at work the air conditioning keeps our work environment at exactly the right temperature, and the lighting is just right for us to see what we are doing. It is only when we come to work one day and discover that the air conditioner is broken or several lights have burned out that the working conditions begin to affect our level of job satisfaction. Certainly, most of us like to work in a clean, neat place, whether indoors or outdoors. We want our work setting to be attractive and pleasant. In fact, many people could earn more money working in less attractive settings but forego these opportunities for a more attractive and comfortable work setting.

Sexual Harassment in the Workplace **Sexual harassment** is any form of unwanted sexually oriented behavior. Although this type of behavior has always existed in the work world, it came to the forefront of American consciousness with the televised Senate hearings on the nomination of Clarence Thomas to the U.S. Supreme Court. During the hearings, law professor Anita Hill described alleged incidents of sexual harassment directed toward her by her former supervisor, the now Justice Clarence Thomas. Sexual harassment can take several forms, from flirtatious sexual advances or propositions to exposing one's genitals to another person or sexual assault and rape.

sexual harassment any form of unwanted sexually oriented behavior

As a result of the country's heightened awareness, numerous companies are retraining their managers and employees in ways to identify and guard against sexual harassment. Webb (1991) in her book, *Step Forward: Sexual Harassment in the Workplace—What You Need to Know,* raises several questions to help determine if a behavior should be judged as sexual harassment:

- Is the behavior directed toward employees of only one gender—only men or only women?
- Is it courting or flirting behavior?
- Has the employee receiving the attention objected in any way?
- Has the employee been asked if the attention is unwanted?
- Is the behavior repeated?
- Does the offending employee behave this way deliberately?
- Does the behavior interfere with the receiving employee's work performance?
- Does the behavior create an atmosphere that is hostile, offensive, or intimidating?
- Does the employee feel demeaned, degraded, or embarrassed by the behavior?

If the answer to any of these questions is yes, then the behavior may be considerd to be sexual harassment.

Managing Stress   Managing our stress in the workplace is another essential aspect of job satisfaction. In a busy workplace we can approach our upper limits of stress (see chapter 4). The National Institute for Occupational Safety and Health warns that the U.S. workplace could grow even more stressful over the next decade. According to the National Council on Compensational Insurance, stress claims related to the workplace are rising dramatically. Stress in the workplace usually results from *boredom, the drive for high achievement, excess competition, ongoing conflict, or feelings of incompetence.* The routine of some jobs can cause apathy. If every day looks like the day before, it is important to build some stimulation into our work. Otherwise, we will become stressed by stagnation and lack of growth and accomplishment. Feeling that we must constantly outperform others to get promotions or other rewards can become stressful and often leads to work inefficiency, suspicion of others, and insecurity. Unresolved conflict can result in long-term resentment toward those with whom we work. Ill feelings toward fellow workers can cause irritation and stress. Failure at some task or a series of tasks can cause a loss of self-confidence. We often become oversensitive to criticism and defensive toward others when our confidence is lacking. Certainly anything that diminishes our self-esteem is quite stressful.

Freudenberger (1980) refers to the stress resulting from the drive for high achievement as the now classic concept of **burnout.** The burned-out person has been overcome by fatigue and frustration, feelings that are often brought about when a job fails to produce a reward equal to the amount of effort. People who suffer from burnout are usually those who are intense about their work, do more than their share on projects, and never admit to their limitations.

The advancement of stress is not always obvious. We often sense that something is wrong, but we are not able to determine what it is. This sense, along with other symptoms, is usually an indicator of excess stress. Severe cases of stress are often referred to as burnout. Some symptoms to look for are:

burnout   job-related stress, usually resulting when high achievers fail to receive expected rewards over a long period of time

- Feeling tired and depressed most of the time.
- Worrying about unimportant things.
- Not being able to relax or sit still.
- Having various aches and pains (back, head, neck, etc.).
- Being irritable with co-workers, family, and friends.
- Experiencing a loss of appetite or wanting to eat always.
- Being unable to sleep.
- Finding it difficult to concentrate.
- Using alcohol, caffeine, and other stimulants excessively.
- Being obsessively concerned about health.

Because of an increase in stress-related lawsuits and insurance claims, employers are becoming more concerned about stress in the workplace.

In chapter 4, we discuss ways in which we can manage our everyday stresses more successfully. One way is to find interests outside of our jobs so we can balance our sources of satisfaction.

<table>
<tr><td colspan="2">

How Employers Can Cut Stress

</td></tr>
<tr><td>

The National Institute for Occupational Safety and Health recommends employers take the following steps to help reduce stress in the workplace.

■ Design work schedules to avoid conflict with out-of-work demands.

■ Allow workers to provide input for decisions and actions that affect their jobs.

■ Watch the workload. Allow for recovery from especially demanding physical or mental tasks.

</td><td>

■ Design tasks to provide meaning, stimulation, and a sense of completion.

■ Define roles and responsibilities clearly.

■ Provide opportunities for social interaction on the job.

■ Avoid ambiguity in matters of job security and career development.

SOURCE: Centers for Disease Control, *Morbidity and Mortality Weekly Report* (October 3, 1986).

</td></tr>
</table>

Outside Interests　Interests outside of the workplace are also important to feelings of satisfaction. For most people, the blend of satisfying experiences both on and off the job is essential to the feeling of completeness in their lives. John Stoltenberg (1985) writes,

> We all pass this way just once, and we have this one chance to make a difference. What we do for the company might well be a significant part of the difference we make, but often as not what we do on our own time adds at least as much to the meaning of how we live (p. 136–137).

Even though the Bureau of Labor Statistics reports that workers are working more hours to maintain their standard of living, our priorities about work and play have shifted over the years. The Protestant ethic, which views leisure as bad, has given way to the contemporary view that play, family relationships, and other activities also have meaning. Making time for leisure has become a major focus in many people's lives.

Career Change

As noted early in this chapter, we must learn to understand and adjust to change. The ever-increasing use of computers, robots, and other high-tech advances has contributed to changes in the way we work and live our lives. John Naisbitt describes in his book *Megatrends* (1990) some of the changes we will be facing in the future. He suggests that there will be change from

■ An industrial/production society to a service/information society;

■ A forced-technology society to a high-tech/high-touch society concerned more with the personal element;

■ A national economy to a world economy;

■ Short-term planning to long-term planning;

■ Centralization to decentralization;

■ Institutional help to self-help;

■ Representative democracy to participatory democracy;

■ Organizational hierarchies (one-way communication flow) to organizational networks (exchanging ideas and sharing);

■ A concentration of economic activity from the North and East to the South and West;

■ Either/or decision making to multiple-alternative decision making.

In recent years our society has had to face the effects of changes that are occurring at an alarming rate. Some of these changes are exciting and in many ways resemble the predictions of science fiction. On the other hand, some of these changes are quite frightening and difficult to live with, especially when they upset the security we have enjoyed through the work that we do. Our ability to adapt to change is essential not only for our survival but for the satisfaction that we get from our jobs.

> Joanne has worked for fifteen years as a secretary to the president of a large bank. It was a good job by the standards most people use to measure a job. The salary was better than that of most of her friends, the fringe benefits were comparable to those for other jobs, and she even got along very well with her boss. However, at age forty, she felt strongly that she was not realizing her full potential. With some encouragement from a friend, she enrolled in some classes at the community college. She was hoping to discover some new interests that might lead to a more stimulating career.
>
> "I started looking forward to the Friday afternoon happy hours and the weekends," said an accountant. "One weekend, I tried to remember what I had accomplished that week that I felt good about. I couldn't come up with anything. I began to realize that each day and each week were the same. I felt like I was on a treadmill."
>
> A thirty-eight-year-old pediatrician, attending a conference on job stress, stood up and stated that he had become a physician to please his father by "following in my father's footsteps." He said, "I hated every minute of it but stayed in it because I was afraid of what he [father] and others might think if I quit." In the presence of over 100 people he announced that he was going to give up his practice and be what he always wanted to be, a charter-boat captain.

Personal Reassessment   Changes occur in our attitudes, our thinking, and our behavior over time. These changes often influence the degree of satisfaction we get from our jobs. As we noticed with Joanne, over time her satisfaction with her job began to lessen, even though by most standards of measurement she should have been happy. For many people, what they hoped would satisfy and challenge them for a lifetime often leaves them without a sense of accomplishment and more importantly without a feeling of worth. It is important for us at different times in our lives to *reassess our goals*. The results of one survey on why people change their jobs indicated that 60 percent changed for advancement, 57 percent to make more money, 38 percent for better job security, 36 percent for more challenging work, 15 percent to move to a better part of the country, 13 percent because the spouse changed jobs, and 9 percent because they were forced to change by their company (Casale, 1986).

age discrimination discriminating against people in a particular age group solely because of their age

Forced Change   Because of illness, personal catastrophe, obsolescence, and **age discrimination,** many people are forced to abandon their current livelihoods and consider something new. Siegmund May (1978), in an essay titled "The Crowning Years," writes about an immigrant plumber who was disabled by a serious accident at age sixty-five. Unable to continue his trade, he created a patented invention that made a considerable contribution to the plumbing trade. In addition, he sent word to all the plumbers in the community announcing that he was starting a weekly class for plumbers' helpers. Soon a dozen would-be plumbers were spending an evening a week absorbing the knowledge and wisdom of a man whose skill and integrity had become a byword in his community. Satisfaction that he had never dreamed of came to him through his own courage and intelligence.

Some of today's and tomorrow's workers are going to find themselves replaced by some form of technology. Machan (1987) reports, "Some 2.2 million big-company jobs vaporized from 1980 to 1985" p. 43. As jobs become obsolete, *retraining* may be the solution for many workers. Being able to foresee an inevitable layoff and do something about it is the worker's key to survival. Through retraining, we can confront change by providing a way to *rechannel* ourselves away from jobs that are becoming obsolete toward other jobs that are growing rapidly in number. This retraining may come at the expense of the employer or at the expense of the worker. Many colleges and universities are responding to the need for retraining by offering pertinent programs designed to meet the needs of employers and workers. Some people will encounter even more change by going to work for foreign-owned corporations. As we mentioned earlier, increasing Japanese investment in U.S. industry has increased the odds that many Americans will find themselves working for Japanese companies. Learning to adjust to Japanese work styles may be quite stressful, at least initially. For example, opportunities for advancement are not as prevalent in Japanese companies. Japanese workers wait much longer than American workers for promotions. The Japanese also expect workers to show greater corporate loyalty by working longer hours and making personal sacrifices. Japa-

Retraining may be the solution for workers facing obsolescence.

consensus management a system of gathering ideas and opinions from workers at all levels of an organization before making a decision

nese workers typically work for one company for their entire lifetime. In addition, sex discrimination is greater in Japanese companies. One of the biggest advantages, though, appears to be in the Japanese system of **consensus management** (Copeland, 1987). Consensus management is a system of soliciting opinions from all levels of the company before making a decision. Although this system requires more time to introduce, actual implementation of the decision is shorter because, having learned about it, workers support it. Ironically, the consensus-management system was introduced to the Japanese by American organizational specialists in the early 1960s.

Some workers are going to find themselves unemployed because of *age discrimination.* The U.S. Labor Department indicates that the number of workers age 55 and older will grow twice as fast as the rest of the labor force and increase 38 percent by the year 2005. (*Occupational Outlook Handbook,* 1992–1993). Older workers increasingly are perceived as rigid, difficult to train, and too expensive to keep on the payroll. The downsizing of numerous corporations has severely affected workers over 50 years of age and is even beginning to affect workers in their forties (Shellenbarger and Hymowitz, 1994). According to the Equal Employment Opportunity Commission (1994), the number of age-discrimination complaints received increased by more than 60 percent between 1980 and 1986. The EEOC reports that the number of age-bias suits continues, increasing during the years 1992 and 1993 by 14 percent as compared to the previous two years. The increase in the number of complaints is due to a growing number of older workers seeking redress under federal law, which protects workers 40 and older from bias in wages and benefits, hiring, firing, and training. It also prohibits mandatory retirement in most occupations.

> Henry, a publishing company supervisor, was honored on the anniversary of his twenty-fifth year with the company. The fifty-seven-year-old man was given a plaque that read "for loyal, faithful, and efficient service." Two months later, he was fired, with no explanation given.

Such dismissals have always been common. Some companies believe that an older person is too costly to retain because of his or her higher salary, accumulated benefits, and perhaps obsolescence. It is cheaper to hire a young person who will accept a smaller salary and work very hard to move up the corporate ladder.

Gray hair may be the norm in the executive suites but is becoming less so in middle management and in the lower ranks. However, the loss of older workers means the loss of their years of experience. According to Harvey Sterns and Michael McDaniel, specialists in industrial gerontology at the University of Akron, dozens of studies comparing older workers to younger workers doing similar jobs show only minor differences in performance. Older workers are equally productive, less likely to change jobs or be absent, more satisfied with their jobs, and have a stronger work ethic than younger workers. A hardware store chain suffering from high turnover with younger workers decided to experiment with older employees by staffing one store entirely with personnel age 50 and older. The turnover at the store was one-sixth that of the other stores. Absenteeism was 39 percent lower, and inventory damage and theft were 59 percent less. In addition, the store had an 18 percent higher performance rating (judged by higher profits each year). One reason cited was that these employees took more time to help the customer (Shellenbarger and Hymowitz, 1994).

It is obvious that the loss of a job creates financial strain. A more subtle effect of unemployment is the strain to our psychological well-being. The daily routine of going to work, the interaction with our colleagues, and the identity with what we do enhances our self-worth. When we find ourselves unemployed, we are removed from this source of fulfillment.

A study of professional men who were laid off during a business slowdown showed that most of them proceeded through four phases of unemployment (Powell and Driscoll, 1973):

1. *The Period of Relaxation and Relief.* Most of the individuals were able to foresee that they might be laid off, and when it actually happened, they were relieved. They were quite certain that they would be able to find a new job, so they decided to postpone job hunting and spend a few weeks relaxing.

2. *The Period of Concerted Effort.* Most of the men became somewhat anxious about finding a job after about a month. They began a concerted effort to find a job by the usual methods—newspaper ads, phone calls, resumes, and employment agencies. Even though they did not find immediate work, they remained optimistic.

3. *The Period of Vacillation and Doubt.* After the men experienced several months of frustration, their search for a job became more sporadic. During this time, they experienced moments of anxiety, depression, anger, and self-doubt. Their self-confidence and self-esteem seemed to diminish. Their relationships with family members became strained as their wives often pushed them to keep looking for a job. Some of the men sought retraining in school. Some who were over thirty-five years of age believed that companies only wanted younger men.

4. *The Period of Malaise and Cynicism.* This period was characterized by hopelessness and despair. The men tended to focus on protecting their self-esteem by narrowing their search for jobs to those that fit their original skills and backgrounds. Sensing that they were losing control over their own fate, their anger and anxiety turned into hopelessness, resignation, and cynicism. They began avoiding contact with friends, and many of their wives were forced to go to work.

A study by University of Southern California sociologist Barry Glassner (1994) found that men fared no better than women when loosing their jobs, and "job leavers" fared no better than "job losers." People he interviewed said that the experience was initially worse than they had feared. They were shocked at being out of work, depressed and embarrassed to tell parents, partners, and children. He discovered that the job loss process unfolds in three steps: cutting loose, hanging out, and moving on.

In spite of these stages of unemployment, we can increase our likelihood of finding other employment by using effective job-seeking skills. A *Fortune* survey of 250 managers who lost their jobs in 1986 indicated that 56 percent found new jobs within a year, and 64 percent of those found jobs within six months. Of those, 45 percent received higher pay, while 20 percent received the same pay (Nulty, 1987). Glassner (1994) found that 70 percent of those who lost their jobs went on to have productive new careers. Of course, these percentages may change as the nation's economy and the demand for workers change.

When those who lose their jobs finally decide to move on, Glassner (1994) believes they must do it on different terms than in the past. Rather than relying on their work to give their lives meaning and structure, they may have to abandon the traditional measure of success found in status, salary, and security.

The same skills discussed earlier in the section on finding the right job may be effective at any stage of job hunting. As the result of many large corporations "downsizing" their employment force, many middle managers have found themselves suddenly unemployed. These layoffs have resulted in the development of *outplacement firms* that specialize in finding other positions for executives who become the casualties of corporate cutbacks (Machan, 1987). Robert Half (1985) suggests that the job interview is one of the most crucial factors in determining who is hired for midlevel and high-level jobs. According to Half, preparing responses to the following interview questions could help the interviewee land the job.

1. Describe your typical day in your previous job.

2. What do you consider to be your single most important contribution to your previous job?

3. What do you think it takes for a person to be successful in the position you are seeking?

4. How would you handle (an appropriate situation) if this happened to you?

5. What specific strength do you bring to this potential job offer that may make you effective?

6. How do you go about making important decisions?

7. What are some of the things your previous company could have done to be more productive?

8. What do you know about our company?

9. Why did you leave your previous job?

10. What risks did you take in your previous job?

11. How did you enjoy working for your previous company?

12. What did you do in your last job to make yourself more effective?

13. Where do you see yourself three years from now?

14. What are your hobbies and interests?

15. Describe the best boss you ever had.

16. Why did you decide to go (or not to go) to college?

17. What salary do you expect to be making three years from now?

18. Do you have any questions?

An interview with similar types of questions, along with an informative resume, should help a potential employer determine how effective the applicant will be if hired. People who are making a career change should capitalize on their years of experience to maximize the potential they have for again finding the right job.

Critical Review 5

1. Job satisfaction is defined as the degree to which our needs are satisfied by the money we earn. T F

2. Herzberg discovered that the hygiene factors in our work come from such things as recognition and job autonomy. T F

3. Money, status, and fringe benefits were found to be in a category that Herzberg called the motivating or maintenance factors. T F

4. We are considered to be in a career path type job if we have opportunities to advance and achieve. T F

5. Job autonomy is a source of motivation because we are given the responsibility to do our jobs as we see fit. T F

6. McGregor's Theory X organizations provide opportunities for the satisfaction of higher-level needs, such as self-esteem and self-actualization. T F

7. Glassner found that seventy percent of workers who lose their jobs go on to find rewarding new careers. T F

8. Advances in technology will mean that in order to remain employed, some of us will have to be retrained to do other kinds of work. T F

9. What measures must we take to ensure that our jobs will be satisfying?

10. How can we best prepare for the possibility that our career jobs will not last a lifetime?

SUMMARY

■ People work for numerous reasons that relate both to traditional and contemporary work values. Traditional work values include money, security, and moral obligation to society. Contemporary work values include personal identity, enhancement of self-esteem, personal growth and fulfillment, and social contact.

■ Today's workers consist of both one-provider and two-provider families, single-parent families, and singles. Families with children must learn to satisfy both the needs and requirements of the job and the needs and requirements of the children.

■ Women are an important aspect of the world of work. Their contribution to the work world is at least as important as men's. We can expect to see more women in management as inequality diminishes.

■ One of the most important decisions facing college students today is the decision about a career. Knowledge about our desired quality of life and desired quality of work is important in helping us make this decision.

■ Several pertinent types of personal information are important when you are considering a career. The career should be one that allows you to express your personality. The career should be compatible with your interests and abilities, or aptitudes. Your likes and dislikes are also important indicators of satisfaction.

■ When making a career choice, you must analyze your personal information in relationship to career information. In this way you will be able to verify correlations that are important to a career decision.

■ When attempting to find the right job, it is important to consider the demand for your desired occupation. You can get help finding a job through your college placement center as well as state and private employment centers. The job interview is perhaps the most important aspect of securing a job. Preparation for the job interview is extremely important.

■ Once you find a job in your career field, it is important to understand your responsibility for adjusting to the career you have chosen. Your job satisfaction depends on how well the job meets your needs for enjoyment, rewards, growth, and any other personal requirements.

■ Many of us will change our careers or jobs several times in our lives for various reasons. Ongoing personal assessment can assist us in adjusting to those changes.

SELECTED READINGS

Bolles, R. *What Color Is Your Parachute?* Berkeley, CA: Ten Speed Press, 1993. Richard Bolles has written one of the most useful self-help books on job hunting and career change. The book also includes job-hunting tips for disabled workers, information on how to use career counselors, and guidance on how to find your mission in life.

Leeds, D. *Marketing Yourself.* New York: Harper Perennial, 1991. Dorothy Leeds describes how you can develop the marketable skills required in today's job market and sell yourself to potential employers. She defines ten of the most desirable strengths employers are looking for.

Naisbitt, J. *Global Paradox.* New York: William Morrow and Company, 1994. A look at the powerful social trends at work in the world in the twenty-first century and how the future may look in terms of global freedom, democracy, and enterprise. The inevitability of change is the major focus of the book, which may help the reader better plan strategies for the future.

Sukiennik, D., Raufman, L., and Bendat, W. *The Career Fitness Program*. Scottsdale, AZ: Gorsuch Scarisbrick, 1986. This book takes the reader from making a personal assessment, which includes attitudes, aptitudes, needs, wants, and values, to developing a career plan.

U.S. Department of Labor, Bureau of Labor Statistics. *Occupational Outlook Handbook, 1992–1993*. The most widely used document on work and career decision making is updated every two years. The source documents future demands for various occupations and forecasts regions of the country where these occupations will be needed.

REFERENCES

Barrett, N. S. "Women in the Job Market: Occupations, Earnings, and Career Opportunities." In *The Subtle Revolution: Women at Work*, edited by R. E. Smith, p. 112–119. Washington, DC: Urban Institute, 1979.

Bottom Line/Personal 8(1) (January 15, 1987): 15.

Briles, J. *Woman to Woman: From Sabotage to Support*. Far Hills, NJ: New Horizon Press, 1989.

Casale, A. M. *USA Today: Tracking Tomorrow's Trends*. New York: Andrews, McMeel, and Parker, 1986.

Castro, J. "More and More, She's the Boss." *Time* (December 2, 1986): 64–66.

Chapman, F. S. "Executive Guilt: Who's Taking Care of the Children?" *Fortune* (February 16, 1987): 30–37.

Copeland, J. B. "How to Win Over a Japanese Boss." *Newsweek* (February 2, 1987): 46–48.

Cordoza, A. *Sequencing*. New York: Macmillan, 1986.

Deutsch, R. Eden. "Tomorrow's Workforce." *Futurist* (December 1985): 8–11.

Drucker, P. *Innovation and Entrepreneurship: Practice and Principles*. New York: Harper & Row, 1986.

Fernandez, J. P. *Childcare and Corporate Productivity*. Lexington, MA: Lexington Books, 1986.

Freudenberger, H. J. *Burn-Out: The High Cost of High Achievement*. Garden City, NY: Anchor Press, 1980.

Gale, L., and Gale, B. *Discover What You're Best At*. New York: Simon and Schuster, 1990.

"Getting Ready for Work in the 21st Century." *USA Today* (August 1986): 10.

Ginzberg, E. "Toward a Theory of Occupational Choice: A Restatement." *Vocational Guidance Quarterly* 20 (June 1972): 169–176.

Glassner, B. *Career Crash: The New Crisis and Who Survives*. New York: Simon and Schuster, 1994.

Guide for Occupational Exploration. Washington, DC: The United States Employment Service, 1979.

Haddock, P. "Living and Working in San Francisco." *Business Week Careers* (October–November 1986): 42–46.

Halbertstam, D. *The Reckoning*. New York: Morrow, 1986.

Half, R. "Essential Skills." *Working Woman* (November 1985): 60–64.

Hellwig, G. "How Working Women Have Changed America." *Working Woman* (November 1986): 129.

Henley, F. M. "Why Being a Mother Made Me a Better Manager." *Working Woman* (November 1986): 268–271.

Herzberg, F. *Work and the Nature of Man*. New York: World, 1966.

———. *Work and the Nature of Man*. London: Staples, 1968.

Holland, J. *Making Vocational Choices: A Theory of Careers*. Englewood Cliffs, NJ: Prentice-Hall, 1973.

Horn, J. C. "Bigger Pay for Better Work." *Psychology Today* (21) (July 1987): 54–57.

Jahoda, M. "Work, Employment, and Unemployment: Values, Theories, and Approaches in Social Research." *American Psychologist* 36 (1981): 184–191

Katzell, R., and Guzzo, R. "Psychological Approaches to Productivity Improvement." *American Psychologist* 38 (1983): 468–472.

Katzenbach, J. R., and Smith, D. K. *The Wisdom of Teams*. New York: Harper Business, 1993.

Koepp, S. "Pul-eeze! Will Somebody Help Me?" *Time* (February 2, 1987): 48–55.

Leeds, D. *Marketing Yourself*. New York: Harper Perennial, 1991.

Lombardo, M. M., and McCall, M. W. "The Intolerable Boss." *Psychology Today* (January 1984): 44–48.

Machan, D. "Pink Slip Time." *Forbes* (February 9, 1987).

May, S., "The Crowning Years." In *The New Old Struggling for Decent Aging*, edited by R. Gross, B. Gross, and S. Seidman, p. 232–243. Garden City, NY: Anchor Books, 1978.

Mayo, E. *The Human Problems of an Industrial Civilization*. New York: Macmillan, 1933.

McGregor, D. *The Human Side of Enterprise*. New York: McGraw-Hill, 1960.

Morbidity and Mortality Weekly Report, Atlanta, GA: U.S. Centers for Disease Control, October 3, 1986.

Morrison, A. M., White, R. P., and Van Velsor, E. "Executive Women: Substance Plus Style." *Psychology Today* 21 (August 1987): 24–26.

Mulholland, D. "Do Women Help Women? Don't Bet on Some at Top." *The Wall Street Journal* (March 29, 1994): A10.

Naisbitt, J. *Global Paradox*. New York: William Morrow and Company, 1994.

———. *Megatrends*. New York: Warner Books, 1990.

Nulty, P. "Pushed Out at 45—Now What?" *Fortune* 115 (April 12, 1987): 26–30.

Powell, B. "Where the Jobs Are: Working for Japan Inc." *Newsweek* (February 2, 1987): 42–46.

Powell, D. H., and Driscoll, P. F. "Middle-Class Professionals Face Unemployment." *Society* 10 (1973): 18–26.

Sawhill, Isabel. "Economic Dimensions of Occupational Segregation." *Signs* 1 (1976): 201–211.

Schor, J. B. *The Overworked American.* New York: Basic Books, 1993.

Sharpe, R. "The Waiting Game: Women Make Strides, but Men Stay Firmly in Top Company Jobs." *The Wall Street Journal* (March 29, 1994): A1.

Shellenbarger, S. "Work and Family: Single Parenting Boosts Career Stress." *The Wall Street Journal* (June 1, 1994): B1.

Shellenbarger, S., and Hymowitz, C. "Over the Hill: As Population Ages, Older Workers Clash With Younger Bosses." *The Wall Street Journal* (June 13, 1994): A1, A5.

Steven, D. L. "Profile of a Good Manager." *Nursing Management* 22 (January 1991): 60–61.

Stoltenberg, J. "Ways to Fall Back in Love with Your Job." *Working Woman* (November 1985): 136–137.

Torgersen, R. E., and Weinstock, I. T. *Management: An Integrated Approach.* Englewood Cliffs, NJ: Prentice-Hall, 1972.

Trost, C. "All Work and No Play? New Study Shows How Americans View Jobs." *The Wall Street Journal* (December 30, 1986): 19.

U.S. Census Bureau. *Statistical Abstract of the United States*, U.S. Government Publication, U.S. Printing Office, Washington, DC, 1990.

U.S. Department of Labor, Bureau of Labor Statistics. *Occupational Outlook Handbook, 1992–1993.* Washington, DC: U.S. Government Printing Office, 1992.

University of Michigan Institute for Research. *Bottom Line/Personal,* 1987, p. 15.

Webb, S. L. *Step Forward: Sexual Harassment in the Workplace—What You Need to Know.* New York: Mastermedia, 1991.

■ *Answers to Critical Review Questions*

Critical Review 1 1. T.   2. F.   3. F.   4. T.   5. T.   6. T.   7. T.   8. T.   9. T.   10. F.   11. T.   12. T.

Critical Review 2 1. F.   2. T.   3. F.   4. T.   5. T.   6. T.   7. T.   8. T.

Critical Review 3 1. T.   2. F.   3. T.   4. F.   5. F.   6. F.   7. F.   8. T.   9. T.   10. T.   11. T.   12. T.

Critical Review 4 1. T.   2. T.   3. T.   4. F.   5. T.   6. T.   7. T.   8. F.

Critical Review 5 1. F.   2. F.   3. F.   4. T.   5. T.   6. F.   7. T.   8. T.

PERSONAL ACTION PLAN
Career Choice

The selection of a career is one of the choices that seems to have a great impact on personal satisfaction, self-esteem, and feelings of happiness and contentment for many people in our society. The exercises in this Personal Action Plan should help you to generate information and insights that may be useful in either your initial choice of a career or your evaluation of your current career.

Step I.

Think about a few career areas that seem interesting and/or exciting to you. It is important here to enter freely into your own world of fantasy. Let your mind wander, and when you come on an area, try to see yourself playing a specific career role. Repeat this procedure several times, each time focusing on a different career area. List the career areas in the spaces below.

_____

_____

_____

_____

Step II.

Having identified several career areas that seem attractive, you are ready to gather pertinent information concerning those areas. A good place to start is with your reference librarian, or perhaps the career counseling department, if your campus has one. The important point is for someone to direct you to useful written information. The answers to three questions are particularly important:

A. What are the future prospects for the career itself? (Is the career area growing or shrinking? Will there be jobs available in that area five years from now? Ten years? Twenty years?)

B. What does a person holding a specific job in the career area actually do? (What is a typical workday like? A workweek? A workyear?)

C. What are the rewards and sacrifices? (What are the salary ranges and fringe benefits? Are there any noneconomic rewards? What are the less attractive aspects of the job?)

After you have gathered answers to these questions from the written sources you have located, you are ready to check them out against verbal reports from people actually working in the career areas. Arrange interviews with at least two people in each area. If possible, interview one relative newcomer to the field and one veteran. Be sure to ask them the same three general questions listed above. Take accurate and complete notes.

Step III.

Study carefully the information you have gathered for each career area. Then analyze each area in terms of the following considerations:

A. What are some of the personality characteristics that seem necessary for a person to succeed in this career?

B. What are the underlying values on which this career seems to be built?

C. What is the capacity of this career to fulfill an individual's needs? (Refer to chapter 2 for a discussion of Maslow's hierarchy of needs.) Describe the capacity of this career to fulfill each of the following needs:

1. Physiological:

2. Safety:

3. Belongingness and love:

4. Esteem:

5. Growth:

Step IV.

A. List your outstanding personality characteristics:

B. List the values that are most important to you:

C. Refer again to chapter 2 for information concerning your needs. Write brief descriptions of the ways you are fulfilling your needs and an estimate of how well you are fulfilling each.

1. Physiological:

2. Safety:

3. Belongingness and love:

4. Esteem:

5. Growth:

Step V.

You are now in a position to make reasonable judgments concerning the suitability of several careers for you and your suitability for several careers. Compare and contrast your responses to steps III and IV for each of the career areas you are investigating. Write answers to the following questions:

A. Do you have the personality characteristics that seem necessary for a person to succeed in this career? _____ Yes _____ No. If you checked No, are you willing to make the sacrifices necessary to acquire those characteristics?

B. Are your personal values esssentially the same as or substantially in agreement with the values you see as underlying this career? _____ Yes _____ No. If you checked No, are you willing to reorient yourself so that your values are consistent with those of this career?

C. Does this career seem to have the capacity to fulfill your needs? _____ Yes _____ No. If you checked No, are you willing to accept the idea that your career will not fulfill some of your needs?

This Personal Action Plan should help you make some important judgments regarding the relative suitability of several careers. Once you have chosen the career you want to pursue, you will be ready to set appropriate goals and begin the process of achieving them.

PART FIVE

PROBLEMS IN ADJUSTMENT AND GETTING HELP

In Part V we consider what happens to the individual when things go wrong and describe several direct coping strategies that may be used to help the person deal more effectively with life circumstances.

Chapter 13 introduces the concept of maladjustment and discusses several categories of maladjustment, including anxiety disorders, disorders of social concern, and psychotic disorders. These categories exemplify the broad range of categories of maladjustment and provide information about several maladjustments commonly suffered by people in our society. Some specific topics covered are irrational fears, substance abuse, sexual dysfunctions, and changing sexual mores, folkways, and customs.

Chapter 14 presents an overview of psychotherapy. It discusses a number of practical questions related to therapy, such as, When should a person consider entering therapy? What are some of the different types of therapists? How does one choose a therapist and a therapy? What does therapy cost? When should therapy end?

The bulk of the chapter comprises brief descriptions of more than twenty different therapies or therapeutic approaches. Each description attempts to capture the characteristic flavor of the therapy. The descriptions of psychoanalysis, Rogerian therapy, behavior therapy, and cognitive therapy complement and round out earlier discussions of the corresponding schools of psychological thought.

13

PROBLEMS IN ADJUSTMENT

Chapter Outline

FOCUS

Maladjustment is the relative failure to meet adequately the psychological demands of oneself, the group, or the situation. There may be some instances in which usually well-adjusted people have a difficult time adjusting. Conversely, a few people may be very maladjusted in most instances but able to adjust very well in a few select circumstances. Thus *everyone* behaves in at least a slightly maladjusted way from time to time, and probably *no one* behaves in a maladjusted way all the time. Most of us, of course, make fairly good adjustments most of the time.

In this chapter we consider a variety of maladjustments, from simple phobias such as a fear of heights to extremely debilitating disorders such as disorganized schizophrenia. Causes and development of the maladjustment discussed are mentioned briefly in some instances, but the general focus of the discussion is descriptive in nature.

MALADJUSTMENT

Causes of Maladjustment

maladjustment   the relative failure to meet adequately the psychological demands of oneself, the group, or the situation

The answer to the question of what causes **maladjustment** has changed substantially over the years and continues to change. It was during the nineteenth century that the *medical* model became widely accepted.[1] This model holds that psychological maladjustment is caused by an underlying physical condition. Hence, brain damage may cause ineffective behavior, and lead poisoning may cause irritability or depression.

The medical model has influenced greatly the treatment of maladjustment in the modern Western world. Generally, treatment has attempted to deal with the cause as well as the symptoms of the maladjustment, and has consisted of medical procedures such as drug therapy and electroshock. The medical model has also influenced how society in general views those who suffer from severe maladjustment—as "sick" persons who suffer because of a condition beyond their control and who need professional help to be "cured."

In the latter part of the nineteenth century, Freud introduced the *psychological* model, which holds that some maladjustments come from underlying psychological causes. Fixations, anxiety, and exaggerated ego defenses may cause the ineffective behavior.

In the twentieth century, both the medical model and the psychological model have been extended. Selye's general adaptation syndrome (see chapter 4) depicts both biological and psychological decay as occurring under excessive stress. In addition, the behaviorists view maladjustment as either the failure to learn effective behaviors or the efficient learning of maladjustive behaviors (that is, the maladjustive behaviors have been reinforced).

Types of Maladjustment

There are many types of maladjustment, each with its own set of symptoms and potential causes. It is important to realize, however, that mental health professionals often disagree concerning the types, symptoms, and causes of maladjustment. Some, Thomas Szasz being the most prominent, even deny that maladjustment exists. In an attempt to remedy this situation, the American

---

1. Prior to the nineteenth century, maladjustment was often assumed to be the work either of evil spirits or of God, who might punish people for sinning by inflicting maladjustment on them.

Psychiatric Association published its first *Diagnostic and Statistical Manual* (DSM) of mental disorders in 1952; the most recent edition (DSM-IV) was published in 1994. DSM-IV is receiving widespread acceptance among mental health professionals, and it is on this edition that we have relied primarily to prepare the following discussion.

DSM-IV specifies a large number of maladjustments (see Table 13–1 for a sample), and it is beyond the scope of this chapter to discuss every one of them. However, to give you an idea of the range of those maladjustments, we will briefly discuss a variety of specific disorders under four general categories we have created for the purpose of the discussion: anxiety disorders, mood disorders, disorders of social concern, and psychotic disorders. It is perhaps important to reiterate that everyone displays maladjustment from time to time. Thus, if you begin to see a little of your own behavior in the following descriptions, do not become overly concerned.

ANXIETY DISORDERS

Anxiety disorders are those disorders in which **anxiety** is the predominant disturbance, or the individual attempts to avoid anxiety by behaving in particular ways. Anxiety disorders are more frequently found in the general population than any of the other disorders listed in DSM-IV. Specific anxiety disorders include panic disorder, phobic disorders, obsessive-compulsive disorder, post-traumatic stress disorder, and generalized anxiety disorder.

anxiety disorder maladjustment in which anxiety is the predominant disturbance or the individual attempts to avoid anxiety by behaving in particular ways

anxiety a fear response to a perceived future threat

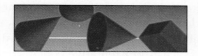

CRITICAL THINKING ISSUE
The Effects of Labels on the Treatment of Persons with Problems in Adjustment

Labels are important and necessary in the treatment of persons with problems in adjustment.

Mental health professionals attempting to treat problems in adjustment usually follow this sequential pattern: (1) diagnose the probem; (2) classify the problem according to the diagnosis; (3) label the person according to the classification; and (4) treat the person according to the label. Thus, some might be called acrophobics, others might be called transvestic fetishists, and still others might be called schizophrenics. But what are the effects of such labeling on the person? For example, how would you behave toward a person introduced to you as a paranoid schizophrenic? Could labels hinder rather than enhance the treatment of the probem?

Labels are unnecessary in the treatment of persons with problems in adjustment.

Labels help mental health professionals understand the adjustment problem. They are shorthand ways of pointing to diagnoses. Labels facilitate communication among mental health professionals. Without effective communication, professionals would be unable to understand and treat the problem. In addition, labels help mental health professionals monitor and treat symptomatic behaviors, thereby containing the problem.

Once a label is attached to a person, there is a tendency to expect certain behaviors from that person, and expectations often lead to fulfillment in two ways. First, the individual viewing the person with the adjustment problem tends to interpret the person's behavior from the perspective of the label. For example, a legitimate complaint about lower back pain from a "hypochondriac" might be dismissed. To make matters worse, this false interpretation tends to reinforce the diagnosis that the person is a hypochondriac. Second, the person with the adjustment problem may begin to believe the label. Ultimately, labels may do more harm than good.

I take the position that:

TABLE 13–1

Categories of Disorders Listed in DSM-IV

Adjustment Disorders
Anxiety Disorders
Delirium, Dementia, Ammestic, and Other Cognitive Disorders
Disorders Usually First Diagnosed in Infancy, Childhood, or Adolescence
Dissociative Disorders
Eating Disorders
Factitious Disorders
Impulse Control Disorders Not Elsewhere Specified
Mood Disorders
Personality Disorders
Psychological Factors Affecting Medical Condition
Schizophrenia and Other Psychotic Disorders
Sexual and Gender Identity Disorders
Sleep Disorders
Somatoform Disorders
Substance-related Disorders

Anxiety is considered normal in many situations. Probably all students have experienced "butterflies" in their stomachs before taking an important final examination. Anxiety is considered abnormal when it repeatedly incapacitates the individual. Such anxiety is intense and may interfere with goals or relationships or cause great pain and consternation. Thus, anxiety disorders are characterized by anxiety that is more intense, frequent, and incapacitating than normal anxiety.

As with all mental disorders, there is more than one theoretical explanation for the causes and development of anxiety disorders. In addition, there is evidence in the form of research, experimentation, and clinical data and experience to support all of these various explanations. However, although each theoretical orientation—physiological, behavioral, cognitive, and psychoanalytic—has its own position, it appears that we may draw at least four tentative conclusions with regard to the causes and development of anxiety disorders (Mehr, 1983, pp. 169–70):

1. Individuals with anxiety disorders seem to be physically overreactive, an apparent predisposition in the development of anxiety disorders that may or may not be genetically transmitted.

2. Learning through both reinforcement and modeling seems to be a very significant factor.

3. Thoughts and self-perceptions are important.

4. Childhood experiences are important.

Critical Review 1

1. Maladjustment is the relative failure to meet adequately the psychological demands of oneself, the group, or the situation. T F

2. During the nineteenth and twentieth centuries, the two primary models for explaining the causes of maladjustment have been the medical model and the physical model. T F

3. Anxiety disorders are those in which anxiety is the predominant disturbance or the individual attempts to avoid anxiety by behaving in particular ways. T F

4. Discuss twentieth-century views of the causes of maladjustment.

5. Define anxiety disorders and discuss factors considered significant in their cause and development.

Panic Disorder

Panic disorder involves recurrent, short-term panic (anxiety) attacks. The attacks are unpredictable in that they are not usually associated with specific objects or situations, and the individual usually does not know in advance when the next one will occur.

    The anxiety in these attacks is experienced by the individual as particularly intense. A sudden onset of severe apprehension, fear, or terror, often linked with feelings of impending doom, virtually immobilize the person for the duration of the attack. Among the most common symptoms are palpitations, chest pain, choking or smothering sensations, feelings of unreality, hot and cold flashes, sweating, faintness, trembling or shaking, and fear of dying or going crazy. Attacks usually last only minutes but may last hours on rare occasions.

panic disorder   a maladjustment characterized by recurrent, intense, short-term anxiety attacks

Phobic Disorders

Phobic disorders involve intense and unrealistic fears, such as fear of being alone, fear of heights, or fear of harmless animals. Phobic disorders seem to be acquired either through conditioning ("I fell from a high place when I was young and to this day I still fear heights") or imitation ("My father always expressed fear when he saw a mouse in the house, and I am afraid of them, too"). Typically, the person relieves the anxiety by avoiding the fear stimulus. The person who fears being alone, for instance, seeks the companionship of others rather than dealing directly with being alone. Being with others relieves the anxiety, encouraging the person to continue seeking the companionship of others. We can easily understand why it is often difficult to break a phobic pattern.

    Clinicians have identified many specific phobias, from a fear of enclosed places (*claustrophobia*) to a fear of blood (*hemotophobia*) to a fear of dirt or germs (*mysophobia*). They have even identified a fear of irrational fear (*phobophobia*)! For purposes of classification, however, phobic disorders are divided into three categories: *agoraphobia, social phobia,* and *simple phobia.*

phobic disorder   disorder characterized by intense and unrealistic fears, such as fear of being alone, of heights, or of harmless animals

Agoraphobia   **Agoraphobia** is the fear of being in places or situations from which escape might be difficult or embarrassing, or in which help might not be available in the event of suddenly developing a symptom or symptoms that could be incapacitating or extremely embarrassing. The agoraphobic fears developing symptoms such as dizziness, loss of bladder control, or vomiting while in a crowd, traveling in a bus or train, and being outside the home alone. Consequently, agoraphobics often either restrict travel or rely on companions when outside the home.

agoraphobia   fear of being overwhelmed or of losing control when alone or in public places

Social Phobia   **Social phobia** is a fear and avoidance of situations in which the person may be carefully observed by others. The person fears that he or she may behave in a humiliating or embarrassing way. Examples of social phobia are fears of speaking, performing, or eating in public; of using public lavatories; and of writing in the presence of others.

social phobia   fear and avoidance of situations in which the person may be carefully observed by others

The person suffering from social phobia usually is concerned that others will detect his or her anxiety. For example, the person who fears speaking in public is concerned that others may detect a voice tremor. Thus, a vicious cycle may be created in which the fear of speaking in public leads to a trembling voice, which further intensifies the fear of speaking in public.

Questionnaire   **Fear Inventory**

What are you afraid of? Use the following scale to indicate how afraid you are of the items listed:

1 = None
2 = Some
3 = Much
4 = Very Much
5 = Terror

_____ 1. Beards
_____ 2. Being alone
_____ 3. Being in an elevator
_____ 4. Blood
_____ 5. Cats
_____ 6. Cemeteries
_____ 7. Crowded places
_____ 8. Dark places
_____ 9. Dead bodies
_____ 10 Death
_____ 11. Dentists
_____ 12. Disapproval
_____ 13. Falling

_____ 14. Flying
_____ 15. Heights
_____ 16. Insects
_____ 17. Lightning
_____ 18. Losing control
_____ 19. Making mistakes
_____ 20. Open spaces
_____ 21. Riding a roller coaster
_____ 22. Snakes
_____ 23. Speaking to a public audience
_____ 24. Spiders
_____ 25. Strangers

---

simple phobia   a persistent, irrational fear of and avoidance of objects and situations other than those included in agoraphobia and social phobia, for example, a fear of insects

Simple Phobia   **Simple phobia** is a persistant, irrational fear and avoidance of objects and situations other than those included in agoraphobia and social phobia. This residual category of phobic disorders includes fears of many objects, the most common of which involve animals such as dogs, snakes, insects, and mice. Fear of heights and fear of enclosed spaces are examples of simple phobias related to situations rather than objects.

Exposure to the phobic stimulus may produce an extreme panic attack, but direct exposure is not necessary for the individual to experience anxiety. Turmoil may be produced when the person thinks about the phobic object or situation.

Simple phobias often begin in childhood, and most disappear without treatment. However, those that remain with us in adulthood rarely disappear without treatment.

obsessive-compulsive disorder   a maladjustment characterized by recurrent obsessions and compulsions

obsession   recurrent, persistent idea, thought, image, or impulse experienced as involuntary and as senseless or repugnant

Obsessive-Compulsive Disorder

As the name suggests, **obsessive-compulsive disorder** involves obsessions and compulsions. **Obsessions** are recurrent, persistent ideas, thoughts, images, or impulses that are experienced as involuntary and as senseless or repugnant. In

A Sampling of Phobias

Acaraphobia: fear of itching.
Acrophobia: fear of heights.
Ailurophobia: fear of cats.
Anthrophobia: fear of human society.
Aquaphobia (or hydrophobia): fear of water.
Aviophobia: fear of flying.
Brontophobia: fear of thunder.
Dromophobia: fear of running.
Erythrophobia: fear of blushing.

Gamophobia: fear of marriage.
Gephydrophobia: fear of bridges.
Graphophobia: fear of writing.
Mysophobia: fear of dirt or germs.
Nyctophobia: fear of the dark.
Phgonophobia: fear of beards.
Triskaidekaphobia: fear of the number 13.
Xenophobia: fear of strangers.
Zoophobia: fear of animals.

other words, senseless or repugnant thoughts keep coming into the person's mind. Common obsessions are thoughts of violence (for example, of killing one's child), of contamination (for example, of becoming infected by shaking hands with someone), and of doubt (for example, by repeatedly wondering if one has performed some action, such as hurting someone in a traffic accident).

Compulsions are repetitive and seemingly purposeful behaviors performed according to certain rules or in a stereotyped fashion. The behavior is designed to produce or prevent some future situation; however, the behavior is either unrealistic or clearly excessive and does not produce pleasure. In short, the person is driven to carry out some ritualized behavior that seems unrelated to his or her current circumstances. Common compulsions include hand washing, counting, and touching.

> **compulsion** repetitive and seemingly purposeful behavior performed according to certain rules or in a stereotyped fashion

Attempts to resist obsessions or compulsions produce anxiety that can be relieved by giving in to the obsessions or compulsions. After repeated failure at resistance, the individual may acquiesce and no longer experience a desire to resist. Fortunately, a combination of drug therapy and behavior therapy (see chapter 14) seems to help persons with obsessive-compulsive disorder (Gelman, 1989).

Posttraumatic Stress Disorder

Individuals who live through psychologically distressing events that are outside the range of usual experience (a serious threat to life or physical integrity, destruction of one's home or community, seeing another person killed or seriously injured) may develop **posttraumatic stress disorder.** This is the persistent reexperiencing of the traumatic event through dreams, recollections, a sense of reliving the experience, or intense distress at exposure to events that resemble or even symbolize an aspect of the experience. Although anxiety and avoidance behavior are not the predominant symptoms, they are commonly experienced by posttraumatic stress disorder victims, and symptoms of increased arousal are invariably present. In some cases symptoms may continue for years following the initial trauma (Buie, 1989). The diagnosis is not made unless the disturbance lasts more than one month.

> **posttraumatic stress disorder** a maladjustment in which the individual persistently reexperiences a traumatic event through dreams, recollections, a sense of reliving the experience, or intense distress at exposure to events that resemble or even symbolize an aspect of the experience

Generalized Anxiety Disorder

The primary feature of **generalized anxiety disorder** is unrealistic or excessive anxiety and worry about two or more life circumstances. The symptoms last for

> **generalized anxiety disorder** a maladjustment characterized by general anxiety about two or more life circumstances that persists for at least six months

at least six months, during which the person is bothered more days than not by the concerns. Specific symptoms vary from one person to the next; however, manifestations of anxiety from each of the following four categories are usually present:

1. Motor tension. Examples: shakiness, trembling, muscle aches, eyelid twitch, strained face, easy startlement.

2. Autonomic hyperactivity. Examples: sweating, racing heart, clammy hands, dizziness, frequent urination, lump in the throat, flushing.

3. Apprehensive expectation. Examples: anxiousness, worry, anticipation that something bad will happen to oneself or others.

4. Vigilance and scanning. Examples: impatience, irritability, distractibility, difficulty in concentrating, insomnia, interrupted sleep, fatigue upon awakening.

Jane has been encouraged to pursue a medical career ever since she can remember. In high school she was able to get excellent marks in the tenth and eleventh grades. However, when she started to take more demanding honors courses in the twelfth grade, she was unable to perform as well. The worse the performance, the more anxious she became.

The following year she entered a pre-med program at college. By this time her level of anxiety had become so high she could get no grade higher than *D*. Physical manifestations of her anxiety included trembling, aching muscles, and dizziness. In addition, she was irritable, had difficulty concentrating, and couldn't sleep at night.

By the end of the second semester, she had become incapable of functioning in school, and her average was too low for her even to consider entrance into medical school. Unable to study, she dropped out of school and, at this time, is barely capable of holding a part-time job.

Critical Review 2

1. An individual suffering from panic disorder always knows when the next panic attack will occur. T F

2. Generalized anxiety disorder differs from panic disorder in that the level of fear is much greater in generalized anxiety disorder. T F

3. Three categories of phobic disorders are agoraphobia, social phobia, and simple phobia. T F

4. Recurrent, persistent ideas, thoughts, images, or impulses experienced as involuntary and as senseless or repugnant are called traumatic thoughts. T F

5. Compulsions are repetitive and seemingly purposeful behaviors performed according to certain rules or in a stereotyped fashion. T F

6. Compare and contrast panic disorder, simple phobia, and obsessive-compulsive disorder.

MOOD DISORDERS

mood a prolonged emotional state that affects a person's thoughts and behavior

Mood disorders are those disorders in which an extreme **mood** is the predominant disturbance. The extreme version of a bad mood is depression, while its opposite is elation (*mania*). All of us experience extreme moods from time to time. They are only considered maladjustments when they are either so prolonged or so intense that they lead a person to harmful or dangerous actions.

DSM-IV contains two major categories of mood disorders: **depressive disorders** (characterized by prolonged or extreme depression) and **bipolar disorders** (characterized by alternating episodes of depression and mania).

Depressive Disorders

Depression has been discussed in detail in chapter 7. You will remember that its primary symptoms are an absence of pleasure, a feeling of sadness, a sense of worthlessness, and self-blame. Additional symptoms may include agitated motor activity such as repetitive pacing or hand wringing; retarded motor activity such as slowed speech and body movements; and increased or decreased sleep or appetite patterns. A DSM-IV diagnosis of a depressive disorder requires that symptoms be prolonged or severe and not be attributable directly to a specific life experience.

There are two classes of depressive disorders. **Major depression** is diagnosed when very severe symptoms occur unabated for a period of at least two weeks. **Dysthymia** is diagnosed when less severe symptoms occur for at least two years. It is not unusual for sporadic periods of major depression to be superimposed over dysthymia, a case in which the person would have *double depression*. Both major depression and dysthymia are diagnosed about twice as often in women than in men.

All of us become depressed from time to time, and most of us are able to work ourselves out of our depression through actions such as thinking positively or becoming actively involved in pleasurable activities. However, a clinically depressed person (someone with major depression or dysthymia) seems to be unable to break a cycle in which mood, thought, and action work together to mire the person in a state of depression: A depressed mood leads to negative thinking and withdrawal from pleasurable activities; negative thinking supports the depressed mood and the withdrawal from pleasurable activities; and withdrawal from pleasurable activities promotes the depressed mood and the negative thinking.

Bipolar Disorders

Bipolar disorders involve alternating episodes of depression (lows) and mania (highs). These episodes last from a few days to several months, with periods of normal mood often occurring in between. There are two primary classes of bipolar disorders: **bipolar disorder** (episodes of severe mood swing) and **cyclothymia** (episodes of less severe mood swing). DSM-IV also recognizes disorders in which there is recurrent mania without depression, which very rarely occur.

Manic episodes often involve positive emotions such as enhanced feelings of power, confidence, energy, ability, and creativity. Some studies support these feelings. For example, a disproportionately high incidence of cyclothymia has been found among creative writers and artists who produced their best work during episodes of mania (Andreasen, 1978, 1987; Hershman and Lieb, 1988). Another study (Richards et al., 1988) indicated that persons who had been clinically diagnosed as having cyclothymia were more creative than those in the control group with no such diagnosis. However, the same study found that persons diagnosed as having bipolar disorder were not more creative than the controls.

depressive disorders maladjustments characterized by prolonged or extreme depression

bipolar disorders maladjustments characterized by alternating episodes of depression and mania

depression a feeling of personal worthlessness, apathy, and hopelessness

major depression maladjustment characterized by very severe symptoms of depression that occur unabated for a period of at least two weeks

dysthymia maladjustment characterized by symptoms of depression that occur for at least two years

bipolar disorder maladjustment characterized by episodes of severe mood swing

cyclothymia maladjustment characterized by episodes of mood swing that are less severe than those of bipolar disorder

Although some episodes of mania involve positive feelings, they may also result in actions that negatively affect the person. For example, it is not unusual for even mild manic episodes to be accompanied by absence from work or spending sprees that the person can ill afford. Extreme episodes can produce even more dangerous actions such as taking undue physical risks in the false belief that one is invulnerable. In addition, some persons with bipolar disorder experience intense destructive rage rather than euphoria when in their manic state (Carroll, 1991).

Seasonal Affective Disorder

Some individuals suffer from **seasonal affective disorder (SAD)** in which they suffer severe depression in fall and winter, followed by normal mood or mild mania in spring. These mood changes seem to be controlled by the quality and quantity of sunlight the person is exposed to from season to season. The depression associated with SAD may be reversed through treatment in which artificial light is administered to the person (Terman et al., 1989; Avery et al., 1993), a treatment that does not work with persons suffering from either bipolar disorder or cyclothymia.

Critical Review 3

1. Depressive disorders are characterized by prolonged or extreme depression. T F
2. Bipolar disorders involve alternating episodes of depression and mania. T F
3. A diagnosis of major depression requires very severe depression that occurs unabated for a period of at least two years. T F
4. Cyclothymia involves mood swings that are more severe than those of bipolar disorder. T F
5. The maladjustment characterized by severe depression in the fall and winter, followed by normal mood or mild mania in the spring, is called seasonal affective disorder. T F
6. Define depressive disorders and discuss the two main types of depressive disorders.
7. Compare and contrast bipolar disorder and cyclothymia.

DISORDERS OF SOCIAL CONCERN

Some behaviors are at least as much a problem for other people as for the person who displays the behavior. Indeed, in some instances the individual may not perceive his or her behavior as a personal problem, even though others directly affected by the behavior do. In this section we consider **disorders of social concern** in two areas: sexual behavior and substance use.

Sexual Behavior

Some aspects of sexual behavior may be intensely private (sexual fantasies, masturbation), while others are clearly of social concern (exhibitionism, sexual sadism). There are two primary groups of sexual disorders: sexual dysfunctions and paraphilias. Other sexual behaviors, such as *homosexuality* and *bisexuality*,

CULTURAL CROSSCURRENTS
A Japanese Disorder

Is there a mental disorder found only in one culture?

There is a psychiatric disorder that is relatively common in Japan but is found in no other culture. The disorder, called **taijin kyofusho** or **TKS,** *is a specific social phobia characterized by a morbid fear of offending others through one's awkward social or physical behavior.* For example, a person with TKS would have a fear of eye-to-eye contact, fear of blushing, fear of giving off an offensive odor, fear of having an unpleasant or tense facial expression, or fear of having trembling hands (Kirmayer, 1991).

Although many Westerners are also concerned about offending others, staring, having offensive body odors, or blushing, TKS is different in that it is a *morbid* fear—in other words, a real phobia. People with TKS behave as if they have a phobia by trying voluntarily to stop these symptoms; since that usually fails, they try to avoid social situations and interactions altogether.

We know that some physical factors, such as blushing easily, having offensive odors, or being quickly aroused, may contribute to TKS. However, physical factors cannot answer the following questions: Why is TKS a common disorder in Japan and no other culture, why is it reported more frequently in men than in women, and why does it begin primarily around adolescence and rarely after age 40? All these questions point to the influence of powerful cultural factors in the development and maintenance of TKS.

CULTURAL INFLUENCES

The Japanese culture places great emphasis on the appropriate way to conduct oneself in public. For example, from a very early age Japanese children are encouraged to have a strong sense of responsibility for the feelings of others. To emphasize the importance of proper behavior in public, mothers often use threats of abandonment, ridicule, and embarrassment as punishment. Through this process of socialization, the child is encouraged to be aware of the impact of his or her social interactions on family members. That is, any loss of face that a person shows in social interactions reflects badly on the person's family and social group.

SOCIAL CUSTOMS

In Japan, individuals are taught to recognize and are expected to know the needs and thoughts of others by reading nonverbal behaviors and not by asking directly, which is considered very rude. One method of such communication is through eye contact and reading another's facial expressions. Westerners often use direct eye contact to show interest, to convey confidence, or to intensify a point in social interactions. However, Japanese people who make too much eye contact are likely to be viewed as insensitive to others, unpleasantly bold, or aggressive. In fact, Japanese children are taught to fix their gaze at the level of the neck of people with whom they are in conversations. Thus, the development of a morbid fear of offending others through one's inappropriate social behaviors is deeply rooted in Japanese customs (Kirmayer, 1991).

TKS is so common in Japan that there are special clinics for treating it. These clinics enjoy the same popularity as weight clinics do in the United States. Although TKS does resemble some Western-type social phobias, its symptoms are specific to the cultural concerns and social customs of the Japanese (Kirmayer, 1991).

The prevalence of TKS in Japan—and nowhere else—points to the powerful influence that culture may have on the development of mental disorders. Next we'll see how some of the phobias that are common in this country are treated.

Taken from Plotnik, R. *Introduction to Psychology,* 3rd ed. Pacific Grove, CA: Brooks/Cole, 1993, p. 531.

---

are not classified as disorders but are matters of concern to some. Let us discuss these various behaviors, and then you may conclude for yourself which are primarily of private concern and which are of social concern.

Sexual Dysfunctions **Sexual dysfunctions** involve inhibitions of sexual desire or psychophysiological functioning that prevent the individual from satisfactorily completing the cycle of sexual response. Good sex requires good nerves, blood vessels, and muscles. Disease or injury in any of these systems can cause sexual difficulties, as can poor nutrition or drug abuse. However, many sexual dysfunctions are psychological in origin.

taijin kyofusho social phobia characterized by a morbid fear of offending others through awkward social or physical behavior

sexual dysfunction maladjustment that involves inhibitions of sexual desire or psychophysiological functioning that prevent the individual from satisfactorily completing the cycle of sexual response

Our physiology predisposes us to be sexually active, but such activity requires an environment that provides a feeling of security for optimal expression. Pressure to be sexually active, creative, and orgasmic to prove masculinity or femininity creates problems. A fear of failure, together with the additional concern that failure will result in the loss of the sexual partner, makes one less able to respond naturally and spontaneously. Power struggles, poor communication, and general tension in a relationship make sexual expression difficult as well. Security and intimacy support each other, and too little of either can destroy the other. Thus, psychosexual dysfunctions are born. The most common complaints today include erectile dysfunction, premature ejaculation, inorgasmic dysfunction, and functional dyspareunia.

Erectile dysfunction is the inability to have or to maintain an erection during intercourse, and it is the most common dysfunction among males. A man's sexual self, his masculinity, is always in peril. If erection does not happen on cue, even once, his concept of himself may become clouded by doubts concerning his potency.

Premature ejaculation is the man's inability to control or delay ejaculation long enough to satisfy his own or his partner's desires, and it is the second most common dysfunction among males. The subjective evaluation of what is normal in this regard is a source of tension because of media-based expectations not grounded in reality. According to one source, most women reach orgasm from five to thirty minutes after the onset of foreplay (Wolfe, 1980). Hunt (1974) found that the median duration of marital intercourse is ten minutes, quite a bit longer than the two-minute median of just a generation ago (Kinsey, Pomeroy, and Martin, 1948).

Inorgasmic dysfunction, the persistent or recurrent delay in, or absence of, orgasm in a female following a normal sexual excitement phase, is the most common dysfunction among females. A woman's sexual self is threatened if she is unresponsive or unable to respond orgasmically. The belief that "frigidity castrates the male" adds tension to this dysfunction.

Functional dyspareunia, painful intercourse, is the second most common dysfunction among females. Lack of knowledge of or insensitivity to physiological cues related to readiness for intercourse accounts for much of this dysfunction. Infection and poorly healed lesions are major causes for pain that is not psychologically based. *Functional vaginismus* is the prevention of insertion of the penis by involuntary muscle spasms around the vaginal entrance; it was once one of the most common female disorders but is now relatively rare. Less fearful expectations of coitus appear to be the reason for the reduction of this disorder.

paraphilia maladjustment in which the individual requires unusual or bizarre imagery or acts for sexual excitement

Paraphilias **Paraphilias** are sexual disorders in which the individual requires unusual or bizarre imagery or acts for sexual excitement. The imagery or acts tend to be involuntary and repetitive and generally involve (1) nonhuman objects, (2) real or simulated suffering or humiliation, or (3) nonconsenting partners. Sexual imagery is common. It becomes a major disorder when the needed image demands a victim, as in *sadism* (in which pain is inflicted on another person), *masochism* (in which pain is inflicted on oneself), or *rape.* It is a minor disorder when it demands an unwilling partner, as in *voyeurism* (viewing of others without their knowledge or consent while they are undressing, nude, or involved in some sexual behavior) and *exhibitionism* (exposing of one's genitals to a nonconsenting person). It may be a minor nuisance (fetishism) or a major nuisance (transvetic fetishism) when the demand is for the image of an inanimate object.

Fetishism involves the use of certain objects (called *fetishes*) as the preferred or exclusive way to achieve sexual excitement. Fetishes are often articles of clothing, sometimes parts of the body, and, rarely, other, nonliving objects. Thus, the fetishist may become sexually excited by a pair of panty hose, a pair of feet, or a pair of bookends.

Transvestic fetishism is an obsession with dressing in the clothes of the opposite sex. Such dress is, at times, required for sexual arousal and for either heterosexual or homosexual performance. Early sexual experiences appear critical in the development of this disorder—for example, the person may have been punished by being dressed in the clothing associated with the opposite sex or may have worn or handled such apparel while masturbating.

It must be pointed out that although there are several theoretical explanations for the origins and development of paraphilias in general, these explanations are supported primarily by generalizations from case histories. Thus, a great deal more research must be done to obtain a clear picture of why paraphilias develop.

The Questions of Homosexuality and Bisexuality   **Homosexuality,** or sexual preference for members of the same sex, is no longer classified as a mental disorder, but it is still illegal in some states. In other states it is legal as long as it represents a private choice between consenting adults. Of course, for many people homosexuality is simply considered an alternative lifestyle.

Personal choice, heredity, and prenatal and postnatal hormonal and environmental influences have all been proposed as the source of homosexuality. Whatever causes it to develop, a strong homosexual identity, once established, tends to resist later social influences that attempt to reshape sexual orientation.

Homosexuality may be considered a problem for the individual if he or she is having difficulty with a desired change in sexual preference or if the individual is having difficulty accepting himself or herself as homosexual. Therapy may be useful under these conditions.

homosexuality   sexual preference for members of the same sex

Bisexuality   **Bisexuality** is not a disorder and requires treatment only for secondary symptoms, should they occur. These are usually the result of a self-imposed or social stigma, and therapy should be directed toward restoring a sense of well-being and acceptance by the individual of whatever sexual preference he or she may desire.

bisexuality   sexual attraction to members of both sexes

What Constitutes Sexual Deviation?   Aberration from statistical, legal, medical, psychological, or moral norms may constitute sexual abnormality or deviation. Freud gave us a psychological perspective from which to judge the normality of sexual behavior. He considered sexual activity instinctive. Sexual instinct had a *source* (tension arising from internal or external stimulation), an *object* (an acceptable adult who can gratify the instinct by reducing the tension), and an *aim* (coitus, an act to reduce tension). For Freud, "normal" sexual behavior is represented by activities toward the reduction of sexual tension through intercourse with an appropriate adult member of the opposite sex. "Deviations" can be classified in terms of their relation to source, object, aim, or a combination of these. For example, prostitution is a deviation because the *source* of the activity for the prostitute is money or power, not sexual tension. Performing sexual acts with certain partners, such as members of the same sex (homosexuality), children (pedophilia), relatives (incest), animals (zoophelia), and inanimate

Do you consider these men to be well-adjusted?

objects (fetishism), is a deviation because the *object* is not an appropriate adult member of the opposite sex. Voyeurism, exhibitionism, and sadomasochism are deviations because the *aim* is not coitus.

While Freud was interested in the discharge of tension as the product of sexual behavior, religion and even the state are sometimes interested in *procreation* as the product that justifies such pleasures of the flesh. Any practice that does not advance the production of legitimate children can thus be considered a deviation. Fetishism, fornication, adultery, homosexuality, incest, masturbation, oral sex, pedophilia, rape, sodomy, voyeurism, and other sexual behaviors fail the test of high religious or state purpose.

In addition, every culture places restrictions even on sexual intercourse between married adults. For example, in some primitive societies coitus is either forbidden or mandated prior to important events such as planting, harvesting, hunting, or war. Failing to abstain during the entire baseball season (April through October) is a deviation for members of the Tokyo Giants.

Finally, anything expressly forbidden or mandated in law is a deviation if prosecution occurs. Marriages can be annulled if they are not consummated. Kinsey, Pomeroy and Martin (1948) found that 95 percent of our male population had at some time violated one or more state or federal statutes pertaining

---

Sexual Variations

What are some of the sexual behaviors you have experimented with?	What do you think and how do you feel when engaged in these behaviors?
_____	_____
_____	_____
_____	_____
Which, if any, do you think are regarded by others as abnormalities or deviations?	What would you think and how would you feel when engaged in these behaviors if you believed others regarded them as variations rather than deviations?
_____	_____
_____	_____
_____	_____

---

to sexual behavior. Laws pertaining to masturbation, fornication, anal intercourse, and oral-genital contact (among others) are not regularly enforced but remain to make potential criminals of us all.

Sexual activity within human groups is extremely varied. One would be hard-pressed to think of an activity that has not been attempted in the search for sexual gratification. The term _sexual variations_, rather than _sexual abnormalities_ or _deviations_, captures this range without placing a stigma on the notion of being sexually experimental.

Critical Review 4

1. Sexual dysfunctions involve inhibitions of sexual desire or psychophysiological functioning that prevent the individual from satisfactorily completing the cycle of sexual response. T F

2. The most common sexual dysfunction among males today is inorgasmia. T F

3. The most common sexual dysfunction among females today is premature ejaculation T F

4. Paraphilias are sexual disorders in which the individual requires unusual or bizarre imagery or acts for sexual excitement. T F

5. Fetishism is an obsession with dressing in the clothes of the opposite sex. T F

6. Homosexuality is sexual preference for members of the same sex. T F

7. Sexual attraction to persons of either sex is called heterosexuality. T F

8. According to Freud, incest would be considered a sexual deviation because the sexual object is not an appropriate adult member of the opposite sex. T F

9. Few cultures place restrictions on sexual intercourse between married adults. T F

10. List and define at least four sexual dysfunctions.

11. How are sexual dysfunctions and paraphilias different from one another?

12. How would you define sexual normality?

Eating Disorders

Dieting has become part of the pattern of eating by many in the United States today. In an attempt to maintain health and to approach the culturally determined ideal of beauty, people try to obtain and maintain a trim body through dieting. Thus, it is normal for people in the United States to diet. But what about a person who diets excessively, whose dieting is so severe that it threatens his or her own life? This person suffers from an **eating disorder,** a pattern of eating that deviates grossly from the norm. In this section we will discuss two eating disorders, **anorexia nervosa** and **bulimia nervosa.**

eating disorder   a pattern of eating that deviates grossly from the norm

anorexia nervosa   an eating disorder characterized by willful maintenance of an abnormally low body weight, a distorted body image, an intense fear of being overweight, and, in females, an absence of menstruation

bulimia nervosa   an eating disorder characterized by recurrent episodes of binge eating followed by purging

Anorexia Nervosa   Anorexia nervosa is an eating disorder characterized by willful maintenance of an abnormally low body weight, a distorted body image, an intense fear of being overweight, and, in females, an absence of menstruation. Anorexia occurs in both females and males, but is predominantly a female disorder that most often affects girls and young women. Typical body weight for an anoretic person is less than 85 percent of normally expected body weight.

Anoretic persons often lose weight rapidly, sometimes as much as 25 percent or more of their body weight within one year. It is this extreme weight loss that triggers an absence of menstruation in females. Psychological symptoms include low self-esteem, anxiety, perfectionist behavior, depression, and denial that a problem exists.

Bulimia Nervosa   Bulimia nervosa is an eating disorder characterized by recurrent episodes of binge eating followed by purging. As is true with anoretic persons, the overwhelming majority of persons suffering from bulimia are females, most of whom were originally inflicted in adolescence or early adulthood. They tend to eat foods rich in carbohydrates and often use self-induced vomiting, laxatives, and/or vigorous exercise to purge the food they have eaten. Psychological symptoms of bulimia include low self-esteem, anxiety depression, and mood swings.

Some persons suffer from both anorexia and bulimia, although bulimia is found more commonly than anorexia. It has been estimated that 15 percent of college-age females might be bulimic (Foreyt, 1986).

Critical Review 5

1. About an equal number of males and females suffer from eating disorders. T F
2. Anoretic persons often lose weight rapidly. T F
3. Some persons suffer from both anorexia and bulimia. T F
4. Why do you think the vast majority of anoretic and bulimic persons are female?

Substance Use

Throughout human history people have used certain psychoactive substances (drugs) to alter their experiences. Such altered experiences usually contain initially pleasurable effects that involve changes in feelings, behavior, or physiological functioning and changes in perception of self and environment. At various times societies have accepted or rejected substance use for such purposes.

Contemporary American society has a decidedly mixed reaction to substance use. The recreational drinking of alcohol is legal in all fifty states, and is commonplace among college students (see Figure 13–1). Although not supported by some groups within the society, alcohol use is widely accepted as normal and appropriate. The recreational use of heroin, on the other hand, is illegal in all fifty states and is considered abnormal and inappropriate by most Americans.

Substance use is considered a mental disorder when it is accompanied by certain behavioral changes such as impairment in social or occupational functioning, inability to control the use of or to stop taking the substance, and the development of serious withdrawal symptoms after cessation of or reduction in substance use. These conditions are distinguished from nonpathological substance use for recreational or medical purposes, which is not considered a disorder. In short, substance use in itself is not a mental disorder; but *substance abuse* and *physical substance dependence* are.

Substance Abuse   **Substance abuse** may be distinguished from nonpathological substance use by three factors.

> **substance abuse**   drug use characterized by impairment in social or occupational functioning caused by a pattern of pathological use that lasts for at least one month

1. A pattern of pathological use. Examples: need for daily use of the substance for adequate functioning; inability to stop or cut down use; intoxication throughout the day; complications of the intoxication (alcoholic blackouts, drug overdose).

2. Impairment in social or occupational functioning caused by the pattern of pathological use. Examples: inappropriate expression of aggressive feelings; erratic and impulsive behavior; failure to meet important obligations to friends and family; missed work or school; inability to function effectively because of intoxication.

3. Duration. The pattern of pathological use causing interference with social or occupational functioning must last at least *one month*.

> **physical substance dependence**
> a substance-use disorder that often involves either tolerance or withdrawal

Physical Substance Dependence   **Physical substance dependence** is generally a more severe form of substance-use disorder than is substance abuse. Physical dependence often includes tolerance or withdrawal, and impairment in social or occupational functioning may also be present. **Tolerance** means that there is a diminished effect with regular use of the same dose of the substance

> **tolerance**   a condition in which there is a diminished effect with regular use of the same dose of a drug or in which increased amounts of the drug are necessary to achieve the same effect

Average number of drinks per week

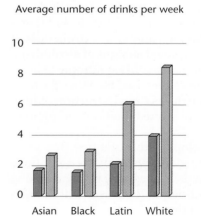

Percent of college students who say they drink to get drunk

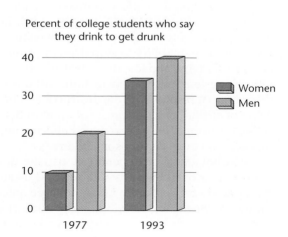

FIGURE 13–1

Increase in College Drinking

SOURCE: Report by Commission on Substance Abuse at Colleges and Universities; Center on Addiction and Substance Abuse at Columbia University, 1994.

withdrawal   a substance-specific syndrome that follows cessation or reduction in intake of a substance

psychological substance dependence   a condition in which the individual needs a drug to cope or to function optimally from a psychological perspective

addiction   a condition in which the individual is either psychologically or physically dependent on drugs, or both

alcohol   a central nervous system depressant that has both immediate and long-term effects on the person

alcoholism   excessive use of alcohol to the extent that it seriously impairs personal, social, or occupational functioning, or physical dependence on alcohol

or that increased amounts of the substance are necessary to achieve the same effect. **Withdrawal** is a substance-specific syndrome that follows cessation or reduction in intake of a substance. For example, a chronic alcoholic who abruptly stops drinking experiences withdrawal symptoms—weakness, anxiety, perspiration, tremors, and nausea—within a few hours.

Psychological Substance Dependence   Some scholars speak of **psychological substance dependence** when referring to a situation in which "the individual needs the drug in order to cope, to function optimally from a subjective perspective" (Mehr, 1983, p. 229). For example, consistent cocaine use produces neither tolerance nor withdrawal, but it may be possible for the user to become psychologically "hooked" on the drug. Mehr points out that psychological dependence "may be present without physical dependence, but is always present when physical dependence exists" (1983, p. 229). Thus, physical and psychological dependence are related terms, and each may be thought of as a type of **addiction.**

There are many categories of substance-use disorders. In an attempt to provide a reasonable sampling, we will discuss disorders as they occur in six groupings: *alcohol, sedatives, opioids, stimulants, hallucinogens,* and *cannabis.*

Alcohol   **Alcohol** is a central nervous system depressant that has both immediate and long-term effects on the user. It is rapidly absorbed into the bloodstream and carried to the brain, where it depresses the activity of cortical centers and allows unrestrained activity of other brain areas.

The initial *subjective* experience of the person who drinks alcohol is stimulation, although the opposite is really happening. For instance, subjective sexual interest may be increased, but the person's ability to be physiologically aroused in a sexual sense is decreased. Intoxication manifests itself in impaired motor coordination and judgment, poor self-control, impulsive behavior, and increased aggressiveness. Once intoxicated, the person who continues to drink in amounts large enough to raise the level of alcohol in his or her blood suffers gross impairment of motor coordination and cognition and ultimately falls asleep. Rapid drinking of large quantities by an individual who is already intoxicated may result in coma and even death.

Alcohol may be abused and may produce dependence. In fact, alcohol abuse is estimated to affect fourteen percent of the adults in the United States (National Institute of Mental Health, 1985). Long-term effects may include the development of tolerance, of an overwhelming sense of need for alcohol (craving), and of an inability to stop drinking after having had the first drink (loss of control). Craving and loss of control are often interpreted as signs of **alcoholism.** Other long-term effects may include withdrawal, Korsakoff's syndrome (a brain disorder that results from the destruction of brain cells caused by either the toxic effect of alcohol or a deficiency of vitamin B_1), cirrhosis (the destruction of liver cells), nutritional deficits, reduced effectiveness of white blood cells in fighting disease, and even chromosomal damage.

Alcohol abuse or dependence usually develops within the first five years after regular drinking is established and usually manifests itself in one of three patterns: (1) regular daily intake of large amounts; (2) regular, heavy drinking limited to weekends; and (3) long periods of sobriety interspersed with binges of daily heavy drinking lasting for weeks or months.

The causes and development of alcoholism, like those of all disorders, are open to debate. It appears that some alcoholics may have a genetic predisposition to drink. Many alcoholics may inherit a capacity to drink relatively large quantities of alcohol without becoming either sick or very intoxicated. In addition, they may inherit a capacity to experience more euphoria from alcohol than others do. Hence, a drinking pattern may emerge in which the individual drinks a lot because it produces pleasant feelings. But alcohol may also produce unpleasant effects—for example, a hangover. Thus, two reinforcers impinge upon drinkers who may have a genetic predisposition to drink: (1) they drink because it produces pleasant feelings, and (2) they drink because it relieves unpleasant feelings. Such reinforcement may ultimately transform a "social drinker" into an alcoholic.

Some alcoholics, however, seem to have no genetic predisposition to drink. Rather, they learn, either through imitation or from their own experience, to cope with stress and emotional problems through alcohol consumption. Emotional problems seem less severe because of alcohol's pain-reducing effect and its effect on the cognitive appraisal of stimuli.

Whether because of physiological or psychological factors, or perhaps some combination of the two, alcoholics develop tolerance that in turn leads to heavier drinking. Heavier drinking leads to increased tolerance and so on until the person develops physical dependence and drinks to avoid the pain of withdrawal.

Sedatives   **Sedatives** are drugs such as barbiturates, tranquilizers, and hypnotics that can induce a relaxed state and sleep. They are usually taken orally in the form of pills or capsules, and they differ widely in rates of absorption, metabolism, distribution in the body, and likelihood of producing intoxication and withdrawal. They may be abused and may produce dependence.

sedative   a drug such as a barbiturate, tranquilizer, or hypnotic that can induce a relaxed state and sleep

The largest subcategory of sedatives is barbiturates, some of which are used medically for the control of epileptic-seizure disorders; others are used to deal with sleeplessness. When abused, barbiturates produce effects similar to those of alcohol—impaired motor coordination and cognition, a release of inhibitions, and so on. Long-term abuse may produce chronic brain damage, and abrupt withdrawal may be fatal.

Barbiturates are more dangerous when combined with alcohol, as these two substances multiply each other's effects. Many accidental overdoses are attributed to this combination. Thus, barbiturates are considered extremely dangerous.

Opioids   **Opioids** are drugs such as opium, morphine, and heroin that produce a floating feeling and can reduce the perception of pain. Like alcohol and sedatives, opioids may be abused and may produce dependence.

opioid   a drug such as opium, morphine, or heroin that produces a floating feeling and can reduce the perception of pain

The most abused opioid is heroin, which may be sniffed (snorted), smoked, taken orally, or injected either subcutaneously or intravenously. The most common form of initial use and long-term occasional use is snorting; intravenous injections are almost always preferred by those who have become physically dependent upon the drug.

Immediate effects are a euphoric "rush" that has been described as being similar in feeling to a sexual orgasm (although some users do not experience the rush) and a milder euphoric high that follows. The mild euphoria typically lasts four to six hours, during which the person is relaxed, withdrawn, and anxiety-free. This euphoria is followed by a slight letdown, a mildly depressed feeling, which tends to encourage the person to take another dose.

Long-term effects include tolerance that requires increasingly larger doses to produce a high equivalent to those obtained from the initial doses. Eventually the high disappears, regardless of the amount used. Users then take the drug to avoid the pain of withdrawal, which, like a severe case of the flu, is extremely unpleasant. Symptoms remain from seven to ten days. Heroin users may contract hepatitis or other infections from unsterile needles, and their resistance to physical diseases is lowered during withdrawal or between doses. In addition, both the individual and society suffer from the effects of crime addicts often commit to get the money to support their heroin habits. Both may also suffer in other ways, as the accompanying box, "He Cheated Us All," illustrates.

stimulant   a substance such as cocaine or an amphetamine that stimulates rather than depresses the central nervous system

Stimulants   **Stimulants** are substances that stimulate rather than depress the central nervous system. The major commonly used stimulants are cocaine and amphetamines. Both may be abused and may produce dependence.

Cocaine, a white powder extracted from the coca shrub, is usually either snorted or injected intravenously, although it is sometimes taken in other ways when used simultaneously with other drugs (see the box entitled "Crack Cocaine"). Immediate effects include a euphoria that lasts from four to six hours, lessened need for sleep, suppressed appetite, heightened alertness, increased intellectual functioning, and heightened sexual pleasure.

"He Cheated Us All"

The theater world was shocked to learn in November 1983 that the actor James Hayden (see picture) had died in his New York apartment, the victim of what was almost certainly an overdose of heroin. Most of his friends and colleagues did not know that Hayden was a drug user. More ironic was the fact that, at the time of his death, Hayden was playing the role of Bobby, a junkie, in David Mamet's *American Buffalo*. On hearing of his tragic death, one of his fellow actors commented, "He cheated us all of the pleasure of knowing him as a human being." James Hayden had cheated himself and society as well.

James Hayden as Bobby with Al Pacino.

> ## Crack Cocaine
>
> Crack is a concentrated form of cocaine that is purified in a process involving cocaine, baking soda, water, and heat. Sold in the form of chunks or "rocks," it is usually smoked in either a cigarette or a pipe. It is called *crack* because of the crackling noise it makes when smoked.
>
> Crack enters the bloodstream through the lungs and can reach the brain in less than ten seconds. Its effects last about five to seven minutes. Because it reaches the brain in highly concentrated dosage, the effects are strong. Some believe that crack is one of the most addictive drugs ever produced.

Cocaine directly stimulates the brain's pleasure center and produces strong feelings of euphoria. However, it also reduces the person's ability to feel pleasure without the drug's stimulus. Thus, users inevitably become depressed and depend on the drug to remove their depression. The resulting addiction can be very strong. For example, given unlimited access to cocaine, animals will consistently seek the cocaine in preference to sex and even to food and water! In short, they will die for it. Cocaine addiction in humans is similar in nature. Thus, one would be well advised never to ingest cocaine.

Long-term effects may include an ulcerated and perforated nasal septum (the wall that divides the inside of the nose), caused by constriction of blood vessels, and cocaine poisoning, which may result in death. In addition, long-term chronic use sometimes results in cocaine psychosis, a mental disorder in which the person loses touch with reality.

Amphetamines may be taken orally or intravenously. Immediate effects include increased alertness and ability to concentrate, reduced fatigue and appetite, and elevated mood. Amphetamines have become popular with some people who need to overcome fatigue to complete a task (such as college students "cramming" for examinations). They are also popular as diet pills for people trying to lose weight.

Amphetamine abuse produces mental excitation, irritability, confusion, tremors, rapid speech, sleeplessness, and hypertension. Abrupt withdrawal may lead to convulsions. Taking large quantities within a short time may produce excitation for several days, followed by exhaustion and several days of sleep. Chronic abuse may lead to amphetamine psychosis, another mental disorder in which the person loses touch with reality.

Hallucinogens **Hallucinogens** are drugs that produce sensory distortion. Mescaline, psilocybin, and LSD are commonly used hallucinogens. These drugs may be abused, but they do not produce physical dependence.

hallucinogen a drug, such as mescaline or LSD, that produces sensory distortion

Immediate effects include sensory distortion, such as seeing sounds or hearing colors; feelings of depersonalization and detachment from reality; and swift changes in emotions. Other immediate effects may include giddiness, weakness, nausea, increased body temperature and blood pressure, and a slight decrease in level of task performance. Individuals sometimes become violent while on a hallucinogenic "trip," committing acts such as mutilation and suicide. Some individuals who have used hallucinogens experience a *flashback,* a sudden, unexpected reexperiencing of parts of a drug trip from their past.

Cannabis **Cannabis** is a preparation of resin taken from the *Cannabis sativa,* or Indian hemp plant. It is commonly called *marihuana* (sometimes spelled *mari-*

cannabis a drug, commonly called marihuana, that is a preparation of resin taken from the *Cannabis sativa,* or Indian hemp plant. Taken in large quantities, it has a mildly hallucinogenic effect

juana). It is usually smoked, but can also be mixed with food and eaten. Taken in large quantities, it has a mildly hallucinogenic effect. Cannabis may be abused and may produce tolerance and psychological dependence, but it does not produce withdrawal symptoms.

Immediate physical effects are virtually the same for all users: heart rate, blood pressure, appetite, and urination frequency increase; eyes become bloodshot; mouth becomes dry; respiratory passages widen. Immediate psychological effects may be positive or negative. Positive effects include euphoria, relaxation, a sense of floating and well-being, and intensified perceptions. Negative effects include dysphoria (unpleasant, unhappy feelings), impaired judgment, and a feeling of going crazy or dying. Most regular users experience primarily positive psychological effects. An additional psychological effect, the slowing down of time, is common for all users. Chronic use may produce more asthma, bronchitis, pharyngitis, sinusitis, and emphysema than does heavy tobacco smoking.

General Factors in Substance Abuse   When considering the question of whether a particular individual is likely to become a substance abuser, we should take into account several general factors (Mehr, 1983, p. 253):

1. *Possible physiological predispositions.* This seems to be particularly important with regard to alcohol addiction. Do you experience a euphoric feeling when you drink? Are you able to consume relatively large quantities of alcohol without becoming sick or very intoxicated?

2. *Social pressure.* This may be a very strong factor, particularly where drugs are readily available. Are you easily influenced by your peers?

3. *Psychological vulnerability.* This seems to be a strong factor in individuals who experience great difficulty in coping effectively with anxiety, depression, and stress. Are you very anxious, depressed, or distressed? Have you developed or are you developing effective coping mechanisms?

Critical Review 6

1. One factor that distinguishes substance abuse from nonpathological substance use is a pattern of pathological use. T F

2. Physical substance dependence requires evidence of tolerance or withdrawal. T F

3. The condition in which the individual needs a drug to cope or to function optimally from a psychological perspective is called psychological substance dependence. T F

4. Alcohol abuse or dependence usually develops within the first five years after regular drinking is established. T F

5. Sedatives are drugs that have a stimulating effect on the central nervous system. T F

6. The most abused opioid is marihuana. T F

7. Cocaine and amphetamines are stimulants. T F

8. Cocaine poisoning may result in death. T F

9. Hallucinogens are drugs that produce sensory distortion. T F

10. Cannabis, also known as marihuana, is a depressant. T F

11. What are the differences between substance abuse and substance dependence?

12. List three good reasons in favor of and three good reasons opposed to recreational substance use.

PSYCHOTIC DISORDERS

Psychotic disorders are maladjustments characterized by disturbances in thinking, feeling, and behaving that are so severe the person loses contact with reality. **Organic psychotic disorders** are associated with brain damage; **functional (nonorganic) psychotic disorders** are not associated with brain pathology, although chemical abnormalities have been found in the brains of some people suffering from functional psychotic disorders.

Characteristics of Psychotic Disorders

Specific characteristics of psychotic disorders vary somewhat from one type to another; however, there are many common factors. One is *inappropriateness of emotional response.* The individual's loss of contact with reality may be manifested in a seemingly total lack of emotional response. Or the emotional response may not fit the situation, as when a person laughs on hearing that a loved one has just been killed in a car accident.

Another characteristic common to most psychotic disorders is *personality disorganization,* in which the person may become disoriented or display grossly inappropriate behavior. The loss of contact with reality may manifest itself in the individual's not knowing who or where he or she is, as in the case of the person holding the proverbial "smoking gun" but not realizing that he or she has committed the murder. Or the person may behave in a totally unacceptable way, perhaps physically attacking another person for no apparent reason.

Two other common psychotic characteristics showing loss of contact with reality are hallucinations and delusions. **Hallucinations** are inappropriate perceptions of sensory phenomena. The person might hear someone talking to him or her when, in fact, no one is there. Or the person might feel the death grip of an imaginary evil spirit. **Delusions** are false beliefs the individual refuses to let go of, despite a wealth of information showing them to be false. Thus, the person might become convinced that she has some terrible, incurable disease, even though ten medical doctors certify that she is in excellent physical health. Or the person may become convinced that enemies are plotting to kill him when, in reality, no such threat exists.

Insanity

Psychotic disorder is a clinical term referring to the characteristics just discussed. **Insanity** is a legal term. It often is used in reference to psychotic disorders but means specifically the state of being unable to be held accountable for one's actions, to manage one's affairs, or to carry out one's social responsibilities. Thus, the individual who has become a threat to himself or herself by continually attempting suicide might be declared insane. The judgment of insanity, however, is made by a judge rather than by a psychiatrist, although the judge might weigh carefully the psychiatrist's assessment of the person's psychological state before rendering the judgment.

Organic Psychotic Disorders

Brain damage may be caused by a variety of factors, from accidental injury to deterioration associated with excessive drinking or old age. Whatever the cause, the result may be some type of psychological disorder. These disorders are usu-

psychotic disorder maladjustment characterized by disturbances in thinking, feeling, and behaving so severe that the person loses contact with reality

organic psychotic disorder psychotic disorder associated with brain damage

functional (nonorganic) psychotic disorder psychotic disorder that is not associated with brain pathology (although chemical abnormalities have been found in the brains of some people with functional psychotic disorders)

hallucination inappropriate perception of sensory phenomena

delusion false belief that the individual refuses to let go of despite a wealth of information showing it to be false

insanity a legal term, often used in reference to psychotic disorders, but meaning specifically the state of being unable to be held accountable for one's actions, manage one's own affairs, or carry out one's social responsibilities

ally referred to as either *acute* or *chronic*, depending on whether they are permanent. Acute disorders are temporary; for example, persons with certain types of tumors or injuries may become disoriented and behave strangely until the tumor or injury has received appropriate treatment. Chronic disorders are permanent, as in the case of primary degenerative dementia, a disorder associated with old age. The condition is not reversible and worsens with time, although the severity of the condition and the speed of its progression may vary tremendously from one person to the next, depending on biological, personality, and situational factors.

Functional Psychotic Disorders

schizophrenia   functional psychotic disorder characterized by a split between cognition and emotion and by the disorientation and confusion one would expect to accompany such a split

Schizophrenia   One type of functional psychotic disorder is **schizophrenia.** It is characterized by a split between cognition and emotion and by the disorientation and confusion one would expect to accompany such a split. People with schizophrenia, for example, may not know where or even who they are at any given time. Sometimes they may not be able to put thoughts together in a logical sequence. They tend to be secretive and unresponsive to other people and to external events. It should be pointed out, however, that symptoms may occur in a variety of combinations and with various intensities. Approximately fifty percent of all persons admitted to mental hospitals are diagnosed as schizophrenic (Torrey, 1988).

Schizophrenia has been subdivided into varying categories by different researchers. Some make a distinction between (1) *process*, or *nuclear*, schizophrenia, which is thought to be based on organic factors; and (2) *reactive* schizophrenia, which is believed to be precipitated by traumatic events in the person's life, such as the sudden loss of a loved one.

DSM-IV divides schizophrenia into four types based on their specific symptoms. The *disorganized* type, for example, is characterized by frequent incoher-

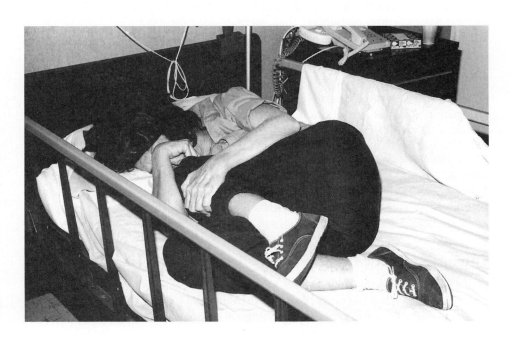

Schizophrenia: losing contact with reality.

ence, absence of systematized delusions, and blunted, inappropriate, or silly affect (feelings). Indeed, the person seems disorganized. The *catatonic* type involves physical immobility, often including mutism (inability to talk) and the absence of most voluntary actions. The person may remain absolutely still for hours, looking more like a statue than a living being. Sometimes this physical immobility is preceded or interrupted by a flurry of movement and excitement. The *paranoid* type involves unrealistic and illogical thinking, including delusions of persecution and/or grandeur, hallucinations, and personality disorganization. The person may become obsessed with the notion that he or she is destined to play some great role in history. The *undifferentiated* type either does not meet the criteria for any of the previously listed types or meets the criteria for more than one. Generally, undifferentiated schizophrenia includes prominent delusions, hallucinations, incoherence, or grossly disorganized behavior.

Delusional (Paranoid) Disorder Another type of functional psychotic disorder is **delusional (paranoid) disorder.** People with delusional disorder become seriously deluded but do not suffer the hallucinations and general personality disorganization usually associated with schizophrenia. The delusions usually involve persecution. The person suffering from delusional disorder is highly suspicious of other people and often misinterprets their actions, remarks, or gestures as intentional insults. Moreover, no evidence to the contrary can convince the person of the falsity of those delusions of persecution. Indeed, a vigorous attempt to convince the deluded person that his or her beliefs are false may result in new suspicion directed at the person attempting to help. In this manner, the delusional system of the individual may continue to expand until it dominates his or her world.

delusional (paranoid) disorder psychotic disorder in which the individual becomes seriously deluded but does not suffer the hallucinations and general personality disorganization usually associated with schizophrenia

Maladjustment and You

It is important for you to understand that it is normal to want to be alone from time to time, just as it is normal to suspect people's motives or to feel unusually happy or sad at times. These are not necessarily signs of maladjustment. The maladjusted person tends to do these things in such an exaggerated fashion that

Disorganized Schizophrenia

Mehr (1983, pp. 300–301) describes some of the behavior of Pam, an institutionalized 24-year-old woman who suffers from the disorganized type of schizophrenic disorder:

1. At night, she often drinks many cups of coffee and then vomits it as she walks.
2. Sometimes she hugs and kisses staff and other patients; at other times, she becomes aggressive.
3. She is usually bizarre and overactive.
4. Her speech is disconnected and confused, and she speaks in fragments about her delusions and hallucinations.
5. She ingests objects such as pens, pencils, and screws.
6. She often sleeps on the floor.

Pam has been treated with psychotherapy, several major tranquilizing medications, and an intensive behavior-modification program, but none has been successful in helping her change her strange behavior.

they begin to dominate his or her life. If, however, you have some serious concerns about your adjustment patterns, it may be worthwhile for you to discuss them with someone who has been professionally trained in human behavior, human relations, or some area of human services. Perhaps a visit to your campus counselor or psychologist would help.

Critical Review 7

1. Psychotic disorders are those in which the individual loses contact with reality. T F

2. Hallucinations are inappropriate perceptions of sensory phenomena. T F

3. Delusions are false beliefs that the individual readily gives up when accurate information is presented to him or her. T F

4. Organic psychotic disorders are associated with brain damage. T F

5. Schizophrenic disorders are characterized by a split between emotions and behavior. T F

6. A person with a paranoid disorder might likely suffer from delusions of persecution. T F

7. Describe the general characteristics of psychotic disorders.

8. Explain the relationship between psychotic disorders and insanity.

SUMMARY

■ Maladjustment is the relative failure to meet adequately the psychological demands of oneself, the group, or the situation. It has been attributed to supernatural, physical, and psychological causes.

■ There are many different types of maladjustment, each with its own set of symptoms and potential causes. The American Psychiatric Association has published a *Diagnostic and Statistical Manual* (DSM) of mental disorders that describes and catalogs maladjustments. The most recent edition (DSM-IV) was published in 1994.

■ Anxiety disorders are those in which anxiety is the predominant disturbance or the individual attempts to avoid anxiety by behaving in particular ways. Specific anxiety disorders include panic disorder, phobic disorders, obsessive-compulsive disorder, posttraumatic stress disorder, and generalized anxiety disorder. Panic disorder includes recurrent, unpredictable, short-term panic attacks.

■ Phobic disorders involve intense and unrealistic fears. Such disorders include agoraphobia, a fear of being alone or being in public places; social phobia, a fear and avoidance of situations in which the person may be carefully observed by others; and simple phobia, a persistent, irrational fear and avoidance of various other objects and situations (e.g., snakes, insects, heights, enclosed places).

■ Obsessive-compulsive disorder involves recurrent obsessions and compulsions.

■ Posttraumatic stress disorder is the persistent reexperiencing of a traumatic event through dreams, recollections, a sense of reliving the experience, or intense distress at exposure to events that resemble or even symbolize an aspect of the experience.

■ Generalized anxiety disorder is unrealistic or excessive anxiety and worry about two or more life circumstances. The symptoms last for at least six months, during which the person is bothered more days than not by the concerns.

■ Mood disorders are those in which an extreme mood is the dominant disturbance. There are two major categories of mood disorders: depressive disorders and bipolar disorders. Depressive disorders include major depression and dysthymia, and bipolar disorders include bipolar disorder and cyclothymia. Another mood disorder is seasonal affective disorder (SAD).

■ Disorders of social concern are at least as much a problem for other people as for the person with the disorder. Two such disorders are sexual disorders and substance use.

■ Sexual disorders include sexual dysfunctions and paraphilias.

■ Sexual dysfunctions involve inhibitions of sexual desire or psychophysiological functioning that prevent the individual from satisfactorily completing the cycle of sexual response. Erectile dysfunction, premature ejaculation, inhibited female orgasm, functional dyspareunia, and functional vaginismus are examples of sexual dysfunctions.

■ Paraphilias are sexual disorders in which the individual requires unusual or bizarre imagery or acts for sexual excitement (e.g., exhibitionism or voyeurism).

■ Homosexuality and bisexuality are not classified by DSM-IV as mental disorders, although they are considered deviations by some people in our society.

■ Eating disorders involve a pattern of eating that deviates grossly from the norm. Anorexia nervosa is characterized by willful maintenance of an abnormally low body weight, a distorted body image, an intense fear of being overweight, and, in females, an absence of menstruation. Bulimia nervosa is characterized by recurrent episodes of binge eating followed by purging.

■ Substance abuse is a maladjustment characterized by impairment in social or occupational functioning caused by a pattern of pathological drug use that lasts for at least one month.

■ Physical substance dependence often involves either tolerance or withdrawal. Psychological substance dependence occurs when the person needs a drug to cope or to function optimally from a psychological perspective.

■ Alcohol, sedatives, opioids, stimulants, hallucinogens, and cannabis are examples of drugs that can be abused and cause dependence.

■ Psychotic disorders are maladjustments characterized by disturbances in thinking, feeling, and behaving that are so severe the person loses contact with reality. Organic psychotic disorders are those associated with brain damage. Functional (nonorganic) psychotic disorders are not associated with brain pathology, although chemical abnormalities have been found in the brains of some people with these disorders. Two classes of functional psychotic disorders are schizophrenia and delusional (paranoid) disorder.

SELECTED READINGS

Barondes, S. *Molecules and Mental Illness*. New York: Scientific American Library, 1993. An introduction to the neurochemical and genetic bases for anxiety disorders, mood disorders, and schizophrenia.

Davison, G. C., and Neale, J. M. *Abnormal Psychology*, 5th ed. New York: Wiley, 1989. A complete and well-balanced text on abnormal psychology.

Diagnostic and Statistical Manual of Mental Disorders, 3rd ed., revised. Washington, DC: American Psychiatric Association, 1987. A manual that is complete, authoritative, and surprisingly easy to understand.

Ray, O., and Ksir, C. *Drugs, Society, and Human Behavior*. St. Louis: Times Mirror/Mosby, 1990. A comprehensive overview of recreational drug use and abuse.

Torrey, E. F. *Surviving Schizophrenia: A Family Manual*, revised New York: Harper & Row, 1988. A description of schizophrenia, including treatment and a consideration of living with schizophrenia from the perspective of both the schizophrenic's family and the schizophrenic.

REFERENCES

Andreasen, N. C. "Creativity and Mental Illness: Prevalence Rates in Writers and Their First-Degree Relatives." *American Journal of Psychiatry* 144 (1987): 1288–1292.

_____. "Creativity and Psychiatric Illness." *Psychiatric Annals* 8 (1978): 113–119.

Avery, D. H., Bolte, M. A., Dager, S. R., Wilson, L. G., Weyer, M., Cox, O. B., and Dunner, D. L. "Dawn Stimulation Treatment of Winter Depression: A Controlled Study." *American Journal of Psychiatry* 150 (1993): 113–117.

Buie, J. "Age, Race, Gender All Influence PTSD." *APA Monitor* (December 1989): 32.

Carroll, B. J. "Psychopathology and Neurobiology of Manic-Depressive Disorders." In *Psychopathology and the Brain*, edited by B. J. Carroll and J. E. Barrett (pp. 328–351). New York: Raven Press, 1991.

[DSM-IV] *Diagnostic and Statistical Manual of Mental Disorders*, 4th ed. Washington, DC: American Psychiatric Association, 1994.

Foreyt, J. P. "Treating the Diseases of the 1980s: Eating Disorders." *Contemporary Psychology* 31 (1986) 658–660.

Gelman, D. "Haunted By Their Habits." *Newsweek* (March 27, 1989): 71–75.

Hershman, D. J., and Lieb, J. *The Key to Genius*. Buffalo, NY: Prometheus, 1988.

Hunt, M. *Sexual Behavior in the 1970s*. Chicago: Playboy Press, 1974.

Kinsey, A. C., Pomeroy, W. B., and Martin, C. E. *Sexual Behavior in the Human Male*. Philadelphia: Saunders, 1948.

Kirmayer, L. J. "The Place of Culture in Psychiatric Nosology: Taijin Kyofusho and DSM-III-R." *Journal of Nervous and Mental Disease* 179 (1991): 19–28.

Mehr, J. *Abnormal Psychology*. New York: Holt, Rinehart and Winston, 1983.

National Institute of Mental Health. *What to Do When a Friend Is Depressed: A Guide for Teenagers*. Washington, DC: U.S. Government Printing Office, 1985.

Richards, R., Kinney, D. K., Lunde, I., Benet, M., and Merzel, A. P. C. "Creativity in Manic-Depressives, Cyclothymes,

Their Normal Relatives and Control Subjects." *Journal of Abnormal Psychology* 97 (1988): 281–288.

Terman, M., Schlager, D., Fairhurst, S., and Perlman, B. "Dawn and Dusk Stimulation as a Therapeutic Intervention." *Biological Psychiatry* 25 (1989): 966–970.

Torrey, E. F. *Surviving Schizophrenia: A Family Manual.* New York: Harper & Row, 1988.

Wolfe, L. "The Sexual Profile of That Cosmopolitan Girl." *Cosmopolitan* (September 1980): 254–257, 263–265.

■ *Answers to Critical Review Questions*

Critical Review 1 1. T. 2. F. 3. T.
Critical Review 2 1. F. 2. F. 3. T. 4. F. 5. T.
Critical Review 3 1. T. 2. T. 3. F. 4. F. 5. T.
Critical Review 4 1. T. 2. F. 3. F. 4. T. 5. F. 6. T. 7. F. 8. T. 9. F.
Critical Review 5 1. F. 2. T. 3. T.
Critical Review 6 1. T. 2. T. 3. T. 4. T. 5. F. 6. F. 7. T. 8. T. 9. T. 10. F.
Critical Review 7 1. T. 2. T. 3. F. 4. T. 5. F. 6. T.

PERSONAL ACTION PLAN
Sexual Reflections

Our sexual identity, preference, and role are largely learned. To understand your current sexual attitudes and practices, it is necessary to reflect upon your sexual heritage. The following questions can guide you in reflectively thinking about your own sexuality. Allow yourself a few hours, and feel free to skip a question, think about it later, and come back to it. An important aspect of this exercise is to allow any feelings that are associated with specific memories to surface and be expressed. Give yourself permission to let the feeling flow, and allow time for this to happen. This self-improvement plan is *for your eyes alone.*

I. Earliest Memories and Associated Feelings:
A. When were you first aware you were a girl/boy?
B. How did your parents act differently toward you because of your sex?
  1. verbally
  2. physically
C. What were your parents' attitudes toward sexual expression?
  1. physical affection
    a. parent to parent
    b. parent to children
  2. dress codes

  a. home nudity
  b. sensual clothing
  3. sex questions and discussion
    a. free or limited exchanges
    b. nature of exchange; parents were:
      i. factual
      ii. supportive
      iii. directing and controlling
D. What were your sexual experiences with your brothers and sisters, friends and neighbors, and relatives?
  1. conversations
  2. jokes
  3. games
  4. other
E. When did you first become aware of being sexually aroused?
  1. When, where, how?
  2. How did you respond to the feeling?
F. When did you first learn of menstruation and/or menstruate?
  1. How did you learn?
  2. Who informed you?

II. My most significant sexual experience of childhood was:

III. Adolescent Memories

A. Bodily exploration

   1. What parts of your body surprised you?

   2. pleased you the most?

   3. displeased you the most?

B. Masturbation

   1. What were the circumstances?

   2. How did you masturbate?

   3. What objects, if any, were used as you masturbated?

C. When did you first begin dating?

   1. group or couples dating

   2. singles dating

D. Describe your petting experiences

   1. What were the circumstances?

   2. How far did you go?

   3. How did your parents respond during this period?

E. Sexual fantasies

   1. sexual scenes (time, place, people, objects)

   2. same-sex fantasy

   3. recurring fantasy

IV. First Coitus

A. What were the circumstances?

B. Was it as expected?

C. What problems arose?

D. Did you have an orgasm?

E. Did your partner?

F. Did you use contraceptives?

   1. What kind?

   2. Were there problems?

G. If prior to marriage, did your parents suspect? How did they (would they have) responded?

V. Religious Background

A. Do you believe religion played a significant role in your sexual training?

1. Were your parents religiously active?

2. Were you religiously active?

VI. My most significant sexual experiences of adolescence were:

VII. My Sexual Self Today

A. Describe your current beliefs, feelings, and practices that are sexual or that center around sexual things:

B. Describe your current position with respect to:

   1. erotic literature, films, art, and so on

   2. pornographic literature, films, and so on

   3. extensive use of sexual fantasy

      a. for solitary pleasure

      b. as an aid during coitus

   4. masturbation

      a. before marriage

      b. while married

   5. foreplay

   6. oral-genital sex

   7. coitus other than face to face, man on top

   8. group sex

   9. contraception

   10. abortion

   11. fornication

   12. adultery

   13. same-sex eroticism

      a. for others

      b. for yourself

VIII. My recent significant sexual experiences:

IX. My happiest sexual moment:

It is not necessary to draw any profound conclusions from this brief sex history. Remember, insight and understanding can help in deciding on a course of action to make your sexual adjustment more rewarding and satisfying. It is in reflective action that we grow.

14

GETTING HELP

Chapter Outline

FOCUS

Psychotherapy is a process involving the use of psychological techniques to help a person achieve better adjustment. There are many types of **psychotherapy** and several types of **psychotherapists.** In this chapter we consider both therapies and therapists and deal with a variety of considerations related to therapy. For example, when should a person consider entering therapy? How does a person choose a therapist? How does a person know whether a therapy is working? What does therapy cost? What is the effect of therapy on family life? When should therapy end? In short, this chapter provides a brief but fairly comprehensive overview of therapy.

psychotherapy a process in which psychological techniques are used to help a person achieve better adjustment

psychotherapist practitioner of psychotherapy

PSYCHOTHERAPY

Entering Therapy

People begin to sense that they may need some kind of help when they realize that things are not going well but that they do not know what to do to improve the situation. Examples might include: (1) *extreme moods,* such as depression, anxiety, hopelessness, continuing guilt, inability to concentrate, or forgetfulness; (2) *problems relating to others,* such as inability to get along with others, compulsive drinking, gambling, drug use, sexual difficulties, repeated trouble with the law, or frequent arguing; (3) *problems with sleep,* such as insomnia, frequent awakening at night, frequent nightmares, or too much sleep; and (4) *stress-related disorders,* such as headaches, ulcers, stomach troubles, or asthma. (See Mishara and Patterson, 1979, pp. 13–15, for a more complete list.)

It is important to emphasize that a person who has one or more of the above-listed symptoms is not necessarily a candidate for therapy. The critical factor in the determination of whether therapy is warranted is the person's perceived need for relief. That is, does the person believe he or she really needs relief? If so, therapy is warranted. Only then is it time to select a therapist.

> Janet is an alcoholic. Her drinking has led to strained relationships with her husband, her children, and her friends. It threatens her physical health and has led to a pattern of absenteeism at work that is placing her job in jeopardy. It would appear that Janet is a prime candidate for therapy.
>
> The problem is that Janet denies that she has a drinking problem. Members of her family, some of her friends, her doctor, the pastor of her church, and even her boss have suggested that she seek help, but to no avail. As long as Janet denies that she needs help, she will not seek it. Janet is not a prime candidate for therapy.

Types of Therapists

There are several types of therapists. They can be differentiated by kind and amount of formal training, licensing requirements, accreditation, services performed, and approaches to therapy.

psychiatrist licensed physician who practices psychotherapy

Psychiatrists **Psychiatrists** are licensed physicians. They have either an M.D. (Doctor of Medicine) or a D.O (Doctor of Osteopathy) degree. Their usual educational and training requirements include four years of undergraduate college study, three or four years of medical school, one year in a hospital internship, and three years of psychiatric residency in which they study the theory and practice of psychiatry. Thus, well-trained psychiatrists should be professionally competent to treat patients through the use of psychological methods as well as through drugs and other physical methods.

Psychiatrists in the United States are certified by the American Board of Psychiatry and Neurology through an approved residency, related work experience, and written and oral examinations. Many psychiatrists do not bother to take the examinations, and only about two-thirds of those who do pass. Consequently, only approximately one-third of psychiatrists are *board certified*. Those who have completed training in approved programs but who have not passed the examination usually refer to themselves as *board eligible*. Psychiatrists may provide many types of therapy, depending on their particular training and interests. They are the only therapists who can legally prescribe drugs or provide electroconvulsive (electroshock) therapy.

Psychologists The usual education and training requirements of **psychologists** include four years of undergraduate college and four to five years of graduate school in which a master's degree (M.S. or M.A.) and/or a doctor's degree (Ph.D., Psy.D., or Ed.D.) are/is earned. Many psychologists are not trained as therapists but instead specialize in research and teaching. Others spend a significant part of their graduate-school training learning and practicing therapy skills, including a one-year internship of full-time supervised clinical work. They are referred to as *clinical* or *counseling* psychologists.

Psychologists are licensed at the state level, and the regulations vary, sometimes considerably, from state to state. Often these regulations require not only an appropriate degree from an accredited university and supervised clinical work but recommendations from superiors and completion of a written examination as well. A small number of psychologists are certified by the American Board of Examiners in Professional Psychology. The *National Registry of Health Services in Psychology* lists all applicants who meet minimum requirements for clinical practice. Generally, psychologists provide all types of psychotherapy as well as several types of psychological testing.

psychologist individual who has earned a master's and/or a doctor's degree in psychology

CRITICAL THINKING ISSUE
Self-Help vs. Professional Help

Most people with problems in adjustment are capable of solving their adjustment problems on their own.

Generally, two factors determine whether problems in adjustment can be solved: (1) knowledge of how to solve the adjustment problem and (2) determination to deal with the adjustment problem. Numerous self-help books and self-help groups are available, and most people are intelligent enough to understand and master the techniques those books and groups employ. Thus, people who are determined to solve most of their problems in adjustment are capable of doing so. Of course, seriously debilitating problems such as schizophrenia may require the services of a professional practitioner, but most people are not schizophrenics.

Most people with problems in adjustment require professional help to solve their adjustment problems.

Self-help books and groups may sometimes play a positive role in helping people to solve some of their adjustment problems, but, in the final analysis, they are inadequate substitutes for professional help. Professionals are trained to diagnose and treat adjustment problems correctly within the context of an organized, formal relationship that facilitates effectiveness in working through adjustment problems. Ultimately, self-help is most effective when it has been prescribed and guided by a professional.

I take the position that:

psychiatric social worker   social worker trained in and practicing psychotherapy

Psychiatric Social Workers   **Psychiatric social workers** complete a four-year undergraduate degree, followed by two years of graduate school to complete either the Master of Social Work (M.S.W.) or the Master of Science in Social Work (M.S.S.W.) degree. Supervised clinical work usually takes up at least half of their training in these programs. A few social workers earn a doctorate in social work (Ph.D. or D.S.W.) by completing a program of approximately three more years of graduate work.

Social workers are licensed by some states, although several states do not issue licenses. The usual licensing requirement includes the master's degree plus approved training and two years of supervised clinical work. In addition, completion of a written examination may be required.

Social workers are certified by the Academy of Social Workers through written examinations to applicants who have a master's degree in social work and two years of clinical experience. In addition, the National Association of Social Workers and the National Federation of Societies of Clinical Social Work publish directories listing approved applicants. Generally, psychiatric social workers provide all types of psychotherapy, some through full-time private practices and others through hospitals, clinics, and family-service organizations.

psychoanalyst   individual who has received advanced training in the psychotherapeutic technique developed by Sigmund Freud

Psychoanalysts   **Psychoanalysts** are therapists who have received advanced training in the treatment technique developed by Sigmund Freud. The training takes place in psychoanalytic institutes such as the New York Psychoanalytic Institute. Most candidates are psychiatrists, although psychologists, social workers, or laypersons may also be trained. The training usually takes at least four years (sometimes as long as ten years), during which candidates take evening and weekend classes while continuing their regular professional work. All candidates must undergo a personal psychoanalysis as part of the training. In addition, they use psychoanalysis to treat, under supervision, two to four patients. There is no licensing for psychoanalysis; however, psychoanalytic associations may accept as members graduates of approved institutes. A few psychoanalysts treat patients only through psychoanalysis. Many, however, use additional approaches according to their patients' needs.

sex therapist   psychotherapist trained in techniques designed to help people overcome sexual dysfunctions

psychiatric nursing   training in psychotherapy, given to all nurses

pastoral counselor   member of the clergy trained in counseling techniques

Others   In addition to psychiatrists, psychologists, psychiatric social workers, and psychoanalysts, there are many other types of therapists. **Sex therapists** help people to overcome sexual dysfunctions. All nurses receive some training and experience in **psychiatric nursing** and may therefore provide psychotherapy to their patients. Psychiatric nurses, of course, do this routinely and may become highly skilled therapists. **Pastoral counselors** are rabbis, ministers, or priests who have been trained in counseling techniques. Most universities have counselors available in student development centers or university services centers. These psychological and school counselors often play important roles in developmental, preventative, and career counseling, in addition to crisis counseling. Other types of therapists include occupational therapists, dance therapists, and vocational therapists. These well-trained professionals, as well as many other types of therapists, provide legitimate therapies, but their backgrounds may or may not include training in psychotherapy or counseling. Some people who call themselves psychotherapists, however, may be charlatans, skilled only at taking money from unsuspecting clients.

Qualities of a Good Therapist

Personally, therapists should have a strong commitment to help. Their work should be more than just a job to them. They should be sensitive, empathic, and accepting. They should really care about the people with whom they work.

Professionally, therapists should have the technical skills necessary to help. They should be able to gather information quickly and efficiently. They should be good listeners willing to discuss any issue that might advance the therapy. They should be fluent in the language the client speaks, and they should have a reasonably good understanding of his or her lifestyle. They should be able to help the client formulate problems and goals and to outline a comprehensive plan for helping. Of course, therapists should be well trained in their particular approach to therapy and familiar with the kinds of problems the people they help are likely to have.

Choosing a Therapist

The best source of information concerning a therapist is a person who has consulted that therapist. Such a person is likely to provide candid information that may be difficult to obtain from other sources. One should realize, however, that many people are reluctant to discuss such highly private matters as their own therapy with others. Therefore, family members and close friends are perhaps the best people to approach and, even with them, prudence dictates a soft touch.

Another good source of information is people who are members of a helping profession. Physicians, nurses, members of the clergy, counselors, and teachers can often provide excellent referrals. The important thing is to talk with someone you know or someone referred to you by someone you know. This direct, informal contact usually provides candid information—the kind that is most useful. Other informational sources include local clinics or hospitals, local professional societies, area mental health associations, telephone hot lines, and various community-service or interagency-council information and referral services. These sources provide information, but the information is not usually very in-depth or specific to the individual's problems and, thus, is restricted in its utility.

One last source of information should be mentioned: a listing in the yellow pages of the telephone directory. This is the least desirable source in that it provides almost no useful information other than the phone number of the therapist. Certainly one can tell very little about the skills and experience of a therapist from a listing in the telephone book.

Eric's problems had been mounting for some time. Over the past year he had suffered from periodic headaches and insomnia, anxiety and depression, and most recently, an increasing inability to get along with others. He needed help and he knew it.

Unfortunately, Eric was reluctant to seek help in choosing a therapist because he thought people would think there was something wrong with him if they knew he was thinking about therapy. So Eric selected his therapist on the basis of an ad in the yellow pages of the telephone directory.

Eight months into his therapy and $1,500 later, Eric is still suffering from headaches and insomnia, anxiety and depression, and an increasing inability to get along with others. He is coming to the conclusion that "therapy doesn't work," a thought that depresses him further. Ironically, he believes the only bright spot in all of this is the fact that no one else knows he has been seeing a therapist.

Critical Review 1

1. Psychotherapy is a process involving the use of psychological techniques to help a person achieve better adjustment. T F

2. People begin to sense that they may need help when they realize that things are not going well but that they do not know what to do to improve the situation. T F

3. The best source of information concerning a therapist is a local clinic. T F

4. Psychologists are the only therapists who can legally prescribe drugs. T F

5. Psychiatric social workers are required to have a Ph.D. T F

6. Psychoanalysis is a treatment technique rather than a type of therapist. T F

7. There is no licensing of psychoanalysts. T F

8. Psychiatrists are physicians. T F

9. Under what conditions is a person a candidate for therapy?

10. Name and describe at least two types of therapists.

11. How would one go about choosing a therapist?

ANALYTIC THERAPIES

There are more than 250 recognized therapies and several ways of classifying them (Meredith, 1986). For example, some therapies are said to be *insight oriented.* These therapies are designed to help clients understand what forces are impinging on them and why their adjustive responses are what they are. It is assumed that the understanding or insight, in and of itself, helps the person to cope better. Other therapies are *action oriented.* These therapies are designed to help clients to act in new, more adjustive ways. It is assumed that understanding alone is not enough (indeed, it may not even be necessary) to change behavior; action is necessary.

Another classification scheme divides the therapies into *directive* and *nondirective* approaches. Directive therapies are those in which the therapist takes an active role in interacting with, interpreting for, and otherwise generally counseling the client. In essence, the therapist either pushes or pulls the client in one direction or another. Nondirective therapies are those in which the client takes much greater responsibility for solving his or her problems. The therapist may provide information and discuss alternatives with the client, but the client decides which courses of action to pursue.

A third classification scheme identifies three approaches—*individual, family,* and *group.* Individual therapy involves only the client and the therapist. Family therapy sessions include two or more family members and the therapist, although family therapists may conduct individual sessions with one family member or another from time to time. Group sessions include several clients and the therapist. Sometimes, because of the nature of a particular therapy, it is useful to have two therapists working together with a group at the same time.

Although each of these three classification schemes is useful in differentiating one type of therapy from another, none is recognized as *the* only way to classify therapies; in fact, there is no universally accepted classification.

Our discussion of therapies is based on a classification scheme developed by Joel Kovel (1976). It progresses along both historical and thematic lines and should serve as a means of both extending and integrating many of the ideas presented earlier in this book. Because the number of therapies in current use is extremely large, our discussion is necessarily selective. Still, we attempt to touch on all major approaches to therapy. This first section deals with the **analytic therapies**—those therapies that rely on verbal means to place the person in greater contact with fragmented parts of his or her mental life. The discussion begins with a consideration of psychoanalysis.

Psychoanalysis

The first psychotherapy to have wide-ranging impact was Sigmund Freud's **psychoanalysis.** As we saw in chapter 2, Freud viewed personality dynamics in terms of the interplay of our desires (the id), our rationality (the ego), and our conception of morality (the superego). Invariably, at times the demands of the id conflict with those of the superego. Generally, we may resolve these conflicts adequately through defensive behavior (unconsciously deceiving ourselves about our true desires). However, fixations (unresolved early childhood conflicts) may be carried unconsciously into our adult lives. Ultimately, the fixated person begins to have adjustment problems because the ego, weakened through its continuous unconscious expenditure of psychic energy in dealing with the id and the superego, becomes too weak to cope with the demands of reality. This weakness manifests itself most often in anxiety and depression.

Free Association   Having conceptualized personality dynamics in these terms, Freud (1969) devised an insight-oriented, directive therapy in which the present is linked inextricably to the past. The analysand (in psychoanalysis today, the patient or client is called the *analysand;* the therapist is called the *analyst*) is taught the method of **free association,** or what Freud called the *fundamental rule* of analysis—to say everything that comes to mind, even if it is disagreeable, nonsensical, or seemingly unimportant. The purpose of free association is to bring repressed thoughts and feelings into consciousness. Of course, the repressed material is rooted in fixations; therefore, the analysand is encouraged to focus on early childhood experiences. Information obtained through free association is interpreted by the analyst, who then explains the interpretation, thus providing the analysand's ego with knowledge of his or her own unconscious. This knowledge, in turn, presumably strengthens the ego and enables it to cope more effectively with the demands of reality.

Resistances   Although free association may be successful in bringing some repressed thoughts and feelings into consciousness, the analysand may be blocked by other, more threatening thoughts and feelings. These blocks are referred to as **resistances.** The analyst helps the analysand to overcome resistances through interpretation, progressing in a slow and deliberate manner. Here Freud was concerned that the analysand's ego might be completely overwhelmed by learning too much too soon about his or her socially forbidden desires. For example, an analysand who became fixated in the phallic stage (see chapter 2) because his mother denied him the physical contact and general love and affection he so desired might maintain an unconscious hatred toward his mother in his adult life. Of course, the hatred would be repressed, because one is supposed to love one's mother, not hate her. This repressed hatred toward the mother might manifest itself in a general suspiciousness directed at all women. In this situation the analyst would proceed cautiously, at first indicating that the

analytic therapy   a therapy that relies on verbal means to place the person in greater contact with fragmented parts of his or her mental life. In essence, the therapist analyzes what has happened or what is happening to the person, who then synthesizes or puts the fragmented parts back together

psychoanalysis   Sigmund Freud's system of psychological thought. It includes both a theory of personality and a therapeutic method

free association   the method whereby the person says everything that comes into his or her mind

resistance   thoughts and feelings severely threatening to the person, who blocks them from consciousness through repression

analysand is repressing something and only later, when the analyst senses that the analysand has enough ego strength to withstand the truth, revealing that he has hated his mother since early childhood.

transference   the process in which the analysand begins to see the analyst as some important figure from childhood and transfers onto the analyst feelings and reactions that applied to that important figure

Transference   A curious phenomenon that occurs during therapy is called **transference.** The analysand begins to see the analyst as some important figure from childhood (often the mother or father) and transfers onto the analyst feelings and reactions that applied to that other person. In essence, the analysand begins to act toward the analyst in ways that are totally unrealistic and outside the range of the therapeutic relationship. For instance, the analysand, in an attempt to win a parent's love, may attempt to win the love and approval of the analyst by acting in more adjustive ways. Freud viewed this affectionate attitude as an advantage, because it tends to strengthen the analysand's ego. That is, under the influence of this affection, the analysand achieves things that would ordinarily be beyond his or her power. In addition, by putting the analyst in the place of one of the parents (who were the origin of his superego), the analysand gives the analyst the power the superego has over the ego. The new superego (the analyst) can reeducate the analysand by correcting the mistakes for which the parents were originally responsible. Freud recognized that the influence of the analyst in this matter is awesome, and cautioned stringently against its misuse.

> However much the analyst may be tempted to become a teacher, model and ideal for other people and to create men in his own image, he should not forget that this is not his task in the analytic relationship, and indeed that he will be disloyal to his task if he allows himself to be led on by his inclinations. If he does, he will only be repeating a mistake of the parents who crushed their child's independence by their influence, and he will only be replacing the patient's earlier dependence by a new one. In all his attempts at improving and educating the patient the analyst should respect his individuality. (1969, p. 32)

Traditional psychoanalysis.

The affectionate attitude is only one part of the transference. Almost inevitably the affection eventually changes to hostility that is also rooted in past experience. As a child, the analysand sought his or her parent as a sex object. At some time during the transference, the same demand will pass forward and seek satisfaction. Freud insisted, however, that real sexual relations between analyst and analysand are "out of the question, and even the subtler methods of satisfaction, such as the giving or preference, intimacy and so on are only sparingly granted by the analyst" (1969, p. 33). The analysand feels rejected and responds with hostility.

Ultimately, transference is useful in that it provides the therapist with an understanding of the analysand's conflicting attitudes toward his or her parents. However, it is also dangerous in that the analysand mistakes reflections of the past for current reality. For example, an analysand who senses the strong erotic desire that underlies the affectionate attitude may believe that he or she has fallen madly in love. If the affection changes to the hostile attitude, the analysand feels rejected, hates the analyst, and wants to quit the therapy. Either way, the analysand's behavior is totally unrealistic. The analyst's task is to show the analysand over and over that his or her thoughts, feelings, and behavior are reflections of the past and have nothing to do with current reality. If the analyst succeeds, the analysand will have taken a great step toward strengthening the ego and breaking down resistances.

Dream Analysis   One more aspect of psychoanalysis should be mentioned: **dream analysis.** In psychoanalysis the analysand is encouraged to tell his or her dreams to the analyst, who interprets them to the analysand. According to Freud, dreams may arise either from the id, as an unconscious wish that makes itself felt by the ego, or from the ego, as a conflict left over from waking life that is supported during sleep by an unconscious element. In either event, a demand is placed on the ego for the satisfaction of an instinct or for the solution of a conflict. The sleeping ego, however, wants to remain sleeping. It accomplishes this by symbolically fulfilling the wish and thus temporarily meeting the demands placed on it, while at the same time allowing itself to remain asleep.

dream analysis   the process in which the analysand tells his or her dreams to the analyst, who interprets them and, in turn, reveals the interpretations to the analysand

In some dreams the symbols are fairly explicit representations of what they stand for. A hungry sleeping person may dream of eating a delicious meal. In this case, if the wish fulfillment is sufficient to meet the person's hunger (temporarily, of course), then he or she will continue sleeping. If the hunger persists, the person will wake up.

In other dreams, the symbols are not so explicit. Suppose, for instance, the sleeper desires a forbidden sexual object, the husband of one of her friends. This desire provokes so much anxiety in her that the ego defends itself by distorting the symbolic content of the wish fulfillment. She dreams of having sex with some other man, one to whom she is sexually indifferent, but who has the same name as her friend's husband. In this case, if the anxiety becomes too great for the wish fulfillment to deal with successfully, the person will wake up.

Summary of Psychoanalysis   To summarize, psychoanalysis involves two steps: strengthening the weakened ego by extending its self-knowledge and breaking down resistances. The analyst gathers material from several sources: direct information supplied by the analysand and information conveyed through free associations, transferences, and the telling of dreams. The analyst then constructs interpretations of this material and gives them to the analysand.

Great care is taken to avoid telling the analysand too much too soon. As a rule, the analyst refrains from providing an interpretation until the analysand is only a single step away from discovering it for himself or herself. Otherwise the information would produce either no effect or a violent outbreak of resistance. When resistances do occur, the analyst must proceed sensitively, patiently, and caringly, always showing the analysand how the present is linked with the past. In this manner, ego strength is restored and the analysand is able to cope more effectively with the demands of reality.

In traditional psychoanalysis, the analyst sits out of view of the analysand, who is lying on a couch, and, as previously described, encourages the unfolding of the analysand's unconscious. A complete analysis usually requires four to five fifty-minute sessions per week for three to five years (Kovel, 1976). At $40 to $125 per session, depending on the analyst and the city in which he or she practices, the costs can be staggering.

Psychoanalytic Psychotherapy

psychoanalytic psychotherapy
a modification of psychoanalysis that attempts to provide the patient with a shorter and less expensive treatment

Psychoanalytic psychotherapy is a modification of psychoanalysis that attempts to provide the patient with a shorter and less expensive treatment. Here, the therapist and patient confront one another, physically sitting up and engaging in a dialogue that focuses more on current problems in living than on fixations. The therapy is classified as psychoanalytic because Freudian principles underlie the general understanding of what is going on and because the goals include strengthening of the ego through the extension of its self-knowledge. The therapy usually consists of only one to two sessions per week, and may be completed in substantially less than the time usually required for traditional psychoanalysis, sometimes in as few as 30 sessions. (Gelman, 1988)

Critical Review 2

1. _____ therapy is designed to help clients understand what forces are impinging on them and why their adjustive responses are what they are.

2. The first psychotherapy to have wide-ranging impact was _____.

3. The condition in which the analysand sees the analyst as some important figure from childhood and transfers onto the analyst feelings and reactions that applied to that other person is called _____.

4. According to Freud, dreams may arise from either the _____ or the _____. In either case, the function of the dream is to help the sleeping ego _____.

5. Psychoanalysis involves two steps: strengthening the ego by extending its _____ and breaking down _____.

6. Explain the fundamental differences between psychoanalysis and psychoanalytic psychotherapy.

Neo-Freudian Analysis

Several of Freud's major disciples broke away from Freud and created therapies of their own. A few of these therapies, although different from one another in

specific details, have enough in common that they may be considered variations of an identifiable type of therapy—**neo-Freudian analysis.**[1]

Neo-Freudian analysis places little emphasis on instinctual drives. Instead, it emphasizes the drive toward self-realization, assuring that each person has a unique, central inner force composed of specific potentialities. This self is influenced by culture in general and interpersonal relations in particular. Ultimately, the needs for security, love, and self-esteem (as opposed to sex) motivate behavior, and repression and unconscious thought are not considered nearly as important as in psychoanalysis. Generally, the neo-Freudians view people's problems as stemming from negative life experiences rather than from unresolved early childhood conflicts related to infantile sexuality.

Neo-Freudian analysis does not insist on strict adherence to the Freudian fundamental rule to say whatever comes to mind. It is much less concerned with exploring the unconscious mind and past relationships. Rather, emphasis is placed on conscious thoughts, feelings, and behavior in the here and now. Sometimes, future orientation in the form of goals is explored.

Generally, neo-Freudian analysis requires less total time, fewer sessions per week, and less expenditure of money than traditional psychoanalysis. There is less emphasis on free association, less use of the couch, and more intervention by the analyst. There is more concern with unrealistic attitudes and self-regard. The therapy tends to produce more immediately discernible change in what neo-Freudians hold to be the most important elements: strategies of living and feelings of self-worth.

neo-Freudian analysis an approach to therapy created by several of Freud's disciples. It emphasizes the realization of self as opposed to instinctual drives, present as opposed to past relationships, and conscious as opposed to unconscious thoughts, feelings, and behavior.

Analytical Psychology

While the neo-Freudians deemphasized the unconscious, C. G. Jung, another major disciple of Freud, attempted to expand the unconscious far beyond what Freud had envisioned. Jung's school of psychological thought, including his method of therapy, is called **analytical psychology.**

Jung (1968) asserted that in addition to the Freudian personal unconscious, there is a vast transpersonal unconscious in which each and every person shares. This *collective unconscious* reflects the cosmic order, including all of human history. It contains mythic themes, such as the Great Mother and the Hero, that recur in one culture after another throughout history. These themes, called *archetypes*, are known through symbols that appear in dreams, in flights of creative imagination, in disturbed states of mind, and in the products of art and science.

Analytical psychology holds that neurosis is caused by a splitting off of parts of the self. The person has lost touch with the archetypes and with other psychological formulations such as the *amina* (split-off female quality in the male), *animus* (split-off male quality in the female), and the *shadow* (a negated or inferior self-image). The overriding goal of therapy, therefore, is the integration of the self with its transpersonal parts.

The therapy is divided into two overlapping phases that usually take one to two sessions per week for a year or more to complete. The first phase is down-to-earth and extremely supportive. The patient and analyst confront one another in a face-to-face dialogue in which the neurosis is dealt with on a conscious

analytical psychology C. G. Jung's system of psychological thought, including his method of therapy

---

1. Among the major contributors to neo-Freudian analysis are Alfred Adler, Otto Rank, Karen Horney, Harry Stack Sullivan, and Erich Fromm.

level. The analyst often provides practical advice and attempts to build a friendly, warm, positive relationship with the patient.

The second phase involves the exploration of the archetypes. This is done primarily through *dream analysis.* Jung, however, did not accept Freud's conception of the dream as a distorted representation of an unconscious wish. Rather, the dream is the vehicle through which archetypes can make themselves known. Thus, Jung devised a technique called *amplification* in which the dream content is first expanded dramatically within the patient's life, then placed within the human tradition of myth and symbol. For example, the patient might be asked to extend the dream by imagining a few additions to it. The analyst could then show how each form of the expanded dream reflected the collective unconscious. In this manner, the analyst puts the patient in contact with the deep unconscious, a process believed by Jung to be intrinsically healing.

The Existential Approach

existential approach   a radical type of analytic strategy based on the idea that the individual is responsible for personal choices

Psychoanalysis, psychoanalytic psychotherapy, neo-Freudian analysis, and analytical psychology have in common a reliance on verbal means to put the person in direct contact with fragmented parts of his or her mental life. The therapist analyzes and the patient synthesizes. This also happens in the **existential approach,** the most radical type of analytic strategy. However, because it is so often woven into the fabric of various other therapies, the existential approach may be more accurately defined as an approach, a technique, or a strategy rather than as a complete therapy.

The existential approach has its roots in twentieth-century European philosophy and psychiatry, both of which include elements that emphasize the themes of personal alienation in mass society, the breakdown of traditional values, and the consequent loss of meaning in our lives. These themes illuminate the chaotic nature of the world in which we live, a world that produces in us a despair and, ultimately, a gnawing anxiety as we encounter the incompleteness, meaninglessness, and nothingness in the here and now.

It is, however, precisely from this encounter that a healthier self can be forged, for an analysis of the human condition reveals that the only certainty is that we can control our own lives. We have the capacity to choose, and it is through our choices that we may construct an orderly and meaningful life for ourselves. In fact, the failure to choose is a choice in itself. The responsibility to choose, then, is inescapable and heavy; but the exercise of that responsibility is the pathway to freedom and wholeness.

The existential approach involves a face-to-face, active dialogue between therapist and patient. The therapist focuses on the conscious, here-and-now relationship between himself or herself and the patient. There is no reference to the unconscious or to anything else other than the dialogue currently taking place. Often the focus of that dialogue is the patient's construction of a personal value system and the consistency of current life choices with that value system.

Critical Review 3

1. Neo-Freudian analysis emphasizes the person's drive toward _____.

2. Analytical psychology holds that in addition to the Freudian personal unconscious, there is a _____ unconscious that reflects the cosmic order, including all of human history.

3. According to the _____ _____ , it is through our own choices that we construct an orderly and meaningful life for ourselves.

4. Compare and contrast neo-Freudian analysis, analytical psychology, and the existential approach.

EXISTENTIAL HUMANISM

A recent and distinctly American trend in therapy is **existential humanism.** This trend, often referred to as *humanist psychology* or the *human potential movement,* is composed of a vast array of therapies—from bioenergetics to encounter groups—that share the following characteristics:

> 1. A blending of the direct-experience component of the existential approach with a deep philosophical commitment to the notion of the perfectibility of human beings.
>
> 2. A shift of concern to ordinary unhappiness and alienation.
>
> 3. A concern with educating the public (that is, the movement tends to promote or sell itself to the public).

Specific techniques vary from one therapy to the next, but a spirit of spontaneous and honest self-expression and the goal of attaining personal happiness can be found at the base of them all.

existential humanism a recent and distinctly American trend in therapy that blends direct experience with the concept of human perfectibility and deals more with ordinary unhappiness and alienation than with the classical neurosis of psychoanalysis

Rogerian Therapy

Sometimes referred to as *client-centered therapy,* **Rogerian therapy** is perhaps the most influential brand of existential humanism. This nondirective therapy was devised by Carl Rogers (1961) and is consistent with his view of personality.

Rogerian therapy an existential humanistic therapy devised by Carl Rogers

In Rogerian therapy, the therapist provides the unconditional positive regard that the client so desperately needs.

As we saw in chapter 2, Rogers believed personality contains two basic components: the *potentialities* (our inherent capacities) and the *self* (a conscious idea of who and what we are). The potentialities are genetically determined and are therefore not subject to modification by social or psychological forces. The self, however, is formed by social and psychological forces and is subject to further modification by those forces.

The basic life force is the drive to actualize potentialities. We also have a drive to actualize the self. When the self is consistent with our potentialities, we are in a state of congruence. As we actualize the self, we also actualize our potentialities. Conversely, when the self is inconsistent with our potentialities, we are in a state of incongruence. As we actualize the self, we do not actualize our potentialities. We are maladjusted.

Rogers saw maladjustment as the last link in a developmental chain that begins when significant others give us *conditional positive regard*. They accept, support, and respect us only when we behave the way they want us to behave. To keep the approval of these significant others, we behave according to their ideas of who and what we should be, and our self develops consistently with those ideas. Next, we translate their "shoulds" into *conditions of worth*—standards by which we judge the value of our thoughts, feelings, and actions. When we fail to live up to these conditions of worth—and inevitably we will fail, because our self is based on someone else's idea of what we should be rather than on our own potentialities—we experience guilt and anxiety. These, in turn, lead to defensive behavior, which is an expression of a state of incongruence and therefore a maladjustment.

The basic technique of Rogerian therapy is for the therapist to encounter the client in an open, honest, and empathic manner, providing the *unconditional positive regard* the client so desperately needs. In such an atmosphere the client is able to experience his or her potentialities and to develop an accurate self while remaining free from the guilt, anxiety, and defensive behavior associated with the old conditions of worth.

The therapist demonstrates unconditional positive regard by listening carefully and reflecting feelings back to the client accurately, always without the slightest hint of negative judgment. For instance, to the client who complains about being unfairly passed over for a job promotion, the therapist might say, "You feel frustrated and angry because you believe it was unfair." To the client who is depressed because she does not have any close friends, the therapist might say, "You feel unhappy because you are lonely." In each case, the cient is being given an opportunity to discuss feelings honestly with an accepting, caring, and understanding person. Note that Rogerian therapy emphasizes the present rather then the past.

As the therapeutic relationship progresses, the therapist encourages a more and more complete description of feelings; as the client's true self emerges, the old neurosis breaks up. In many instances, the complete therapy may take only one session per week for a year or less.

Gestalt Therapy

Gestalt therapy an existential humanistic therapy that places the body on the same level as the mind

Like Rogerian therapy, **Gestalt therapy** emphasizes human perfectibility; however, the Gestaltists place a much greater emphasis on nonverbal experience than do the Rogerians. In fact, as articulated by its principal founder, Frederick (Fritz) Perls (1969), Gestalt therapy places the body on the same level as the mind.

The basic idea of Gestalt therapy is that any organism seeks to maintain its internal organization through exchanges with its environment. It does this through the process of *awareness:* first, an awareness of an imbalance in its internal organization; second, an awareness of something in the environment that can restore balance. The organism's recognition of the relationship between itself and its environment as an integrated unit, an organized, meaningful whole, is called a *gestalt.* Perls explains as follows:

> Let's assume that I walk through the desert, and it's very hot. I lose, let's say, eight ounces of fluid. Now how do I know . . . this? First, through self-awareness . . . called "thirst." Second, suddenly . . . something emerges as a gestalt, as a foreground, . . . say, . . . a pump—or anything that would have plus eight ounces. This minus eight ounces of our organism and the plus eight ounces in the world can balance each other. The very moment this eight ounces goes into the system, we get a plus/minus water which brings balance. We come to rest as the situation is finished, the gestalt is closed. (1969, pp. 14–15)

The situation may be finished and the gestalt closed, but only to be replaced by another unfinished situation, another incomplete gestalt. Thus, life is an unending series of incomplete gestalts. When we are living well, we are aware of our needs. As these needs express themselves through our thoughts, feelings, and actions, we become aware of what in the environment will satisfy them, and we move to close the gestalt.

When we are not living well, we are unaware of our needs. Consequently, we are unaware of what will satisfy our needs, and we do not move to close the gestalt. Failure to close the gestalt leads to a psychological fragmentation, that in turn, leads to the anxiety, frustration, and conflict we experience as we blindly grope to put the pieces together again.

Gestalt therapy seeks to help by expanding conscious awareness so that the person can recognize needs and, through the process of gestalt formation, be restored to psychological wholeness. The therapist's job is to get the patient to focus awareness on the present so that the natural process of gestalt formation will take place. Attempts by the patient to interpret what is happening or to refer to the past or future are strictly prohibited. Gestalt therapy may be practiced on an individual basis; however, treatment is usually in groups. The function of the group is usually limited to providing approval for emotional expression by the patient. Also, treatment often takes place in workshops in which many hours of contact are concentrated into a small time frame (for example, a weekend). This workshop approach often allows therapy to be completed in a relatively short time.

The therapist usually works with only one patient at a time within the group setting, watching and listening to the patient carefully, keeping awareness focused on the here and now, and prodding the patient to express thoughts and feelings. When a conflict is uncovered, the patient is asked to act it out by alternately playing its different parts. Similarly, images from fantasies and dreams may be acted out. The parts of a conflict and images from fantasies and dreams are considered fragmented parts of the patient, and the dramatizations serve to heighten awareness that, despite the fragmentation, there is only one organism.

Critical Review 4

1. Existential humanism is concerned more with ordinary unhappiness and alienation than with the classical neurosis of psychoanalysis. T F

2. The basic technique of Rogerian therapy is for the therapist to provide the client with conditional positive regard. T F

3. Usually Rogerian therapy takes longer to complete than psychoanalysis. T F

4. In Gestalt therapy the therapist's job is to get the patient to focus awareness on the present so that the natural process of gestalt formation will take place. T F

5. Gestalt therapy is always provided in traditional fifty-minute sessions between therapist and patient. T F

6. Compare and contrast Rogerian therapy and Gestalt therapy.

Biofunctional Therapy

biofunctional therapy   an existential humanistic therapy that places the body above the mind

While Gestalt therapy places the body on the same level as the mind, **biofunctional therapy** goes a step further by placing body above mind. There are a variety of biofunctional therapies, but all of them assume that both psychological health and neurosis are expressed directly through the body. Hence, the therapist works directly with the body of the patient.

The originator of biofunctional therapy is Wilhelm Reich, a disciple of Freud who rejects the later Freudian view that anxiety is a signal of impending disaster to the ego. Instead, he retains the earlier Freudian view that anxiety is an expression of blocked sexual energy (Kovel, 1976, pp. 128–129). Reich maintains that our attempts to defend ourselves against stress are expressed in the development of muscular armor, body postures such as the stiff neck, the ramrod back, or the fixed smile, which become more rigid with time. This muscular armor blocks the free flow of sexual energy, thus producing anxiety, frustration, psychological conflict, and neurosis.

The goal of Reichian biofunctional therapy is to release the flow of sexual energy, and the criterion of the therapy's success is sexual orgasm. The therapist carefully observes the patient's body and then begins to knead, squeeze, press, stick, and prod muscles. Sometimes there is an exchange of words; often there is not. Therapy progresses in a sequence, moving from blockages in the forehead down through the eyes, mouth, throat, neck, shoulders, thorax, diaphagm, belly, perineum, and genitals. Treatment sessions usually take place once a week, and the therapy continues for an undetermined time (until a completely satisfactory orgasm can be achieved by the patient). It is important to note that Reich, like Freud, is expressly opposed to sex between the therapist and the patient. Therefore, orgasm is to be sought outside the therapeutic relationship.

As mentioned, Reich's is not the only biofunctional therapy. A pupil of Reich, Alexander Lowen (1976), originated his own approach, called *bioenergetics*. Lowen devised a series of exercises to facilitate the flow of energy, and he does some analytic as well as biofunctional work with his patients. Another biofunctional therapy is *Rolfing*, or *structural integration*, developed by Ida P. Rolf, which is closer to the original Reichian approach in that no analytic work is done.

Primal Therapy

primal therapy   an existential humanistic therapy designed to rid the person of the hurt feelings carried over from early childhood when rejected by his or her parents

A recently conceived but notable existential humanist therapy is Arthur Janov's **primal therapy.** According to Janov (1970), neurosis is rooted in early childhood experience, specifically the rejection of the child by the parents. What a child needs more than anything else is to be loved by his or her parents. Children who are accepted and loved grow into well-adjusted adults. However, children who are not accepted and loved experience a Pain (Janov often capitalizes terms to emphasize their significance) that sets the neurosis into motion. Janov conceptualizes the neurosis as consisting of symbolic attempts to avoid the Pain (for example, defensive behavior) and the chronic tension that inevitably engulfs the person.

The goal of primal therapy is to transform the patient's state of feeling. The therapy is divided into two phases, and the treatment is highly structured. The first phase takes three weeks to complete. During this phase, the patient isolates himself or herself from usual relationships and regular activities, abstains from drugs and tension-reducing diversions, and concentrates only on the treatment. There is an open-ended session with the therapist each day. The session ends when the therapist decides the patient has had enough (usually after two to three hours). Each session has as its specific goal to get the patient to express deep feelings toward his or her parents. Sessions tend to be highy emotional, including crying, moaning, and screaming, as the patient confronts Primal Pain (the pain of having been rejected by parents). The therapist does not let anything interfere with the patient's expression of feelings toward the parents—no thoughts, feelings, or actions related to anything else.

The second phase lasts approximately six months. The patient resumes normal life activities but continues therapy in a Primal Group. There is little interaction in the group; each patient works in isolation. Ultimately, the patient experiences his or her real self and is able to live autonomously.

The Transcendent Approach

One more aspect of the human-potential movement is the **transcendent approach.** Like existentialism, the transcendent approach is used in conjunction with a variety of therapies, although it has at times taken the form of a complete therapy in itself (Watts, 1961). Whether in the form of Yoga, Zen, Sufism, Tibetan Buddhism, variants of Judeo-Christian mysticism, or mind-expanding drugs, the transcendent approach is concerned with the attainment of altered states of consciousness in which the usual boundary between subject and object becomes blurred.

transcendent approach an approach to therapy that uses altered states of consciousness as a new perspective from which to view everyday life

Having transcended the usual state of consciousness, the person allows the emergence of a potential spectrum of experiential states.

> At the one end is the attainment of the blissful state of reunion and unity; while the other faces the terror of repressed demonic fantasies. The situation is very much the same as having a good or bad drug trip. The agent of change, be it the drug or meditative ritual, succeeds in disengaging the person from everyday expectations and perceptions. (Kovel, 1976, p. 152)

Thus, the transcendent approach provides a new perspective from which to view everyday life. This new perspective, when supported by an effort to change life circumstances, may produce therapeutic effects.

Critical Review 5

1. The goal of Reichian biofunctional therapy is to release the flow of sexual energy, and the criterion of the therapy's success is sexual orgasm. T F

2. Primal therapy holds that neurosis is caused by dysfunctional relationships between either spouses or friends. T F

3. Like existentialism, the transcendent approach is used in conjunction with a variety of therapies. T F

4. How is biofunctional therapy distinctly different from other existential humanist therapies?

5. How does primal therapy attempt to transform the patient's state of feeling?

6. Briefly explain the transcendent approach.

GROUP THERAPY

The therapies discussed thus far focus either on the mind or on the body as a means to help the person change. Each of these therapies also has a social dimension, but it receives little or no attention as an agent of change.

Conversely, **group therapy** uses the social dimension as the predominant change agent. Within a group the individual becomes part of an ongoing system of relationships. Over time this web of relationships develops a set of objective realities (customs, social norms, belief and value systems, and so on) that may be powerful influences that can be brought to bear on the individual's thoughts, feelings, and actions.

group therapy   a type of therapy in which one or more therapists meet with several patients or clients who form a social group that becomes a powerful influence that may be used to help change the behavior of its members

Traditional Group Therapy

traditional group therapy   a group-therapy version of psychoanalysis

Traditional group therapy is most often associated with the psychoanalytic schools of therapy. Although the therapist must deal with both the individual patients within the group and with the group itself, there is a tendency to focus primarily on one factor or the other. Thus, some therapists are said to do psychoanalysis in groups, while others are said to do group psychoanalysis (see the box entitled "Two Approaches to Traditional Group Therapy").

In traditional group therapy, transference feelings toward the therapist provide the opportunity for group members to act out their neuroses both as individuals and as a group. Extreme idealization of the therapist, truculence, provocation, jealousy, and flattery are grist for the mill of therapy.

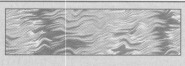

CULTURAL CROSSCURRENTS
Approaches to Therapy

Psychologist Juan Abascal often treats his Latino and Anglo clients differently, based on their cultural orientations. For example, Dr. Abascal tells us that Latinos typically revere the authority of a physician, a respect for authority that they transfer to the psychologist, whom they expect to tell them how to solve their problems. "They usually expect answers from me, not realizing the answers are within them. I'm expected to tell them what's good for them." On the other hand, Anglo clients do not expect the therapist to be so directive. "They are much more likely to expect me to guide them to self-discovery."

Because he values self-discovery and because it is an important part of his approach to therapy, Dr. Abascal deals with his Latino clients by presenting himself initially as an authority figure but moving toward less direction and the establishment of more egalitarian relationships with them as the therapy progresses. "This approach usually facilitates faster progress for Latinos. If I relinquished authority too rapidly, they would become confused and possibly upset. This would become just another obstacle to overcome in the therapy."

Two Approaches to Traditional Group Therapy

A therapist focusing on the individual might note that patient A is behaving in a hostile manner and interpret this as the result of a slight received from patient B, who has been lavishing attention on patient C. The therapist might then refer this interpretation back to some specific facts known about patient A's childhood.

A therapist focusing on the group might note that the group was extremely passive as the dynamics of the A-B-C triangle unfolded before it. The therapist might interpret this passivity as members' need to behave as helpless infants because they fear their own jealousy and hostility. Here, the therapist would be relating the group members' behavior to a phase in their development as a group.

Additional advantages are afforded by traditional group therapy. As the group progresses, the therapist can begin to withdraw from the position of dominance. This allows group members the opportunity for personal maturation. They can become less dependent on the therapist's authority and also can facilitate their identification with the therapist by helping other group members.

Encounter Groups

The human-potential movement is represented in group therapy by **encounter groups.** These groups tend to be more concerned with adding something positive (such as joy, warmth, spontaneity) to their members' lives than with removing something negative (such as neurosis). Indeed, encounter-group leaders often indicate that the group activities are designed for normal people who want to get more out of life and not for emotionally disturbed people seeking a cure for their adjustment problems.

encounter group an existential humanistic group that tends to concentrate on adding something positive to rather than removing something negative from the lives of participants

There have been so many encounter groups representing such a great variety of goals and activities that it is virtually impossible to define them in any precise manner. However, whether small (six to ten members) or large (twenty to forty members), whether led by one therapist or by two or more, and whether focusing on body, mind, emotion, or spirit, encounter groups provide experiences in which the individual may approach life on new levels. The group itself becomes an instrument of support to encourage the individual to try out new thoughts, feelings, and actions.

Although encounter groups have no doubt been of great benefit to many people by helping them discover hidden potentialities, they have also produced negative results for others (Lieberman, Yalom, and Miles, 1973). We therefore recommend that you get appropriate information and referrals before joining an encounter group.

Transactional Analysis

Although often used in individual therapy, **transactional analysis** (TA), a creation of Eric Berne (1961), may be used just as effectively with groups. In fact, TA is one of the more popular group therapies.

transactional analysis a popular group therapy that focuses on the way people interact with one another and the way they behave toward themselves

TA focuses on the way people interact with one another and the way they behave toward themselves. According to Berne, a person's behavior at any given time is dominated by one of three *ego states:* the *Parent,* which expresses prejudicial, critical, and nurturing behavior; the *Adult,* which tests reality, esti-

Encounter groups provide experiences in which the individual may "try on" new thoughts, feelings, and actions.

mates probabilities, and computes dispassionately; or the *Child,* which acts impulsively, creatively, and selfishly. Although all three ego states are considered essential in a healthy personality, the Adult should be in charge. Thus, TA places a premium on rational, conscious behavior. Of course, it is acceptable to be critical or impulsive at times, but only when appropriate (that is, when the Adult has flashed a green light). Therefore, adjustment problems are to be approached through the individual's Adult.

In TA therapy, clients learn to identify their ego states and to determine which one seems to be taking control at any given time. This allows them to exercise greater choice in their behavior.

> Tina has always suffered from a terrible case of the "shoulds." She seems to have rules to govern all occasions and judgments concerning how well the rules are being followed. She is highly critical and overly responsible, and she rarely lets herself have fun, even when there is nothing wrong with what she keeps herself from doing.
>
> Recently, Tina joined a TA group. Now, when her "critical Parent" begins to take charge, her Adult makes a rational decision about the propriety of her desired behavior. If she believes there is nothing wrong with what she wants to do, then she does it—without guilty feelings.

Three additional major concepts of TA are *life scripts, life positions,* and *games.* Life scripts are much like theatrical scripts. Both include a cast of characters, dialogue, scenes, acts, plots, themes, and so on. The difference is that life scripts are for real. We go through life as though we were actors in a play, acting out our hopes, fears, desires, likes, and dislikes according to a drama that was written when we were young children.

Life scripts are jointly produced by parental teachings and early decisions we make about ourselves. Among these early decisions are the life positions we adopt; they concern how we relate to ourselves and others. There are four life positions: (1) I'm OK—you're OK, (2) I'm OK—you're not OK, (3) I'm not OK—

you're OK, and (4) I'm not OK—you're not OK. According to TA, most of us settle upon one of the life positions in early childhood and continue to act from that position unless something unusual happens.

Games are manipulative ploys used to induce "payoffs," which always are reactions that support the negative component of our life position. For example, a person with an *I'm not OK—you're OK* life position might express this position's negative component by believing "I'm stupid." One way of verifying this belief is to manipulate someone else, particularly someone whose intellect is respected, such as a teacher, into saying "You're stupid." Of course, games are never played from the *I'm OK—you're OK* life position, because this position has no negtive component.

TA clients are taught to recognize their life scripts and life positions and the games they play and are encouraged to make positive changes in their lives (that is, to avoid games, to adopt the *I'm OK—you're OK* life position, and to "rewrite" the life script).

TA groups usually meet once a week for a predetermined length of time (often ten weeks). The therapist teaches the group the basic concepts of TA and then facilitates group interaction (transactions). The emphasis is on analysis of conscious behavior as it is displayed in transactions. The group provides emotional support, feedback, and help in analyzing these transactions.

Family Therapy

Since the mid-1950s, **family therapy** has steadily expanded to become one of today's most important treatment modes. Unlike the other groups discussed thus far, the family is a natural group; it contains the set of relationships within which the individual lives and within which his or her neurosis probably has its roots. Thus, the family is an excellent setting within which to deal with maladjustment.

family therapy the only type of group therapy that involves the natural group—the family—that contains the set of relationships within which the individual lives and within which his or her neurosis probably has its roots

Family therapists use various techniques. A psychoanalytically oriented therapist, for instance, might approach the therapy from either or both of the perspectives described in the section dealing with traditional group therapy. Many family therapists, however, are thoroughly grounded in *systems theory.* These therapists view the family itself as the primary unit of analysis and treatment. In this view, neurosis in one family member is an indication that something has gone wrong within the family and that the family itself needs treatment (Beck, 1989).

A usual approach taken by a systems family therapist is to observe the family as interaction takes place within it. This can be done either in the therapist's office or in the family's home. Once the therapist has inferred the rules governing the family's behavior, he or she can begin to intervene, focusing on interaction as it takes place. "The goal is to interrupt the circular feedback of pathological communications, then replace it with a new pattern that will sustain itself without the crippling limitations imposed by the rules of the original setup" (Kovel, 1976, p. 188).

Suppose Johnny asks Father if he can stay out late on Saturday night and Father says no. When Johnny asks again, Mother tells him not to ask his father that question again. Then Father tells Mother not to tell Johnny not to ask that question again. Then Johnny asks again and Father says no. In this case, the therapist would intervene, point out the dysfunctionality of the circular communication, and suggest some alternative. Perhaps some new rules concerning how late Johnny can stay out on certain nights need to be negotiated. In taking the family through the negotiation of the new rules, the therapist would be teaching a process for resolving disputes as well as helping to produce a more functional set of rules to govern future behavior.

Couples Therapy

couples therapy a variant of family therapy that deals with the relationship between two people

A variant of family therapy that has grown recently is **couples therapy.** The couple might be any two people, married or not, who share a significant relationship. The basic methods of couples therapy are essentially the same as those employed in other family-therapy approaches, including an emphasis on communications and techniques designed to manage or eliminate conflicts. Couples therapy is of particularly great potential benefit to couples who are thinking about getting married. Such therapy allows the opportunity to look objectively at an emerging relationship at a time when people are not usually objective. And that might save a lot of problems in the long run.

Critical Review 6

1. Group therapy differs from individual therapy in that group therapy uses the _____ dimension as the predominant agent of _____.

2. Traditional group therapy is most often associated with the _____ schools of therapy.

3. _____ groups tend to be more concerned with adding something positive to people's lives than with removing something negative.

4. Transactional analysis was created by _____.

5. Transactional analysis holds that behavior at any given time is dominated by one of three ego states: the _____, the _____, or the _____.

6. The _____ contains the set of relationships within which the individual lives and within which his or her neurosis probably has its roots.

7. Many family therapists treat the family as a social _____.

8. _____ therapy might include any two people, married or not, who share a _____ _____.

9. How does traditional group therapy differ from encounter groups and TA?

10. In what ways is family therapy a unique form of group therapy?

BEHAVIORAL-DIRECTIVE THERAPIES

behavioral-directive therapy a therapy that assumes emotional problems have observable sources

Behavioral-directive therapies assume that emotional problems have an *observable* source. Once the source is located, therapeutic activity is directed toward it so that it may be eliminated, or at least controlled. Thus, therapists using a behavioral-directive theapy would not concern themselves with whether patients having problems getting to sleep at night have unresolved conflicts from early childhood, lack self-esteem, feel unloved by parents, or have any other unobservable source of the sleep problem. Rather, such a therapist would carefully observe the antecedents to the problem behavior (what came before it) and its consequences (what followed it). Then, after having identified what he or she believed to be the observable source of the problem, the therapist would prescribe an appropriate treatment, which, in this case, might include rearranging the antecedents, teaching the patient relaxation techniques, or even directing the patient to take sleeping pills. There are many behavioral-directive therapies, and the following discussion surveys only a few.

Somatic Therapy

Somatic therapy defines the source of the emotional problem as biological and attempts to treat the problem through some biological means such as drugs, shock treatment, or psychosurgery. There seems to be little doubt that a distinct, inherited somatic predisposition exists for schizophrenia and that some forms of severe depressive illness are inheritable (Kovel, 1976). Thus, there is a definite link between biology and some forms of extreme emotional disturbance. In these instances, drugs may be much more useful than other techniques in managing the disorders (for example, phenothiazine is used for schizophrenia; lithium for mania; tricyclic antidepressants for psychotic depressions, and so on).

Sometimes, *electroconvulsive,* or *shock therapy* (ECT) is used to treat serious depressions and extreme states of excitement when the patient fails to respond to drug or other treatment (Thompson and Blaine, 1987). ECT involves the application of an electric current for a fraction of a second through two electrodes placed on the sides of the patient's head. The patient is unconscious throughout the procedure and does not feel any discomfort. The treatment usually requires two to eight sessions and is administered at the rate of three sessions per week. The usual effects after two or three sessions include a return to a more normal emotional mood and general mental state, improved appetite and sleep, and temporary difficulty in remembering. The memory lapses usually go away gradually over several weeks after treatment stops, although some patients claim to have persistant memory difficulty after the therapy.

Psychosurgery is a surgical procedure in which seemingly healthy brain tissue is destroyed or nerve pathways severed to change brain functioning and, consequently, behavior. This radical therapy has been used primarily to treat prolonged severe depression, abnormal excitement, severe anxiety, and violent outbursts of anger. Psychosurgery is relatively rare today and is usually regarded as an experimental procedure, although it was used more frequently in the 1950s. The infrequency of use today is the result of permanent negative side effects that have been observed, including loss of motivation for constructive activities and deterioration of ordinary social habits such as concern for others or concern for personal appearance.

Although biologically based treatment may be the only therapy that works in some of the cases just mentioned, it is not the only workable treatment in many instances in which some doctors prescribe it. This is particularly true of drugs. It is likely that everyone suffers from tension, frustration, anxiety, and slight depression from time to time. In the case of a brief crisis, taking a sedative might be a reasonable treatment. However, for a crisis of longer duration, psychological or social therapy is the preferred treatment. In short, drugs do not help you cope with life; they simply postpone your ultimate confrontation with reality.

Sex Therapy

While somatic therapy attempts to influence mind, emotions, and behavior by treating the body, **sex therapy** attempts to influence the body by treating mind,

somatic therapy   a behavioral-directive therapy that defines the source of emotional problems as biological and that attempts to treat the problem through some biological means, such as drugs, shock treatment, or psychosurgery

sex therapy   a behavioral-directive therapy that attempts to influence the body (that is, sexual dysfunction) by treating mind, emotions, and behavior

emotions, and behavior. Sex therapy seems to work best for couples who, because of the effects of inhibition or ignorance, are sexually frustrated. They have fairly intact relationships and reasonably good capacities for communication. There is a clear, behavioral aspect to their difficulty.

Many approaches have been taken to treating sexual dysfunctions, from simple reeducation programs for transient problems to lengthy and intensive psychotherapy. Knowledge of the physiology of sex, simple techniques of arousal, and contemporary sexual practices may alter the attitudes of the sexual partners and thus improve their sexual lives. For example, knowing that an extensive use of fantasy during coitus is effective and widely practiced may enable one or both partners to respond more effectively. If sexual dysfunctions are found to be based on interpersonal conflicts or poor communication, couples counseling can help change the bedroom from a battleground to a focal point for mutually supportive activities. Personal problems rooted in past experiences may contribute to the couple's problems, and insight-oriented therapies may help the affected partner to gain an understanding of the unconscious conflicts relating to current sexual problems. Insight can improve performance.

Perhaps the most widely practiced sex therapy is the behavioral-directive therapy based on the work of William Masters and Virginia Johnson (1966, 1970), who employ an intimate educational approach. A treatment consisting of a female and a male therapist interact with an involved couple. (Single people are not allowed into therapy because of legal and moral considerations.) After a complete background study has been completed, a relaxed atmosphere is established and training begins. Treatment consists of education pertaining to the sex organs and their functioning, sets of suggestions for pleasurable explorations leading to, but short of, intercourse, and a new awareness of the nature of a sound sexual relationship.

Certain concepts are introduced and reinforced during treatment:

1. No one is uninvolved and no one is at fault; it takes two to make love.
2. Sex is a natural function that requires relaxation, not heroics.
3. Each partner must learn self-arousal and communication skills.
4. Each must give as well as receive stimulation.
5. Orgasm will come in time, and there is nothing to be gained by seeking it anxiously.

Behavior Therapy

behavior therapy   a behavioral-directive approach to therapy that is strictly psychological

Behavior therapy is a behavioral-directive approach that is strictly psychological. It is a natural outgrowth of behavioral psychology, the academic tradition that focuses on observable, testable, quantifiable, and reproducible behavior. Thus, behavior therapy begins with analyzing a pattern of behavior and identifying an observable component such as a phobia. Then a set of directives is aimed at altering the behavior pattern so that the observable component is eliminated or controlled. The key to this method is to narrow the problem by continually defining and redefining it so that it can eventually be brought under control. Once the problem is narrowed sufficiently, treatment can begin.

There are many behavior-therapy techniques. Generally, they involve the application of control over one piece of behavior, then another, then another, and so on until the whole problem as been brought under control. For example, a technique created by Joseph Wolpe (1969) for the treatment of phobias is *systematic desensitization.* This technique is often used when the patient suffers from some overt anxiety. The general notion is to construct a hierarchy of fear-inducing situations, beginning with one the patient can handle and then proceeding, step by step, to the target situation. Suppose, for instance, that the patient is fearful of flying in a plane. Over a period of several weeks the patient might look at pictures of people flying in a plane; go to the airport and watch planes take off and land; get on a plane and imagine that it is taking off, flying, and landing; and finally, actually fly in a plane.

An integral part of systematic desensitization is relaxation training. One widely used relaxation technique is *progressive relaxation,* in which the alternate tensing and relaxing of muscles, together with breathing exercises, relaxes first one part of the body and then another, until the person is in a highly relaxed state (see chapter 4 on stress). A variation of this technique involves the use of relaxing images rather than the tensing and relaxing of muscles. These techniques can be taught to the patient so that he or she can attain states of calm whenever desired, or they can be used to relax the patient, making him or her more susceptible to suggestion. (Another technique that can accomplish either of these objectives is *hypnosis,* although hypnosis does not appear to be widely used by behavior therapists.)

One of the main currents of behavior therapy mixes Skinnerian operant conditioning and respondent conditioning. For example, a behavior therapist working with a couple might observe their interaction carefully and then show how a behavior emitted by one is a reinforcement for a negative response by the other, which in turn reinforces the reinforcer and so on, until they are literally at each other's throats. Here again, the behavior pattern can be broken down into small parts, which can be changed through conditioning until a new functional behavior pattern has been constructed to replace the older, dysfunctional one. See chapter 2 for more on Skinner's work.

Cognitive Therapy

One more type of behavioral-directive therapy is **cognitive therapy.** This therapy has several versions, including Albert Ellis's (1962) *rational-emotive therapy,* William Glasser's (1965) *reality therapy,* and Aaron Beck's (1976) *cognitive therapy.* All of them are concerned with concepts, assumptions, and values.

cognitive therapy a behavioral-directive therapy concerned with correcting incorrect or unrealistic concepts, assumptions, and values

The general notion is that the patient displays maladjustive behavior because of some error or confusion with regard to beliefs or values (Ellis, 1987). For example, we can easily understand the depression of a person who believes he or she should be thoroughly competent and adequate and who has just made a terrible blunder. The real blunder, according to the cognitivists, is not in making a mistake but in believing one has to be perfect. The truth of the matter is that *everyone* makes errors from time to time; although we do not look forward to making errors, doing so does not justify depression.

Cognitive therapists, therefore, point out to their patients faulty thinking and confusion with regard to value judgments. Then, they attempt to correct these errors by teaching more realistic and effective ways of thinking and methods by which patients can work out their own value systems. This approach is demonstrated in the Personal Action Plan at the end of this chapter, which provides a self-help model based on cognitive therapy.

Questionnaire

Which Therapy Appeals to You?

Respond to each of the following statements by marking A in the space provided if you agree more than disagree with the statement. Mark D in the space provided if you disagree more than agree with the statement. The scoring key on page 563 will indicate which of three specific therapies might be more appealing to you.

Mark A or D

_____ **1.** What happened in the past determines what happens in the present.
_____ **2.** In order to understand a particular behavior by a person, one must understand the whole person.
_____ **3.** A person's character is largely determined before the individual reaches adulthood.
_____ **4.** We are unaware of most of the factors that direct our behavior.
_____ **5.** When given alternatives and support, people can make important changes in themselves in relatively short periods of time.
_____ **6.** All of our values are learned through living.
_____ **7.** It is not a good idea to look within the person (as opposed to the social environment) for the causes of behavior.
_____ **8.** Therapists should be personally involved in therapy sessions.
_____ **9.** The relationship between therapist and client is critically important to the client's success in therapy.
_____ **10.** People are free to be what they want to be.
_____ **11.** The best way to understand human beings is to focus on the observable.

Critical Review 7

1. Behavioral-directive therapies assume that emotional problems have observable sources. T F

2. A somatic therapist would never treat a patient with drugs. T F

3. Psychosurgery is a popular new type of surgery. T F

4. Sex therapy attempts to influence the body by treating mind, emotions, and behavior. T F

5. Behavior therapy is a behavioral-directive approach that is strictly psychological. T F

6. A widely used behavior-therapy technique that was originally created for the treatment of phobias is systematic desensitization. T F

7. Progressive relaxation tends to make the person more susceptible to suggestion. T F

8. Cognitive therapy is nondirective in nature. T F

9. What do all behavioral-directive therapies have in common?

10. In what way are somatic therapy and sex therapy directly opposed to one another?

11. What is the essential difference between behavior therapy and cognitive therapy?

A FEW REMAINING CONCERNS

Thus far in this chapter we have explored concerns related to the appropriate time to enter therapy, different types of therapists, qualities of a good therapist, methods of choosing a therapist, and a variety of specific therapies. Now, in this last section, we tie together the loose ends by answering a few remaining questions.

Choice of Therapy

The choice of a particular therapy may not be as important as the choice of a particular therapist or the decision to enter therapy in the first place. Once a person has willingly chosen to seek help and has selected a therapist who meets the criteria discussed earlier in this chapter, the chances of success are good regardless of the therapy employed.

Still, some therapies may be better suited than others to deal with certain problems. A person who wants to quit smoking, for example, might be well advised to try a behavioral-directive approach to therapy, rather than one of the analytic or existential humanistic approaches. By the same token, the person who has deeply rooted internal conflicts and who suffers the pangs of great anxiety and guilt might be a more likely candidate for an analytic therapy, and the person who is mildly depressed because he or she believes that "life is passing me by" might better seek an existential humanistic therapy.

It is also important to point out that the pure models of therapy discussed earlier are often not precisely followed. Although some therapists use a "strict" approach and do not deviate from it, others are more **eclectic** in approach, and may use aspects of more than one therapy when working with clients. Cognitive therapy, for example, is often blended with behavior therapy in the treatment of anxiety, and both of these are often coupled with somatic therapy in the treatment of depression. Thus, eclectic therapists are able to tailor therapy to the specific needs of their clients; because of this, there is a growing trend for therapists to become eclectic (Beitman, 1989). Ultimately, common sense dictates that the selection of a particular therapy should be based on information gathered about that therapy, including factors such as time and money spent.

eclecticism   an approach to therapy in which the therapist tailors the therapy to the needs of the client by selecting for use aspects of more than one therapy

Price of Therapy

Therapy costs what the market will bear. Because of the relatively large fluctuation in inflation rates in the United States in recent years, prices for therapy have been unstable, and it is difficult to quote accurate figures. However, even if prices remain stable, the variation in price from one therapy to another can be great, depending on whether the therapy treats individuals or groups and on whether it is provided through private practice or a practice supported by public funds. For example, in some places in the United States individuals are willing to pay private practitioners as much as $125 an hour for therapy. In other parts of the country people are not willing to pay that much, and the same type of therapy may be bought from private practitioners for $40 an hour, or perhaps even less. Some group therapies tend to be relatively inexpensive (for example, TA or encounter-group therapy may cost as little as $15 to $20 per session), while others may cost more. Therapy provided through a practice supported by public funds (by some community agency or a public university or college, for example) may cost little or nothing. The main point here is that, because prices vary greatly, one should investigate them thoroughly before making a commitment to a particular therapy.

Other Costs of Therapy

Therapy may have other costs. The general expectation is that a person who enters therapy will achieve better adjustment. Thus, a person in therapy can expect to change. This change may involve thoughts, feelings, or actions and may manifest itself in the way the person treats himself or herself, others, or life in general.

Successful therapy may cost the person a relationship. Suppose the wife in therapy should discover that she has grown apart from her husband and that this growth threatens and may ultimately destroy their relationship. Costs such as this are inherent in the process of therapy. Certainly, not all of the changes are so dramatic, but changes will occur. The change may "cost" the person in therapy and/or those who are close to him or her. Thus, the risks of successful therapy extend to family members and friends as well as to the person in therapy.

Evaluating Therapy

By definition, successful therapy helps the person to achieve better adjustment. Thus, to judge whether a therapy is successful, we can evaluate how well the goals of the therapy are being achieved. For example, the person who suffers frequent, severe anxiety attacks would, no doubt, want to eliminate the anxiety attacks. This person might conclude that the therapy is working well if the anxiety attacks decrease in both intensity and frequency.

Note that in our example there is an implicit division of the goals of therapy into long-range and short-range goals. The long-range goal is the elimination of anxiety attacks. The short-range goal is a decrease in the intensity and/or frequency of the attacks. This division of goals is useful because it is through the achievement of short-range goals that we ultimately achieve our long-range goals, and it is through the evaluation of short-range goals that we can make reasonable judgments about whether the therapy is helping us to achieve our long-range goals.

One method of evaluating goal achievement is self-assessment. Ask yourself, "What evidence do I have that I am achieving my goal?" Another method is discussion with the therapist. Ask the therapist, "What evidence do you see that I am achieving my goal?" A third method is discussion with a family member or friend. Ask this person, "What evidence do you see that I am achieving my goal?" Gather information from all three sources, examine it carefully, and make a judgment.

Therapy should end either when the goals have been achieved or when there has been no progress toward the achievement of goals for an inordinately long time. In either case, you have achieved what is possible for the time being, and it is time to move on.

Critical Review 8

1. Some therapies may be better suited than others to deal with certain problems. T F
2. Many therapists today blend elements of two or even more approaches in an attempt to tailor a therapy to the unique needs of their clients. T F
3. The monetary costs of all types of therapy are the same. T F
4. Generally, a person in therapy can expect to change. T F
5. The risks of successful therapy extend to family members and friends as well as to the person in therapy. T F
6. Therapy should end only when the goals of therapy have been achieved. T F
7. On what basis should one choose a type of therapy?

8. How can successful therapy be risky?

9. How should one evaluate therapy?

SUMMARY

■ Psychotherapy is a process involving the use of psychological techniques to help a person achieve better adjustment. There are many types of psychotherapy and several types of psychotherapists.

■ People should consider entering therapy when they realize that things are not going well and that they do not know what to do to improve the situation.

■ Therapists can be differentiated by kind and amount of formal training, licensing requirements, accreditation, services performed, and approaches to therapy. They include psychiatrists, psychologists, psychiatric social workers, psychoanalysts, sex therapists, psychiatric nurses, and pastoral counselors. Good therapists are sensitive, empathic, and accepting, in addition to being well trained.

■ The best source of information concerning a therapist is a person who has been in therapy with that therapist. Other sources of information include members of helping professions, local clinics or hospitals, local professional societies, area mental health associations, telephone hot lines, and community-service or interagency-council information and referral services. The least desirable source is the yellow pages of the telephone directory.

■ A therapy may be classified as insight oriented or action oriented; as directive or nondirective; or as oriented toward individual, family, or group treatment. This chapter classifies therapies as analytic, existential humanistic, group, or behavioral-directive. There is some overlapping among these categories.

■ Analytic therapies rely on verbal means to place the person in greater contact with fragmented parts of his or her mental life. These therapies include psychoanalysis, psychoanalytic psychotherapy, neo-Freudian analysis, analytical psychology, and the existential approach.

■ Psychoanalysis involves two steps: strengthening the weakened ego by extending its self-knowledge and breaking down resistances. Using direct information supplied by the analysand and information conveyed through free associations, transferences, and the telling of dreams, the analyst acts as interpreter for the analysand.

■ Psychoanalytic psychotherapy is a modification of psychoanalysis that focuses more on current problems in living than on fixations. The treatment is shorter and less expensive than traditional psychoanalysis.

■ Neo-Freudian analysis emphasizes the drive toward self-realization and views adjustment problems as stemming from negative life experiences rather than from unresolved early childhood conflicts related to infantile sexuality. Therefore, the treatment focuses on conscious thoughts, feelings, and behavior in the here and now.

■ Analytical psychology is based on the notion that there is a collective unconscious, shared by all people, that reflects the cosmic order and contains archetypes that recur in human cultures and that can be known through dream symbols, creative imagination, disturbed mental states, and the products of art and science. It is assumed that neurosis results when the person has lost touch with the archetypes and other psychological formations such as the anima, the animus, and the shadow. The goal of treatment is to integrate the self with its transpersonal parts.

■ The existential approach emphasizes the themes of personal alienation in mass society, the breakdown of traditional values, and the consequent loss of meaning in our lives. It assumes that we can control our own lives through the individual choices we make. The treatment involves an active dialogue between therapist and patient that focuses on the patient's current choices.

■ Existential humanistic therapies share the following characteristics: (1) a blending of the direct-experience component of the existential approach with a deep philosophical commitment to the notion of the perfectibility of human beings, (2) a concern with ordinary unhappiness and alienation as opposed to the classical neurosis of psychoanalysis, and (3) a concern with educating people. Existential humanistic therapies include Rogerian therapy, Gestalt therapy, biofunctional therapy, primary therapy, and the transcendent approach.

■ Rogerian therapy aims at getting the client to experience his or her potentialities and to develop an accurate self-concept. The therapist works toward these ends by providing unconditional positive regard in an open, honest, and empathic encounter.

■ Gestalt therapy assumes that maladjustment is the result of a person's failing to recognize and satisfy his or her needs. The therapist attempts to get the patient to focus awareness on the present so that needs and the means to satisfy them will come into focus. There is a distinct emphasis on nonverbal as well as verbal behavior.

■ Biofunctional therapy assumes that both psychological health and neurosis are expressed directly through the body. Hence, the therapist works directly with the body of the patient.

■ Primal therapy asserts that neurosis is rooted in early rejection of the child by the parents. The goal of treatment is to transform the patient's state of feeling. The therapist accomplishes this by getting the patient to express deep feelings toward his or her parents.

■ The transcendent approach is concerned with the attainment of a new perspective of life through altered states of consciousness in which the usual boundary between subject and object becomes blurred.

■ Group therapy uses social dynamics as the predominant change agent. Group therapies include traditional group therapy, encounter groups, transactional analysis, and family therapy.

■ Traditional group therapy is most often associated with the psychoanalytic schools of therapy. The therapist tends to focus on either the individual patients within the group or on the group itself.

■ Encounter groups tend to be more concerned with adding something positive to members' lives than removing something negative. The group functions as an instrument of support to encourage the individual to try out new thoughts, feelings, and actions.

■ Transactional analysis (TA) focuses on the way people interact with one another and the way they behave toward themselves. The therapist draws attention to people's interactions (transactions) and emphasizes the value of reality testing, probability estimating, and dispassionate computing in the establishment of adjustive behavior patterns.

■ Family therapy focuses on group dynamics within the family itself, which comprises the living set of relationships that probably gave rise to the patient's neurosis in the first place. A growing variant of family therapy is couples therapy.

■ Behavioral-directive therapies asume that emotional problems have observable sources. Once the source is located, therapeutic activity is directed toward eliminating, or at least controlling, it. Behavioral-directive therapies include somatic therapy, sex therapy, behavior therapy, and cognitive therapy.

■ Somatic therapy defines the source of emotional problems as biological and attempts to treat the problem through such means as drugs, shock treatment, or psychosurgery.

■ Sexual therapy attempts to treat sexual dysfunctions, such as premature ejaculation, by dealing with attitudes, expecta-

tions, emotions, and behavior. Treatment is usually given to a couple, with both partners being taught various techniques for enhancing erotic arousal.

■ Behavior therapy is a strictly psychological behavioral-directive approach that begins with analysis of a pattern of behavior and identification of an observable component, such as a phobia. Therapy is aimed at altering the behavior pattern so that the observable component is eliminated or controlled.

■ Proponents of cognitive therapy believe maladjustive behavior is caused by some error or confusion with regard to beliefs or values. The therapist points out the faulty thinking to the patient and then attempts to correct it by teaching more realistic and effective ways of thinking and of establishing values.

■ The choice of a particular therapy may not be as important as the choice of a particular therapist and/or the decision to enter therapy in the first place. Still, some therapies may be better suited than others to deal with certain problems. Common sense dictates that the selection of a particular therapy should be based on information gathered about that therapy, including factors such as time and money to be spent.

■ Therapy costs what the market will bear, from literally nothing, as in the case of some therapy provided through practices supported by public funds, to as much as the $125-an-hour rate charged by some private practitioners.

■ A person in therapy can be expected to change in various ways. Thus, the risks of therapy, particularly successful therapy, extend to family members and friends as well as the person in therapy.

■ We can judge whether a therapy is successful by evaluating how well the goals of therapy are being achieved. This evaluation might include self-assessment, discussion with the therapist, and discussion with a family member or friend.

■ Therapy should end either when the goals have been completely achieved or when there has been no progress toward the achievement of goals for an inordinately long period of time.

SELECTED READINGS

Beck, A. T. *Love Is Never Enough*. New York: Harper & Row, 1989. An overview of cognitive therapy that includes examples of its use in treating marital problems.

Corey, G. *Theory and Practice of Counseling and Psychotherapy, 3rd ed*. Monterey, CA: Brooks/Cole, 1986. An excellent practical guide to the processes and applications of therapy.

Corsini, R., and contributors. *Five Therapists and One Client*. Itasca, IL: F. E. Peacock Publishers Inc., 1991. A demonstration of how five therapists, each with a different approach, would work with the same fictitious client.

Engler, J., and Goleman, D. *The Consumer's Guide to Psychotherapy*. New York: Simon and Schuster, 1992. This book provides answers to many questions usually asked by a person considering therapy.

Kaminer, W. *I'm Dysfunctional, You're Dysfunctional*. Reading, MA: Addison-Wesley, 1992. A critical analysis of the self-help movement in popular psychology.

Kottler, J. *The Compleat Therapist*. New York: Jossey-Bass, 1991. An examination of the common characteristics and techniques of all good therapists.

Ramirez, M. *Psychotherapy and Counseling with Minorities*. New York: Pergamon, 1991. A consideration of differences in the preferred techniques of psychotherapy and counseling of various minorities.

REFERENCES

Beck, A. *Cognitive Therapy and Emotional Disorders*. New York: International University Press, 1976.

_____. *Love Is Never Enough*. New York: Harper & Row, 1989.

Beitman, B. D., Goldfried, M. R., and Norcross, J. C. "The Movement Toward Integrating the Psychotherapies: An Overview." *American Journal of Psychiatry* 146 (April 1989): 138–147.

Berne, E. *Transactional Analysis in Psychotherapy*. New York: Grove Press, 1961.

Ellis, A. *Reason and Emotion in Psychotherapy*. New York: Lyle Stuart, 1962.

Freud, S. *An Outline of Psycho-Analysis*. Revised, translated, and edited by James Strachey. New York: Norton, 1969. (First German edition, 1940).

Gelman, D. "Where Are The Patients?" *Newsweek* (June 27, 1988): 62–66.

Glasser, W. *Reality Therapy*. New York: Harper & Row, 1965.

Janov, A. *The Primal Scream*. New York: Putnam, 1970.

Jung, C. G. *Analytical Psychology: Its Theory and Practice*. New York: Pantheon Books, 1968.

Kovel, J. A. *Complete Guide to Therapy: From Psychoanalysis to Behavior Modification*. New York: Pantheon, 1976.

Lieberman, M. A., Yalom, I. D., and Miles, M. B. *Encounter Groups: First Facts*. New York: Basic Books, 1973.

Lowen, A. *Bioenergetics*. New York: Penguin, 1976.

Masters, W. H., and Johnson, V. E., *Human Sexual Inadequacy*. Boston: Little, Brown, 1970.

_____. *Human Sexual Response*. Boston: Little, Brown, 1966.

Meredith, N. "Testing the Talking Cure." *Science* 86 (June 1986): 30–37.

The Miami Herald (November 16, 1980): 4b.

Mishara, B. L., and Patterson, R. D. *Consumer's Handbook of Mental Health: How to Find, Select and Use Help*. New York: Signet, 1979.

Perls, F. *Gestalt Therapy Verbatim*. Lafayette, CA: Real People Press, 1969.

Rogers, C. *On Becoming a Person*. Boston: Houghton Mifflin, 1961.

Thompson, J. W., and Blaine, J. D. "Use of ECT in the U.S. in 1975 and 1980." *American Journal of Psychiatry* 144 (1987): 577–582.

Watts, A. *Psychotherapy East and West*. New York: Pantheon Books, 1961.

Williams, R. L., and Long, J. D. *Toward a Self-Managed Life Syle*, 2d ed. Boston: Houghton Mifflin, 1979.

Wolpe, J. *The Practice of Behavior Therapy*. New York: Pergamon Press, 1969.

■ *Questionnaire Scoring Key*

Which Therapy Appeals to You?

To figure your score:

	P	R	B
1.	A	D	A
2.	A	A	D
3.	A	D	D
4.	A	D	D
5.	D	A	A
6.	D	D	A
7.	D	D	A
8.	D	A	D
9.	A	A	D
10.	D	A	D
11.	D	D	A

First, if you agreed with a statement, circle all the As in that line; if you disagreed, circle all the Ds in that line. For example, if you agreed with statement 1, you would circle the As on line 1 under the headings P and B.

Next, count the number of circles in each of the three columns and record the totals: P R B.

P = psychoanalysis   R = Rogerian therapy   B = behavior therapy

Which therapy seems to have more appeal to you?

■ *Answers to Review Questions*

Critical Review 1 1. T. **2.** T. **3.** F. **4.** F. **5.** F. **6.** T. **7.** T. **8.** T.

Critical Review 2 **1.** Insight-oriented. **2.** psychoanalysis. **3.** transference. **4.** id, ego, remain sleeping. **5.** self-knowledge, resistances.
Critical Review 3 **1.** self-realization. **2.** collective. **3.** existential approach.
Critical Review 4 **1.** T. **2.** F. **3.** F. **4.** T. **5.** F.
Critical Review 5 **1.** T. **2.** F. **3.** T.
Critical Review 6 **1.** social, change. **2.** psychoanalytic. **3.** Encounter. **4.** Eric Berne. **5.** Parent, Adult, Child. **6.** family. **7.** system. **8.** Couples, significant relationship.
Critical Review 7 **1.** T. **2.** F. **3.** F. **4.** T. **5.** T. **6.** T. **7.** T. **8.** F.
Critical Review 8 **1.** T. **2.** T. **3.** F. **4.** T. **5.** T. **6.** F.

PERSONAL ACTION PLAN
Self-Help

The first section in this Personal Action Plan provides a model for self-help. This model is a modification of William Glasser's reality therapy combined with Watson and Tharp's ABCs of behavior. The second section applies the model to an area in which many people openly acknowledge they need help: cigarette smoking. Many of the remarks in this section are based on the discussion contained in chapter 5 of R. L. Williams and J. D. Long, *Toward a Self-Managed Life Syle, 2nd ed.* (Boston: Houghton Mifflin, 1979).

A Model for Self-Help

Step I.

Make friends with yourself. People who realize that things are not going well, but who do not know what to do to improve the situation, often treat themselves poorly. This tendency must be overcome if effective self-help is to be provided. Making friends with yourself might include the use of relaxation techniques, fantasy, or positive self-talk. The important thing is to see yourself as an OK person. You may need some help, but you are OK nonetheless.

Step II.

Ask yourself, "What am I doing now?" This is simply a way of focusing awareness on the target behavior.

Step III.

Ask yourself, "Is it helping?" This is a critical step because a thorough consideration of the answer to this question should provide the motivation to change your behavior. Think about it. If you have a clear picture of what you are doing (Step II), and what you are doing is not helping, then why not change your behavior?

Step IV.

Make a plan to do better. This step involves: (A) gathering information about the kind of behavior you want to change; (B) studying carefully not only the behavior itself, but the antecedents and consequences of the behavior; and (C) applying the information from (A) to the conditions of (B) in the construction of a plan designed to change the target behavior.

Step V.

Make a commitment. A plan to change behavior is worthless unless you carry it out. Thus, it is important to make a commitment to do what you have planned to do. Here, it is probably best to make the commitment to at least two people—to yourself and to some other person who cares about you. Choose a person whom you respect, who has known you for some time, and who is willing to spend time talking with you about what you are attempting to do.

Step VI.

Do not accept excuses. If you fail to carry out the desired behavior change, accept the fact that you have not done what you wanted to do and try again.

Step VII.

Do not punish yourself, but do not interfere with reasonable consequences of your behavior. If you continue to try but also continue to fail in changing your behavior, go back to Step IV and make a new plan to do better.

Step VIII.

Never give up.

A Self-Help Plan to Quit Smoking Cigarettes

Step I.

Using one or more of the techniques suggested in the model for self-help, make friends with yourself. You are really an OK person, but one who has a habit that is not good for you or for anyone else.

Step II.

Ask yourself, "What am I doing now?"

Step III.

Ask yourself, "Is it helping?"

Step IV.

Make a plan to do better.

A. Getting information. Some things you ought to know about smoking and smokers.

   1. There are no physiological benefits to be gained from smoking. Smoking is positively correlated with higher rates of heart attack, stroke, and lung cancer—three of the greatest causes of disability and death in our society. In fact, smoking does not even calm you down. It constricts blood vessels, raises blood pressure, and places the body in a condition of stress.

      Research indicates that the attitudes of smokers toward their own smoking range from smoking without regret to smoking with considerabe conflict. In all cases, however, smokers tend to resort to defensive coping to maintain their habit. Those who smoke without regret, for example, tend either to deny or to minimize the hazards of smoking.

      You may often hear smokers making statements such as the following: "I just had a complete physical exam and my doctor says I am as healthy as a horse. Smoking does not bother me." "I cannot understand why they make such a big deal about smoking. A person can get killed crossing the street." "If smoking is so bad for you, how come some doctors and nurses smoke?" Those who smoke with conflict often attempt to resolve the conflict by reducing their smoking, by telling themselves and others that

they intend to quit in the future, by contending that if they quit smoking they will suffer some negative effect such as gaining weight, and by emphasizing that they simply lack control over the problem.

   2. There is an alternative to all of the above rationalizations: One can quit smoking. In fact, millions of people have quit smoking and so can you. Some succeed with a gradual approach, reducing the amount of smoking little by little over a period of time. Others succeed by quitting "cold turkey." Thus, there is more than one way to quit smoking.

B. Focusing on the ABCs. Construct a log in which you record answers to each of the following questions for each cigarette you smoke during the day:

   1. Amount smoked (whole cigarette, 3/4, 1/2, 1/4)?
   2. Time of day?
   3. Place?
   4. Who was present?
   5. What were you doing?
   6. What were the consequences of your smoking?

   Continue to log information for one week. At the end of the week, study your log carefully. Look for patterns. When are you most or least likely to smoke? Where? With whom? Doing what? When was smoking most or least satisfying for you?

C. Applying information. Our suggested strategy combines aspects of the gradual and "cold turkey" approaches. When you begin, apply the following guidelines. For the next two weeks you will use the gradual approach to reduce your smoking. You will:

   1. Set a long-range goal for the number of cigarettes you want to be smoking two weeks from now. We suggest that the number be about half the number you are currently smoking. If you now smoke two packs a day (forty cigarettes), your goal will be to smoke only one pack a day (twenty cigarettes) two weeks from now.

   2. Construct a schedule that reflects short-range goals for the number of cigarettes you want to be smoking at three- to four-day intervals during the two-week period. If you currently smoke forty cigarettes a day, you will want to cut down by at least five cigarettes every three to four days to achieve your long-range goal.

   Your schedule will look like this:

Sunday (today)	40 cigarettes
Wednesday	35 cigarettes
Sunday	30 cigarettes
Wednesday	25 cigarettes
Sunday	20 cigarettes

3. Use information obtained from your smoking log to devise tactics that alter the antecedents and the consequences of your smoking. The following list of suggestions and examples might be useful to you.

   a. *Antecedents.* (1) Alter the antecedents so that you become more aware of your behavior and thus eliminate impulsive smoking. For example, do not carry matches or a lighter (so you will have to ask someone for a light whenever you smoke), or change the place you usually carry your cigarettes (so you will have to think about what you are doing to find a cigarette). (2) Reduce the range of stimuli associated with smoking. For example you might find that there are six or seven situations in which you are more likely to smoke (after eating, while studying, when driving, and so on). Try to break these associations. Deliberately do not smoke immediately after eating or while driving your car. Another excellent tactic is to confine your smoking to a limited number of places (perhaps one place at home, one at school, one at work). (3) Replace the antecedents with other antecedents over which you have no control. For example, you could set a time interval between cigarettes and gradually increase the interval. You might begin with an interval of at least half an hour between cigarettes and, three days later, increase the interval to forty-five minutes, and so on. In this manner, you would be controlling when you smoked.

   b. *Consequences.* (1) Apply aversive consequences so that smoking is an unpleasant experience for you. For example, each time you light a cigarette, force yourself to think about the most disgusting and dehumanizing experience you have ever had. (2) Positively reinforce nonsmoking behavior. For example, each day you smoke less than the day before, reward yourself with something you really like. (3) Combine aversive and positive reinforcement tactics. Combining

(1) and (2) is often a more effective tactic than applying either (1) only or (2) only.

4. While you are gradually reducing your smoking during the next two weeks, you will also be devising tactics to use when you quit completely. You will:

   a. Devise tactics for dealing with the antecedents. You could: (1) Remove or reduce environmental cues that trigger impulsive smoking. For example, remove all ashtrays and table lighters from your home and office. (2) Avoid people, places, and activities that are most frequently associated with smoking. For example, if smoking is always a part of your behavior when you and a couple of your classmates stop at the campus cafeteria for a cup of coffee following your psychology class, then go to the library or some other place when your psychology class ends. (3) Concentrate on alternatives to the usual smoking antecedents. For exampe, become more involved in activities that you have never associated with smoking.

   b. Devise tactics for altering the consequences. Here, you will focus on tactics that positively reinforce nonsmoking behavior. For example, construct a list of reinforcers, any of which can be used to reward yourself at predetermined intervals (say, once a day or once a week) for not smoking. It is important to continue to reinforce your nonsmoking behavior for some time after you have quit competely. We recommend indefinite periodic reinforcement. So, even if you have not smoked for ten years, give yourself a reward. You deserve it. Also, you should be aware that it takes about one week from the time you quit completely for your withdrawal symptoms to disappear. Thus, each time you crave a cigarette during that week, you will have moved one step closer to never craving a cigarette again.

5. Two weeks from now, you will quit smoking completely and put into action the tactics you have devised to use when you have quit.

Step V.

Make a commitment. Make a solemn commitment to yourself to carry out the plan specified in Step IV. Also, locate another person to whom you can make the same commitment. Tell the person what you are attempting to do and explain carefully the plan you have constructed. Ask the person to be available to you for the support and encouragement when needed and to help you evaluate your progress at predetermined intervals.

Step VI.

Do not accept excuses. If you have not lived up to your commitment, do not despair. Put your nose to the grindstone and try again.

Step VII.

Do not punish yourself, but do not interfere with reasonable consequences of your behavior. If you repeat- edly do not live up to your commitment, go back to Step IV and make a new plan.

Step VIII.

Never give up. Smoking is usually a difficult habit to break. But millions of people have broken the habit and so can you. Like those who have succeeded in breaking the habit, you too, will quit if you keep trying. We repeat, *never give up.*

INDEX